Aphorisms, the Arts, and Late Writings

THE COMPLETE WORKS OF SANGHARAKSHITA include all his previously published work, as well as talks, seminars, and writings published here for the first time. The collection represents the definitive edition of his life's work as Buddhist writer and teacher. For further details, including the contents of each volume, please turn to the 'Guide' on pp. 803–11.

FOUNDATION

1 A Survey of Buddhism / The Buddha's Noble Eightfold Path
2 The Three Jewels I
3 The Three Jewels II
4 The Bodhisattva Ideal
5 The Purpose and Practice of Buddhist Meditation
6 The Essential Sangharakshita

INDIA

7 Crossing the Stream: India Writings I
8 Beating the Dharma Drum: India Writings II
9 Dr Ambedkar and the Revival of Buddhism I
10 Dr Ambedkar and the Revival of Buddhism II

THE WEST

11 A New Buddhist Movement I
12 A New Buddhist Movement II
13 Eastern and Western Traditions

COMPLETE WORKS 26 **POETRY AND THE ARTS**

Sangharakshita

Aphorisms, the Arts, and Late Writings

EDITED BY VIDYADEVI

Windhorse Publications
38 Newmarket Road
Cambridge CB5 8DT

info@windhorsepublications.com
www.windhorsepublications.com

First published in 2022.

Cover design by Dhammarati
Cover images: Front: *Saint Jerome in His Study*, detail. Vincenzo Catena, circa 1510, The National Gallery, London.
Back flap: Sangharakshita, Madhyamaloka, 2012.
Photo: Mahasiddhi.

Typesetting and layout by Tarajyoti
Printed by Bell & Bain Ltd, Glasgow

British Library Cataloguing in Publication Data:
A catalogue record for this book is available from the British Library.

ISBN 978-1-911407-85-0 (paperback)
ISBN 978-1-911407-84-3 (hardback)

CONTENTS

FOREWORD: ART FOR OUR SAKE

I cycled to the London Buddhist Centre (LBC) on a cold November evening in 1985. I was 25. My degree at Goldsmiths College of Art had ground to a halt. I'd believed art could change the world, and that somehow my artwork would play a part in that. I'd made a painting based on *The Sun*'s infamous headline about the bombing of the Belgrano during the Falklands War: 'GOTCHA!' I'd stuck an Airfix model of a Blackburn Buccaneer on a picture inspired by semiotics. I'd marched hand in hand with my new boyfriend across London Bridge alongside Lesbians and Gays Support the Miners. But I was unhappy. I oscillated between depressed anxiety and life-and-soul mania. I was smoking too much dope, worrying about AIDS, and I didn't really know how art could help anyone, least of all myself. A fellow student at Goldsmiths was doing performance pieces that involved walking in circles, naked, and dragging a bloody pig's head. That about summed it up.

A friend suggested meditation. I cycled from my squat in Brixton to the LBC. As soon as I learned the Mindfulness of Breathing I knew I was a Buddhist. That's how it felt – immediate, instinctual. This 'Buddhism' was what life was *for*. Without realizing it Sangharakshita had become my Teacher (capital T). Not that I knew anything about him at the time. Soon enough I heard the name 'Bhante' bandied about, but I felt no real connection with him. I'd assumed 'Bhante' was an affectionate nickname until someone pointed out it meant 'venerable teacher'. No one ever called him Sangharakshita. It was always 'Bhante'.

I'd read Christopher Isherwood's *My Guru and His Disciple* and, in my naivety, assumed that Buddhism and Vedanta were pretty much the same thing. I even asked where the swami was. There was nothing particularly mystical or incense-laden about the LBC. No one was wearing robes. No one fixed me with a hypnotic stare. It was all pretty ordinary, except for the large golden Buddha statue which I thought absurdly patriarchal and Victorian (I was at Goldsmiths after all!) and at the same time rather wonderful. Despite my disappointment at the general lack of exoticism – just the breath to focus on, and, at half time, a cup of tea and a biscuit – I knew I had changed my life.

My artwork changed almost overnight. I stopped making sloganeering political statements and started allowing myself to enjoy making paintings, something I'd always dismissed as bourgeois. I began to paint the natural world – at least in the form of a few bushes and trees in Myatt's Fields, the park next to the college. I started to listen to classical music, visit galleries, and read novels. I went to see foreign-language films. All this was new to me. I discovered culture alongside meditating every morning, going on retreat, cycling regularly to the LBC, and making new friends. Sangharakshita's vision of Buddhism and art had changed everything.

Four years later, having moved into the community above the LBC, I was on a four-month ordination retreat in the Spanish mountains. I'd explained to my concerned parents that I was not about to become a monk. What I was doing was nothing less than following up that – what to call it? 'vision' is too grand, 'hunch' is too petty – that initial conviction that the truths of the Dharma were the truths of life. In the final month of our retreat we were asked to prepare a short talk. I chose to talk about *The Religion of Art*.

One of the things that had kept me cycling back and forth between Goldsmiths and the LBC was that Buddhism – whatever *that* was – seemed a natural extension of art. It felt like my art practice taken into my life, something like that. What I hadn't known was that the arts in general – music, literature, art, theatre – were part of Bhante's vision of the Dharma, part of his understanding of the true meaning of Buddhism, its *inner* meaning beneath the cultural accretions and historical vicissitudes that had amassed around the Buddha's Enlightenment. Written in the early 1950s, while Bhante was living in Kalimpong on the border of India and Tibet, its four essays explored the meaning of Buddhism and the value of art. Struck by Bhante's passionate belief in art's transcendent value, I focused my short talk on the title essay and his definition of art:

> Art is the organization of sensuous impressions into pleasurable formal relations that express the artist's sensibility and communicate to his audience a sense of values that can transform their lives.

When I returned from my ordination retreat with my new name and my new life, I tried to carry on painting. I painted in my room in the community. I painted on retreat. I made oil pastels in Victoria Park. But there was a conflict between my commitment to Buddhism and my feeling for art. I tried to resolve that conflict by teaching *The Religion of Art*. Initially, I thought we'd just study the essay, but some participants found Bhante's writing too dense. Some thought it highfaluting and rhetorical. It was written when Bhante was still a young man and it is full of passionate intensity. And it pulls no punches when it comes to what Bhante considers to be art and not art. So I created a course exploring Bhante's fundamental ideas. I took people to galleries to help them look at paintings. I got them to listen more deeply to music.

But my own conflict never really went away. I even feared that my commitment to Buddhism – by now I was living and working at the LBC – was an escape from the loneliness and frustration of the studio. An escape from trying to get a gallery to take my work. A kind of cowardice. It felt that both Buddhism and art wanted all of me and I'd chosen Buddhism.

Meanwhile I was tentatively getting to know Bhante. I was so overawed the first time I met him that I started a conversation about William Blake, about whom I knew next to nothing. At the end of our short meeting – Bhante having looked so bored – I decided I didn't like him. But occasionally I'd bump into him in the community (he lived in a small flat next door), and once, not long after I got home from my ordination retreat, I nearly knocked him over in the stairwell. I'd been upstairs studying *The Religion of Art* (I must have been preparing a course) and I swung down the bannisters to the kitchen in such a state of ecstatic high spirits that I very nearly crashed into him. After that I'd chat to him as he went through the community to his flat. One morning,

I was examining a poster for a gay men's retreat I was planning. At the time, the idea of running a retreat for gay men was quite controversial. (Bhante told me he'd received a letter of complaint from a Sinhalese *bhikkhu*.) The poster said: 'Get Away from the Stress and Strain of London'. Suddenly Bhante was at my shoulder. He read the headline, turned to me and said 'Yes, and all those gay bars!'

I decided that what was needed was a book exploring art's relationship to Buddhism, based on Bhante's thinking. By then he'd been interviewed by J. O. Mallander for what was to become a short and beautiful book, *In the Realm of the Lotus*, and anyway Bhante's insights into the arts were everywhere to be found in his transcribed seminars. I went next door to ask him about it. 'You're going to update me,' Bhante said with a twinkle. He asked had I read Plotinus? No. Had I read Schopenhauer? No. Had I read...? Eventually I said, 'Bhante, it's probably not worth asking me if I've read someone. I almost certainly haven't.' I left with an armful of books. The next day I received a photocopy of a few pages of Plotinus with a note saying that this was a more accessible translation. I put the pile of books on my desk. But I never managed – despite three or four attempts – to write the book.

I gave it a good go. Everything I read for the non-existent book seemed to echo Bhante's thought. I read George Steiner's *Real Presences*: 'The archaic torso in Rilke's famous poem says to us: "change your life". So do any poem, novel, play, painting, musical composition worth meeting.' I read Bryan Magee's *The Philosophy of Schopenhauer*: '"What is life?" Every genuine and successful work of art answers this question in its own way....' I read Roger Scruton's *An Intelligent Person's Guide to Modern Culture*: 'Art has grown from the sacred view of life. And this is why art suddenly leapt into prominence at the Enlightenment, with the eclipse of sacred things.' More recently I have read Iain McGilchrist's *The Master and His Emissary*: 'There are, it seems to me, four main pathways to the truth: science, reason, intuition and imagination. I also believe strongly that any world view that tries to get by without paying due respect to all four of these is bound to fail.' Anyone reading Sangharakshita's work, in this volume or any other, will recognize echoes.

This volume contains much more than Bhante's writings on art and culture. It contains, for instance, two books of remarkable aphorisms.

I still have my treasured copies with Dhammarati's beautiful cover designs, black-and-white photos inside – Bhante in robes reading, everyone lined up and solemn at the first ordination, a young Aloka with a mallet making the Buddha image for the LBC – and some of Bhante's poems. One of them, *Peace is a Fire*, is dated 1995 and signed 'With much love on your birthday, Maria'. Maria was the friend who first suggested I try meditation. Aphorisms are an aristocratic form: you either get them or you don't. They are little shocks, tiny lightning conductors. They are meant to provoke you, or light you up. Once again there are wonderful insights into art: 'Milton's *Paradise Lost* is an imaginative statement of the whole dilemma of modern man.' 'Art is an object through which we find our way back to the subject.'

Bhante's late writings are also to be found here, some written, or rather dictated, at Madhyamaloka, in Birmingham – Bhante's macular degeneration meant his eyesight was very poor in his later years – and some composed at Adhisthana, his final home (another small flat) in Herefordshire. In the late writing what I see, again and again, is how ever-present the Dharma was in Bhante's life, a kind of ground-note you can hear in any and every piece of writing. Whether he's describing Roy, his neighbour's dog when he was a child, or a blackbird singing from a chimney pot in Bethnal Green, whether he's paying tribute to Ayya Khema or rejoicing in his literary heroes, something indefinable – some hint of the mysteries of the Dharma – subtly pervades his words, like a rare perfume.

The very late writing, painstakingly dictated in his lounge overlooking the duck pond at Adhisthana, with the background sound of diggers preparing his burial site in the garden outside, are remarkable for their concision and range of subject matter: reflections on Green Tārā, the fourth *lakṣaṇa*, and the *Gārava Sutta* rub shoulders with descriptions of his uncles, William Morris's *News from Nowhere*, and a sexual encounter with an American hippy. But what stays in my mind are two recurring themes. The first is an inquiry into the nature of evil. Buddhists have thought long and hard about suffering, but not perhaps about the nature of human malevolence. Near the end of his life, evil seemed to be on Bhante's mind: how could people act so evilly to one another? Another theme (and in my own small way this had been a theme in my own life) was his experience of homosexuality:

> In subsequent years, thanks to my wide reading, I had become aware that there were, and always had been, men like me, among them being some of the brightest names in poetry, literature, music, and the visual arts. By the time I entered the army, therefore, I knew just where I stood, sexually speaking. I also knew what the majority of people thought of sexuality such as mine. Homosexuality was unnatural. It was wicked, sinful, and perverse and a homosexual was a moral leper. This was not the worst. In my own country, as in other civilized countries, any kind of homosexual activity was a criminal offence, and there were countries in which it was punishable by death. It therefore behoved me to be very careful what I did or said, or even how I looked at other men. This was not without its consequences for my emotional life. Keeping my feelings to myself became a habit, especially when those feelings were very strong and directed to another man. Many years were to pass before I was able to give expression to such feelings even to a limited extent.

Bhante was thinking about art, poetry, and culture right up to the end of his life. On 15 March 2018 he woke to the news that Stephen Hawking, the theoretical physicist and cosmologist, had died. This prompted him to buy an audiobook of Hawking's *Brief History of Time*, followed by Carlo Rovelli's *Reality Is Not What It Seems*. The latter struck him in particular. He quotes Rovelli: 'I believe that this example demonstrates how great science and great poetry are both visionary, and may even arrive at the same intuitions. Our culture is foolish to keep science and poetry separated…' That was music to Bhante's ears.

Along with *The Religion of Art*, it was *Advice to a Young Poet*, inspired by the German poet Rainer Maria Rilke's *Letters to a Young Poet*, that finally resolved (to the degree it can be resolved) my conflict between a committed Dharma life and my need, amounting at times to an obsession, to make art. I was on a seven-month sabbatical in Spain. I'd gone with the express intention of finally writing that book on Bhante's vision of art. This time, secluded in the Spanish mountains, away from my life at the LBC, I'd finally get it written. I shipped over volumes of cultural theory and art criticism. I had a computer and printer rigged to a generator. Every day I wrote for hours on end, re-reading Bhante, comparing his thought to other writers. Halfway through my sabbatical a friend visited me, read my manuscript, and declared it a dud. He was right. I promised not to work on it any more. I dedicated more time to meditation and study. I painted watercolours and, for the first time in my life, typed up my poems. I never looked at the book manuscript again.

By now I was visiting Bhante whenever I could. If I was spending time with my family near Birmingham, I'd make an appointment to see him at Madhyamaloka. When he moved to Adhisthana, I'd try to see him there. In the old days I'd needed an excuse. I'd need to talk to him about such and such.... But I didn't need an excuse any more. I'd just ask to see him because I wanted to spend some time with him, to talk and laugh – he would often tease me. Each time I'd thank him for all he'd given me. Near the end of his life I visited him again. I was just thanking him for something when he suddenly said, 'And I want to thank *you*! 'What on earth for?' I said. 'For your poem.' I'd spent what had felt like forever (six years) writing a long narrative poem called *The Travellers from Orissa*. It was about the first two disciples of the Buddha. I'd recorded it for him to listen to. He told me he'd been waiting for a time when he felt in the mood to listen to contemporary poetry. When he'd finally got around to listening to it, he told me, he found it wasn't as contemporary as he'd feared! We talked about Robert Frost's 'conversational style', something, at least, I knew something about. And he encouraged me to write more.

Bhante has been dead for almost three years now. His simple burial mound, overlooked by Oyster Hill, is surrounded by roses. It's a place of pilgrimage. I can't shake his hand any more or laugh at his jokes, but every time I read him he's still there – that mysterious *something* is still there, that unobtrusive majesty. I have a picture of him on the shrine in my bedroom under a bookcase of his writings and too much, far too much, poetry. He's sitting on the steps of a fairground ride – jet planes to ride and scream in. He's wearing a buttercup-yellow T-shirt, a purple jacket, and blue jeans. He looks like an anarchist, or a Beat poet, or an artist.

Maitreyabandhu
Samaggavasa Community
London
September 2021

A NOTE FROM THE EDITOR

Believe it or not, this was originally going to be a slim volume, but it has grown substantially. First, we realized that we needed to find a home for the collection of late writings called *A Moseley Miscellany*, which was originally to appear elsewhere in the *Complete Works*. The book was originally published as a carefully assembled combination of prose pieces, poems, and book reviews, but unfortunately the sheer number of words in this volume meant that there wasn't room to allow us to keep the Miscellany intact. The poems can be found in volume 25 of the *Complete Works* and the book reviews in volume 8, so nothing has been lost. The parts of the book which appear here have been retitled *Madhyamaloka Reflections*. More is explained in the introduction to this part of the book.

The reason why we ran short of space is because Sangharakshita's late writings didn't end there. In the last few years of his life, which he spent at Adhisthana, the Triratna centre in the Herefordshire countryside, he kept writing, the final piece in this collection being composed just three weeks before his death. Hence a companion volume to *Madhyamaloka Reflections*, called *Adhisthana Writings*, which appears in print for the first time in this volume.

One of the consequences of these additions is that the volume spans nearly seventy years of Sangharakshita's work, the essays in *The Religion of Art* dating back to the early 1950s, showing how his writing style changed over time. The elaborate style of *The Religion of Art* is very much of its period, and from an editorial point of view it was tempting to update it, but we have resisted that temptation, deciding that we had better present the work as originally published, in line with the policy we have adopted for the *Complete Works* as a whole. Similarly, the style of the aphorisms in the first part of the volume is very much of its time. There are many considerations here, but apart from anything else, even if we had edited the work in line with contemporary taste, that would itself have become outdated within the life of these volumes, long as we hope it will be.

I am very grateful to Dhivan (Dr Thomas Jones) for his permission to include his introduction to the 2010 edition of *The Religion of Art*, which lights the way into that work. Likewise, much gratitude to Ratnaprabha for permission to include his illuminating piece on the reading of aphorisms, a literary form which Sangharakshita much enjoyed, but which (at the time I am writing this, anyway) is perhaps not well understood.

Many thanks also to Ratnagarbha, the founding editor of the Buddhist arts magazine *Urthona*, for his permission to include several interviews with Sangharakshita. For more of Sangharakshita's writings on the arts, you may be interested to consult the third section of *Complete Works*, vol. 6, the anthology *The Essential Sangharakshita*, which contains among other extracts an article from the magazine *Dharma Life*, 'Entering a Spiritual Dimension Through Writing'. I must also thank the venerable compilers of the collections of aphorisms which appear here, decades after they were first published, Ananda and Abhaya. (*Peace is a Fire* was first published in 1979 and *A Stream of Stars* in 1998.) Many thanks also to Kalyanaprabha, who edited *A Moseley Miscellany* so beautifully; her thoughtful notes still accompany the excerpts from that work included here; my introduction to *Madhyamaloka Reflections* says more about her involvement with that work. Many people in Sangharakshita's support team helped with the writing down, digitizing, and editing of *Adhisthana Writings*; thanks to them too. And heartfelt gratitude, as ever, to Shantavira and all the *Complete Works* team for this labour of love, with special thanks to our wonderfully unflappable typesetter Tarajyoti, who coped with late changes to the layout with grace and flair.

Vidyadevi
Herefordshire
February 2022

Reflections and Aphorisms

GRABBING A FIREBRAND: APHORISMS AND SANGHARAKSHITA

In 1976, when I was a student, I used to go along to a Buddhist centre in the back streets of Brighton not far from the sea. The first book I picked up there was a pamphlet with a yellow cover, called *Sangharakshita: Sayings, Poems, Reflections*. The very first quotation was: '*One cannot be what one should be merely by closing one's eyes to what one is.*' That aphorism really grabbed me. 'Wow!' I thought. It worked. I was very struck. I had to think about it.

But you can't get Sangharakshita's teachings just from aphorisms. An aphorism is like a firebrand – if you grab the wrong end, you will get burnt. Sometimes, you are bound to grab the wrong end.

> The world will be different only if we live differently.[1]

Aphorisms, like this one from Humberto Maturana, are short, pithy statements trying to communicate a truth of general import. The etymology is from the Greek *apo-* 'from' + *horīzein* 'to bound', source of the English word 'horizon'. So an aphorism is perhaps 'from a horizon'. It helps you to a particular perspective by indicating the horizon, the boundary, of that perspective. It adopts a viewpoint and identifies what can be seen only from that perspective, rather than trying to describe the viewpoint from outside, as would a longer explanation.

Friedrich Nietzsche was one of the great aphorists. He wrote, in *Thus Spoke Zarathustra*,

> In the mountains the shortest route is from peak to peak, but for that you must have long legs. Aphorisms should be peaks, and those to whom they are spoken should be big and tall of stature.[2]

His biographer comments:

> The aphorism is a provocation, a springboard, a stimulus to further and deeper questioning.[3]

Aphorisms are bound to be ambiguous because they are short and striking. And to work, they should really hit you, so it's best if they sound rather controversial, against the run of normal opinion. Sangharakshita is a controversial aphorist. But here are a couple of warnings. 'An aphorism can never be the whole truth; it is either a half-truth or a truth-and-a-half.'[4] And from Dr Johnson: 'In lapidary inscriptions a man is not upon oath.'[5] (Lapidary inscriptions are the short sayings carved into tombstones and the like.)

Whenever we're presented with a statement, it's so tempting to take it literally, not to look *through* it for truth, but to think it *is* the truth. But aphorisms can flag the dangers of literalism so much more forcefully:

> Art is a lie that makes us realize truth.[6]

> Words, like eyeglasses, blur everything
> that they do not make more clear.[7]

Quite a while ago, there was a period when challenges to Sangharakshita's ideas reached something of a crescendo within the Buddhist organization he founded. I remember that he remarked at the time, 'Before deciding that you disagree with me, clarify your understanding of what I've said.' It's so easy to assume that one disagrees – or indeed that one agrees. But consider, what does the statement you wish to challenge actually mean?

A powerful example of the importance of clarification is connected with a very controversial little booklet written by Subhuti, *Women, Men and Angels*.[8] Its title comes from a strange saying by Sangharakshita: '*Angels are to men as men are to women – because they are more human and therefore more divine.*' What on earth does that mean? It sounds like it's saying that men are superior to women in some sense. If so, in what sense? But what is an angel? Is it good to be more divine? What about the Buddhist idea of the *deva* realms (where divine beings live) being a dead end? In any case, what is the background to this weird little saying – how does it fit in with traditional Buddhist teachings? How does it fit in with other ideas of Sangharakshita's, and his life and behaviour? How does it fit in with your experience? There are so many questions. If you can, ask questions, get clarification, before you get indignant.

Here's another example: 'One should not waste time helping the weak. Nowadays it is the strong who need help.' If, like me, you sometimes bristle at an outrageous statement, you might say, 'Hey, what's this about ignoring suffering and defenceless people, and only nurturing some master race of the strong?' When I thought more deeply about this aphorism, I decided that it was suggesting that the most effective way of making a difference in the world is to band together with others who seem to be *capable* of making a difference in the world, referred to here as 'the strong' because of that capability. Help the strong in order that the world – which includes everybody, weak or strong – can be genuinely transformed in a radical and lasting way. It could also be hinting that it is a waste of time helping the weak in the sense that you need a certain amount of strength to be able to *accept* help. But don't be cowed by this idea. If you have an altruistic project in your life, in my opinion, you need to feel that you own it personally. Your heart, your vision, is so important. If that vision is to be involved intimately with people who are weak and in need of assistance, then that is admirable. For example, they might be dependent on harmful drugs in extreme ways. You have found something to do that is very challenging but very rewarding. Wouldn't it be appalling if you were put off from engaging in a project like that by some little saying in *Peace Is a Fire*!

Finally, some advice from Sangharakshita himself on how you might respond to teachings or Dharmic ideas that you come across. 'It is not enough to sympathize with something to such an extent that one agrees with it. If necessary, one must sympathize to such an extent that one disagrees.'

Ratnaprabha
London
January 2022

SAYINGS, POEMS, REFLECTIONS: EXCERPTS

In 1976, FWBO Surrey published this booklet of Sangharakshita's sayings and poems. Most of the sayings were included in a later publication, Peace is a Fire; *those that were omitted are included below. The booklet provides no information about the contexts in which they were said or written.*

One is not really human unless one has at least a spark of awareness.

One must work towards a state of harmony
through states of positive conflict.

Truth that is repeated becomes untruth – or else another truth.

A spiritual community is not a group.

It is not advisable to be as harmless as the dove unless one also has the wisdom of the serpent. In fact if you don't have the wisdom of the serpent it is difficult even to be harmless.

It may be that one day we will have to conclude that, in sticking to conventional religious forms, we are being unrealistic (in that we are) excluding certain people from the truth

If there is an experience about which we can think: 'This is my experience,' then that experience is not ultimate.

THE TANTRIC VERSION OF THE FIVE PRECEPTS

1. Do not obstruct the energy of any other person.
2. Do not drain the energy of others. Give freely of your own energy.
3. Do not misuse energy.
4. Use for any given purpose the energy appropriate to that purpose, not one which is inappropriate.
5. Do not allow energy to become turbid. Keep it clear and bright.

Nirvāṇa cannot wait for Saṃsāra to exhaust itself.

For the Bodhisattva, Nirvāṇa represents a failure.

PEACE IS A FIRE

THE SPIRITUAL PATH

Buddhism is a universal teaching. It speaks to all men. It speaks to them, moreover, not as belonging to any particular social group, e.g. clan, tribe, caste, race, nation, but as individual human beings. What it tells each one of them is that he can grow – that he can grow from manhood to Buddhahood, or from unenlightened humanity into enlightened humanity. It also tells him how he can do this.

Buddhism and William Blake (essay)

Some are attracted to Buddhism because they find in it the confirmation of their ideas. It would be better if they were attracted by it because it refutes their ideas.

Aphorism

You cannot be a Buddhist unless you are free *not* to be a Buddhist. A Sinhalese, apparently, is not free not to be a Buddhist.

Aphorism

One supremely important fact [is] that we *can* change. Consciousness *can* be restructured; negative states like hatred *can* be converted to positive states like love.

A Method of Personal Development (talk)

Buddhism is misunderstood if it is identified with just one or another of its specific forms, its particular cultural variants. It is rather like identifying a whole oak tree with just one single branch, or even, in some cases, with one single acorn.

A Method of Personal Development (talk)

There is no such thing as natural man. Any attempt to treat man as other than a spiritual being distorts him.

Aphorism

Any kind of life which is making no effort to evolve is escapism.

Aphorism

What every living thing, what every living being, wants to do most of all is to fulfil the law of its own being, and the law of our being is – as it is the law of the being of every living thing – that we should develop.

A Method of Personal Development (talk)

How terrible it would be if in a year's time we were just the same people that we are today! And in five years' time, the same people! Ten years' time, or when we came to die!... None of us, surely, likes to think that even in a year's time – or maybe even next week, if we are sufficiently idealistic! – we'll be exactly where we are just at this moment.

A Method of Personal Development (talk)

Buddhism is not yet really known in the West at all.

A Method of Personal Development (talk)

In reality Buddhism is neither pessimistic nor optimistic. If compelled to label it in this way at all we should borrow a word from George Eliot and call it melioristic, for though asserting that conditioned existence is suffering it also maintains, as the Third Āryan Truth teaches, that suffering can be transcended.

The Three Jewels

If one is unhappy, one wants to know the reason why. But it never occurs to one to ask why one is happy. It is therefore unhappiness, rather than happiness, that causes us to reflect upon our condition. It is unhappiness that makes us think.

Aphorism

The tragedy is not that we don't get what we want, but that we *do* get what we want, and then we're stuck with it, and very often we find that it's not what we wanted at all.

Seminar on Nāgārjuna's Precious Garland

What the third *lakṣaṇa*[9] really means is, in positive terms, that Nirvāṇa alone is peace, and negatively that conditioned things are painful because we seek in them for that absolute bliss which only the Unconditioned can bestow and have, therefore, inevitably to experience disappointment and frustration.

The Three Jewels

Mankind progresses for the same reason that the amoeba evolves – from irritation. There was never any flower of human achievement but some great sorrow lay at its root.

Crossing the Stream

Sometimes, of course, we just try – we may even do our best – to forget the whole bothersome question of personal development. Especially when it's a fine summer day, and the beach is calling, and your friends, maybe, want to take you out, you think, 'Why bother? Why not just be an ordinary human being and forget all about this question of the Higher Evolution and personal development?' But, fortunately or unfortunately, luckily or unluckily, once you've reached a certain point, once self-consciousness has really started to emerge, once you've really started to think, once you've really started to *feel*, once you've really started to *imagine*, you cannot really do that.

A Method of Personal Development (talk)

The happiness that you feel when you satisfy a desire is not due to the satisfaction of the desire but to the momentary cessation of the desire. But the desire returns. Therefore desires can never be satisfied: they can only be overcome, abandoned.

Seminar on Geshe Wangyal's The Door of Liberation

The Sanskrit word being translated as 'suffering' is *duḥkha*, the 'ill-fitting chariot wheel': the sort of discomfort that arises when things don't fit or work together properly, the jarring quality that we experience in the course of our everyday life.... Things are never one hundred per cent right. There's always something that goes wrong, even if it's only a small thing. Even on the most beautiful day, only too often a cloud has to float across the face of the sun. Something goes wrong. Maybe you've been looking forward to this day: you're going to meet someone you like, you imagine things are going to be so lovely. But then some absurd incident happens and it all goes wrong, and you feel utterly jangled. This is how we go through life. Nothing quite lives up to our expectations – or at least not for long. This is what is meant by *duḥkha*, unsatisfactoriness or suffering.

The Stages of the Spiritual Path (talk)

We have a responsibility for our own life, a responsibility for our own growth, a responsibility for our own happiness.

A Method of Personal Development (talk)

Happy is the man whose needs and whose wants coincide.

Aphorism

People who suffer are not necessarily nearer to the realization of the Āryan Truth of suffering than those who do not. One can, indeed, have insight into the truth of suffering while experiencing happiness (e.g. when meditating), for in the transcendental perspective even happiness is suffering – not in the sense of being actually painful, as a sensation or a feeling, but in the sense of being a conditioned thing.

Correspondence

Experiences are rarely satisfying in themselves:
only in anticipation and recollection.
Seminar on Geshe Wangyal's The Door of Liberation

RELIGION AND BELIEF

It is best not to believe in God. If one does believe in him, one should at least disobey him. To believe in him *and* obey him is pitiable.
Aphorism

We ceased to believe in God the day he was proved to exist.
Aphorism

The meaning of life is to be found only beyond life.
Aphorism

Ultimate spiritual choices are not to be
determined by cultural considerations.
Aphorism

Religions, as they have come down to us, are gold mixed
with ore. Sometimes the quantity of gold is so small,
compared with the quantity of ore, that it is not worth
the labour of extraction. Better open up a new mine.
Aphorism

An ethnic religion is one whose members have a common past;
a missionary religion, one in which they have a common future.
Aphorism

Religions that have gone rotten with age
are good for compost, not food.
Aphorism

Better to end up on the dung heap than in a museum.
Aphorism

If Christianity is of supernatural origin, I fail to see how it can be 'part' of our cultural heritage. One is therefore not being untrue to the heritage if one rejects Christianity.

Aphorism

Religion is essentially the experience of egolessness; the truly religious life is the life of egolessness; and genuinely religious beliefs and practices are those by which the realization of egolessness can be achieved.

The Religion of Art

It seems to me that if you use the words 'religious consciousness', it's a total consciousness. It's when all of your being – your head and your heart and your will – is directed, totally and integrally if possible, onto those things or that thing which you regard as of the highest importance and significance: then you can speak in terms of the 'religious consciousness'. It's not a sort of separate faculty, which needs a separate satisfaction. It's your own total commitment to, or total preoccupation with, what is, as far as you can see, of absolute importance – or of the greatest importance, if you like. It's not a *separate kind* of consciousness.

Seminar on D. T. Suzuki's Outlines of Mahāyāna Buddhism

To be a pagan is to have a positive attitude towards Nature and towards oneself as a part of Nature.

Aphorism

I think it is, in a way, very suspect (to say) that there is a separate religious sense, or a separate religious consciousness, and that some people have it and some people don't.... If you use the word religious it seems to indicate a sort of coordination of all one's faculties and one's whole being in a certain direction which you recognize to be ultimate.

Seminar on D. T. Suzuki's Outlines of Mahāyāna Buddhism

The besetting sin of organized Christianity is intolerance, that of Islam fanaticism, of Hinduism inhumanity, and of Buddhism laziness and indifference.
Aphorism

Universalism does not mean comparing the letters of different traditions, but trying to get through to the spirit.
Aphorism

In a traditional civilization ... religion (to use the narrow modern term) is not something from which a man can escape, even if he wants to; for it encounters him at every step, with the familiar objects of home and the accustomed routine of daily life. Nurtured in such an environment, in which the whole of existence appears to be a great Smaragdine Tablet, constantly reminding us that 'the things below are copies' and that the originals are above, sensitive hearts and minds become more subtle and sensitive still. To them 'rocks, and stones, and trees', and other natural objects, are not simply lumps of matter of various shapes and sizes, but 'huge cloudy symbols of a high romance' traced, not by the 'magic hand of chance', but by the irresistible finger of omnipresent spiritual law. Nature is not dead, but alive with many voices, and to an eye accustomed to see and to hear things that point beyond themselves, even

An old pine tree is preaching wisdom
And a wild bird is crying out truth

A Survey of Buddhism

WORK AND ACTION

Outer achievements should be expressions of inner abundance, not compensation for inner poverty.
Aphorism

People who have no real work of their own to do will always interfere with that of others. They may even make it their 'work' to interfere.
Aphorism

Find the truth, and then live by it.
Aphorism

'Work makes the companion,' says Goethe. Therefore, if you have no work you have no companion. Those are not companions with whom we merely amuse ourselves.
Aphorism

That one is able to do a thing is no reason for doing it.
Aphorism

There is no such thing as the will. What we think of as the will is simply our idea of ourselves as performing an action. To say that we *will* to do something is meaningless. We do it – or do not do it. The will is a myth.
Aphorism

One should be useful – but useful only within the much larger context of complete uselessness.
Seminar on the Ratnaguṇa-saṃcayagāthā

One should try to be too big to be used.
Seminar on the Ratnaguṇa-saṃcayagāthā

It's a virtue to be ornamental as well as useful.
Seminar on the Ratnaguṇa-saṃcayagāthā

Success in any field is not without its drawbacks.
Correspondence

I sometimes quite happily do nothing! But when I'm doing nothing, I don't mean 'not doing anything'! Not sort of sitting there in a slightly negative mood feeling that you're not doing anything but maybe you ought to be doing something. If there is something to be done, well, of course, do it! But if there is nothing to be done, well, *positively enjoy* that state of not doing anything!
Seminar on Trevor Ling's The Buddha

To be able to do one thing at a time is the whole art of life.
Aphorism

It is not a sign of spirituality to allow oneself to be exploited. Sooner or later you begin to start resenting it.
Seminar on Geshe Wangyal's The Door of Liberation

You can't help helping others when you are truly helping yourself.... One can help others even simply by providing facilities whereby they can help themselves. The importance of being able to help others in a supportive way is also very great. In a way, even people in the forefront of our activities are only supporting the whole activity of the Sangha. This is developing the faculty of rejoicing in merit.
Seminar on Geshe Wangyal's The Door of Liberation

We should consider not so much how our actions stand in relation to one another as how they stand in relation to Reality.
Aphorism

Surely we are very near to heaven, if not to Nirvāṇa, if we enjoy our work, and if our work is our life!
Correspondence

You learn what it is that you are trying to do in the process of trying to do it.
A Method of Personal Development (talk)

The deeper the internal realization, the broader and stronger should be the outflow of energy. A spirituality that is sterile in respect of 'good works' is highly suspect. Of course, there is such a thing as purely spiritual action on higher levels of consciousness, and this is far more effective than ordinary action, but for most treaders of the spiritual path it is many, many years before this stage is reached, and meanwhile we have to busy ourselves with humble, everyday tasks of service on the mundane level.
Correspondence

Unless your work is your meditation, your meditation is not meditation.
Aphorism

It is wrong to distinguish between what a man is and what he does. There are no mute inglorious Miltons. If he is mute he is not Milton. That one does *not* do something is part of one's character.
Aphorism

A skilful act is one that is an expression of will-to-growth rather than neurotic need, which is emotionally positive, which is an act of the total individual, and which is orientated towards a higher state of being.
Aphorism

The true revolutionary does not play other people's games – including the game of violence.
Aphorism

In the minds of those who prefer evolution to revolution there is always a conflict between loyalty to the past and loyalty to the future.
Aphorism

When the old order dies, two possibilities reveal themselves: one, that the old order shall be restored under a new name; two, that a genuinely new order shall come into existence. At the beginning, it is very difficult to distinguish between the two.
Aphorism

Some say they experience the will as 'free'. But one who experiences it as free and one who experiences it as unfree, as determined, have in fact the same experience. Both have the experience of *acting*. On this experience they superimpose the ideas – not to say the fictions – of freedom and bondage.
Aphorism

If one does not dream, one becomes a monster.
Aphorism

Perfect work comes from the unification of
pure wisdom and pure deeds.
Seminar on Geshe Wangyal's The Door of Liberation

Most of our friends find that they need to alternate between exertion and relaxation, work and meditation. Eventually the two must become one, or rather must interfuse, the one not getting in the way of the other. Meanwhile, we need to pursue both, at different times. Both are necessary to our spiritual development.
Correspondence

POLITICS AND THE STATE

While other people are busy making up our minds for us in small matters, we are at liberty to make up our own in great.
Aphorism

Nowadays there's quite a lot of talk about freedom, and most people, it seems, think that freedom means simply doing what one likes. But the Buddhist conception of freedom is rather different.... In the first place it's ... complete freedom from all subjective emotional and psychological bias, from prejudice, from all psychological conditioning. Secondly [it is] freedom from all wrong views, all ignorance, all false philosophy, all opinions. This complete freedom of heart and mind at the highest possible level is the aim and object of Buddhist life and practice.
The Stages of the Spiritual Path (talk)

The fact that the second precept[10] is worded in terms of not taking the not-given suggests that, ethically speaking, there is no such thing as rights. All rights are based upon power, i.e. on capacity to exert force.
Aphorism

Buddhism, properly and deeply understood, and thoroughly and extensively applied, is *revolutionary*. It is revolutionary, that is to say, within the context of the established order. It is in this realization that our breakthrough consists: in the realization of the fact that Buddhism has to transform every aspect of our lives and be not just something that we theoretically understand, not just a little hobby with which we occupy ourselves once or twice a week, but the transforming agent, the transforming influence – the catalyst, if you like – of our lives.

Breaking Through into Buddhahood (talk)

Awareness is revolutionary.

Aphorism

In what does the extension of the FWBO consist? Not in the publicizing of a personality, not in the popularization of an idea, but in the growth of a new society and a new world.

Aphorism

Negative emotions are much stronger in man than positive emotions. Any individual or organization that wants to influence or control people in large numbers, in the mass, therefore does so by manipulating their negative emotions. The Catholic Church plays upon fear, the Communist Party on hate, Capitalism on greed, totalitarian states on feelings of inadequacy and inferiority. One may also say that in time of peace the state plays more on people's greed, in time of war more on their fear.

Aphorism

A state is governed by a combination of force and inertia – force, on the part of the minority; inertia, on the part of the majority.

Aphorism

Tradition was once innovation; what is now innovation may one day be tradition.

Aphorism

Your power should be the function of your being.

A System of Meditation (talk)

Art is the organization of sensuous impressions into pleasurable formal relations that express the artist's sensibility and communicate to his audience a sense of values that can transform their lives.
The Religion of Art

It has been recognized even in the West (by Schopenhauer) that all great Art contains an element of self-transcendence akin to that which constitutes the quintessence of religion. When this element of self-transcendence is consciously cultivated in poetry, in music, or in painting and sculpture, instead of the element of mere sensuous appeal, art ceases to be a form of sensuous indulgence and becomes a kind of spiritual discipline, and the highest stages of aesthetic contemplation become spiritual experiences.
Crossing the Stream

One cannot be an artist without at the same time participating in the Higher Evolution.
Art and Spiritual Life (talk)

All art is (among other things) expression. But not all expression is art.
Aphorism

Perhaps only in the field of poetry have the English been truly great.
Aphorism

Coleridge, as a thinker, was a sublime abortion. He had greater mental endowment than any Englishman perhaps ever had, and he would have been one of the greatest religious thinkers of all time. But he was severely hampered, crippled even, by his attachment to orthodox Christianity. His inability to reconcile the Trinitarian Christian in him with his own true, original genius was the cause, not the effect, of his famous indolence.
Aphorism

Coleridge was the greatest thinker the English have produced, only his Christianity did not allow him to think.
Aphorism

D. H. Lawrence's writings are not works of art, but the works of an artist. When he does achieve a 'work of art', therefore, it seems both natural and miraculous.
Aphorism

Commentaries on Living, by J. Krishnamurti – the title gives the whole show away completely.
Aphorism

Milton's *Paradise Lost* is an imaginative statement of the whole dilemma of modern man.
Aphorism

Paradise Lost has claim to be considered the most important work in English literature.
Aphorism

If you are looking for evidence of rebirth, listen to Mozart's Symphony No. 1 – composed at the age of eight.
Aphorism

Beethoven at his worst – and perhaps at his most characteristic and popular – is will pretending to be power.
Aphorism

The myth of Perseus and Medusa: he could cut off her head only by looking at it not directly, which would have petrified him, but indirectly, at the reflection in his shield. Similarly we cannot confront reality, especially our own psychic reality, directly: it would kill us. Art, etc. is the medium.
Aphorism

The more creative someone is the less predictable he is.
Seminar on the Ratnaguṇa-saṃcayagāthā

When we experience a work of art we momentarily experience the same state of mind that the artist experienced when he created that work. Thus ... the artist contributes to the Higher Evolution of other people and of the race.
Art and Spiritual Life (talk)

The spiritual aspirant is like Shelley's Skylark: while his understanding soars, his emotions sing. It is in this singing and soaring, in the simultaneous expansion of the understanding and the emotions, that we find the meaning of Buddhism and the value of art, and, in fact, the secret of spiritual life.
The Meaning of Buddhism and the Value of Art

FRIENDSHIP

Very few people know the real meaning of friendship. More often than not, there is too much emphasis on sentiment, and too little on action. *Metta* is something that must be *lived*.
Correspondence

We should have strong feelings of *mettā* towards our own self – don't forget that! – and towards others, strong feelings of spiritual fellowship. And when I say 'strong feelings' I mean *strong* feelings, not something tepid and lukewarm and half-hearted and faint-hearted, but really warm; even, if you like, a little hot! And strong, not feeble.
A System of Meditation (talk)

Paradoxical though it may seem, being less concerned with oneself (in the selfish sense) and loving oneself (in the sense of directing *mettā* to oneself) are not incompatible. It is, in fact, the person who does not truly love himself who is concerned with himself in an egocentric, even a neurotic, sort of way.
Correspondence

The cynic feels less than is justified; the sentimentalist more than is justified.
Seminar on Zhiyi's Dhyāna for Beginners

Only individuals can practise true friendliness.
Seminar on Zhiyi's Dhyāna for Beginners

It is impossible for people to live together without mutual forgiveness.
Aphorism

You must not relate to a neurotic person
on the basis of his neurosis.
Seminar on The Stability of Societies

Have sympathy for those who are going through a difficult phase – nearly everybody goes through it some time or another: if not this year, next year; if not this week, next week. Some of you, I know very well, were going through it last week – not to say the day before yesterday! We know this! Everybody has his turn. Everybody has a difficult phase to go through occasionally. So if you yourself are not going through a difficult phase, and somebody else is, be sympathetic – I mean, wisely sympathetic, not indulgent. Don't use the occasion as an opportunity for asserting your own relative, temporary superiority to that sort of thing.
A System of Meditation (talk)

I think one should distinguish between: (1) neurotic craving for company as a means of escape from your own inner emptiness; (2) a healthy human desire for human contact; (3) a wish, or aspiration, for spiritual fellowship. We should have nothing to do with the first stage, a modest place for the second, and develop the third as much as we can.
Seminar on The Stability of Societies

Speaking in an ordinary sort of way – leaving aside transcendental things – positive emotion is the lifeblood of the Order. If there's no positive emotion in the Order, there is no life in it at all, and no life, therefore, in the Movement. So the development of positive emotion in each one of us and in all of us in association with one another is absolutely crucial.
A System of Meditation (talk)

If you are not happy with yourself, if you are not at ease with yourself, if you don't like yourself – and many people nowadays, unfortunately, don't like themselves – you can't like other people. Your so-called liking of other people mustn't be what Nietzsche called 'your bad love of yourself', by which he meant your disliking of yourself.

A Method of Personal Development (talk)

If a normal, healthy person loses someone who is near and dear to him, this is not neurotic suffering, this is real suffering.... And one can genuinely and wholeheartedly sympathize with that person, and know that he will get over it in due course, because he is healthy. In a healthy person, there might be a slight element of neurosis, but nothing to speak of, as it were. In such a case, you know that time will heal the wound. Neurosis is not healed by time.

Seminar on The Stability of Societies

I'd even go so far as to say that without strong positive emotion, no spiritual progress is possible at all. This means that many people's first duty, to themselves and to others, is simply to be happy: to develop friendliness, compassion, sympathetic joy, equanimity, and devotion.

A Method of Personal Development (talk)

It is hardly possible to have a neutral attitude towards [parents], I think, which means that if one's attitude is not positive it is negative, and if one's attitude to those who are so closely connected with one as one's parents are is negative it is likely to have a deleterious effect on one's whole attitude towards life, including other people.

Correspondence

Getting truly to know another human being is like exploring a new continent – or another world. One plunges into abysses, wanders among lofty mountains, is lost in the depths of mysterious forests, rests in bowers of roses with the brook sparkling beside one and the birds singing in the branches overhead, and stands on lonely shores gazing out over the illimitable expanse of sunlit waters.

Aphorism

The Four Limitless States.[11] *Metta* is the basis of them all. When our friendliness comes into contact with suffering, compassion arises. When our friendliness comes into contact with other people's happiness, sympathetic joy arises. When friendliness, compassion, and sympathetic joy are developed equally towards all, then equanimity arises. Equanimity is not indifference; there's no equanimity without friendliness. We can also add reverence or devotion. This is experienced when the *mettā*, the friendliness, is directed as it were upwards towards the ideal, the spiritual ideal.

A Method of Personal Development (talk)

Having once met, we can never really be separated, even though we may be physically apart, and though no spoken or written word may pass between us for a long time.

Correspondence

It is absolutely wrong to say that by 'isolating' oneself from the opposite sex in single-sex communities one loses the opportunity of contacting the 'other side' of one's nature, which the other sex symbolizes. The precise opposite is the case. In single-sex communities men and women tend to develop, and integrate into their own spiritual life and practice, the 'feminine' and 'masculine' qualities which are normally projected on to the opposite sex and which normally *stay projected.*

Correspondence

As for friendship, it is probably true that you have never – or only very fleetingly – experienced the nature of real friendship, and have never been anyone's friend. *Real friendship is very rare indeed*, and if you haven't experienced it, neither have a lot of other people, including many who would like to think they have. The fact that real friendship is so rare should not make us cynical, of course, but only more determined to develop real friendship, and be a real friend, ourselves, and the first step towards developing a quality is realizing that we don't have it.

Correspondence

More and more I think that communication cannot be hurried, and that friendship needs time and patience for its development.
Correspondence

'What do you do for a living?' I asked. His hand shook so badly, as he lit another cigarette, that he knocked over the whisky bottle at his elbow. 'Oh, I'm a psychiatrist,' he said. 'I help people who have problems.'
Aphorism

Unless you are a healthy, growing individual – unless, as it were, you love yourself – you can't love others.
Seminar on Trevor Ling's The Buddha

Unless one has lived completely alone for a while one hardly knows what life is all about – certainly unless one is able to live alone one is not really able to live with other people.
Correspondence

It is not enough to sympathize with something to such an extent that one agrees with it. If necessary, one must sympathize to such an extent that one disagrees.
Aphorism

Angels are to men as men are to women – because they are more human and, therefore, more divine.
Aphorism

The best relationships ... are surely those which are based on sincerity and straightforwardness, on mutual trust and confidence, which grow stronger and more satisfying with the years, and into which the element of game-playing never enters.
Correspondence

So long as you are aiming at Enlightenment, you will be relating, directly or indirectly, to everybody else who is aiming at Enlightenment, and that is the only form of relating that really matters.
Correspondence

In the FWBO we do not have a puritanical attitude towards sex, but at the same time it must be recognized that it belongs to the lower, not to the higher, evolution of man, and that its place is at the periphery rather than at the centre of our existence. Nowadays people tend to 'over-invest' in the sexual-romantic type of relationship, with the result that their emotional balance is constantly being threatened and peace of mind becomes impossible of achievement. So long as this state of affairs continues, no real spiritual progress is possible.

Correspondence

Positive human relationships have their own value, but a *spiritual* relationship, i.e. a relationship based on the effective pursuit of a common spiritual ideal – in our case the ideal of Enlightenment – is an entirely different matter, and the one must never be mistaken for the other.

Correspondence

So far as I can see, the 'woman question' is a difficulty only to the extent that men are weak, i.e. are emotionally dependent on women. If men are 'strong', i.e. are not emotionally dependent in this manner, then they can provide women with the kind of support that most of them seem to need, as well as get on with the task of their own spiritual development. Paradoxically, a woman can really rely on a man only if he is committed to something that is more important to him than she is. If she is the most important thing in his life, then heaven help her – and him.

Correspondence

Whether in the case of men or women, I am not convinced by the argument that one needs sex in order to keep in touch with one's emotions. It is true that sex does give one, momentarily, a feeling of warmth towards others, but this is really no more than the 'good mood' into which any kind of sense satisfaction is able to put one. It bears no resemblance to the experience of *mettā*, which takes place on quite another level, and it is a great mistake to confuse the two, or to think that the one brings one any nearer to the other.

Correspondence

Between male and female there will always be war, or at least tension. The only solution is for both men and women to try to develop both 'masculine' and 'feminine' qualities within themselves and relate to one another as individuals. This may well involve the separation of the sexes, so that neither is tempted to project onto the other the qualities which it lacks.

Correspondence

To the extent that one is dominated by the sex-instinct one is not an individual.

Aphorism

In the case of a mentally healthy person his or her principal support is always within, so that even when, owing to changed circumstances, external supports in the form of personal relationships are no longer there, he or she is able to go on functioning as before with little or no difficulty.

Correspondence

A married man is like a donkey tethered to a post: within a restricted area he can move about as he wishes. An unmarried man, who carries on a succession of 'affairs', is like a convict carrying a ball and chain: he is free to go wherever he pleases, but he has to carry with him the iron ball, and this is so heavy that every now and then he has to stop and rest, temporarily immobilized.

Aphorism

Any normal person ought to be able to live alone.

Seminar on Geshe Wangyal's The Door of Liberation

You can't really live with other people unless you can live without them. If you're happy on your own, you can be happy with others. If you can't be happy on your own, you can't be happy with others. In that case you're with them, not because you want to be with them, but because you don't want to be on your own. Your being with them isn't a real being with them. It isn't positive. It is only an escape from yourself

Seminar on The Stability of Societies

There is not much point in giving up sex as a sort of discipline when the neurotic craving and dependence is still there, and maybe finding outlets in other ways. You may be still just as neurotically attached to your dog or cat.

Seminar on the Sutta-Nipāta

To a man, celibacy means that he is deprived of sex; to a woman, that she is not wanted.

Aphorism

I sometimes say that there are two kinds of sexuality: neurotic and non-neurotic. The non-neurotic is when there is sexual activity, not through any need for security – for example, through sex, or through the 'relationship' – but just because you are young and healthy. Neurotic sexuality is where there is not only the actual sexual urge, but also an infantile craving for security, contact, warmth, and so on, through sexual relationship or activity. It may be, in the case of some people, that they do experience higher states of consciousness ... yet at the same time a certain amount of sexual activity may go on, but this will certainly be non-neurotic. However,... the great test is how you feel if the relationship breaks up. If your partner, or lover, or whatever, says 'Bye-bye! I've found someone else,' if you can say, 'That's great! See you some time,' and just accept it happily, then you had no neurotic craving along with your sexual relationship and activity. But if you are 'cut up', upset, and disturbed, and can't meditate for months, well, obviously there has been a strong neurotic element. So that is the criterion,... whether one can remain happy whatever happens, whatever storms may come.

Seminar on the Sutta-Nipāta

We are not kept going by abstract ideas, we are kept going by our emotions. It is our positive emotions which keep us going on the spiritual Path - which give us inspiration, enthusiasm and so on - until such time as we can develop Perfect Wisdom and be motivated by that.

A System of Meditation (talk)

A group is united by its lowest common denominator, a spiritual community by its highest common factor.
Aphorism

An orchestra is a spiritual community – at least while it is playing.
Aphorism

The relation between the individual and the 'positive community' should be like that between soloist and orchestra in a concerto.
Aphorism

Lay life may be said to be any situation that prevents one's higher development. This may occur even within the context of a formally monastic situation.
Seminar on Nāgārjuna's Precious Garland

In a spiritual movement you can have a teacher but you can't have a leader.
Seminar on Geshe Wangyal's The Door of Liberation

One should try to avoid close association *only* with those with whom one feels close affinities: one should attempt to go beyond this level – this affords great opportunities to see one's own reactions at work.
Aphorism

Despite their different lifestyles, Order members in particular should be able to relate to one another in a thoroughly positive manner, on the basis of their common commitment to the Three Jewels[12] – a commitment which far transcends all social differences.
Correspondence

You can't really commit yourself to something that you know. To commit yourself to the known is a contradiction in terms. You always commit yourself to the unknown. At least there is always an unknown element in that to which you commit yourself.
Seminar on the Ratnaguṇa-saṃcayagāthā

If you have seen through something, you're no longer involved in it. You withdraw from it. It's just like seeing a mirage in a desert. At first we may be very interested in those palm trees and that apparent oasis, and we may be hastening in that direction. But as soon as we see that it's a *fata morgana*, and isn't really there, then we're no longer really interested. We stop, and don't hasten in that direction any longer.

The Stages of the Spiritual Path (talk)

This is the root, this is the foundation, this is the absolute bedrock of our spiritual life; this is how we really start practising the Path: by Going for Refuge.

The Path of Regular Steps and the Path of Irregular Steps (talk)

Usually it is assumed that ordination means monastic ordination, that is, we think it means becoming a *bhikṣu*,[13] or *gelong*. But this is a great misconception and it is high time we sorted it out. Monastic ordination is only one kind of ordination. The Sanskrit word for ordination is *saṃvara* – literally a 'binding' – and we therefore speak of *upāsakā-saṃvara*, *bhikṣu-saṃvara*, and even *bodhisattva-saṃvara*, as well as the feminine equivalents of the first two – *upāsikā-saṃvara* and *bhikṣuṇī-saṃvara*. In other words we speak of lay ordination, monastic ordination, and even bodhisattva ordination.[14] But all three are ordinations, the same word, *saṃvara*, being applied to each of them.

Upāsaka/upāsikā,[15] *bhikṣu/bhikṣuṇī*, and bodhisattva all equally go for Refuge – the bodhisattva, perhaps, in a deeper sense than the other two. All three commit themselves to the Three Jewels. Any difference between them is simply as regards the number and, in the case of the bodhisattva, the kind of precepts observed. So what the monk and the layman, the *bhikṣu* and the *upāsaka*, have in common is far more important than what they do not have in common. What they have in common is the Three Jewels, or the Three Refuges, and for the Buddhist nothing can be more important than that.[16] Thus the real line of demarcation is not between monks and laymen but, properly speaking, between those who have gone for Refuge and those who have not.

The Path of Regular Steps and the Path of Irregular Steps (talk)

Question: Can a Mitra[17] who joins in with the chanting of the Refuges and Precepts, be said to go for Refuge, even though he is not an *upāsaka*?
Answer: There is no question of an absolute difference, as between light and darkness, between one who has gone for Refuge and one who has not. Intermediate degrees exist. Even if one merely thinks about going for Refuge – even merely hears about it – to an infinitesimal degree one has gone for Refuge.

Questions and answers on Going for Refuge, Tuscany 1986

Honest collision is better than dishonest collusion.

Aphorism

MORALITY

If values do not exist one must create them.
Otherwise one cannot evolve.

Aphorism

Hitler's killing the Jews was an evil action; but it was evil because they were human beings, not because they were Jews.

Aphorism

It is easy to forgive people their vices. What is sometimes more difficult is to forgive them their virtues.

Aphorism

One stone divides the whole stream.

Aphorism

For 'confession' to be possible, there should be no feeling of guilt.

Aphorism

It is the spirit of renunciation that renders
fruitful all one's religious observances.

Seminar on Geshe Wangyal's The Door of Liberation

Better a live sinner than a dead saint.
Aphorism

I am much worse than people think I am, and also much better.
Aphorism

One cannot be what one should be merely by closing one's eyes to what one is.
Aphorism

Sometimes we think we are being patient when we are only being persistent.
Aphorism

To a truly honest man, it is a source of no satisfaction whatever to be credited with successes he has not achieved or virtues he does not possess.
Aphorism

You can only lead a simple life if you remember what life is really for. The purpose of simplicity is not to let the business of living get in the way of the things that are of importance.
Seminar on Geshe Wangyal's The Door of Liberation

Unless one solves the problem of right livelihood (or rather, the problem of wrong livelihood), to some extent at least, spiritual development can be quite difficult.
Correspondence

Hardly anybody is willing to give. Everybody wants to get. We search for someone without 'needs' so that we can obtain from him everything for nothing, as it were. Is this, perhaps, the reason why Gurdjieff insisted that everything must be paid for? Perhaps it is immoral to give something for nothing – one is encouraging greed and selfishness. At the time of Tantric initiation one has to make a cash payment to the guru. How much one is prepared to give shows how much – or how little – one values the initiation.
Aphorism

Giving is the natural, unforced interchange of one's energy with that of others. In this sense real giving is receiving.
Seminar on Nāgārjuna's Precious Garland

We should receive rather than take, give rather than impose, share rather than divide.
Aphorism

We often think that people are behaving most characteristically when they are behaving most badly. We often think the same thing about ourselves.
Aphorism

One should not waste time helping the weak. Nowadays it is the strong who need help.
Aphorism

There is no feeling of joy without a feeling of strength. The weak, therefore, cannot be joyful.
Aphorism

If we want a definition of faith we may say that it is the response, even the emotional response, of what is ultimate in us to what is ultimate in the universe.
The Stages of the Spiritual Path (talk)

Faith is one's emotional response to something higher than oneself. And because it is higher one cannot possibly understand it.
Seminar on Geshe Wangyal's The Door of Liberation

Genuine devotion dissolves whatever is not genuine in the object of devotion. You can't be taken in, can't be deceived, if you enter into a situation with genuine feelings, with true integrity.
Seminar on Geshe Wangyal's The Door of Liberation

Faith is innate, doubt acquired.
Aphorism

According to the *Abhidharma*, faith (*śraddhā*) is present in all skilful mental states. Faith consists in being aware of, and responsive to, that which is higher. All skilful mental states are, therefore, essentially progressive. The terrifying corollary of this last fact is, of course, that all unskilful mental states have an inherent tendency to deteriorate, i.e. to become still more unskilful. There is never a state of perfect equilibrium between the skilful and the unskilful. One either ascends or descends in the scale of consciousness. Once one has passed the 'point of no return', however, there is only the possibility of ascent.[18]
Aphorism

Monks should appear to come from another world, not just another country.
Aphorism

There are four kinds of disciples: disciples who are like patients, disciples who are like friends, disciples who are like sons, and disciples who are like lovers.
Aphorism

There is no question of our making sacred cows of anything, but rather of trying to develop a spirit of reverence.... One might go so far as to say that it is better to have sacred cows, even in the literal sense, than to hold nothing sacred.
Correspondence

Gurus are the middlemen of religion.
Aphorism

In all traditional civilizations the relation between master and disciple was one of the basic facts of life, and to be without a teacher was synonymous with being without education or culture of any kind.
A Survey of Buddhism

The good is very often the enemy of the best.
Seminar on The Stability of Societies

The early stages of the career of a spiritual aspirant are a period of unceasing struggle between the lower and higher impulses of his nature. On the outcome of this struggle depends the success or failure of his vocation. If he is able to resist the solicitations of the objects of perception and turn his senses as it were inside out, like the five fingers of a glove, thus reversing their direction, they will merge into a single inner sense, and with this subtle inner sense he will be able to perceive spiritual realities.

The Path of the Inner Life

The over-developed intellect and the under-developed emotions – it's really a pathetic sort of combination; but most people have this combination in some degree, don't they? In your conscious mind you're a great big man, but unconsciously you're just a little child – possibly, in some cases, crying for mother – or even a baby just howling for the breast.

Seminar on Trevor Ling's The Buddha

I was reading a book the other day that had a chapter called 'The Pathology of Thinking', and it said – and this is one of the things that I've been saying lately – that excessive thinking is pathological.

Seminar on Trevor Ling's The Buddha

One of the ways in which one can counterbalance excessive thinking is through contact with Nature and the elements. One can develop one's sense consciousness (for want of a better term) by contact with earth, fire, water, air – it's as simple as that. This will take a lot of the tension and one-sidedness out of one's mental development, and out of one's will.

Seminar on Trevor Ling's The Buddha

It is very important to develop a very positive emotional counterpart to one's intellectual understanding, and this is where the development of *maitrī, karuṇā, muditā, upekṣā* – to say nothing of faith and devotion – comes in.

Seminar on Trevor Ling's The Buddha

If your emotions are here and your reason as it were there, then it's a question of being guided either by your reason or by your emotions – which means you're not an integrated person. The integrated person acts as a total person. There is emotionality in what he does, and also reason – meaning a sort of aware recognition of certain objective facts and circumstances and possibilities.

Seminar on the Ratnaguṇa-saṃcayagāthā

When we are totally integrated, and our reason is our emotion and our emotion our reason, it's quite difficult for us to say, sometimes, whether we do things on account of certain reasons or just because we feel like doing them. We have become as it were one: one whole.

Seminar on the Ratnaguṇa-saṃcayagāthā

Inasmuch as our emergence as individuals, or at least as the beginnings of individuals, has been via the development of independent thinking, we have above all else to be on the lookout that our one-sided thinking doesn't develop too disproportionately, and that we give a great deal of attention to the development of all the other sides of ourselves, especially the emotional: that we reinforce that as much as possible and lift our emotions to a correspondingly high level. Otherwise there will be no development, no emergence of true individuality. We shall all have dragons' heads and snakes' bodies.[19]

Seminar on Trevor Ling's The Buddha

It seems to me that the strength of the Tantric tradition, the Vajrayāna tradition, Tibetan Buddhism generally, is the presence in it of symbols.[20] But it seems that in Japanese Buddhism, at least as presented by Suzuki and others, you've got philosophy on the one hand and emotion on the other, and what should be symbols, traditionally, have become converted simply into objects of emotion. So there's no unification taking place.

Seminar on D. T. Suzuki's Outlines of Mahāyāna Buddhism

Opposites are not to be eliminated, but
reconciled within a higher unity.

Aphorism

When you start thinking, you start thinking of what is possible. But the mere fact that it is possible does not mean that it is desirable. When you develop, or over-develop, the thinking faculty, you tend to think that because you can *think* of doing something, that is sufficient reason for doing it. In this way, imbalance develops. A very good example of this in modern times is the space programme. It's as though, if you can think of doing something, you should do it. But the capacity for abstract thinking runs far ahead of the development, or even the needs, of the organism as a whole.

Seminar on Trevor Ling's The Buddha

Seeing is active, hearing is passive. When one visualizes the form of a Buddha or bodhisattva, and hears the sound of their mantra, one is being simultaneously active and passive, 'masculine' and 'feminine'.

Aphorism

THE INDIVIDUAL

To begin with, when we come – I might even say, staggering – along to our first meditation class, maybe from the office, from home, or wheresoever, we don't have any real individuality. We are usually just a bundle of conflicting desires and selves, both conscious and unconscious, loosely tied together with the thread of a name and address! When we practise Mindfulness of Breathing, it helps bring them together; it at least tightens the string a little bit so that they aren't so loose in the middle; it makes of these different cravings and selves more of a definite, recognizable, identifiable bundle.

A System of Meditation (talk)

The teaching of the Buddha was concerned with the development of the individual. Admittedly that development had, through ethics, a social dimension, but the Buddha was not concerned with 'something much wider, the whole realm of sentient Being' in opposition, as it were, to the individual. He was not concerned with the development of the group as such, or the well-being of the group as such: he was concerned with the development of individuals *as* individuals.

Seminar on Trevor Ling's The Buddha

In the individual, when you force your organism to go along in accordance with something that you've merely thought, *because* you've thought it, then there's great strain on the organism. And this is the nature of mind; this is the nature of rational thinking. So inasmuch as it is through rational thinking that the individual begins to be emancipated from the group, the person who is emancipated from the group is, to begin with, an *unbalanced* person, a person whose thinking is in excess of his emotional development and so on. That is individualism. To become an individual, what you have to do is to restrain your one-sided intellectual development and cultivate your emotional side, and thus develop as an individual in a more integrated way – on a higher level, on a more conscious level – than the primitive member of the tribe. Once you've achieved that more all-round development which is covered in Buddhist teaching by the teaching of the five spiritual faculties – then you can go on to develop your true individuality.

Seminar on Trevor Ling's The Buddha

You can't commit yourself unless there is just one individuality to commit itself.

A System of Meditation (talk)

Because one is in a minority of one, it does not necessarily follow that one is more of an individual.

Aphorism

When we speak of the emergence of the individual from the group, we are not to think of an all-round-developed individual emerging from the group. It doesn't seem to happen that way. What happens is that, usually, emancipation from the group occurs via the intellect, via the development of independent thinking, and that, therefore, what emerges is an unbalanced person, a one-sidedly developed person, and that one-sidedly developed person we still have very much with us. Therefore one of the most pressing tasks, within the context of individual development, is to bring the emotions up into harmony with the intellect, and have a more all-round development.

Seminar on Trevor Ling's The Buddha

Every true individual is a whole species in himself.
Aphorism

Individuals are incommensurable.
Aphorism

It is usually your thinking faculty which is the means of your emancipation from the group, but, because it is on account of the over-development of the thinking faculty that you've emancipated yourself from the group, when you are emancipated, or at least to some extent emancipated, you find yourself a one-sidedly developed person. And very often you find yourself in a situation of conflict, because mentally you have emancipated yourself from the group, but emotionally, to a great extent, you still belong to it! So, having prised yourself free from the group and the group consciousness, to some extent, by means of your developed intelligence, you haven't got to continue developing just your intelligence more and more – you've almost got to stop developing your intelligence – that has developed sufficiently for the time being – and develop the rest of you and achieve a sort of *emotional* independence of the tribe: a development of emotion as a true individual.
Seminar on Trevor Ling's The Buddha

Nowadays we've got quite a lot of individualists: people who are mentally emancipated from the group, though still belonging to it emotionally; people who are capable of a great deal of mental activity, and who sometimes try to gear the whole of their being to the purely one-sided ideals of that over-developed intellect. But it would seem that this is a necessary stage of development. For most people development in any other way is difficult – they start thinking independently, usually, before they become independent in any other way.
Question: You say that it's a necessary intermediate step. Can't you go straight to work on your emotions without going through this intellectual phase?
Answer: It would seem not. I don't say that you can't. I mean, if you've got favourable conditions, yes, I think you could; but in the modern world those favourable conditions hardly ever exist.
Seminar on Trevor Ling's The Buddha

One can legislate for the group, but not for the individual.
Aphorism

One can generalize about people only to the extent that they are not individuals.
Aphorism

Jewels are produced only by the collision of immense forces.
Aphorism

Truth is more likely to be with the individual than with the group.
The Individual, the Group, and the Spiritual Community (talk)

The group is always wrong.
The Individual, the Group, and the Spiritual Community (talk)

TEACHING AND STUDY

What is needed so far as [real help in the actual spiritual development of the individual] is concerned is not books, but the living context of a spiritual fellowship and concrete spiritual teachings appropriate to one's actual requirements. In other words, there is a great deal that we do not need to know, that we can safely ignore. Then why is it that we go on reading? Only too often, I suspect, it is because reading, including the reading of religious literature, has become a form of mental distraction. However, if even the reading of good religious books does not help us much, what is one to say of the reading of bad books – books that are the product of ill-digested information, muddled thinking, unconscious rationalization, and downright spiritual delusion and confusion? And such books are in the majority.
Correspondence

There is a great deal to be said for a thorough knowledge of a small number of works, rather than a superficial knowledge of many.
Seminar on Geshe Wangyal's The Door of Liberation

The Dharma is the Buddha's Enlightenment objectified, and therefore falsified.

Aphorism

Many years ago, I constantly asked myself: 'How does this teaching relate to one's actual spiritual experience, spiritual life, and spiritual development? Why did the Buddha say this? Why was the Buddha concerned with this? Where does it connect up with spiritual life?' And I found that very, very few scholars ever thought in those terms. In many cases it didn't even seem to occur to them to do so – even to Buddhists themselves, very often – as though it was just a sort of game, you know, that had no relevance to life and no bearing on the spiritual life or on spiritual development as an individual.

Seminar on Trevor Ling's The Buddha

It is fashionable among some modern 'intellectuals' to run down the intellect. In this way they seek to give the impression that they have transcended its limitations. However, their understanding of the limitations of the intellect remains – purely intellectual.

Seminar on Trevor Ling's The Buddha

One of the biggest sources of confusion and misunderstanding here in the West, so far as Buddhism is concerned, is that we have talked in terms of 'monks', 'monasteries', etc., which gives a totally wrong impression of the Buddhist spiritual life. I really do wish we could get rid of all these terms once and for all – including the word 'religion'.

Correspondence

Only from the intellectual or dogmatic scientific point of view is it possible to regard Buddhism as being merely one among hundreds of other possible subjects of scholarly research and doctoral dissertation. To one who studies it with some attempt at approximation to the fully traditional method … it can appear as nothing less than what it actually is, the dominating and controlling influence of the whole of life.

Seminar on Trevor Ling's The Buddha

To people immersed in worldly states of mind, the Dharma will inevitably appear negative because it opposes what they have based their lives on.[21]

Seminar on Geshe Wangyal's The Door of Liberation

The quest for holiness, which the study of the Dharma subserves, is a quest for spiritual wholeness, for complete integration of the 'personality' not with any subjective principle merely, but with Reality.

Seminar on Trevor Ling's The Buddha

The more committed should *help* the less committed rather than feel impatient with them; the less committed should *revere* the more committed and be grateful to them, rather than feel inferior and resentful.

Correspondence

One is able to communicate the Dharma, through any medium, only to the extent that one has realized it in one's own heart and mind, one's own life. Realization of the Dharma must therefore logically – and spiritually – precede the expression and communication of the Dharma. This is not to say that only a fully Enlightened being is able to teach, but simply that before communicating one must have something to communicate, even though one discovers what that is only in the process of communication.

Correspondence

People should be encouraged to rely on themselves to the extent that they are really *able* to rely on themselves. But it is no use expecting the baby to walk on his own two feet before his limbs are strong enough to support his body. It is the same with psychological and spiritual babies as with physical ones. Mother must not get impatient. Help and encourage them to grow up, by all means, but don't try to thrust independence on people who are not ready for it and who need, in fact, a further period of 'dependence' (perhaps 'apprenticeship' would be a better word) before being in a position to set up on their own.

Correspondence

We are usually able to bear much more than we – and others – think we can.

Correspondence

If we could only *realize* a hundredth part of what we *understand* we should all become Buddhas on the spot.

Correspondence

One can only speak the truth to one person. The larger the number of people to whom you are speaking, the more will what you say become an approximation to the truth.

Seminar on Geshe Wangyal's The Door of Liberation

An academic is not an intellectual. An intellectual has a strong creative element in his thought.

Seminar on Geshe Wangyal's The Door of Liberation

Theology is to mysticism as literary criticism is to poetry.

Aphorism

Philosophy is the rational construction of reality.

Aphorism

Genuine emotional involvement in the spiritual life, as distinct from the initial sensation of excitement and discovery, usually requires much more time for its development than intellectual involvement.

Correspondence

The Higher Evolution consists in the conscious acceptance of the action of the Absolute upon oneself and others.

Aphorism

The teachings contained in the *Dhammapada* are literal truth, and deserve to be engraved on our hearts in letters of gold – or fire.[22]

Aphorism

Commentary must itself be creation, or it is not even commentary.

Aphorism

The truth does not scorch you nearly as fiercely as the suffering you bring upon yourself when you ignore the truth.
Aphorism

The Buddha taught and influenced people by what he was, far more than by what he said.
Aphorism

MEDITATION

Meditation is the uninterrupted production of skilful mental states.
Seminar on Geshe Wangyal's The Door of Liberation

When we are completely happy, and all our emotional energies are unified, then we are concentrated, in the true sense. Hence we may say that a concentrated person is a happy person, a happy person is a concentrated person, and the happier we are, the longer we shall be able to stay concentrated. We find it difficult to stay concentrated for very long because we are not happy with our present state. If we were really and truly happy we wouldn't need to do anything else: we would just stay still enjoying that happiness. But we are not happy, we are dissatisfied, and so we get restless, and go searching for this, searching for that – for some distraction, some diversion – and in this way there is no concentration.
The Stages of the Spiritual Path (talk)

The four superconscious states, the four so-called lower *dhyānas*, are within the reach of everybody who meditates systematically and regularly.
A System of Meditation (talk)

In the period of sleep, one's mindfulness is impeded. Meditation helps one to maintain the creativity of the dream state into waking life, blending the richness of the dream state with the clarity of the waking state.
Seminar on Geshe Wangyal's The Door of Liberation

Sloth is the weight of one's actual existence
resisting further evolving.
Seminar on Zhiyi's Dhyāna for Beginners

In a sleep you come to the class, in a sleep you listen to the lecture, in a sleep even you meditate.... You may not actually be dead but all these activities are carried on in a sleep.
Meditation: the Expanding Consciousness (talk)

Concentration ... is a union, or a marriage if you like, of the forces of the depths with the forces of the heights.
Meditation: the Expanding Consciousness (talk)

Heaven, the ultimate goal of so many faiths, since it is a mode of contingent and hence of transitory existence, is accounted no more than a pleasant interlude in a pilgrimage fundamentally of more serious import.
The Three Jewels

The object of meditation is to transform oneself, not to have good meditations.
Aphorism

It would appear that, for some people at least, the experience of causeless, nameless fear, often prolonged, and of great intensity, is a necessary part of the process of spiritual self-development. But the function of experience, however dreadful, is positive. Indeed one might say, the more dreadful, the more positive.
Correspondence

When one mentions 'meditation without any steps at all' people usually become rather interested. They are not at all interested in 'meditation by regular steps', which sounds rather dull and prosaic. 'Meditation by irregular steps' appeals to them quite a bit. But what *really* captivates and fascinates them is this idea of 'meditation without any steps at all'... Unfortunately, people are usually attracted to this kind of meditation for entirely the wrong reasons.
The Path of Regular Steps and the Path of Irregular Steps (talk)

Śūnyatā could well be rendered 'death' because it is the death of everything conditioned. It is only when the conditioned individuality dies that the unconditioned individuality ... begins to emerge.[23]

A System of Meditation (talk)

In meditation, as we go deeper and deeper, we often experience a great fear. Sometimes people shy away from this fear, but it is good to allow oneself to experience it. That fear occurs when we feel what may be called 'the touch of *śūnyatā*', the touch of reality, on the conditioned self. The touch of *śūnyatā* feels like death. In fact, for the conditioned self it *is* death,. So the conditioned self feels – *we* feel – afraid.

A System of Meditation (talk)

To say that matter is evil is to say that it is not material.

Aphorism

For Buddhism, no less than for modern physics and psychology, all the apparently stable and solid material and mental objects in the universe are in reality temporary condensations of energy. Hence despite what some have assumed the use of such words as 'states' and 'elements' to mean, seeing conditioned things as impermanent does not consist in conceiving them as chopped up into bits (which would raise the artificial problem of how the bits were to be joined together again), but rather in seeing them as so many phases of one or the other of two pure, absolutely continuous, interdependent streams of energy which can be locked up in the atom, in the one case, and trapped in the individual mind, in the other.

The Three Jewels

Śamatha develops and refines our conditioned individuality; *vipaśyanā* breaks down that individuality, or rather it enables us to see right through it.[24]

A System of Meditation (talk)

A *dhyāna* is not a 'state' in which 'we' are, but a way in which we reorganize our being.

Aphorism

When we see that the Path of the Inner Life, the true esoteric path, the way of emptiness and the way of compassion, and the middle way, are all aspects of the One Way, the Way taught by the Buddha, we begin to glimpse the profound truth of the saying that 'The Path is one for all, the means to reach the goal must vary with the Pilgrims.'[25]

The Path of the Inner Life

We swivel round and round in time on the pivot of eternity.

Aphorism

True, time is short; but that is no reason for being in a hurry.

Aphorism

Time is part of our structure of consciousness.

Seminar on Geshe Wangyal's The Door of Liberation

Time, like space, is curved. To go forwards in time
is, therefore, to go backwards, and vice versa.

Aphorism

The true Esoteric Path, the true Secret teaching, the true Doctrine of the Heart, the true Master, is not to be found in any book, or, indeed, anywhere at all in the outside world, but in the heart-depths of the spiritual experience of the individual devotee.

The Path of the Inner Life

There is no infallible criterion by means of which the unenlightened can recognize the Enlightened.

Aphorism

Any practice which heightens one's ego-sense, howsoever holy in popular estimation it may be, is unspiritual, and any practice which attenuates it, howsoever mean and despicable outwardly it may seem, is spiritual in the truest and best sense of the term.

Crossing the Stream

Death is ... a state of enforced meditation.

A System of Meditation (talk)

The figure of a Buddha or Bodhisattva, sublime and glorious though it may be, is, in fact, you: is the new you – you as you will be if only you allow yourself to die.

A System of Meditation (talk)

To state the matter axiomatically, we may say that a higher stage of the Path cannot be developed in its fullness, or even to a moderate extent, before a lower stage of the Path has been developed in its fullness. This is the basic principle.

The Path of Regular Steps and the Path of Irregular Steps (talk)

WISDOM AND COMPASSION

The activity of emptiness is compassion.

Crossing the Stream

We purify ourselves truly by waking up to the fact that we have never become impure.

Aphorism

Since the Path of the Inner Life consists essentially in a series of experiences, and since all experiences are by their very nature ineffable, it is also an Esoteric as opposed to an Exoteric Path. Nothing in the religious life is truly esoteric save spiritual experience. The most private ritual, the abstrusest philosophical doctrine, the most jealously guarded scripture, the most secret society or organization, are all exoteric. They belong to the domain of 'head-learning' rather than to the domain of 'soul-wisdom', and, as *The Voice of the Silence* emphatically admonishes us, it is above all things necessary to learn to separate the one from the other, to learn to discriminate between 'The Doctrine of the Eye' and 'The Doctrine of the Heart'.

The Path of the Inner Life

A tiny speck of dust in the eye can prevent one from seeing. A single misunderstanding can obstruct one's vision of the Truth.

Aphorism

The individual self is a centre from which all lines of discrimination radiate in all directions. It is the innermost citadel of separateness. Only when this centre expands to infinity, only when the walls of this citadel are razed to the ground, is the consummation of the spiritual life achieved.

Crossing the Stream

Every single thing in the universe, however mean or insignificant it may outwardly seem, bears deep within itself ... the trace of absolute purity and perfection. This is the famous Jewel which the great Sanskrit mantra *oṃ maṇi padme hūṃ*, so beloved of the people of Tibet, informs us lies hidden in what is, microcosmically speaking, the heart-lotus of every being, and what is, macrocosmically speaking, the world-lotus of mundane existence itself.

Thus it is possible to analyse every single object in the universe into an Absolute, nirvāṇic, or perfect aspect, and a relative, saṃsāric, and imperfect aspect. In Tantric Buddhism the former is often spoken of as the *vajra* or diamond aspect of existence. Everything possesses a diamond or noumenal aspect corresponding to its material or phenomenal aspect. Corresponding to the simple earthly flower springing up from the soil there is a transcendental diamond flower, which is that aspect of the flower in which it is perfumed by, or in which it reflects and is reflected by, the reality of suchness.[26] Similarly, as the transcendental aspect of our fickle and unsteady mundane mind there exists the mind which is 'pure and hard as flaming diamond', the *vajracitta* – human personality in its highest possible aspect of freeness, mutuality, and interpenetratingness with regard to all other things in the universe. That highest and most real aspect of existence in which everything interpenetrates every other thing, and wherein everything reflects, and is in turn reflected by, every other phenomenon (offering no obstruction to each other whatsoever, like the mutual interpenetration of innumerable beams of coloured light) is called the *Dharmadhātu*, the realm of Truth, or the *Vajradhātu*, the Diamond World. The bodhisattva aspires to live in this world, the world of realities, instead of in that presented by the ordinary mundane consciousness, the world of illusions.

Crossing the Stream

You are pure from the beginning, pure from the beginningless beginning, pure by nature, pure essentially; in the depths of your being you are pure of all conditionality, or rather you are pure of the very distinction between conditioned and Unconditioned.

A System of Meditation

The culmination of wisdom is freedom from all views. You have nothing to say. When all the answers are in your being, you have no need to keep them in your head.

Seminar on Geshe Wangyal's The Door of Liberation

We have the potentiality; if we make the effort we can reach Enlightenment. But we are not destined in the sense that we *must* gain Enlightenment, whether we like it or not, as it were! No. The *saṃsāra* can go on and on indefinitely.[27] You can remain in it indefinitely. You can remain indefinitely unenlightened and go on, you know, to eternity, as it were. You are not 'destined' for Enlightenment! *You don't have to have Enlightenment if you don't want it!*

Seminar on D. T. Suzuki's Outlines of Mahāyāna Buddhism

No accumulation of karma can get you to Nirvāṇa.

Seminar on D. T. Suzuki's Outlines of Mahāyāna Buddhism

According to Buddhism a man is not, strictly speaking, reborn as an animal, neither is he reborn as a man, nor as a god. What is 'reborn', in the sense of becoming temporarily linked to an appropriate form, is the continuously changing stream of psychical energy.

The Three Jewels

Energy is primary, form secondary. It is not that man wills, but rather that will 'mans'.

The Three Jewels

To dedicate oneself to the salvation of others with the conviction that there in reality exist others who need saving is as much a source of bondage as to devote oneself to the task of one's own liberation under the impression that one has a real self to be liberated.

The Three Jewels

One does not feel compassion for beings because they suffer. One simply feels compassion.
Aphorism

Purity is power.
Aphorism

The one root-illusion which prevents us from seeing things as they really are, and which it is the primary business of spiritual practice to remove, is the belief in ourselves as separate, perduring individual selves or ego-entities.
The Path of the Inner Life

I have no before or after, neither beginning nor end.
Aphorism

Growth in holiness is essentially growth in emptiness.
Crossing the Stream

He who conceives the spiritual life as a means of attaining eternal bliss has not understood. The whole conception of attainment is fundamentally wrong. One has simply to break down the barriers of his separative individuality and allow himself to be penetrated by everything that exists. Then he will himself penetrate everything. This mutual penetration is liberation, is happiness.
Crossing the Stream

Peace is a fire.
Aphorism

A STREAM OF STARS

BUDDHISM IN MINIATURE

A Buddhist does not 'represent' Buddhism. If you represent Buddhism, you are not a Buddhist. A Buddhist *is* Buddhism – in miniature.
Aphorism

If you treat non-violence as the highest principle you can't go far wrong; so much follows from that. But, of course, non-violence isn't just a question of abstaining from killing and from eating meat. To follow the principle of non-violence is to be brought into the very heart of the spiritual life.
Questions and Answers: Tuscany 1981

Ever since the dawn of history ... two great principles have been at work in the world: the principle of violence and the principle of non-violence or, as we may also call it, the principle of love.... The principle of violence is a principle of darkness, the principle of non-violence a principle of light. Whereas to live in accordance with the principle of violence is to be either an animal or a devil or a combination of the two, to live in accordance with the principle of non-violence is to be a human being, in the full sense of the term, or even an angel.
Buddhism, World Peace, and Nuclear War

More and more I see the spiritual life in terms of learning to switch from the power mode to the love mode. If one can do that, everything else will follow.

Correspondence

To be a Buddhist in name only is worse than useless. A real Buddhist should change a little every day – should grow a little every day.

Correspondence

Religion cannot be taught; it can only be caught. You have to catch the spirit of religion, and you do that through the influence of other people.

Buddhism and Education (talk)

Let us do away with the divisions between monastic and lay Buddhists, between men and women Buddhists, and between the followers of different sects and schools of Buddhism. Let us have an integrated Buddhism and an integrated Buddhist community. Let us base ourselves firmly and unmistakably upon our common Going for Refuge to the Buddha, the Dharma, and the Sangha.

Buddhism and the West

Women should stop looking over their shoulders at men and trying to prove themselves equal to men. This does not mean that the sexes are unequal. It means that the concepts of equality and inequality are inappropriate. Women should simply do what is best for their own development as individuals without bothering about whether or not men are doing the same things or about where it leaves them in relation to men.

Correspondence

To me it seems more obvious than ever that if we are to generate enough enthusiasm and inspiration to enable us to break through the bonds of our own individualism, as well as through the strongly anti-spiritual tendencies of modern life itself, we need the bodhisattva ideal. Only the bodhisattva ideal can carry us beyond ourselves and the world – and back again into them on a totally different basis.

Correspondence

If our deeper and more powerful emotions are still tied up with things of a worldly nature, our involvement with the Dharma can only be superficial, however sincere we may be. If we are to be truly Buddhist, our involvement with the Dharma must be truly passionate.
Correspondence

The whole criticism of religion as escapism is ridiculous. If you are suffering why shouldn't you get out? What's wrong with escaping? It's the sensible thing to do.
Seminar on the Udāna

The more deeply we get into the spiritual life the more our sense of reality changes. What seemed very real before now seems relatively unreal, and vice versa. Things seem more or less real according to the degree of our emotional investment in them. In any case, experiences – strange or otherwise – come and go, and we should not allow ourselves to become attached to them or even to take much interest in them. The main thing is to go on deepening our Going for Refuge in whatever way we can.
Correspondence

Four basic propositions: (1) Man can change. (2) He can change himself. (3) He can help others to change. (4) Together they can change the world.
Aphorism

It is crucial to keep the transcendental element in Buddhism in mind. If you lose sight of that, you lose sight of Buddhism itself – and run the risk of getting bogged down in psychology.
Seminar on the Itivuttaka

Some people like Zen (so they say) because it is iconoclastic. They become quite upset, however, should anyone venture to be iconoclastic about Zen.
Aphorism

The more 'scholarly' a Buddhist is, the more firmly he needs to base himself on Going for Refuge, ethics, and meditation. Otherwise his influence may be disastrous.

Aphorism

Buddhists are tolerant in the sense that they are able to differ profoundly from the followers of other religions on certain issues without regarding those followers with feelings of hostility, and without behaving violently toward them. Buddhist tolerance is not based on a belief in the oneness of all religions.

Correspondence

In order to reconcile Buddhism and Christianity you've got to know Buddhism and to know Christianity. You've got to be honest. You've got to be true to Buddhism and true to Christianity and reconcile the real Christianity with the real Buddhism. If you have an imaginary version of Christianity and an imaginary version of Buddhism, it might be easy to reconcile the two, but have you really reconciled Buddhism and Christianity? To do that you must know them really well; know them in depth; know them thoroughly. Only then might it be possible to suggest a framework vast enough to include them both – and that framework would have to be very vast indeed.

Seminar on the Mahāparinibbāna Sutta

The only real advantage that Christianity has over Buddhism is that it is more poetic.

Aphorism

A spiritually barren period is not unusual in the life of even the most committed Buddhist. What is important is that we realize it is only a phase and wait for it to pass, and, in the meantime, do nothing that we may later on regret.

Correspondence

We can perhaps summarize the position of traditional ethics today by saying that it consists in not doing what we want to do, and doing what we do not want to do, because – for reasons we do not understand – we have been told to by someone in whose existence we no longer believe.

The Buddha's Noble Eightfold Path

Rest on your laurels and they will wither.

Aphorism

Strictly speaking there is no such thing as moral or spiritual stagnation. Contrary to what people usually think, stagnation is not a state in which, while things do not get any better, they at least do not get any worse. It is a state in which things get worse without our doing anything to make them worse.

Aphorism

Sometimes it is difficult to distinguish a
temptation from an opportunity.

Aphorism

It's much easier to deal with external pressures when there is no conflict within oneself. If you are relatively integrated, even when the whole of you is under pressure you have a better chance of resisting temptation. But if you've got a traitor within that is going to cooperate with the enemy without, you're in a much more difficult position.

Seminar on the Sūtra of Golden Light

It is a very dangerous thing to regard oneself as the instrument by which God, karma, or whatever, punishes other people. It could be called the Genghis Khan complex.

Aphorism

It is not that one is dishonest, but that one is only honest up to a point.

Aphorism

Never promise anything which it is not in your power to perform. That is, never promise anything for the performance of which you have to rely on other people.
Aphorism

We may have to leave our roots behind, in a sense, but it is a question of growing beyond them, not severing them abruptly by an act of will. I once wrote a poem entitled 'The Root Speaks'. Sometimes we have to listen to that Root.
Correspondence

Not everything that is legal is moral, and not everything that is illegal is immoral.
Aphorism

Faith is the capacity for being emotionally moved – at least for the time being – by something that transcends the senses and even the rational mind.
Seminar on The Way to Wisdom

If you won't get under the shower you can't complain if it isn't wetting you.
Aphorism

In a sense, to live from one day to the next requires a leap of faith, so it is hardly surprising that a step as momentous as committing oneself to the Three Jewels should require such a leap.
Correspondence

The hindrance of doubt isn't a sort of suspension of belief until such time as you have sufficient grounds to be able to make up your mind. Doubt is almost deliberately refusing to make up your mind – allowing yourself to be in a vacillating mental state, even, so that you will not have to commit yourself one way or the other.
Seminar on Nāgārjuna's Precious Garland

There is no doubt that spiritual development is sometimes a slow and painful process. It is not difficult to have 'insights' of a general kind, but it is very difficult to apply them to oneself.

Correspondence

It is certainly possible to think of spiritual growth in terms of removing imperfections and becoming more pure, and many people find this approach helpful. But that does not justify dismissing the complementary method – trying to develop – as 'trying to make oneself into something else'. Both models have their limitations, and neither should be understood too literally.

Correspondence

Humility is the pride of the weak.

Aphorism

What does 'accept' mean? I wanted to be quite sure of this, so I consulted my old friend Dr Johnson, on whom I find I can rely. In his dictionary he defines the verb 'to accept' as 'to receive with approbation, with approval'. But surely there is much in ourselves of which we don't approve, much of which perhaps we strongly disapprove. We shouldn't want to hang on to that personal characteristic, whatever it is. We should want to reject it. So we should modify the popular statement about accepting ourselves and say, 'Let us accept what is skilful in ourselves, but let us reject what is unskilful.'

Fifteen Points for Old – and New – Order Members (talk)

Humiliation may even be counted among the ways in which Perfect Vision might arise – being cut down to size by reality itself – so it can be a very positive experience indeed. If you can take it as such, you find you can survive it. Life goes on. You pick yourself up, dust yourself down, and start all over again.

Wisdom Beyond Words

One of the most important aspects of the spiritual life is that one should be aware of the consequences of one's own actions.

Seminar on the Sūtra of Golden Light

We should not underestimate the role of the will in spiritual life. It is not enough to have feeling for the Buddha. We have to will to be like the Buddha. One might even say there is no spiritual life without will. Indeed, spiritual life could be defined as the constant willing of the good in all circumstances.

Talk at the opening of the Manchester Buddhist Centre

Many people experience themselves in a purely passive way, feeling that they are victims of circumstances. Sometimes the important thing is to do something: to experience your own energy, experience yourself in action. Otherwise you don't really feel alive. No real spiritual progress is possible until you start experiencing yourself as acting rather than acted upon.

Seminar on The Jewel Ornament of Liberation

By itself, experiencing suffering doesn't teach one anything. If there has been no insight into the truth of suffering, one can very quickly forget, even if one has suffered a great deal. And, of course, insight into the truth of suffering can be gained even when one is happy.

Seminar on The Jewel Ornament of Liberation

We may not be able to shut out all the input all the time, but we can be much more selective about what we choose to let in.... Be more selective, and try to make sure that the influences that are impinging on you are positive.

Fifteen Points for Old – and New – Order Members (talk)

True confession is very important in the spiritual life, and very rare. In true confession there is no feeling of irrational guilt and no fear of rejection or any other form of punishment. On the contrary, one has complete trust in the person to whom one is making the confession, which means that one does not see him or her as an authority figure or as wielding any sort of 'power'. It is very difficult for a Westerner, and an ex-Christian, not to see the Buddha as God, i.e. as the embodiment of the power mode rather than of the love mode, and for this reason it is very difficult for a Western Buddhist to practise true confession and engage in true worship.

Seminar on The Sūtra of Golden Light

Compromise is the enemy of the spiritual life,
besides being psychologically undermining.
Correspondence

THE COURAGE OF ONE'S POSITIVE EMOTIONS

Wherever there is a wish to repeat an experience there is craving.
Aphorism

Buddhism distinguishes between *kāmachanda*, 'worldly desire', and *dhammachanda*, 'spiritual desire'. So the aim is not to eliminate desire, but to eliminate craving.
Correspondence

A human being is a stream of consciousness
deeply imbued with the dye of craving.
Seminar on the Dhammapada

Our everyday life may be pleasurable or painful; wildly ecstatic or unbearably agonizing; or just plain dull and boring much of the time. But it is here, in the midst of all these experiences, good, bad, and indifferent – and nowhere else – that Enlightenment is to be attained.
Wisdom Beyond Words

Some people, it seems, don't regard enjoyment as a natural thing. They almost have to teach themselves to enjoy life. André Gide, the French writer, had to discipline himself into enjoying the sun, the air, and the sea. It was quite an effort on his part.
Seminar on The Jewel Ornament of Liberation

Pleasure is a passive state, happiness an active one. We usually think of ourselves as lying back and enjoying happiness, but it isn't like that. We experience true happiness when we are active. And we are active when we meditate successfully, for then we are powerfully generating skilful mental states, and what can be more active – more creative – than that?
Seminar on The Jewel Ornament of Liberation

If what we see is the utilitarian value of something, we are relating to it from a need, which becomes desire, which turns to craving for the object conceived as fulfilling that desire. The tree is seen not as existing in its own right, for its own sake, but as something to fulfil our own need. If, however, we have no desires to be fulfilled, there is no subject and no object. That is the state of the bodhisattva – empty of any desire to use things for any particular purpose. All that is left is aesthetic appreciation. If you are a bodhisattva you enjoy the world much as you enjoy a work of art or an artistic performance – with the difference that you do not experience a division between yourself and something 'out there'.

Wisdom Beyond Words

The worldly-minded person thinks in terms of happiness, the spiritually-minded person thinks in terms of liberation.

Seminar on Nāgārjuna's Precious Garland

In the search for freedom, happiness is a by-product.

Seminar on Nāgārjuna's Precious Garland

It has been said that Buddhism is an ascetic religion and this is very true. But it is ascetic in the original Greek sense of getting into training, to enable yourself to reach the goal of Enlightenment. You won't reach that goal if you are flabby or out of condition, spiritually speaking.

Seminar on The Nature of Existence

The more you enjoy life the more ascetic you will be, and the more ascetic you are, the more you'll enjoy life.

Seminar on The Nature of Existence

Happiness is to be irreversibly creative.

Seminar on The Nature of Existence

It's a bit ironic to talk about giving up worldly pleasures when you take up the spiritual life. It's much more like giving up worldly miseries and taking up spiritual happiness.

Seminar on the Sāmaññaphala Sutta

It was desire that dashed from my hands the
chalice that love raised to my lips.
The Veil of Stars (poem)

You can no more confine love within the limits of human hearts
Than you can catch the showering moonlight in cups of gold.
The Veil of Stars (poem)

One can love people only as far as one understands them, and be ready to love them more when one understands them better.
Aphorism

It is better to establish real, living contact with our negative emotions (which means acknowledging them and experiencing them but not indulging them) than to remain in that alienated state and not experience our emotions at all.
A System of Meditation

Despite what the Dharma says, or is supposed to say, I don't think grief (*soka*) is invariably, under all circumstances, a negative (i.e. unskilful) state, though of course undue indulgence in grief is negative. In any case, no negative mental state should ever be repressed (repression being an unconscious process), as distinct from being consciously suppressed, in the sense of not being allowed to dominate the mind or to find inappropriate outward expression.
Correspondence

Passivity is not to be mistaken for receptivity.
The wet clay is not the open jar.
Aphorism

It is often said that one should have the courage of one's convictions. Perhaps one should also have the courage of one's positive emotions.
Correspondence

The only way to avoid hating one's fellow men is to love them.
Aphorism

We only too often find it easier to hate the wicked than to love the good.
Aphorism

Love ... is no mere flabby sentiment but the vigorous expression of an imaginative identification with other living beings.
The Ten Pillars of Buddhism

Love is a self-giving of person to person, or ... a surrender of person to person ('surrender' here meaning the complete abandonment of any advantage derived from the power mode).
The Ten Pillars of Buddhism

Personal development is not an easy matter for anyone, and there are times when we must bear with others, just as there are times when they must bear with us.
Correspondence

THE HEAT OF THE FURNACE

Culture is the preserved remains of what others before us have achieved, experienced, or discovered. By appreciating, understanding, and appropriating it we enrich our own lives and contribute to our own development.
Seminar on The Tibetan Book of the Dead

Culture is a rainbow bridge thrown from the material world to the spiritual world.
Aphorism

On finding itself in a western environment, [Buddhism] has become the focus for an interaction between the timeless truths of the Dharma and the language of the secular Western culture through which it seeks to express those truths. Western Buddhism is/will be the creation of that interaction.
The FWBO *and 'Protestant Buddhism'*

The fact that there is Buddhist culture does not necessarily mean that there is Buddhism, although there may be. Very often what people from the East bring to the West is Buddhist culture rather than Buddhism proper.
Seminar on The Precepts of the Gurus

Art is a means of overcoming alienation. We repossess ourselves of what we have lost by recreating it from within us.
Aphorism

Art is an object through which we find our way back to the subject.
Aphorism

Religious art is that kind of poetry, music, painting, or any other species of art, which conduces to the experience of egolessness. Much conventionally religious art ... is not religious art in [this] sense ... because it not only fails to induce the experience of egolessness, but even positively strengthens the ego-sense.
The Religion of Art

The arts capture crude, egoistic energy and process it until it's more refined. It can then be utilized, so to speak, for the purposes of the spiritual life.
Aphorism

Religion has been defined as what a man does with his solitude. Art might be similarly defined.
Aphorism

Every creative writer is the founder of a new religion.
Aphorism

The fact that an author is dissatisfied with his work does not mean that the critics have the right to be.
Aphorism

One does not write a book. One writes sentences.
Aphorism

Aesthetic appreciation is pure delight in the object of contemplation for its own sake. This is the difference between lust, which is stimulated by the sensuously attractive, and the aesthetic sense, which is stimulated by pure beauty. If you look with craving, you see things in terms of sensuous attractiveness, but if you look with *mettā*, with loving kindness, you see things in terms of beauty. *Mettā* is disinterested. When it's a question of lust you want to grab; when it's a question of aesthetic appreciation, you just want to stand back and contemplate.

Seminar on Nāgārjuna's Precious Garland

Only too often people think the poets do not mean what they say. They think it is 'just poetry'. The poets, however, mean exactly what they say.

Aphorism

One of the signs of a great writer is that even his bad work is interesting – more interesting than the best work of a mediocre writer.

Aphorism

Writing memoirs is the penance one performs for having lived – or not lived.

Aphorism

The writer invites you to read his book, the artist to look at his painting; the religious teacher invites you to share his life.

Aphorism

When poetry is no longer enjoyed it ceases to be poetry – at least for the one reading it or listening to it.

Aphorism

With so many masterpieces of world literature to read it is a pity to waste one's time on trivia. Indeed, it is a pity to waste one's time on anything that does not genuinely enhance the quality of one's life, that does not deepen one's positive emotions – that does not, in short, help one to become Enlightened.

Correspondence

Speaking personally, I never show what I am writing to anybody, and never discuss it. I do not even really like to be asked how I am 'getting on with my writing'. Authorship is an essentially solitary business, and any outside interference, whether from government censors or well-meaning friends, is rightly to be resented.

Correspondence

Diaries can be very misleading – especially
when they contain nothing but facts.

Aphorism

At the moment of the creation of a work of art, the feelings experienced may be very intense and powerful. They may come welling up from the depths quite uncontrollably. Should anything get in your way, or should there be any sort of interruption or disturbance, you can react quite violently, just because you are so absorbed in what you are doing. In the process of artistic creation you are bringing together into a unity a whole mass of materials, by virtue of the intensity of your feelings, even of your Insight, and great psychic pressure is needed to do that. Milton's artistic inspiration has been described as being like a great furnace which he kept banking up until it was just a mass of glowing coals. Into it he flung all sorts of things – his knowledge, all the materials he had gathered – but such was the heat of the furnace that he could melt down all those materials and cast them into a mould of his own.

Seminar on The Jewel Ornament of Liberation

Creative writing in the true sense is a spiritual discipline that calls for the same kind of seriousness and dedication as the spiritual life itself.

Correspondence

What we need is a new generation of writers and artists who are committed to the spiritual life, as well as dedicated to their particular art, and for whom the former inspires the latter while the latter provides the former with a means of expression. This is, of course, something much more subtle than simply using the arts as a vehicle of religious propaganda.

Correspondence

The written word remains. Even the noblest actions and the wisest utterances are known to us only by their being – eventually – written down.

Correspondence

Writing is no substitute for face-to-face communication – unless one can write a whole book.

Correspondence

Sometimes we use words very loosely and inaccurately, because we do not ask ourselves what they mean. Our speech is laden with jargon from various sources, and that does not conduce to clarity. So let us understand the meaning of the words we speak, and especially the words we write, and consult the dictionary if necessary. I think the most useful book in the world, leaving aside the scriptures, is the dictionary.

Fifteen points for Old – and New – Order members (talk)

I plead for a greater, more vivid realization of the poetic nature of speech. This should be our approach to language all the time, because language, as applied to non-material realities, is essentially metaphorical, poetry rather than prose.

Seminar on The Jewel Ornament of Liberation

Cultivate an aphorism as you would cultivate a rose; but be careful not to remove the thorns.

Aphorism

In metaphor language begins to transcend itself. Metaphor offers us a clue to the nature of reality.

Wisdom Beyond Words

Language – even abstract language – is essentially metaphorical. Of course, one can ask how, if this is so, words can describe reality. But that assumes that reality is not metaphorical, that it is somehow abstract, as science usually thinks of it. But if language is metaphorical, this suggests that reality too is metaphorical, and that one can get closer to reality by *realizing* that language is metaphorical.

Questions and Answers: Tuscany 1984

Children aren't just members of the family; they are eventually going to be members of society. They have to be brought up to consider other people's feelings and respect other people's property.

Fifteen Points for Buddhist Parents (talk)

One of the most important things we can teach our children is to empathize with others – with other children, with animals, with all living beings. Otherwise their recognition of the distinction between right and wrong will be purely theoretical.

Fifteen Points for Buddhist Parents (talk)

Parents will always be deeply affected by anything that concerns their children, whether for good or ill; but we have to try to remain detached, without losing our human feelings. In fact we should try to universalize our feelings, and feel as much for our neighbour's child as for our own.

Correspondence

The first purpose of education is to enable the individual to take his place as a functioning, responsible member of the wider society to which he belongs.

Buddhism and Education (talk)

The group is a collectivity organized for its own survival, in which the interests of the individual are subordinated to those of the collectivity. The group is also a power structure in which the ultimate sanction is force.

New Currents in Western Buddhism

Group attitudes die very hard.

Correspondence

The truly human, consciously evolving individual is characterized by awareness, emotional positivity, responsibility, intelligence, creativity, spontaneity, imagination, and insight.

The Bodhisattva Principle

The Buddha's teaching is concerned solely with the individual, both alone and in free association with other individuals. It shows the individual how to grow, shows him or her, by means of actual methods, how to develop awareness, how to develop emotional positivity, how to live spontaneously and creatively, how to accept responsibility for oneself and for others.... Gautama the Buddha, the original teacher, was and is an example of a true individual. Indeed, he was an individual of the highest kind: an Enlightened individual.
New Currents in Western Buddhism

If one is healthy, one has energy, and if one has energy, one naturally wants to put it into something – that is, one wants to work, whether the work consists in digging the soil or painting a picture.
Correspondence

Without unremitting effort nothing truly great is ever achieved. All the great artists seem to have been great workers. Perhaps this was because they loved their work.
Correspondence

Sometimes I think work – real work, work in which one believes – is the greatest enjoyment in life.
Correspondence

Work should be an expression of one's life, not simply the means to one's existence.
Correspondence

'A load of sandalwood is still a load,' said the camel.
Aphorism

Much of what is thought of as history is really myth. Not that it is necessarily any the worse for that, of course, but it would be better if things were called by their right names.
Aphorism

Equality is a concept that has a place only in arithmetic.
Aphorism

Though rights and duties are reciprocal, one should place the emphasis on one's duties rather than on one's rights. If you faithfully discharge your duties, the chances are that other people will observe their duties towards you, and you will in fact get your rights. If there is a mutual recognition of duties, there is no need to speak of rights at all. Other factors being equal, people start claiming their rights only when other people have been very remiss in the performance of their duties.

Seminar on The Duties of Brotherhood in Islam

Rights exist only within the group: within the spiritual community there are only duties.

Aphorism

From a Buddhist point of view, your duty is what you see as incumbent upon yourself in view of the principles in which you believe, and the situation in which you find yourself.

Questions and Answers: Tuscany 1982

It is not on ideological grounds that one tries to break down class barriers. One tries to break them down simply because one wants to be able to relate to other people as individuals.

Questions and Answers: Tuscany 1982

The remedy for any injustice or inequality in human relationships, whether domestic, social, civic, political, cultural, racial, or religious, is an insistence not upon the rights of one party, but on the duties of the other.

Crossing the Stream

Formerly one needed courage to attack institutions. Now one needs courage to defend them – and still more courage to create them.

Aphorism

It would seem that there will always be a minority of people in society who will try to harm others. The majority will therefore need to invoke force, at least to restrain them from their antisocial conduct. I don't think one can get round that.

Questions and Answers: Tuscany 1982

Inequality is life. Equality is death.
Aphorism

A good man sometimes helps to perpetuate
a bad system, and vice versa.
Aphorism

The larger society needs to have a set of shared values, in however dilute a form. Otherwise it could not cohere – could not be a society at all. At the same time, there is little doubt that the truly ideal society could exist only on a small scale, in a number of different embodiments within the larger society.
Correspondence

'Political correctness' is one of the most pernicious tendencies of our time – far more pernicious than pseudo-liberalism, of which it is probably the extreme form.
Correspondence

Liberalism is the belief that life should be fair. Pseudo-liberalism is the belief that fairness can be achieved by unfair means.
Aphorism

It is in the interests of Buddhists to work wherever possible for a pluralistic society; a threat to any minority is a threat to Buddhism. But for there to be a pluralistic society, the adherents of the religions and other ideologies that exist within that society must recognize the possibility, even the desirability, of their peaceful coexistence. That does imply a certain common ethical outlook, certain ethical values, such as the ideal of tolerance, or the spirit of live and let live.
Questions and Answers: The Noble Eightfold Path

It is sometimes said 'There is no revolutionary like an old revolutionary.' The young revolutionary is just hot blooded, just impulsive, and usually he gets over it and settles down and conforms, but the real revolutionary is one who, the older he gets, the more revolutionary he gets.
Seminar on the Sevenfold Puja

If everyone bears his or her full share of responsibility, there will be no room for authoritarianism. Unfortunately, people criticize others for authoritarianism while at the same time they are reluctant to recognize their own responsibility within a given situation. They want others to accept all or most of the responsibility, and do all or most of the work; at the same time, they want to be able to control those others.

Correspondence

NO LAST-MINUTE METHODS

'All worldlings are mad,' said the Buddha, and in the long run a mad person may do anything. Hence the importance of developing insight into reality.

Correspondence

There are no last-minute methods. Since one is, in principle, facing death every minute, all insight meditation practices are methods of 'coping' with the problem of death and consequently with the fear of death. At times when death seems near one should therefore do whatever practice one is most familiar with, or has most faith in. One should be careful not to relax one's efforts when the crisis has passed, or appears to have passed, which is what usually happens.

Correspondence

Meditation is essentially the willing of the Good.

Aphorism

Without regular meditation, our spiritual life has no sheet anchor.

Correspondence

Most people either repress fear completely or allow it to diffuse itself throughout the whole of their experience in the form of a vague feeling of anxiety or dread. But fear is inseparable from one's consciousness of oneself as a separate individual. As one advances in the spiritual life, and especially as one practises meditation, one is sure to have to face it.

Correspondence

The optimism of the creative mind persists despite unpleasant stimuli.... [It] loves where there is no reason to love, is happy where there is no reason for happiness, creates where there is no possibility of creativity, and in this way 'builds a heaven in hell's despair'.
Mind – Reactive and Creative

As what we fear approaches, we realize it is not really this that we are afraid of after all. What it is that we are afraid of, we do not know.
Aphorism

Logic is a highly irrational phenomenon.
Aphorism

A philosophy cannot be founded on reasons.
Aphorism

Reason must be supreme in all human affairs, say the Rationalists. But on what grounds do they accept the truth of this statement? If it is on authority, reason is not supreme; if on rational grounds, then they assume the supremacy of reason in order to establish the supremacy of reason.
Aphorism

The development of positive emotions ... is absolutely crucial to our development as individuals. It is, after all, our emotions that keep us going; we are not kept going by abstract ideas. It is our positive emotions that keep us going on the spiritual path, giving us inspiration, enthusiasm, and so on, until such time as we can develop Perfect Vision [i.e. Insight or *vipaśyanā*] and be motivated by that.
A System of Meditation (talk)

The problem of how to combine reason and emotion, so that we think what we feel and feel what we think, at ever higher levels, is one that all who are concerned with personal development have to face sooner or later. In their most developed forms, reason is *vipaśyanā* or insight and emotion is *śamatha* or calm – though by that stage of development they have already begun to coincide.
Correspondence

'External understanding' is an understanding which is not part of yourself, which is dissociated from yourself. It is that alienated intellect which in Blake's symbolism is represented by the figure of Urizen. Not only is one not able to understand the Buddha's teaching with alienated intellect: one can't understand anything with it. From Blake's point of view the whole of modern science is an attempt to understand life by the alienated intellect.

Seminar on Milarepa's Heartfelt Advice to Rechungpa

Unless your alienated intellect is transformed by being brought into contact with very strong emotion so that the two are fused, there is no possibility of developing Insight. Insight is no nearer to intellect than it is to emotion.

Seminar on Milarepa's Heartfelt Advice to Rechungpa

When we get on to the spiritual path, the conflict between the rational and the emotional has been virtually resolved, so that you have a sort of unified energy, still mundane but unified, and orientated in the direction of the Transcendental.

Seminar on D. T. Suzuki's Outlines of Mahāyāna Buddhism

It is true that one needs to unify one's energy. But if one's energy is not unified one should not worry about it, otherwise energy will be wasted in worrying and unification will be further away than ever.

Correspondence

Positive emotion is emotion which is pleasurable and at the same time skilful.

Aphorism

Only when a man feels strongly will he act effectively. It is for this reason above all others that Buddhism starts not with a concept but with a feeling, not with intellectual postulation but with emotional experience.

Crossing the Stream

Nowadays people don't have friends; they have psychotherapists, lawyers, and hairdressers.
Aphorism

Spiritual fellowship is indeed the whole of the spiritual life, as well as being the panacea for ordinary psychological problems.
Correspondence

'Take rhetoric and wring its neck,' said Arthur Rimbaud, the French poet. Charisma, one might add, is the psychological equivalent of rhetoric.
Aphorism

'Joviality' sometimes masks competitiveness and even antagonism. Thus it is the near enemy of *muditā* (sympathetic joy).
Correspondence

Friendship is certainly a vital part of Buddhism, but non-exclusiveness is equally a vital part of friendship.
Correspondence

Our real friends are indeed people who welcome us with a warm hug however long we have been away, and who are not interested in what they can get out of us for themselves. Such friends are bodhisattvas in the form of ordinary human beings, as Gampopa calls them.[28]
Correspondence

Friendships must certainly be kept up. They can't look after themselves, or be kept in cold storage.
Correspondence

The Enlightenment experience is not self-contained in a one-sided way. It contains an element of communication and therefore an element of spiritual friendship, even transcendental friendship – friendship on the highest conceivable level.
Correspondence

True competition is a form of collaboration.
Aphorism

The emotions connected with friendship are skilful but weak; the emotions connected with sex are unskilful but strong. The former therefore need to be cultivated, the latter gradually eliminated.
Aphorism

A sexual relationship is like a lobster pot – easy to get into but difficult to get out of.
Aphorism

Without chastity it is difficult to experience spiritual androgyny, and without the experience of spiritual androgyny it is difficult to achieve a vision of the Truth.
Aphorism

It is difficult to know which is worse: not to be believed when you speak the truth, or to be believed when you tell a lie.
Aphorism

Not to be believed means to be cut off from communication. It means to be treated as an object.
Aphorism

The primary meaning of *kalyāṇa* in *kalyāṇa mitratā* (spiritual friendship) is 'beautiful'. In spiritual friendship we take delight in the spiritual beauty of our dear friend. This aspect of 'taking delight' means that we not only see a person as a person, but also like what we see, enjoy and take delight in what we see, just as we do with a beautiful painting or poem – except that here the painting or poem is alive: the painting can speak to you, and the beautiful poem can answer back. This makes it very exciting and stimulating indeed.
Correspondence

It is appalling to think how much time, energy, and initiative it takes to get to know even one person very well.
Correspondence

A fool can give more advice in a day than
a wise man can follow in a year.
Aphorism

It seems extraordinary that people should have such difficulty understanding what seems to be a straightforward point. Perhaps it is because they are thinking of something else.
Aphorism

Things that are allowed to remain unspoken eventually build up an insurmountable barrier to communication. Either one communicates or one is blocked. There is no middle way.
Correspondence

'Manner' is such an elusive thing. Different people can perceive a person's manner in quite different ways and therefore have quite different reactions to it. So, it is usually better to pay attention to the substance of someone's communication, not to its manner.
Correspondence

Speaking personally, I do not want disciples who are meek and obedient and afraid to speak their mind. I want disciples who are bold, self-confident, and independent and who are capable of standing against the whole world if necessary.
Correspondence

In spiritual life there will always be ups and downs,
and during the down periods our spiritual friends
are our main source of help and inspiration.
Correspondence

We have to try to appreciate people's positive qualities,
without dwelling on their weaknesses.
Correspondence

Authoritarianism and spiritual life are completely
incompatible. Most 'gurus' are simply exploiters.
Correspondence

Criticism is not condemnation. Personally I never condemn anyone, since I believe that human beings are capable of change. Criticism, if taken in the right spirit, helps us to grow.
Correspondence

Don't be impatient, especially with other people. Realize that sometimes they have their problems too. Though they may want to be friends, in practice they may find it difficult. Try not to think in terms of what other people should be giving you, but rather in terms of what you can give them.
Correspondence

When people make you more than human they in effect make you less than human. The only important thing is for us to be friends; and whatever teaching is to happen will come over naturally in the course of the friendship.
Conversation

Few are great enough to serve.
Aphorism

If in each generation the disciples fall below the level of attainment of the guru, in a few generations what's going to be the state of affairs? So a guru should consider that he has not been successful as a guru until his disciples do better than himself. Otherwise the chances are that the whole tradition will degenerate very quickly.
Seminar on Milarepa's Heartfelt Advice to Rechungpa

It is sometimes necessary to criticize the weaknesses of others, but people often seem to find it difficult to do so without doing it in a 'hard' sort of way that excludes compassion. Perhaps, in some cases, people criticize others as a way of paying homage to the ideal without actually having to practise that ideal.
Correspondence

Where there is trust, explanations are unnecessary.
Where there is no trust, explanations are useless.
Aphorism

As Buddhists, we have to learn to live, work, and communicate together on the basis of our common commitment to the Three Jewels, without attaching too much importance to differences which are, after all, only part of our general psychological and social conditioning.
Correspondence

One of the great disadvantages of the mass media is that trivialities can be given an importance that they absolutely don't possess. People need to be delivered not just from tragedy and disaster, but from triviality. Triviality, in fact, is one of the greatest disasters that can happen to us.
Questions and Answers: Combined Order Convention 1985

Sound judgement is a very rare quality. People do not necessarily possess it because they are sincere and well meaning and spiritually committed, or because they have one's interests (where it is a question of giving personal advice) genuinely at heart. In refusing to accept someone's judgements one is not, therefore, questioning their integrity or their spiritual development.
Correspondence

There is no time in life for misunderstandings.
Correspondence

If you do not wear your heart on your sleeve for daws to peck at, the daws will accuse you of having no heart.
Aphorism

Don't argue; discuss. When you get into an argument, what you are concerned with is to win, to beat the other person. But the aim of discussion is to find out between you the truth of the matter. If you are not very careful, what starts off as a genuine discussion can become an argument.
Fifteen Points for Old – and New – Order Members (talk)

There is no wound that man can give
That nature cannot heal.
The Veil of Stars (poem)

To understand all is perhaps to forgive all. But sometimes we have to forgive without understanding.
Aphorism

One of the problems facing the religious teacher is that literal-minded people want literal answers to literal questions.
Aphorism

Fooling other people can be dangerous,
but fooling oneself is fatal.
Aphorism

THE CIRCLE OF ETERNITY

If one always tries to explain the unknown by the known one will never learn anything.
Aphorism

Beware of premature syntheses.
Aphorism

Only those who experience death in life can experience life in death.
Aphorism

The fundamental principle of my philosophy is that power and value do not coincide.
Aphorism

A perfect sphere on a perfect plane: are they or are they not in contact?
Aphorism

Time is unable to square the circle of eternity.
Aphorism

Security is insecurity. 'That which is supported has no support.'[29]
Aphorism

A white dot against a black background: how does one tell whether it is revolving or stationary?
Aphorism

It is not that there are two worlds which, while distinct, both have ontological status. The distinction is between the ontological and the —?
Aphorism

Soul is reticulated into souls.
Aphorism

Change your consciousness and you will see a different world.
Change your consciousness and you will see the world differently.
What is the difference between these two statements?
Aphorism

Intellectual clarity is not everything, but it counts for a great deal, especially when one remembers that right view constitutes a basis for the development of Perfect Vision.
Correspondence

Perhaps dreams have no explanation in the ordinary sense. They are their own explanation. Probably the best thing one can do is to reflect upon the images of which the dream consists and try to retain and intensify the distinctive emotional quality of the dream experience. The dream, after all, is you, though a part of yourself which you do not usually experience, and with which you need, perhaps, to be more in touch.
Correspondence

To distinguish between thoughts and things, between the concepts which merely indicate realities and those realities themselves, is an art belonging to a highly advanced stage of philosophical discipline and spiritual culture.
A Survey of Buddhism

The Pāli scriptures speak of multiple consciousnesses associated with single bodies, besides the more usual one consciousness to one body. I suppose that in this area, as in so many others, we have to beware of thinking too much in terms of fixed patterns, and be open to the possibility of there being patterns different from those with which we are familiar.
Correspondence

'There is nothing in the mind that was not previously in the senses.' If this were true, the recollection of former lives would be impossible.
Aphorism

There can be no absolute duality between dualism and non-dualism. The absolute truth is the absolute truth of the relative truth. They are inseparable.
Wisdom Beyond Words

The doctrine of 'no-self' represents the possibility of change, radical change – change from reactive to creative, conditioned to unconditioned, mundane to transcendental.
Seminar on The Nature of Existence

Thought is incommensurable with reality and reality with thought.
Seminar on The Nature of Existence

The Arts

THE RELIGION OF ART

CONSCIOUS SURRENDER TO THE BEAUTIFUL: AN INTRODUCTION TO *THE RELIGION OF ART*

Imagine that the arts are important in your life – that your engagement with the arts and your pursuit of aesthetic beauty is the thing that gives your life its deepest meaning. Now, imagine that religion, in the form of Buddhism, is something that also makes a claim upon your heart, that also gives your existence its sense and purpose, with its teaching of a path to liberation and truth for those who commit themselves. Now, how will you choose between Buddhism and the arts? In *The Religion of Art*, Sangharakshita explores the possibility of a unifying vision that embraces both passions to find the truth in beauty, and the beauty in truth.

Sangharakshita's interest in the arts goes back to his childhood when, made to stay in bed because of a supposed heart condition, he read great poetry, such as Milton's *Paradise Lost*, and pored over reproductions of Renaissance paintings. His interest became a passion, and this passion did not diminish even when he travelled to India and became a Buddhist monk. While he was living in Benares, studying with Bhikkhu Jagdish Kashyap, this passion for a life devoted to beauty came into conflict with his passion for a life devoted to spiritual truth. In his first volume of memoirs, he describes this inner conflict in terms of a struggle between what seemed two very different sides of himself:

> Sangharakshita I wanted to enjoy the beauty of nature, to read and write poetry, to listen to music, to look at paintings and sculpture, to experience emotion, to lie in bed and dream, to

> see places, to meet people. Sangharakshita II wanted to realize the truth, to read and write philosophy, to observe the precepts, to get up early and meditate, to mortify the flesh, to fast and pray. Sometimes Sangharakshita I was victorious, sometimes Sangharakshita II, while occasionally there was an uneasy duumvirate.[30]

The conflict turned nasty: Sangharakshita II burned Sangharakshita I's poetry notebooks. Out of the shock of such inner violence these two sides of the one man sought reconciliation. Later, like the nations of Europe, they established a peaceful and prosperous union. This union was established when Sangharakshita came to the realization, while explaining some poems by Shelley to a young student and friend, that the innermost meaning of Buddhism and the true meaning of art were essentially the same:

> The greater the number of times we went through a poem, the more deeply we were able to penetrate into its meaning – a meaning that seemed, in the case of some poems, to coincide with the meaning of Buddhism itself. Once again I realized that ... in explaining a poem – a poem such as Shelley's 'The Cloud' or one of Keats' Odes – I was in fact teaching Buddhism, especially when I was explaining it to, or studying it with, a dear friend.[31]

The reconciliation process recorded in his memoirs tells us something important about Sangharakshita's way of being. Many of us would readily admit to an interest in, and even a love for, the arts; many of us also consider ourselves committed to a spiritual path. But this combination in itself does not provoke the kind of conflict that Sangharakshita describes. For that to happen one's devotion to art has to become a requirement of existence; the quest for beauty through poetry, music, or painting has to become a driving force. One's commitment to the spiritual life also has to become something absolute and uncompromising. Only when such a driving force meets such an absolute commitment does the burning of poetry notebooks begin. Sangharakshita's subsequent realization of the essential unity of Buddhism and art was therefore more than an interesting idea to him. It was the higher synthesis of opposing passions, forged in a crucible of his inner life.

Hence the sense of intensity and even urgency in the four essays comprising *The Religion of Art*, since they attempt to give conceptual expression to this pacifying realization of the essential similarity of Buddhism and art. They were written in the early 1950s while Sangharakshita was living in a hermitage in Kalimpong, and have an ardour and rhetorical drive about them typical of his writings of that time, such as *A Survey of Buddhism*. What was for Sangharakshita a distinct and living experience of art and Buddhism, after the integration of what had been distinct parts of his personality, he now attempted to argue for, with bold generalizations, adventurous logic and the passion of some highly informed convictions. The essays thrive on an inspired simplicity of vision and the confidence of a young man of great intellectual power.

It is the title essay and the other long essay, 'The Meaning of Buddhism and the Value of Art', that carry the main weight in the collection. The other two are of more particular value. 'Advice to a Young Poet' is clearly inspired by the German poet Rilke's *Letters to a Young Poet*, in which the author (himself only about 28, the same age as Sangharakshita at the time of writing) provides guidance on the spirit of poetry rather than on its form. Sangharakshita elsewhere tells us that the essay was written for the young student friend with whom he had realized that poetry could share a common essence with Buddhism; but he tells us that the essay was written as much for his own benefit as for his friend.[32] Its message is that the poet, in order to improve his poetry, should develop his personality by developing certain qualities: the capacity for concentrated observation; a sensitive depth of feeling; a universal sympathy; and a taste for solitary reflection. Artistic creativity is therefore not separate from self-development. The final essay, 'Paradox and Poetry in *The Voice of the Silence*', is a wide-ranging commentary on a theosophical text supposedly translated by Madame Blavatsky from secret teachings. Its relevance to this volume is its message that poetry, as imagery, along with paradox, is a more effective vehicle for spiritual teachings than rational discourse alone.

The first two essays attempt an ambitious synthesis of the deepest meaning of Buddhism and the true meaning of art, and go on to proclaim 'the religion of art' as a spiritual force for modern times. In this they are practising the art of the essay in its original sense: 'essay' comes from the French *essayer*, to attempt or try; an essay is an attempt or trial.

Essays are supposed to be daring, to try out a new line of thought. These essays are pioneering attempts, inspired by Sangharakshita's passionate engagement with both Buddhism and art.

Sangharakshita was not, however, the first to attempt an essay on the relation of art and Buddhism. His friend Lama Govinda, originally from Germany, and an accomplished artist as well as an experienced Buddhist, had in 1936 published a small book entitled *Art and Meditation*.[33] Lama Govinda gave a copy to Sangharakshita when he and his wife visited him in his Kalimpong hermitage.[34] Sangharakshita was sufficiently impressed by some of Lama Govinda's ideas to reproduce them in his memoirs:

> Art and meditation are creative states of the human mind. Both are nourished by the same source, but it may seem that they are moving in different directions: art towards the realm of sense-impressions, meditation towards the overcoming of forms and sense-impressions. But the difference pertains only to accidentals, not to the essentials.[35]

Lama Govinda's ideas, however, are not developed very far, and his essay goes on to explain the symbolism behind his own abstract paintings rather than to explore more general themes. But he does go on to make a couple of resonant points:

> Art and religious life meet in a sphere of consciousness where no such distinctions exist. Therefore wherever religion is a living force there it finds its natural expression in art, in fact, it becomes art itself – just as art in its highest attainments becomes religion. Art is the measure of the living quality of a religion.... The more the artist expresses himself the nearer he comes to others, because our real nature is that of egolessness (*anattā*) or unlimited relationship (*suññatā*).[36]

The idea of the essential unity of art and religion as a living experience, and the idea that art is connected with egolessness, are the germs from which Sangharakshita's essays begin.

In his essay 'The Meaning of Buddhism and the Value of Art', Sangharakshita develops this conception of egolessness in terms of a spatial metaphor: that both Buddhism and art involve an expansion of consciousness beyond the usual limitations of the ego. Buddhism expands consciousness vertically in terms of a greater understanding of reality, and horizontally in terms of increased compassion for other beings, while art expands consciousness vertically in terms of increased sensibility and appreciation of beauty, and horizontally in terms of greater sympathy for experience beyond our own. Therefore both art and Buddhism expand consciousness in two dimensions, but practically speaking Buddhism expands consciousness via the mind and the will, while art does so via the emotions and through beauty. In the second and longest essay, 'The Religion of Art', Sangharakshita similarly identifies the essence of art and Buddhism as egolessness, but develops this idea in terms of the possibilities of transformation inherent in each. Egolessness is the centrifugal tendency into the unknown that characterizes both the spirit of the artist and the effect of art upon the enjoyer. Art, therefore, involves a conscious surrender to the beautiful, a process of transformation that parallels the infinite creativity of the Buddha's 'spiral path' to Enlightenment.

It should be obvious that Sangharakshita's ideas involve a conception of Buddhism that has little to do with 'religion' in the conventional sense, but more to do with a living spirit of individual development. His conception of art is similarly unconventional. Not everything that is said to be 'art' in today's world would meet the exacting definition that Sangharakshita presents in 'The Religion of Art':

> Art is the organization of sensuous impressions into pleasurable formal relations that express the artist's sensibility and communicate to his audience a sense of values that can transform their lives.

Great art communicates transformative values, which are essentially the same as the core values implicit in Buddhism as a living spiritual tradition: this is Sangharakshita's vision. As a definition of art, the one given above would probably exclude much of what is usually described as art – for instance Sangharakshita deliberately excludes popular art as mere entertainment. We should perhaps understand Sangharakshita's definition of art as what one philosopher has described as a 'persuasive definition':

> A 'persuasive' definition is one which gives a new conceptual meaning to a familiar word without substantially changing its emotive meaning, and which is used with the conscious or unconscious purpose of changing, by this means, the direction of people's interests.[37]

Sangharakshita wishes not only to characterize Buddhism and art, but to cause us to attend to art differently – with eyes and ears opened to how the arts can expand and transform us. Whether or not we regard ourselves as Buddhists, art can bring about an effect upon us essentially similar to the effect of meditation.

* * *

How do all these fascinating ideas work in practice? Let me explore them by taking an imaginary walk around Cambridge, England, where I live. (It is an unusually beautiful city, full of medieval architecture and alive with culture, at least in term-time, when all the students are here. So it is a particularly good city to walk around, thinking about the religion of art.) I first visit King's College Chapel, a world-famous example of sacred architecture. This is an example of architectural art that, in Sangharakshita's terms, is both formally and essentially religious. Its huge, high windows fill the simple space of the interior with a sublime light, illuminating highly decorated carved stonework. Roofing the high space is a woven pattern of fan vaulting so delicate you can hardly understand how its many tons stay up. My heart responds to the magnificence of the medieval imagination in planning this building, and to the builders' skill; when I am in it, thoughts of the force of history, commitment to the Christian religion, the symbolism of stone vaulting, its combined weight and poise, all press upon me, placing my own life in a much bigger perspective. I feel my little ego subjected to much greater forces, and a greater vision of life all around me.

Then, as I walk up the nave and under the chapel's organ, peculiarly situated in mid-air on top of the oak choir screen, I see that at the east end of the chapel, above the altar, is a huge painting. It is *The Adoration of the Magi*, by the Flemish painter Peter Paul Rubens. The three wise men are humbly offering their gifts to the child Christ, who is presented to them by his holy mother. The effect of hanging such a work directly above the high altar in the chapel makes me think about what I am being invited to worship. Is it the baby Jesus, the Saviour of the World, who is represented so warmly in the dramatic gestures of Rubens' baroque style? Or am I being invited to worship the artwork itself, such a famous and magnificent creation of the European artistic tradition? Either way, my attention is drawn to aesthetic features of the painting: the rich red robes of the nearest king, the gold robes of the one behind him, the purple ones behind him – all in complete contrast to the delicate flesh of the entirely naked baby. This vulnerable weak being is held into the light, and every gaze in the picture converges upon it, just as my own does as a viewer. I have become part of the scene, joining in with the abasement even of the wise before the reality of the divine. The artwork has taken me into its imaginative world, and suggested something to me, in the form of a beautiful symbol, about reality.

Contemplating the painting makes me think that the chapel is now as much concerned with a somewhat secularized religion of art as with the Christian religion. The effect is strengthened when I stay on to attend sung evensong: robed and gentle choristers loft gorgeous harmonies up into the dim vaulting, harmonies of such sophistication that they seem as much a celebration of the art of music as of the Christian religious beliefs hidden somewhere underneath the chords and lyrics. For me, a Buddhist, attending such a service, the sheer beauty of it all is a sudden reminder of the importance of the arts in the religious life, somehow transcending the limitations of doctrine and belief. And then they start singing again, and my heart is briefly elevated to bliss by the beauty of it, all thought is laid aside, and for a while I enter a realm of unworldly purity not so different from states of meditative concentration that I occasionally experience while on retreat.

As I leave the chapel I think about how I am an inheritor of the beauty and richness of the European artistic tradition going back centuries, back ultimately to the architecture and literature of ancient Greece. Sangharakshita does not mention this in his essays, but western Buddhists are in a peculiar situation, and his idea of a 'religion of art' helps to sort it out. Probably all of us who have been exposed to Western culture have found ourselves moved and inspired at some point by a piece of music, a poem or a painting, produced in the context of traditions of Western art. At the same time we have chosen to become enthusiastic and even effective practitioners of an Asian religious tradition that comes to us complete with its native *sūtras*, thangkas, and haiku. The tangle of inspiration and influence is a positive challenge: how should we sort out the competing claims on our emotions?

With all this in mind I walk along the Trumpington Road, heading for the Fitzwilliam Museum, an imposing neo-classical building in dove-grey limestone, similar to the British Museum in London, but smaller. I go up wide steps, past tall pillars, under a carved portico. Even the building itself is a monument to world-crowning Victorian confidence. Downstairs, past the sarcophagi and ceramics, I am suddenly confronted with a life-size Buddhist figure. It is a thirteenth-century Chinese sculpture of Guanyin, seated in the posture of 'royal ease'. He leans on one arm, the other arm resting upon his upraised knee. Although the wooden statue is knocked and worn, with both feet and one hand missing, the face and posture are striking. His gaze shines out with relaxed alertness, his face almost lighting into a smile. His body is comfortable and without tension – his pot belly shows he has an abundance of *chi* – but he also has the poise of one who knows full well his status and power.

It is disconcerting to find such an overtly religious image among all the old and interesting stuff in a British museum. Guanyin is the Chinese equivalent of the bodhisattva Avalokiteśvara, 'the Lord who looks down': an embodiment of transcendental compassion. (Most later figures of Guanyin are female.) A friend once told me that he had prostrated himself (on a quiet day) at Guanyin's feet. The sculpture was obviously made to live in a Buddhist temple; there must be some sad tale of how it came to Cambridge. Yet seeing him in the Fitzwilliam makes me take in the sculpture as a piece of art: how the sculptor has created an ideal form embodying some of Buddhism's fundamental values, and succeeded in balancing alertness and relaxation in the face, and poise and ease in the belly and chest; how that same artist has placed two little polished black stones just so, to make his eyes. I sense that Song Dynasty China must have been just as civilized as Europe to have produced such a figure. I feel my conditioning ease off, and my sense of identity expand – another step towards egolessness.

As I turn away from Guanyin I find myself thinking that the examples of art I've contemplated are both formally and essentially religious, and how with such examples it is relatively easy to sense an essential connection between religion and art. I walk upstairs to find a painting that is not at all religious. My attention alights on one of Cézanne's studies of apples. How can such secular artwork lead to a transcending of the ego? I first take in the bold slanting brushstrokes. Cézanne's art is not trying to create any illusion. Here are seven apples, yes, but it is quite clearly a painting, made of patches of colour on a flat canvas. I keep looking. Despite – or perhaps because of – the lack of illusion, the apples start to come alive in my imagination. The artist has managed to paint the particular colour and shine of their skins: the plump redness, the juicy green, ripe yellow. The apples press on each other and on the plain surface on which they have been carelessly placed. They are there. I realize that Cézanne has really gone into apples, allowed apples to fill his senses, his mind, his hand – and I have been pulled into the same lively contemplation of reality. Is this egolessness? It is at least another window onto a world beyond self-centred concern.

* * *

Something that needs to be emphasized in relation to Sangharakshita's vision of the religion of art is that the reader, hearer, or viewer of art needs to be receptive to the artist's communication, and ready for art's transforming power. Some training is necessary. His essays on the religion of art are a spur to train oneself in just such receptivity and readiness. They culminate in Sangharakshita's own definition of the religion of art as 'conscious surrender to the beautiful'. By bringing a mind that is receptive to art and ready to be changed by it, one's experience of art can be a wholehearted plunge into the higher pleasures of colour, sound, and form, a plunge that touches you deeply and will have you thirsting for more.

I have hardly touched on the creation of artworks in relation to Sangharakshita's ideas. In fact almost everything said applies to the creation as well as the enjoyment of art. In fact, an active engagement with the arts is one of the best ways to learn to appreciate the power and potential of art for personal transformation. Hence a further value in these essays on the religion of art, which lies outside this book itself and instead in the life of the Triratna Buddhist Community, the movement that he founded. If we suppose that writing these essays was in itself an important part of the work of integration of Sangharakshita I and Sangharakshita II, those warring parts of a highly idealistic young man, then we might look at what followed from the conclusions that Sangharakshita reached. The first result was that Sangharakshita continued to immerse himself in great art as well as in Buddhist study and practice.[38] He continued to write poetry, his own chosen art form, poetry that strove to meet his own criteria and values.[39] And he deliberately emphasized, and continues to emphasize, the importance of the arts in the spiritual life.

The importance of the arts for the spiritual life is in fact one of the six distinctive emphases of the Triratna Buddhist Community. There are retreats and gatherings for Buddhist poets and artists to learn and practise together. I know from my own participation in *Wolf at the Door* creative writing workshops and retreats how powerful a tool for development creative writing can be – and how this participation has increased my appreciation of poetry. There have been arts festivals, operas, and oratorios on Buddhist themes, a musical composition competition, and several anthologies of poetry produced by Buddhists. The magazine *Urthona* continues to explore themes in Buddhism and the arts. None of these activities presupposes the particular theories about the relation of Buddhism and art explored in Sangharakshita's essays in *The Religion of Art*, but in one way or another they are inspired by the same conviction and passion that produced them.

What remains as relevant now as when the essays were written is an attitude that underlies them, the attitude that is convinced that there is some necessary and profound connection between the impulse to create and appreciate art and the practice of the Buddha's teachings. It may be that ultimately it is impossible to exactly articulate what there is in common between the great traditions of art and Buddhism. One has its source and continuity in European culture and thought; the other is a universal religion originating in Asia. Both traditions are too old and extensive to tolerate very many generalizations. The attitude that Sangharakshita's convictions encourage, however, is this. Engaging with the arts gives Buddhists the chance to develop and refine their emotional lives. The beauty, inspiration, and self-transcendence accessible through participation in western artistic traditions are of great benefit to us as we seek to understand reality beyond our limited egoic concerns. The arts can lift us and lead our imaginations beyond what we know. The pleasure they give directly educates the heart and mind. We should therefore wholeheartedly immerse ourselves in the aesthetic life, give ourselves over to music, poetry, and the visual arts; we should try out new artists, so as to expand our experience and taste. In this way we ourselves will come to experience the religion of art, and engage for ourselves in the exploration begun so energetically by Sangharakshita in Kalimpong.

Dhivan Thomas Jones
Cambridge
January 2010

AFTER RILKE

The poet is the world's interpreter,
At least to his own self. He recreates
In his own heart the things he contemplates,
And brings them forth transformed from what they were
Into a beauty-truth that cannot err,
That cannot fade or die. Though dull ingrates
May mock, no vile disparagement abates
The benefits the poet's words confer.

A tree is not a tree, unless within
The poet's all-transmuting mind it grows
Refined, reborn, – by his own power redeemed
Into a truer life. The poet's kin
Are Memnon, Orpheus, Merlin. History shows
The best but live what once the poet dreamed.

Sangharakshita

THE MEANING OF BUDDHISM AND THE VALUE OF ART

It was about a century ago that Schopenhauer, who, more deeply than any other Western thinker, was influenced by and imbued with the spirit of ancient Indian philosophy, ventured to predict that the renaissance that would be brought about by the discovery, in the nineteenth century, of the treasures of oriental literature, would be incomparably more glorious than that which had been ushered in during the fifteenth and sixteenth centuries by the rediscovery of the classics of Greece and Rome.[40] This bold prediction of the nineteenth century is being fulfilled, or at least beginning to be fulfilled, in the twentieth. What was merely political and commercial contact between the nations of the East and the West has begun to deepen into cultural exchanges and interreligious fellowship. Throughout every Western land, men and women are now to be found – few in number, indeed, but increasingly influential – who are convinced that, now as ever, light comes from the East: *Ex Oriente lux*.

Of the rays into which that light, shooting through the spectrum of human understanding, is broken up, none confronts occidental eyes with a steadier radiance, or shines forth with a more blindingly brilliant effulgence, than the hitherto unknown splendour to which the West, startled into awareness of a whole new world of values, has given the name 'Buddhism'. Yet often is that splendour dimmed by the opacity of the medium through which it is transmitted. Even today, when the Pali Text Society of London and other bodies, as well as distinguished scholars working independently in the field of Buddhist studies, have between them published a small library of Pāli, Sanskrit, Chinese, and Tibetan Buddhist texts and their translations, the writers of articles and compilers of popular handbooks on Buddhism, ignoring this mass of authentic material, are frequently found repeating the same old misunderstandings about Nirvāṇa and other points of Buddhist doctrine.

Such misunderstandings, when they are not due to ineradicable religious prejudice, such as still animates many Christian writers on non-Christian religions, may be traced to a misconception of the very nature of Buddhism. This misconception has its roots deep down in the history of Western thought. Briefly stated, it consists in regarding Buddhism as a system of philosophy in the modern academic sense.

To the ancient Greeks and Romans, philosophy was not merely an opinion, but a passion; it meant not only loftier thinking, but nobler living. A philosopher was expected to leave his hair and beard untrimmed, to wear but one long simple garment, to sleep on the bare ground, and to eat sparingly. With the irruption of Christianity into the Graeco-Roman world, the old classic ideals of moderation, balance, and harmony were destroyed. Wisdom was replaced by faith, while for the harmless and helpful philosophic life was substituted one of aggressive good works (which included the conversion of the heathen, by force, if necessary, and the burning of heretics). Between faith and works some kind of harmony was indeed sought to be maintained, but, covering as these did only a small part of the scale of human potentialities, this harmony was not rich or full enough to be long sustained, and, before many centuries had passed, the shrill note of faith first dominated and then drowned all others.

The modern scientific attitude of mind developed in part as a protest against the unverifiable dogmas of medieval Christianity, and every advance in scientific knowledge was made in the teeth of determined ecclesiastical opposition; for the schoolman, no less than the scientist, was aware that the victory of science spelled the defeat of faith. With the abandonment of Christian doctrine came the tacit repudiation of the Christian way of life, and, though individual thinkers continued to conform to Christian ethical standards and even, in some cases, professed to accept the Christian revelation, Western thought came more and more under the influence of science and developed with increasing freedom from religious preconceptions. The introduction of psychological and epistemological interests strengthened still further the theoretical and speculative tendencies in modern thought, and, by the time Schopenhauer arose to challenge the academic and professorial conception of philosophy, despite artificial attempts at reconciliation, the divorce between religion and philosophy had been made absolute.

A division between concrete living and abstract thinking continues to characterize modern Western culture. Philosophy is taught at universities as a purely theoretical subject; it does not demand from its votaries the adoption of a distinctive mode of life, neither does it have as a whole any bearing upon practical affairs. For the philosophic life, as it was understood by the Greeks and Romans in even their most degenerate days – the passionate pursuit of beauty, truth, and goodness, and the endeavour to reflect them in one's own life – has been substituted the detached and barren study of the history of philosophical opinions.

When the star of Buddhism first rose above these icy academic horizons, its dependence on reason rather than faith, its freedom from credulity and superstition, not unnaturally caused it to be regarded as an ethico-philosophical system rather than as a religion in the Christian sense of the term. Owing to the congenitally abstract proclivities of Western thought, the close connection between the practical and the theoretical aspects of Buddhism was gradually ignored, and topics such as the nature of Nirvāṇa came to be discussed as though they had a simply theoretical import that could be determined by the exercise of the speculative reason. The fact that Buddhism is, above all, a way of life was forgotten.

Most of the problems, and many of the misunderstandings, that have arisen in connection with Buddhism may be traced to this wrong habit of considering the significance of its profoundest teachings in complete dissociation from their pragmatic consequences in the actual Buddhist way of living. Owing to the introduction of a Western-style system of university education, such misunderstandings have taken root, and are flourishing, even here in the soil of India, despite the fact that in this country, even more decidedly than in Greece or Rome, philosophy was traditionally regarded as the theoretical side of religion, and religion as the practical side of philosophy. It therefore becomes necessary to stress the fact that Buddhism is not a system of abstract thought, and that it does not attempt to satisfy mere intellectual curiosity by giving a rationally coherent account of the universe.

Buddhism is a way of life that leads to a spiritual experience; in fact, to a number of experiences. These experiences link up into a series that culminates in the supreme experience of Nirvāṇa. Since it is not only a certain kind of thinking, but also a special way of living, the Dharma of the Enlightened One cannot be adequately understood by the reading of books, even Buddhist books, but only by practising it and making an effort to absorb its spirit into one's life. The teaching of Buddhist philosophy as part of a course of studies the principal aim of which is to 'qualify' the student for secular employment, by professors who make no attempt to put it into practice in their own lives, is really an abuse of Buddhism that will do both teacher and pupil, perhaps, as much harm as good.

Partly by way of a precaution against the danger of regarding Buddhism exclusively from the theoretical point of view, and partly because of the difficulty of giving, briefly, an adequate account of two such vast subjects as Buddhism and art, I propose to elucidate the meaning of Buddhism not by attempting to make a summary of its doctrines, but by endeavouring to present it in a more concrete and poetic manner. The Chinese have a proverb that one illustration is worth a thousand words. I shall seek to make clear the meaning of Buddhism not with one illustration only, but with three. Metaphors, similes, parables, and other literary forms have long been among the recognized vehicles of religious instruction, and, owing to their semi-poetic character, they often make a deeper and more enduring impression on our hearts than more learned but more prosaic treatment of the same theme can do.

The following parables, drawn from sources widely separate in time and place, may be considered as illustrating the meaning of Buddhism from what is the most deeply spiritual and, at the same time, the most truly practical standpoint from which it can be viewed.

The first of these may be called the parable of the well frog and the ocean frog. So well known to the people of India is this instructive fable that its hero has passed into a proverb, and 'well frog' (*kūpa maṇḍūka*) is an expression often applied, not without a touch of humour, to persons of narrow intelligence and bigoted views. The story is given in the words of Swami Vivekananda, by whom it was related, not without effect, at a session of the World's Parliament of Religions held in Chicago on 15 September 1893.

> A frog lived in a well. It had lived there for a long time. It was born there and brought up there, and yet was a little, small frog.

> Of course, the evolutionists were not there then to tell us whether the frog lost its eyes or not, but, for our story's sake, we must take it for granted that it had its eyes, and that it every day cleansed the water of all the worms and bacilli that lived in it with an energy that would do credit to our modern bacteriologists. In this way, it went on and became a little sleek and fat. Well, one day another frog that lived in the sea came and fell into the well.
> 'Where are you from?'
> 'I am from the sea.'
> 'The sea! How big is that? Is it as big as my well?' – and he took a leap from one side of the well to the other.
> 'My friend,' said the frog of the sea, 'how do you compare the sea with your little well?'
> Then the frog took another leap and asked, 'Is your sea so big?'
> 'What nonsense you speak, to compare the sea with your well!'
> 'Well then,' said the frog in the well, 'nothing can be bigger than my well; there can nothing bigger than this; this fellow is a liar, so turn him out.'[41]

The parable of the prisoners of the cave is as permanent a part of the cultural heritage of Europe as that of the well frog and the ocean frog is of the religious traditions of India. Unlike its popular Eastern parallel, it is not anonymous, but exhibits to a superlative degree that wonderful combination of truth and beauty, of philosophic insight and literary art, forever associated with the incomparable genius of Plato.

> 'Imagine a number of men living in an underground cavernous chamber, with an entrance open to the light, extending along the entire length of the cavern, in which they have been confined, from their childhood, with their legs and necks so shackled that they are obliged to sit still and look straight forwards, because their chains render it impossible for them to turn their heads round: and imagine a bright fire burning some way off, above and behind them, and an elevated roadway passing between the fire and the prisoners, with a low wall built along it, like the screens which conjurors put up in front of their audience, and above which they exhibit their wonders.'
> 'I have it,' Glaucon replied.

'Also figure to yourself a number of persons walking behind this wall, and carrying with them statues of men, and images of other animals, wrought in wood and stone and all kinds of materials, together with various other articles, which overtop the wall, and, as you might expect, let some of the passers-by be talking and others silent.'

'You are describing a strange scene, and strange prisoners.'

'They resemble us,' I replied. 'For let me ask you, in the first place, whether persons so confined could have seen anything of themselves or of each other, beyond the shadows thrown by the fire upon the part of the cavern facing them?'

'Certainly not, if you suppose them to have been compelled all their lifetime to keep their heads unmoved.'

'And is not their knowledge of the things carried past them equally limited?'

'Unquestionably it is.'

'And if they were able to converse with one another, do you not think that they would be in the habit of giving names to the objects which they saw before them?'

'Doubtless they would.'

'Again, if their prison-house returned an echo from the part facing them, whenever one of the passers-by opened his lips, to what, let me ask you, could they refer the voice, if not to the shadow which was passing?'

'Unquestionably they would refer it to that.'

'Then surely such persons would hold the shadows of those manufactured articles to be the only realities.'

'Without a doubt they would.'

'Now consider what would happen if the course of nature brought them a release from their fetters, and a remedy for their foolishness, in the following manner. Let us suppose that one of them has been released, and compelled suddenly to stand up, and turn his neck round and walk with open eyes towards the light and let us suppose that he goes through all these actions with pain, and that the dazzling splendour renders him incapable of discerning those objects of which he used formerly to see the shadows. What answer should you expect him to make, if someone were to tell him that in those days he was watching

> foolish phantoms, but that now he is somewhat nearer to reality, and is turned towards things more real, and sees more correctly; above all, if he were to point out to him the several objects that are passing by, and question him, and compel him to answer what they are? Should you not expect him to be puzzled, and to regard his old visions as truer than the objects now forced upon his notice?'
>
> 'Yes, much truer.'
>
> 'And if he were further compelled to gaze at the light itself, would not his eyes, think you, be distressed, and would he not shrink and turn away to the things which he could see distinctly, and consider them to be really clearer than the things pointed out to him?'
>
> 'Just so.'
>
> 'And if someone were to drag him violently up the rough and steep ascent from the cavern, and refuse to let him go till he had drawn him out into the light of the sun, would he not, think you, be vexed and indignant at such treatment, and on reaching the light, would he not find his eyes so dazzled by the glare as to be incapable of making out so much as one of the objects which are now called true?'
>
> 'Yes, he would find it so at first.'[42]

Such is the tremendous myth that Plato puts into the mouth of Socrates at the beginning of the seventh book of *The Republic.*

Our third and last parable carries us from Greece to India; from the house of Polemarchus in the Piraeus, outside Athens, to the Jeta Grove, in Anāthapiṇḍika's Park near Sāvatthī; from the noise and excitement of the Thracian festival in the fifth century BCE, back to the quarrels and disputations of recluses and *brāhmaṇas* in the sixth. So serious had these quarrels and disputes at one time become that they attracted the attention of certain *bhikkhus*, who came to the Buddha and reported the matter to him. After condemning the behaviour of those sectarians in strong terms, the Buddha related the parable of the blind men and the elephant. This parable was subsequently included in the repertoire of Indian storytellers, and appears frequently in popular religious literature. By a strange twist of interpretation, however, it is now quoted as an illustration of the belief that all religions are equally true. An examination of the Buddha's own words will reveal the fallaciousness of such an interpretation.

Formerly, monks, there was a certain rājah of this same Sāvatthī. Then, monks, that rājah called to a certain man, saying, 'Come thou, good fellow! Go and gather together in one place all the men in Sāvatthī who were born blind!'

'Very good, sire,' replied that man, and in obedience to the rājah gathered together all the men born blind in Sāvatthī, and having done so went to the rājah and said, 'Sire, all the blind men of Sāvatthī are now assembled.'

'Then, my good man, show the blind men an elephant.'

'Very good, sire,' said the man, and did as he was told, and said to them, 'O blind, such as this is an elephant'; and to one man he presented the head of the elephant, to another its ear, to another a tusk, to another the trunk, the foot, back, tail and tuft of the tail, saying to each one that that was the elephant.

Now, monks, that man, having thus presented the elephant to the blind men, came to the rājah and said, 'Sire, the elephant has been presented to the blind men. Do what is your will.'

Thereupon, monks, that rājah went up to the blind men and said to each, 'Well, blind man, have you [perceived] the elephant?'

'Yes, sire.'

'Then tell me, blind men, what sort of thing is an elephant.'

Thereupon those who had been presented with the head answered, 'Sire, an elephant is like a pot.' And those who had observed an ear only replied, 'An elephant is like a winnowing-basket.' Those who had been presented with a tusk said it was a ploughshare. Those who knew only the trunk said it was a plough; they said the body was a granary; the foot, a pillar; the back, a mortar; the tail, a pestle; the tuft of the tail, just a besom.'

Then they began to quarrel, shouting, 'Yes it is!' 'No it is not!' 'An elephant is not that!' 'Yes, it's like that!' and so on, till they came to fisticuffs over the matter.

Then, monks, that rājah was delighted with the scene.

Just so are those Wanderers holding other views, blind, unseeing, knowing not the profitable, knowing not the unprofitable. They know not dhamma. They know not what is not dhamma. In their ignorance of these things they are by nature quarrelsome, wrangling and disputatious, each maintaining it is thus and thus.

> Thereupon the Exalted One at that time, seeing the meaning of it, gave utterance to this verse of uplift:
>
> O how they cling and wrangle, some who claim
> Of brāhmin and recluse the honoured name.
> For, quarrelling, each to his view they cling.
> Such folk see only one side of a thing.[43]

These three parables illustrate different aspects of one truth. Each of them contains two different characters, or sets of characters, one representing a wider, more illumined, and more comprehensive state of consciousness; the other, a state of mind comparatively narrow, unillumined, and exclusive. In the first parable, the parochial outlook of the well frog, who dwells within a limited range of consciousness represented by the waters of the well, is sharply contrasted with the ampler vision of his visitor, the ocean frog, who inhabits a realm of consciousness which is infinite. Between those who, in the parable of the prisoners of the cave, are still fettered and can perceive only shadows flitting across the rear wall of their prison, and the released prisoner who has been dragged out of the cave and compelled to behold the light of day, a similar difference may be observed. The third parable contrasts the correct idea of an elephant possessed by a man of normal sight with the erroneous notions entertained by the blind, thus illustrating the enormous discrepancy between the all-embracing wisdom of the Buddha and the one-sided opinions of the sectarian teachers of his time. Thus we have on the one hand an infinite consciousness, represented by the waters of the ocean, the light of day, and the eyesight of a healthy man, and on the other a narrow state of consciousness, illustrated by the waters of the well, the gloom of the cave, and the lack of eyesight of the blind.

This difference renders possible two movements in consciousness, a movement of expansion from a narrower to a wider state, and a diametrically opposite movement of contraction from a wider to a narrower state.

Buddhism, as a way of life, as a practicable scheme of spiritual development, is based on the first movement, the movement of expansion. It aims at lifting us out of the well and plunging us into the ocean; at leading us from the darkness of the cave into the glorious light of the sun; at healing us of our spiritual blindness and restoring to our eyes the divine vision that they have lost. Ethically speaking this expansive movement in consciousness consists in a continual renunciation of the self, in a constant progression from egoism to selflessness. Though twenty-five centuries of history have led Buddhism to many new developments, particularly in the field of spiritual practice and meditational technique, the validity of such developments is to be tested by this criterion. If they lead to an expansion of consciousness, to an illumination of mind and purification of heart, to a higher degree of spiritual sharp-sightedness, to emancipation from the fetters of egoism, then they may be considered as the teaching of the Master himself. The Buddha stands alone among the founders of religions in not merely permitting, but even demanding, that instead of accepting his words on trust, we should believe them only after having verified their truth in our own spiritual experience, testing them, in his own expressive simile, as on the touchstone the goldsmith tests his gold.[44]

Our spatial metaphor may be elaborated, and the meaning of Buddhism rendered still more explicit, by pointing out that expansion takes place in two planes, the vertical and the horizontal. By an upward or downward movement of expansion in consciousness is meant a heightening or deepening (the two expressions come to much the same thing) of experience, an increase of insight, or augmentation of understanding; by a movement of expansion outwards is meant a constant multiplication of our points of contact with the external world, a ceaseless enlargement and elaboration of that delicate network of sympathy and affection by which we are connected in a thousand ways not only with all other human beings, but with every other form of life. To the upward and downward movement of expansion in consciousness, Buddhism gives the name 'wisdom' (*prajñā*); the movement of expansion outwards, it terms 'compassion' (*karuṇā*). We shall not greatly err if, from a strictly practical and spiritual point of view, we find in a life dedicated to the expansion of consciousness through the development of wisdom and compassion the ultimate meaning of Buddhism.

Having made the meaning of Buddhism clear at least for practical purposes, we must now investigate its relation to art. By art is not meant, as people so often suppose, merely the art of painting, but the sister arts of music and poetry, architecture and sculpture, as well. That Buddhism is justly famous not only for the richness and beauty of its artistic flowerings in India, but also for the fertility and vigour of the seeds it scattered all over Asia, is a commonplace of the history of oriental art that need not be repeated here. What we propose to trace, however, is not the relation between Buddhism and art on the historical level, but their connection on the immeasurably deeper levels of psychology and the spiritual life. We do not intend to trace the vicissitudes of Buddhist themes as the subject matter of art, or to give either a description or a critical account of Buddhist painting, sculpture, architecture, or literature, but simply to ascertain the nature of the inner connection, as two independent branches of human experience, between Buddhism as Buddhism and art as art. For only then shall we be able to estimate the value of art from the spiritual point of view.

Neither the relation of art to Buddhism nor its spiritual value can, however, be determined, until we have first acquainted ourselves with the precise nature of the subject of our inquiry. The word 'art', like all other general ideas, is a mere abstraction, and no more denotes an actually existing object than the words 'liberty', 'freedom', 'independence', and similar terms of which newspapers make such lavish use, denote concrete things existing either in the world of facts or in the realm of ideas. There is no such thing as art. Only works of art exist. No investigation into the nature of art can be fruitful that does not begin and end with a consideration of the nature of concrete pictures and poems.

Back to earth, then, we come from the cloudy heavens of abstraction and proceed to plant our feet firmly on the ground with an analysis of the individual artwork into its two component parts. These parts may be described, if a not too exact usage of scholastic terminology be permitted us, as substance and as form. By the substance of a work of art we mean the degree of sensitiveness or sensibility, the state of consciousness, the kind of experience or realization, which it expresses and communicates. Form, on the other hand, is the pleasurable pattern of sensations into which the rarefied thoughts and emotions of the artist condense and crystallize themselves and through which they find embodiment and expression. A refinement of analysis may help to define the second part more clearly. Even as the work of art is divisible into substance and form, so is the form in turn susceptible of a further division into a sensuous content and an organization of that sensuous content by means of pattern and rhythm. Eye and ear being the most prominent of the organs of sense, it follows that sensations of colour and shape (really we should telescope the words and say 'colourshape', as the two 'things', though distinguishable, are inseparable), and sensations of sound, provide the artist with the raw material of his creations. Brooding upon the chaos of visual sensations, the spirit of the artist begets dove-like the cosmos of painting, sculpture, and architecture; spreading wings over the abyss of sound, it produces the universe of poetry and music. At the fiat of creative genius the discordant atoms of sensation 'in order to their stations leap',[45] and obey, not the power of music, but the power whence music itself derives its influence.

Through their organization of visual sensations by means of the harmonious arrangement of colours, shapes, and surfaces, and of auditory sensations by means of rhythm and melody, the painter, the sculptor, and the architect, on the one hand, and the poet and the musician, on the other, make patterns that are beautiful and which produce pleasure. These pleasurable patterns of sensations, which compose the form of a work of art, are in turn arranged in such a way as to express the artist's feelings and sense of values, which make up what we have termed its substance.

Without entering into the psychology of artistic creation, or attempting to investigate the nature of that mysterious urge by which his life is dominated and sometimes destroyed, it may be affirmed that from the viewpoint of the artist there is a movement from substance to form, from the feelings that arise so irresistibly within him to the ultimate embodiment of those feelings in metal, wood, and stone, in pigment, words, and notes. This movement is creation. From the viewpoint of one who reads a poem, looks at a picture, or listens to a song, there is a movement from form to substance, from patterns made of certain visual and auditory sensations, from patches of colour and snatches of sound, to participation in the experience they embody. This movement is one of enjoyment or appreciation. But whether, in respect of the creative and appreciative experience of a work of art, there takes place a movement from substance to form, or from form to substance, it is of far greater importance to our present inquiry that there occurs in both cases that stretching of the mind 'some distance beyond the limits of the understanding', which Herbert Read has clearly recognized as 'the function of art',[46] and which we have already discovered and described, in the form of an expansion of consciousness, as constituting the spiritual meaning of Buddhism. In the case of the artist, the stretching or expansion is the cause of which the work of art is the effect. In the case of the enjoyer or appreciator (we would use the less clumsy appellation 'critic', if it had not acquired such an unsympathetic connotation), the stretching of the mind beyond the limits of understanding, or the expansion of consciousness beyond the boundaries of selfhood, is the effect whereof the work of art is the cause.

As with the expansion of consciousness through Buddhism, so, with its expansion by means of art, the movement of expansion takes place in two directions, on two planes. In Buddhism there is a movement of wisdom upwards or downwards, and a movement of compassion outwards. Corresponding to this, there is in art an intensification or heightening of sensibility, as well as an extension or widening of sympathy. Some forms of art have a tendency to expand our consciousness in one direction rather than in another, while others expand it in both. Lyric poetry, for instance, lifts our gross human emotions of love and anguish, hope and despair, to so high a pitch of intensity that earthly passions are refined into spiritual raptures, and our whole emotional being keyed to a higher and purer octave of feeling. Classical music, whether Eastern or Western, often produces the same kind of effect. Dramatic poetry, on the contrary, by introducing us to men and women of every imaginable age and country, with every conceivable variation of character and circumstances; by compelling us to watch with interest and concern the vicissitudes of their fortunes; by forcing us to weep with them in their day of sorrow and rejoice with them in their hour of mirth, extends and enlarges the house of our sympathies by a thousand ramifications into the many mansions of other lives. Epic and narrative poetry generally stretch the mind in the same direction as the dramatic; and so, on a lower level, do the novel and the short story.

Such a distribution of functions between the fine arts should not, however, be taken in too literal and exclusive a sense, or regarded as being of very great importance to our present inquiry. All that we now wish to insist upon is the fact that every genuine work of art enlarges the circle of our consciousness, and that in this enlargement of consciousness the value of a work of art, from the spiritual point of view, consists.

Just as there are two kinds of expansion of consciousness, so within each kind are there infinite degrees of expansion. Some works of art lift us, as it were, only a few inches above the ground; others transport us to the empyrean. This difference of degree, whereby we distinguish the palpitations of Tom Moore from the authentic thrill of Shelley, is due to a difference in the quality of their inspiration. It is one of the great merits of Sri Aurobindo's literary criticism that he so clearly distinguishes the different levels whence the flow of poetic inspiration may descend. Without necessarily endorsing all the details of his stratification of existence, we can both recognize and make use of the truth enunciated in the following passage:

> The originating source may be anywhere; the poetry may arise or descend from the subtle physical plane, from the higher or lower vital itself, from the dynamic or creative intelligence, from the plane of dynamic vision, from the psychic, from the illumined mind or Intuition – even, though this is the rarest, from the Overmind widenesses. To get the Overmind inspiration is so rare that there are only a few lines or short passages in all poetic literature that give at least some appearance or reflection of it.[47]

Coupling Sri Aurobindo's doctrine with our own discovery, we may say that the higher the source of artistic inspiration the greater is the expansion of consciousness involved and the higher the spiritual value of the work of art produced. Care should be taken, though, not to confuse the essentially spiritual function of art as art with the didacticism of conventionally religious art. To make the matter clearer, it will be convenient to summarize a classification that we have made elsewhere.

From the dual viewpoint of subject matter and quality of inspiration, four categories of art can be distinguished. The first is neither religious in form nor spiritualizing in effect. Spawned as it is in the slimiest depths of our psychic nature, it not only fails to expand our consciousness, but, pandering to our lust for sex and crime, thrusts us down into the hell of an even lower and narrower range of consciousness. In modern life examples of this kind of art are legion, and specification would be almost invidious. Tabloid newspapers, pulp magazines, and the majority of popular films may be mentioned as the principal purveyors of this pseudo-artistic trash. The second category of art is that which is formally, but not essentially, religious. Such are the lithographed pictures of gods and saints and religious teachers which one finds in the possession of devout people all over the world. Though religious in theme, they are either technically inept or executed in mechanical fashion, without feeling, and do not produce an expansion of consciousness so much as condition a devotional reflex. Thirdly, we have a type of art that is essentially, though not formally, religious. Chinese landscape painting springs at once to mind as the almost classic example of this category of art. Though devoid of any formally religious content, such paintings are in the deepest sense spiritual, the extraordinary sense of liberation and infinite expansion of consciousness that they produce in the spectator being sufficient proof of the tremendous height of inspiration whence, like a cataract that 'smokes upon the mountainside', they descend through brushes and black ink onto rolls of silk.

The fourth and last of our categories includes works of art that are both formally and essentially religious. Enough has been said of the three previous categories to make clear, without need of further explanation, the nature of this one, the crown and flower of them all. The ancient Buddhist art of India and Ceylon, China and Japan, Tibet and Cambodia, may without reproach of partiality be allowed the honour of representing this supreme class. Though it is difficult, even impossible, to single out any one type of Buddhist art as being more typical of the whole group than are others, it will no doubt be conceded that the sedent image of the Buddha in meditation is the most popular and widely known of all. Here the meaning of Buddhism and the value of art coalesce upon the lips of the Buddha into a smile that expresses what is, perhaps, the greatest expansion of consciousness that it is possible for the plastic arts to mediate.

From how high a quality of inspiration the work of art issued, we hardly dare to guess. How tremendous an effect it can have upon the whole character may be understood from a story that we heard a few weeks ago from a French lady, a scholar in Sanskrit and poetess in her own language, now a Buddhist nun in India, who had received so deep an impression – a spiritual shock of such high voltage – from an image of this kind that she had seen in the Musée Guimet in Paris that she resolved to consecrate her whole life to the study and practice of Buddhism, so as to experience for herself, to however small an extent, that liberation of consciousness, that wisdom and compassion, which shone through those stone features as though they had been transparent to a light within.[48]

An archaic torso of Apollo that the poet Rilke saw in a museum seems to have produced a similar transformation in his consciousness; but, since he was a poet, the transformation was not so much reflected in his life as registered in his art. Not that he was unaware of the spiritual significance of deep aesthetic experience. He was, perhaps, more conscious of the inner relations between the experience of the saint and the experience of the artist than any modern poet, and this consciousness makes him, in an age when external contact between religion and art has been broken off, an artist whose work is of very special significance and value. If the first twelve and a half lines of his sonnet, 'An Archaic Torso of Apollo', show how deep, how heartfelt, was his experience of beauty, the concluding one and a half lines, which mark an abrupt, almost a violent, transition from the descriptive to the reflective mood, reveal how clearly he understood the ethical and spiritual demands of that experience, and how little afraid he was to meet and grapple with them. His meaning is unmistakable, as feeling abruptly deepens into insight and he cries out,

> ... for here is no place
> That does not see you. You must change your life.[49]

This change of life, this transformation of character and attitude, constitutes not only the message of the Buddha image and of the archaic torso of Apollo, but, as we have tried to show, the essence and meaning of Buddhism and the real value of art as well.

Buddhism and art both effect a two-dimensional expansion in consciousness; the practical results that they achieve are of the same kind, however greatly such results may vary in degree, and however dissimilar may be the methods employed by Buddhism, on the one hand, and art, on the other, to bring them about. Buddhism effects an expansion of consciousness by acting directly on the understanding and the will. Art produces a change of life indirectly, by appealing to our sense of beauty. Since man possesses an emotional as well as an intellectual and a volitional nature, and is capable of response to beauty no less than to truth and goodness, it is necessary for him to develop and expand simultaneously the emotional, intellectual, and volitional aspects of his personality. Buddhism and art, therefore, are both indispensable to a balanced spiritual life. Not that we intend to suggest an absolutely exclusive distribution of functions between them, allotting to Buddhism the sole responsibility for developing the mind, and to art the sole responsibility for developing the emotions. Every thought possesses emotional colouring, however obscure. Buddhism, though acting primarily on the intellect, certainly makes a powerful secondary appeal to the emotions, especially to the devotional feelings, which are developed as fully, though not so one-sidedly, in members of the Buddhist community as in people belonging to religions that appeal more to the heart than to the head, to faith rather than to reason. Art, though it operates on the imagination directly, does not fail to influence the understanding. In poetry especially, it is impossible to dissociate the emotional impact of a work of art from the framework of objective reference to which it is attached and which constitutes its 'meaning' for the intellect.

Whether the life of any particular person will be dominated more by interests pertaining to Buddhism, or more by interests pertaining to art, is a question that will be determined by the relative strength in him of reason and of emotion. We are concerned only to insist, first of all, that the meaning of Buddhism coincides with the value of art; and secondly, that the development of understanding and insight through the one, and of imagination and sensitiveness to beauty through the other is, for modern men and women, in whom the emotional life and the intellectual life are of almost equal vividness and vigour, not only a need, but almost a necessity.

Despite the obviously spiritualizing influence of many great works of art, there may be found, in different communities and religious bodies, people who think that religion and art are mutually exclusive, and that one who takes his religious life seriously ought to have no more to do with art than with drinking, dancing, and gambling. Puritans of this brand believe that since art makes its appeal through the senses – through eye and ear – its content is necessarily sensual and even sexual. To their way of thinking, which is wholly incapable of visualizing the wider horizons into which a life of genuine spirituality may open, an artistic life is practically synonymous with a career of immorality.

Whenever a reaction against puritanism sets in, its supporters generally go to the other extreme and proclaim the doctrine of art for art's sake. The middle way between these two extreme views is indicated by Sri Aurobindo, who in some published letters to his poet-disciples has advanced what appears to be a satisfactory solution of the problem. All four extracts given below have been taken from Section Eight (dealing with *Poetic Creation and Yoga* and with *Utility of Literature, etc. in*

Sadhana) of the Third Series of his letters, to which those interested in the subject are referred for further information.

> (1) A 'literary man' is one who loves literature and literary activity for their own separate sake. A Yogi who writes is not a literary man, for he writes only what the inner Will and Word wants him to express. He is a channel and an instrument of something greater than his own literary personality.[50]
>
> (2) I have always told you that you ought not to stop your poetry and similar activities. It is a mistake to do so out of asceticism or with the idea of *tapasyā*. One can stop these things when they drop of themselves, because one is in full experience and so interested in one's inner life that one has no energy to spare for the rest. Even then, there is no rule for giving up; for there is no reason why the poetry, etc., should not be a part of sadhana.[51]
>
> (3) It would be a mistake to silence the poetic flow on principle. Creative activity is a tonic to the vital and keeps it in a good condition, and a strong and widening vital is helpful as a support to the practice of sadhana. There is no real incompatibility between the creative power and silence; for the real silence is something inward and it does not or at least need not cease when a strong activity or expression rises to the surface.[52]
>
> (4) The Vedic poets regarded the poetry as *mantras*, they were the vehicles of their own realisations and could be the vehicles of realisation for others.... Anything that carries the Word, the Light in it, spoken or written, can light this fire within, open a sky, as it were, bring the effective vision of which the Word is the body.... In all ages spiritual seekers have expressed their aspirations or their experiences in poetry or inspired language, and it has helped themselves and others. Therefore there is nothing absurd in my assigning to such poetry a spiritual or psychic value and effectiveness of a psychic or spiritual character.[53]

This firm and emphatic vindication of the spiritual function of poetry, and, by implication, of the arts in general, could hardly be bettered, and may be allowed to stand as an adequate reply to all the objections which puritanism may urge against the creation and enjoyment of works of art.

But one serious difficulty still remains to be faced. Granting that the inner relation between Buddhism and art is such as we have described, and that art is, or at least can be, as Sri Aurobindo maintains, a part of *sādhana*, are we justified in assuming that such a view of the matter is correct from the standpoint of orthodox Buddhism? Are we not guilty of misrepresenting the Buddhist doctrine of the value of art? Buddhist art is undoubtedly a glorious achievement from the artistic point of view. But can it be regarded as a strictly Buddhist achievement? Is it not rather a beautiful excrescence on the trunk of Buddhism, like the mistletoe on the oak, or the orchid on the elm?

Some Buddhists do, in fact, seem to be of this opinion. They believe that the arts stimulate sexual desire, and that the Buddha, therefore, prohibited his *bhikkhu* disciples from enjoying works of art. For them this prohibition is implicit in the eighth precept, observed by all *bhikkhus*, and by lay devotees on the *uposatha* days: *Nacca-gīta-vādita –visukadassanā veramaṇi sikkhāpadaṃ samādhiyāmi*,[54] which is generally translated as 'I observe the precept of abstaining from dances, songs, instrumental music, and theatrical performances.' This precept, they maintain, in effect excludes not only the enjoyment of the arts of singing, dancing, and music, but also of poetry and painting, sculpture and architecture, from all of which a true follower of the Buddha should hold himself rigidly aloof. Buddhism is, in their opinion, puritanical in its attitude to art. An enlightened mind, which is free from even the slightest taint of desire, is by its very nature incapable of aesthetic enjoyment, for such enjoyment, they believe, is of a fundamentally sensuous and even sexual character.

Whether Buddhism agrees with this puritanical evaluation of the nature and function of art, or whether its view of the relation between the spiritual life and the artistic life approximates to that which we have taken above, is a question which can be answered firstly, by referring to Sri Aurobindo's teaching about the different levels, from the subtle physical to that of the overmind, whence artistic inspiration can originate, and secondly, by an appeal to the personal example of the Buddha.

From information available in the three baskets (*tripiṭaka*) of canonical scriptures, and in their commentaries, it is evident that the dancing, singing, instrumental music, and theatrical performances of the eighth precept belonged to the first of our four categories of art:

that is to say, they were neither religious in form nor spiritualizing in effect. Like the songs, dances, and orchestral music of the contemporary film, they originated from what Sri Aurobindo terms the subtle physical and vital planes, and it may be contended that the Buddha required his disciples to abstain from such kinds of entertainment not because they were art, but because they were not art of that deeper and more genuine kind that we have included in the third and fourth of our categories. The prohibitions of the eighth precept can no more be generalized into a total exclusion of all kinds of art from the purview of the spiritual life than, for example, a contemporary spiritual master's disapproval of cinema-going could be construed as a condemnation of classical music, or of poetry and painting. Sri Aurobindo, whose views on the spiritual function of art we have quoted so extensively, says of novel-reading in *sādhana*: 'If novels touch the lower vital or raise it, they ought not be read by the sadhak.'[55] No contradiction is involved in prohibiting one kind of art to the spiritual aspirant and permitting him the other. Indeed, it is just what might have been expected.

But even though, in imparting the eighth precept to his monastic disciples and lay devotees, the Buddha intended no more than a prohibition of the ancient Indian equivalent of dance-music, what evidence is there (it may be demanded) that he regarded the appreciation of art, the enjoyment and creation of painting, poetry, and music, as being compatible with the demands of the spiritual life? If the records of his life and teaching contain even one reference to his appreciation of the beauties of art, it will be sufficient to prove that such appreciation is not impossible to the Enlightened mind and that, therefore, the content of art is compatible with the content of spirituality. We shall cite not merely one but three such references, the first demonstrating his appreciation of music, the second his approval of poetry, and the third his sensitiveness to visual beauty.

The Buddha's appreciation of music is recorded in the *Sakkapañha Sutta* of the *Dīgha Nikāya*, the first of the five great divisions of the Sutta Pitaka or 'Basket of Discourses'. Sakka, king of the gods, wished to ask the Buddha certain questions, but seeing that he was absorbed in meditation hesitated to approach him. He therefore sent in advance one of the *gandharvas*, or celestial musicians, of his court, whose skill in music and song is in Indian literature as famous, though not as fatal, as that of the Sirens in the literature of the West. We quote the whole of this charming episode, which provides an introduction of great literary beauty to the more serious discussions between the Buddha and Sakka which make up the bulk of this *Sutta*.

> Then Sakka, King of the Gods, spoke to Pañcasikha the musician: 'My dear Pañcasikha, it is hard for someone like me to get near to the *tathāgatas*; they live in solitude, continually enjoying deep absorption in meditation. But, my dear Pañcasikha, if you were first to gain the Blessed One's attention, then afterwards I might myself be able to get near the Blessed One, whose attention you had engaged, that worthy and fully Awakened One, so as to see him.'
>
> 'Certainly, and all the best,' replied Pañcasikha the musician to Sakka, King of the Gods; and taking his pale bilva-wood lute he approached the cave [where the Buddha was sitting]. Having arrived, he decided to stand neither too far from the Blessed One, nor too near, but to one side where his voice would be heard. So, standing to one side, Pañcasikha the musician played his pale bilva-wood lute, and recited these verses about the Buddha, the Dharma, the Sangha, about Arahants and about love:
>
> Lovely Lady Sunshine, source of my joy,
> I honour Timbaru, your father, through whom you came to be.
>
> You're like water for the thirsty, or like a cool breeze;
> Radiant Goddess, I love you, like Arahants love Dharma.
>
> Be medicine for my sickness, for my hunger be food;
> Put my fire out, Lady, be cool water where I burn.
>
> Let me plunge down onto your belly and breasts,
> Like an over-heated beast into a flowering lotus pool.
>
> Like a crazed elephant, heedless of sticks, spears or work,
> I've gone blank, maddened by your amazing thighs.
>
> My heart's tangled up with you, my mind's turned upside-down;
> I'm hooked like a fish, and I can't leave you behind.

Delightful thighs, wrap me; soft-eyed Lady, hold me;
Lovely one, embrace me – how I pray for this!

There wasn't much love in me but now, because of your curls,
My love's become infinite, like a donation made to Arahants.

Whatever merit I've made in relation to such Arahants,
May it ripen in my being with your complete loveliness.

Whatever good I've done on this wide earth,
May its fruition be my being with your perfect beauty.

Just as Śākyamuni – focused, wise and aware – through meditation
Sought the deathless, so I want you, sweet Sunshine;

And as the sage rejoiced, attaining the highest enlightenment
So I'd be delighted, my lovely, to be making love with you.

If Sakka, Lord of heaven, were to grant me a wish,
Ah, Lady, my love's so strong I'd choose you.

Saluting him I honour your father, woman of wisdom, as I would
A suddenly-blooming Sāl-tree, for such a daughter's sake.

When it was over, the Blessed One said to Pañcasikha the musician: 'The sound of your strings harmonizes so well with that of your singing, and the sound of your singing harmonizes so well with that of your strings, that the sound of your strings does not dominate that of your singing, nor the sound of your singing that of your strings. Where, Pañcasikha, did you compose these verses about the Buddha, the Dharma, the Sangha, about Arahants, and about love?'

'At one time, Lord, the Blessed One was living at Uruvelā, on a bank of the river Nerañjarā, at the root of the Goatherd's banyan, before you were awakened. Now at that time I very much wanted this lovely Lady Sunshine, called Bhaddā, daughter of Timbarū, the king of the musicians. But, Lord, the lady was with someone else, Sikhaddi, the son of Mātali the charioteer. Then, Lord, since I couldn't find any way to have the lady, I took up my pale bilva-wood lute and went to the house of Timbaru, the king of musicians, and there I played my pale bilva-wood lute, and recited these verses about the Buddha, the Dharma, the Sangha, about Arahants and about love… [The text here repeats the verses].

'When it was over, Lord, the Lady Sunshine, said to me: "I have not seen this Blessed One personally, but I heard him mentioned when I was dancing in the Sudhammā Hall of the Heaven of the Thirty-Three. Because you, my friend, have praised that Blessed One, let us get together right away." And indeed, Lord, that lady and I got together, and we've been so ever since.'[56]

At the end of the *sutta* Sakka, the king of the gods, having obtained from the Buddha satisfactory answers to all his questions, and having gained 'the stainless spotless Eye for the Truth', in return for the services he had rendered made Pañcasikha king of the musicians and bestowed upon him the hand of the Lady Sunshine. This idyllic episode reveals not only the Buddha's appreciation of music, but also his tender humanity. One can almost imagine the smile of amusement with which the Passionless One listened to the woes of the lovelorn *gandharva*.

The Buddha's appreciation of poetry has been recorded in the *Vaṅgīsa-saṃyutta*, the eighth section of the *Saṃyutta Nikāya* (*Book of the Kindred Sayings*). Vaṅgīsa was one of the most gifted of the Buddha's disciples, and each of the group of twelve *suttas* bearing his name contains a piece of poetry together with a prose introduction narrating the circumstances that led to its composition. The poetry is included, without the prose, in the *Theragāthā*, or 'Songs of the Elder Bhikkhus', one of the books of the *Khuddaka Nikāya*, which also contains verses by Vaṅgīsa from the *Sutta-Nipāta* not found in the *Saṃyutta*. The first four poems are verses of self-condemnation, of repentance for lust and pride, and express the poet's determination to attain to the extinction of all mental impurities in the passionless peace of *nibbāna*. The following seven *suttas*, most of which contain verses of great literary beauty, reveal the Buddha and, in one case, Sāriputta also as encouraging Vaṅgīsa in the exercise of his poetic gift. *Sutta* 11 is short and poetic enough to be quoted in full as a typical example of the Buddha's attitude.

> At one time the Blessed One was living in Campā, on the banks of the lotus pond at Gaggarā, with a large group of monks, numbering 500 *bhikkhus*, 700 male lay followers, 700 female lay followers, and several thousand deities, though the Blessed One outshone them with his beauty and glory. Then Venerable Vaṅgīsa thought, 'This Blessed one is living in Campā, on the banks of the lotus pond at Gaggarā, with a large group of monks, numbering 500 *bhikkhus*, 700 male lay followers, 700 female lay followers, and several thousand deities, and the Blessed One outshines them with his beauty and glory. Should I not praise the Blessed One in his presence with appropriate verses?'
>
> Then Venerable Vaṅgīsa, rising from his seat, arranging his robe over his shoulder, and saluting the Blessed One with folded hands, said this to him: 'Blessed One, inspiration has struck me! Joyful One, inspiration has struck me!'
>
> 'Share your inspiration, Vaṅgīsa,' said the Blessed One.
>
> Then Venerable Vaṅgīsa praised the Blessed One in his presence with appropriate verses:
>
> Like the full moon on a cloudless night,
> Or the sun shining in a clear blue sky,
> You, great sage, like a God of Fire,
> Outshine the whole world with your glory.[57]

In each of the other six *suttas*, also, Vaṅgīsa is encouraged to make use of his by no means inconsiderable poetic talents, and he improvises verses on 'speech that is well spoken', in praise of Sāriputta, on occasion of the *pavāraṇā* ceremony, on the preaching of the Buddha, on Aññāsi-Koṇḍañña's homage to the Master, and in recognition of the psychic power of Moggallāna. *Sutta* 8 contains not only the permission to improvise for which Vaṅgīsa asks, and the Buddha invariably grants, but a few additional lines of dialogue, not found in the other *suttas*, which prove how emphatic was the Blessed One's approval, and how unambiguous his encouragement, of the type of poetry in which Vaṅgīsa excelled. After Vaṅgīsa, in a burst of enthusiasm, had compared the

Buddha preaching the Dharma to his disciples to a great storm cloud pouring down plenteous rain upon the earth and had concluded with a stanza in adoration of the Master, the Exalted One said:

> 'These verses of yours, Vaṅgīsa, had you already thought them out, or did inspiration just strike you spontaneously?'
> 'Lord, these verses of mine were not already thought out, but inspiration just struck me spontaneously.'
> 'Well, Vaṅgīsa, might you be inspired to share some more of these verses not already thought out?'
> 'Of course, Lord,' Venerable Vaṅgīsa replied to the Blessed One, and he praised him with still more verses not already thought out:
>
> Overwhelming Māra's misleading ways,
> You go on bursting every boundary.
> Behold him, unbound liberation-maker,
> Quite detached, sharing his discoveries.
>
> For the sake of ferrying over the flood,
> You have shown the path with its several parts.
> Those who see Dharma stand immovable
> In the same Deathless that you have declared.
>
> Lighter-up of every crack and corner,
> You saw through every standpoint for views.
> Having yourself known and realized the truth,
> You taught it at first to the group of five.
>
> Now the Dharma has been well demonstrated,
> Who could be unheeding who knows about it?
> Therefore, always heedful and devout, we
> Will train in the teaching of the Blessed One.[58]

In the sixth century BCE Indian painting had not yet embarked upon the career which was to culminate in the frescoes that glorify the caves of Ajanta, and we are, therefore, precluded from referring to any instance of the Buddha's appreciation of visual art in its more refined and developed forms. At least one example, however, can be cited of his sensitiveness to the beauty of the human body in motion, and to the harmonious effect of contrasted colours; and, inasmuch as form and colour constitute the two basic elements of the visual arts, the Buddha's appreciation of them as they occur in nature may be understood as being in principle not different from the appreciation of the arts of painting and sculpture. Our example is taken from the *Mahāparinibbāna Sutta* of the *Dīgha Nikāya*, which is admitted to contain some of the oldest and most authentic material found in the Pāli canon. The passage throws an interesting sidelight on contemporary sartorial fashions.

> Now the Licchavis of Vesāli heard that the Exalted One had arrived in Vesāli, and was staying at Ambapālī's grove. And ordering a number of state carriages to be made ready, they each mounted one of them and went forth with their train from Vesāli. Some of them were dark, dark in colour, and wearing dark clothes and ornaments: some of them were fair, fair in colour, and wearing light clothes and ornaments: some of them were red, ruddy in colour, and wearing red clothes and ornaments: some of them were white, pale in colour, and wearing white clothes and ornaments....
>
> When the Exalted One saw the Licchavis approaching in the distance, he addressed the brethren and said: 'O brethren, let those of the brethren who have never seen the Tāvatiṃsa gods, gaze upon this company of the Licchavis, behold this company of the Licchavis, compare this company of the Licchavis – for they are even as a company of Tāvatiṃsa gods.'[59]

The simile implied by this passage is not present by an accident. Aesthetic emotion naturally tends to express itself, on the literary side, in figures of speech of various kinds. That the Buddha, moved by the beauty of the richly dressed and ornamented Licchavis, should have compared them to a company of celestial beings, is not attributable to any desire on his part for the edification of the brethren, but rather to the spontaneous outburst of his aesthetic emotions.

In addition to these specific instances of the Buddha's own appreciation of art, it is possible to adduce in support of our contention that, even from the orthodox Buddhist point of view, the content of art is not incompatible with the content of spirituality, and that the religious life does not exclude artistic interests, a number of general considerations. Since the Buddha's teachings were preserved not by means of pictures of musical notation, but in words that were subsequently written down in books as works of literature, it is inevitable that these considerations should be of a predominantly literary character. One of the first things that arrest our attention when we take up any canonical Pāli book is that a great deal of it is in verse. Some books, indeed, such as the *Dhammapada* and the *Sutta-Nipāta*, consist either entirely of verses, or contain only a small intermixture of prose passages. The *Thera-* and *Therī-gāthās* or 'Psalms of the Elder Brethren and Elder Sisters', many of them extemporized after their composer's Enlightenment, are, perhaps, the most outstanding examples of the former class. Besides being spiritual documents of rare value, they contain gems of spiritual poetry of the first water, and Caroline Rhys Davids, in the Introduction to her pioneer work of translation, *Psalms of the Early Buddhists – 1: The Brethren*, has not hesitated to compare the most poetically gifted of the *theras* with Keats and Shelley. Though felicity of verbal music is the basis of her comparison, it is by no means the only point of similarity between the verses of the Indian and English poets. Like the Romantics, the *theras* had an eye for the beauties of nature, and Caroline Rhys Davids goes so far as to suggest – the idea might shock an 'orthodox' Buddhist – that they sought the solitude of the forests as much for aesthetic as for spiritual reasons.[60]

It is even possible to claim the Buddha himself for a poet. The Pāli scriptures contain thousands of verses that are traditionally believed to have fallen from the lips of the Master. One whole book, the *Udāna*, consists of a number of verses, each followed by a narrative in prose of the circumstances that led to its composition, which the Buddha 'breathed out' (the literal meaning of the title-word) in moments of intense emotional pressure.

The bulk of the sacred canon, though prose in form, is frequently poetical in spirit. Enriched with vivid and appropriate metaphors, similes, parables, and other figures of speech, which delight the imagination as well as illumine the understanding, the discourses of the Buddha often glow with a subdued and serene loveliness that makes his words as beautiful as they are true. The undeniable fact that the Buddha and his Enlightened disciples could appreciate and enjoy the beauty of nature and of art, and that they could even add to the sum of that beauty by their own aesthetic activities, is, we believe, sufficient proof of our contention that religion and art both are manifestations of the same movement of self-transcendence, and that the genuine devotee and the true artist travel along ultimately converging paths.

For the benefit of those who, though knowing that the passages we have cited from the scriptures are authentic, may doubt whether the interpretation we have given of them is correct, we shall set the final seal of orthodoxy upon our views by quoting a modern writer of unquestionable reliability whose expositions of Buddhist doctrine are based on the strictest commentarial tradition. Referring to mental culture (*bhāvanā*), the second of the three stages into which, according to one scheme, the path to Nirvāṇa is divided, Dr C. L. A. de Silva says,

> The volitions arising in the processes of thought during the time of learning the Dharma Vinaya (the doctrine) or any arts, sciences, and so on too are included under the heading of mental culture or *bhāvanā*.'[61]

The inseparability of Buddhism and art arises out of the nature of our psychic life. Though will, intelligence, and emotion may be distinguished in thought from one another, and spoken of as if they were separate 'faculties', in reality they can no more be divided in this way than can the shifting green and gold and purple that shimmer on a pigeon's neck. Consequently, the spiritual development of man must either take place on all levels of his being, in all aspects of his personality, practical as well as theoretical, emotional no less than intellectual, or not at all. One 'part' of him cannot soar eagle-like in the empyrean while another wallows pig-like in the mire; for ultimately there are no 'parts', and it is not piecemeal, but as a whole, that the life of man must either rise or fall in the scale of values. Spiritual practice – taking the expression in the widest sense as whatever conduces to expansion of consciousness, to self-transcendence – must develop to the full all the 'faculties' with which human personality is endowed; and it must develop them not one-sidedly but in a manner so harmonious that, at every stage of the spiritual ascent, they balance each other and approximate as nearly as possible to that condition of perfect equilibrium which will be theirs when consciousness has been expanded to its farthest limits, the ego utterly transcended.

Modern man, by which we mean modern Western man and his imitators in Eastern countries, suffers from a dissociation of intellect and emotion so chronic that it has almost paralysed his will for spiritual good. A kind of psychological elephantiasis has made him monstrous with an overdeveloped intellect and underdeveloped emotions. By this we do not mean that he is emotionally inactive; far from it! But that his emotional life, if so crudely spatial a metaphor may be pardoned, is on a much lower level than his intellectual life. His emotions are not non-existent, but undeveloped. Intellectually mature, he remains in feeling a child. The scientist, whose intellectual curiosity is not satisfied until he has numbered all the stars of the Milky Way, or measured as though with a rod the immensities of the heaven, seems to find full satisfaction for the affective side of his nature in the emotional muck-heaps of the popular film, in detective fiction, or in an occasional sexual embrace. One of the results of this rupture between the intellectual and the emotional life is that even the intellect is not developed with reference to a scale of values external to itself, but only with reference to the degree of its own internal complication. The need of modern man is, we conclude, for a development in his emotional nature which will render spiritually fruitful the intellectual development which has already taken place, and which will, by restoring the long lost equilibrium between his faculties, render possible for the whole personality that movement of ascent, of expansion of consciousness and self-transcendence, the secret of which seems to have been lost to Western civilization for so many centuries.

One of the normal instruments of emotional development in the past was religious devotion. But religion in the dogmatic Western Christian sense of the term has become so repugnant to modern man that the use of this instrument is often impossible. The discovery of some other means of refining his emotional life, therefore, becomes an imperative necessity. Such a method, we believe, may be found in the creation and enjoyment of works of art, provided that these activities are carried on with a vivid awareness of their spiritual function and significance. The desiderative nature of man clamours for satisfaction, and its demands cannot be ignored. If an outlet is not found for it on a higher level, then it will force one for itself on a lower. Sublimation of desire is, perhaps, the central problem of ethics, for sublimated desire is the dynamo that generates the energy whereby the machinery of the whole spiritual life is kept in motion. Art is important and valuable, in some cases even necessary, to the spiritual life, because it provides a channel for the emotional energies, leading them from lower to ever-higher levels of expression. At each level the emotions galvanize the whole personality into activity: on the lower levels, into the innumerable activities whereby the ordinary man seeks to gratify his petty lusts and vanities; on the higher, as compassion, into the infinitely diverse expedients whereby Buddhas and bodhisattvas seek to deliver mankind.

For the sublimation of the emotions, two things are necessary: a consciously imposed check on the lower, and a consciously opened outlet on the higher, levels of experience. The first is generally provided for the individual by the society in which he lives through a system of taboos. Of these taboos, the most important are those that, by checking the expression of the two primary emotions of love and hate, regulate the creative and destructive functions of emotion. Unfortunately, modern society often imposes the checks on one level without opening the outlets on the other. The individual, lacking any view of life which enables him to understand the possibility of attaining to a higher and wider kind of experience, is irritated by the constant imposition of what appear to him quite arbitrary checks to his natural impulses, and ultimately rebels against them. Psychological facts such as these help to explain a great deal of 'student indiscipline', juvenile delinquency, and other destructive manifestations of emotions that have been denied creative expression, and point to the necessity of giving a more prominent place in the educational curriculum to interests and activities by which the emotions are refined and sublimated. If the kind of education we receive should be determined, to some extent at least, by the kind of people we are, and if emotion is agreed to be no less a component of human nature than reason, then no denial of the necessity of finding a place for art in the scheme of education can logically be made.

Inasmuch as the ideals governing the educational system of a given society are generated by the application, within the narrower field of educational theory and practice, of ideals that govern not only that society but the whole civilization to which it belongs, it is to be expected that the absence of art today from our schools and colleges is but the reflection of a death of beauty in modern life. Since the Industrial Revolution the cities in which the countries of the West have gradually concentrated their populations have been dominated by an ever-increasing ugliness. Through political and commercial channels the products of this ugliness have flooded not only the Western but the Eastern world as well, and even now, high on the shores of traditional civilizations like those of India, Ceylon (Sri Lanka), and Burma, the retreating tide of imperialism has left a noisome deposit of ugliness which, putrefying in the tropic sun, continues to infect the lives of most Asian peoples. Modern man, whether of the East or of the West, is suffering from starvation of beauty, and until he again receives and assimilates that divine pabulum there is little hope of his being restored to spiritual health. Before the Second World War, the Moral Re-Armament movement was launched in England.[62] The inauguration on a global scale of a movement for Aesthetic Re-Armament, the launching of a worldwide Battle for Beauty, is today no less necessary. Until an outlet for the emotions of man is found on those higher levels of experience, to which art and religion alike give access, they will continue on the lower their turbulent and destructive career. Like the two wings of a bird, reason and emotion are both indispensable to the spiritual flights of man.

> Higher still and higher
> From the earth thou springest
> Like a cloud of fire;
> The blue deep thou wingest,
> And singing still dost soar, and soaring ever singest.[63]

The spiritual aspirant is like Shelley's skylark: while his understanding soars, his emotions sing. It is in this singing and soaring, in the simultaneous expansion of the understanding and the emotions, that we find the meaning of Buddhism and the value of art, and, in fact, the secret of spiritual life.

ADVICE TO A YOUNG POET

The utility of giving advice to a young poet may be questioned. One gives advice with the intention of improving, in some way or other, the person to whom it is addressed. Such a procedure may be admissible when we are concerned with an art or science that can be taught and learned; but with regard to poetry we have the assertion of Horace that poets are born, not made (*Poeta nascitur, non fit*).[64] Let us at the beginning of these remarks disclaim the fond hope that they will help make a poet out of anyone who is not a poet already. All that they hope to do is to tend what nature has planted; to suggest to the young poet ways in which the capacities he possesses may be developed; to indicate the discipline by which his still inchoate inspiration can be transformed into the deliberate creativity of the mature artist.

Poetry, like other things, has two distinguishable, though indivisible, aspects: substance and form. Our hints on the cultivation of these aspects will be given separately; but it should be borne in mind that the distinction is made for the sake of convenience in exposition, and does not correspond to any division of parts in the subject. In the fire of creative genius substance and form are made to coalesce into the partless whole which is a work of art.

By the substance of poetry, we mean the experience that it contains. This experience is emotionally rather than intellectually toned, for although poetry contains definite thoughts and ideas, in its essence it does not consist of these. Even the most abstract and philosophical statement possesses emotional value, however little that may be. Conversely, even the most intensely emotional poem contains intellectual elements. In the best poetry, however, these elements occupy a strictly subordinate place, and appear to function solely as aids to the exhibition of a non-intellectual experience. But here, too, we must beware of contrasting too sharply what are the coexistent aspects of poetry rather than its mutually exclusive parts.

By the form of poetry we mean the different species of poetic composition (lyric, epic, dramatic, etc.), together with the various metres, stanza forms, and styles in which the predominantly emotional content is expressed. From our previous remarks it will be obvious without further explanation that the substance of poetry is not related to its form as wax to a seal, but in a manner so intimate that it is strictly impossible to speak of a relation at all.

Poetry expresses the personality of the poet. It records his deepest feelings and sublimest thoughts, his tears and smiles, anguish and delight, frustration and fulfilment. In short it is the more or less complete embodiment of his whole experience of life. As the poet is, so also will his poetry be. Any change or development in the one will inevitably be paralleled in the other. To improve the poetry we must therefore, first of all, improve the poet whose expression it is. This improvement will not be ethical but artistic – or at least not directly ethical; for, if Plato is to be believed, since beauty, truth, and goodness are equally aspects of Reality, an approximation to one is also, indirectly, an approximation to each of the others.

The personality of the poet has, like the personalities of other men, two aspects: emotional and intellectual. The advice we are about to offer the young poet therefore relates first of all, more to the culture of his emotions, from which is created the substance of his poetry, and secondly, more to the culture of his intellectual faculties, whence it derives its form. Once again, however, distinctions should not be mistaken for divisions. It should also be noted that the emotional and intellectual culture with regard to which our advice is offered is of a strictly limited kind, being simply what is significant and valuable from the poetic point of view. Moreover, our remarks are not exhaustive but suggestive. They do not provide a ready-made programme of poetic self-improvement, but simply point out some of the qualities which, in the writer's opinion, a young poet should take special pains to develop.

There are five predominantly emotional qualities – aspects of the poet's experience of life – which, when developed, will enrich the substance of his poetry. These are: observation, sensitiveness, sympathy, solitude, and reflection.

All our knowledge and feeling begin from the impressions we derive from our five senses. Those derived from the eye, the organ of vision, are, however, more prominent and important than those entering through the ear or other senses, and we have, therefore, chosen the word 'observation' to cover the poet's intensified awareness of the whole external world. Everyone sees mountains, trees, flowers, houses, people's faces, and a thousand other things, every day. But the poet – or artist – should not be satisfied with merely seeing things: he must learn to observe them. Observation of course implies concentration. A poet should be prepared to spend a whole day looking at a flower, for only then will he be able to observe it. Observation means a vivid awareness of the unique individuality of things. A poet should be alive to the subtlest differences of colour, shape, contour, tone, touch, and smell, and should know the exactly right, the inevitable, word with which to describe every one of them. He should mark the different ways in which trees, in accordance with the stoutness or slenderness of their trunks and branches, and the relative scarcity or abundance of their leaves, dance and sway in the wind. He should be able to detect the change in the cuckoo's cry from month to month, while the personalities of different kinds of flowers should be as distinctly recognizable to him as those of individual human beings. This faculty of intense observation has been beautifully illustrated by Shelley, who says of the poet:

> He will watch from dawn till gloom
> The lake-reflected sun illume
> The yellow bees in the ivy-bloom.[65]

Incidentally, the description of bees as 'yellow' is a fine example of the kind of observation of which we are speaking. Any ordinary person, if asked to describe in one word the colour of a bee, would reply either that it was brown, or that he had never noticed the insect's colour. The poets quite often startle us with epithets so fresh and original, yet withal so apt and vivid, that we realize with shame that we had never troubled to observe the objects to which their genius so triumphantly applies them.

Those who are not poets can generally see nature much more vividly through the eyes of the poets than with their own. Who had really seen the blackness of ash-buds in March, or the greenness of the evening sky, until a Tennyson or a Coleridge had taught them to do so?[66]

Second-hand observation may suffice for the ordinary person; but a poet cannot be satisfied with seeing nature through the eyes of another poet, however great. For him, in so far as he is a poet, not to see Nature with his own eyes is not to see her at all. Though he appreciates and admires the beauties of description found in poets of long ago, he does not simply purvey them at second-hand in his own poems. On the contrary, he observes Nature with his own eyes as clearly as he can, and describes what he has seen as strikingly as he is able. Few evidences of a decline in poetic vitality are more unmistakable than when poets slip into a habit of drawing their knowledge of natural objects not from life but from literature. Such bookish poets merely describe descriptions. Hence their poetry, though it may possess other great and noble qualities, does not impart to us the sensation of immediate impact with life. It may possess sweetness, artistry, and charm, but is lacking in freshness, vigour, and reality. Similes and metaphors, which are of the very essence of poetry, are born of personal observation. The more accurate and truthful is the poet's observation of the beauties of Nature, the more readily will he apprehend the deeper relations and subtler interconnections which exist between them. The more ready this apprehension, the more original, impressive, and illuminating his similitudes will be.

By 'sensitiveness', which is an entirely emotional quality, we mean depth and delicacy, or strength and refinement, of feeling. Most people consider those emotions to be powerful which are accompanied by violent physical action; but in fact the opposite of this belief is more nearly related to the family of truth. The subtler an emotion grows, the less adequate become the normal bodily means of its expression. A blow or an embrace may suffice to embody the full content of the grosser forms of hatred and desire, but by what motions, save by those of poetry, music, and the visual arts, shall the finer feelings of the human soul find expression? The poet is compelled to give vent to his emotions in verse because they cannot be realized through any human relation: they refuse to terminate, in the noble words of Plato, on finite and particular objects, but protract themselves into the infinite and universal realm of poetry and Truth.[67] It is in this capacity of protraction or penetration into Reality that the strength of an emotion truly consists. Subtlety and strength of feeling are, therefore, fundamentally one quality. This quality we have indicated by the term sensitiveness. The poet is aware of, and responds to, not only the grosser vibrations of the world of sense, but the immeasurably higher and finer vibrations of a world which lies beyond; a world that metaphysicians describe as a world of values, but which the poet generally prefers to describe as a world of ideal forms of Beauty. It should not be thought, however, that the poet's aspiration takes wing on a world-transcending flight of the alone to the Alone. If there be mysticism in poetry, it belongs more to the *via affirmativa* than to the *via negativa*. And if the poet possesses, as Aldous Huxley finely says of D. H. Lawrence (and his words have been applied with equal justice to Rainer Maria Rilke), 'a capacity of experiencing unknown modes of being',[68] he experiences them not by abstracting himself from sensible objects, but rather by interpenetrating their essence with his own. Most poets would echo the words with which Wordsworth concludes his famous Ode:

> To me the meanest flower that blows can give
> Thoughts that do often lie too deep for tears.[69]

The last words of these lines are significant. No outward and visible sign of emotion, such as tears, is capable of expressing the full depth of the inward and spiritual grace of the poet's thought, or the extreme intensity of his feelings.

Experience of this kind may be natural enough to a poet of Wordsworth's eminence, but by what means can the young poet of today even approach the altitudes at which they are possible? How is he to subtilize his feelings to the point at which they can become sensitive to the delicatest touches of the eternal beauty? The solution of this problem lies in the domain of what may be termed the asceticism of art. Aesthetic and religious experience belong to a common order, and in the former no less than the latter the higher and subtler reaches are to be attained by the renunciation of those which are, in comparison, low and gross. The philosophy of this ascesis, and the manner in which the lover of Beauty ascends from the experience of its lowest to the experience of its highest forms until, in the last supreme flight of his soul, he soars into the presence of Beauty Ineffable, has been for all time unfolded with matchless artistry in Plato's *Symposium*, wherein the incomparable genius of the Athenian poet-philosopher has magisterially blended the scattered rays of Philosophy, Religion, and Art into a single dazzling beam that penetrates far, far into the obscure depths of Reality.[70]

In these remarks it is our more modest intention to offer only one or two suggestions (apart from advising the young poet to read and re-read the *Symposium*) concerning the cultivation of sensitiveness; for the subject is so intensely personal, and depends so much more upon the sincerity and integrity of the poet than upon the mechanical application of rules, that even these are advanced with hesitation. To begin with, it should be clearly understood that emotion is essentially a force, and that it has a natural tendency to express itself in some outward form. If this force is consciously checked, so that it is no longer able to express itself in the normal manner, the inhibited energy will assume a subtler and more powerful form, and therefore tend to find expressions on a higher plane of experience. Feelings are like fountains, in which the water, unable to find an outlet on its own level, shoots up through a narrow aperture to leap a hundred feet into the air.

It should be noted that the 'check' of which we speak is a conscious and deliberate process; were it unconscious, then the inhibited emotion would simply be pressed down beneath the conscious surface of the mind into the unconscious depths below, and what psychic disturbance a repressed emotion is capable of creating has been too strongly insisted on by psychoanalysts to need repetition here. The poet, like the mystic, has at all times to be aware of his feelings: he must saturate them with consciousness. For, like the breath, thought and emotion are naturally inhibited when the unwavering beam of awareness falls upon them, and at once resolve themselves into subtler forms, just as the dew melts, in the warm rays of the early morning sun, into the mist and air. These subtler forms are the raw material not only of art but also of spirituality. From them the poet, the painter, and the musician create, in their respective media, images of imperishable beauty; while the mystic, repeating the process of inhibition over again, rises to even sublimer heights of experience. Such are the principles to be followed in the cultivation of sensitiveness, or delicacy and depth of feeling. The exact manner of their application must be determined by the young poet, no less than by the novice in mysticism, for himself.

Supremely important as the cultivation of sensitiveness is, it should not be supposed that in the previous paragraph we have advised the young poet to isolate himself in an ivory tower of rarefied personal emotion. The varieties of poetry are multitudinous, and by no means all of them deal with the poet's private feelings. Epic, narrative, and dramatic poems, for instance, are generally concerned with the thoughts, feelings, and actions of people far remote in time and place, and of widely different circumstances, from the poet who narrates them. Even lyric poetry, into which the poet's deepest and most intimate experiences naturally flow, is sometimes in a manner dramatic, being written by the poet not in his own character but in that of some other person, real or imagined. Here, however, our concern is not so much with the form as with the manner in which this is done. Descriptions must possess liveliness and poetic truth. It is not enough for the poet to observe accurately, and delineate naturally, the external effects of strong feelings; for as we have already said, such feelings cannot be adequately expressed by any bodily movements. By an act of sympathy he must project himself out of his personality into that of another being, and experience the emotions of that being because, for the moment at least, he has become one with him. This capacity for universal sympathy, wherein the joys and sorrows of others are felt as keenly as our own, is yet another quality which has to be developed by the poet no less than by the religious devotee. The secret of art is identical with the secret of spirituality. Shelley writes in 'A Defence of Poetry':

> The great secret of morals is love; or a going out of our own nature, and an identification of ourselves with the beautiful which exists in thought, action, or person, not our own. A man, to be greatly good, must imagine intensely and comprehensively; he must put himself in the place of another and of many others; the pains and pleasures of his species must become his own.[71]

The emotion to which Shelley, in this passage, from his more general point of view, has given the name 'love', corresponds with what we, from the special point of view of poetry, have called 'sympathy'. We would go further than Shelley only in advising the young poet not merely to make the pleasure and pains of the human species his own, but to cultivate a feeling of identity with, and sympathy for, every kind of sentient being. '...If a sparrow come before my window I take part in its existence and pick about the gravel,' wrote Keats in one of his letters.[72] The poet's sympathies must be universal. He must be able to enter into the existences, and share the feelings, not only of human beings, not only of birds and beasts, but even of trees, flowers, mountains, streams, and stones. A poet in whom this quality of sympathy is highly developed will be able to describe the thoughts and emotions of others with peculiar force and vividness. For he will be describing not what he has observed from without but what he has experienced from within.

It is for this reason that supreme poetry, no less than the higher kind of Religion, possesses the capacity to lift us out of the littleness of our individual being into an infinitely deeper, richer, and wider kind of life. To read poetry of this exalted type is much more than witnessing unfamiliar situations and novel sentiments: it is an initiation into a new mode of being. Momentarily we experience what the poet experienced when with his 'glassy essence' he interpenetrated the essence of another form of life and felt the pulsation of its existence as his own. Sympathy is therefore closely allied to self-transcendence, to the power of getting beyond one's personal ego.

A self-centred man may be a competent versifier; but he can never be a great poet. Beauty and goodness once more join hands. The cultivation of sympathy implies the adoption of a selfless attitude towards life. As remarked at the beginning of these suggestions, we entertain no hope that they will be able to make a poet of anyone who is not a poet already. The utmost they can accomplish is to help in the development of a congenial aptitude. Sympathy, even more, perhaps, than any of the qualities already mentioned, is a natural endowment; and we are therefore able to offer less advice on its cultivation than on that of any other quality. All that can be suggested in this regard is that the cultivation of observation and sensitiveness will naturally contribute to the enlargement of the poet's sympathies. Since we generally find it easier to sympathize with the sorrows than the joys of our fellow men, the young poet may in addition be recommended to direct his attention first of all to the miseries and misfortunes of others, and only afterwards to their consolations and blessings. For if they are contemplated in reverse order, he may feel not sympathy but envy. More than this cannot be said on the subject without trespassing beyond the uncertain boundary which divides the life aesthetic from the life spiritual, and exchanging the realm of poetry for the sister realm of Religion.

The qualities which the young poet should develop are not only interrelated, so that the cultivation of one leads indirectly to the cultivation of others, but also linked serially, so that each springs naturally into existence out of the very abundance of the quality preceding it. Observation flowers into sensitiveness, and sensitiveness ripens into sympathy. The mind of the young poet is at this stage replete with vivid impressions of forms and colour; his heart responds immediately to the subtlest nuances of feelings; the horizons of his soul have widened until he can begin to say, with Sir Edwin Arnold, 'Forgoing self, the universe grows I'.[73] But, before the work of poetic creation can begin, the richly diverse products of these three qualities must be mingled and fused as elements are fused in a crucible, the dross of irrelevancies purged from them by fire, and the imperishable poetic essence extracted. The crucible is *solitude*; the fire *reflection*.

Without some degree of solitude reflection is impossible, and without prolonged reflection no great work of art was ever brought forth. The poet needs solitude as the lungs need air. By solitude is meant not so much physical loneliness as inner isolation, for the time being at least, from all that does not directly concern the process of poetic creation. Physical withdrawal from normal human activities and interests can be included in the definition of solitude only to the extent that the latter is dependent on it. In the urbanized and industrialized societies of the present age this is, with increasing frequency, the case. Without withdrawing externally from the hurry and bustle of modern life, the poet may not be able to find the internal solitude necessary for the progress and perfection of his work. At the same time, the necessity of earning his own livelihood – on its own level a no less urgent problem – again and again draws him from solitude back into society. In a world wherein poetry as a profession is no longer recognized or remunerated, the young poet has to find a way of life that will enable him to provide for both the lower and higher necessities of his nature.

The religious mystic, to whom opportunities for solitude are as necessary as to the poet, can find them in the solemn hush of monastery or hermitage; but corresponding facilities are not offered by an indulgent society to the poet. Perhaps it is just as well they are not. Opportunities for sympathy are no less precious or necessary to him than opportunities for solitude, and it cannot be denied that through the complex network of mutual ties and obligations woven in the course of earning a livelihood they are most easily and naturally secured. Having already refused to allow sensitiveness to open for the young poet the portals of the ivory tower, it would be strange if we permitted solitude to usher him through them. The kind of solution which we envisage should be neither unbalanced nor one-sided: it should exemplify poetically what Baron von Hügel said of the spiritual life:

> The great rule is, *Variety up to the verge of dissipation: Recollection to the verge of emptiness*: each alternating with the other and making a rich fruitful tension.[74]

The extremes of variety and recollection, dissipation and emptiness, of which von Hügel speaks, correspond with the extremes of sympathy and solitude between which the young poet has to pursue a middle path, and for both of which we have urged him to provide opportunities in his life. As circumstances will tend to force him into the first extreme, and as opportunities for solitude are in modern times the rarer of the two, we shall, however, consider the problem from one side only and, after enunciating a general rule, put forward a few more detailed suggestions with regard to the cultivation of solitude.

The general rule is negative in form, and consists in the simple reminder that the young poet should not embrace any means of earning his living which does not grant him regular periods of respite from its preoccupations. The longer and more frequent such periods, the more congenial the employment will generally be to him. Prospects of financial gain (above what is actually needed for the maintenance of himself and his dependants, if any), hopes of worldly advancement, and consideration of social prestige, must the poet no less than the contemplative brush resolutely aside. The temptation of commercializing his literary gifts must be no less uncompromisingly resisted. This is not to say that he should refuse to accept payment for his work; for in this field, as in any other, the labourer is worthy of his hire. But the poet should not resort for his livelihood to journalism, or to the production of novels, short stories, and newspaper articles from motives predominantly commercial. Should he prostitute his talent in this way he will eventually lose even his poetic integrity. He cannot divide his literary character into two separate personalities. The more money he needs, the more work he is compelled to produce; the more he produces (beyond a certain point), the more slipshod it becomes; slipshod work results in a general lowering of standards and this, in the end, will vitiate even the quality of his poetry.

If a young poet desires an avocation which, while not unconnected with his literary interests, will nevertheless involve no degradation of his art, he perhaps cannot do better than adopt an academic career, and teach languages and literature, history, or some other humane subject. Otherwise, farming or bricklaying is preferable to journalism. For it should not be thought that a poet is necessarily unfit for manual labour, or incapable of practical activity of any kind, or that the sensitiveness of his heart has in any degree impaired the dexterity and usefulness of his hands. The annals of poetry are no more wanting in the names of politicians, statesmen, administrators, engravers, apothecaries, ploughmen, doctors, and traders, than in the names of writers and teachers.

Matthew Arnold's famous description of Shelley as 'a beautiful and ineffectual angel' is applicable to no other poet of equal stature, and is less than fair to Shelley himself.[75] The popular picture of the poet as a long-haired, effeminate, and incompetent creature was never more than a late-nineteenth-century caricature of a group of minor poets, and is now less true than it ever was. There is nothing in the poet's constitution to prevent him swinging a pick or handling a shovel, and such a means of livelihood may be, for some, no less conducive to the pursuit of poetry than any other. The sole question which the young poet, as such, has to ask himself regarding any form of employment is: does it give me opportunities for solitude? If it does, he can, as a poet, ask of it nothing more.

It should not be thought, however, that the suggestions we have offered are an infallible and universally applicable solution of the problem of solitude. The poetic temperament is rarely amenable to the rules of reason. Even though the young poet succeeds in finding work which provides him with opportunities of withdrawal from the world, of experiencing those periods of inner isolation so necessary to the progress of his work, he may find that his creative moods refuse to synchronize with office hours or college vacations; that just when his whole being cries out to be alone, to be free to concentrate on the shaping of a poem, some trivial detail of the daily round claims his attention.

Contrariwise, he may spend weeks and months in apparently ideal surroundings and yet feel his heart as dry as dust and his soul incapable of producing even the thinnest trickle of inspiration. The wind of poetry, like other winds of spirit, bloweth where it listeth. Again, there are social obligations and family ties to be considered. Like the mystic, the poet has often felt them to be a hindrance; and, like the mystic, he has often not hesitated to snap them when they have become too restricting. The mystic's renunciation of such obligations and ties is usually recognized and approved by society, but the poet's repudiation, being much more haphazard and unsystematic, is usually considered as evidence of a disposition to immorality. Though, as D. H. Lawrence says, 'The true artist [or poet] doesn't substitute immorality for morality. On the contrary, he *always* substitutes a finer morality for a grosser.'[76] To all these problems we can offer no cut-and-dried solution. All that we can do is to reiterate the necessity for solitude, and leave the young poet to make provision for it, in the light of our suggestions, as amply as he can.

Once the crucible has been prepared, the fire may be kindled beneath it. When the poet finds himself in solitude, in conditions favourable to the cultivation of inner isolation, the process of *reflection*, of extracting the shining gold of poetry from the drossy ore of experience, can begin. About this process we need say little. Not that it is unimportant, though. Bagehot indicates its position when he writes 'One of the reasons of the rarity of great imaginative art is that in very few cases is this capacity for musing solitude combined with that of observing mankind';[77] and Wordsworth does likewise in his famous definition of poetry as 'emotion recollected in tranquillity'.[78] The word 'musing' in the first quotation, and 'recollection' in the second, both refer to the process we have termed reflection. If we have less to say about this quality than about the four preceding ones it is not, therefore, because of its relative insignificance, but because of the obscurity and mysteriousness of this part of the poetic process. How, from his experience of life, from his observations, feelings, and thoughts, he produces, like the musician, 'not a fourth note, but a star',[79] is known only to the poet himself, and even he is rarely able to offer an adequate description of the process, to say nothing of giving an explanation of it which will satisfy the philosopher. His definitions and descriptions are usually figurative, and more often than not in the end themselves become poems.

It will therefore hardly be an occasion for surprise if the few words of advice which we intend to offer the young poet on the cultivation of reflection are figurative rather than scientific in character. The fire of reflection must be kindled as often, and kept burning for as long, as possible. In one who is by vocation a poet this flame of slow quiet musing is always present, however deeply it may be hidden under the ashes of external activities and events, and only waiting for the breeze of solitude to fan it into a blaze. This sacred fire of reflection must the young poet learn to tend as carefully as though he was a Zoroastrian priest, feeding it with the sandalwood of his thoughts, and stirring the ore of his experience in the crucible of inner isolation until the fine gold of poetry, separated from the dross of irrelevant circumstances, glitters at the bottom like a star.

Having offered our suggestions on the cultivation of the five predominantly emotional qualities which will enrich the content of his poetry, we shall now suggest to the young poet three predominantly intellectual acquisitions which will help give precision and definition to its form. None of these may be adequately designated by any single word, but they may be provisionally indicated by the terms 'appreciation', 'understanding', and 'technique'.

The word 'poet' means, literally, a maker, and like all other makers or craftsmen the poet has to undergo a period of apprenticeship to those more skilled than himself in the gentle craft which he aspires to master. During this period of training he learns to know and appreciate the work of his predecessors. This *appreciation* is not a mere spark produced by the cold collision of the flint and steel of criticism, but a flame begotten on the tinder of his heart by the fiery seed of their greatness. Neither is it mere imitation. It does not, or should not, teach him the mannerisms, however magnificent, or tricks of style, however effective, of 'poets dead and gone'. The chief function it has to perform is to fan into brightness the flame of his poetry with the mighty breath of inspiration which blows through their song.

Nor should it be thought that this breath can come only through the mouth of his native language. In these days of close international contact, if not always of cooperation, the poet, no less than other men, has to keep himself open to the impact of multitudinous influences. The English poet, for instance, must learn to appreciate, at least in translation, the best poetic work which has been done not only in French, German, and Italian, but also in Arabic, Persian, and Chinese. No non-English poet, on the other hand, especially if he is working in one of the undeveloped minor languages of the world, can afford to neglect the unequalled riches of English poetry. Such a commerce between the languages and literatures, but especially the poetic literatures, of many times and lands will contribute to the growth of a newer and more truly international kind of poetry which will embody the ideals and aspirations, not of any single race or people, but of humanity.

Though we have spoken only of poetry, it should not be thought that we are implying any limitations on the young poet's appreciation to the progeny of his own peculiar muse. The daughters of Clio and Euterpe must be as dear to him as the sons of Calliope and Erato. Without suggesting that every poet should attempt to follow in the footsteps of Blake and Rossetti – for the mastery of two arts is more than twice as difficult as the mastery of one – it should at least be pointed out that the scope of poetry is often considerably enlarged when the poet is familiar, not with poetry alone, but with the sister arts of music and painting as well. Poetry is a limpid mountain lake into which flow the streams of every branch of knowledge and invention. The greater the volume of such tributary waters that it receives, the deeper and fuller will its own waters become.

Among the many streams which feed the tarn of poetry is that of philosophy. Not that an academically adequate acquaintance with the subject is essential to a poet. But of the course of that particular channel by which they are connected, he should have at least some knowledge. This channel is the philosophy of art, or aesthetics. Familiarity with the philosophy of beauty on the theoretical side will not ensure that his poetic work will be beautiful, but it will help give him an intellectual understanding of the metaphysical nature of poetry, and this *understanding*, the second of the intellectual qualifications with which the young poet should be equipped, will strengthen the structure of his verse and, while it is incapable of making him a good poet, may be able, by sharpening his faculty of self-criticism, at least to prevent him from being a very bad one.

Not much more than this can be said of the third qualification, that of *technique*, which consists in a working acquaintance with the details of rhetoric and prosody such as may be found in standard manuals on the subject. Such acquaintance may not be sufficient to set the young poet's heart on fire with the flame of inspiration, but it will at least enable him to be sure that the fuel is dry. Though the shortest, this is not necessarily the least valuable part of the advice we have endeavoured to offer those who have apprenticed themselves to one of the most difficult and delightful of arts.

THE RELIGION OF ART

Art and religion overlap. Just as there is in religion an element which is aesthetic, so there is also in art a constituent which is religious. In these days, when the decay of religious belief has led to the decline of that part of religion which is also a province of art, it might be possible, by developing the implications of that part of art which is also a province of religion, to promote a way of life dedicated to the realization of values in a manner attractive to those who are only repelled when it is presented to them from a formally religious point of view. It might even be possible to inaugurate for such people a Religion of Art.

By the Religion of Art we do not mean the use of art as one of the substitutes for religion in the Huxleian sense. Just as there are some things belonging to religion which have nothing to do with art, so also are there many things of much importance to art which have no place in religion. The coincidence between the areas of these two spheres of human activity is partial, not complete. Some religion is some art, and some art some religion. All religion is not all art. Mr Huxley makes it clear that while he uses the word religion in the fuller sense that includes an aesthetic constituent, the term art is used in the narrower sense that excludes any element of religion. Art-without-religion is set up as one of the substitutes for religion-with-art. Although admitting that 'to minds whose religious needs have been denied their normal fulfilment, art brings a certain spiritual satisfaction', the author of the penetrating essay on 'The Substitutes for Religion' is not blind to the fact that 'where beauty is worshipped for beauty's sake as a goddess, independent of and superior to morality and philosophy, the most horrible putrefaction is apt to set in', and he concludes his section on 'The Artistic Substitute' with the caustic observation: 'The lives of the aesthetes are the far from edifying commentary on the religion of beauty.'[80]

The 'horrible putrefaction' which ensues when art is sundered from religion and metaphysics was the subject of a poem written almost a century earlier than Huxley's essay. In the dedication to 'The Palace of Art' Tennyson described with his usual abundance of vivid pictorial detail the fate of

> A glorious Devil, large in heart and brain,
> That did love Beauty only

and who had therefore planned to devote his life to the solitary enjoyment of whatever masterpieces of painting, music, and poetry had been produced by man.[81] Historically speaking, the poem is prophetic of the Aesthetic Movement which was to spring up in the latter half of the nineteenth century, and which was to flower most gorgeously and most corruptly during the decade preceding the arrest and conviction of Oscar Wilde, when the dew was abruptly shaken from the black rose and the wasp-bodied butterflies rudely scattered from their green carnations.[82] Psychologically, it is an eternally true study of the feelings of dissatisfaction and frustration into which a life of self-indulgence, even aesthetic self-indulgence, eventually disintegrates.

At the beginning of the poem the 'glorious Devil' is described as building for his soul

> a lordly pleasure-house,
> Wherein at ease for ay to dwell.

and is reported as inviting her to 'make merry and carouse'. She is to live alone in her high palace, indifferent to what is happening in the world outside, and caring nothing for the joys and sorrows of men. Indeed, to her fastidious taste the uncultured commonalty appears no better than 'darkening droves of swine', and with a little delicate shudder of disgust she watches them as they 'graze and wallow, breed and sleep'. But the day of retribution is at hand. The opium-eater's dream lasts but for three short years. In the fourth year, tormented by despair and doubt, she begins to loathe solitude and to hate herself. The pleasure-house becomes her prison; remorse scorches her like fire; and at the conclusion of the poem she abandons her palace for a cottage in the valley where she can 'mourn and pray'. She begs her master not to pull down her palace towers, which have been so lightly and beautifully built. It was not Art that was at fault, but the soul's misuse of Art. When she has purged her guilt, she says, perhaps it will be possible for her to return there and dwell, not alone, but this time in the company of other people.

Though 'The Palace of Art' is a poem, and not a treatise on ethics or an excursus into psychology, the moral which emerges from its dream-like sequence of brilliant word-pictures is almost nakedly apparent, and has in fact been stated explicitly in the dedication which Tennyson prefixed to the poem. He that shuts out Love from his life

> in turn shall be
> Shut out from Love, and on her threshold lie
> Howling in outer darkness.

This is the sentence of what Buddhists would call karma: not blind fate or destiny, but that reaction of one's own action whereby the justice of the universe is asserted and the equilibrium of Nature restored. By love is meant not 'a meaty acquaintance' or a jealous emotional preference but that spirit of self-abnegation, that entire absence of selfish desires, which is the beginning and end of every virtue, the base and crown of all spirituality, and which according to Dante is so mighty that it 'moves the sun in heaven and all the stars'.[83] Though at a high stage of spiritual development it may be possible to speak, with Rilke, of 'love without the beloved',[84] for most of us this emotion, like the rest, can be achieved only through our association with other men and women. The aesthete shuts out love from his life because he shuts out people, because his soul dwells 'alone unto herself', indulging in the refined selfishness of artistic pleasures. The sin he commits, the guilt which in the end he feels he must purge away, is the primal sin of attachment to one's separate selfhood. He finds to his horror that the much-vaunted doctrine of 'Art for Art's sake' is reversed in practice and becomes, though probably in a sense different from that intended by Lawrence, 'Art for my sake.'[85] He discovers that he has failed to distinguish what have been called 'the pleasures of poetry', which first satisfy, then satiate, and finally disgust the soul, from 'the ardours of poetry', by which the soul is quickened, purified, and in the end liberated from the bondage of its own separateness. It is regarding works of art as an amusement, or employing them merely as a means of egoistic pleasure, that constitutes the distinguishing feature of Art as one of the Substitutes for Religion. The Religion of Art, on the contrary, views the creation and enjoyment of paintings, musical compositions, and poems as primarily a means of liberation from the egoistic life and looks upon Beauty as one of the three great initiators into the mysteries of the life of egolessness. But before attempting to gain a clear understanding of the nature of the Religion of Art we must first of all examine separately the meaning of Religion and the meaning of Art.

No one who has attempted to reduce into a semblance of order the swarm of indistinct ideas and confused emotions which cluster about 'religion' can have failed to be struck by the vagueness and ambiguity of this protean word. Like the Apostle to the Gentiles, it has endeavoured to be all things to all men; but instead of meaning something to everybody, it has now come perilously near to meaning nothing to anybody. In so thick an obscurity, indeed, has the word now become involved, that Mr Aldous Huxley, who introduces his collection of substitutes for religion with a description of what he calls 'the genuine article', very wisely refrains from attempting a formal definition of religion, remarking: 'Such definitions are mostly so vague and abstract as to be almost meaningless.' Instead of a definition he gives 'a catalogue of the principal states of mind and actions recognized as religious, together with a brief account of the most characteristic features of the religious doctrines which are the rationalizations of these states and acts.'[86]

'But recognized as religious by whom?' one may pertinently enquire. 'Most characteristic from what point of view, or in the eyes of which observer?' A description that highlights certain details of an object at the expense of certain others can be almost as misleading as a definition that submerges all alike in the double darkness of abstraction and generalization. Though not untrue, it does not tell the whole truth, and is therefore not wholly true. Moreover, description and definition cannot be divorced so absolutely as Mr Huxley's remarks appear to suggest. Definition is always of a specific thing which has been isolated for the purpose from the multiplicity of other things in the midst of which it exists. The isolation of a highly complex phenomenon like religion is impossible without some criterion of which elements are to be excluded and which are not. In other words, you cannot describe a thing unless you have first of all at least some knowledge of *what* is to be described. No description of religion can be attempted without formulating a provisional definition of the nature of religion. Such a provisional definition does in fact lurk somewhere at the back of Mr Huxley's mind, and betrays its presence as soon as he talks about 'rationalization'. Far from casting over the religions of the world a glance of Olympian impartiality, all that he offers us is a view of the subject that is asquint with selective prejudice. However, some of the characteristics he describes are undoubtedly characteristics of religion from the standpoint of the Religion of Art, and we shall therefore examine them one by one in the hope that this procedure will enable our own definition of the word to emerge with greater clarity. The description of 'the genuine article' which he has given in this essay certainly will be in any case more helpful to us than his researches in more recent years, which have extracted from the diversity of religious beliefs a Highest Common Factor as vague and abstract as the most impenitent intellectual, even, could wish for.

First in the Huxleian catalogue is 'a sense of awe in face of the mysteries and immensities of the world', which, he supposes, 'is the most fundamental religious state of mind.' The definition of religion implicit in his mind has already set in motion the machinery of selection, and by the time we have recovered from the jolt it is grinding away vigorously. 'This feeling is rationalized in the form of belief in supernatural beings, both kindly and malevolent, as is the world in which men live.' The wheels are now fairly whizzing round. 'In the higher religions the rationalization is very elaborate and constitutes an account, complete and coherent, of the whole universe.' The ambiguity of the word 'fundamental', which can be understood in a historical, psychological, or metaphysical sense, may be overlooked. What cannot be overlooked is the incompleteness of the facts whereon the generalization is based, and the consequent precariousness of an explanation reared on such a slender foundation. Like almost all generalizations about religion it ignores completely that vast area of belief and practice designated Buddhism. 'A sense of awe in face of the mysteries and immensities of the world' is not the 'fundamental' Buddhist state of mind in any sense of the word. Awe is a species of fear, and the fundamental Buddhist state of mind is not one of fear, but of complete freedom from fear. All fear is basically hatred of death, just as every kind of hope is essentially desire for life. Desire and hatred, attraction and repulsion, are rooted in the ego-sense, in the false conception that the word 'self' denotes an unchanging entity separate from all other 'selves'. The fundamental Buddhist state of mind is a state of freedom from fear because it is also a state of freedom from the ego-sense. When the Buddha, before his Enlightenment, experienced a 'panic fear and dread' while dwelling alone in the terror-haunted jungle, so that the hair rose bristling on his scalp, he did not rationalize the feeling, as according to Mr Huxley he ought to have done, but remained where he was until he had subdued and conquered it.[87] This spirit of 'heroic valour, firm and unmoved'[88] he not only breathed himself but inspired into the hearts of his disciples, and exercises for the control of fear have remained through the centuries an integral part of Buddhist spiritual practice. It is hardly reasonable to explain the beliefs of a religion as rationalizations of an emotion which it does its utmost to subjugate. Even a teaching that has suffered as much as Buddhism has from the misrepresentations of critics would not expect to be treated so unfairly. Though references to 'supernatural beings, both kindly and malevolent' do occur in the Tripiṭaka quite frequently, their occurrence cannot be regarded as a manifestation of awe in the face of natural phenomena on the part of the compilers of the sacred volumes. Without necessarily asserting the non-existence of 'supernatural' beings – a dogma which appears to be one of the Thirty-Nine Articles of modern 'scientific' belief – we would point out that such beings occupy an entirely subordinate position on the mythological fringe of Buddhism, so that even if their objective existence were definitely disproved the basic truths of the Dharma would remain unshaken. Indeed, it could be argued with considerable plausibility that the *devas*, *yakṣas*, and other species of non-human beings who from time to time make their appearance in Buddhist apologue and anecdote are the rationalizations of the fears, not of the Buddha and his disciples, but of the peoples of pre-Buddhist India. The argument seems to be strengthened by the fact that even Māra, the chief of the malevolent beings, is never represented as a really dangerous or even formidable antagonist of the Buddha. He is a mischievous rather than an evil spirit, and totally lacks the dignity and grandeur of Milton's rebel angel. His wickedness vents itself by playing petty tricks and giving small annoyances; it does not explode in cosmic disaster or entail universal ruin. Like the emotions of which he and his myrmidons are supposed to be rationalizations, he is rendered harmless as soon as he is recognized, and has no refuge from ignominious punishment other than equally ignominious flight amid the laughter of the *arhants* who are the witnesses of his discomfiture.[89] Ridicule is a powerful solvent of fear, and the fact that they could laugh at the silly blundering wickedness of poor Māra shows that those early Buddhists were not afraid of him; perhaps it shows that they no longer really believed in his existence. The position occupied by the Prince of Darkness in the Pāli scriptures is far from enviable. After all, it is not easy to tempt or frighten those who insist upon regarding you as a piece of obsolete psychology, or as an out-of-date literary convention.

Buddhism could, we suppose, without exaggerating its own importance, claim to rank among those 'higher religions' to which Mr Huxley's selective machinery rattles out a reference. But the inclusion serves only to make the uniqueness of the Dharma still more strikingly evident. Far from obediently toeing the line that Mr Huxley draws for the higher religions, and advancing a rationalization of the feeling of awe so 'very elaborate' that it constitutes 'an account, complete and coherent, of the whole universe', Buddhism withdraws into a position so aloof from that occupied by all other religions that some of them even consider it as no more belonging to their company. If interrogated on the subject it would agree (having in fact maintained the principle for five-and-twenty centuries) that complete and coherent accounts of the universe were if not all the direct outcome of fear, certainly at bottom the joint product of egoistic craving and ignorance. Indeed, being nothing if not practical, it would go much further than this and insist that all such accounts (*diṭṭhi*, or views, in its own terminology) must be abandoned if ever the mind is to attain to a condition of absolute freedom.[90]

Buddhism is a method of resolving the disharmonies of life. In the oft-recurring formula of the sacred books, it teaches only 'suffering and the cessation of suffering'.[91] It is not science, so that it has nothing to say concerning the origin of the material universe. It is not philosophy in the merely speculative or academic sense, so that it is silent on metaphysical differences which do not, in William James' expressive phrase, 'make a difference'.[92] It is not religion in the Huxleian connotation of the term, because it not only fails to rationalize feelings of awe into a belief in good and evil spirits, but also refrains from elaborating them into a systematic explanation of the universe. Buddhism proclaims not merely freedom from fear, but also freedom from religion, for religion is based on fear. Needless to say, the belief in a personal Creator-God, which occupies a central position in all other higher religions, is regarded by Buddhism simply as a more ambitious, and therefore more harmful, result of the same process of rationalization which, at the other end of the scale, was responsible for the production of poor Māra. *Diabolus Deus inversus est.*[93] Indeed Brahmā cuts in the Pāli scriptures a figure no less ridiculous than that of his infernal counterpart, and for precisely the same reason. The fear of the Lord is, according to Buddhism, not the beginning of wisdom but the crown of folly. True wisdom cannot be attained until fear in all its forms has been conquered. What more effective means of dissipating this particular 'fear of the Lord' could there be than the delicate mockery of the Pāli scriptures?

The second item in Mr Huxley's catalogue of 'the principal states of mind and actions recognized as religious' is ritual.

> The religious feeling finds its active as opposed to its intellectual expression in the form of propitiatory ritual. Ritual, as soon as it is invented, occupies a position of prime importance in all religions. For the rite evokes by association those emotions of awe which are, for the individual who feels them, the god himself. And these emotions are accompanied by others no less exhilarating, and therefore no less divine. Chief among these is what may be called the social emotion, the feeling of excitement caused by being in a crowd.

Once again we are made aware of the enormous discrepancy between Buddhism and other religions. Gods and demons are, according to Mr Huxley, rationalizations of fear, and this feeling of fear is, as we have seen, absent from the representatively Buddhist mind. Yet, ignoring this fact, he rushes into a generalization to which, as the most elementary manual of Buddhism would have informed him, there is at least one very important exception, and sweepingly asserts that rituals for the propitiation of gods and demons occupy 'a place of prime importance in all religions', among which it must be supposed he intends to include Buddhism.

Let it be said at once that although such rituals are known in most Buddhist lands, and indeed are upon occasions resorted to by most Buddhists, they are merely survivals of primitive beliefs that have been affiliated to Buddhism, and in no sense form part of the original Dharma of the Buddha which, as we have already observed, on the contrary confines itself to resolving the disharmonies of life, to the attainment of a state of mind, usually designated Nirvāṇa, whence fear and all other egocentric emotions have been prescinded. Buddhist religious feeling finds its 'active as opposed to its intellectual expression' not in propitiatory ritual but in the practice of ethics (*śīla*), concentration (*samādhi*), and intuitive wisdom (*prajñā*); in following the Noble Eightfold Path which leads to arhantship, and in cultivating the ten perfections of the bodhisattva. It is a stranger to 'exhilarating' emotions of the Dionysian sort. What Mr Huxley calls 'the social emotion, the feeling of excitement caused by being in a crowd', far from being chief among Buddhist emotions, is deliberately excluded by it from their number. One of the signs by which the Dharma might be recognized, the Buddha told Mahāpajāpatī, was that it conduced 'to solitude, not to company'.[94] The bliss arising in the concentrated mind of the disciple is said, according to one interpretation of the word, to be 'born of solitude'. 'Wander alone, as the horn of the rhinoceros is single,' sings the refrain of a poem in the *Sutta-Nipāta* which celebrates the delights of, and enumerates the spiritual advantages which accrue from, a life of solitariness.[95] Not excitement but silence, the Āryan silence wherein not words merely, but also the perturbations of the mind, are stilled, is the emotion evoked by those assembled either in the presence of the Buddha or, after the disappearance of his earthly body, to do honour to his memory. When the physician Jīvaka took Ajātasattu, the raja of Magadha, on a nocturnal visit to the Master's abode, so deep a silence surrounded the place that the king became suspicious and accused the physician of leading him into an ambush. The story is told with all the dignity and quiet beauty of the Pāli scriptures thus:

> Now when His Majesty Ajātasattu was close upon the Mango Grove, there came upon him fear and trembling, so that every hair upon his body stood on end, and he exclaimed to Jīvaka: 'Surely,

> master Jīvaka, you are deceiving me! Surely, master Jīvaka, you are playing a trick upon me! Are you not delivering me into the hands of mine enemies, Jīvaka?'
> (Being reassured by Jīvaka he went on) 'How is it, then, that there is not a sneeze, not a clearing of the throat, not a single sound to be heard in all this company of brethren, numbering (as you say) twelve hundred and fifty?'
> 'Fear not, Maharajah. Fear not, Maharajah. I am not deceiving your Majesty, nor playing you a trick, nor am I delivering your Majesty into the hands of your enemies. Go right on, Maharajah! Go right on, Maharajah! See! Yonder in the pavilion the lamps are burning.'
> Then the rajah went on, riding his elephant as far as the path allowed, then went on foot to the pavilion door. Then he said to Jīvaka: 'Where, master Jīvaka, is the Exalted One?'
> 'Yonder, Maharajah, is the Exalted One! Yonder, Maharajah, is the Exalted One, sitting up against the midpost pillar, facing east and surrounded by the brethren.'
> Then the rajah of Magadha, Ajātasattu, drew near to the Exalted One and stood aside. So standing he gazed upon that company sitting there in perfect silence, calm as a translucent pool. And he exclaimed: 'O that my boy Prince Udayi, the Lucky Lad, may be blessed with the peacefulness wherewith this company of brethren is now blessed!'[96]

The apprehensiveness of an ancient Indian despot, who went in constant fear of betrayal and assassination, is in this passage strikingly contrasted with the calm and untroubled bearing of the Buddha and his disciples who, far from abandoning themselves to 'the feeling of excitement caused by being in a crowd', were enjoying tranquillity of mind so great that the king could imagine for his darling son no blessing more desirable.

'Asceticism is common to all religions,' says Mr Huxley of the third of his 'recognizedly' religious states of mind and actions. Had he ended with these words as well as begun with them, and permitted the reader to understand the word asceticism in whatever way he would, all would have been well, and with one statement at least we should have had no cause for disagreement. Unfortunately, in the next sentence he makes it clear that by asceticism he means the belief that men could 'win the favour of the gods by abstaining from pleasure and comfort'. We have already shown that to the Buddha and his disciples the gods were not objects of fear, and from that for which no fear is felt obviously no attempt will be made to win favours. Abstention from pleasure and comfort for the mere sake of abstinence, or with the wrong view that self-torture could lead to Enlightenment, was one of the two kinds of extreme methods tried and rejected as useless by the Buddha, and was afterwards condemned by him as 'painful, unworthy, and unprofitable' at the commencement of his first sermon at Sarnath.[97] The world-honoured one taught instead a middle path which consists, on the level of ethics, in an equally scrupulous eschewal of self-indulgence and self-mortification. Mental purity can be won neither by pleasure nor by pain, but only by that special kind of wisdom – third of the three ascending stages into which the Noble Eightfold Path or middle way is divided – mention of which has already been made. Asceticism can be considered as an integral part of the Buddhist way of life, as a factor which contributes to the growth of wisdom, only if we use the word in its original Graeco-Roman sense of that 'training' or 'discipline' which, as J. Evola says, 'aims at placing all the energies of the human being under the control of a central principle'.[98] This kind of asceticism is not confined to 'religion' but is one of the chief instruments whereby physical, intellectual, or artistic excellence of any kind is achieved. It is the blade which, pruning the exuberance of nature into the restraint of art (in the widest sense of the term), renders possible the unfolding of perfect blossoms of human culture. And Buddhism, it may be added, does not confuse the blade with the blossom. Asceticism is very definitely regarded only as a means to an end, and that this end has nothing to do with winning the favours of gods we now hardly need insist.

The next neatly cartoned product shot out by Mr Huxley's selective machinery is labelled 'future compensatory states' or, in plainer language, heavens and hells. Belief in the existence of these states or places he lays before us as 'one of the most typical religious doctrines', and accounts for its prevalence by saying: 'Human misery is so great and so widespread that one of the principal functions of religion has been that of consolation.' This explanation of course suffices only for the heavens, not for the hells, but be that as it may, the fact that human beings suffer has never been denied by Buddhism, which indeed on the contrary directs its attention primarily to 'pain and the cessation of pain'. However, though it teaches rebirth or 're-becoming' (*punabbhava*) after death, either in this world or another, the process of compensation goes on in strict accordance with the law of moral equity, whereby selfish volitions result in suffering, and unselfish ones in happiness. We are compensated not for what others have done to us but for that which we have done to others. Our sufferings on this earth, far from being in need of future compensation, are themselves generally the retribution of our misguided volitions in previous existences. Buddhist teaching on the subject of compensatory states can hardly be described as consolatory, in fact it can scarcely be described as essentially and specifically Buddhist. What may be termed the higher teaching of Buddhism points out that suffering is inseparable from sentient existence, and that true happiness is to be attained, not by seeking rebirth in any heaven-world, however glorious, but by eradicating that craving for continued individual existence which is the cause of rebirth, and by attaining, not after death but in this very life itself, the imperishable bliss of Nirvāṇa.

Of the fifth item in his catalogue. Mr Huxley says,

> Absoluteness is a quality typical of religious beliefs. Religious doctrines are held with a passionate tenacity. If what is believed is absolutely true, then it is of vital importance that the believer should cling to his belief and refuse to admit the contrary beliefs of others. Conversely, absoluteness of belief, resulting from whatever cause, tends to create a certainty of the absolute reality of the thing believed in. The quality of the faith is transferred to its object, which thereby becomes absolute and consequently worthy of worship.

Nowhere else, perhaps, does Buddhism so clearly tower with supreme transcension above all other 'religions' than when it teaches, not the absoluteness, but the relativity of all religious beliefs and practices whatever, its own included. Of the supreme experience of Nirvāṇa no attribute can be predicated, no quality affirmed. All that can be said is that certain beliefs and practices conduce to its achievement, while others do not. The former are collectively termed 'Dharma', which is the correct word for what is popularly called 'Buddhism'; the latter *adharma*, or that which is contrary to Dharma. Far from encouraging his disciples to hold his doctrines 'with a passionate tenacity' the Buddha time and time again reminded them that, in the words of the famous parable of the raft, the Dharma was 'something to leave behind, not to take with you'.[99] One who thought that ethics, concentration, and wisdom were ends in themselves, and not simply a means for the attainment of Nirvāṇa, and who endowed them with absolute value, was in the Buddha's opinion no less foolish than a man who, after crossing a great river, should bear away on his shoulders the raft whereon he had paddled over, instead of hauling it up onto the shore, or sinking it in the water and going about his business. Since for the Buddhist none of his own beliefs is 'absolutely true', it is not of vital importance that he 'should cling to his belief and refuse to admit the contrary beliefs of others'. Typical as this attitude is of the followers of other 'religions', it is quite unfamiliar to those who truly follow the Buddha.

The Buddhist attitude is that of the sharp-sighted man in another parable, the parable of the elephant, who saw with a smile of amusement a group of blind men disputing about the nature of that lordly pachyderm, one seizing its trunk and declaring it to be like a ploughshare, another grasping its ear and maintaining that it resembled a winnowing-basket, and so on one after the other until they all fell into a rage and began fighting among themselves.[100] 'Views' are, in Huxleian language, rationalizations of egocentric emotions, and Enlightenment cannot be attained until they are abandoned. Even 'right views', the intellectual formulation of the conditions precedent to the attainment of Nirvāṇa, are not to be understood as metaphysically true or clung to as though they possessed absolute validity, but simply to be used with discrimination for the attainment of those ends to which they are in the nature of things best adapted. Absoluteness of belief being absent from Buddhism, there is no question of it tending to create 'a certainty in the absolute reality of the thing believed in'. The kind of 'faith' and 'worship' ensuing from this certainty are therefore meaningless words to it.

Almost equally meaningless, from the Buddhist point of view, is the word 'priest', despite the fact that Mr Huxley introduces the last item of his catalogue with the generalization: 'All religions have priests, who fulfil a double function.' 'They are,' proceeds his description, 'in the first place, to use M. Paul Valery's expressive phrase, *les preposes aux choses vagues* – mediators between man and the surrounding mystery, which they understand and can propitiate more effectually than ordinary folk. Their second function is earthly; they are confessors, advisers, casuists, spiritual doctors; at certain periods they have also been rulers.' Though 'priest' is hardly a correct rendering of the Aryan word *bhikṣu*, which originally meant a mendicant friar, the life of the *bhikṣu* has two aspects which are in a sense analogous to the double function which, according to Mr Huxley, priests fulfil. He 'mediates between man and the surrounding mystery' not by propitiating malevolent beings on man's behalf, but by revealing through his own actions the greatest of all mysteries, the mystery of holiness. The *bhikṣu* mediates between the ideal and the real, and enables mankind to see the highest spiritual truths in terms of ordinary human life. He does more than this. By his practical instructions he enables people to know the mystery of holiness for themselves; he helps them make it a part of their own experience. In this twofold way, combining example and precept, he makes the mystery to them a mystery no longer, and irradiates the darkness of the unknown with the light of realization.

It has been truly said that a complete account of Buddhism could be given by simply denying one after another the statements made about it by non-Buddhist writers. Similarly, we have allowed our own descriptions of 'the principal states of mind and actions recognized as religious' to emerge into view by laying bare the shortcomings of Mr Huxley's account of them. These shortcomings are all due to the fact that in spite of his disparagement of formal definitions of religion he had lurking at the back of his mind a definition which was not broad enough to include Buddhism. The exclusion is significant, though with the exploration of that significance we are not now concerned. We are concerned instead with the discovery of a definition of religion which will be of service to us in our task of making clear the nature of the Religion of Art. Such a definition will necessarily deal not with adventitious frills and trimmings but with the barest essentials of the thing, and even those essentials it must present, not in incipient or half-developed shapes, but only in the perfection of their fully articulated forms. If it should be objected that our attempt to elicit a definition of religion from a consideration of Mr Huxley's catalogue was in fact nothing but an exhibition of the differences, both partial and complete, by which Buddhism is separated from all other faiths, we shall reply that such a proceeding was unavoidable, because Buddhism is not merely a religion among religions, but Religion in its classical and archetypal form, disentangled from all irrelevant additions, so that a complete unfolding of the characteristics of religion inevitably results in a description of what, historically speaking, is the Dharma of the Buddha. The truth of this statement may be made more evident by abstracting our observations from their Huxleian context and presenting them as an independent description of recognizably religious states and actions, after which we shall allow the rotundities of description to crystallize into the straighter lines and acuter angles of one of those abstract definitions which Mr Huxley affected so much to despise. Our own catalogue, then, is briefly as follows.

The fundamental religious state of mind is a sense of absolute fearlessness. This feeling is the result of freedom from selfish attachments and desires, which is itself the consequence of having abandoned the misconception that one is essentially a separate, unchanging individual being. Interpretations of existence which have been elaborated from rationalizations of egocentric emotions such as hope and fear dissolve like mist, and the emancipated mind shines forth in its intrinsic purity unclouded by even the shadow of a concept.

The religious feeling finds its active as opposed to its theoretical expression in the practice of ethics, the development of the mind through concentration, and the intuitive realization of higher wisdom, all of which are necessary steps on the path leading to liberation from the ego-idea and, consequently, to those emotions of fearlessness which are, for the individual who feels them, a proof of the authenticity of his realization. These emotions are accompanied by others no less tranquillizing, and therefore no less genuinely spiritual. Chief among these is what may be called the solitary emotion, the feeling of bliss and peace caused by being alone.

Asceticism is not an end in itself, but only a means of concentrating the total energies of the personality along a single line of development. Self-torture is not only of no use in the spiritual life, but is even positively harmful.

Human suffering is the result of selfish desires, of craving, and can cease only when those desires cease. Rebirth in a heaven after death, as the result of living virtuously, is possible, but since such a state is not everlasting, being subject to the universal law of impermanence, it also is eventually a source of suffering. Permanent happiness, the happiness of Nirvāṇa, can be obtained in this life itself by the destruction of craving.

Relativity is a quality typical of religious beliefs. Religious doctrines should be followed but they should never be made a basis of attachment. If what is believed is only relatively true, then it is of vital importance that the believer should not cling to his belief and refuse to admit the contrary beliefs of others. Conversely, tentativeness of belief, resulting from whatever cause, tends to create a conviction of the merely relative and instrumental value of religious doctrines and practices. Faith is belief in the efficacy of the means employed after we have put them to the test in our own life and experience. It is 'confidence based on knowledge'.

Buddhism is the only religion which has *bhikṣu*s, who fulfil a double function. They are in the first place living embodiments of the Buddhist ideal, and in the second the teachers of that ideal to the world in general, and the Buddhist community in particular, as well as the conservators of the entire great heritage of Buddhist culture, the whole body of which collectively, and each part individually, is intended as a means of orienting human life in the direction of its highest goal.

Having now given our own description of the archetypally religious states of mind and actions, it will not be difficult for us to telescope them into a definition of religion. The central principle stands out among the multiplicity of its applications with unmistakable pre-eminence. Religion is essentially the experience of egolessness; the truly religious life is the life of egolessness; and genuinely religious beliefs and practices are those by which the realization of egolessness can be achieved. Like most definitions, this one that we have given of religion is abstract and contentless in the extreme, and although nobody, perhaps, would be inclined to deny its correctness, not one of them, probably, would find it of much practical use. Definition is the result of comparison, abstraction, and generalization, all of which are intellectual operations. Warm, living, concrete things are fed into one end of the intellectual machine and emerge at the other cold, dead concepts with every drop of emotion squeezed out of them. These concepts reason may manipulate in a ghastly puppet-dance of argument, spinning round her 'unearthly ballet of bloodless categories'[101] in a complicated choreography of syllogisms; but though the performance may convince the head, it is powerless to move the heart. The heart can be moved only by emotions, and only the heart can move man. Intellectual recognition of the fact that religion consists in a life of egolessness is not sufficient to inspire anyone actually to live such a life, because his emotional energies have not been involved.

To know what is good is not the same as to do what is good because, as Aristotle remarked in his unanswerable criticism of the ethical theory of Socrates, it fails to take into consideration 'the irrational parts of the soul'.[102] Every religion therefore attempts, not only to justify its teachings to the intellect, but also to recommend them to the feelings. Through myth, ritual, literature, painting, sculpture, and music each tries to canalize emotion into the arid fields of the doctrines in which they wish us to believe and the practices they desire us to follow. In this way arises what is generally known as religious art. But, as might be expected, an ambiguity lurks in the word 'religious', and in order not to be confused by it we shall have to bear in mind the description of truly religious mental states and practices we have already given, and the definition of religion which we elicited from that description. Religious art is that kind of poetry, music, painting, or any other species of art, which conduces to the experience of egolessness. Much conventionally religious art, particularly Christian art, is not religious art in the sense that we have defined the term because it not only fails to induce the experience of egolessness, but even positively strengthens the ego-sense. The kind of pseudo-religious art that we have in mind is represented by sensually attractive Madonnas such as the Italian Renaissance painters so abundantly produced, and by literary works such as the *Rāmacaritamānasa* of Tulsidas, which despite its poetical beauties is only the hot air of devotional frenzy inflating the bladder of brahminical egoism.[103] The direct contrary of such pseudo-religious art, which is religious in subject but non-religious in sentiment, is what may be termed naturally or essentially religious art, which is religious in sentiment, though non-religious in subject. Examples of this kind of art might be multiplied indefinitely: Chinese landscape painting, the best of Shelley's poetry, and much of the music of Beethoven, are sufficient to represent it. Two more permutations of the terms 'religious art' and 'non-religious art' it is possible to obtain. The first of these is religious both conventionally and naturally, in subject as well as sentiment, while the second is religious in neither, a work of art of this type being merely a profane subject profanely treated. The Buddha-image is perhaps the finest example of the one, and almost all contemporary popular art among the worst examples of the other.

Further refinements of classification it would be possible to introduce, but since they are irrelevant to our present purpose we abstain from making them. Of the four categories of art already mentioned our concern is with the second only, for it is this which supplies the raw material, as it were, of the Religion of Art. We are not concerned with artworks of the first category because their ostensible religiosity often prevents them from appealing to modern sensibility, while their lack of truly religious sentiment – their failure to impart the experience of egolessness – renders them valueless from the point of view adopted in our present inquiry. With the fourth kind of art we have no concern not only because it is not in any sense religious, but because it is perhaps only superficially art. The domain of the Religion of Art, as demarcated at the beginning of our inquiry, is that province of art which is also a province of religion, and that part of true religion which is also a part of art. But before attempting to deal with the Religion of Art it will be necessary for us to deal separately with the nature of art, just as we had already to deal separately with the nature of religion.

Art is essentially creative. Like the general creativity of human life, civilization, and culture, of which it is the highest and most intensified development, it creates, not out of nothing, but by impressing its own ideal forms upon the chaos of sensuous experience. The *materia prima*, the stuff and raw material that an artist subdues and adapts to his creative purpose, is compounded of outlines, colours, masses, words, and sounds with which all men are familiar, and which are indeed themselves products of the rudimentary artistic activity if not of humanity at least of an important section of the human race. These sensuously given elements the painter, sculptor, poet, and musician organize into formal relations which, by some mysterious resonance of the human spirit, are capable of imparting a pleasure more intense and rare than that given by sensuous experiences which have not been so organized. But however intense the pleasure given by works of art it would be a mistake to suppose that art gives nothing but pleasure. Poetry, for example, which is the most fully developed form of art, even as Buddhism is the archetypal form of religion, is not only pleasurable but meaningful: besides expressing the poet's emotions it communicates his sense of values. It is the organ not merely of his feelings, much less still only of his thoughts, but of the whole unified sensibility with which he explores undiscovered regions of experience. Though the terms 'sensibility' and 'experience' have been allowed to stand for the subjective and objective aspects of artistic realization it should not be thought that a rigid line of demarcation can be drawn between them. Experiences are not possessions like pieces of furniture, but states and modifications of our own being, or, in more Buddhistic language, of our own becoming. The poet experiences things directly, by assimilating them into his spiritual being in much the same way as he assimilates material food into his physical body. For this reason some philosophers of art have thought that art was adequately defined as intuition, in which the subject and object of experience coalesce as it were into one. What the poet, or any other artist, tries through his special medium to express is not so much an unfamiliar kind of experience as a new mode of being. As Rilke says at the end of his sonnet 'Archaic Torso of Apollo':

> ... for here is no place
> That does not see you. You must change your life.[104]

The 'you' to whom the poet addresses his exhortation is what Indian Aesthetics has termed the *rasika* (a much better word than either the 'aesthete' or 'critic' of European artistic tradition), the 'taster' or 'enjoyer' of the *rasa* or aesthetic relish which saturates a work of art. For art is not only expression but communication as well. According to Herbert Read it communicates a sense of values.[105] Values are things that are desirable not as means to the attainment of other things, but for their own sakes. Modes of being or states of consciousness (in Buddhist philosophy being and consciousness are equated) which are expressed in, and communicated by, works of art, are not values from the point of view of the artist – for he has already attained them – but only to his audience, who are first of all startled into an enhanced awareness of life by the impact of a sensibility infinitely more refined and powerful than their own, and then confronted with the terrible necessity of renouncing their old self and transforming it into a new personality by the assimilation of a wholly unfamiliar experience. Often they shrink from what their natural egoism regards as the stress and pain of such transformation. They feel only the terror of death, and not the joy of birth into a richer and larger life. J. B. Leishman compares the lines which we have just quoted from Rilke with the description in the poet's *Malte Laurids Brigge* of a certain actress, probably Eleonora Duse, who

> tried to distract the gaze of the audience from herself to the immense reality that filled her. *But they were already breaking into applause in their terror of the extreme: as though at the last moment to deflect from themselves something that would compel them to change their lives.*[106]

At this stage of our inquiry, which has now brought us to the point at which the realm of art begins to overlap the realm of religion, we may fittingly condense our findings into a formal definition of the nature of art before attempting to gain admittance to the fascinating domain of the Religion of Art or to continue our journey through its unexplored interior. *Art is the organization of sensuous impressions into pleasurable formal relations that express the artist's sensibility and communicate to his audience a sense of values that can transform their lives.* The completeness of this definition becomes clearly apparent when we compare it with fragmentary definitions according to which art is 'an attempt to create pleasing forms' (Herbert Read), 'significant form' (Clive Bell), or, most simply of all, 'intuition' (Croce).[107] It moreover illuminates the significance of definitions of beauty as modern as Herbert Read's 'Beauty is a unity of formal relations among our sense perceptions,' or as ancient as the scholastic 'Beauty is the splendour of form reflected on the proportioned parts of matter.'[108]

Having now formed a clear, even if rather abstract, idea of the nature of religion and the nature of art as independent lines of human activity, we must now trace out the parallels between them, as well as determine, if possible, their exact points of intersection. First of all we shall have to examine the relation between egolessness and art; but the examination will be fruitful only if we load every rift of our conception with the ore of concrete meaning.

In spite of its negative form, the word egolessness, or in unmixed Anglo-Saxon 'unselfishness', is far from devoid of positive content, as we shall presently see, though our effort to reveal that content may well begin with an explanation of the principle which it negates. This principle, strange to say, is in truth itself a negation, a suppression of reality; that is to say, it is a delusion. The ego does not really exist; it is not a thing but a thought; not a metaphysical entity but an epistemological error. It is simply the idea of separate individuality. Since ideas are themselves things (not in the sense of being material objects, but in the sense that they are capable of producing tangible effects) the idea of separate individuality does not remain ineffectually floating about in the ether of consciousness but descends upon the earth in a storm of consequences. Being a wrong idea it proliferates effects which are wrong. The first of these effects is the attraction and aggregation of material particles into a human body endowed with sense-organs through which the nucleating 'ego' will be able to gratify that craving for individual existence, that longing for experience as a separate 'self', which it has carried over unsatisfied from previous births and which is the cause of its present 'reincarnation'. In this new body it experiences sensations that enhance its feeling of separateness, and sensations which diminish it and even threaten the existence of its physical basis. The former it describes as pleasurable, the latter as painful. These simple sensations of pleasure and pain are connected with the idea of external cause, and in this way the automatic responses of attraction and repulsion are transformed into conscious desire and aversion, together with all the elaborate variations and permutations of these two great feelings which constitute the self-centred emotional life of ordinary people.

Since men live not in solitude but in society, their efforts to maintain and augment their own separate selfhood inevitably bring them into conflict with all the millions of other men who are engaged in the same attempt. Interests differ, and therefore individualities necessarily clash. Different social groups come into conflict with one another. 'Religions' disagree, and holy wars are preached. National existences are threatened, and armies march to the battlefield. Bodies of men, women, and children are hideously mutilated or blown to pieces. Blood flows like a river. The details of such scenes of human conflict are nowadays too familiar to require further particularization. As Spinoza long ago understood, individuals, nations, and all other things endeavour to persist in their own mode of being,[109] or, as we should ourselves phrase it, to prolong their own stream of becoming, to go on repeating, over and over again, the same old pattern of experience. The colours may vary from time to time, the threads be changed from coarse to fine, but all are woven into the same unchanging pattern. If (to use a more dynamic metaphor) some new experience rushes comet-like from the unknown immensity of the surrounding universe, the ego steadies itself grimly on its axis, and, putting forth all its powers of attraction, endeavours to draw the intruder from his path and swing him round like a planet at the circumference of its own little solar system.

Selfishness is simply unwillingness to face new experiences. A radically new experience which we cannot weave into the pattern of our life demands the changing of the pattern and the working out of a fresh design in which it can form a part. The ego resists the onrush of new experiences because of the changes they involve, for a change in experience means a modification of existence; and though, in relation to the new life, such a modification is a birth, in relation to the old life, to the ego, it is in fact a death. Unselfishness, on the other hand, is an openness to new experiences, a willingness to die for the sake of being born anew. If egoism is a centripetal tendency, a movement of contraction upon its own centre, egolessness, on the contrary, is a centrifugal tendency, a movement of expansion not only towards its own circumference (for this has no meaning except in relation to a centre) but towards something absolutely outside the orbit of its own being. If a new experience appears comet-like in the sky, it eagerly abandons its own planetary system and spins towards it singing, with Shelley's Moon,

> I must hurry, whirl and follow,
> Through the heavens wide and hollow.[110]

This is the spirit of the true artist. Possessing from his birth an extraordinary sensitiveness to what Wordsworth called 'unknown modes of being'[111] – a capacity to experience what Mr Aldous Huxley, writing of D. H. Lawrence, describes as 'the dark presence of the otherness that lies beyond the boundaries of man's conscious mind'[112] – he is passionately eager to widen and deepen the range of his experience to the farthest possible limit.

Now experience is of two kinds: that which relates to the external world of flowers, trees, people, mountains, and stars; and that which relates to the internal world of emotions, thoughts, imaginations, and intuitions. Our use of the words 'widen' and 'deepen' refers to the possibility of developing experience in these two directions. The artist widens his experience by continually increasing the number of his points of contact with the material universe in which he lives; for, like Antaeus in the myth, contact with the earth strengthens him. He deepens his experience (or heightens it, for both words connote refinement and intensification) first of all by becoming aware of it and then by subjecting it to a process of prolonged incubatory reflection in which essentials are separated from accidents and the significance of the experience gradually disclosed.

Contact with the earth is of course possible only through the body, by means of the five senses, particularly the eye, and to the poet's awareness through this highly sensitive organ of what we have elsewhere described as 'the unique individuality of things' we have already given the name observation.[113] When an object is observed intently for some time sympathy for it will begin to be felt, for in the act of pure observation self-awareness is suspended and, at least for an instant, subject coalesces with object and feels the pulse of its existence beating indistinguishably from its own. Contact with 'unknown modes of being', on the other hand, is possible not through any external sense but only through an internal organ of experience – by means of refined and subtilized emotion. As we have explained in our *Advice to a Young Poet*, emotion, which is a force, can be subtilized by what we have there called the asceticism of art, wherein conscious inhibition of the normal outlets of emotional energy succeeds in making it seek expression on higher and more refined levels of existence.[114]

Though we have spoken of the two kinds of experience, one having the external, the other the internal, world for object, it should not be supposed that they exist side by side without any deeper or more intimate relation than that of mere external juxtaposition. They are not so much two worlds as two hemispheres of experience within the one world of the artist's personality. Between these two hemispheres a continual traffic goes on. Facts are forever crossing over into our personal life as feelings, and experiences which are both thoughts and feelings, as well as something more significant than either, go forth into the external world not as fugitive words and deeds but as immortal works of art. The poet (to change the metaphor) is rooted in the objective world as a plant is rooted in the soil. The nutriment that he derives therefrom is transformed into the invisible sap of aesthetic experience and creative potency, re-emerging thence into visibility not as earth and water but as the marvel of a leaf or the miracle of a flower. For the true poet seeks not only to enrich his experience through observation of, and sympathy with, life in all its multitudinous forms, but also to refine it, to raise it to the highest possible pitch of intensity, by solitary reflection on its meaning. Poetry which has not been enriched by the continual influx of sensuous impressions lacks vitality, while that which has not been refined by prolonged meditation is drossy and impure, and incapable of imparting to the *rasika* that sudden shock of delight which transports him into a hitherto unknown region of experience. The rhythm of the poet's life is dominated by the systole and diastole of receptiveness and creativity, absorption and transmutation, enrichment and refinement. Sometimes his heart expands until it embraces the universe; sometimes it contracts into a point. Both movements are necessary, and the soul of the poet can no more exist with one only than his physical body can live with a heart that only pumps blood in or only pumps it out.

The first kind of poetic experience, the necessity for that subtle alchemy whereby objective fact is transmuted not merely into subjective feeling but into the very stuff of the poet's personal life, has found poignant utterance in Rilke's well-known description of poetry in *The Notebooks of Malte Laurids Brigge*:

> But alas! [he exclaims] one does not get very far with verses if one writes them too early. One should wait and collect sense and sweetness during a whole lifetime and if possible a long one, and then, right at the end, one might perhaps be able to write ten lines that were good. For verses are not, as people suppose, feelings (one has them soon enough) – they are experiences. For the sake of a verse one must see many cities, men and things, one must know animals, one must feel how birds fly, and understand the gestures with which little flowers open in the morning. One must be able to look back upon roads in unknown regions, on unexpected meetings and on partings that one long foresaw, on days of childhood that are still unexplained, on parents whom one had to hurt, if they brought one a pleasure and one did not comprehend it (it was a pleasure for someone else), – on childish illnesses, that begin so strangely with so many deep and difficult changes, on days in still, subdued rooms and on mornings by the sea, on all that the sea can mean, on seas, on nights of travel that rushed away on high and flew with all the stars – and even if one is able to think of all that, it is not yet sufficient. One must have memories of many nights of love, of which not one was like another, of cries of women in labour and of light, white sleeping

> women in childbed, who are closing. But one must also have been beside the dying, must have sat beside the dead in the room with the open window and the intermittent sounds. And still, even to have memories is not sufficient. If there are many of them one must be able to forget them, and one must have the great patience to wait till they return. For the memories themselves are not yet what is required. Not till they become blood within us, look and gesture, nameless and no longer distinguishable from ourselves, not till then is it possible, in some very rare hour, for the first word of a verse to arise in their midst and to proceed from them.[115]

The second kind of experience, the indispensable complementary process in which the enriched poetic personality is elevated to hitherto unscaled heights of being by the deliberate refinement of its emotional energies, has been admirably described by J. B. Leishman in his Commentary on Rilke's *Later Poems*:

> Here we have the very kernel of what might be called Rilke's philosophy of love. He felt that the immense reserve of emotional energy developed or released by that experience ought not to be squandered on a transient and comparatively trivial satisfaction, but suppressed, repressed, dammed up like a stream, until it reached an almost unbearable intensity, and then used as the propulsive force for some journey to the infinite, to undiscovered regions of thought and feeling. It might, perhaps, be objected that here art was encroaching upon life; that, while the exhortation to sublimate his emotional experiences, to divert and convert them into means of imaginative discovery and creation, may be valid for the artist, it is only partially valid for humanity in general. I feel there is something in this objection, but, at the same time, I also feel that (like many other objections to Rilke) it tends to flatter too much our satisfaction with ourselves as we are.[116]

Inasmuch as love is the basic emotion, even as desire is the fundamental feeling (love being, according to Spinoza, pleasure accompanied by the idea of an external cause),[117] Rilke's philosophy of love is no less a philosophy of all the emotions, and his technique of sublimation can therefore be applied not to one emotion alone but to the whole affective life. This process of sublimation is for the artist not only valid, but an indispensable part of his artistic experience. If it is only partially valid for humanity in general the reason is that ordinary men and women are only partially artists. Their sensibilities are coarse, their imagination weak, and their creative power constantly frittered away on 'transient and comparatively trivial satisfaction'. Whatever their nominal religion may be, such people more often regard their physical body as the centre of the universe, and the gratification of the senses, together with the occasional titillation of the lower mind, as the highest aim of existence. As yet no spark of divine discontent has fallen from the stars to set their hearts ablaze. The winds of spirit search for them in vain from end to end of the sky. They sit snug all the while in the cosy cottage of individual selfhood, huddling over the smoky flame of desire, and are quite content to be shuttered in from the airs of truth that blow so clean and cold outside. Any interruption of the 'noiseless tenor of their way', to say nothing of any quickening of their dormant spiritual life, or any drastic modification of their own being, is farther from their thoughts than flying to the moon. They do not want to change their lives; they are, as Leishman phrases it, satisfied with themselves as they are. Most human beings are content to be human beings, just as a pig is content to be a pig, and long indeed is the coming of that 'spiritual dawn' when

> By vengeful working of mysterious codes
> An angel wakens in the drowsy beast.[118]

That dawn can come either from religion or from art (in the sense that we have defined them), and one might as well blame light for encroaching on darkness as object to art that it encroaches upon life. It is the function of art to encroach upon life. For a great work of art embodies an unfamiliar experience, and this experience confronts us, as the archaic torso of Apollo confronted Rilke, with a challenge and a demand, with the flat imperative: 'You must change your life.' If in our terror we refuse to accept that challenge, to meet that demand, then the world of art is in reality closed to us. Then we either have not intercourse with it at all, or else attempt to enjoy works of art without permitting them to transform our lives. In the first case we become philistines, in the second aesthetes of the type satirized in 'The Palace of Art'. Tennyson's

glorious Devil, large in heart and brain,
That did love Beauty only.[119]

was simply a man who thought of art as a comparatively refined means of sensuous pleasure, as an elegant cup-bearer at the feast of life, rather than as a bare skeleton grimly announcing the necessity of terrible transformations. (Death and art are terrible for the same reason: both represent change.)

Religion, we have already seen, is essentially a life of egolessness; and egolessness, we have found, is fundamentally a willingness to accept new experiences. The Religion of Art may therefore be defined as conscious surrender to the Beautiful, especially as manifested in poetry, music, and the visual arts, as a means of breaking up established egocentric patterns of behaviour and protracting one's experience along the line of egolessness into the starry depths of Reality. It will be noted that we speak not merely of experiences but of new experiences, for only a new experience is capable of making a breach in that thick wall of selfhood with which most of us are surrounded. By 'new' we do not mean, however, the relative newness of, for instance, a young man's first experience of love, which is new only to him, but of what is, within the limits of average human experience, the absolute newness of a symphony of Beethoven or a sonnet by Keats.

According to some ancient Indian poets the essential quality of Beauty is that it remains from moment to moment ever new (*tadeva rūpaṃ ramaṇīyatāyāḥ kṣaṇe kṣaṇe yannavataṃ vidhatte*).[120] Since every new experience compels a fresh modification of character it might be possible to describe Beauty not only as that which is always new, but also as that which, far from allowing us the luxury of remaining satisfied with ourselves as we are, demands from moment to moment a fresh transformation of our lives. Absolute Beauty (to plunge for a minute into the stormy sea of metaphysics) would then be that Beauty whose demands upon us are inexhaustible, which never allows us to rest in any perfection, and which even beyond what seems to us the highest transformation calls for another higher still.

This conception of the aesthetic life as being fulfilled in a perpetual progress, rather than in a definite arrival at a fixed point of achievement, is paralleled by an early Buddhist teaching, the significance of which was first emphasized by Dr Beni Madhab Barua in his lecture on *Buddhism as*

Personal Religion. According to this teaching (which, though attributed to the nun Dhammadinnā, was approved by the Buddha himself),

> Buddha's Causal Genesis admits of two different trends of things in the whole of reality. In one of them the reaction (*paṭibhāga*) takes place in a cyclical order between two opposites (*paccanīkas*), such as pleasure and pain (*sukha-dukkha*), virtue and vice (*puñña-pāpa*), good and evil (*kusala-akusala*). This is aptly termed by Buddhaghosa *visabhāga-paṭibhāga*. In the other, the reaction takes place in a progressive order between two counterparts or complements, or between two things of the same genus, the succeeding factor augmenting the effect of the preceding one. This is what Buddhaghosa terms *sadisa-paṭibhāga*. By the term 'world', as distinguished from *Nirvāṇa*, we are to understand the first trend in the causal genesis where we revolve within the cycle of reaction between the opposites. *Nirvāṇa* represents the other trend in the causal genesis in which the course of reaction lies from strength to strength, good to further good, from that to still greater good, from pleasure to joy, from joy to gladness, from gladness to happiness, from happiness to bliss, from bliss to beatitude, from intuitional knowledge (*vijjā*) to the feeling of emancipation (*vimutti*), from that to self-mastery (*vasībhāva*) or self-consciousness as to the acquisition of the free state, and from that to the fullest enjoyment of the bliss of *Nirvāṇa*. In reply to the question as to what follows by way of the reaction from *Nirvāṇa* Dhammadinnā wisely said that *Nirvāṇa* was generally regarded as the final step of the process in order to avoid an infinite regress – for the sake of *pariyantagahaṇam* in her own language. But she has not failed to indicate that even if there be any further reaction, that also takes place in the line and that whatever follows therefrom will also appertain in *Nirvāṇa* and, therefore, will partake of its nature.[171]

Less than five hundred years after Dhammadinnā these ideas received their full development in the Prajñāpāramitā *sūtras*, wherein the principle of infinite regress is accepted, and wherein the bodhisattva is time and again exhorted not to rest in any *dharma*, not to regard any attainment as ultimate, including the attainment of Nirvāṇa, and wherein he is in fact even required to abandon the idea of attainment altogether.[122] The greatest mistake an aspirant to the life of egolessness could make would be to think of egolessness as though it was a kind of attainment. For it is not so much a state or an experience as an attitude to all states and experiences whatsoever. This attitude reveals itself as a readiness to renounce old experiences and to face and embrace new ones. Egolessness is thus not any state of existence, howsoever exalted, but essentially a condition of will. Neither the saint nor the artist – the artist in goodness nor the saint of the beautiful – should allow himself to become attached to his experiences, attainments, or realizations. For to rest in any particular experience of the good, or of the beautiful, would mean nothing less than the collapse of his spiritual or aesthetic career.

Art adores that Absolute Beauty which, since it is ever new, demands of its votaries the perpetual transformation of their lives, offering as reward for the terror of incessant death the joy of repeated birth into a life infinitely enriched and refined 'beyond all that is comprehensible and embraceable here'.[123] It does not allow them to settle down in any perfection, for, as Lama Govinda has pointed out, perfection itself is not 'an absolute value or a fixed condition', and 'neither exists as an end at the top of a scale, nor as an absolute or fixed measurement, but as an infinitesimal moment of harmony in movement.'[124] The true artist understands this relativity of perfection no less thoroughly than the true saint does. He beholds beauty rising and shining beyond beauty as the mountaineer sees range upon range of hills rising up one behind another, each one loftier and grander than that beneath it. The traveller's eye must come to rest somewhere in the end, either on the last and loftiest range as it stands silhouetted against the sky, or on the blue depths of haze, indistinguishable from the sky itself, into which the contours of ridge and peak melt and fade away. But the eye of the artist never comes to rest, for beauty is inexhaustible. She is the ever attained, and yet remains the ever unattainable, and therefore the artist's longing and desire for her, though perpetually satisfied, are perpetually unsatisfied, so that he presses eagerly on through keener satisfactions, diviner discontents, and intenser longings, until he realizes, if he had not realized it before, that the prize is in the race, and beauty in truth nothing but the rhythm of delight within his own experience.

Such is the natural egolessness of true artists, of the genuine devotees of Beauty, the sainted souls of Art. But here, just as we touch the highest point of our inquiry, two or three difficulties might arise, or one or two objections could be voiced, which must be resolved and answered before we can pursue the Religion of Art round into the full circle of its conclusion.

The first of these difficulties arises out of the apparent instability and irregularity which often distinguishes the lives of artists – poets, painters, and musicians – from the lives of non-artists. In the minds of most tax-paying, form-completing citizens art and immorality are almost synonyms, and it is more or less tacitly assumed that moral laxity is prerequisite to artistic achievement. Though our contention that egolessness is the substance of art no less than of religion might be at least theoretically acceptable to such people, our assertion of its corollary – that the true artist, far from being immoral, is in fact a spiritual being, and the genuinely aesthetic life essentially a life of spirituality – would, therefore, probably appear in their eyes not only unacceptable but even positively absurd. Shrill voices would at once be raised to remind us of Byron's philanderings, while indignant fingers would point out to us the direction of Reading Gaol.[125]

The misconception out of which these difficulties arise is twofold. In the first place, it should not have passed unnoticed that, in our foregoing remarks, we have been careful to speak not of the artist – not just of any practitioner of poetry or painting, music or sculpture – but always of the *true* artist. What we intended this distinguishing epithet to convey has already been made partially clear by our fourfold classification of art into the (1) neither conventionally nor essentially religious type, the (2) conventionally but not essentially religious type, the (3) essentially but not conventionally religious type, and the (4) essentially as well as conventionally religious type. As soon as it is realized that our subsequent definition of Art as *the organization of sensuous impressions into pleasurable formal relations that express the artist's sensibility and communicate to his audience a sense of values that can transform their lives* excludes the first and second types (which, as we had already hinted when discussing them, were not only not essentially religious, but even only superficially art) our conception of the true artist, as distinguished from the false practitioner of the arts, is one who produces art of the third and fourth types, that is to say, art which, either with or without the aid of accepted and understood religious symbols, communicates an experience that compels us to change our lives. As Carlyle finely says in *On Heroes, Hero-Worship, and the Heroic in History*:

> Poet and Prophet differ greatly in our loose modern notions of them. In some old languages, again, the titles are synonymous; *Vates* means both Prophet and Poet; and indeed at all times, Prophet and Poet, well understood, have much kindred of meaning. Fundamentally indeed they are still the same; in this most important respect especially, That they have penetrated both of them into the sacred mystery of the Universe; what Goethe calls 'the open secret'.[126]

What is here said of the poet is essentially true of the painter and musician, for Carlyle is really not concerned to point out the historical connection between the poetic and prophetic functions, so much as to vindicate the existence of a common spiritual element wherein both art and religion live and move and have their being. We believe that one who inhabits, as the true artist does, this spiritual element, who leads a life of egolessness by means of continual surrender to the incessant demands of the Beautiful, is hardly more liable to instabilities and irregularities of conduct than is that other swimmer in spiritual deep waters, the genuine saint, who leads a life of egolessness by unfailing surrender to the demands of the Good. This is not to say that the true artist may not sometimes behave egotistically; but this is due to the fact not that he is an artist but that he is a man, and constitutes a lapse from art no less than a fall from spirituality. We believe that to the extent that he is faithful to Art he will be not only a truer artist than ordinary people but also much better as a man. That the lives of those who are not true artists, who produce art of the first and second types should, on the contrary, frequently be disfigured by intemperance or passional excess, is only what might have been expected, since it is but natural that the same lack of egolessness manifested by their art should also be exhibited in their lives. Moreover, just as in certain Shamanist rites (of a psychic rather than of a spiritual order) a state of trance can be induced in the celebrant by means of intoxicants, so in art which is not essentially religious (which stands in the same relation to true art as Shamanism does to true spirituality) a mood of seeming inspiration, or emotional excitation, can sometimes be induced by the abnormal stimulation of inordinate sensuous indulgence.

The difficulty of recognizing that the truly aesthetic life is also a life of spirituality arises in the second place out of a misconception of the nature of ethics. Those unbending moralists to whom art and immorality are practically synonymous terms are generally found adhering to an external and legalistic conception of morals. To them the moral life consists in the undeviating observance of an 'eternal and immutable' moral code, and this moral code is regarded not as a means to some sublimer spiritual end, but as being an end in itself. By its imperatives all human conduct is to be governed and judged: those who conform to them are moral, the salt of the earth, the elect of God; while those who cannot or will not conform are immoral, accursed, and forever reprobate. We have no intention of questioning the utility of such prescribed patterns of behaviour. Neither society nor civilization could exist without them, and in the earlier stages of the spiritual life of the individual devotee they are indispensable. All we wish to point out is this: that however useful for practical purposes a moral code may be, the criterion of ethics is, nevertheless, fundamentally not external but internal. Although, generally speaking, a conventionally immoral action is at the same time an egoistic action, and therefore not only immoral but unspiritual as well, exceptional cases do occur which are conventionally immoral but in truth both egoless and spiritual. Sometimes it happens that a man may be compelled to shatter moralities out of the sheer intensity of his spiritual life. This is not antinomianism, for, as D. H. Lawrence has finely said, 'The true artist doesn't substitute immorality for morality. On the contrary, he *always* substitutes a finer morality for a grosser.'[127] The grosser immorality of which Lawrence speaks corresponds with the moral codes to which we have referred, and his finer morality to our life of egolessness and spirituality. Many spiritual masters appeared immoral in the eyes of their contemporaries because they had outgrown current notions of right and wrong. Socrates was sentenced to death for 'corrupting' the youth of Athens.[128] Jesus was rebuked by the Pharisees for allowing his disciples to pluck ears of corn (which technically was 'working') on the Sabbath, and for setting them the example of eating with unwashed hands.[129] The Buddha scandalized the orthodox brahmins of his day by disparaging the purifying power of ceremonial bathing, and by bluntly denying the value of animal sacrifices, both of which practices were then considered as being of the very essence of religion.[130] All three masters were not behaving immorally but simply substituting a finer morality for a grosser one. Even while promulgating moral codes, both Jesus and the Buddha were careful to emphasize that such sets of rules possessed at the most a purely instrumental value: to Jesus, love of God and one's neighbour was the ultimate value; to the Buddha, the realization of Nirvāṇa.

We may therefore conclude that the widespread impression that art and immorality are practically synonymous terms has been produced by a combination of three causes: firstly, by a general failure to discriminate the true artist from the false; secondly, by the fact that, unlike the religious ascesis of the Buddhist devotee, the aesthetic ascesis of even the truest artist is rarely a conscious process, so that a fall from egolessness, and the consequent performance of an immoral action, is more to be expected of him than of his fellow pilgrim on the parallel path of Goodness; and thirdly, by the fact that true artists, like genuine spiritual masters, do quite often substitute a finer morality of their own for the grosser moralities of the crowd. But in any case, there is no connection whatsoever between Art and immorality. All true Art in both essence and effect is egoless.

The remaining difficulty relates to the value of the Religion of Art not for the artist but to one who is simply a lover of works of art, whether in the form of poems or paintings, pottery or architecture, musical compositions or sculptures. Such people may possess a deep and genuine love of beauty, and may be keenly sensitive to at least some of its numerous manifestations; but the necessity of earning a livelihood, the cramping pressure of daily routine, and, above all, the exhausting strains and tensions of modern life, usually combine to prevent them from responding to the perceived beauty as actively and as ardently as they desire. Those to whom it is given to be saints of Art will always be a minority, even as among those who are called by religion few will be chosen as artists in the spiritual life. The major portion of any given human community is doomed by limitations of character, no less than by restrictions imposed through external circumstances, to stand not in the inner sanctuary of Egolessness but in its outer courts. As one might have expected, the predicament of the average art-lover runs almost exactly parallel to that of the ordinary religious-minded person. In the case of those who possess both artistic and religious interests, the parallelism is of course between twin aspects of their own personality. For whether one enters the temple of Egolessness by 'the gate which is called Beautiful',[131] or through the portals of the Good, or whether one enters in by both simultaneously, the difficulty of how the average worshipper, with the dust of the world's roads still white upon his feet, can be enabled to participate, at least for a few moments, in the mysteries of the inner shrine, remains the same.

The first step to be taken towards the resolution of this difficulty is to understand that between saint and sinner, artist and critic, creator and enjoyer, expert and amateur, there is a difference not of kind but only of degree. Just as there may be even in the true artist an element of egoism which sometimes makes him act like an ordinary mortal, so there is in the average man an element of egolessness which enables him upon occasions to experience Beauty as it is experienced by the true artist. With regard to their participation in egolessness through the mediation of the Beautiful, the most devoted artist and the most casual enjoyer of works of art stand upon higher and lower rungs of the same golden ladder. With regard to the mode of their participation, however, there exists not a simple difference of degree but, at least from the point of view adopted at this stage of our inquiry, the far more radical difference of kind. The artist's participation in the Religion of Art is a predominantly active participation. He explores realms of experience before unknown, and reveals beauties hitherto unseen. The art-lover's participation, on the other hand, is passive rather than active. Not that active creation necessarily excludes passive enjoyment. All that we wish to point out is that whereas, in the artist's life, active participation in the Religion of Art by means of aesthetic creativity occupies a position of greater centrality than passive participation through mere enjoyment of works of art, in the experience of the art-lover the relative positions of these two modes of participation are reversed, and enjoyment predominates over creation. Once more an analogy between Art and Religion discloses itself. The relation between the creator and the enjoyer of a poem or statue is paralleled by that between the Master who gives and the disciple who receives a religious teaching.

> The Tathāgata, brethren, who, being arahant, is fully enlightened, he it is who doth cause a way to arise which had not arisen before; who doth bring about a way not brought about before; who doth

> proclaim a way not proclaimed before; who is the knower of a way, who understandeth a way, who is skilled in a way. And now, brethren, his disciples are wayfarers who follow after him. That, brethren, is the distinction, the specific feature which distinguishes the Tathāgata who, being arahant, is fully enlightened, from the brother who is freed by insight.[132]

In these words does the Buddha contrast his own creative role in the drama of Buddhism with the comparatively passive part played by his followers. Since the ordinary person participates in the Religion of Art more as a disciple than as a Master, passively rather than actively, we shall deal with his enjoyment of the beauty of works of art first, and only afterwards with his own creation of beauty through personal aesthetic activity.

Beyond the very limited point to which merely untrained and instinctive appreciation of the fine arts can carry him, the value of the Religion of Art to the average man depends upon the clarity with which he understands the distinction between false art which purveys the stale taste of ordinary egoistic human desire, and true art which caters to our deepest spiritual needs the rich and substantial diet, the unique savour, the unsurpassed relish, of emotions which, as they are without precedent in our experience, are an initiation into the mysteries of egolessness. This distinction between what may be provisionally termed 'good' and 'bad' art has to be made not so much for its theoretical value as for its practical consequences, just as in the religious life which parallels the life of art the distinction between ethically 'good' and 'bad' actions is drawn less for the satisfaction of the philosopher than for the guidance of the devotee. He who becomes a devotee of the Religion of Art is required to discriminate works of false art from works of art which are genuine not merely that he may understand but that he may eschew them. Just as the thief must stop stealing before he can become an honest man, and as it is necessary for the debauchee to abandon his impure line of conduct before he can become chaste, so is the renunciation of the enjoyment of bad art an indispensable prerequisite to the full enjoyment of good art. Egoism and egolessness are contradictory attitudes, and poems or pictures ensouling them cannot but inspire in the hearts of their 'enjoyers' emotions no less mutually contradictory than they are. Throughout the whole vast range of nature we see exemplified the law that when the great gods come, the lesser gods depart. Unless the bud bursts the flower cannot unfold its petals, and unless the flower withers and dies in its turn no fruit can ever swell and ripen on the bough. In human life, too, childhood and adolescence, with all their charm, must pass away before maturity can be attained. Humanity must transcend itself in order to achieve superhumanity. Prince Siddhārtha must die so that a Buddha may be born. The Religion of Art's insistence that all pseudo-artistic rubbish must be swept from the highways of the soul before the car of Beauty can drive in triumph there is an application within its own domain of the same immutable law.

What practical difference does this prohibition make in the aesthetic life of the art-lover? If he accepts the authority of the Religion of Art, it will compel him to protect himself from bad art as carefully as he would take precautions against being infected by a particularly dangerous and virulent disease. He will have to stop reading almost all newspapers (which are generally bad literature in a state of putrefaction), pulp-magazines, and that vast mass of tenth-rate fiction which the printing presses of the world turn out in such abundance. From second- and third-rate poetry, even, he should rigorously abstain, for although the quantity of first-rate poetry which has been written since the world began is small compared with that of other forms of literature, it is more than big enough to supply the utmost demands that may be made upon it by any single person. Cheap 'religious' lithographs, shoddy reproductions of popular paintings, and badly printed commercial calendars in all their gaudy hideousness, should be ruthlessly banished from the walls of his home. Inartistic furniture, carpets, curtains, and crockery should be dealt with in the same kind of way and replaced, if not by things which are genuinely beautiful, at least by articles which are well made, functionally appropriate, simple, and not so much an offence to the eye as such articles usually are. The devotee of the Religion of Art should be as much ashamed of being found with a sensational tabloid newspaper in his hand, a pair of unsightly factory-produced vases on his mantelshelf, or with two or three volumes of cheap fiction in his bookcase, as he would be if he was caught picking someone's pocket.

Turning from the contents of the home to the home itself, such a devotee should do his best to ensure that his house is as beautiful outside, in materials, structure, and setting, as it is inside. In this matter, the Indian peasant who lives in a thatched hut, with grey mud-plastered walls, cow-dunged courtyard, and threshold ornamented with intricate designs in rice-paste, amid groves of plantain and mango, and with, perhaps, a pool or a tank nearby wherein to grow blue, red, or white lotuses, is more fortunate than the well-to-do city-dweller who lives in a house like thousands of other houses, in a street like thousands of other streets, with the smell of factory smoke in his nostrils and the noise of traffic thundering in his ears, with a balcony (if he is lucky!) or a grubby back yard instead of a garden, a compartment in a brick box instead of a home and, more likely than not, a bundle of nerves instead of a soul. In the countryside it is easy for a poor man to live beautifully, but in a city it is difficult even for a very wealthy person to do so. Things cannot escape from one another. Beauty and ugliness are both contagious; both spread and influence their surroundings. It is difficult for the city-dwelling art-lover to beautify his own house without beautifying the houses of his neighbours also, for their ugliness casts as it were a dark shadow over the beauty of his own abode. Similarly, ugly houses cannot be eschewed without rebelling against an ugly street, and a rebellion against an ugly street cannot succeed in a town given over to ugliness. It would seem as though the efforts made by the devotee of the Religion of Art to eschew bad works of art cannot be wholly successful without the cooperation of the entire community. Aristotle has said that the function of the state is to provide the conditions upon which the good life depends:[133] it is no less the function of the state to assist its citizens to lead an aesthetic life. Offences against beauty are no less reprehensible than offences against morals, and hence no less deserving of punishment. A businessman who inflicts a hideous factory upon the skyline is as much a menace to society as an embezzler of public funds, and the architect who designed it, the contractor who built it, and the workmen who mixed the cement and swung the girders into position should be treated as his accomplices in crime. In a truly cultured community the unsightly buildings which disfigure most of our modern cities would not be tolerated for a day. Unfortunately, such communities have become rare almost to the point of extinction, and in the anguish of his soul the modern art-lover often thinks wistfully of the lovely cities of Ancient Greece, especially of Athens, city of the violet crown,[134] with the Acropolis gleaming white upon her brow, and wonders whether Beauty will ever reign upon the earth as she reigned in those days over Hellas. Perhaps she will, if the Religion of Art succeeds in attracting a large enough following. Meanwhile the art-lover, despite his inability to pull down ugly houses or replan unsightly streets, can at least eschew, within the walls of his own dwelling, false painting, literature, and music in at least some of their innumerable contemporary forms. Without taking this preliminary step, without cleansing his heart of the egoistically toned emotions which false art induces, deep and genuine appreciation of true art, together with all that such appreciation means for his spiritual life, will be impossible.

Before elucidating the significance of this appreciation, which will enable us to understand the value of the Religion of Art for its average devotee, we should briefly notice another form which, in modern civilization, the eschewal of ugliness often quite spontaneously takes: those periodical exoduses from town to country which seem to have become almost an institution in many Western lands. Even admitting that people who spend weekends in the country or at the seaside are looking for health, amusement, or merely a change of scene as much as they are in search of natural beauty, still it cannot be denied that an unconscious urge to escape from the drabness and squalor of their everyday surroundings, and to gaze upon the face of a beauty untouched by man, impels them no less strongly than other motives. Unfortunately, as Aldous Huxley says in one of his earlier essays, 'Beauty-spots accessible to whole populations cease to be beauty-spots and become Blackpools.'[135] Regrettably true as this statement is, we are now concerned, not so much with appreciation of the beauty of nature as one aspect of a modern social phenomenon, as with the place of that appreciation in the life of the average devotee of the Religion of Art. Kant points out the close connection between the aesthetic and religious aspects of existence, thereby indicating their common fundamental spirituality, when he says that 'to take an immediate interest in the beauty of nature ... is at all times a mark of a good soul'.[136] For Kant, the interest in the beauty of nature is 'immediate' in the sense that it aims to admire and love, while not intending any use or purpose. We may thus speak of appreciation of natural beauty for its own sake, and from our present standpoint the qualification 'for its own sake' is important. Since spirituality, or what the moralistically inclined Kant calls 'goodness', is, as we have seen, essentially an egoless attitude to life, there follows the consequence that only a selfless, that is to say a disinterested, appreciation of the beauties of nature is capable of expressing aesthetically the selflessness of the truly ethical character. In a passage on the love of flowers D. H. Lawrence discriminates with remarkable insight between the interested and the disinterested appreciation of natural beauty:

> Now the love of flowers is a very misleading thing. Most women love flowers as possessions, and as trimmings. They can't look at a flower, and wonder a moment and pass on. If they see a flower that arrests their attention, they must at once pick it, pluck it. Possession! A possession! Something added on to me! And most of the so-called love of flowers today is merely this reaching out of possession and egoism; something I've got; something that embellishes me.
>
> Yet I've seen many a collier stand in his back garden looking down at a flower with that odd, remote sort of contemplation which shows a real awareness of the presence of beauty. It would not even be admiration, or joy, or delight, or any of these things which so often have a root in the possessive instinct. It would be a sort of contemplation; which shows the incipient artist.[137]

A sort of contemplation! Yes, and how unmistakably does Lawrence indicate the connection between Religion and Art, between the aesthetic and the ethical expressions of spirituality, when he makes this disinterested contemplation of a flower's beauty the sign of dawning artistic sensibility! Paradoxically, the value of natural beauty to the devotee of the Religion of Art is in inverse ratio to his merely egoistic consciousness that it has any value for him at all. The value of an inaccessible mountain peak, or of a serenely floating cloud, consists in its very valuelessness. It has no relevance to our material needs. We cannot turn the snow-clad peak into a human habitation; neither can we harness the white cloud to any earthly chariot. Nature is most beautiful when most aloof. Perhaps it is because of their sheer irrelevance to the needs of man, their utter indifference to his petty hopes and fears, that upon the face of gigantic mountain ranges, with their dreadful sunlit peaks and terrifyingly precipitous plunges into gloomy gorges, plays the intense and terrible light of a beauty never seen in fields or orchards, or in any other aspects of nature which have been brought in relation with the necessities of human life. Not that fields and orchards are unbeautiful. Formally speaking, they may be no less significant aesthetically than wilder and sterner scenes; but what the tabloid newspapers call 'human interest' generally obtrudes itself, like the moon between the earth and the sun in a solar eclipse, so that we see not the brightness of their beauty but only the dark shadow of their utility. For the same reason that he eschews bad art the art-lover would therefore be well advised, at least during the early years of his apprenticeship, to avoid the more domestic kind of natural beauty and to cultivate, instead, appreciation for those aspects of nature which, since they have no connection with ordinary human interests, are most capable of liberating him from the bondage of selfish desires. Egoism is natural to man, and to be overcome only with the utmost difficulty. Only too readily do we stop to pluck the flowers of the world's beauty, instead of wondering and passing on. A mountain, or a starry sky, offers no foothold to our desires. We are left as it were naked in the midst of a great empty space full of sweeping winds. Consequently, our enjoyment of their beauty is of the truly aesthetic order, and a faint anticipation of that intenser enjoyment to be offered us by the still brighter beauty of works of true art.

As we have already said, the artist's enjoyment of Beauty is more intense and active, while that of the *rasika* is less intense and comparatively passive. The artist is masculine, and plays the lover's role; the *rasika* is feminine, and assumes the part of the beloved. These differences will have to be borne in mind when assessing the value of the Religion of Art for the ordinary person, though, as we shall presently see in greater detail, they indicate not so much the presence of contradictory qualities as the predominance of one quality over another in a single individuality. Such differences apart, however, the value of the Religion of Art, for those who wait in its outer courts no less than for those who stand in the inner sanctuary, more than anything else consists in the broadening of their sympathies, in the enrichment and refinement of their experience, and in the uplifting of their transformed personality to new heights of being. Says Herbert Read:

> It has always been the function of art to stretch the mind some distance beyond the limits of the understanding. That 'distance beyond' may be spiritual or transcendental, or, perhaps, merely fantastical; somewhere it will overstep the limits of the rational.[138]

The distinction here made (rather diffidently, it seems) between the spiritual or transcendental, and the merely fantastical, aspects of the 'distance beyond' is, from the special viewpoint of the Religion of Art, without significance. If the fantastical does succeed in stretching the mind 'some distance beyond the limits of understanding', then the fantastical also is truly spiritual. For the presence of spirituality is revealed not by any outward sign but simply by that readiness to accept new experiences, that willingness to modify the pattern of one's existence, which is implied whenever we speak of transcending the limits of the understanding. To us the most interesting and significant part of the passage quoted is the concrete and expressive term used to describe the relation of art to the mind. Art *stretches* the mind.... How difficult it would be to find a more appropriate verb! It connotes a continuity, and, at the same time, a progressive development, of experience through higher and higher levels of subtilization not suggested by cruder and more abstract terms such as 'transcend', or even by concrete ones like 'overstep' and 'pass beyond', all of which imply that the mind is somehow lifted up bodily over the 'limits of the rational', like a small boy over a fence, and dumped down safely on the other side. The rational is not external to the mind, but is the mind itself at one stage of its development, and to transcend the rational does not mean to transfer the mind unchanged from the rational to the super-rational plane (such transferrals are possible only for physical bodies), but to continue changing it until a complete transformation takes place and it enters the super-rational stage of its development by becoming itself super-rational.

Time and again the literalness and abstractness of philosophic and religious terminology introduce confusions which vitiate the spiritual strivings of humanity. Most of these confusions, like that from which Herbert Read saves himself by speaking of stretching the mind, arise from the misconception that the mind, or soul, or whatever else it may be called, is not a flux, a process – a *santāna*, as the expressive Pāli word has it – in a state of continuous change and development, but an inert, unchanging *thing* subject only to external changes of time and place, and therefore differing from a stone in no observable particular. From this fatal misconception, which is in fact the rationalization of ordinary human egoism, the Religion of Art, no less than other forms of spiritual culture, promises to deliver us. If within the sphere of art itself the delusion that the mind is an immutable non-material 'substance' arises, the possibility of transforming the mind through art is precluded, and works of art are regarded not as engines of delight but solely as instruments of selfish pleasure, with the consequence that the pseudo-aesthetic life depicted by Tennyson in 'The Palace of Art', together with the ruin which inevitably overtakes such a life, of necessity ensues in place of the train of lofty consequences set in motion by the Religion of Art.

We should do well, therefore, to think of the function of art as being quite literally to stretch the mind (the implied comparison with a piece of elastic is far less objectionable than a covert comparison with a stone) further than the limits of its own rationality into the 'distance beyond' of Beauty, as this will enable us to see more clearly in what consists the value of the Religion of Art to its average devotee. Works of art are valuable to him because they stretch his mind. Usually, his mind is stiff and unyieldingly rigid; changes take place in it, but there is no development. The egoistic pattern of his life remains the same, though the elements composing it may vary from time to time. To a 'tough' mind like this, conventional religion nowadays often appeals in vain. Tug and pull as she may, it stubbornly refuses to be stretched or, even if she does succeed in stretching it for just a fraction of an inch, the minute her grip is relaxed it flies back to its former position more obstinately than ever. Then along comes the artist. Gently, very gently, he takes hold of the reluctant mind; slowly, oh so slowly, he starts drawing it out of itself, caressing and coaxing it all the time. Then, little by little, with infinite patience and inexorable firmness, he stretches and stretches it until it passes, no longer coarse and thick but delicate as the thread of a spider's web, over the limits of selfhood into that realm of selflessness which is the homeland of true art no less than of true religion.

At first the mind shrinks from the artist's touch; but it soon discovers that to be stretched is, after all, not such an unpleasant experience as it had supposed. Eventually, the experience becomes a positive delight, dearer, perhaps, and more rewarding, than any hitherto known. The spiritual life claims another devotee. So irresistible are the charms of Art. As Irwin Edman has written, 'Values translated into immediately loved images have a powerful suasion on the imagination.'[139] A single smile of Beauty can bring about greater transformations of character than all the frowns of Righteousness. Shelley gives fuller expression to the same idea when, in a famous passage of 'A Defence of Poetry', he declares:

> The great secret of morals is love; or a going out of our own nature, and an identification of ourselves with the beautiful which exists in thought, action, or person, not our own. A man, to be greatly good, must imagine intensely and comprehensively; he must put himself in the place of another and of many others; the pains and pleasures of his species must become his own. The great instrument of moral good is the imagination; and poetry administers to the effect by acting upon the cause. Poetry enlarges the circumference of the imagination by replenishing it with thoughts of ever new delight, which have the power of attracting and assimilating to their own nature all other thoughts, and which form new intervals and interstices whose void for ever craves fresh food. Poetry strengthens the faculty which is the organ of the moral nature of man, in the same manner as exercise strengthens a limb.[140]

What Shelley describes as a 'strengthening' of the mind corresponds to what Herbert Read speaks of as its 'stretching'. Despite dissimilarities – for illustrations do not agree in all particulars with their object, much less still with each other – both figures bring out an important fact. Just as a limb is strengthened, not merely during the period of exercise, but for the time when the exercise is no longer being performed, so the mind, even after being stretched by art beyond the limits of the rational, does not relapse into quite the same degree of rigidity as it was habituated to formerly. In plain language, the impression produced by looking at a painting, listening to a symphony, or reading a poem, does not disappear when we cease to look at the picture, or when the symphony ends, or when we put the poem by, or even when the memory of the delight they gave us has vanished, but remains a permanent part of our character modifying, in however slight a degree, the whole course of our life and conduct.

Since the experience of Art, like the experience of Religion, is essentially an experience of egolessness, the impression produced on the soul by the enjoyment of works of art will be of the same nature. The man who bears on his soul, as it were, the stamp of egolessness, whether derived from Religion through the will, or from Art by means of the imagination, will tend to act egolessly in all the relations of life. Such a one will be a good man in the noblest sense of the term, sensitive to the sufferings of others, sharing their sorrows and their joys, ready to help in time of need, not moved by 'greed or hate or fear', and ever seeking to share with his fellow men the joy of the Beauty which he has known. In this way, as Irwin Edman says,

> Aesthetic enjoyment and artistic creation are anticipations of what the Good Life would really be. Such happiness as is present among our contemporaries is the happiness of those who are doing work that is itself delightful to them and enjoying things that are themselves a delight.[141]

The value to the ordinary man of participation in the Religion of Art through the enjoyment of beautiful things can be questioned only when the value of goodness, and the value of happiness, are questioned too.

The second way in which the average man participates in the Religion of Art is through his own creative activities. Here the difference between the saint and the devotee of Beauty is a simple difference of degree. All men have emotions; in fact, of such importance is the affective side of human life that it might be more truthfully said that men are what their emotions are. Since emotion has a natural tendency towards self-expression – towards the creation, on the physical, aesthetic, or spiritual level, of an object either in its own likeness, or in the likeness of the thing, person, or event by which it was aroused – all men have a natural tendency towards the expression of emotion through creative activity. This expression may take two forms, one being achieved vicariously – for 'we are all poets when we read a poem well'[142] – through the contemplation, the other personally through the actual creation, of works of art. Herbert Read clearly indicates the cathartic function of art when he writes:

> The work of art is in some sense a liberation of the personality; normally our feelings are inhibited and repressed. We contemplate a work of art, and immediately there is a release; and not only a release – sympathy is a release of feelings – but also a heightening, a tautening, a sublimation.[143]

While not denying that this vertical release of feeling (as distinct from the horizontal release of mere sentimentality) can be effected by aesthetic contemplation as well as by aesthetic creation, we believe that the release effected through personal creative activity is generally more satisfactory and complete than any other. Probably most artists, poets, and musicians would agree with us. The average man, with whose needs we are now concerned, often discovers that his own artistic achievements, however clumsy and inept they may be, give him a strange feeling of satisfaction, a peculiar thrill of delight, such as he was never able to derive from the greatest works of art. Even a mud-pie, if he has made it with his own hands, may give a child more genuine pleasure than a costly painted toy. We therefore believe that, in much the same way as, for the religious devotee, vicarious attainment of sainthood by reading the lives of saints cannot make up for his own actual shortcomings, so even the widest and richest enjoyment of works of art will not be able to compensate the art-lover for the poverty of his own creative life.

Not that it is possible for any man to be absolutely uncreative, for then he would be totally lacking in emotive energy, and such a being would be an even greater freak than a man without a head. Our creative instinct is in fact generally more alive than we realize, and every day manifests itself in a hundred different ways. Dressing and adorning the body; furnishing a room; arranging books symmetrically on a shelf, or flowers in a bowl; planning a garden; laying the table for a meal; writing a letter; sewing a dress; embroidering a cushion; knitting a pullover; painting the woodwork of the house; making a kennel for the dog; icing a cake – all these activities, and countless others, provide us with outlets for our creative energies. The more consciously and deliberately we make use of them, the greater will be the satisfaction they give us. Nevertheless they have their limitations. An ardent lover of Beauty will not be content with touching the fringe of her robe, but will want to lift up his eyes and behold her face. Such a person will feel surging within him energies too impetuous and vast to be confined within the narrow channels of the domestic creativity just described. He will long for a more quiveringly intense experience, a more purely ardent enjoyment; for that 'quintessential, keen, ethereal bliss'[144] which, within the limits of the Religion of Art, only the actual creation of a work of art can give him. At first, his heightened creative activity may take the form, not only of combating ugliness in his surroundings – a subject which has been dealt with as preliminary to the enjoyment of works of art – but of trying to render them positively more beautiful. Sooner or later, however, he will feel compelled to start writing stories or poems, or to learn how to play a musical instrument, or how to paint or carve. Once he has reached this point, and begins creating works of art (however inferior or valueless they may seem in comparison with the productions of artistic genius) as well as enjoying them, he becomes a fully-fledged devotee of the Religion of Art, and worthy to stand, not merely in the outer courts of the temple of Beauty, but within the inner precincts and the secret shrine.

With the various kinds of creative activity, from poetry to pottery, or with the means whereby the skills necessary to the production of a work of art may be acquired, we shall make no attempt to deal. Information on these subjects is within the reach of those who really want it. Having briefly indicated the value of the Religion of Art to the average man, and having suggested ways in which he can deepen his participation in it through the enjoyment and creation of works of art, all that now remains to be done is to round off our remarks on the value of creative activities with two observations more, and then to conclude our inquiry into the Religion of Art with a few general reflections.

Enjoyment of an object is often enhanced by a sense of obstacles surmounted and difficulties overcome. In art, the difficulties and obstacles by which the artist is confronted are generally technical; they arise out of the intractability of his material, whether it be words, sounds, or pigments, out of the resistance it offers to the fiat of his creative will. The artist has to wrestle with his medium as Jacob with the Angel; but in the end it blesses him. One who knows naught of the struggle will not savour to the full the unction of that final benediction. This is the position of the man-in-the-Art-Gallery, or in-the-library, or any other repository of finished works of art. He enjoys them mildly, like a cow in a field munching a daisy, for he knows nothing of the sweat which dropped from the giant thews of genius producing them; he knows nothing of the anguish of struggling with that which, while it is the greatest obstacle to the artist's achievement, is also the indispensable condition of his success; he knows nothing of the triumph of technique. The man-in-the-studio, on the other hand, the man who has at least tried to paint a picture or write a poem, knows from experience how difficult the task is, knows from his own bitter pains the problems of composition, the inexorable requirements of metre and rhyme. When he looks at a picture, or reads a poem, he will not only thrill with delight at beauties achieved, but rejoice at difficulties overcome. His enjoyment will be heightened and intensified to a degree that one ignorant of artistic technique will hardly be able to imagine. The actual creation of works of art is therefore of value to the average man, not only as an outlet for his emotional energies, but because it enhances his delight in the works of art produced by men whose genius is immeasurably superior to his own.

Inasmuch as men live not in solitude but as members of society, their activities and interests affect not merely themselves but others too. The value of the enjoyment and creation of works of art as outlets of emotional energies is not restricted to the individual artist or art-lover, but on the contrary possesses a significance which extends to the whole community. Emotion has a natural tendency to express itself. If it can find no outlet on the cultural level it will sink to the level of the physical and force an outlet there. Should opportunities for constructive expression be denied, then it will seize the first chance of expressing itself destructively. A child who is not encouraged to create will naturally learn to destroy. But destruction does not bring the same kind of joy as creation. After a few minutes of savage delight comes a reaction, a feeling of frustration sets in, and eventually the culprit feels even more miserable than he did before indulging in his bout of destructiveness. Many causes of juvenile delinquency and adolescent gangsterism are directly traceable to the fact that neither at home nor in school are sufficient outlets for the emotional energies of youth provided. For nearly all adults, the most frequently used outlet is the lowest and grossest, that of sexual intercourse. Such an outlet the conventions of society quite rightly close to the young. But society errs in providing for its younger members insufficient cultural and constructive means of releasing their emotional energies. Education generally places a stronger emphasis on the gaining of knowledge, or the acquisition of technical skills, than on the cultivation of the emotions. Art is certainly the Cinderella of education. Without going so far as to say that the intellectual and practical aspects of education are its Ugly Sisters, we do certainly wish to emphasize that if Cinderella is not allowed to go to the ball she will not stay quietly at home washing the dishes; probably she will set the house on fire instead.

Though the problem of untrained emotion is acutest for adolescents, it is by no means absent from the life of adults (whose predominantly sexual solution is almost as big a confession of failure as the antisocial solution of wayward youth), and in fact is found in one form or another in practically every department of modern life. As Erich Heller's striking image reminds us, 'The workshops in which our truths are manufactured are surrounded by swarms of unemployed affections' and, as he goes on to warn us, 'Unemployment leads to riots.'[145] Not the smallest part of the value of the Religion of Art is that it restores our individual and social life to order by giving work to our unemployed affections, transforming them from not only lazy and yawning, but positively dangerous, drones into 'singing masons building roofs of gold'[146] – the million-tiled golden roofs of the Temple of Beauty.

In these days when, all over the world, conventional religion so often fails to move the hearts of men, the Religion of Art may enable some people at least to experience, through the instrumentality of Beauty, those supreme values of life which in former centuries were generally mediated by Religion. That in its present nascent condition the Religion of Art can mediate those values as fully and as effectively as the great historic faiths are even now able to do, we would not be justified in claiming. Whether in future it will ever be sufficiently developed so to mediate them, we hesitate to assert. But we believe that our inquiries have revealed no *a priori* reason why the Religion of Art should not be able, when consciously developed and utilized as a means of leading the spiritual life, the life of egolessness, to take for many people the place of religion; not, indeed, by becoming a Huxleian substitute, but through its mediation of those values which constitute the very lifeblood of religion truly understood. Indeed, were the claims of the Religion of Art to be too invidiously weighed against those of conventional religion, in at least one respect the pan of the former would be found preponderating: the Religion of Art has never preached a holy war, or burned a heretic at the stake, whereas all religions except Buddhism have at one time or another been guilty of some form of persecution. History contains ample justification of Swift's celebrated aphorism that we have just enough religion to make us hate, but not enough to make us love, one another.[147] May it never be said that the Religion of Art has ever tried to stifle the impulse of any noble soul!

Conventional religions may be organizationally strong, whereas the Religion of Art is organizationally weak; but their strength is their greatest weakness, while in its very weakness lies its greatest strength. The Religion of Art has no temple and no church; wherever men feel the touch of Beauty, there is holy ground. It possesses no scriptures; the whole of nature is its sacred book. It has no priests, for those who enjoy and those who create works of art behold Beauty face to face and have no need of any mediator or intercessor. It has no membership, for the brotherhood of Beauty recognize one another at a glance; no fees, for her devotees are prepared to offer the sacrifice of their lives. By its very deficiencies, no less than because of its actual endowments, does the Religion of Art recommend itself to the hearts and minds of modern men and women. On account of its absolute freedom from institutional and credal bonds, as much as by reason of its irresistible appeal to all that is best and brightest in humanity, is it not only of supreme value to the constantly growing number of the creedless and unchurched, but also a useful supplement to the spiritual life of those who can still find in one established religion or another the main sources of their inspiration.

Deeply and firmly do we believe that, despite its present undeveloped condition, the Religion of Art is peculiarly fitted to produce in these troublous days a kind of character, a type of spiritual personality, which will be the living embodiment of the fact that Religion and Art are in essence one, and that Beauty is not merely Truth, but Goodness as well.

PARADOX AND POETRY IN *THE VOICE OF THE SILENCE*

Buddhist canonical literature, which subsists not merely in volumes but in libraries, falls quite naturally into two main groups, each possessing certain distinctive features. The *sūtras*, as the works comprising the first and more important group are designated, purport to be discourses delivered by the Lord Buddha himself or, in a few cases, those given by *arhant* and bodhisattva disciples speaking either with his approval or under his inspiration. The *śāstras*, the works comprising the second group, are treatises composed by the great *ācāryas*, founders and exponents of the various Buddhist schools, in order to elucidate and systematize the teachings of a particular *sūtra* or group of *sūtras*. The distinctive features of these two groups of works, which we have differentiated at length elsewhere,[148] will for our present purpose be sufficiently indicated by saying that whereas the method of the *sūtras* is direct and intuitional, aiming at spiritual awakening rather than intellectual conviction, that of the *śāstras* is definitely more discursive and logical.

The Voice of the Silence,[149] though it does not claim to be the utterance of a Buddha, is nevertheless akin to the *sūtra* rather than to the *śāstra* group of texts. Like the longer and more celebrated discourses, it seeks more to inspire than to instruct, appeals to the heart rather than to the head. To make use of De Quincey's classification, it belongs not to the literature of information, the purpose of which is to augment knowledge, but to the literature of power, the aim of which is to move.[150] So important is a clear understanding of the difference not merely between the kinds of effect they are calculated to produce but the organs upon which they are intended to act that, according to *The Voice of the Silence* itself, the disciple at the very outset of his quest is admonished:

> Learn above all to separate Head-learning from Soul-wisdom, the 'Eye' from the 'Heart' doctrine.[151]

By Head-learning is meant, of course, a merely intellectual understanding of spiritual truths. Not that such an understanding is deprecated, much less still condemned: the Master simply insists on the necessity of recognizing its limitations, a task which most people – even religious people – seem to find extremely hard. Soul-wisdom on the other hand signifies what the Prajñāpāramitā corpus of *sūtras* calls simply *prajñā*, wisdom, and the *Laṅkāvatāra Sūtra āryajñāna*, noble knowledge, a purely transcendental faculty for the apprehension of spiritual truths which, when fully developed, is identical with the *bodhi* or Enlightenment of a Buddha. Just as it is the function of the 'Eye' doctrine of the *śāstras* to impart Head-learning, so it is the function of the 'Heart' doctrine of the *sūtras* to stimulate the development of Soul-wisdom. We are not to suppose, however, that there are two doctrines, in the sense of two different bodies of teachings: it is a question of a difference of attitude, of approach. Inasmuch as it conforms to the *sūtra* rather than to the *śāstra* type of literature, *The Voice of the Silence* seeks to awaken Wisdom by appealing to the heart – not a physical organ but a transcendental faculty – and by encouraging the disciple to adopt an attitude in which the intellectual will be subordinated to the spiritual.

How does it do this? Buddhism, it is well known, upholds the equal validity of reason (*anumāna*) and experience (*pratyakṣa*). The latter is twofold, consisting on the one hand of the contact of the five sense-organs and the mind (regarded as merely a sixth sense) with their respective objects, and on the other of the various levels of *dhyāna* or *samādhi* wherein, though consciousness is intensified, the senses and the mind no longer function. This second type of experience is itself subject to further subdivision. If the object of the *dhyāna* or *samādhi* is, though good (*kuśala*), still mundane (*laukika*), the experience itself, despite the fact that it transcends the physical and mental levels, is necessarily mundane too, and as such incapable of directly conducing to liberation (*mokṣa*). If the object of the *dhyāna* or *samādhi* is transcendental (*lokuttara*) the *dhyāna* or *samādhi* is also transcendental and its development therefore equivalent to the attainment of a stage of the transcendental path leading directly to Nirvāṇa.

This distinction between the two types of meditational experience, one mundane, the other transcendental, is of the utmost importance, and had it been more widely known and uncompromisingly insisted upon, the world would have been less at the mercy of teachings which, though claiming to issue from the Absolute, in fact proceeded only from the upper reaches of the phenomenal. Whether transcendental or mundane, however, *samādhi* in the full sense involves not only a holding of the senses in abeyance but also a complete suspension of mental activity, and it is perhaps this very fact which, by acting as an occasion for a misapplication of the principle of the identity of indiscernibles, has been chiefly responsible for the confusion of these two radically different modes of experience.

Since in *samādhi* the mind is transcended, it follows that the various functions of the mind, such as perception, memory, and ratiocination, are transcended too. Consequently, the possibility of giving an account of *samādhi*, in terms of the concepts which the mind has either generalized from sense-impressions or evolved spider-like from its own entrails, is by the very nature of the meditational experience precluded. The superconscious, as the mystics of all religions have insisted, is beyond reason. This does not mean that it contradicts reason. For it could contradict reason only if they occupied a common level; if it diverged from reason as it were on the horizontal plane, instead of being separated from it, as with the mundane *samādhi*, vertically, or as with the transcendental *samādhi*, by the abrupt disappearance of the latter into a 'fourth' dimension which, since it is transcendental, hence absolute, stands in no relation to reason at all. Only reason can contradict reason. In fact, as Nāgārjuna and his followers maintained, reason is inherently self-contradictory.[152] We should therefore be on our guard against the very common error of assuming that by the mystical is meant anything irrational and illogical. As T. S. Eliot sardonically remarks, before one can go beyond the intellect one must have an intellect.[153]

But meanwhile the problem of communication remains. How is it possible to convey the nature of *samādhi* to one who has no personal experience of it when language, the main vehicle of communication, is derived from those very levels of experience which *samādhi* transcends? Certain Zen masters, of course, solve the problem in their own way by endeavouring to dispense with language altogether. The traditional Buddhist solution of the problem is much less drastic. One group of *sūtras*, of which those constituting the Prajñāpāramitā corpus are the most prominent, places its reliance mainly on the method of systematic paradox. Another group, which includes the *Saddharma Puṇḍarīka* and the *Larger* and *Smaller Sukhāvatī-vyūha Sūtras*, has recourse to poetry, especially in the highly developed form of cosmic myth. *The Voice of the Silence* is probably unique in making use of a combination of both methods, a procedure which no doubt has much to do with the extraordinary effectiveness of this little treatise in awakening the dormant Soul-wisdom of the qualified disciple. Before proceeding to illustrate this thesis with examples from the text itself it will be necessary for us to try to gain a clearer understanding of the nature of both paradox and poetry.

A paradox has been facetiously defined as a truth standing on its head to attract attention. As far as it goes the definition is not a bad one, for in its own way it does attempt to bring out two highly relevant points: firstly, that a paradox involves a contradiction and, secondly, that it contains an element of truth. In the case of a paradox in the merely rhetorical sense of the term the contradiction is only apparent, and the truth it is intended to emphasize quite capable of being stated logically: the paradoxical form is no more than a literary trick to excite attention. The paradoxes of the Buddhist scriptures, however, are what may be termed paradoxes per se; the contradictions they involve are real contradictions, and the truths that, through those contradictions, they try to convey, or better to indicate, are truths not susceptible to logical analysis. Buddhist paradox, in other words, is an attempt to express in terms of logical contradiction that which transcends logic. Exactly how this is done cannot be understood without at least passing reference to the so-called laws of thought.[154]

According to the first of these, the law of identity, A is A, which means that it cannot be not-A, or that a thing is identical with itself. The second law, the law of non-contradiction, states that A is not not-A. The third, the law of excluded middle, states that A either is or is not B; meaning that between two contradictory statements there is no middle ground, so that if one is denied the other must be affirmed.

These laws or principles of thought constitute, at least in theory, the ultimate foundation not only of all philosophy but of every field of human achievement in the development of which reason has played a part, and to deny them at that level would produce on civilization and culture an effect comparable to that of a violent earthquake upon a town. So disastrous a denial as this is never contemplated, of course, by the genuine mystics (who usually display sterling common sense in their attitude to the affairs of everyday life) for, as the Mahāyāna so emphatically maintains, the absolute truth is not to be realized except in dependence on the relative truth.[155] But whatever their other differences may be, probably all mystics without exception refuse to commit what would be for them the elementary mistake of trying to abide by the Laws of Thought when speaking of those things which transcend logic because they transcend the rational mind. Spiritual experience, they unanimously insist, is as it were three-dimensional, the intellect two-dimensional. Even as a number of 'contradictory' projections of a portion of the globe can give us, when compared, a more adequate idea of its true size, shape, and contours than only one, so a statement which involves a logical contradiction stands a better chance of being able to describe the content of the *dhyāna-samādhi* experience than one which is logically self-consistent.

For this reason do the religious geniuses of all times and ages, attempting to describe the indescribable, speak of the dark light, the dazzling darkness, the nothing which is everything, the voidness which is full. Hence, admonishing the spiritual aspirant, do they urge him to lose his life in order to find it. In all these paradoxes, though, expressive and effective as they are, lurks still some residue of the merely literary and rhetorical. Only in the Buddhist *sūtras*, perhaps, especially in those of the Prajñāpāramitā corpus, can we find the paradox of unmitigated logical contradiction in all its glory employed on a grand scale to express the experiences not merely of mundane *samādhi*, but of the Transcendental.

Says the *Vajracchedikā Sūtra*, describing the attitude to be developed by the bodhisattva:

> One who has set out on the career of a Bodhisattva should reflect in such a wise: As many beings as there are in the universe of beings, comprehended under the term 'beings' – egg-born, or born from a womb, or moisture born, or miraculously born,

> with or without form, with perception, without perception, with neither perception nor non-perception, – as far as any conceivable universe of beings is conceived; all these I should lead to Nirvāṇa, into the realm of Nirvāṇa which leaves nothing behind. But, although innumerable beings have thus been led to Nirvāṇa, no being at all has been led to Nirvāṇa. And why? If in a Bodhisattva the perception of a 'being' should take place he would not be called a 'Bodhi-being'. He is not to be called a 'Bodhi-being', in whom the perception of a self should take place, or the perception of a being, or the perception of a living soul, or the perception of a person.[156]

This boldly paradoxical passage makes it clear that since he has his being in a sphere describable only in terms of logical contradiction, the bodhisattva, as he manifests in the world of the senses and the mind, is himself a contradiction, a living paradox.

Even more tersely explicative of the Prajñāpāramitā's 'logic of contradiction' is a text from the *Saptaśatikā* in which the Buddha says:

> 'Beings, beings', O Subhūti, as non-beings have they been taught by the Tathāgata. Therefore are they called 'beings'.[157]

Greater havoc could hardly be played with the Laws of Thought than this!

The Voice of the Silence uses paradox as a method of awakening Soul-wisdom in much the same way as the Prajñāpāramitā, though of course it does not use it on nearly so grand a scale. Even the title of these chosen fragments from 'The Book of the Golden Precepts' is, as a moment's reflection will show, profoundly paradoxical. It is as though the hand which transcribed them for the good of humanity, and dedicated them 'To the Few', had written in letters of fire above the sanctuary portal an awful warning that here was ground upon which the intellect could not tread, where only a chastened and sublimated spiritual intuition that worked not within the narrow bounds of formal logic could possibly hope to gain admittance. May that warning not go unheeded as we attempt to bring to the surface a few of the pearls of meaning which lie hidden in the abyss of this paradoxical juxtaposition of the contradictory terms 'Voice' and 'Silence'.

Madame Guyon, the great seventeenth-century French mystic who was the friend and spiritual adviser of Fénelon, makes a distinction which will be of use to us in approaching our subject. There are, she says, four kinds of silence: the silence of sound, the silence of desires, the silence of thoughts, and the silence of the will.[158] These are of course not unknown to Buddhist tradition. In the *Saṃyutta Nikāya* of the Pāli Sutta Piṭaka, for example, occurs a passage which makes it perfectly clear that the *ariya-mona* or 'noble silence' of the Buddhist texts corresponds to the third of Madame Guyon's four silences (not to the first, the silence of sound, as generally imagined). After relating to the brethren how, when he was secluded and living all alone, there had occurred to him the discursive thought, 'The Ariyan silence! they say. Now what means this Ariyan silence?' Moggallāna the Great, one of the two chief disciples of the Buddha, proceeds:

> Then, friends, I thus thought: 'Herein a brother, by the suppression of discursive thought and investigation, enters on and abides in the Second Trance ... a state of internal calm of heart, concentrated on its object, free from discursive thought and investigation, born of mental balance, a state of zest and ease. This is called *the Ariyan silence*.'[159]

Here *ariya-mona* is plainly equated with the second *jhāna* (Sanskrit *dhyāna*), wherein, in contradistinction to the first *jhāna*, there is no discursive thought and investigation (*vitakka-vicāra*) but only concentration (*samādhi*), zest or joy (*pīti*), and happiness or ease (*sukha*).

More germane to our present inquiry, however, is the fourth kind of silence, the silence of the will. By will Madame Guyon presumably understood self-will, that is to say, any movement of the soul that was not in accordance with the will of God. So much must the will of the creature be one with that of the Creator that, according to her doctrine of disinterested love, the soul must love God even though he decrees its damnation. Obviously the conception of will is closely linked with that of self. In a sense they are correlative. If the one is grossly conceived, the other will be grossly conceived too; if subtly, with corresponding subtlety. Immured as she was within the Christian tradition, Madame Guyon, for all her acuteness, could hardly be expected to perceive the finer shades of selfhood so palpable to Buddhist eyes, long accustomed to the minutest psycho-spiritual analysis. Consequently her conception of self-will is in comparison gross (fine as it may be in its immediate Christian context), and her silence of the will not the ultimate silence of the will. If *śūnyatā* is described as the absolute cessation of even the faintest vestige of self-consciousness or ego-sense, however, and if from the cessation of self-consciousness the cessation of self-will necessarily follows, then obviously it should be possible to regard the complete cessation of self-will as equivalent to the realization of *śūnyatā*. Silence in its profoundest sense is thus *śūnyatā*, and *śūnyatā* is the Absolute Silence.

No less deep is the ultimate meaning of 'Voice'. In almost all religions and cultures the voice, speech, or utterance of man, as he expresses his thought in words, has been regarded as symbolizing the creation of the world by God, the involution of the spiritual into the material, the manifestation of the Absolute as the relative. *Śūnyatā*, the ultimate principle according to Buddhism, is not regarded as exercising creative functions: it is neither the First Cause nor the existential ground of things. But it would be a grave mistake to assume that it is therefore devoid of a dynamic aspect. This dynamic aspect is *karuṇā*, compassion. According to the Mahāyāna school, compassion is much more than an emotion. Three kinds of *karuṇā* are distinguished. In the words of Henri de Lubac, who prefers to render *karuṇā* by 'pity':

> The first sort of pity has as its object the beings who suffer; it is *sattvālambana karuṇā* – the ordinary, inferior kind of pity, tainted by the vulgar error of believing in the reality of living beings. The second sort, which is higher, has as its object painful sensations in themselves; this is *dharmālambana karuṇā* [phenomena, including sensations, are technically known as Dharma in Buddhist philosophy] and the person who experiences it knows that beings do not exist, but only their *dharma* [or constituent psycho-physical phenomena]. But this is still only an approximation to true knowledge, for the painful sensations do not exist in or by themselves; and so this second sort of pity still involves *avidyā* (nescience). There must therefore be a third kind of pity – pure pity, the pity which has no object; *anālambana karuṇā*. A virtue is all the higher, the more it is in this sense pure. Perfect pity, ideal pity – 'the great pity' – will therefore arise, not from the love of

creatures nor to put an end to suffering, but quite gratuitously, from the love of pity itself. And, at this highest level, just as it is no longer directed towards any living being or any reality, so it is not the possession of any particular person.[160]

It is of this third kind of *karuṇā* that *The Voice of the Silence* itself speaks in the well-known passage: 'Compassion is no attribute. It is the Law of LAWS – eternal Harmony....'[161] Strictly speaking, compassion, in this sense, is no more an aspect of *śūnyatā* than it is an attribute of the thinking, feeling self. To describe it as an aspect of *śūnyatā* means in effect to assert that, unlike *śūnyatā*, which possesses independent reality, compassion possesses merely dependent or derivative reality, which in turn implies the assertion that it is not fully real. A number of Mahāyāna texts make it clear that *śūnyatā* is as much an aspect of *karuṇā* as *karuṇā* is of *śūnyatā*. In fact in the *dharmakāya*, or whole 'body of reality' in the ultimate sense, *śūnyatā* and *karuṇā*, the conditioned and the Unconditioned, *saṃsāra* and Nirvāṇa – in fact all possible pairs of logically contradictory terms – are related in a manner inconceivable to the intellect, so that the relation cannot be described in terms of unity or of difference, nor yet in terms of neither unity nor difference. Only from the purely relative standpoint is it permissible to speak of *śūnyatā* manifesting as *karuṇā*, or of one being static, the other dynamic, as though they were two distinct or even distinguishable entities. Both transcend the reach of logic. The only way in which their relationship can be described is by some such paradoxical, that is to say logically contradictory, expression as 'the Voice of the Silence'. Speaking again from the relative standpoint, it may be said that the fact that these precious fragments from 'The Book of the Golden Precepts' bear such a profoundly paradoxical title may be taken as an indication that they emanate from, and are intended to help the disciple attain to, a state beyond the power of reason to describe.

The contents of *The Voice of the Silence* are, in parts, no less paradoxical than is its title. Only two examples will be given here, the reader, we believe, preferring to enjoy the excitement of discovering and studying others for himself.

In Fragment I the neophyte is warned, 'Thou canst not travel on the Path until thou hast become that Path itself.'[162] The path referred to is, of course, the spiritual path. In all religions, but perhaps most of all in

Buddhism, where the figure of the Way reigns supreme, is the spiritual life depicted as a progression through a series of stages – the first lying beneath one's feet, the last glimmering hardly discernible through the mists of the far distance – and the spiritual aspirant as a pilgrim or traveller. While the analogy has many advantages, as its worldwide popularity attests, it is by no means exempt from the danger that dogs every metaphor employed to elucidate religious or philosophical themes – the danger of being understood too literally and too logically, so that it becomes not the stimulus of a spiritual response but merely the starting point of a chain of deductions. In the present case, the danger lies in pushing the metaphor of the path so far as to think that because, in actual fact, the path and the traveller on the path are two different entities the spiritual path and the spiritual aspirant are two different entities too. From this there follows a conclusion diametrically opposed to the fundamental principles of Buddhism – the conclusion that just as the traveller, from the beginning to the end of his journey, remains unchanged in relation to the portions of the road over which he travels, so the self or ego or principle of personal identity persists unchanged as it passes through the succession of spiritual experiences or stages intercalated between the mundane starting point and the transcendental goal. Against this perfectly logical but absolutely wrong deduction the paradoxical statement that, in reality, you cannot travel the Path until you have become that Path itself launches a vigorous protest.

As all schools of Buddhism maintain, the idea of an unchanging soul or self or *ātman* distinct from the various mental processes is a delusion, in fact the greatest of all delusions, so that only from the standpoint of relative or conventional truth is it possible even to speak of the attainment of Nirvāṇa by this or that person. Spiritual progress consists not in the acquisition of spiritual attainments by the ego as though they were a species of personal property, but in the attenuation of the ego, or rather of the false idea of egohood, in such a way that from gross it becomes subtle, from subtle more subtle still, until in the end the aspirant becomes as it were an impersonal stream of spiritual energy which, becoming progressively wider and deeper, eventually discovers that it coincides with the fathomless ocean of Nirvāṇa. By its paradoxical identification of Path and pilgrim *The Voice of the Silence* in effect reminds us that just as the 'individual' or 'person' is merely a name for certain psychosomatic states, so 'Path' is no more than a convenient designation for a succession of thoughts, words, and deeds oriented in the direction of 'Enlightenment'. Whether at a higher or a lower level, there is in reality no question of personal acquisition at all.

This links up with the vitally important teaching, found in Fragment II, concerning 'The Two Paths'. These are the path of the *śrāvaka* and the *pratyekabuddha*, on the one hand, and that of the bodhisattva on the other. In *The Voice of the Silence* the first is called 'The Open Path' and 'The Path of Liberation', the second 'The Secret Path', 'The Path of Renunciation', and 'The Path of Woe'. According to the popular interpretation, the difference between the two paths is that while one aims at individual emancipation, the other aims at universal emancipation. Whereas the *śrāvaka* is content to become an *arhant*, to gain Nirvāṇa for himself alone, the bodhisattva is not satisfied unless he achieves Supreme Buddhahood, for in this case he will be able to lead a multitude of other beings to Nirvāṇa. But as we have already pointed out, Nirvāṇa is not something that can be owned, either individually or collectively. The bodhisattva's renunciation of the Open Path, the path of personal liberation, is therefore not to be construed as meaning that this path represents an actually realizable possibility. What it means is that the bodhisattva resists the temptation of thinking of Nirvāṇa as a personal acquisition. In Prajñāpāramitā language, he realizes that Nirvāṇa is to be attained by means of a non-attainment. With this lapse into paradox we remind ourselves that, after all, of all methods of giving expression to transcendental realities, that of logical contradiction is perhaps the safest and least open to misunderstanding. A metaphor may be taken literally, a paradox never. Without some appreciation of the reason why *The Voice of the Silence* gives so profoundly paradoxical a twist to the time-honoured figure of the Way, we shall be able to understand neither the message of this marvellously meaningful little treatise nor the implications of the bodhisattva ideal.

Our second example of the use of paradox in *The Voice of the Silence* is taken from the end of Fragment III, where the bodhisattva, now on the threshold of Enlightenment, is told:

> If thou would'st be Tathāgata, follow upon thy predecessor's steps, remain unselfish till the endless end.[163]

This is profound doctrine, but we are not now concerned with the passage as a whole but only with the paradoxical phrase with which it concludes. It is no mere coincidence that the expression 'the endless end' should have been used in association with unselfishness of the most exalted kind – the unselfishness of a Tathāgata or Buddha.

Now there are some who understand Nirvāṇa so crudely as to imagine that it does in the gross literal sense stand at the end of the spiritual path, as it were waiting to be reached, or realized, by the aspirant. Besides bringing Nirvāṇa, which is eternal (*dhruva*) in the sense that it transcends time, within the time-series, such literal-mindedness in effect commits the far graver mistake of treating Nirvāṇa as though it could in reality be the object of personal attainment and possession. As we have already shown at sufficient length in the case of the first paradox, that of the Path, the Bodhisattva does not and cannot treat Nirvāṇa as a personal possession, for it is of his very essence to have transcended those false notions of absolute selfhood, of real personal identity, upon which the idea of possession is necessarily grounded. Since he is incapable of thinking of Nirvāṇa as a possession, or as being in the ultimate sense an attainment, the bodhisattva cannot regard it as in reality constituting the end of his career. We do not wish to labour the point, for to those who followed the previous paragraph with attention it will already be sufficiently obvious: *The Voice of the Silence* speaks of 'the endless end' for what is basically the same reason that it speaks of the pilgrim becoming the Path. Adopting a slightly different point of view, however, it may be said by way of supplementary explanation that if, to speak in accordance with the relative truth, the attainment of Wisdom is the 'end' of the bodhisattva's career, that end is 'endless' because Wisdom is ultimately non-different from Compassion which has for object the uninterrupted succession of birth, old age, disease, and death in the *saṃsāra* which, as a process, is without end.

From paradoxes we pass to poetry. The poetry of *The Voice of the Silence* is, in places, as beautiful as its paradoxes are startling. By poetry we do not mean verse, for in their English dress, at least, these inspired utterances fail to observe the rules of classical prosody. But what is poetry? For the purposes of our present discussion – enough ink has already been spilled in attempts to define the indefinable – we shall take it that the essence of poetry is imagery. The poetic image, or more simply the image, is defined as 'anything concrete or abstract introduced figuratively to represent something which it strikingly resembles, as sleep for death.'[164] Imagery, of whatever kind, is thus based on comparison. Not on any kind of comparison, however. An image is made only when the objects compared are of different kinds but possessed of the same attributes. Thus in the case of the metaphor 'golden sunset' we compare a phenomenon of sun and clouds and sky with a metal because, though the objects are of quite different kinds, they share a common quality, in this case, a colour.

Despite the fact that in its decline poetry, or what by courtesy continues to be styled poetry, either uses the old figures of speech mechanically or manufactures new ones artificially, the comparisons between one object and another which constitute as it were the lifeblood of the image are not arbitrary. In the section 'Transition to the Tantra' of *A Survey of Buddhism* we tried to show how the sacramental action of the tantras was based on the *Avataṃsaka Sūtra*'s conception of the universe as a gigantic system of correspondences.[165] The poetic image is similarly based. And just as the efficacy of the sacramental action of the tantras is ultimately due to the essential truth of the *sūtra*'s teaching, so does the power of the image to induce poetic experience ultimately derive from the fact that its comparisons are not merely fanciful but strike a deep root into the very nature of things.

Images are perceptions of real correspondences. These correspondences the true poet – not the mere versifier or wearer of poetic reach-me-downs – perceives intuitively. The intuitive perception of a correspondence through an image constitutes poetic truth. It is because they possess the power of perceiving correspondences, or imagination in the Blakean sense, that the great poets of the world are not merely 'the idle singers of an empty day' but 'the hierophants of an unapprehended mystery'.[166] Not unoften, indeed, are we delighted by the discovery that there is more Soul-wisdom in the pages of the poets than in those of the academic philosophers and the professionally devout. The poet, as the Romantics clearly saw, and as Carlyle so magnificently dinned into the ears of an unbelieving generation, is a prophet and a seer.[167] Hence we need not be surprised to find that the prophets and seers are poets. The Vedic rishis, the authors of the poetical books of the Old Testament, and the Sufis of medieval Iran, were poets as true as any that ever breathed. Mohammed, Christ, and the Buddha – to go higher still in the scale of spiritual attainment – all made extensive use of metaphor and simile in their teachings. That this should be so is undoubtedly due to the fact that images based on a system of correspondence are more easily able to arouse the imagination, to stimulate the intuition, or (to revert to the term beloved of our present text) to awaken Soul-wisdom, than more rational methods.

Hence *The Voice of the Silence* abounds in imagery. One can hardly turn a page without encountering at least one strikingly beautiful figure of speech. What could be more vigorous than the image in which it is said that the Disciple's sins '...will raise their voices, like as the jackal's laugh and sob after the sun goes down....'[168] or more vivid than the picture of the Hosts of Souls hovering bird-like over 'the stormy sea of human life',[169] or more solemnly beautiful than the simile which says of the newly arisen Buddha that he stands

> like a white pillar to the west, upon whose face the rising Sun of thought eternal poureth forth its first most glorious waves.[170]

Examples could be multiplied indefinitely. An assiduous student might well compile for *The Voice of the Silence*, as E. M. Hare has done for the *Sutta-Nipata*,[171] an index of similes.

But imagery, though the essence of poetry, is not the whole of it. Other elements are also needed. For instance, rhythm. Though it is nowadays generally admitted that poetry can dispense with metre and rhyme, it would be difficult to imagine it existing without some kind of rhythm, either regular or irregular. This may well be because rhythm is essentially a periodicity, a reflection of sameness and difference within the order of time, and as such indirectly in correspondence with imagery, their reflection in words. Be that as it may (for it is no more than a speculation), there is no doubt that the poetry of *The Voice of the Silence* is strongly rhythmical and that its marvellous effects are owing, in some cases at least, as much to rhythm as to imagery. Consider, for instance, the following sublime passage, arranged in stanza form so that the reader may be the better able to appreciate how strongly, indeed regularly, rhythmical it is:

> Let thy Soul lend its ear
> To every cry of pain
> Like as the lotus bares its heart
> To drink the morning sun.

Let not the fierce Sun dry
One tear of pain before
Thyself has wiped it
From the sufferer's eye.

But let each burning human tear
Drop on thy heart and there remain,
Nor ever brush it off, until
The pain that caused it is removed.[172]

The prosodist will observe that the stanzas scan perfectly. In the first stanza two iambic trimeters are succeeded by two iambic tetrameters, the second is composed of trimeters and dimeters, while the glorious third stanza consists of four iambic tetrameters.

That merely rhyme should be needed to make this 'poem of pity' acceptable not only as poetry but as perfectly good traditional English verse is no accident. Shelley, in an inspired moment, spoke of 'the incantation of this verse'.[173] All great poetry is incantation. It produces its effect more by sound than by meaning. The classic illustration of this profound truth is the famous first line of Keats' 'Endymion': 'A thing of beauty is a joy forever'. According to a story, probably apocryphal, Keats originally wrote 'A thing of beauty is a constant joy', and showed the line to his friend Leigh Hunt, whom it failed to satisfy. Keats thereupon thought again, and wrote the line previously quoted. The difference in meaning between the two lines is negligible; both are iambic pentameters; but one is poetry, the other prose. Why so tremendous a difference? The answer can lie only in the fact that, whereas the meaning is the same, the associated sounds, including the respective rhymes of the two lines, are different. A poem is a kind of mantra. We might even say that while imagery is the content of poetry, the mantra is its form. Indeed, just as poetry can sometimes substitute a meaning for an image and still remain poetry by retaining its mantraic form, so it can substitute meaning for mantraic quality and remain poetry in that case too. In other words, though poetry in the fullest sense combines image, mantra, and meaning, a combination of image and mantra, or of meaning and mantra, alone, is also poetry. Meaning by itself is prose; the addition of metre merely condemns it to be verse. Such distinctions should not, however, be mistaken for divisions. A poem, as we have insisted in 'Advice to a Young Poet', is a whole, and its 'parts', though distinguishable, are inseparable.[174]

In passages like the one quoted above, which is one of the loftiest peaks of that Himalayan range of spiritual truths that is *The Voice of the Silence*, all the constituents of poetry in the full sense of the term are present. It is as though, whenever it has anything of special importance to impart, the text either explodes in paradox or erupts into the imagery and starts shaking with the mantra-like vibrations of poetry. The fact that *The Voice of the Silence* consists of, or at least contains, what are really mantras in English, incidentally may account for the circumstance that as a whole it does not correspond to any known Tibetan text, though individual verses seem to have been identified. For, as an eminent Tibetologist has suggested to the writer, if the translator of these three fragments from 'The Book of the Golden Precepts' was as much concerned to reproduce the mantraic effect of the original as to translate its literal meaning, she may well have found some sacrifice of the letter to the spirit of the text inevitable.

The Voice of the Silence is not, however, all paradox and poetry – a mercy for which the weakness of human nature is doubtless sufficiently thankful. Little valleys of rationality and prose do intervene, for even the Himalayas are not all peak and precipice. But, as he rests in them between bouts of spiritual mountaineering, even the most casual reader should remember that the message of *The Voice of the Silence* is not to be understood unless we realize that it appeals to the heart, that it strives to develop intuition, to awaken Soul-wisdom, and that in so doing its principal methods are paradox and poetry.

IN THE REALM OF THE LOTUS

A Conversation About Art, Beauty, and the Spiritual Life

Sangharakshita in conversation with J. O. Mallander

FOREWORD

Meetings with a Remarkable Man

The Venerable Sangharakshita has been my friend and mentor for the last twenty years. The first time I met him – in this life at least – was when he visited Finland in 1974. I still have a strong mental image of this oddly familiar yet utterly strange figure. He looked like a beggar monk and a hippy at the same time.

After our meeting, wanting to get more deeply involved in Buddhism, I went to the local FWBO centre and learned to meditate. At that time I was immersed in the arts, writing criticism, running a gallery – trying to change as much as I could in a system I found unbearably conventional, spiritually dull, and full of inauthentic people with cowardly views. The big revelations of my early life came through the arts: pop art, minimal art, experimental poetry, films, books, and music: particularly jazz, which I found had an intense transforming power. John Cage was also a seminal force, as the Eastern world opened up to us in the West.

Over the next few years Sangharakshita came to Finland twice, and our private talks had a profound effect on me. I read whatever of his writings I could lay my hands on. In 1976 I was involved in starting *Aura*, an alternative magazine which published an interview with Sangharakshita as well as his essay on William Blake and his talk 'What Meditation Really Is'. I also reviewed *The Three Jewels* when it appeared in Finnish. But the book that affected me most was *Peace Is a Fire* – a collection of condensed sayings, witty aphorisms, paradoxes, and tantric utterances which were very much on my wavelength.

But the man behind these writings remained a mystery to me. What his marvellous mindstream contained I could only guess; but what he revealed was enough to set me marvelling at his unique insights.

In 1978 I went on a magic journey to Padmaloka, a retreat centre in Norfolk, England. I can still remember the mood of those days: Padmaloka's old-fashioned garden, the serene shrine-room, Sangharakshita's study and books, the strange forest, the river, the pungent smell of the fields. The lotus pond was just being made, and I worked on it between meditation sessions – not very effectively. I could never be sure which roots were essential parts of the complex whole and which were weeds to be discarded.

Towards the end of the retreat I met Sangharakshita for a long interview. It turned out well, and I was happy. From Padmaloka I went to stay at the London Buddhist Centre, which was then under construction. The fervour of the people working on the project impressed me. On my last day in London I had a mystical experience. For about an hour that evening in Berkeley Square the gates of Heaven were opened to me, and I beheld the eternal endless light behind this creation.

In the eighties things changed for me. With a family, but no income, I had many problems, and felt compelled to put my spiritual life on hold. In 1986 I had a retrospective show of my art work: a death-and-rebirth experience of a kind.

Sangharakshita did not come to Finland again, but now and then I wrote him a letter or card, and sometimes I received a reply, or a new book – for example a signed copy of his poems which I still treasure. Towards the end of the eighties I visited him in London: a deeply meaningful encounter, although he did not say much. I felt a longing to interview him again. I knew he had more to say – and I had matured. I wanted to interview him on the subject I knew most intimately: the arts.

In 1991 I was in New York to see some modern art and the Tibetan Art exhibition, as well as to attend the Kalachakra ceremony. I sent Sangharakshita a card with enthusiastic greetings, asking him if I could interview him once again. When I arrived back in Finland I found a card from Sangharakshita agreeing to the interview and suggesting a date. I rushed to my producers, Pekka and Pamela Mandart, with whom I had discussed a series of documentaries on contemporary artists. To my surprise they were interested.

So I travelled to Padmaloka in May 1992 to make what was to me a historic documentary. I felt as though I was going to see Plato, or some other ancient wise man – perhaps Nāgasena.... Sangharakshita was in good spirits: collected, relaxed, and ready to share his wealth of knowledge. I had a plan or leitmotif for the interview, but he changed the score right from the start, and I went along with his wishes. In the course of three days his vision unfolded before my eyes. Any subject that came up was handled with precision and elegance, and woven into the fabric of the screenplay. My job was easy; the themes just unfolded. But I also felt a little awkward about my role. We barely touched on many issues; there was so much more that I wanted to ask.

Still, I was happy with the way things went. During those days in the Padmaloka garden I could feel the wings of history and the muses, and a host of *ḍākinīs*, in the air. The birds were singing; the weather was fine. Two lotuses bloomed in the pond, and a frog sat contemplating not far from the Buddha statue. The film crew rose to the occasion splendidly, especially the cameraman, Raine Kuisma, who was inspired to catch some hauntingly beautiful moments.

'Now the real work begins,' Sangharakshita said softly as we parted. How right he was! The problem was that, knowing full well the unique value of every word Sangharakshita says, I found it difficult, even painful, to leave anything out, to trim the material down to television size.

But it was worth all the effort. On reading Sangharakshita's volume of memoirs, *Facing Mount Kanchenjunga*, and re-reading his *Religion of Art*, I was pleased to find that many of the central issues were included in the film. When it was finally shown on Finnish television, I felt that a milestone in the spiritual history of Finland had been passed.

How *In the Realm of the Lotus* will fare in the wider media world I cannot know, but it is my hope that East and West may unite in art, and that the Enlightened ones may be seen more on television in the future!

I am very happy to see the edited transcript of this unique occasion in print. Many thanks to the Venerable Sangharakshita and all those involved.

J. O. Mallander[175]
Helsinki
January 1995

1
A PASSION FOR COLOUR

OLLE MALLANDER: We know you as a Buddhist scholar, a prolific writer, a teacher with many thousands of disciples around the world – and a reformer, if I may say so. There are many different streams in your life and work which we could explore. But I would like to take up, as the subject of this interview, a particular stream in your spiritual life that has had a profound effect on the rest of your very active life. What I would like to ask you about is your experience of art and symbols and visions. To begin with, where does this stream come from?

SANGHARAKSHITA: Where it ultimately originates I don't really know, but from a more limited point of view it has its source in my childhood. When I was about eight years old I was diagnosed as having heart disease, and confined to bed – in fact, I was not allowed to move – and I stayed in bed for three years. So for three years the only thing I could do was read. At first my parents were hard pressed to keep me supplied with reading material, but then our next-door neighbour gave me a copy of a children's encyclopaedia, in twelve thick volumes. And in those volumes there were a number of articles about art, with illustrations. So far as I can recollect, that was my first experience of art.

When I was reintroduced to that particular encyclopaedia a few years ago, and I looked through it to see what had interested me as a child, I remembered that it was the section on ancient Egyptian art that I had found especially fascinating. As I flicked through the volumes, I also discovered a section called 'The Wise Men of the East' – the wise men being Zoroaster, Confucius, Laozi, and the Buddha. There were pictures too, including a photograph of the famous image of the Buddha at Kamakura in Japan. I think the brief account of Buddhism given in this section must have been my first contact with Buddhism as a teaching. So this children's encyclopaedia gave me my first experience of art, both Eastern and Western, and also my first acquaintance with Buddhism. From when I was eight until I was ten or eleven, that encyclopaedia was a very important part of my life.

Thus far, my experience of art was limited to small, reproduced images in books, and I can still vividly recollect my subsequent encounters with the real thing. When my health had improved and I had learned to walk for the second time, I started going to museums and art galleries in London, and there was one painting that caught my imagination more than any other. This was Titian's *Bacchus and Ariadne* in the National Gallery. Years later, I asked myself what it was in the picture that had made such an impression on me, and I came to the conclusion that it was simply the colour, the vivid, vibrant colour. I think that must have been what it was, because not long after that I became very interested in the art of the Pre-Raphaelites – the early Millais, Rossetti, Burne-Jones, and others – and of course in their paintings colour does play a very important part.

It was not just Western art to which I responded. I remember in particular a Persian miniature – from the Victoria and Albert Museum – which depicted the ascent of the prophet Mohammed to heaven. This was an important theme of Sufi mysticism as well as of Persian Islamic art, but it was not the theme itself which really interested me. What I think struck me about this miniature were the angel figures in it, because angel figures did become very important to me at about this time.

However, generally speaking, I was fascinated not so much by the subject matter of a painting, nor by the design or the composition, but definitely by the colour.

OLLE MALLANDER: Consciously?

SANGHARAKSHITA: No. I was not aware of this at the time. But a little later the theme of colour re-emerged in my life too compellingly to be overlooked. In 1943 I had been conscripted and shipped off to India with the Army. After the war I stayed on, and my wanderings there eventually took me to Kalimpong, a town not far from Darjeeling, in the foothills of the eastern Himalayas, about 4,000 feet above sea level.

From Kalimpong you can see Tibet, and the snows of the Himalayas. I lived in Kalimpong for fourteen years, and saw those mountains every day. The principal peak visible from Kalimpong – actually a double peak – was Mount Kanchenjunga.

OLLE MALLANDER: What does the name mean?

SANGHARAKSHITA: Kanchenjunga means 'the five treasures of the snow'. According to Tibetan legend, four of the treasures were gold, silver, crystal, and grain; as for the fifth, some said it was books, some that it was weapons.

The snows weren't visible all the time – sometimes the tops of the mountains were veiled in cloud – but often enough they were revealed, and the colours were remarkable. At sunrise you would see the snows just glimmering in the dawn, white against the grey-blue, and then, as the sun rose, although you couldn't see the sun, the mountains would become a sort of pink, and then they would change to a fiery red, a sort of crimson, like a heap of glowing embers. Then they'd become a pure gold, and then a pure, dazzling white. By that time, if it was a clear day, the sky would be a deep, vibrant, rich blue.

OLLE MALLANDER: It sounds almost as though you did nothing but look at the mountains.

SANGHARAKSHITA: I did sometimes feel like doing nothing but look at the mountains, but of course I did many other things in Kalimpong. I studied, I meditated, I taught, and I also wrote a number of poems, some of which, admittedly, were about mountains, but even those weren't always *just* about mountains. I wrote a number of poems which were, so to speak, just poems – and these included haiku – but I used to feel very often that it is not enough just to write poems. I used to feel that a poem ought to have a message to it – even a moral – something inspiring and uplifting.

OLLE MALLANDER: I see you as an essentially solitary figure at this time, at least as far as contact with the Western world is concerned. But from the evidence of the second volume of your memoirs, *Facing Mount Kanchenjunga*, it seems that you found some kindred spirits while you were in Kalimpong.

SANGHARAKSHITA: Yes. When I had been in Kalimpong for a few months, I started up a Buddhist magazine called *Stepping-Stones*, and sent copies all over the world. Copies of it even found their way to some of the early Zen Beat people, including Gary Snyder, whom I finally met up with in the USA two years ago. But one of the most important friends I made through that magazine was Lama Govinda. As we began to correspond, we found that our ideas about Buddhism were very similar. He had experience of several forms of Buddhism, and did not wish to identify himself exclusively with any one form. As for me, even though I had been ordained as a Theravādin Buddhist monk, I accepted the whole of Buddhist tradition, in all its richness. Theravāda, Mahāyāna, Tibetan Buddhism, Zen, Shin – in principle I accepted everything.[176]

In 1951, after we had been writing to each other for a while, Lama Govinda came to Kalimpong and spent some time with me. The friendship that then sprang up between us lasted for many years – indeed, the last letter I received from him was written just four days before his death. During our first meetings, he and his wife, Li Gotami, told me about some of the experiences that are described in his classic account of the trip they had made a few years earlier to Tsaparang in western Tibet – *The Way of the White Clouds*.

In particular, I remember Lama Govinda was very impressed by the clarity of the atmosphere of Tibet, in which colours showed up so vividly. In fact, he devotes a whole chapter of *The Way of the White Clouds* to the subject, entitling it 'The Living Language of Colours'. In this chapter – among many other things – he says this:

> I realized the tremendous influence of colour upon the human mind. Quite apart from the aesthetic pleasure and beauty it conveyed – which I tried to capture in paintings and sketches – there was something deeper and subtler that contributed to the transformation of consciousness more perhaps than any other single factor. It is for this reason that Tibetan, and in fact all Tantric, meditation gives such great importance to colours.[177]

This is a very significant point. In Tantric visualization you usually begin by visualizing a vast expanse of blue sky, which symbolizes the Void, *śūnyatā*. It isn't easy to do this if you've never seen a really blue sky. In England we're much more familiar with grey clouds, but in Tibet the sky is a rich blue all the time, and colours stand out with wonderful vividness. Lama Govinda believed that this contributed to the development of Tantric Buddhist visualization: against the rich, vibrant blue background, you visualize the figure of a Buddha or bodhisattva in brilliant, radiant, jewel-like colours.

That kind of awareness of and sensitivity to colour is reflected in Lama Govinda's own paintings, perhaps especially in his painting of a lake on the caravan route from India to Lhasa. He didn't use oil paints – he didn't particularly like oils as a medium, and they would have been cumbersome to carry about on his wanderings. Most of his work is in pastels, which he used to say could produce effects of colour impossible to achieve even with oils.[178]

Lama Govinda's reflections led me not only to develop my own interest in colour, but also to understand why I was interested in colour in the first place. For instance, I have always taken pleasure in semi-precious stones – the sheer luminosity of their colours – and have accumulated quite a little collection of them over the years. I think it was Aldous Huxley who suggested that we value jewels not because of their monetary value but because they give us a glimpse of some higher archetypal realm.[179] Certainly many scriptures and mystical writings, from Buddhist, Christian, and other traditions, describe higher worlds in terms of brilliant, jewel-like colours.

This reminds me of an occasion when I went to church with my grandmother. I must have been about 16 at the time, and although I had ceased to be a Christian when I was 14, my grandmother liked me to go to church with her, so I used to go. One Sunday the sermon was on a verse from the Book of Revelation, the Apocalypse: 'And every gate was one pearl.' What interested me about this sermon was not its Christian content but its imagery: that every gate was one pearl. This alone stuck in my mind; I don't remember anything else of the discourse.

Another person I got to know fairly well in Kalimpong was George Roerich, the elder son of the artist Nicholas Roerich, who of course had died by this time. He often spoke about his father, whom he had accompanied on his explorations in Central Asia.

Nicholas Roerich was a Buddhist devoted to the cult of Maitreya, and he wrote a lot on the subject. He claimed that he had seen in Tibet many signs that the Buddha Maitreya would soon be coming; and this was also the theme of many of his paintings.[180] In some respects his work was similar to that of Lama Govinda, although Lama Govinda specialized in paintings of Tibetan landscapes and monasteries, whilst Roerich's scope was much broader. Roerich had, after all, played a prominent part in various artistic movements in the West. He had designed stage sets for Diaghilev in Paris. So there had been for him all sorts of connections with the Western artistic world which Lama Govinda had never enjoyed. Roerich's range of subject matter is therefore very much wider, and it must be said that his vision in artistic terms is also much broader. His colour sense was perhaps not so well developed as Govinda's, but he had a much more powerful dramatic sense. His work is very scattered, nowadays. A lot of it is in India, and there is a Roerich Centre in New York. I have a volume of reproductions of his paintings published fairly recently in Moscow, so it could be that there is some recent interest in his work in Russia as well.

His wife Helena still lived in Kalimpong when I was there. I didn't meet her, because she didn't meet anybody – she never left her room. I became aware of her existence, though, when I visited her son George. As I entered his room, I was conscious of a strong downward pressure, a sort of psychic pressure, coming from above, and I learned later that his mother lived upstairs.[181] She was what they call a 'spiritual medium', that is, she received spiritual messages – which she wrote down and had published. She was the founder of a branch of the theosophical movement called Agni Yoga, 'Yoga of Fire', about which Nicholas Roerich also wrote extensively.

There was a younger son, Svetoslav, who died recently. He too was an artist, and he married a famous Indian film star. I must say that the glamorous world of artists and film stars is not a social milieu I am at all familiar with, but in India I did know the mother of this film star, and it seems to be a feature of Indian social life that if you know one person, then you come to know all the people *they* know. It doesn't quite happen like that in England.

2

DREAMS, VISIONS, INITIATIONS

OLLE MALLANDER: Talking about your experience of art we almost inevitably touch upon the world of dreams and visions. Can you tell us something about your dream world?

SANGHARAKSHITA: Dreams are an ineluctable part of our lives. We sleep so many hours every night, and when we sleep we cannot but dream. I have often thought that we have two parallel lives, a waking life and a dream life. We sleep for so many hours every night, and our sleep is always full of dreams, whether we remember them or not. But when we do remember, it is as if that dream world interpenetrates to some extent with the world of our waking experience, to produce another – different and enriching – level of experience. Sometimes, of course, dreams follow certain patterns; one can have the same kind of dream over and over again, over a period of many years.

When I was in India, I had a series of dreams of this kind which finally erupted into a dream experience that was something more than just a dream. For many years I used to dream of two houses – or rather, hermitages. One of these hermitages or monasteries was a public one which was open to everybody, and somewhere behind it was a very much smaller one that very few people knew about. In the dream I would usually be going from the big public monastery to the small private one, up some secret path, sometimes on my own, and sometimes with a few other people. I had this dream every now and then for about ten or twelve years, culminating in what was not actually a dream, I think, but more a visionary experience – what one might call a 'dream-vision'.

I have sometimes thought that we can reach higher states of consciousness not just from the waking state, but also from the dream state – only, note that I say *from* the dream state: it's not that we have those experiences *in* the dream state, but that we attain them *from* the dream state, which is a rather different matter. This culminating experience of mine was of that nature, and even though it took place thirty or forty years ago, it remains vividly in my memory.

The scene seemed to be South India. After being in the big monastery for some time, I made my way, up a little path, into the mountains, and came to the second, much smaller monastery. I entered a sort of shrine-room, and in this shrine-room a man was standing. He was in early middle age, perhaps 40 or 45. He was clad in white, a sturdy-looking figure – stocky, as we would say – with long grey hair and a long grey beard. And I knew that this was the rishi Agastya. Agastya, according to the Hindu tradition, was the sage who led the Aryan people down to southern India, and he is associated, in that tradition, with many esoteric teachings.[182]

Immediately behind Agastya there was a Tibetan-style shrine – that is to say, one in the form of a sort of glass-fronted cupboard, with images and stupas and pictures behind the glass. And I was thinking, 'It's strange that even though this rishi is a Hindu figure, he is standing in front of a Tibetan Buddhist shrine, with all these Buddha images behind the glass.' But I was also conscious that in this shrine-room there was a very, very powerful atmosphere. At the same time, the rishi was giving me various teachings – teachings which could not be put into words – and I had a strong sense of transmission, of energy being transmitted. It was as though I was being given some kind of initiation.

I don't know how much time passed, but afterwards I went out of the back door of this second hermitage to find myself in an open courtyard between two mountain peaks, one behind me and one in front. There was a sort of balustrade or parapet around the courtyard and I looked over this low wall down to the plains far below. In the distance there was a small town with factory chimneys. Later, when I woke up, I had a strong feeling that the town was an actual place somewhere in southern India which I would be able to discover if I searched for it long enough.

So this was the visionary experience I had – not just a dream, but an experience in some other world, on some other plane of existence.

This seemed to me clear enough. The real mystery was – why Agastya? Granted, the setting of the dream was appropriate: the Hindus have the same kind of belief about Agastya as some Buddhists have about the Buddha's disciple Kaśyapa – that even though he supposedly died thousands of years ago, he is in truth still living secretly in some mountain hermitage. But why should this Hindu sage have taken such a central role in the dream-vision of a Buddhist?

For many years, this remained a complete mystery to me. Then, on my most recent visit to India, I discovered a clue – a possible connection. It is well-known that the language spoken in South India, Tamil, is very ancient; and it is said that the oldest extant Tamil literature is influenced by Buddhism. But there is a curious detail to this ancient cultural traffic which had, up till now, escaped my attention. I discovered that there are Hindu legends to the effect that Agastya was taught the Tamil language by the bodhisattva Avalokiteśvara. So here perhaps was the reason for this particular Hindu sage conferring some kind of initiation on a Buddhist.

It was a few years before this encounter with Agastya that I had what I like to call my 'vision in the cave'. This really did take place in South India. It took place in a cave where Ramana Maharshi – who is probably the most famous Hindu teacher and yogi of this century – had lived for many years. In 1949 I spent six weeks at Mount Arunachala, in or near the ashram of Ramana Maharshi, and much of that time I was staying in this cave, called the Virupaksha Cave.

Buddhist cosmology tells of four guardian kings, one for each quarter, and Virupaksha is the guardian king of the western quarter; which is interesting in view of what happened to me in that particular cave. For there I saw a vision of Amitābha, who is the Buddha of the western quarter.

I have described this vision in the volume of my memoirs entitled *The Rainbow Road*:

> One night I found myself, as it were, out of the body and in the presence of Amitābha, the Buddha of Infinite Light, who presides over the western quarter of the universe. The colour of the Buddha was a deep, rich, luminous red, like that of rubies, though at the same time soft and glowing, like the light of the setting sun. While his left hand rested on his lap, the fingers of his right hand held

> up by the stalk a single red lotus in full bloom, and he sat, in the usual cross-legged posture, on an enormous red lotus that floated on the surface of the sea. To the left, immediately beneath the raised right arm of the Buddha, was the red hemisphere of the setting sun, its reflection glittering golden across the waters.[183]

Many years later I commissioned from one of my disciples a sort of thangka representing what I saw there in the cave. And this, of course, is how Tibetan thangkas – painted scrolls – originate. They are not just artistic productions in the ordinary Western sense. What happens is that a yogi has a vision of a Buddha or bodhisattva or guardian deity, and then either paints a picture of it himself, or else gets an artist to paint it for him according to his precise description. Of course, other painters will copy it and then the copies are copied by other artists, and very often contact with the original visionary experience is lost. But originally thangkas derive from visionary experiences. They are a form of visionary art.

The most obvious characteristic of such visionary, archetypal experiences is the luminosity of the colour in them. This is why so much of the religious art of the world has a rich, glowing, luminous, jewel-like quality. Tibetan thangkas, Persian miniatures, the mosaics of Ravenna – they all have this in common.

I myself have had just a few visionary experiences, but several of my own teachers had a great many; and the one who had the most of all was Kachu Rimpoche. Kachu Rimpoche was the head lama of Pemyangtse Gompa, the oldest Nyingmapa establishment in the state of Sikkim, but he was a very free and easy lama. Many Tibetan lamas are rather formal, even a little stiff, but Kachu Rimpoche wasn't like that. He was very informal and friendly, and was kind enough to take considerable interest in me. He would come to stay from time to time, bringing along his nephew, who afterwards remained with me as my pupil for quite a while.

Kachu Rimpoche used to meditate every morning, and usually he'd see some kind of vision. But what was really characteristic of him was that he would then act on it. His visions weren't, as far as he was concerned, just visions; they were signs of things he was to do. I remember that one morning when we were having breakfast, he said, 'What do you think I saw in my vision this morning?' I said 'I don't know.' 'What I saw' he said, 'was a banner of victory on the roof of your vihara. We've got to have a banner of victory on the roof.' So straight after breakfast he went into the bazaar, found a carpenter, and got him to make a wooden frame. Then he went to the cloth merchant and bought different coloured silks. And then he brought the whole lot back to the vihara, and very quickly manufactured a huge multi-coloured banner of victory. He put it up on the roof, and performed various ceremonies – pujas, blessings, invocations.... So this is the kind of thing he was always doing – he was very spontaneous, never acting from thought or calculation, but always from his visions. He was very much a meditating lama.

Tibetans have a great belief in astrology. When Kachu Rimpoche came down from Tibet to take up his post at the Pemyangtse Gompa, he had to enter the monastery on a certain date at a certain time – all according to the astrological signs. So he camped out in the jungle in a little tent, waiting for that time to come. He had travelled all the way from Tibet, but he just waited out in the jungle, all on his own, meditating.

Now at that time in Kalimpong there was a Frenchwoman who was the disciple of Dhardo Rimpoche, another of my Tibetan teachers – indeed, the one with whom I had the longest and most constant association. We worked together for many years, and I received a number of initiations from him. Anyway, this Frenchwoman who was a disciple of his – in fact he had made her a nun, a *śrāmaṇerī* – was giving him a lot of trouble. She was a very difficult, quarrelsome woman, and after studying with Dhardo Rimpoche for about six months she quarrelled with him, left him, and went up to Sikkim looking for another teacher. She happened to wander through the jungle where Kachu Rimpoche was staying in his tent, and came across him quite unexpectedly. So she thought, 'Oh, this is wonderful! I've found another lama,' and as she knew some Tibetan, she got talking to him. He asked her whose disciple she was, and she said she was a disciple of Dhardo Rimpoche. Then he asked her what spiritual practice she was doing, and she told him that she was doing a certain kind of meditation. Kachu Rimpoche looked at her and said, 'No, you haven't been doing that meditation for six months.' And it was true. She told me herself that she had told him a lie – she hadn't done that practice for six months.

I quickly saw for myself that he could read people's thoughts. Once, when he was staying with me, an American couple came to see me and wanted to talk with him, so I acted as interpreter. After a while, though, he was answering their questions before I was able to translate. Some of the questions were quite difficult, but he knew what they were asking without my translating, and gave the answers straightaway.

He was also an artist – a painter, and an excellent caster of images. After he became head lama, I went to see him at Pemyangtse, and found him in his room sitting on the bed. Underneath the bed were the pieces of a life-sized silver image which he was in the process of casting. And what was interesting from my point of view was that this image was of Padmasambhava, because it was Kachu Rimpoche who initiated me into the practice of Padmasambhava (along with that of Amitāyus, the Buddha of Long Life). He was casting this particular image of Padmasambhava in memory of Jamyang Khyentse Rimpoche, who had died not long before. Kachu Rimpoche was a staunch follower of the Nyingma tradition, and a staunch disciple of Jamyang Khyentse Rimpoche, from whom I too received a number of initiations. Jamyang Khyentse was said to be the greatest Tibetan scholar of this century, a vastly learned man of great spiritual experience – and something of a visionary too.

When a lama gives the initiation of a Buddha or bodhisattva, he is, at the same time, supposed to meditate on that Buddha or bodhisattva and visualize him (or her). In the course of my own initiation, as Jamyang Khyentse performed the ceremony, I noticed that he was looking up, and I had the strong impression that he could actually see the various bodhisattvas whose initiations he was giving me – Mañjuśrī, Avalokiteśvara, Vajrapāṇi, and Tārā. He had a smile on his face as though he was recognizing them while he was performing the ceremony.

I also received initiations from Dilgo Khyentse, who died not so long ago, and from Chattrul Sangye Dorje, a remarkable lama who spent many years wandering about Tibet and meditating. He wasn't an incarnate lama – or rather I should say he *isn't*, because he is the only one of my principal teachers who is, at the age of 82, still alive.[184] I received my first Tantric initiation from him, which was that of Green Tārā, so he occupies quite an important place in my spiritual life. In fact, all my teachers occupy an important place in my life; and I certainly remember them all the time. Some, perhaps, more than others, but they are at the back of my mind all the time, I could say.

Dudjom Rimpoche, another of my Tibetan teachers, once explained to me that when the lama gives the initiation of a Buddha or bodhisattva, it's as though he is introducing you, the one to the other. He is, as it were, saying to the bodhisattva, Tārā, as it might be, 'Tārā, here is my disciple so-and-so.' And then he says to the disciple, 'This is Tārā.' In this way he makes the introductions; he creates a connection. To be able to do this, of course, he must first establish his own connection with Tārā, or whoever the deity is. It's as though he puts himself in contact with that experience, and because he is in contact with it, he can be the means of putting you in contact with it. He can't give what he hasn't got himself. So there can't really be any such thing as a purely formal initiation. An ordinary lama who hasn't got much spiritual experience may go through the motions of the ceremony – this occurs all too frequently, I'm afraid – but in this case really not very much happens.

Usually visions are seen by one person. When they are seen by a number of people then they become something more than just visions. In the case of Lama Govinda's teacher, Tomo Geshe Rimpoche, one of the most famous visionary Tibetan lamas, it was as though his visions materialized so that they could be perceived by other people – on one famous occasion, by hundreds of other people. I heard about this incident from Tibetans in Kalimpong before I met Lama Govinda. They said that when Tomo Geshe Rimpoche was once travelling in a particular area of Tibet, the people there saw Buddhas and bodhisattvas in the sky, and then very large, lotus-like flowers started raining down, so real that people could touch them and take them up. These strange flowers apparently survived about half an hour, before they melted away. I was told that the whole episode has been depicted in a fresco on the walls of the Dungkhar Gompa in the Chumbi Valley of southern Tibet, where the Dalai Lama stayed for a while after the Chinese invasion of Tibet.

Tomo Geshe Rimpoche is not the only person credited with this spectacular gift. I heard a strange story recently concerning the contemporary Hindu yogi, Satya Sai Baba, who is famous for materializing things. The story was related to me by some of my Western disciples who had made the trip to Kalimpong. While they were there they visited a small shrine where a Tibetan disciple of mine, called Sherab Nangwa, used to live. He died just a few years ago. He was much older than me, but he had wanted me to ordain him, so I did. Anyway, on the altar of his shrine there was a picture of Satya Sai Baba, and the local people told my disciples that when Sherab Nangwa was living there, this photograph of Satya Sai Baba used to produce holy ashes. It apparently stopped doing this when Sherab Nangwa died.

I just don't understand these strange occurrences – which is no reason, of course, to believe that they don't happen. In Buddhist eyes they have no great spiritual value, but they do suggest that the laws of nature are more profound and complex than we usually think.

OLLE MALLANDER: The East seems to provide more fertile ground for such occurrences than the West does. Maybe, though, they do also happen in the West, only people don't know how to perceive them, or they don't pay attention.

SANGHARAKSHITA: They don't pay attention. In the West we don't perceive such things, even when they happen before our eyes, simply because we just don't pay attention. Similarly, when small children start talking about experiences before they were born, we're inclined in the West to dismiss it as just childish imagination, but in the East it would be taken seriously as recollections of a previous life.

Later on in my time in India I came to know the new Tomo Geshe Rimpoche, the reincarnation of Lama Govinda's guru. At the time of the Chinese invasion he was arrested by the Chinese, because he was supplying the Khambas with *ribus*, magic pills, to protect them. The Chinese imprisoned him, and treated him very badly. But he had been born in Sikkim, which was a protectorate of India, so the Indian government applied for him to be returned to Sikkim and the Chinese agreed, so eventually Tomo Geshe Rimpoche came to Kalimpong. We became quite good friends – I would have been about 35 then, and he was 22 or 23.

He was a strange person. To begin with, he was very small. The Sikkimese, especially the Lepchas, are often small, but he was exceptionally small and thin, and he had a very quiet voice. Despite his diminutive stature, however, people had great respect for him. He also had a sly sense of humour, and he was fond of pulling my leg. Sometimes it was difficult to know whether he was joking or not, because his sense of humour was so subtle. Although he was only in his twenties, his movements, his bearing, and his speech, were just like those of an old man. And he was very fond of little animals; he kept a number of dogs and cats and birds. This was not unusual – many incarnate lamas did the same: Dhardo Rimpoche had lots of little dogs and cats and birds as well.

I have been very fortunate in my teachers. As well as the valuable contact I had with the Tibetan lamas I have mentioned, I was fortunate enough to be able to learn from Yogi Chen, a master of Chan Buddhism. Mr Chen was a hermit who lived in a little house on the edge of the Kalimpong bazaar. He never came out. He spent most of the day meditating and saw very few people. I came to know him quite well, however, and got into the habit of visiting him once a week, on a Saturday evening. He was a mine of information about Chinese Buddhism, and all sorts of yogic practices. His spiritual experience was vast. He was also a very eccentric person. He did strange things, and he was constantly seeing visions.

My first teacher, however, was neither Tibetan nor Chinese, but Indian. This was Bhikkhu Jagdish Kashyap, who was a very learned man, a master of the Tripiṭaka. I studied Pāli, Abhidhamma, and Logic with him in Benares in 1949 and 1950, and he it was who took me to Kalimpong, and told me to stay there and work for the good of Buddhism. He was a great scholar, but very kindly and unpretentious; I was very fortunate to be able to study with him.

3
ASPECTS OF ENLIGHTENMENT

OLLE MALLANDER: In your study, besides pictures of your teachers and friends, you have many images and thangkas of archetypal forms. Would you say something about the meaning of these symbols?

SANGHARAKSHITA: When one is initiated into the 'cult' of a bodhisattva, especially of an archetypal bodhisattva, one is being introduced to an image of a particular aspect of Buddhahood or Enlightenment. We may say that Enlightenment has three principal aspects: the aspect of wisdom – or insight into ultimate reality, the aspect of spiritual vigour or energy, and the aspect of compassion. These three aspects of Enlightenment are embodied in the forms of the three bodhisattvas known to Tibetan Buddhists as the 'three family protectors': Mañjuśrī, Vajrapāṇi, and Avalokiteśvara.

Mañjuśrī is the embodiment of wisdom, of insight into reality. His name means 'gently auspicious one', and he appears in many forms. Sometimes he appears as Mañjughoṣa, 'gentle-voiced one', a manifestation with slightly different iconography. But the best-known form of Mañjuśrī is probably Mañjuśrī Arapacana. Here he is depicted as a youthful warrior or prince who holds aloft the flaming sword of wisdom, with which he cuts asunder the bonds of ignorance that prevent us from realizing Enlightenment.

Spiritual energy is embodied in the figure of Vajrapāṇi. He is sometimes depicted in peaceful form, but the best known image of him is his wrathful manifestation, a massive dark blue figure with bulging eyes and a fierce expression, with an aura of flames, stamping to the right, and holding in his right hand a vajra, the diamond-thunderbolt, symbol of unstoppable power.

The third of these three protectors is Avalokiteśvara, sometimes called Padmapāṇi (which means 'lotus in hand'). He is the embodiment of the compassion aspect of Enlightenment, and is popularly said to have 108 different forms (108 being a highly auspicious number in Tibetan Buddhism). The Dalai Lama, of course, is believed to be the manifestation in particular of Avalokiteśvara. The mantra of Avalokiteśvara is the famous *oṃ maṇi padme hūṃ*, which is usually translated as 'the jewel in the lotus', although it should be said that it is in the nature of a mantra that it cannot properly be translated at all.

All these various bodhisattvas come to us as various depictions of Enlightenment, but they depict that spiritual ideal in an ideal form. In this they contrast strikingly with the depiction – particularly in Chinese Buddhist art – of *arhants*, that is, those who have gained Enlightenment through following the teachings of the Buddha. The tradition is for most bodhisattvas to appear as radiant and beautiful 16-year-olds, whereas *arhants* are represented as being old and ugly, even deformed. So why this contrast? I gave quite a bit of thought to this question some time ago, and I came to the conclusion that bodhisattvas represent the spiritual ideal in its perfection, as it exists in another world, on another plane, whereas *arhants* represent that same ideal as embodied under the conditions of history, as limited by space and time. For time and space *are* limitations: when the ideal becomes embodied in actual life, it cannot exhibit the full perfection that it has in a higher, more ideal realm.

The depiction of bodhisattvas in Buddhist art is meant to give us a glimpse of that ideal realm, free of the limitations of space and time, and some very exceptional works do succeed in this endeavour. I was in Ajanta recently, and had the opportunity to examine each of the thirty caves there quite closely. As it happened there were not many visitors there that day, and the caretakers, being Buddhists, made very helpful use of lights and mirrors in order to show us the paintings. These have, of course, deteriorated badly even since they were discovered. They are going to be restored by a Japanese team soon, and the caves will be closed to the general public for several years while that is being done. But what is visible is extremely beautiful, especially the famous

Padmapāṇi figure with the blue lotus in his hand. This painting was still vivid in my memory from my first visit to the caves more than twenty-five years previously, but I was even more pleased to see it on this occasion. The expression of the face is really quite remarkable. It's compassionate and it's sad – and yet 'sad' is too strong a word, and even 'compassionate' is too strong a word. It's so much more refined and delicate than that. I don't think there is anything comparable in Western art as regards delicacy and refinement of expression except in the work of Leonardo da Vinci. The sculpture in the caves, by contrast, is very solid and – one couldn't exactly say crude – massive is the word to use, I think. In fact, 'massive' will do for the appearance of the caves generally: the columns are fat and squat, with cushion capitals.

Padmapāṇi is an example of an archetypal bodhisattva, a depiction of a particular facet of Enlightenment, as envisioned by a meditator in the course of his meditation. However, there are also living practitioners of Buddhism whose spiritual practice is of such a high standard that they may be thought of as living bodhisattvas. I have mentioned that the Dalai Lama is thought of as the emanation of Avalokiteśvara, the quintessence of compassion. I myself have no doubt that I have met living bodhisattvas, Buddhist practitioners par excellence – like, for example, my teacher Dhardo Rimpoche.

There is one figure who is regarded both as having had a human, historical existence and as being an archetypal embodiment of the qualities of Enlightenment. This is Padmasambhava, and there is a traditional account of his life, *The Life and Liberation of Padmasambhava*,[185] which fuses the human and the archetypal aspects of this bodhisattva by spectacularly interweaving historical and mythical strands of biographical material. Padmasambhava was a great Indian Buddhist teacher who lived round about 800 CE, at a time when Buddhism was first being introduced into Tibet. The king of Tibet had been converted to Buddhism, and had commissioned a huge monastery to be built, but the walls kept falling down, because, it was said, the local gods and spirits objected to being displaced by the new religion. Padmasambhava was invited to Tibet in order to subdue these local gods and spirits, so that the monastery could be completed.

Before going to Tibet, Padmasambhava visited many parts of India and the adjacent regions, and, according to legend, in each of the regions he visited, he assumed a particular form suited to the inclinations and temperament and spiritual needs of the people of that particular region. He assumed very many forms but, later, eight forms in particular were recognized, and these eight forms of Padmasambhava are commonly depicted in Tibetan thangkas.

The form known as Guru Padmasambhava is the one in which Padmasambhava went to Tibet. Here he is found in the robes of a Buddhist monk, and wearing the so-called 'pandit cap', signifying a master of the Buddhist scriptures. Thangkas conventionally depict snow peaks in the background, which probably represent the snows of Tibet to which he journeyed.

The *Śākyasiṃha* form of Padmasambhava represents him as the 'lion of the Śākyans', which is, of course, the title of the Buddha himself, Śākyamuni – the historical Buddha. The followers of Padmasambhava, the Nyingma sect of Tibetan Buddhism, go so far as to say that the Buddha Śākyamuni was one of the eight forms of Padmasambhava – a view which most Buddhists would not, of course, accept.

The 'esoteric' form of Padmasambhava comprises a male Buddha form and a female Buddha form locked in embrace. The male Buddha form represents compassion and the female form wisdom, so the figure as a whole represents the union, so to speak, of compassion and wisdom within the Enlightened mind of Padmasambhava.

Next, the form of Padmasambhava known in Tibetan as 'the thoughtful coveter of the best' depicts him as a lay teacher. He is carrying a *ḍamaru*, a little Tibetan drum, which represents the sound of the Buddha's teaching; and he also bears a bowl full of nectar, to represent the blissful experience that results from practising that teaching.

There are two wrathful, demonic forms that Padmasambhava assumes. In one he is riding on a tiger and wielding the diamond or thunderbolt sceptre in order to counteract the negative influence of false teachers. The other is called 'the Roaring Lion', in which form he again subdues the forces of evil.

Then there is Padmasambhava as the 'Lotus King' In this form he is sounding a *ḍamaru* and he has a bowl with what in some depictions is shown as a moon. Here he represents a righteous ruler – that is to say, a king who rules his country in accordance with the principles of the Dharma, the Buddha's teaching.

Finally, Padmasambhava appears as a yogi. He wears just a tiger skin round the waist, and a very meagre upper garment, and he carries his characteristic staff, with the five skulls to represent the five wisdoms, which are, of course, sometimes personified as the five Buddhas. The very graphic image of the skull signifies, I would suggest, insight into the ultimate nature of all existence, the Void, *śūnyatā*.

OLLE MALLANDER: Recently we in the West have been treated to a major exhibition of Tibetan art.[186]

SANGHARAKSHITA: Yes. And it is certainly of more than historical interest. Many of the items are of very great artistic value as well. I personally like the thangkas with the pure red background and the figures picked out in gold. I'm told that this particular style was a characteristic of Kham Tibetan Buddhist art. The contrast of the red and gold produces a definitely visionary and non-realistic kind of impression.

4
RETURN TO WESTERN CULTURE

OLLE MALLANDER: After about twenty years I believe you returned to the West and in many ways rediscovered for yourself Western, European art.

SANGHARAKSHITA: When I came back to England in 1964, after having been away for twenty years, there were many things that were strange to me. People's way of life had changed very much; and especially I noticed that they seemed much more prosperous than before. New services and utilities had sprung up – things like supermarkets and launderettes, which had simply not existed before the war.

Of course, these were not the aspects of Western life which most interested me on my return, though their pervasive impact could not be ignored. My main concern was to establish my own connections with Western culture. So after I'd been back in England for about a year and a half, I embarked on a sort of cultural pilgrimage to continental Europe with a friend of mine who drove me around. We went through Belgium, France, and Switzerland, down to Italy and across to Greece, and I took in a lot of monuments, art galleries, churches, cathedrals, temples, and so on.

In Italy it was the brilliant colours of the mosaics of Ravenna which made the strongest impression, together with the mosaics in St Marks – partly because I hadn't heard of them before. And the catacombs of Rome were quite a profound experience for me. However, it was in

Greece that I found myself moved most deeply – by the sacred places of ancient Greece: Delphi, Epidaurus, and Olympia, and by Delphi most of all. Shortly before I left Kalimpong, I'd read Henry Miller's *The Colossus of Maroussi*, in which he gives a very inspiring description of Delphi, so I was well prepared to be inspired, and I was not disappointed.[187] The natural beauty of the place combined exquisitely with the beauty of the archaeological remains. And I remember sitting on the hillside looking down at the ruins of the temple of Apollo and reading Euripides' *Ion*, written two-and-a-half millennia before, the action of which is set in that very place – the temple of Apollo at Delphi.[188]

In Epidaurus, which was the great healing centre of ancient Greece, I really did feel a calm, healing influence. And in Olympia, it was, of course, the archaic sculpture I responded to. Indeed, of all the ancient sculpture I saw in Greece – and I saw a lot – I think I was more impressed by the archaic sculpture than by the works of the classical period. I hadn't really expected this, but then I hadn't really known anything about archaic Greek sculpture before.

In 1981, quite a while after the foundation of the FWBO, we started holding ordination retreats in Tuscany, at a place called Batignano, which is not too far from Siena. That gave me the opportunity of renewing my contact with Italian medieval and Renaissance culture. I became particularly fond of Siena and Sienese art, but I also visited Florence, Rome, Naples, Venice, and Pisa.

Going round museums and art galleries I encountered certain symbols again and again. Needless to say, there were hundreds and hundreds of Madonnas and Crucifixions, but these didn't appeal to me very much. The image that did appeal to me was the figure of St Jerome – so much so that I wrote two essays about him.[189] St Jerome was, of course, the author of what eventually became known as the *Vulgate*, the Latin translation of the Bible used throughout medieval Christendom. And I found that there were very many paintings of St Jerome, including examples from some of the greatest artists, like Dürer and El Greco. Usually he was depicted either in his study, working at his translation, or in the wilderness doing penance.

St Jerome became an important symbol to me because he was a translator, and I thought a good deal about what being a translator means. It isn't just a question of translating from one language to another. Translation is making known something that was unknown, bringing something up from the depths, from – if you like – the unconscious, bringing it into the light of consciousness, and in that way making it generally available. I thought in this connection of the Buddhist figure Nāgārjuna, who receives the teachings of the Perfection of Wisdom from a dragon princess – she comes up from the depths of the ocean and hands these scriptures to him.[190] That was a translation, in a way, and Nāgārjuna was a sort of translator. You could even say the same thing about Asaṅga, because translation is not just a question of bringing up from the depths, but also of bringing down from the heights. Asaṅga is believed to have ascended in meditation to the Tuṣita *devaloka*, the higher spiritual realm where Maitreya, the future Buddha, was living – and still is, according to Buddhist tradition. There he received teachings from Maitreya, which he then brought down to earth.[191] So he also is a translator.

OLLE MALLANDER: Another subject which is also very close to your heart, and which you also must have encountered in the art galleries of Italy, is the subject of angels.

SANGHARAKSHITA: Yes. Angels occupy quite an important place in Western religious art, especially perhaps in medieval religious art. Coming upon so many examples of this type of painting I started remembering that when I was about 13 or 14 I made a whole series of detailed drawings of angels. We all know in a general way what is meant by an angel. An angel is a being belonging to a higher sphere of existence – an intermediate being, half in the realm of absolute reality and half in the ordinary, everyday world. In some ways, angels correspond – very roughly, very approximately – to bodhisattvas in Buddhism. And angels function as messengers (the word 'angel' in Greek meant originally just 'messenger') which is perhaps why they are winged. The angel represents the messenger coming from the world of higher reality, even the world of ultimate reality, bringing a message about that higher reality to us, down here on this earth. So the angel is also a sort of translator, perhaps in a more direct way than St Jerome.

Angels appear in all spiritual traditions. I've mentioned the bodhisattva as the Buddhist equivalent of the angel figure in Christianity. Angels also appear in Islamic – especially Persian – art, where they are portrayed in much the same way as in Christian art. They are, though, very colourful, often with very beautifully coloured wings, and in this respect they are like Fra Angelico's angels rather than the more sentimental type from later Western art – a type one can never quite believe in. But Fra Angelico clearly did believe in his angels. They are quite credible in imaginative terms, and notable for the beautiful peacock-like colouring of the wings.

When they appear in modern art, angels seem less likely to conform to the sentimental stereotype. In the Ateneum gallery in Helsinki, for instance, there is a painting by a Finnish artist of a 'wounded angel'. The angel's head is bandaged, and he is sitting on a stretcher being carried along by two boys. The message in this painting is clear enough. It suggests that some sort of higher faculty – maybe the imagination – has been badly damaged in our modern era. Angels also feature prominently in the work of a contemporary English artist – Cecil Collins – who depicts angels in a quite non-realistic, almost abstract way, which is at once strange and also quite evocative and meaningful. There are twentieth century literary angels as well – one thinks, for example, of the very dramatic appearance of the angel in Rilke's *Duino Elegies*.[192]

So as regards the Western cultural and spiritual tradition, the figure or symbol of St Jerome and the figure or symbol of the angel are both important to me personally. Both of them are translators, in their different ways; both of them are messengers. Both of them, in other words, bring to us spiritual riches we might not otherwise have access to.

5

BEAUTY AND THE HIERARCHY OF ART

OLLE MALLANDER:

> As stars, a fault of vision, as a lamp,
> A mock show, dew drops, or a bubble,
> A dream, a lightning flash, or cloud,
> So should one view what is conditioned.[193]

These words of the Buddha suggest a strong appreciation of nature. Would you say something about the Buddhist view of nature and your own relation to nature?

SANGHARAKSHITA: These comparisons are taken from a well-known Buddhist text, the *Diamond Sūtra*, and they are meant to illustrate the impermanence of all conditioned things. The lightning flash doesn't last very long, the dewdrop doesn't last very long, the cloud drifts by, the dream comes and goes. All these things are evanescent, impermanent. Life is like that.

But there is something else to notice about these comparisons: they are all beautiful. They may be illustrating impermanence, but they also illustrate the beauty of the world. The cloud is beautiful as it floats through the sky. The dewdrop is beautiful as it glistens in the early morning sunlight. The lightning flash is beautiful in its brief, awesome power. The bubble on the stream, reflecting myriad hues – like a rainbow sometimes – is also beautiful. So to my mind there is a twofold message in that particular verse: life is fleeting, life is transient, but life is also beautiful.

In the early Buddhist scriptures – those, that is, which can be said to reflect the historical circumstances under which the Buddha taught – there is evidence of a very great sensitivity to the natural world. The Buddha himself, as also his immediate disciples, lived close to nature. He was actually born in an orchard – his mother holding on to the branch of a tree. He gained Enlightenment at Bodh Gaya sitting underneath a tree. He died in the *sāl* tree grove of the Mallas, stretched out between two *sāl* trees. And of course he spent much of his time wandering from place to place, from village to village, in the open air.

So Buddhism had its origins in the open air, and this open air background to the scriptures inevitably affected the way the Dharma was taught by the Buddha and experienced by his disciples. For instance, there is a set of verses in the *Theragāthā* ('Verses of the Elders'), attributed to one of the Buddha's senior disciples. In it he describes a cloud – a heavy, black, or rather, dark blue, cloud – and how a white bird flies across the dark cloud. And it seems that the beauty of this sight sends him into a sort of ecstasy.[194]

Scholars have a tendency, perhaps, to overlook this aspect of Buddhism in their intent to present Buddhism as a *teaching*, sometimes, even, as quite a dry, methodical, analytical teaching. But if you look at the *life* of the Buddha, the life of his close companions, you see the natural world very much *there* in their lives, in their practice of the Dharma. And there is therefore a close connection, I would say, between early Buddhism and the natural environment.

OLLE MALLANDER: Also the different spiritual stages culminating in Enlightenment are very often presented in terms of natural phenomena.

SANGHARAKSHITA: Yes. The most common symbol in Christianity is the cross, even the crucifix. But the most common symbol in Buddhism is the lotus flower. It goes right back to the time immediately after the Buddha's Enlightenment, when he was wondering whether or not he would ever be able to communicate his experience to others. He looked out over the world and saw human beings as lotus flowers growing in a pond. Some were deep down in the mud, some had just raised their petals above the water, and some were standing completely free of the water, opening their petals to the sunlight. This was the Buddha's vision of humanity. And through it he knew that human beings could grow and expand and open up to receive the sunlight of the Dharma – and that like blossoms, some individuals were more developed and mature – and therefore more receptive to the Dharma – than others.

So it does seem that the Buddha himself was not just conscious of the natural environment but felt deep sympathy with it. The Buddhist scriptures are full of references to nature spirits – spirits of the trees, spirits of the ponds, spirits of the streams, even spirits of flowers. There's a story in one of the scriptures of a monk who goes and smells a lotus flower growing in the water, and the spirit of the flower comes out and says, 'Why are you stealing my scent?' – which obviously gives the monk something to think about. In future he won't thoughtlessly take from nature without asking permission in some way. He won't even think to smell a lotus flower without the flower's permission. After all, it isn't *his* scent – it's the flower's scent.[195]

This does, perhaps, convey to us some kind of environmentalist message about the way we exploit nature. The idea that we shouldn't so much as smell a flower without seeking the flower's permission might seem a bit sentimental, but there is a philosophy underlying it which has some quite far-reaching implications for us today, and this is that there can be a sort of imaginative identification between man and nature.

OLLE MALLANDER: There is that Zen saying: 'An old pine preaches wisdom, a wild crane cries out the Truth.'

SANGHARAKSHITA: Yes. And Wordsworth says much the same thing, of course in his own way:

> One impulse from a vernal wood
> Can tell us more of man
> Of moral evil and of good
> Than all the sages can.[196]

Unfortunately, the way it is put can make what Wordsworth says seem trite and sentimental, but it is nonetheless true. One certainly doesn't want to be sentimental about it, but if one reflects on nature, if one is in sympathy with nature, then yes, one can learn.

OLLE MALLANDER: From love of nature, it is a small step to the subject of art and poetry. Beauty is always a unifying factor. And you have made an important statement of your views on the subject in your book *The Religion of Art*.

SANGHARAKSHITA: Nowadays, of course, beauty is regarded as rather an old-fashioned idea. Many modern artists and art critics would not accept the validity of talking in terms of beauty; they have other criteria. But personally I believe that the concept of beauty is very important and valid. We are all susceptible to beauty. And one of the characteristics of appreciation of beauty is that it is quite disinterested. When you see a beautiful flower, you appreciate it just for its beauty. You don't want to *do* anything with it. You don't want to own it, possess it, take it to pieces, analyse it. You just want to contemplate it and appreciate it. In this way it lifts you out of your usual preoccupations, it lifts you even beyond your ordinary usual self, into a different kind of world, in which one is concerned with *values* rather than with interests in the economic sense. Unless you are a market gardener, you are not going to be thinking in terms of making money out of the flower. You just value it for its own sake.

OLLE MALLANDER: The more selfless people are, the more possible it becomes to appreciate beauty.

SANGHARAKSHITA: Yes. And the more you appreciate beauty, the more selfless you become. In the book you mentioned I quote Kant to the effect that to appreciate natural beauty is a sign of goodness in man.[197]

But as I say, quite a few people nowadays would not agree that beauty had anything to do with art. It depends, of course, on how you define art. In that book, which I wrote many years ago, I tried to work out my own definition, and this is what I came up with: 'Art is the organization of sensuous impressions into pleasurable formal relations that express the artist's sensibility and communicate to his audience a sense of values that can transform their lives.'

It's as if one goes up step by step in a sort of hierarchy of experience. Art begins with sensuous impressions – impressions of sound, colour, and shape mainly, because art is not concerned with touch, smell, or taste, except in a subordinate sense. And what do we do with these impressions? They are usually chaotic to begin with, so the first thing we do is organize them – and we generally organize them into pleasurable formal relations. To put it simply, we organize them into patterns. However, that is to put it very simply indeed, because then there arises the question of what has been called 'significant form'. It's not just that we bring about these pleasurable formal relations; these relations also have a relation to the artist himself. They express the artist's sensibility – his awareness, his consciousness, of nature, perhaps, or of other people. More than that, they communicate to his (or her) audience a sense of values, a deep underlying philosophy. And they communicate that sense of values in such a way that the lives of that audience are transformed.

So as I see it, any art which is worthy of the name finds itself in a sort of hierarchy. At the lowest level there is art that simply organizes sensuous impressions into pleasurable formal relations. Above this level you can then find art that expresses, through those formal relations, the artist's sensibility. A still higher form of art communicates, through that sensibility, the artist's sense of values. And in the very highest form of art, that sense of values, communicated in that way, is capable of transforming the lives of the observer, listener, or reader.

OLLE MALLANDER: Could you perhaps mention some names here?

SANGHARAKSHITA: As an example of the lowest level of this hierarchy I think of Moorish tilework of the kind to be seen at the Alhambra. In Islamic art of this period there was a ban on the representation of living things (a ban which was broken by Persian artists) so that what you find in mosques is just lots of very beautiful patterns – in tilework, and calligraphy. And that is, to my way of thinking, the lowest or most basic form of art.

I would say that the Pre-Raphaelites don't go far beyond the first two levels. Yes, there are beautiful patterns, beautiful formal relations which are pleasurable, and yes, a sensibility is expressed, but despite the medievalism, despite the moralism, there is not really much of a deeper communication of values.

In the case of some of the Renaissance artists like Botticelli, or like El Greco, there is an underlying Neoplatonic philosophy, and some communication of values through their work. But to go right to the top of the hierarchy, I would say that in his paintings on the ceiling of the Sistine Chapel Michelangelo definitely expresses a profound philosophy. He was a thinker. He wasn't merely illustrating Bible scenes; those scenes – interspersed with the figures of the sybils and *ignudi* and the prophets – had a significance for him which, I think we may say, transcended their immediate Christian connection. Take, for example, *The Creation of Adam*. It is a familiar, even hackneyed image, nowadays, but it is really an extraordinary interpretation of the old biblical myth. Because the two figures don't make physical contact, it really does seem as if a current of energy is flowing into the comparatively inert and flaccid body of the newly created Adam. It does seem to represent a sort of influx of divine inspiration into humanity. It is, if you like, a symbol of spiritual communication. Michelangelo's art is not just pretty patterns. He is not just expressing his sensibility, even. He is expressing his vision, his sense of values, and expressing it in such a way as to transform the life of the onlooker.

6
THE CONFLICT BETWEEN RELIGION AND ART

OLLE MALLANDER: In the first volume of your memoirs you give a hint about there being not one Sangharakshita, but maybe several. Can you elaborate a little on this disclosure?

SANGHARAKSHITA: In *The Thousand-Petalled Lotus* I wrote about the conflict I experienced fairly early on in my Buddhist life between two aspects of myself whom I called 'Sangharakshita I' and 'Sangharakshita II'. Sangharakshita I was the more 'religious-minded', even ascetic, aspect, while Sangharakshita II was the more aesthetic aspect, who was interested in the arts and literature. Sangharakshita I wanted to meditate and realize the truth; Sangharakshita II wanted to experience life....[198]

I was reminded of this recently when someone asked me whether there had been a reconciliation between Sangharakshita I and Sangharakshita II, or whether they were still in conflict. My reply was that it isn't possible for Sangharakshita I to get rid of Sangharakshita II, and it isn't possible for Sangharakshita II to get rid of Sangharakshita I. They have to co-exist. There has to be, it seems, a sort of fruitful tension, or even a fruitful conflict, between the two, as they interact with each other.

OLLE MALLANDER: Is that the creative spur?

SANGHARAKSHITA: Yes and no: because if one thinks of creativity in purely aesthetic terms, creativity belongs to Sangharakshita II, not to Sangharakshita I. The tension is not between two types of creativity, but between creativity in the aesthetic sense and something quite different from creativity.

Shortly after he was condemned to death by the Ayatollah Khomeini, Salman Rushdie gave a lecture in which he made the point that there are two absolutes, the religious absolute and the artistic absolute. The religious absolute takes religious values as being absolute: for Islam, Islamic values are absolute, and there can be no compromise. If Salman Rushdie blasphemes against the prophet, as Muslims see it, there can be no compromise: he must just be killed. But Salman Rushdie's attitude is different. He represents the aesthetic absolute, according to which the artist must have complete freedom to express whatever he wishes to express, regardless of any religious or ethical considerations.[199] Here there are two absolutes in conflict, neither prepared to give way to the other. In medieval times, it was the religious absolute which had the power, but in modern times, at least in the West, the aesthetic absolute has the upper hand.

In my own case there is the same kind of conflict – Sangharakshita I representing the religious absolute and Sangharakshita II representing the aesthetic absolute – and it seems that there has to be conflict between them. However, this conflict can be considered in some sense creative, or at least productive – if not in a narrowly aesthetic sense. Because nowadays you cannot really have the religious teacher in the old sense, as representing the religious absolute. Some people in the Buddhist world are not very happy with the way in which I'm doing things, but they have to recognize that the FWBO is successful – which surely has something to do with this 'conflict' of mine.

When I was in Spain two or three years ago, I was invited to speak to a Tibetan group. In discussion with them, I found they were experiencing a great difficulty, which was that according to the Tibetan tradition they were supposed to accept whatever their lama said, without question. In other words, they were up against the religious absolute. Being good Buddhist disciples they wanted to follow the lama's teaching, but being modern Westerners they could not, in their hearts, accept the religious absolute.

I tend to think that we need a sort of synthesis – for want of a better word – between the two positions. We need a person who is not a lama, who doesn't represent just the religious absolute. And we need a person who does not uphold the aesthetic absolute, who does not break *all* the rules, cross *all* the boundaries. We need a new sort of person.

I think Lama Govinda was a bit like that. He was an artist and at the same time he was something of a mystic. He was an artist and a writer and a poet, as well as being a Buddhist devoted to meditation, Buddhist thought, and Buddhist philosophy. There was nothing absolute about him; he seemed to synthesize the two very well, without any conflict.

The days of the religious absolute are finished. We don't any longer really need teachers – whether they are Christian or Muslim or Buddhist – who stand for a religious absolute. Nor do we need any longer artists, painters, and writers who stand for the aesthetic absolute and refuse to consider moral and spiritual values. It's not that the artist cannot break rules, from the spiritual point of view, but there is no value in breaking rules for the sake of it. Many artists and writers seem to set out with the idea that they can extend the scope of artistic expression just by breaking rules. In my view this is not the case. The aesthetic absolute is no more valid than the religious absolute. The dogmatism of art insists that the rules must be broken, while dogmatic religion insists that the rules must be obeyed, and they are equally dogmatic.

OLLE MALLANDER: What sort of energy nourishes your writing? For instance, you have said about Beethoven that 'at his worst – and perhaps at his most characteristic and popular – is will pretending to be power'.[200] I thought of this as a comment on Western culture in general. Will-power is very much the kind of energy used by Titans like Picasso. The Eastern artistic attitude seems to be more subtle.

SANGHARAKSHITA: A lot of the characteristically oriental artistic temperament comes from contemplation, and the rapport which develops between the artist and the object of his contemplation. This comes out clearly in Chinese art, especially Chinese landscape art. There is a well-known story of a man who wanted to paint bamboos, and was advised to go and look at bamboos for seven years. So he did. He just looked at bamboos for seven years, before he ever lifted a paintbrush to paint one. What was the point of that? Well, if you contemplate, say, a bamboo, then a sort of empathy springs up between you and it. You have a contact with the bamboo, a feeling for it, and out of that feeling you create. It is as though you and the bamboo come together in a kind of marriage, out of which something is born – a painting of the bamboo, in this case.

OLLE MALLANDER: In Chinese landscape art humanity is very clearly reduced in scale against the vast presence of nature.

SANGHARAKSHITA: This sometimes happens in Western art too. One sometimes has to look very hard to see the human figures in the landscapes of Claude, for instance.[201]

OLLE MALLANDER: How do you find that your meditation practice benefits your own work as a writer?

SANGHARAKSHITA: I find that meditation helps me to write in that it makes my mind calmer and clearer. When I was writing *The Three Jewels*, for example, and came to a point where I wasn't clear, I used to stop and do the meditation of Mañjuśrī, and I used to find that very helpful.

OLLE MALLANDER: The book didn't come from heaven. You had to write it still.

SANGHARAKSHITA: I had to write it still.

OLLE MALLANDER: Do you work from inspiration?

SANGHARAKSHITA: I suppose, yes, it does start with inspiration. An idea just comes into my head – I don't know where it comes from – and then I start thinking. I connect it with other ideas; I connect it with literary material and with Buddhist material. Sometimes I carry all this in my mind for years before I write it down. I usually have several different lines of thought going on in my mind, things I've been thinking about and reflecting on for many years, and eventually, at some suitable opportunity, they get written down. I reflect a lot.

OLLE MALLANDER: What would you say is the nourishing or fuelling energy when you actually start writing?

SANGHARAKSHITA: I think the important thing for me is clarity; I want to make things clear, either to myself or to others.

OLLE MALLANDER: Clarity is very rare nowadays.

SANGHARAKSHITA: Yes. I get a little annoyed when people are confused in their thinking and use words clumsily. I consider this as a sort of intellectual laziness, and perhaps spiritual laziness as well.

7
A NEW RENAISSANCE?

OLLE MALLANDER: Many of your books and articles on Buddhism are illustrated by the works of Western artists, particularly from the Renaissance period. What is it in this period do you think that appeals so much to the Buddhist mind?

SANGHARAKSHITA: Often, it is to do not so much with the Buddhist mind as with the designer's mind! But it is certainly true that as far as possible we want to present the message or the teaching of Buddhism through the medium of Western culture. The Renaissance does represent a peak in Western culture, at least as regards painting and architecture, so it is quite natural to take illustrations and images from that particular source. Just recently, for example, I finished writing a book, and the designer and I came up with the idea of using Botticelli's painting *The Calumny of Apelles* for the cover design. In the book I am replying to criticism and appealing to the truth about the nature of Buddhism, and in the painting there is a female figure pointing upwards, appealing to truth against calumny. Thus it fitted in with the theme of the book quite nicely, though in the event we chose to highlight on the cover a different aspect of the theme of the book.[202]

OLLE MALLANDER: You have written a small pamphlet which perhaps deserves wider circulation. It's called *The Artist's Dream*, and it's a story or parable about an artist who goes through various trials and tribulations and then wakes up to the vision of a new world.[203] Would you say it was something of a self-portrait?

SANGHARAKSHITA: It could be taken as such, although the medium is different, of course. You might say that in my case the artist's dream was the FWBO, because I wrote the story about twenty years ago.

OLLE MALLANDER: You didn't have any particular artist – a visual artist – in mind?

SANGHARAKSHITA: No, I didn't. I deliberately laid the scene in Italy, in the Middle Ages. If I was influenced by anything in writing the story, it was probably by a little-known story of Rossetti's called 'Hand and Soul', written when he was quite young, and which I read many years ago.[204]

OLLE MALLANDER: You have said that it is the colour in paintings to which you respond most directly, and you have mentioned Titian in this regard. But the Renaissance period as a whole seems to be characterized by mastery of colour, compared, for instance, with baroque and rococo painting.

SANGHARAKSHITA: The Venetians were the great colourists, of course, Titian above all. And Tintoretto brings a realistic and dramatic handling of subject matter to the Venetian tradition. El Greco came under the influence of Tintoretto when he spent some time in Venice, so he can be seen as continuing that tradition, although he has a much more spiritual outlook – a more spiritual philosophy – as well as a much better colour sense than Tintoretto.

OLLE MALLANDER: Would it be fair to say that he is more exalted and in that way more spiritual?

SANGHARAKSHITA: Yes, he is more exalted. He is also more visionary. You could even say of his work that it is sometimes ecstatic; this effect is, of course, very often heightened by the elongated nature of his figures and their upward movement. In El Greco's art there is not so much a uniting of the forces of heaven and earth or hell as a complete escape from the forces of earth. There is an upward soaring to heaven – the sort of movement often associated with Gothic architecture.

OLLE MALLANDER: In the English visionary, William Blake, who I know is very dear to you, we find even more of a sense of the dramatic.

SANGHARAKSHITA: In Blake's work, by contrast with that of El Greco, there is a very definite meeting of the forces of heaven and hell. And here I don't have in mind his famous work, *The Marriage of Heaven and Hell.* What I particularly have in mind is an engraving of his, *The Reunion of the Soul and the Body*, in which a masculine figure is rising up from the ground and a female figure is descending from above, and the two are clasping each other.[205] In Blake's work one gets a strong sense of line, of linear rhythm. Blake isn't much of a colourist, but his line is always vigorous, fluid, and expressive. He took a conscious delight in what he called 'the wiry, bounding line' (by 'bounding' he means, of course, 'boundary-defining').[206]

Art critics have mixed feelings about Blake. He can be very good indeed, but he can also be very bad, and I think most historians of English art would give the highest place not to Blake but to Gainsborough or Turner. Turner captures the dramatic qualities of the elements – mountains, chasms, skies, storms, and sea, and particularly the sea – with perhaps unequalled authority. But to my mind he is at his most interesting when he relates the physically insignificant human being to the much more powerful elements. I'm thinking, for instance, of his *Fire at Sea*, in which a ship has caught fire and human beings are in peril, caught 'between the devil and the deep blue sea'. Turner is very good at depicting that sort of situation; you are conscious of the physical helplessness of man, confronted by the infinitely more powerful elements by which he is surrounded and almost crushed.

But there is also another side of Turner which I like very much: his classical and mythological, or legendary, paintings. I like his paintings of Rome and Naples, with their southern Italian scenery: blue skies and peaceful landscapes. His paintings of Venice are probably influenced by Canaletto, or can be seen as in some way continuing that tradition. Turner is a many-sided artist, a very great genius indeed. He was a remarkable man, who cared only for his painting. There are some very interesting stories told about him. It is said, for instance, that when he was due to exhibit a painting, he would very often paint the picture at the last moment, actually in the gallery where it was going to be exhibited. He would just arrive, very shabbily dressed, put up his easel, take out his paints, and start to scrabble colours on the canvas. People would think 'What a mess!' and 'What on earth is he doing?', but gradually it would change and develop to become a beautiful picture. He took no notice of anybody. He told Ruskin once that he never bothered to reply to criticism; he just went on in his own way.[207] He refused to have anything to do with fashionable society; he just lived to paint.

Another artist who can be said to have sacrificed his life for art is the Pre-Raphaelite painter Holman Hunt. In his search for authenticity he went all the way to the Dead Sea in order to paint *The Scapegoat*, his famous portrait of a goat which has been, according to ancient and annual Judaic tradition, dedicated to God and then driven out into the wilderness to die 'for the people's sins'. In the first version of the painting Hunt added a rainbow, which is the Biblical symbol of hope (inasmuch as it represented God's promise to Noah that he would not send any more floods upon the earth). But the final version has no rainbow – some say because Hunt had lost hope in the world in the meantime. The symbolism of the painting appeals to me very much, although, perhaps predictably, I was originally attracted to it because of its colours.

OLLE MALLANDER: Blake, Turner, and Hunt are of course all English. What then of the German romantic school? For me, after the greatest Italian masters, Caspar David Friedrich is always there.... He has subtlety and precision, a sense of man in a landscape....

SANGHARAKSHITA: One could say that Friedrich is quintessentially northern. If Titian, for example, is the epitome of the southern artist, filling his works with light and colour, beauty and joy, then Friedrich is very definitely northern: melancholy, capturing not bright sunlight but mist, darkness, and gloom. The qualities of their work are antithetical. When I was last in Germany I visited the art gallery in Düsseldorf, which has a very impressive collection of German romantic paintings. They are generally of this same kind: the product not of beautiful, sunlit Italian landscapes, but of the northern forests and the grey northern skies – melancholy, reflective, mystical. In Friedrich, as in Japanese painting and in Turner, one discovers, as you say, the isolated figure in a huge landscape, the sense of man in relation to his surroundings – in mysterious relation to an unfathomed cosmos.

The work of the German romantic writers also evokes this kind of feeling. I once told Lama Govinda that I had the impression that his writings were influenced by the German romantics (whose work I had got to know in my teens). Lama Govinda said that actually he was not just influenced by these writers; he had certain recollections which led him to believe that he himself was the incarnation of one of them. I later came to understand that he believed that he had been the poet Novalis in a previous lifetime.[208]

It is perhaps not too far-fetched to think that artists are working on a story that takes them many lifetimes to write – even if artists themselves rarely think in these terms. D. H. Lawrence, for example, thought of the novel as a 'thought adventure'.[209] He saw himself not so much as a writer but as a preacher; he wanted to communicate certain insights, certain ideas, and he didn't mind spoiling his novels from an artistic point of view if he could do this. Some people have criticized him for being too much of a preacher, but he would not have regarded that as a criticism; a preacher was what he wanted to be.

OLLE MALLANDER: In a paper you delivered in 1985, *The Glory of the Literary World*,[210] as well as in your book *The Religion of Art*, you have spoken of the possibility of a 'second Renaissance', a Renaissance in which the West would discover the treasury of Eastern art and literature. Does this not seem to have become more and more of a reality as Eastern religious teachers have come to the West in ever-increasing numbers, and with so many more texts being made available in translation?

SANGHARAKSHITA: In my view, this Renaissance has not yet really begun. Many of those who take up some Eastern religion take it up almost as a substitute for Christianity. For instance, in taking up Tibetan Buddhism, some people accept everything the lama says at face value, just as a Christian might accept everything the Bible says, quite literally – or everything the Pope says. There is no real difference. They have found refuge in an authority; they have found a security system, and that is quite a different thing from Enlightenment – or even just knowledge. There seem to be, very broadly, two groups of people, both looking for a security system. Some go back, or try to go back, to the Christian religion: they may go straight back to the traditional view of the Bible as being true both symbolically and literally; or they may decide gently to drop the literal interpretation; but they go back, or part of the way back, to the old security system. Others look for a new security system; but they are looking for the same thing, essentially.

Even though Eastern religions are becoming better known in the West, they are often approached wrongly, and used for wrong purposes. I doubt, therefore, whether there is yet a real Renaissance comparable to the Renaissance that took place in Europe in the fifteenth century as the result of the rediscovery of classical literature, art, and culture. So far, the influx of Eastern teachings into the West has not produced any great art – nothing outstanding, nothing to compare with the great artistic achievements of the Renaissance.

OLLE MALLANDER: Should we expect it, even?

SANGHARAKSHITA: I don't know if we can expect, but at least we may hope.

OLLE MALLANDER: Don't Buddhists build a better world?

SANGHARAKSHITA: They put up buildings. We ourselves in India are constructing some very big and beautiful buildings, in Pune and other places – more so than we do in Britain, anyway.

OLLE MALLANDER: Are they Buddhist in style?

SANGHARAKSHITA: Yes, one could say that they are in a neo-Buddhist style. We have put up at least four or five buildings of some architectural value, I think, designed by an American architect.[211]

OLLE MALLANDER: The introduction of meditation in the West could surely contribute to a possible cultural rebirth? Meditation is a household word, nowadays.

SANGHARAKSHITA: Indeed. When I returned to England in 1964, meditation was known to only a few people, but now it is an ordinary, everyday thing. If you tell your friends that you meditate, they are not going to be surprised. People are also much more familiar with the idea of vegetarianism; when I was a boy there was only one Indian vegetarian restaurant in London, but now there are hundreds. Hatha yoga too is widely known now, and people who practise it, even if they belong to what we call the 'health and beauty brigade', are usually aware that yoga has some connection with the East.

OLLE MALLANDER: There must be millions of Westerners who have learnt meditation. I could imagine that meditation would help to tune people's sensibilities in such a way as eventually to issue in an artistic renaissance of some kind.

SANGHARAKSHITA: Meditation can certainly be a contributory factor, although by itself it is not enough. You can be a good meditator, but the creative impulse is something quite different. In some ways, you could say, meditation may even inhibit the creative impulse.

On the other hand, if you look at the work of great writers and artists, you can see a sort of spiritual development (to use that expression) taking place. Human beings are rarely completely unified personalities; there are usually a number of personalities fighting for supremacy, now one being uppermost, now another. In the work of Shakespeare, for example, or Dickens, you can see different personalities emerging in a sort of developmental sequence, so that a more and more mature personality emerges, a personality which is more aware of the different subpersonalities, or integrates them more.

OLLE MALLANDER: Then there are, of course, more direct artistic influences from the East – Ravi Shankar for example.

SANGHARAKSHITA: Certainly, there are some Eastern influences already to be discerned in Western art forms. Even the Beatles were influenced to a small degree by Indian classical music. And there is Messaien's *Turangalila Symphony* – *turaṃgalīla* being the Sanskrit for 'the far-going play'.

OLLE MALLANDER: I would like to ask a general question about the sacredness of art, or the degree of sacredness in art. When does a work of art function on a sacred level? There must always be an amalgam of many layers, but sometimes one can get a strange feeling of holiness and sacredness.... These are strong words and I rather hesitate to use them; but I suppose what I am talking about is a sense of the sublime.

SANGHARAKSHITA: We must not take the idea of developing 'religious art' too literally. In *The Religion of Art* I distinguish between conventionally religious art and art which is genuinely religious.[212] You can take a picture of a so-called sacred subject, the Madonna and Child for instance (to take an example from Christian art), painted without any real feeling. What you will have is a painting that is religious only by tradition or association, not by virtue of its inner spirit, or the artist's insight and realization. On the other hand, someone with real insight can take the same subject, and make it not only formally but genuinely religious. Then again, you can have a painting that is genuinely religious, in that it is the product of real spiritual insight, but not associated with any specific formally religious imagery – it could be a landscape, or a painting of a flower.

In modern times, maybe since the Renaissance, artistic inspiration has tended to flow less and less in conventionally religious channels. The English critic Middleton Murry said, 'When Roman Catholicism died in Britain, then English literature was born.'[213] By this he meant that the spiritual energies which formerly flowed through the church were now free to flow outside it and find expression in secular art and literature. If people today are looking for inspiration – let's say in literary terms, leaving aside the visual arts – unless they are definitely Christian they don't read the Bible, or other formally religious literature. They look to the great poets and novelists. They will get their spiritual nourishment from *those* sources, not from ostensibly religious ones. We have always to distinguish between art which is not genuinely religious in feeling, whether it is formally religious or not, and art which is genuinely religious in feeling, even when it is expressed in secular terms.

THE JOURNEY TO IL CONVENTO

As the opening paragraphs make clear, this paper was presented in the context of a three-month ordination retreat held in Tuscany, Italy, in 1984.

We have all made the journey to Il Convento.[214] Most of you have made it for the first time, a few for the third or even the fourth time. Of those who have made the journey for the first time most have made it in the hope of being ordained during the three months we shall be together here, and it is to them in particular that these remarks are addressed, even though what I have to say will also be applicable to those who have made the journey to Il Convento not in the hope of being ordained, for they are already ordained, but in order to help others to prepare themselves for ordination.

Addressing myself, then, to those of you who have made the journey to Il Convento for the first time, I wonder to what extent you realize the significance of this journey, and the real nature of its connection with your being ordained here. Initially, when you received your invitation to this pre-ordination course, it might have seemed to you that the journey to Il Convento was no more than a means to an end, the end being, of course, to participate in 'Tuscany 84', and, hopefully, to be ordained. It might have seemed that the process of getting here had no special significance. It was, perhaps, something to be got through as quickly and cheaply as possible, the main idea being that one should transport oneself from London or Glasgow or wherever to Il Convento with the minimum of fuss and bother. On the other hand, when you received your invitation it might have occurred to you that the journey to Il Convento presented an opportunity of enjoying something you had not, perhaps, been able to enjoy for a long time, especially if you had been working in an FWBO co-op, i.e. a holiday, either with one of your spiritual friends or, less mindfully, in company of a rather different type. But even if you were concerned simply to get here, or simply to enjoy a little holiday en route, it will almost certainly have dawned on you, sooner or later, that the journey to Il Convento was more than just a means to an end, more than just an agreeable interlude, and that it had a significance of its own that it was not easy to formulate in conceptual terms. Indeed, for some of you it might have seemed that the more familiar you became with those magic words Il Convento, Batignano, Grosseto, and the more mantra-like the way in which they rolled off your tongue, the more the phrase 'the journey to Il Convento' came for you to assume overtones of a mysterious and even archetypal nature.

That this should be so is not surprising. On more than one occasion I have spoken in terms of our acting out, in the course of our lives, what I have called our personal myth, and the various journeys we make are often an important part of that myth. The journey is, in fact, a myth in its own right, or rather it is an archetype which finds expression in many myths and symbols, legends, and stories, though without being exhausted by them and without being identical with any or all of them. Thus we have the voyage of the Argo, or Jason's journey in quest of the Golden Fleece; Odysseus's ten-year journey from 'the ringing plains of windy Troy' back to his home in rocky Ithaca;[215] the Chosen People's still more protracted journey up from Egypt into the Promised Land; Monkey's journey to the West, i.e. from India, from which he and his companions returned to China with the *false* scriptures, the ones that had writing on them; the prophet Mohammed's Night Journey from Mecca to Jerusalem up through the heavens; Dante's journey through the Inferno, Purgatorio, and Paradiso; Christian's journey from the City of Destruction to the Heavenly Jerusalem; Bashō's journey to the Far North; and many other journeys by land and sea, through the air and through worlds and even universes. All these journeys possess, some of them more obviously than others, a significance that is not exhausted by their literal, surface meaning. This being the case it is only to be expected that a journey as crucial as the journey to Il Convento, that is to say, the journey to the venue of ordination, with all that ordination implies, should be imbued with a very special significance, even though that significance might not be immediately apparent.

To begin with, the journey to Il Convento is a journey from West to East. Most of you started your journey in England, and even those of you who did not actually start it there spent some time in England before setting out on the journey to Il Convento. The East is, of course, the source of light, for that is where the sun rises, and from time immemorial a journey towards the East has been a journey towards the light, or a spiritual journey. In medieval Iran there was even a school of mystic philosophers known as the Orientals (*ishrāqīya*), in the sense of those who were 'oriented' or who turned themselves in the direction of, and travelled towards, the 'Orient' or world of supersensitive realities, and who spoke of entry into that world in terms of arriving at an 'oriental' knowledge (*'ilm ishrāqī*).[216] In more recent times a distinguished German author has spoken of a mysterious 'Journey to the East' undertaken not by one person only but by a number of people, and has even written a book with that title.[217] Thus the journey to Il Convento is significant in that inasmuch as it is a journey to the East, it is a spiritual journey, or a pilgrimage. One might, of course, object that Il Convento is not very far east of England and that a real journey to the East would take one not to Italy but to India, not to Batignano but to Bhaja.[218] That would be quite true, in a sense, and perhaps there is something to be said for our holding these pre-ordination courses further afield than we do, so that it would be a question not of a journey to Il Convento, or even a journey to Bhaja, but of a journey to Sarnath or Bodh Gaya. Nevertheless it must not be forgotten that the journey to the East does not really terminate at any particular point, either in the literal or the metaphysical sense. All that is really necessary is that our journey, whether long or short, should be a journey to the East, i.e. in the direction of the East, and that it should be a journey to the East in the *real* sense of the term. Whether it is a journey to Il Convento, or to Bodh Gaya, or even to Padmaloka, is of secondary importance.

Though the journey to Il Convento is a journey from west to east, it is also a journey from north to south. It is a journey from the Protestant north to the Catholic south, or even, to some extent, to the pagan south. It is a journey from cold to warmth, from gloom to sunshine, from pink complexions and blond hair to swarthy complexions and black hair, from pine forests to olive groves, from barley fields to vineyards, from the grim figures of Thor and Wotan to the more pleasing ones of Ceres and Dionysius. It is a journey from skies and seas that are nearly always grey to seas and skies that are rarely anything but blue. In another sense it is a journey from the surface of things to the depths, from the conscious to the unconscious mind, from brain cells to bloodstream (as D. H. Lawrence might say), from the modern to the archaic, from the present to the past, from the rational to the irrational. In order to go forward we have to go back, or rather, we have to go forward and back at the same time. In order to move in the direction of the east we have to move in the direction of the south. In order to travel towards the region of light and life we have to travel towards – and through – the region of darkness and death.

Besides being a journey from west to east, and from north to south, the journey to Il Convento is not a straight journey but a crooked or zigzag journey. Most of you have made all sorts of detours to get here, so that if all your different routes were to be plotted on a map of Europe it would show not a single beaten track but a complicated network of lines all of which eventually converged on Il Convento. But if you took advantage of the journey to Il Convento to do a little sightseeing, why did you decide to see something of Rome and Naples (I am taking hypothetical examples, since I do not know exactly where each one of you went), rather than Venice and Ravenna? What was it that drew you to the red-ribbed dome of the Santa Maria di Fiore in Florence, as it seemingly floats above a sea of red roofs? Why were you so keen to see the Leaning Tower of Pisa? What sort of mental picture did you have of these places, or what did they mean to you, that you decided to visit this one rather than that? Practical considerations played a part, no doubt, but in the ultimate analysis the deciding factor must have been subjective or even largely unconscious. Nor is that all. In Rome and Naples, as in Venice and Ravenna and any of the innumerable other places you may have visited, there will have been many churches and palaces, art galleries and museums, gardens and grottoes. What led you to one rather than to another of them, or caused you to linger in front of this painting or piece of sculpture rather than in front of that? Last year an Order member who saw Michelangelo's *David* in the Academy at Florence afterwards reported that he was so overwhelmed that he felt like prostrating himself before it. Why did he not (apparently) feel like prostrating himself before Orcagna's tabernacle – or, for the matter of that, before Donatello's *David*? In making your way from one city or town of Italy to another, from one church or museum to another, and from one painting or sculpture to another, you were no doubt directed not so much by logic as by a sort of irrational wisdom, an obscure awareness of an inner need, and it was because you were so directed that your journey to Il Convento was crooked in both the literal and the metaphysical sense, for as Yeats tells us:

> Wisdom is a butterfly
> And not a gloomy bird of prey.[219]

It is a butterfly because a butterfly floats from flower to flower, or flutters aloft in the air, in zigzag fashion, as you must have observed in the course of your walks in the vicinity of Il Convento, where the butterflies are apparently more abundant than they are in most parts of England, as well as sometimes being of an unfamiliar species. I remember reading somewhere that in China the streets used to be built not straight but crooked, with many sudden bends, because people believed that evil spirits moved only in straight lines, and could not go round corners. In modern times, of course, many Western cities have been laid out on a grid plan, with one perfectly straight avenue crossing another exactly at right angles. Paris, for instance, was rebuilt on this kind of plan in the middle of the nineteenth century, the reason being that in the event of an armed uprising the broad, straight avenues would enable the government to bring is artillery to bear on the revolutionary masses with maximum effect. Bullets and artillery shells, like evil spirits, cannot go round corners.

To return to the journey to Il Convento, in the course of your sightseeing you will have been led to one building rather than another, and have lingered in front of this sculpture or painting rather than that, not so much because you found it of special historic or artistic interest (though this may have been the case at times), but rather because you were deeply moved by it and because it possessed for you a significance that you were at a loss to explain. Perhaps you were affected more by sculptures and paintings than by buildings, and more by individual sculptured or painted figures than by groups of figures or by landscapes, but be that as it may, the likelihood is that a certain work of art moved you so deeply because it represented an image or symbol, and because this image or symbol embodied an archetype – though it is important not to make too hard and fast a distinction either between the image or symbol and the sculptured or painted form by which it is represented, or between the archetype and the image or symbol in which it is embodied. Moreover, if you were sufficiently receptive to what you saw, and sufficiently sensitive, the irrational wisdom that directed you to a particular sculpture or painting will have been clarified and strengthened by your contact with that work of art to such an extent as to be transformed into imagination, by which I do not mean fancy but a faculty for the perception of images, in the sense of images that are the embodiments of archetypes. That faculty once developed, you will have moved from one work of art to another, or from one image to another, finding each work of art, and each image, more deeply moving and more highly significant than the last. Thus the journey to Il Convento is not only a crooked journey from one image to another. It is a journey through a world of images, or through an imaginal world, and herein lies its greatest significance.

All this obviously requires explanation, and you may be thinking that I am moving ahead far too rapidly. You may even be thinking that your own journey to Il Convento does not correspond very closely to the journey to Il Convento as described by me. Perhaps the best thing I can do, therefore, is to give you one or two examples, from my own experience, of the sort of thing about which I have been speaking. These examples are not drawn from any of my own journeys to Il Convento, but they are at least drawn from a journey to Italy. This journey took place in the summer of 1966, when I passed through Italy on my way to Greece, entering the country by way of the Gothard Pass and leaving it from the port of Brindisi. It was my first visit to Italy, and since I had been intensely interested in Italian art, especially Italian Renaissance art, ever since my childhood, I wanted to make the fullest possible use of my opportunity. Wherever I went I tried to see every church, palace, museum, and art gallery, and every sculpture and painting that each one of these contained. In this way I traversed northern Italy, passing through Milan, Bergamo, Verona, Vicenza, Venice, Padua, and Ravenna. Probably I saw hundreds of buildings and thousands of sculptures and paintings. As the days went by, however, I became aware that I was being drawn to some paintings much more than others, and that the attraction often had more to do with the theme of the paintings than with the quality of their execution or the reputation of the artist.

One of the subjects by which I was most drawn was St Jerome. One of the Four Fathers of the Latin Church, St Jerome lived in the latter half of the fourth and the first quarter of the fifth century, and was a contemporary of St Augustine, another of the Fathers, with whom he had an acrimonious correspondence. When he was already middle-aged St Jerome left Rome and went to live in the Holy Land, at Bethlehem, and it is at this stage of his career that he is usually depicted in Christian art. In the course of that journey in 1966 I must have seen two or three dozen St Jeromes, and I have seen many others since, either in the original or in reproduction. He is usually represented either in the desert, or in his cell, and either on his knees in front of a crucifix, or at his desk. I was drawn most of all by those paintings which represented him in his cell or study, with an hourglass in front of him, a lion (which he had tamed) sleeping at his feet, his red cardinal's hat hanging on the wall (due to his association with the reigning pope he was traditionally regarded as a cardinal, though cardinals as such did not come into existence until many centuries later), a large volume open before him, and a quill pen in his hand. St Jerome was responsible for the production of the Vulgate, the standard Latin version of the Bible, which was in use throughout the Middle Ages, and when represented in his study he is generally understood to be engaged in this great work. He is represented as a very old man, with a long white beard. Sometimes his cell-study is practically bare, sometimes furnished with every scholarly comfort and convenience.

Somehow this theme, or image, took hold of my mind. St Jerome was the wise old man, one of Jung's archetypes of the collective unconscious. That he was engaged in the work of translation, especially that of rendering the word of God into ordinary human speech, meant that something hidden in the depths was being brought to the surface, or brought from darkness into light. Thus St Jerome was the alchemist – another embodiment of the wise old man. His cell-study (sometimes depicted as a cave) was the alchemist's laboratory. Indeed, it was the alchemist's alembic, in which the Red King united with the White Queen, or his crucible, in which lead was transmuted into gold. In this way the image of St Jerome in his study tended to merge with other images, not only of the alchemist in his laboratory, but also of the philosopher in his study – especially Rembrandt's philosopher, as he sits with the staircase spiralling up through the darkness behind him.[220]

No doubt I was drawn to the image of St Jerome partly because of my personal situation at the time. I was living in the desert. I had left the 'Rome' of collective, official, even establishment, Buddhism, and was seeking to return to the origins of Buddhism in the actual life and experience of the Buddha and his immediate disciples. Not only that. I was trying to teach Buddhism in the West, which meant I was trying to communicate the spirit of the Dharma in terms of Western rather than in terms of Eastern culture. I was thus a translator, with all that that implies in the way of seeking to fathom the uttermost depths of what one is trying to translate so that one may translate it faithfully, i.e. bring its meaning to the surface, or from darkness into light. Thus I was drawn to the image of St Jerome, and was able to see that image as an embodiment of the archetype of the wise old man as 'translator' and alchemist, because I had a personal affinity with that image, or because there was something in me that corresponded to that image. In other words, I had possessed, or had developed, a faculty for the perception of that kind of image. I possessed an imagination or, since the word imagination is often used in a pejorative sense, I possessed at least the rudiments of what has been termed the imaginal faculty. This imaginal faculty enabled me to see in the figure of St Jerome more than what was given by the paintings themselves, whether considered as 'works of art' in the modern sense or as examples of traditional religious iconography. It enabled me to see the figure of St Jerome – who in a sense was no longer St Jerome – as in fact belonging to a completely different plane. It enabled me to see him as an image that had its existence in a world of images or in an imaginal world – a world to which one has access by virtue of the imaginal faculty.

Another image to which I was drawn at that time was the image of the angel, though I was not drawn to it as much as to the image of St Jerome. Indeed, I must have been drawn to this particular image quite early in life, for I can remember executing a whole series of pencil drawings of angels when I was 13 or 14. These angels I depicted as hovering in, or flying through, the air, and since one of them carried a sword he was, I suppose, the archangel Michael. Some years later, during my stay in Kalimpong, I was deeply impressed by the image of the angel as he appears in Rilke's *Duino Elegies*.[221] More recently, having allowed my interest in angels to lapse for a number of years, I have taken up the study of this image again and have devoted a certain amount of thought to it. Some of you may recall that thanks to reproductions of the well-known painting in the National Gallery, London, the image of *Tobias and the Angel* is now well established in the FWBO as an image of *kalyāṇa mitratā* or spiritual friendship.[222] You may have encountered other versions of the same subject in the course of your journey to Il Convento, as I myself did in the course of both my 1966 visit to Italy and my four journeys to Il Convento. That you should see paintings of *Tobias and the Angel* on the way to Il Convento is wholly appropriate, for your journey to Il Convento parallels Tobias's journey to Rages, and like him you need to be accompanied by an angel, whether in visible or invisible form. Indeed, unless you are accompanied by an angel the journey to Il Convento is not the journey to Il Convento at all, but only a journey.

Now both the image of St Jerome and the image of the angel are Christian images, and you may be wondering to what extent they can be of significance to a Buddhist. The difficulty is more apparent than real, and is perhaps best resolved by a reference to Jung's archetypes of the collective unconscious. As I think is well known, in studying the dreams of his patients Jung discovered that these often reproduced, quite spontaneously, themes and motifs that play an important part in the various mythologies of mankind, as well as in the teachings of the different religions. Some patients, for instance, described, and even painted, circular figures which bore a remarkable resemblance to Buddhist mandalas. From all this Jung eventually concluded that there were various basic psychic patterns, or archetypes, which were common to the whole human race, both past and present, and which found expression in myths, in religious beliefs, in dreams, and in works of art. These common psychic patterns he termed the 'archetypes of the collective unconscious'. Though the patterns or archetypes were common to the whole human race, however, the various forms in which they expressed themselves were not. The forms were culturally determined, and therefore extremely varied. Thus, although the images of St Jerome and the angel are Christian images, they are Christian only in the sense that in them an archetype which is of universal significance and value has been clothed in a Christian, Italian, Renaissance form – even in a form peculiar to a particular artist. It is for this reason that it is possible for a Christian image to be of significance to a Buddhist. What the Buddhist is drawn to is not so much the Christian form of the image as the archetype of which that image is an embodiment, and it is therefore really the archetype that is of significance to him. In some cases, of course, the form taken by a Christian image, e.g. the Crucifixion, will be so repugnant to Buddhist sentiment as to render it quite impossible for a Buddhist to be drawn to the image and, therefore, in this instance at least, to the archetype of which it is the embodiment. In other cases, such as the images of St Jerome and of the angel, the fact that the form taken by the image is conditioned by, or belongs to, a culture with which the (Western) Buddhist happens to be familiar, and with which he feels a definite emotional connection, may even mean that he is drawn to it to a greater extent than he is drawn to its traditional Buddhist counterpart, where such exists, so that he is in the uncomfortable position of finding the Christian image of significance to him on account of its being the embodiment of an archetype of which he has a better intellectual understanding, and even a keener spiritual appreciation, in specifically Buddhist terms. In yet other cases, both the Christian image and its Buddhist counterpart may be of significance to a Buddhist, and it may be clear to him that both images are embodiments, within their respective cultures, of one and the same archetype, even though he is at the same time fully aware that in Buddhism the archetype is incorporated within a much broader and more meaningful context.

For me this was especially so with regard to the image of the angel, which was probably one of the reasons I was drawn to it. The image of the angel, though Christian, not only has its immediate antecedents in classical antiquity, but also its counterparts in practically all other religions and cultures, as a glance at the illustrations to Peter Lamborn Wilson's well-known book, *Angels*,[223] will be sufficient to show. In the case of Buddhism, the principal counterparts of the image of the angel are the *deva* and the bodhisattva, as represented in traditional Buddhist art. The Buddhist may well feel that the image of the bodhisattva is the embodiment par excellence of the particular archetype in question. Indeed, he may feel that the archetype of which the bodhisattva is the embodiment, and which the image of the angel reflects in a different cultural context and on a lower spiritual level, is nothing less than the archetype of Enlightenment, as it may be termed, and as such immeasurably transcends the archetypes that were the subject of Jung's discoveries. This implies an enlargement of the meaning of the term 'archetype' far beyond the significance it possesses for any current system of psychology. It also implies a stratification, so to speak, of images, in accordance with the degree to which they are the embodiments of a particular archetype, and even, perhaps, a stratification of the archetypes themselves. This in turn implies a stratification, in the sense of an arrangement in a progressive, hierarchical order, of the faculty by which the images themselves are perceived, or rather, a stratification of the successive stages of its unfoldment or manifestation. Thus one arrives at the conception of a hierarchy of levels of the imagination, or imaginal *faculty*, corresponding to a hierarchy of levels of images and archetypes, or imaginal *world*. In Buddhism this imaginal world is known as the world – or worlds – of the gods, access to the different planes and sub-planes of which can be obtained through the cultivation of the corresponding mental state, in the form of a particular 'concentration' (*dhyāna*) or sublime abode (*brahma vihāra*).

But though I have spoken of the imaginal faculty, the expression should not be taken too literally. The imagination, or image-perceiving faculty, is not so much a faculty among faculties as the man – the spiritual man – himself. It is spoken of as a faculty because, in the case of the vast majority of people, it exists in such a rudimentary form that it appears to be simply a 'faculty' like, for instance, reason or emotion, or because it has not yet been developed or manifested at all. The imaginal faculty is, in reality, the man himself, because when one truly perceives an image one perceives it with the whole of oneself, or with one's whole being. When one truly perceives an image, therefore, one is transported to the world to which that image belongs and becomes, if only for the time being, an inhabitant of that world. In other words, truly to perceive an image means to become an image, so that when one speaks of the imagination, or the imaginal faculty, what one is really speaking of is *image perceiving image*. That is to say, in perceiving an image what one really perceives is, in a sense, oneself.

By this time you may be thinking that I have got rather a long way from the journey to Il Convento, but that is not really the case. Buddhism sees mundane existence as stratified into three great planes or 'worlds', each with its subsidiary worlds or sub-planes. These three worlds or planes (*loka, dhātu*) are those of (1) desire for sensuous experience (*kāma*), (2) archetypal form (*rūpa*), and (3) no archetypal form (*arūpa*) or, perhaps we should say, extremely subtle archetypal form. 'Beyond' these three worlds there lies the unconditioned or transcendental. In terms of spiritual cosmography the spiritual life consists of a journey from the world or plane of sensuous desire, through the worlds or planes of archetypal form and extremely subtle archetypal form, to the unconditioned or transcendental, and it is of this archetypal journey that the journey to Il Convento is an image or symbol. Thus when you start your journey by leaving England you are not just leaving grey skies. What you are really doing is leaving your old interests and activities, your old habits and attachments, your old way of life, and even your old self. What you are really doing is leaving the world of sensuous desire. Similarly, when you visit this or that town or city en route, and do your sightseeing, you are not just looking at churches and palaces, museums and art galleries, gardens and grottoes, not just admiring buildings, sculptures, and paintings. What you are really doing is moving from one image, i.e. archetype-image, to another, or travelling through a world of images. What you are really doing is traversing the world or plane of archetypal form. (The world or plane of extremely subtle archetypal form falls outside the scope of the comparison – except, perhaps, in the case of those who spent some time in the Alps.) In the same way, when you arrive at Il Convento you arrive at the threshold of the Transcendental, for you have made the journey to Il Convento in the hope of being ordained or, in more traditional language, of being able to go for Refuge to the Three Jewels, and not only are the Three Jewels essentially transcendental but the act of going for Refuge to them is, ultimately, transcendental too.

Thus the journey to Il Convento is not only a journey from west to east, and from north to south, not only a crooked or zigzag journey, not only an opportunity for sightseeing. It is also an inner journey, an inner exploration, that takes one through the three great worlds or planes of mundane existence up to the very threshold of the Transcendental. Of course, I hardly need tell you that however successfully you might have accomplished the journey to Il Convento in the literal sense – and the fact that you are here at all means that you have done at least that – in the metaphorical sense you have probably accomplished the journey only in the most rudimentary fashion. In particular, your journey through the world of images will probably have been of a very sketchy nature and have taken place at a comparatively low level. Indeed, it may have consisted in little more than a series of brief forays into unfamiliar regions where images loomed as though through mist rather than revealing themselves in brilliant sunshine against skies eternally blue. But even if this should have been the case it does not matter very much. The real journey to Il Convento has to be made not once but many times. Each time you make the journey you make it in a more thoroughgoing fashion or, so to speak, at a higher level. It is like making your way up a mountain by a spiral path. Each time you circle the mountain you circle it at a higher level, but it is the same mountain that you are circling. Thus each time you make the journey to Il Convento and leave the world of sensuous desire, traverse the world of images, and arrive at the threshold of the Transcendental, you do so in a fuller and more effective manner than you did before. Your old way of life, and your old self, is increasingly abandoned, while far from being a series of brief forays into unfamiliar regions, your journey through the world of images is a more and more protracted sojourn among archetype-images of ever-increasing refinement, richness, beauty, and sublimity among which you feel more and more at home. Christian images will, no doubt, eventually be left far behind, and perhaps Buddhist images too, and one will find oneself in the presence of the archetypes which those images embody, and even in the presence of the archetypes of the archetypes.

But before that happens one will perhaps have realized that images are not such fixed and definite things as one originally thought. Images are fluid. They can change, which means that their significance can change. Perhaps I can best illustrate what I mean with the help of a short story. In the course of my life I have written only six or seven short stories,[224] though I have had ideas for many more, and the short story to which I refer has not actually been written down. The idea of it came to me a few weeks ago as a result of the sightseeing Prasannasiddhi and I had been doing in Pisa in the course of our latest journey to Il Convento. As you know, sightseeing can be quite tiring, especially when one is getting on in years, and I think the story must have come to me as a result of the tiredness I experienced one day after we had visited the National Museum of St Matthew, the cathedral and baptistery, the Leaning Tower, the Museum of the Sinopias, and several churches. The story began with two people coming to Italy on a sort of cultural tour. I imagined them visiting all the famous Italian cities, and seeing the great churches and palaces, the museums and art galleries, much as I had done in 1966. One day they happen to find themselves inside a particularly fine cathedral (and this is where the story really begins), equipped with the usual Crucifixions, Madonnas (both with and without Child), Annunciations, saints, and martyrs (being grilled, beheaded, sawn in two, broken on the wheel, shot full of arrows, torn with pincers, skinned alive, etc.), Nativities, Ascensions, Assumptions, and Last Judgements, together with sundry cherubs and putti. Since the place is so vast, and there is so much to see, the two friends spend several hours looking round the cathedral. Moreover, they are so interested in all the paintings and sculptures, which are of excellent quality, that they fail to notice that the place has gradually emptied and that the sacristan, thinking that everyone had left, has locked the massive bronze doors for the night. The younger of the two friends goes in search of a side entrance that might still be open, while his older companion, feeling in need of a rest, sits down on a bench at the foot of one of the enormous Gothic pillars of the nave. By that time it is practically dark, and he has not been sitting there for more than a few minutes when he hears a confused sound of footsteps and voices. It is almost as though a party of sightseers had entered the cathedral. But it is not a party of sightseers. On lifting his head he sees in the dim light that now pervades the whole building an extraordinary sight. The sculpted and painted figures at which he and his friend had gazed so intently only a short while ago are now stepping down from their marble pedestals, and out of their carved and gilded frames, on to the floor of the cathedral. There are hundreds of them, and after a momentary pause some of them start moving down the aisle in his direction. The sound of footsteps and voices grows gradually louder as they approach.

What followed was the main part of the story, and was to have taken up the greatest amount of space, but since I have not worked it out in detail I can give you only a rough sketch of what happened. No doubt this will be enough for my present purpose. The idea was that once they had stepped down from their pedestals, and out of their picture frames, the figures should start behaving in a way that was not completely in accordance with their official character, so to speak. They were off duty, now that the cathedral was closed, and were free to behave as they liked. Christ stretches his arms and says that he is glad to get down from that cross for a few hours, while the Virgin Mary complains that the Child gets heavier every day and she does not know how much longer she will be able to stand here holding him. As for the Child himself, he is playing with some of the more mischievous-looking putti, and they are actually trying to use one of the cherubs, who is of course all head and wings, as a football. The Archangel Michael lays aside his sword and his scales, takes off his shining armour, and starts doing press-ups in the middle of the nave. God the Father then comes along, having stepped down out of an enormous fresco of the Last Judgement. He is rather worried, and mutters into his beard, saying that he is fed up with judging people, and in any case thinks he has made quite a few mistakes. As if to confirm his suspicions, a crowd of figures out of the same fresco surround him and indignantly complain about the treatment they have received. Some of those who have been sent to heaven complain that it is a dull and boring place, and ask to be sent somewhere more interesting, while some of those who have been sent to hell complain that the devils do not give them any attention. They could stand anything except that, they say. Even poor old St Jerome is there. His back is stiff from spending so many hours at his desk, and he is glad to have a respite from that endless work of translation. As for the lion, having woken up, shaken himself, and followed St Jerome out of the picture frame, he takes a leisurely stroll down the aisle, pausing to rub himself against the legs of various saints and martyrs, all of whom have something to contribute to the proceedings. St John the Baptist remarks that it is nice to have his head back on again, while St Agatha makes a similar remark about her breasts. St Lawrence hopes that no one will mind him mentioning that his gridiron is in need of repair. St Agnes confesses to St Mary Magdalene that she is tired of looking after all those lambs, while St Mary Magdalene confides to St Agnes that she thinks hair shirts don't really suit her any more. Salome, who is of course neither a saint nor a martyr, asks her mother whether she ought to learn a new dance, since Herod seems to be getting tired of the old one after all these years.

How the story developed from that point onwards I found it difficult to decide. Perhaps the complaints that the figures from the Last Judgement make to God the Father become so loud that the elder of the two friends, sitting there on his bench in the nave, gives a start, rubs his eyes, and finds that the sculpted and painted figures have returned to their pedestals and picture frames, and that the place is again practically dark. Or perhaps the figures suddenly become aware of his presence and make a concerted rush at him, or try to drag him up on to a pedestal, or into a picture frame. Anyway, it has all been a dream, and he is now awake. His young friend is standing beside him, shaking him vigorously by the shoulder. He has found a side entrance still unlocked, he says, and they must hurry or it will be too late. Thus the short story ends. It is not, of course, very original. I have read one novel, and at least two short stories, in which the statues in a museum all come to life and have various adventures, and these may have influenced me. Moreover, to make one's principal character undergo some highly unusual experience which in the end turns out to have been a dream is a rather hackneyed device. Nonetheless, I hope that despite its shortcomings this story of mine has illustrated the point that images are not such fixed and definite things as one might have thought, and that their significance can change. Images and their significance are, in fact, changing all the time. The angel as represented in Italian Gothic art is very different from the angel as represented in Italian Renaissance art, and both are very different from the angel as represented in Italian Baroque art, besides which there are within each of these periods great differences as between the angel as represented by one artist and the angel as represented by another. Thus over the period of a few hundred years the image of the angel, together with the significance of that image, is seen to undergo a whole series of developments and transformations even within the limits of a single national culture.

Images can not only change; they can also be broken. They are broken when they have lost all significance for us, a process which begins when we no longer perceive them with the imaginal faculty or, what amounts to much the same thing, when we no longer respond to the particular archetype they embody. In the literal sense, images are broken when the paintings and sculptures which are their embodiments are smashed or burned. This usually happens when the images themselves no longer have significance for us, as was the case with the Puritans when they smashed and burned the 'superstitious' paintings and sculptures that adorned the cathedrals and churches of England, or when their meaning is completely misunderstood, as was the case with the Muslim invaders of India who smashed and burned the 'idols' they discovered in the Buddhist temples and monasteries. Perhaps it is not without significance that the journey to Il Convento should be a journey to what was formerly a Christian monastery. Il Convento di Santa Croce, to give the place its full title, until a little less than two hundred years ago was occupied by a community of brown-robed Franciscan friars who in theory, at least, had 'come together' – the literal meaning of the word from which convent is derived – in order to live in accordance with the ideal of Christian perfection as exemplified by St Francis, the founder of their order. How long Il Convento di Santa Croce had by that time been in existence I do not know. It may have dated back to the Middle Ages, or it may have been a recent foundation. Whichever may have been the case, the friars were expelled, and the building itself was badly damaged, about two hundred years ago, during the Napoleonic Wars – presumably at the time of Napoleon's conflict with the Papacy. Whether the friars returned to their monastery after the downfall of the great tyrant I do not know, but if any of them did return, and if they did so without delay, it must have given them great satisfaction to look – as we can still look today – from the olive groves of Il Convento down to the great coastal plain, and from there to the island of Elba, lying a dim grey shape on the horizon, behind its strip of blue sea, and to think that Napoleon was confined there. It must have given them still greater satisfaction when, after the escape from Elba and the Hundred Days, he was finally confined to the island of St Helena, a much less pleasant place. On the other hand, human nature being what it is, they may have lamented his fall, and even offered up prayers on his behalf, for he had eventually made his peace with the Church and signed a concordat with the Pope, as many a tyrant had done before him, and as tyrants have done since.

Thinking about Napoleon, I remember that last year my own journey to Il Convento included four days in Paris. Among the places I went to see with Prasannasiddhi, as well as with Subhuti and Silabhadra, who were giving us their company as far as the French capital, was Napoleon's tomb. As might have been expected, this was a large and imposing structure in extremely bad taste, seemingly dedicated not just to the glorification of Napoleon Bonaparte but to the glorification of the spirit of militarism or, to put it more crudely, the spirit of war. To walk round inside the tomb, with its clumsy neo-classical sculptures and its vulgarly expensive marbles, was to make a foray into the world of the *asuras* or anti-gods, or into that world of aggression, competition, and conflict that has to be left behind by anyone engaged on the journey to Il Convento. To make matters worse, a shop next door to the Tomb was doing a brisk business in Napoleonic postcards and souvenirs of every kind, including swords, suits of armour, and model soldiers. After visiting the tomb I felt a strong urge to write an open letter to President Mitterand pointing out that if he really was a socialist, and really believed in peace, he should close down the tomb of Napoleon forthwith, since it was the negation of everything he stood for. However, I did not write the letter, since I found it difficult to believe that anything so contrary to French national sentiment would be allowed to reach him. All the same, I am unwilling to give up the idea entirely, and may yet find a way of carrying it out. But that is another story.

The reason why it is not without significance that the journey to Il Convento should be a journey to what was formerly a Christian monastery is that that monastery is in a state of disrepair and dilapidation. What happened to it after the monks returned, if they ever did, I am unable to tell you. At some time during the last two hundred years the place was a glass factory, as the lumps of green vitreous material that strew the surrounding area testify. More recently it was used for agricultural purposes until it passed into the hands of the present owner, who uses the place during the summer months for putting on small-scale productions of seventeenth-century Italian operas and other works – a fact which is also not without significance, though what that significance is I shall leave you to discover for yourselves. Yet despite having been put to such a variety of uses, Il Convento remains in much the same condition as, I imagine, it was left by Napoleon's troops after the expulsion of the friars. What was once the church is hardly even a shell, the roof having been ripped off and the façade reduced to a heap of rubble. Though the cloister is more or less intact, several of the brick pillars are damaged, while hardly a trace remains of the frescoes that once covered the walls. The journey to Il Convento is thus a journey to a place of broken images. In the literal sense there are, indeed, not even any broken images, though on the occasion of my first journey to Il Convento I did see, before someone put it away in a cupboard, a cracked wooden figure of St Anthony of Padua that looked as though it was badly in need of a coat of paint. Since the journey to Il Convento is a journey to a place of broken images, the Going for Refuge which is the whole purpose of that journey takes place – and this is the point I really want to make – in the midst of broken images. We become Buddhists, in fact, in the midst of the ruins of Christian civilization and culture, and though the images of that culture may still draw us to some extent, in their specifically Christian sense they no longer have any significance for us. That is in fact why we go for Refuge. That is why in the midst of the ruins of Christian culture, in the midst of broken images, we set up our own Buddhist images, which will, we hope, eventually take over and reconstruct the whole place.

As I have said more than once, the journey to Il Convento takes us from the world of sensuous desire, through the world of archetypal form, to the threshold of the Transcendental. The real journey to Il Convento is therefore a journey that must be made not once but many times, each time at a higher level. So much, perhaps, has already been made clear. What also needs to be made clear is that it is possible to make the journey to Il Convento without coming to Il Convento in the literal sense at all. We can make it without leaving England, without seeing Italy, for since the journey to Il Convento is an inner journey it is a journey that we can make staying in our own house and sitting in our own room. As Laozi says, 'Without looking out of the window, one can see the Way of Heaven.'[225] But although this is true it is no more than half the truth, or even less than half. Man has not only an inner but an outer being; he consists not only of mind but also of speech and body. Consequently, if one really wants to make the journey to Il Convento – if one really wants to leave the world of sensuous desire, traverse the world of images or the imaginal world, and arrive at the threshold of the Transcendental – then one will want to do so in the most complete and total manner possible. One will not be content to go forth metaphorically. One will want to go forth literally too. Thus one's inner journey will be paralleled by an outer journey, and this outer journey will not necessarily be a journey from London or Glasgow to Il Convento. It may be a journey from Bombay to Bhaja, or from Manchester to Padmaloka. But wherever it begins and wherever it ends, it will be a journey to a place where one can be ordained, a place where one can go for Refuge to the Three Jewels with body, speech, and mind.

Even though one's outer journey does not necessarily take one to Il Convento, there is no doubt that at the present juncture in the history of the FWBO those who are in a position to make the journey to Il Convento in the literal sense are particularly fortunate. I am therefore glad that this year fifteen of you have been able to make that journey for the first time, and to make it in the hope, now about to be fulfilled, of being ordained here. I hope that you will be able to make the real journey to Il Convento many, many times. I hope that each time you make the journey you will be able to make a more decisive break with the world of sensuous desire. I hope that each time you make it you will be able to explore the world of images at ever higher and more refined levels. Above all, I hope that as you truly arrive at the threshold of the Transcendental your Going for Refuge will be transformed into a transcendental Going for Refuge. When that happens, the purpose of the whole journey to Il Convento will be fulfilled.

SAINT JEROME REVISITED

This paper is a sequel to The Journey to Il Convento, and was presented on the same 1984 retreat.

In the course of the paper on 'The Journey to Il Convento' which I read to you a few weeks ago I spoke of our being drawn to one image or symbol rather than another, often without understanding why, and by way of illustration I described how in the course of my journey to Italy in 1966 I was myself drawn by two images. One of these was the image of St Jerome. Since I described him at some length in the paper, and moreover tried to explain why the image of St Jerome – especially St Jerome in his study, translating the Bible into Latin – should have been of significance to me at that time, I was under the impression that for the time being at least I was finished with that particular image and could forget all about it. But this did not turn out to be the case. Within a few days of reading the paper I found myself thinking about St Jerome quite a lot, and the more I thought about him the more significant the image of the old man bending over his desk in his cell, study, or cave seemed to be. It was as though an archetype-image, once activated, possesses a life of its own, and forces itself upon your attention, so to speak, whether you like it or not, and insists on continuing the conversation which, so far as you are concerned, is finished. I therefore decided that the best thing I could do would be to write another paper, devoted exclusively to the image of St Jerome, in the hope that once I had written it, and perhaps read it, I really would be finished with this particular image for the time being.

At first I thought I would write the paper when I was back at Padmaloka, and comfortably settled in my own study again. At Padmaloka I have all my books, and I would be able to look up all sorts of references to St Jerome, as well as to the various images and symbols with which the figure of the saint is traditionally associated. In the end, however, I decided to write the paper here at Il Convento, partly because the image of St Jerome refused to leave me in peace and partly because the thought occurred to me that it might, in fact, be an advantage if I was not able to look up any references, since then I would have to rely entirely on my memory and my imagination, which might mean that my imagination would be able to play a more active part in the writing of the paper. True, I might make mistakes in matters of historical fact, but that would not matter very much. There are one or two mistakes in 'The Journey to Il Convento'. After writing the paper I realized that although in my short story I had described the figure of God the Father stepping down from the fresco of the Last Judgement I had not, in fact, seen any such fresco. In all the frescoes of the Last Judgement which I had seen the judge was not God the Father but Christ, in accordance with the words of the Apostle's Creed, 'From whence he (i.e. Christ) shall come to judge the quick and the dead'. Similarly, after I had read the paper one of you questioned whether Il Convento di Santa Croce was originally occupied by Franciscan friars or Augustinian canons, since he had seen a reference to Augustinian canons on the back of one of the present-day Il Convento's opera programmes. Whether God the Father or Christ should have been described as stepping down from the fresco, and whether Il Convento was originally occupied by Franciscans or Augustinians, does not affect the validity of the points I was trying to make, so that so far as the paper is concerned the 'mistakes' have no significance. They may, however, have a psychological, or even a spiritual, significance of their own, but that is a matter into which I do not propose to enter on the present occasion. Instead, now that those of you who made the journey to Il Convento in the hope of being ordained have had your hope fulfilled, let us go back over some of the ground that we have already covered and examine it more thoroughly. Let us revisit St Jerome.

As I mentioned last time, St Jerome is usually represented either in the desert or in his cell – that is to say, when he is represented in his own right, so to speak, and not simply as one saint among many in an altarpiece or predella – and it is in his cell, or study, that we shall be visiting him. Before doing so, however, let us pay a short visit to St Jerome in the desert. Paintings of St Jerome in the desert exhibit a much greater variety than do paintings of St Jerome in his study, almost as though the traditional iconography was not so definitely fixed and the artist had greater freedom, at least in certain respects. Paintings of this sort sometimes represent, according to the title, not St Jerome in the desert but St Jerome performing penance. What they all really represent, however, is simply St Jerome in a landscape, and this is the best and most accurate way of describing them. Since the landscape was that of the Holy Land, to which St Jerome had retired from Rome, what the artists of the Italian Renaissance should have depicted was presumably the kind of landscape that Holman Hunt depicts in *The Scapegoat* – a dreary expanse of salt marshland with the bottle-green streak of the Dead Sea in the distance backed by a low range of weirdly glowing pink and mauve foothills.[226] In order to paint this landscape the Pre-Raphaelite artist had to make a journey to the Holy Land, but the artists of the Italian Renaissance made no such journey, and never thought of making it. They simply painted whatever landscape lay nearest to hand. The result is that, more often than not, St Jerome is seen not in the desert, or what the King James Bible calls the wilderness, but in the midst of an extremely beautiful, typically Tuscan or Umbrian landscape, with plenty of luxuriant Mediterranean vegetation and an abundance of picturesque rock formations. The landscape is not cultivated but wild, but it is wild with the wildness not of the desert but of Paradise before the Fall.

Sometimes St Jerome is shown performing penance, dressed in a sort of loincloth, often tattered, and either kneeling before or clasping a rude crucifix. Sometimes he sits on a rock, his head resting on his hand, as though deep in meditation. More often than not, his faithful lion can be seen somewhere in the picture, usually fast asleep, though in some of the more naive representations of the scene he appears to be sharing in St Jerome's devotions. In quite a number of paintings of St Jerome in a landscape the figure of the saint is quite tiny in comparison with the rest of the picture. In a few such cases it takes a minute or two to find the figure of St Jerome, which in relation to the surrounding countryside appears not only tiny but insignificant. What the artists had depicted was not St Jerome in the desert, or St Jerome doing penance, or even St Jerome in a landscape, but simply man in the midst of nature, and in these paintings nature, in her richness and abundance and beauty, appears serenely indifferent to the existential anguish of man – an anguish which she is, in fact, incapable of comprehending. Man and nature are strangers to each other. Though he lives in the midst of her, he is not *of* her. She knows him, if she knows him at all, only as a physical body, and as a physical body he is infinitely smaller than she is, and infinitely less powerful. What these representations of man in the midst of nature seemed to say is that viewed from the outside, or simply as a material object among material objects, man is a very insignificant creature. In order to appreciate his greatness, or what an Italian Renaissance philosopher calls 'the dignity of man',[227] it is necessary to view him from within, as a spiritual being among other spiritual beings, or at least among objects of spiritual significance. In other words, it is necessary to turn from St Jerome in the desert to St Jerome in his study.

St Jerome's study or cell is often depicted as a cave, the mouth of which can sometimes be seen in paintings of St Jerome in the desert or performing penance, either quite near at hand or up on the mountainside, depending on the scale of the painting. This cave thus constitutes a link between the two different representations of St Jerome or, one might even say, between the two different images of St Jerome, i.e. St Jerome in the desert, or performing penance, and St Jerome in his study translating the Bible. Now I have said that in order to appreciate the greatness of man it is necessary to view him from the inside, from within, as a spiritual being among spiritual beings. But it is only man himself who can view man in this way. Nature cannot do it. *She* is able to view him, if she views him at all, only from the outside: she sees him only as a physical body. In order to see himself as a spiritual being man has to stop viewing himself only as a physical body, as nature does, and *enter into the cave of the heart*. To begin with, the heart will appear to him as an object, even as a physical object or physical organ. That is why in paintings of St Jerome in the desert the cave can be seen, but it is seen from the outside, since there it is part of nature, part of the material universe. When man, as represented by the figure of St Jerome in a landscape, enters the cave, the cave is no longer object but subject. Man has turned himself inside out, as it were. St Jerome is no longer in the desert. He is in his study, and we are there in his study with him.

The first thing we notice about the study is that except for a few spiritually significant items such as a red hat, an hourglass, and a human skull, it is completely bare. (I am speaking of what may be termed the 'typical' representation of St Jerome's study in Italian Renaissance art.) In particular, it does not contain – apart from one important exception, which I shall mention in a minute – any natural object. There are no flowers in vases, and no food – not so much as a crust of bread or a cruse of wine. Moreover, there are no windows and therefore no view, so that St Jerome cannot look out at the surrounding desert when he gets tired of translating the Bible and the Greek and Hebrew characters start dancing in front of his eyes. In the cave of the heart man cannot see nature, and nature cannot see man. There must, of course, be a door, but it cannot be open, for no sunlight streams through it into the cave, which is filled with a mysterious glow of its own. (Sometimes St Jerome is depicted working by the light of a candle.) What the typical representation of St Jerome in his study really gives us is a cross-section of an inner world. In this inner world man is not insignificant, as he is when viewed from the outside, as part of the material universe, and this is why in paintings of St Jerome in his study the figure of St Jerome himself looms extremely large. Indeed, it sometimes practically fills the entire painting. If when St Jerome is depicted in a landscape, in the midst of nature, there is hardly room for St Jerome, in images of St Jerome in his study there is hardly room for nature. As I have already said, with one exception St Jerome's study or cell does not contain any living natural object, although presumably his desk is made of wood that was once part of a tree and the pages of the Bible he is translating are of parchment that was once part of a sheep. One might even say that St Jerome's study contains nothing but St Jerome, for every one of the spiritually significant items is in a sense an extension of the saint's own personality – as is even the one natural object that the study contains.

This natural object is the lion. He is always with St Jerome in his cell or study, just as he is nearly always with him in the desert, or when he is doing penance. Like the cave, he is a link between the desert and the study, the objective world and the subjective world, matter and spirit. How St Jerome came to be associated with the lion, I do not recollect ever reading. Tucked away in an obscure corner of the legendary life of the saint there is in all probability an episode of the type made familiar to us by the story of Androcles and the Lion – an episode, that is to say, in which St Jerome removes a thorn from the paw of a lion who, out of gratitude, thereafter stays with him as his attendant. Even if there is such an episode, however, the artists of the Italian Renaissance do not seem to have represented it in any way. It is as though they felt that the lion's presence in the painting – whether of St Jerome in the desert or St Jerome in his study – needed no explanation. He was simply there, and he was there not for biographical reasons but for psychological and spiritual reasons that were perfectly obvious to anyone in whom the imaginal faculty was awake and who could understand the language of images and symbols. Translated from the language of images and symbols into the language of concepts the significance of the lion is not difficult to appreciate. The lion is the king of beasts. Apart from man, who in reality belongs to a different order of existence, the lion is the highest of all natural objects. Just as the vegetable kingdom is higher than the mineral kingdom, so the animal kingdom is higher than the vegetable kingdom, and in the animal kingdom the lion is supreme. In the lion, therefore, all the energies and powers of the natural world are gathered together and given their highest and most perfect embodiment. Thus the lion is nature par excellence, which in fact means that the lion represents not so much nature herself as nature as she exists in man. The lion accompanies St Jerome because he is part of St Jerome. He is St Jerome's lower nature, so to speak. He is the lower evolution as taken up into, and incorporated with, the Higher Evolution. Thus the lion not only stays with St Jerome in the desert, where he is a natural object among natural objects, but also follows him into the cave – the cave of the heart – where he is a natural object among objects of spiritual significance, and stays with him there.

In paintings of St Jerome in the desert the figure of the lion is often as tiny and insignificant as that of St Jerome. Indeed, sometimes he disappears altogether, as though merged into the landscape, for since he represents nature, albeit nature par excellence, it is hardly necessary for him to be present in his individual capacity. In paintings of St Jerome in his study, however, the figure of the lion looms almost as large as that of the saint. True, as depicted in medieval Italian art he often looks more like a large yellow dog than a lion, but as depicted by the artists of the Italian Renaissance, who often studied him from life (Italian princes of the period liked to keep lions in their menageries), he is in both form and feature the king of beasts indeed. Usually he is curled up quite close to St Jerome. When the figure of St Jerome threatens to fill the entire painting such proximity is a practical necessity, and the artist has to have recourse to some ingenious foreshortening to get them both in. Sometimes, indeed, the lion lies stretched out beneath St Jerome's desk, so that the saint is able to use him as a foot-warmer. Sometimes his eyes are wide open, and regard the spectator with a steady, level stare, but more often they are closed in sleep. But howsoever he is depicted, whether as more like a large yellow dog or more like a real lion, whether curled up or stretched out, awake or asleep, St Jerome's lion represents not only nature as a part of man but also nature as a part of man that has been tamed. Because he has been tamed the lion does not disturb St Jerome in his work of translation, and how important it is that St Jerome should not be disturbed we shall be able to appreciate only when we have a better understanding of the true nature of that work.

Meanwhile, we have by no means finished with the lion, or exhausted the significance of his association with St Jerome. When I first found myself thinking about St Jerome, shortly after reading my last paper, I did not pay much attention to the lion. But after I had decided that we should revisit St Jerome I found myself thinking about the lion almost as much as about St Jerome himself. Nor was that all. As I thought about St Jerome and the lion I found that I was thinking of other instances of close association between man and lion and that their images too were forcing themselves upon my attention. These instances came from both the Judaeo-Christian and the classical traditions and involved images belonging to ancient myth and legend that were no less familiar to me, from art and literature, than the image of St Jerome himself, and imbued with hardly less significance. To begin with there were images of Samson slaying the lion and Daniel in the lion's den. Both these images came from the Old Testament, and I encountered them for the first time when, at the age of 4 or 5 or even earlier, I started spelling my way through Grandmother's Bible. This was a massive leather-bound volume with huge gilt clasps that my father had inherited from his maternal grandmother. In the front it contained the names and dates of birth (and in some cases dates of death) of great-grandmother's and great-grandfather's children and grandchildren, to which, I believe, my father had added the names and dates of birth of myself and my sister. It also contained numerous full-page illustrations, all printed in the most vivid colours imaginable. Apart from Moses breaking the Tablets of the Law, the ones I remember most clearly are those of Samson slaying the lion and Daniel in the lion's den. In the first, a bright pink Samson wrestled with a bright yellow lion against an emerald green background. In the second, a Daniel in a deep-blue robe knelt in prayer while a pale yellow light streamed down onto his head from the open heavens. Around him were strewn human skulls and bones (I particularly remember a set of ribs), while an enormous grey lion regarded him from the shadows. From the classical tradition came the image of Hercules and the Nemean lion. The strangling of this enormous lion was the first of the famous Twelve Labours of Hercules, and after killing it the hero wore its skin as a sort of cloak, with the head forming a rough hood, and the paws dangling down in front like empty sleeves. In the case of all three images – Samson slaying the lion, Daniel in the lion's den, and Hercules and the Nemean lion – there is an association between a man and a lion, and in each case the man tames or subdues the lion. Samson tears the lion's jaws apart, Daniel renders the lion powerless by virtue of his faith in God, and Hercules strangles the lion to death. Thus in each case there is a close parallel with the association between St Jerome and the lion. At the same time, there are differences. In Samson's case, he actually destroys the lion. Daniel manages to keep the lion at bay. Hercules kills the lion and wears its skin. The three heroes may therefore be regarded as representing the three different attitudes which it is possible for man to adopt towards his own lower nature. He can destroy it, i.e. repress it completely, he can keep it at a safe distance, i.e. suppress it by religious and other means, or he can tame it and turn it into a companion, i.e. integrate it into his higher nature. The third possibility is represented by St Jerome and the lion, as well as by Hercules who, having strangled the Nemean lion, wears its skin on his shoulders. In all four cases, however, the lion is subdued. Man's lower nature is not allowed to disturb him as he pursues his distinctively human activities.

Once images of lions, and men in association with lions, had started forcing themselves on my attention, there seemed to be no stopping them. Since we still have to consider the significance of the various items contained in St Jerome's study there is time for no more than a brief reference to a few of these images, with some of which you will already be familiar, though you may not have attached to them the kind of significance with which we are at present concerned. These more insistent images come from even further afield than the images of men and lions which we have so far encountered. They come not from the Judaeo-Christian and classical traditions but, originally, from the treasury of Indian Buddhist culture. The first such image is that of the Teaching Buddha and the two, sometimes four, lions which support his throne in the same way that elephants support the throne of the Earth-Touching Buddha and peacocks the throne of the Meditating Buddha, and so on.[228] There are, of course, biographical and doctrinal reasons why the throne of the Teaching Buddha should be supported by lions rather than by animals of any other kind, but at present all I want to do is draw attention to the association between Enlightened Man and lion and to suggest that, on its own much higher level, it has the same general significance as the association between St Jerome and the lion or, for the matter of that, between the heroes of the Old Testament and of classical legend and their respective lions.

From the Buddha and his lions to Mañjuśrī, the Bodhisattva of Wisdom, and his, is no more than a short step. Lions support the throne of Mañjuśrī in exactly the same manner that they support the throne of the Teaching Buddha (those of you who are acquainted with the symbolism of the Five Buddhas will know the reason for this),[229] but the best known and most typical example of the association between Mañjuśrī and the lion is that which represents the great bodhisattva as using a single lion as his vehicle or mount. Such representations seem to have been particularly abundant in Buddhist China, where Mañjuśrī was known as Wenshu and where the Manchu or Qing dynasty – the last of the dynasties of China – supposedly took its name from him. In China, however, either there were no lions or Chinese artists did not care to study them from life, for in Chinese Buddhist art Mañjuśrī is represented as riding on an animal that looks much more like an enormous dog than like a lion. Indeed, under Manchu dynasty the Chinese actually succeeded in breeding a dog that looked like a lion, the famous 'lion-dog', in the West better known as the Pekingese, after its place of origin. These dogs were semi-sacred, and could be kept only by the emperor, who was regarded as an emanation of Mañjuśrī in much the same way that the Dalai Lama was regarded as an emanation of Avalokiteśvara. When the lion-dogs died their skins were made into chair-coverings for the imperial apartments, and I remember my father telling me that his stepfather, who was present at the sack of the Summer Palace,[230] had brought several of these chair-coverings back to England with him as souvenirs. Two or three decades earlier, however, the first pair of lion-dogs to be seen in the West had been sent – I believe by the celebrated Dowager Empress – as a present to Queen Victoria.

I had intended that these images of lions, and images of men in association with lions, should be the last that I would allow into this paper, but even as I was writing about them yet another image, from a completely different culture, positively forced itself upon my attention and insisted on finding a place here. Since it is high time we returned to St Jerome's study, and started considering the significance of the red hat hanging on the wall there, I shall do no more than mention this final instance of close association between man and lion. The image in question does not come from so far afield as the images from Indian and Chinese Buddhist culture, but it comes from a culture perhaps more alien in spirit. It is an image belonging to the myths and legends of ancient Assyria, as illustrated by the bas-reliefs preserved in the British Museum and elsewhere. The image is that of a powerfully built man, either a hero or a king, who stands with both arms extended to their full length, so that his body forms a Latin cross. He grasps a lion by the hind legs, so that it hangs down head foremost with its whiskers almost touching the ground. Once again man and lion are in close association, and once again man has subdued the lion.

The red hat hanging on the wall of St Jerome's study is a cardinal's hat, that is to say, it is a round red hat with a broad brim over which red tassels hang down on either side. In more than one painting of St Jerome in his study it contributes a splash of vivid colour to what would otherwise be a sombre scene, sometimes piercing through the gloom with a rich ruby gleam. As I mentioned in the previous paper, due to his association with the reigning pope of his day, St Jerome was traditionally regarded as a cardinal, and when depicted in alterpieces and predellas along with other saints he usually wears not only his red cardinal's hat but also red cardinal's robes, so that what with these and his long white or grey beard and the large, richly bound volume he holds clasped beneath one arm, he is a colourful and picturesque figure. In his study, however, St Jerome puts aside his cardinal's hat and robes. Indeed, the robes are nowhere to be seen. Only the red hat hangs there on the wall, where the warmth of its colour harmonizes with the warm orange-tawny hues of the lion asleep at St Jerome's feet, as though to suggest that there is some kind of connection between the two. A connection, indeed, there is. In the same way that the lion represents nature, or the natural order, so the red cardinal's hat represents human society, or the social order. This social order has not actually followed St Jerome into his cell, or study, or cave, as the lion has followed him, because unlike the lion it is not really part of St Jerome and it is possible for St Jerome to separate himself from it in a way that he cannot separate himself from the lion. But though St Jerome has separated himself from the social order – though he has left Rome and come to Bethlehem, to the desert – there is a sense in which the social order, while not exactly a part of him, is nevertheless present in him. It is present in him as his capacity to function within the social order – a capacity which he continues to possess even when he does not actually exercise it. It is his social self, or even his group self. The red hat represents not so much human society, or the social order, as it is in itself, as this social self. For the time being it hangs on the wall. St Jerome hung it there when he entered his study, or cell, or cave, and he can put it on again whenever he chooses to leave his study and resume his rightful place in the world.

Originally, a cardinal was a priest in charge of one of the Roman churches who, as well as running his own church, assisted the Bishop of Rome, i.e. the pope, in the administration of his diocese. (At that time, of course, the titles of cardinal and pope were unknown.) Later, when the pope had become the ruler of the whole western Church, the cardinals assisted him in the administration of his vast ecclesiastical empire and, though they were no longer responsible for the running of the Roman churches, on his appointment every cardinal was attached to one of these churches in a titular capacity – a practice which I believe still exists. Thus the cardinals were 'princes of the Church'. With few exceptions they lived in sumptuous style, in magnificent palaces, possessed great personal wealth, and wielded enormous political influence. Most important of all, it was they who elected the pope, and they usually elected him from among themselves. By the time the artists of the Italian Renaissance came to represent St Jerome in his study a cardinal was a very important person indeed, so that to be presented with a red hat by the pope was the eventual aim of every ambitious cleric in Christendom. All that was well understood by the artists of the Italian Renaissance, and sometimes the red hat on the wall of St Jerome's study seems to glow with a sinister and lurid splendour. In theory the deep crimson of a cardinal's hat and robes symbolized his readiness to shed his blood in the service of the Church, but only too often it symbolized the blood he had had to shed in order to become a cardinal – not to speak of all the blood shed by the Church in the furtherance of its interests and the establishment of its power. Seen in the light of these developments, the red hat hanging on the wall of St Jerome's study represents not just human society, or the social order, not just St Jerome's social self. It represents the worldly ambition whose realization the social order makes possible. When he withdraws into the cave, when he devotes himself to the work of translating the Bible, or to bringing what was hidden in the depths up to the surface, or from darkness into light, St Jerome not only separates himself from the social order and keeps his social self in abeyance. He also renounces all worldly ambition, especially ambition which wears the cloak of religion and professes to sacrifice self for others when in reality it is sacrificing others to self. He renounces all thought of doing evil that good may come of it (the image of St Jerome as I see it does not necessarily correspond at all points with the Jerome of history), or seeking to achieve spiritual ends by worldly or unspiritual means.[231] In other words, the red hat hanging on the wall of St Jerome's study represents the fact that having subdued his lower nature so that it does not disturb him as he pursues his distinctively human activities man separates himself from the social order and its temptations, at least for the time being, in order to pursue those activities in ever higher and more refined forms.

After the red hat come the hourglass and the human skull. These usually occupy a small shelf along the wall from the hat, though sometimes one or both of them stand on the top of St Jerome's desk, which is not a modern desk with a flat top but a sort of reading desk or lectern. According to the dictionary, an hourglass is a device consisting of two transparent chambers linked by a narrow channel, containing a quantity of sand that takes a specified time to trickle to one chamber from the other. When the chamber is empty and the lower chamber full the hourglass is reversed and the whole process is repeated. The significance of the hourglass is obvious. It represents time, just as the skull represents death. St Jerome is translating the Bible. The Bible is a very big book, and St Jerome is a very old man, and he has no time to lose if the work is to be finished before his death. Perhaps he has set himself to translate so many lines of Greek or Hebrew text for every reversal of the hourglass. Be that as it may, when I started thinking of the image of the hourglass, as it stands on a shelf in St Jerome's study, I found that images of hourglasses from other cultures were far from forcing themselves upon my attention in the way that images of the lion had done. The only images that came to mind were the semi-human hourglass in one of Hieronymus Bosch's paintings of hell and the vague and shadowy figure of Father Time – complete with hourglass and scythe – in various allegorical paintings by artists whose names I could not remember. This relative paucity of images may have been due to the fact that in modern times the hourglass has been replaced by the clock, so that we are familiar with it only in the miniature form of the egg-timer, which measures not the passing of the hours but the three minutes it takes to boil an egg. Or it may have been due to the fact that the hourglass was not really ubiquitous in the traditions and cultures of the world (in many cultures its place was taken by the clepsydra or water clock) and that it was therefore not a universal image. Since it was not universal, and to that extent not truly an image, it was unlikely that images would arise when I reflected upon its significance.

But if images did not arise, ideas certainly did, and I was soon made aware that if the artists had not often depicted Time in their paintings the poets had often alluded to him in their poems. Within a matter of seconds half a dozen well known quotations from the English poets had floated into my mind. The first to come were the pathetic and haunting lines from Marvell's 'To His Coy Mistress', in which after pointing out to the lady at some length that if they only had more time at their disposal her coyness would be less reprehensible, he exclaims:

> But at my back I always hear
> Time's wingèd chariot hurrying near,

thus conveying in an unforgettable manner the feeling we get, especially as we grow older, that time is actually overtaking us.[232] This was followed by Shakespeare's memorable couplet:

> Like as the waves make towards the pebbl'd shore,
> So do our minutes hasten to their end.[233]

and by Walter Raleigh's solemn lines, supposedly written on the eve of his execution:

Even such is Time, which takes in trust
Our youth, our joys, and all we have,
And pays us but with age and dust;
Who, in the dark and silent grave,
When we have wandered all our ways,
Shuts up the story of our days.[234]

After a brief interval came the lines in which the young Milton gives touching expression to the mingled surprise and regret with which he realizes that he is now 23:

How soon hath Time, the subtle thief of youth,
Stol'n on his wing my three-and-twentieth year.[235]

From a much lesser poet, but one whom Dr Johnson esteemed highly enough to recommend his inclusion in the series of English poets for which he was writing his 'little prefaces', came the verse:

Time, like an ever-rolling stream,
Bears all its sons away;
They fly forgotten, as a dream
Dies at the opening day.

This is, of course, a verse from the well-known hymn, 'O God, Our Help in Ages Past', by Isaac Watts, which I remember singing as a boy at school in morning assemblies. It might be interesting to speculate to what extent this verse helped to instil into me the Buddhist idea of universal impermanence.

No doubt many more quotations would have come if I had let them, and no doubt I would have tracked down still more, and not from the English poets alone, if this paper had been written at Padmaloka and I had been able to consult my books. But even the half dozen quotations which floated into my mind when I started thinking of the image of the hourglass, all but one of which I have reproduced here, should be sufficient to illustrate the extent to which allusions to death occur in the works of the poets. It will be noticed, however, that in two, possibly three, of the quotations I have given, Time seems to be personified or semi-personified, while in the two others he is compared with water in motion. Marvell imagines him as borne in a chariot equipped with wings instead of wheels, Milton as being himself a winged creature of some kind (at this point the image of a winged hourglass I have seen somewhere flashes into my mind), Raleigh as an invisible presence that takes everything from us and gives us nothing. As for Shakespeare and Watts, the one compares the minutes of which time consists to waves that come surging up the shingle, the other to a river in constant flow. (Though Watts' hymn is, I believe, a version of one of the Psalms, in the verse I have quoted there may be a submerged reference to the Cronos of Greek mythology, who devoured his own children as soon as they were born.)

Thus we find in these quotations not only ideas but also images. True, the images are not so vivid or so concrete as they would be if represented in painting, but that is because of the nature of time itself. According to Plato, time is the moving image of eternity, and it is because time is something that moves that it is impossible to depict it in painting in a satisfactory manner. The best the artist can do is to represent time as a winged old man with an hourglass and scythe; but the wings do not beat the air, the sands in the hourglass do not trickle down, and the scythe does not mow anything. What has been depicted is not time so much as the objects that symbolize time. In the case of poetry, however, the poet not only describes time as winged, or as borne in a winged chariot, but makes use of words that are not simultaneous, like the different parts of a painting, but themselves successive. In other words, the poem itself moves with the movement it is describing. Thus Marvell's 'wingèd chariot hurrying near' actually does hurry: it is not merely depicted in a state of arrested motion. Moreover, with the word 'near' we actually hear the downward beat of its wings and feel their wind on the back of our necks. In the same way, though perhaps less successfully, Milton's 'subtle thief of youth' actually does perform the act of silently filching the poet's twenty-third year: he is not merely depicted frozen in the posture of performing it. Likewise, Shakespeare's waves actually make towards the pebbled shore, and Isaac Watts's stream actually rolls ever on, in accordance with the movement of the verse itself.

From these examples it should be clear that poetry is better adapted to the representation of movement than is the sister art of painting, and therefore better adapted to the representation of time. Perhaps the reason why so few images came to me when I started thinking of the image of the hourglass was that I expected them to come from the visual arts rather than from the performing arts or those arts which exist in time rather than in space and which include literature considered as that which is not only written but also read, whether aloud or to oneself. Such being the case, it was not surprising that following on the quotations from the English poets there should come into my mind ideas about time from Buddhist literature rather than images of time from the Buddhist visual arts. Indeed, it would appear that in the Buddhist visual arts images of time hardly exist (the demon who grasps the Tibetan wheel of life represents impermanence rather than time), and that in Buddhist culture time has not been personified even to the extent that it has been personified in the classical and Judaeo-Christian cultures of the West. The only really noteworthy personification of time that came to me from Eastern sources came from Hinduism, from the twelfth chapter of the *Bhagavad Gītā*, in the course of which Sri Krishna reveals himself to Arjuna as Time the All-Destroyer, down whose flaming gullet disappears not only the entire human race but everything in the universe. But however deficient Buddhism may be in images of time it is certainly not lacking in ideas about time. Buddhism itself could be described as a meditation on time, or on impermanence (it could perhaps be argued that in Buddhism these two concepts are not distinguished in quite the same way that they are in the West), or as a reflection on the shortness and preciousness of human life. Allusions to time occur even more frequently in Buddhist literature, both canonical and non-canonical, than they do in English poetry, and if I was to reproduce here all the quotations that came to me from this source as I thought of the image of the hourglass they would take up a quite disproportionate amount of space in this paper. Let me therefore quote just one passage, as an example of the kind of ideas to which I refer. It is a passage from the *Sūtra of Forty-Two Sections*, renowned as the first Buddhist scripture to be rendered into Chinese.

> The Buddha said to a Śramaṇa, 'How long is the span of a man's life?' 'It is but a few days,' was the answer. The Buddha said, 'You have not understood,' and asked another Śramaṇa, who replied, 'It is (like) the time taken to eat (a single meal).' To this the Buddha replied in the same way and asked a third: 'How long is the span of a man's life?' 'It is (like) the time taken by a (single) breath,' was the reply. 'Excellent,' said the Buddha, 'You understand the Way.'[236]

Translating this idea into the language of the images and symbols of St Jerome's study, one could say that the span of human life is not a few days, nor even the time taken by the sands to trickle to one chamber of the hourglass from the other, but the time taken for a single grain of sand to fall. Man therefore has no time to waste. It is not enough for him to pursue his distinctively human activities, even in ever higher and more refined forms. He must pursue them with full awareness that time is passing, and in the knowledge that unless he works unremittingly he will not be able to bring them to a successful conclusion.

If the hourglass is not a universal image, the skull most certainly is. With its empty eye-sockets and grinning jaw it is indeed one of the most universal and most powerfully evocative of all images, and its significance can be understood immediately. Having come from Rome to Bethlehem, to the desert, and having taken up the work of translating the Bible into the vulgar tongue at a comparatively advanced age, St Jerome is not only acutely aware of the passing of time but also aware of the fact that, for mortal men, the passing of time inevitably brings death. Time and death are inseparable, and for this reason hourglass and skull usually stand side by side on the shelf in St Jerome's study, where he can see them all the time and from whence they admonish him, in the words of one of those classical authors that he loved too well, that art is long, and human life short: *ars longa, vita brevis*.

Since the image of the skull is so universal, it was natural that when I thought of it as it stands in St Jerome's study, where it is depicted with such grim realism by the artists of the Italian Renaissance, there should have come to my mind images of skulls and skeletons of every kind, from the skeletons that decorate Christian tombs to the garlands of skulls that hang round the necks of Buddhist Tantric divinities, and from complex images such as that of the medieval Dance of Death, Holbein's woodcuts of which I knew and admired as a boy, wherein death in the form of a skeleton dances with lord and with lady, with prince and with prelate, and even with the very pope himself, to simple images such as the pairs of dancing skeletons depicted on Tibetan temple banners and the pyramids of skulls heaped on battlefields by conquerors like Tamerlane and at the feet of bloodthirsty gods by the priests of pre-Columbian Mexico. So many images of skulls and skeletons came crowding into my mind from the different traditions and cultures of the world that it is quite impossible for me to describe them all, or even to enumerate more than a fraction of them. Instead, I shall describe just one image, and this can be taken as representing the rest. It comes from the fourteenth-century frescoes in the Campo Santo in Pisa, which I saw two months ago in the course of my journey to Il Convento. One of these frescoes, which is by an unknown master, depicts the Triumph of Death, who is represented as a kind of female devil with a scythe which she directs against a group of young men and women sitting in a grove, ignoring the pleas of those who regard death as a deliverer. More interesting still, in the bottom left hand corner of the fresco a party of fashionably dressed men and women on horseback, out for a ride in the forest, suddenly come upon three open coffins, containing the bodies of three kings, one who has just died, one who is in an advanced state of decomposition, and one who is no more than a skeleton. Beside the coffin stands the figure of St Macarius the Hermit, pointing to a long scroll and reading the party a lesson on the vanity of earthly existence. One cannot but be reminded, in the most forcible manner, of the well-known story of how the youthful Buddha-to-be, on driving out from his palace in his chariot accompanied by his faithful charioteer, was successively confronted by an old man, a sick man, a corpse, and, finally, a saintly ascetic. As if to underline the resemblance, above the figure of St Macarius other hermits are shown living among rocks and trees, in caves and cottages, occupying themselves with simple daily tasks, spiritual exercises, and religious discussion. The significance of the 'four sights' seen by the Buddha-to-be, as of the corpses of the three kings and the figure of St Macarius, is the same as that of the skull in St Jerome's study. Confronted by the fact of inevitable death, man has no alternative but to devote himself wholeheartedly to the pursuit of his distinctively human activities in their purest form.

Since St Jerome's study contains an object symbolizing time and an object symbolizing death, one might have thought that it would also contain an object symbolizing human suffering, and in a sense it does. It contains a crucifix. As we have already seen, when depicted in the desert, or performing penance, St Jerome is often represented as kneeling before, or clasping, a rude crucifix, but when at the hands of the artists of the Italian Renaissance the desert turns into a pleasant Tuscan or Umbrian landscape, and the figure of St Jerome shrinks into insignificance, the crucifix either becomes so small as to be unrecognizable or disappears completely. It is as though the artists who depicted St Jerome's anguish as he performs his penance in the midst of the countryside, or man's existential anguish in the midst of an uncomprehending and indifferent nature, felt that this anguish was enough, and that it did not really need to be duplicated by the anguish of the figure on the cross. When St Jerome is depicted in his study, however, the scale of the painting changes, and to the extent that the figure of St Jerome becomes more prominent the crucifix becomes more prominent too. Nevertheless, the artists rarely give it the degree of prominence they might have done, considering the central importance of the Crucifixion in the Christian scheme of salvation, and sometimes they do not depict it at all. Again it is as though they were trying to universalize the image of St Jerome in his study, and therefore wanted to universalize the various images and symbols with which he is traditionally associated. When they do depict the crucifix, which usually either stands on the top of St Jerome's desk, or hangs on the wall facing him, what confronts the saint's gaze, when he lifts his eyes from the volume that lies before him, is not so much a representation of the crucified Saviour as an image of suffering humanity. In withdrawing into his cave or study, St Jerome has taken the sufferings of humanity with him, and it is in order to help alleviate those sufferings that he is translating the volume that lies before him. Even though man may separate himself from the social order and its temptations, and even though he may devote himself to the wholehearted pursuit of his distinctively human activities in their highest, most refined, and purest form, it is impossible for him to forget the problem of human suffering. Indeed, it is to solve the problem of human suffering that man withdraws from the social order in the first place.

The volume St Jerome is translating is, of course, the Bible, and together with the figure of St Jerome himself, as he leans over it with slightly knitted brows, it naturally constitutes the centre of interest of paintings of St Jerome in his study of every type. As depicted by the artists of the Italian Renaissance it is no mere pocket volume but an enormous folio of practically the same dimensions as the desk on which, or against which, it rests. Sometimes it is closed, as though St Jerome was on the point of opening it and beginning his day's work, or even as though he would never be able to open it and that it was, in fact, impossible to translate. Much more usually, however, it lies wide open, and we can see on either page the double columns of black text, enclosed, more often than not, within a colourful border of interlacing foliage, flowers, and fruit, from which peep out strange figures of animals and men; we can see the illuminated capital letters, some of them of burnished gold, and the figures of prophets, saints, and angels. In short, from the size of the volume, and the extent to which it has been decorated, we can see its importance. 'What you love, you adorn,' a very wise friend of mine once said to me many years ago (he was referring to my literary style, which some of my more austere friends considered much too 'flowery'), and the fact that the artists of the Italian Renaissance adorned the volume that lies on St Jerome's desk shows that they loved it. But what did they love? Technically, of course, the volume is the Christian Bible, beginning with the Book of Genesis and ending with the Revelation of St John the Divine, for it is the Christian Bible that St Jerome is translating. But the word 'bible' (from Byblos, the city where the papyrus used by the Greeks for the manufacture of books came from) means book, so that the Bible simply means 'the Book'. What the artists of the Italian Renaissance depicted – what they loved and adorned – was therefore not so much the traditional Christian Bible as the Bible in a more universal sense. The volume that lies on St Jerome's desk is in reality the book par excellence. It is the archetypal book. But what is a book?

The answer to this question can be found, at least by implication, in an image or symbol with which you are all familiar: the image of the wheel of life, particularly as depicted in Tibetan Buddhist art. The wheel of life consists of four concentric circles, the third of which (reckoning from the hub outwards) is divided into five or six segments, one for each of the five or six principal classes of sentient beings. In each segment there appears a Buddha of a certain colour who bears in his hands an object that is of special significance to the beings of that class or 'world'. The Buddha who appears in the animal world is light blue in colour, and bears in his hands a book. This book is not a Western-style volume but one of the Indo-Tibetan type, that is to say, it consists of a stack of loose oblong sheets held between two wooden boards of roughly the same dimensions. Sometimes the sheets are connected by strings passed through holes punched at either end, two or three inches from the edge. These details are not visible in actual paintings of the wheel of life, but the object the light-blue Buddha bears in his hands is clearly a book of the Indo-Tibetan type, and he is clearly offering it to the different kinds of animals by whom he is surrounded. The book symbolizes knowledge, both sacred and profane, for it is knowledge that distinguishes man from the animals, so that if animals want to become human beings they must acquire knowledge. Here by 'animals' is meant not only animals in the literal sense but also those animal-like human beings whose interests are confined to food, sex, and sleep, and who are devoid of knowledge in the sense of having no consciousness other than that of the sense-objects that confront them in the present moment. The reason why it is the book that symbolizes knowledge, rather than any other object, is that it is by means of the book – which is essentially a device for the preservation and transmission of information – that we are enabled to extend our consciousness far beyond the limits imposed by our own experience. By means of the book we are enabled to transcend time and space and to communicate with human beings living in other ages and other climes, many of whom are far more highly developed than we are. We are enabled to enter into their experiences, and to share their knowledge. Thus the book is the golden key to the treasury of human culture. The book makes us more truly human. Hence it is not surprising that the object which the light blue Buddha offers to the animals should be a book, as representing the means by which they will rise to the human level and enter the human world. Similarly, it is not surprising that the mighty volume that lies on St Jerome's desk should be not so much the traditional Christian Bible as the Bible in a more universal sense, and not surprising that the artists of the Italian Renaissance, when depicting St Jerome in his study, should have adorned it to the best of their ability.

But if the volume that lies on St Jerome's desk is, in reality, the book par excellence, or the archetypal book, what is it that St Jerome is translating? In what sense can he be said to translate at all? According to Christian tradition, which in this case is based on the facts of history, St Jerome is translating the Bible, and on this level there is no difficulty. St Jerome is translating the Hebrew of the Old Testament and the Greek of the New Testament into the Latin of what came to be known as the Vulgate. But if the Bible means the Book, and if the Book symbolizes knowledge, what is it that St Jerome translates, or in what sense does he translate? In other words, how does one translate knowledge? What does one translate it into? Obviously, knowledge can be translated only into knowledge, just as one language can be translated only into another language, so if knowledge is to be translated there must be another knowledge for it to be translated into, just as if a text in one language is to be translated there must be another language for it to be translated into. Thus translation implies plurality, whether of languages or of knowledges, and to speak of translating knowledge is to speak of different kinds of knowledge. These kinds can be differentiated either horizontally or vertically. Differentiated horizontally, knowledge is either conceptual or symbolic, i.e. either a knowledge of concepts or a knowledge of symbols or images. Differentiated vertically, it consists of a knowledge of sense-objects, a knowledge of ideas or mental objects, a knowledge of archetypes, and a knowledge of ultimate spiritual realities. Knowledge of the highest kind is identical with its object. From all this it is clear that knowledge is translated either from one mode to another, as when what was expressed in terms of symbols and images is expressed in terms of concepts, or vice versa, or when it is translated from one degree to another, as when knowledge of ultimate spiritual realities is translated into knowledge of archetypes, or knowledge of archetypes into knowledge of ideas or mental objects. Since the Bible on St Jerome's desk is the book par excellence, it follows that the knowledge which it symbolizes will be knowledge par excellence, i.e. knowledge of ultimate spiritual realities. Thus St Jerome is translating in the sense that he is translating knowledge of ultimate spiritual realities into knowledge of the archetypes, and knowledge of the archetypes into knowledge of ideas or mental objects, so that those who have risen no higher than the level of ideas or mental objects will be given at least some intimation of the existence of those archetypes and those ultimate spiritual realities and be inspired to orient themselves accordingly.

To be a translator in this sense is to be more than a translator. It is to be an interpreter: an interpreter of one degree of knowledge, or one level of reality, to another. It is to be, even, a mediator between different planes of existence or different worlds. A parallel to the figure of St Jerome as translator in this more exalted sense is to be found within the Buddhist tradition in the slightly earlier figure of the great sage Nāgārjuna, the Second Founder of Buddhism, who after retrieving the 'Perfection of Wisdom' *sūtras* from the kingdom of the *nāgas*, where the Buddha had deposited them, not only propagated the teaching far and wide but also expounded it in numerous works of his own, thus inaugurating a new era in the history of Buddhism. According to Buddhist tradition, the kingdom of the *nāgas* is situated in the depths of the ocean, and Tibetan Buddhist art loves to depict the saffron-robed figure of Nāgārjuna, wearing the pointed cap of a master of the Tripiṭaka or 'three collections' of Buddhist scriptures, seated on a raft in mid-ocean and receiving the massive Indo-Tibetan type volume of the 'Perfection of Wisdom' from the hands of the mermaid-like *nāga* princess who has brought it up to him from the palace of the *nāga* king, where it has lain concealed for more than a thousand years (according to modern historical research, more than five hundred years). Since the ocean symbolizes deeper levels of knowledge (what is seen externally as 'higher' is seen internally as 'deeper'), the kingdom of the *nāgas* symbolizes the realm of ultimate spiritual realities, and the significance of Nāgārjuna's achievement consists in the fact that he has made the knowledge of those realities accessible to ordinary human consciousness by 'translating' it into knowledge of ideas or mental objects – at least to the extent that the limitations of that kind of knowledge permit. Thus Nāgārjuna is an interpreter of one degree of knowledge, or one level of reality, to another. He is a mediator between the plane or world of the *nāgas* and the human plane or world, or between the world of the Buddhas and the world of ordinary, unenlightened men and women. He is a human – as distinct from an archetypal – bodhisattva, mysteriously hovering between the Transcendental and the mundane.[237]

Besides providing a parallel to the figure of St Jerome, the more remote and legendary figure of Nāgārjuna as the retriever and propagator of the 'Perfection of Wisdom' enables us to appreciate, perhaps more deeply than would otherwise have been possible, the significance of the image of St Jerome as the translator not simply of the Bible in the traditional Christian sense but as the translator – or the interpreter – of one degree of knowledge, or one level of reality, into another. There are within the Buddhist tradition other parallels to the figure of St Jerome as translator in the more exalted sense with which we are at present concerned. There is Kumārajīva, who was almost the exact contemporary of St Jerome, and Xuanzang, who lived about two hundred years later, both of whom in addition to translating Buddhist scriptures from Sanskrit into Chinese explained them in Chinese for the benefit of Chinese audiences. To the best of my knowledge, the figure of Xuanzang in *his* study, after his return from India, is not depicted by the artists of the Tang and Song dynasties with nearly the same frequency that the image of St Jerome in his study, after his retirement from Rome to Bethlehem, is depicted by the artists of the Italian Renaissance. I did, however, once see a block print (as I think it was) of Xuanzang seated cross-legged behind a low desk across which lies a long scroll on which, with brush poised and a thoughtful expression on his face, he is inscribing row after vertical row of Chinese characters – presumably the text of one of the *sūtras* he has translated. Paintings of Xuanzang on his way back to China are fortunately more common. One of the best of them depicts the great translator in the guise of a pilgrim, with robes girt to the knee, and a staff in his hand. His whole body is bent forward, partly because of the weight of all the books and images he is carrying on his back, and partly because of his eagerness to complete his journey. Neither the block print of Xuanzang 'in his study' nor even the best of the paintings of Xuanzang as pilgrim give us, however, any reason to suppose that the artists of the Tang and Song dynasties ever saw in either of these figures anything that would have enabled them to transcend the facts of the immediate historical situation and to transform the figure of Xuanzang into an image of universal significance. Whether they ever saw anything in any of the other famous figures in Chinese Buddhist history that would have enabled them to transform them in this way, by concentrating on one crucial and representative episode in their career, it would be interesting to enquire.

But perhaps we have strayed too far away from the image of St Jerome in his study, or cell, or cave, as depicted by the artists of the Italian Renaissance, and it is time we started drawing together the main threads of this investigation. Before we do so, however, I would like to touch on one more point. I said that knowledge of the highest kind was identical with its object. By knowledge of the highest kind I meant, of course, knowledge of ultimate spiritual realities or, in other words, knowledge of Nirvāṇa or Enlightenment, which is identical with its 'object' because, at this level of reality, the difference between subject and object no longer obtains. But all knowledge is, in a sense, identical with its object, since otherwise knowledge would be impossible. Thus when one 'translates' knowledge of one degree into knowledge of another degree, as when one translates knowledge of archetypes into knowledge of ideas or mental objects, one is not only translating the archetypes as, so to speak, objects completely distinct and separate from oneself. One is also translating them as, to some extent, identical with oneself. In other words, one is translating what one has experienced on one level of consciousness into terms appropriate to another level of consciousness. One brings what one has experienced on the mountain top down into the valley or, to change the metaphor, one brings what one has experienced in the depths up to the surface, from darkness into light. It is in this bringing down, or bringing up, of what one has experienced on the heights, or in the depths, of one's own being, and giving it concrete form, as St Jerome does when be produces the Vulgate, that the essence of creativity consists. St Jerome is therefore not only the translator and interpreter but also the creator and artist, and because he is the creator and artist he is the true individual; for the corollary of the fact that all knowledge is, in a sense, identical with its object, and that what one translates is one level of one's own being into another, is that all translation is essentially an individual and even a solitary activity.

It is because the translator is also the individual, as well as the interpreter and the creator, that the artists of the Italian Renaissance, in depicting St Jerome in his study, depict him as having no companion except the lion, who in any case represents his own lower nature. This is all the more significant in that it is at variance with both ecclesiastical tradition and the facts of history. When St Jerome left Rome and went to live in the Holy Land he did not go alone but accompanied by a number of disciples, prominent among whom were a devout Roman matron and her daughter who, between them, were responsible for the construction of the small monastic establishment in Bethlehem where St Jerome eventually settled and where he translated the Bible. It would not have been difficult for the artists of the Italian Renaissance to depict St Jerome with these two ladies, thanks to whose generosity he was able to carry on his work, as well as with the various personal attendants, research assistants, and amanuenses upon whose services he was likewise dependent. Yet they never did so. Instead, they chose to depict him in a study that was completely bare, except for a few significant items, and they chose to depict him alone. From this it is obvious that in depicting the figure of St Jerome what they – and perhaps their patrons – were in fact doing was working, whether consciously or unconsciously, towards the creation of an image of universal significance. What the artists of the Italian Renaissance depict is not so much St Jerome in his study, translating the Bible, as man in the cave of his own heart where, having subdued his lower nature and separated himself from the social order, he devotes himself to the pursuit of his distinctively human activities. What they depict is man as interpreter and creator, bringing up into consciousness what he has experienced in the depths of his own being and giving it appropriate expression for the benefit of all. What they depict, and what I have tried in this paper to show them as depicting, is man as a spiritual being who, in the shadow of time and death, strives to fathom the mystery of existence.

A NOTE ON *THE BURIAL OF COUNT ORGAZ*

In the autumn of 1990 I spent two weeks visiting Madrid and its environs and some of the most ancient and historic cities of southern Spain. There were mainly two reasons for my embarking on this little tour. I wanted to see the great mosque of Córdoba and other monuments of the Moorish civilization of Spain; and I wanted to see the paintings of El Greco – especially his *Burial of Count Orgaz*.

My acquaintance with El Greco had begun early, when I was still in my teens. It was an acquaintance at second hand, for with the National Gallery virtually closed for the duration of the war, my knowledge of the master's œuvre was confined to monochrome reproductions in art books and literary descriptions by such writers as Aldous Huxley and Sacheverell Sitwell. Perhaps the closest I got to El Greco at this time, in purely visual terms, was when I saw, in the window of a bookshop in Torquay, a folio art book that was open at a full page colour plate of one of his paintings – a painting in which two richly clad ecclesiastics supported, between them, the body of a man in black armour, while behind was a row of white-ruffed faces and above were Christ, the Virgin Mary, and all the host of heaven. It was the famous *Burial*. But though I was acquainted with El Greco only at second hand, and even then only to a very limited extent, there must have been something about the man and his work that fascinated me greatly, for the novel I wrote in my eighteenth year contained descriptions of his paintings, and of those of no other artist. A year later I found myself in the East, where I remained for twenty years and where I had no opportunity of furthering my acquaintance with El Greco, even at second hand, but after my return to the West in 1964 I saw such of his works as were in the National Gallery and the Metropolitan, notably *The Agony in the Garden* and *The Storm over Toledo*, thus at last making the master's acquaintance at first hand. The bulk of El Greco's production, however, was still in Spain, especially in Toledo, and to Spain I would have to go if I wanted to extend my acquaintance with the artist. During the late eighties I visited Spain several times, but it was only in the autumn of 1990 that I could devote two weeks to the monuments of Moorish civilization and the paintings of El Greco.

In the Prado I saw the *Baptism* and the *Resurrection*, and some thirty other paintings by El Greco, and in the Escorial I saw *St Maurice and the Theban Legion*, which was rejected by Philip II but described by Sacheverell Sitwell in 1950 as the artist's masterpiece. Thus by the time I reached Toledo I had seen quite a lot of El Greco's work, but this only made me eager to see more – especially *The Burial of Count Orgaz*. Having checked in at the hotel we immediately made our way, my companion and I, to the church of Santo Tomé, only a few hundred yards up the cobbled street. By a happy accident, we arrived just after opening time and there were only a couple of dozen people in the small, uncluttered chapel that housed the famous painting. Before long we found places on one of the benches in front of the altar, above which the *Burial* was displayed, and so were able to sit contemplating it for as long as we wished. That evening, and in the course of the following day, I saw in the Cathedral, in the Hospital de Santa Cruz, and in the museum of the Casa del Greco, three or four dozen more paintings by the Cretan-born master (including copies and alternative versions), but these I shall not particularize. I shall stay with *The Burial of Count Orgaz*. Not that I shall attempt to describe the painting or even give a general account of it. I shall stay with it only to the extent of making a single point.

A few weeks after my tour, when I was back in England, I happened to dip into James A. Michener's best-selling *Iberia*, and in particular into the chapter on Toledo. Originally he had not intended saying anything about *The Burial of Count Orgaz*, the author tells us, it having been so well and so repeatedly described that there seemed little he might add; but happening to revisit Santo Tomé one afternoon with a party of English tourists (apparently he was actually writing the book at the time) he decided simply to look at 'the magisterial painting' as if he had never seen it before. The result, as one might have expected, is that he has quite a lot to say about it after all.

'Like most universal masterpieces,' he declares, with American forthrightness, 'this one has many fine passages and others that are frankly bad.' Michener does not ignore the fine passages. Slowly studying the canvas as he sits before it in his Renaissance chair, he in fact finds hidden beauties which had escaped him on previous visits (the naked figures throwing rocks, in the right-hand panel of St Stephen's cloak, if painted on a full scale canvas of their own would have anticipated Cézanne's *Bathers* by three hundred years), and having described them he gives us some useful information about the Conde de Orgaz, about the origin of the painting, and about the painting itself. Michener's most trenchant comments, however, relate to the 'bad' passages in 'this monumental work' of El Greco's.

> There are three glaring defects [he assures us]. The picture breaks into two unrelated halves, an upper and a lower; the yellow-robed angel that is supposed to unite them is one of the sorriest figures El Greco ever drew and fails completely in his mission (in Spain all angels must be male); and the clouds of little bodiless angels consisting only of head and wings are ridiculous and, unlike the similar putti of Raphael and the other Italians who used the convention with charm, accomplish nothing. The unresolved breaking into two halves is caused by that much-vaunted line of heads which is one of the glories of the work but which in its excellence creates a problem that El Greco could not surmount. The faulty angel is poorly designed, poorly placed and poorly executed, which is curious, since El Greco used the same device with success in other paintings.... What I object to most, however, is that the putti are badly painted, and as one looks at the canvas with a fresh eye unimpeded by what others have seen, they merely add to the general clutter of a work that was poorly organized to begin with.'[38]

I have nothing to say in defence of the putti (not that they necessarily need defending), and nothing to say about the drawing of the yellow-robed angel, though I shall have something to say about the failure of his supposed mission of uniting the upper and lower halves of the painting. The point I want to make relates to what Michener considers the poor organization of the work, in particular his allegation that the line of heads breaks the picture into two unrelated halves, an upper and a lower, and this creates a problem that El Greco could not surmount.

But is *The Burial of Count Orgaz* in fact broken into two halves? This view, it seems to me, attributes far too much weight to the part played in the organization of the painting to the line of heads. It also fails to do justice to the fact that the painting is held together as much by colour as by design. The greys on the friar's habit on the left and the whites of the priest's surplice on the right, in the lower half of the painting connect with the diagonal grey-and-white of the two cloud forms which, in the upper half, converge to support the figures of the Virgin Mary and St John the Baptist and, at their apex, the white-robed figure of Christ. Moreover, the golds of St Stephen's dalmatic and St Augustine's cope, as the two saints bend to lower the dead Count into his grave, in the lower half, are echoed by the golds of the angel's robe and the robes of St Peter and other saints, in the upper half. The painting could in fact be described as a symphony in grey-and-white and gold, on a ground of black, varied here and there, in the upper half especially, with notes of purple and red. In terms of abstract design the painting is held together by the fact that the figures of Christ, the Virgin Mary, St John the Baptist, and the angel, in the upper half of the painting, form a mandorla, and that this mandorla has a common axis with the sphere formed by the figures of St Stephen and St Augustine directly underneath, in the lower half of the painting. Moreover, the point at which the 'much-vaunted line of heads' bisects this axis is midway between the bottom of the mandorla and the top of the sphere, while the convergent cloud forms of the upper half protract themselves beyond their apex and pass behind the figures of the Virgin and St John to describe a St Andrew's cross. The geometric centre of the mandorla and the apex of the convergent clouds or the centre of the St Andrew's cross are thus coincident. Far from being badly organized, as Michener claims, *The Burial of Count Orgaz* is extremely well organized, with both colour and design contributing to the welding of the various figures and forms of the painting into one uniform pattern. The work is in fact no less rigorously schematic than are the icons of El Greco's native Crete.

Nor is that all. The halves into which the *Burial* is 'broken' are held together not just by means of colour and design; they are also held together by what may be described as the painting's underlying philosophy. Looking at the line of heads, one notices a number of things about them. Including the heads of the two friars and the two priests, there are altogether twenty-five of them, not all of which are fully visible. Some of the heads are portraits of contemporaries, as Michener tells us; one of them may even depict El Greco himself. One also notices that the head of the grey-robed friar on the left, just within the border of the painting, and the head of the white-surpliced priest on the right, are on a slightly higher level than the line of heads in between (not counting the four rather shadowy heads in the background), which they seem to enclose in a sort of parenthesis. Midway between the friar's head and the priest's, however, there is a head that is on a slightly higher level again than theirs. This head is on the same axis as the mandorla, in the upper half of the painting, and the sphere, in the lower, and occupies the space between the bottom of the one and the top of the other. Mandorla and sphere are thus joined together by a second, much smaller, mandorla. In other words, the painting is united not just by colour and design but, in particular, by means of the middle head in that same 'much-vaunted line' which, according to Michener, breaks it into two unrelated halves. What does this mean? Why does the head occupy the position in the line – and in the painting – that it does? In order to answer these questions we shall have to study the head itself more closely.

It is the head of a young man. The Ancient Greeks would probably have styled him 'a beardless youth', with all that that implied, for in marked contrast to the bearded and moustached worthies on either side of him, some of whom are grizzled and balding, he has only an incipient moustache. The young man is handsome, even beautiful. His ruff-surrounded face, which is fully visible, is perhaps a shade less beautiful than that of the even younger-looking St Stephen who, in contrast to the wrinkled, white-bearded St Augustine, appears in the very bloom of youth. But then St Stephen has come down from heaven in order to help bury Count Orgaz: like the Virgin Mary and the other saints he belongs wholly to heaven. The unknown young man, on the other hand, belongs to the earth. Or rather, he belongs partly to earth and partly to heaven, which is perhaps what gives him his pensive, almost melancholy expression. He belongs partly to earth and partly to heaven on account of his beauty, for there is a beauty that is of the earth, earthly, and a beauty that is of heaven, heavenly, the former being the latter's reflection. Because he belongs to both earth and heaven, he is the means by which they are joined together, and he is beautiful. Thus the two halves of the *Burial* are held together by colour and design *and* by the painting's underlying philosophy. They are held together by its underlying philosophy because, in that philosophy, it is beauty that holds together the two halves of the universe, beauty that holds together heaven and earth.

Beauty is the object of love, for as Diotima tells Socrates in Plato's *Symposium*, Love is a lover of Wisdom because Wisdom is beautiful and 'Love is love of beauty'.[239] Like beauty itself, love is of two kinds, the earthly and the heavenly. Earthly love is the love of earthly things, while heavenly love is the love of the things of heaven. The soul ascends from earth to heaven as it learns to love the things of heaven more than the things of earth, and it loves the things of heaven more than the things of earth as it perceives the greater beauty of the things of heaven, earthly beauty being but the faint, distorted reflection of heavenly beauty in the mirror of sense. The classic description of the soul's ascent to heaven – to the goal of the mysteries of love – is that found in the *Symposium*. As Diotima explains to Socrates:

> The man who would pursue the right way to this goal must begin, when he is young, by applying himself to the contemplation of physical beauty, and, if he is properly directed by his guide, he will first fall in love with one particular beautiful person and beget noble sentiments in partnership with him. Later he will observe that physical beauty in any person is closely akin to physical beauty in any other, and that, if he is to make beauty of outward form the object of his quest, it is great folly not to acknowledge that the beauty exhibited in all bodies is one and the same; when he has reached this conclusion he will become a lover of all physical beauty, and will relax the intensity of his passion for one particular person, because he will realize that such a passion is beneath him and of small account. The next stage is for him to reckon beauty of soul more valuable than beauty of body; the result will be that, when he encounters a virtuous soul in a body which has little of the bloom of beauty, he will be content to

love and cherish it and to bring forth such notions as may serve to make young people better; in this way he will be compelled to contemplate beauty as it exists in activities and institutions, and to recognize that here too all beauty is akin, so that he will be led to consider physical beauty taken as a whole a poor thing in comparison. From morals he must be directed to the sciences and contemplate their beauty also, so that, having his eyes fixed upon beauty in the widest sense, he may no longer be the slave of a base and mean-spirited devotion to an individual example of beauty, whether the object of his love be a boy or a man or an activity, but, by gazing upon the vast ocean of beauty to which his attention is now turned, may bring forth in the abundance of his love of wisdom many beautiful and magnificent sentiments and ideas, until at last, strengthened and increased in stature by this experience, he catches sight of one unique science whose object is the beauty of which I am about to speak....

The man who has been guided thus far in the mysteries of love, and who has directed his thoughts towards examples of beauty in due and orderly succession, will suddenly have revealed to him as he approaches the end of his initiation a beauty whose nature is marvellous indeed, the final goal, Socrates, of all his previous efforts. This beauty is first of all eternal; it neither comes into being nor passes away, neither waxes nor wanes; next, it is not beautiful in part and ugly in part, nor beautiful at one time and ugly at another, nor beautiful in this relation and ugly in that, nor beautiful here and ugly there, as varying according to its beholders; nor again will this beauty appear to him like the beauty of a face or hands or anything else corporeal, or like the beauty of a thought or a science, or like beauty which has its seat in something other than itself, be it a living thing or the earth or the sky or anything else whatever; he will see it as absolute, existing alone with itself, unique, eternal, and all other beautiful things as partaking of it, yet in such a manner that, while they come into being and pass away, it neither undergoes any increase or diminution nor suffers any change. When a man, starting from this sensible world and making his way upward by a right use of his feeling of love for boys, begins to catch sight of that beauty, he

> is very near his goal. This is the right way of approaching or being initiated into the mysteries of love, to begin with examples of beauty in this world, and using them as steps to ascend continually with that absolute beauty as one's aim, from one instance of physical beauty to two and from two to all, then from physical beauty to moral beauty, and from moral beauty to the beauty of knowledge, until from knowledge of various kinds one arrives at the supreme knowledge whose sole object is that absolute beauty, and knows at last what absolute beauty is.[240]

Thus the underlying philosophy of *The Burial of Count Orgaz* is broadly Platonic, even though the painting's subject matter is a fourteenth century local legend and though its images are drawn from Catholic Christian mythology. It could also be said to be basically Buddhistic, the soul's ascent from a lower to a higher beauty being exemplified by the well-known episode in which the Buddha transports the monk Nanda, who had been troubled by thoughts of his beautiful ex-girlfriend, to the Heaven of the Thirty-Three and shows him five hundred nymphs. In comparison with the nymphs, Nanda declares, his ex-girlfriend is like a scalded she-monkey with her nose and ears lopped off, the nymphs being infinitely more lovely and beautiful and alluring.[241] That the underlying philosophy of the *Burial* is broadly Platonic does not necessarily mean that El Greco has read Plato. In any case he would have had to read him either in the original Classical Greek or in Latin, complete Greek editions having been published in Venice (1513) and Paris (1578) and Latin versions in Florence (1496) and Paris (1578). Not that El Greco needed to read Plato in order to be influenced by him. Since the Renaissance Platonism had been in the air, like a delicate perfume, and though it was Florence and not Venice that was, or had been, the great centre of Platonic studies, it is not unlikely that during his sojourn in the city of the Doges El Greco should have breathed in some particles of the Platonic essence. Moreover, as his art itself suggests and as stories that have come down to us about him testify, El Greco was something of a visionary, a man who saw more clearly in the darkness than in the light and who found in the words of a modern writer on Spain, 'no use for the splendid Spanish sun'.[242] Like many poets and artists both before and after his time, he was a Platonist by nature. To him it was self-evident that there existed a higher, spiritual world and that the right contemplation of human beauty was a means of access to that world.

Which brings us back to the head of the unknown young man. Though it is entirely feasible that El Greco, Platonist by nature that he was, should have evolved the underlying philosophy of his great painting from the depths of his own experience, certain features in his treatment of the young man's head suggest that this was not the case and that he had, in fact, read Plato, even read the *Symposium*, or at least been privy to the latter's ideas on love and beauty. It is not just that the head joins together the two halves of the painting, or that the young man is beautiful. El Greco seems to want to emphasize these facts. While the tip of the rear half of St Augustine's mitre points upwards to the young man's chin, almost touching his ruff, the twin folds of the angel's robe, pointing downwards, form a right-angle just above his head; the saint's mitre is gold and white, the angel's robe gold (or yellow). The young man's head is thus at the point of intersection between a black and white horizontal and a gold and white vertical; it also occupies a position, vertically, exactly midway between the dead Count's heart and the naked white infant onto which the angel is holding and which is, presumably, the Count's recently departed soul.

But what of the gold-robed angel himself? Does he fail completely in his mission of uniting the two halves of the picture, as Michener asserts, and is he 'one of the sorriest of figures El Greco ever drew'? Is he 'poorly designed, poorly placed, and poorly executed'? How well or how badly he is drawn compared with El Greco's other figures I cannot say, nor can I say if he is poorly designed or poorly executed. What I can say, in the light of my previous observations on the painting, is that the angel neither succeeds nor fails in his mission of uniting the upper and lower halves of the picture. He neither succeeds nor fails because it is not his mission to unite them. The two halves of the painting are united by the head of the young man. It is the young man, not the angel, who is the intermediary between heaven and earth, and he is the intermediary between them because he is beautiful and because, in the underlying philosophy of the *Burial*, it is with the right contemplation of *human* beauty that the soul commences its ascent from earth to heaven. The figure of the angel is therefore not poorly placed at all. Since not he but the young man is the intermediary he is rightly placed, not between heaven and earth, as the young man is, but in heaven, where he forms a mandorla with Christ, the Virgin Mary, and St John the Baptist, and El Greco makes use of the folds of his gold robe to emphasize the fact that it is the young man's head that unites the two halves of the painting. When Michener looked at the *Burial* he should have noticed this. He indeed thinks it 'curious' that 'since El Greco used the same device with success in other paintings' the angel should be 'poorly designed, poorly placed, and poorly executed'. What he ought to have asked himself was whether the artist was, in fact, using the same device in the *Burial* as in other paintings, that is, using the figure of the angel to unite the upper and lower halves of the picture. Had he asked himself this question he might have perceived that the two halves were united by the head of the young man, and perceiving this he might have gone on to ask himself why El Greco should have given the mission of uniting them to the young man's head rather than to the figure of the angel. Proceeding in this way he might even have realized that at least one of the 'glaring defects' that he attributed to *The Burial of Count Orgaz* existed only in his mind and that actually the artist had solved the problem created by the 'unresolved' breaking of the picture into two unrelated halves by the line of heads.

But we have not quite finished with the angel. Though it is not his mission to unite the two halves of the picture – to join together heaven and earth – he does have a function. His function is to be the midwife, so to speak, of the deceased Count's soul, which seems to be ascending to the judgement seat of Christ up a narrow passage between the two diagonal cloud forms – a passage that has reminded at least one commentator of the human birth canal. The Virgin Mary looks down in compassion, while St John the Baptist and the other saints, as well as sundry angels and blessed spirits, intercede for it with Christ. All this is in full accordance with Catholic Christian teaching. But the Count's soul – the naked white infant (actually it may not be naked but wearing a ghostly white integument) is vertically aligned with the head of the beautiful young man and with the Count's heart, the young man's head being situated exactly midway between the Count's heart and his soul. What does this mean?

The answer to the question is to be found in the *Symposium*. Earlier in their conversation, before her great speech on the ascent from the contemplation of physical beauty to the knowledge of absolute beauty, Diotima tells Socrates that the function of love is to procreate in what is beautiful, and that such procreation can be either physical or spiritual. Procreation, she says, is the nearest thing to perpetuity and immortality that a mortal being can attain. 'Those whose creative instinct is physical have recourse to women, and show their love in this way, believing that by begetting children they can secure for themselves an immortal and blessed memory hereafter for ever; but there are some whose creative desire is of the soul, and who conceive spiritually, not physically, the progeny which it is the nature of the soul to conceive and bring forth.' Diotima continues:

> If you ask what that progeny is, it is wisdom and virtue in general; of this all poets and such craftsmen as have found out some new thing may be said to be begetters; but far the greatest and fairest branch of wisdom is that which is concerned with the due ordering of states and families, whose name is moderation and justice. When by divine inspiration a man finds himself from his youth up spiritually pregnant with these qualities, as soon as he comes of due age he desires to bring forth and to be delivered, and goes in search of a beautiful environment for his children; for he can never bring forth in ugliness. In his pregnant condition physical beauty is more pleasing to him than ugliness, and if in a beautiful body he finds also a beautiful and noble and gracious soul, he welcomes the combination warmly, and finds much to say to such a one about virtue and the qualities and actions which mark a good man, and takes his education in hand. By intimate association with beauty embodied in his friend, and by keeping him always before his mind, he succeeds in bringing to birth the children of which he has been long in labour, and once they are born he shares their upbringing with his friend; the partnership between them will be far closer and the bond of affection far stronger than between ordinary parents, because the children that they share surpass human children by being immortal as well as more beautiful. Everyone would prefer children such as these to children after the flesh.[243]

Does it not appear, in the light of this passage, that the naked white infant might be not just the soul of Count Orgaz but the spiritual child that he has brought to birth by intimate association with beauty embodied in his friend and that his friend is none other than the beautiful young man whose head occupies a position exactly midway between the Count's heart and his soul? Should this be the case, it could also be that the little page standing in the foreground of the picture, to the extreme left, who is believed to be a portrait of El Greco's son, represents physical procreation, just as the naked white infant represents spiritual procreation. The page holds in his left hand a torch, symbolizing mortality, the flame of the torch being echoed by the flames of the torches at either end of the row of heads, as well as by the vertical arms of the red Maltese crosses on the cloaks of two of the gentlemen in the middle of the row, one behind St Augustine and the other between St Augustine and St Stephen. With the forefinger of his left hand the page points to the centre of the white rose embroidered on the sleeve of St Stephen's dalmatic. What this means I cannot say, unless the rose is the snow-white rose of celestial love described by Dante in Canto 30 of the *Paradiso*, in which case the page's gesture would indicate that earthly beauty, rightly contemplated, points to heavenly beauty, physical love to spiritual love.

Finally, could it not be that the head of the beautiful young man is a portrait of someone personally known to El Greco, and that the *Burial* itself is a child brought forth by the artist 'by intimate association with beauty embodied in his friend and by keeping him always before his mind'? This is only a speculation, but it is a speculation fully in accordance with the underlying philosophy of the painting. What is certain is that, universal masterpiece or no universal masterpiece, *The Burial of Count Orgaz* does *not* break into two unrelated halves and is *not* poorly organized, its two halves being held together not only by colour and design but by the painting's broadly Platonic underlying philosophy. When he looked at the canvas Michener looked not so much with a fresh eye as with a raw eye. For my own part, I would like to pay a second visit to Toledo and see *The Burial of Count Orgaz* again. Perhaps I, too, would find hidden beauties that had escaped me on my previous visit. In which case there might be another Note.

CRITICISM EAST AND WEST

When Keith Sagar invited me to take part in this weekend school I hesitated a long time before accepting.[244] *Criticism in Crisis* was indeed an exciting topic, but I was conscious that I knew very little about the present state of literary criticism and was therefore hardly in a position to make a positive contribution to the proceedings. However, Keith Sagar seemed not to share these misgivings, or rather, was inclined to dismiss them as irrelevant. He was sure I didn't know any less about the present state of literary criticism than he did, he cheerfully assured me, and in any case the school would be hearing enough about *that* from the first two speakers. What was wanted from me, as the speaker 'with a perspective from outside our culture altogether', was much more on what criticism ought to be doing.

My role was therefore clear. I was to be present among you as a belated avatar of that once well-known figure, the outsider, and it was as an outsider that I was to contribute to the weekend's proceedings. But before trying to do this perhaps I had better explain in what sense, exactly, I am an outsider. Firstly, I am an outsider in that my life's work has lain not in the field of English, whether university or non-university, but almost entirely in the field of Buddhism, with only occasional excursions into other areas. In pursuit of my Buddhist studies I spent twenty years uninterruptedly in the East, mainly in India, returning to England for good only in 1967. Secondly, I am an outsider in that I have never held a permanent academic post, though I have to confess that I was once a lecturer at an American university. There were, of course, mitigating circumstances, and in any case I was only a visiting lecturer, and not in the department of English but only in the department of philosophy, besides which I stayed there for no more than a single semester.

But though a genuine avatar of the outsider I am not so much of an outsider as not to be aware, however vaguely, that there is something wrong in the field of English and particularly, perhaps, in the field that deep-browed Leavis once ruled – or tried to rule – as his demesne.[245] Only a few weeks ago, leafing through a collection of essays on poetry by that cantankerous and opinionated bard Robert Graves I happened to light upon the following anecdote. It comes at the end of the fourth of Graves's Clark Lectures, which were sponsored by Trinity College, Cambridge.

> Before closing I must tell you about a girl who is reading English here under Professor X. I asked her: 'What poems do you enjoy most?' and she answered with dignity: 'Poems are not meant to be enjoyed; they are meant to be analysed.'[246]

Graves adds that he hoped his listeners did not think he subscribed to that heresy.

That was more than thirty years ago and in the meantime the situation seems to have become worse rather than better. A few days after I happened to light upon the Robert Graves anecdote there appeared in *The Times* an interview with Professor Allan Bloom of Chicago, whose book *The Closing of the American Mind*, a hard-hitting attack on cultural illiteracy, had 'shaken America's academic establishment'. If the interview was anything to go by, it was a pity the American academic establishment had only been shaken. Stanford University had become embroiled in controversy over a decision to drop its compulsory beginners' course of Western culture, while at Duke University Shakespeare was taught as 'a vehicle to illuminate the way seventeenth-century society mistreated women, the working class, and minorities'.[247]

Now let there be no misunderstanding here. I am not saying that poetry should never, under any circumstances, be analysed (I am sure Graves did not mean to suggest this), and neither am I saying that

Shakespeare is too sacrosanct to be utilized as a source of information about the way seventeenth-century society mistreated women, the working class, and minorities. Indeed, a certain amount of analysis may well enhance our appreciation of a poem, just as information regarding the way seventeenth-century society mistreated women, the working class, and minorities may reciprocally illuminate Shakespeare – provided, of course, we can be sure that seventeenth-century society really did mistreat these social groups as alleged. What I am saying is that literary criticism is concerned primarily with the enjoyment of poetry rather than with its analysis (not that the two need be mutually exclusive), and concerned with Shakespeare as an outstanding literary phenomenon rather than as an important source of sociological information.

In speaking of literary criticism in this way I am of course defining it, at least by implication, and definition is no doubt premature at this stage. After all, in formal terms literary criticism is simply the criticism of literature. But what is literature? Surely it is not really possible for us to say what literary criticism is without first saying what literature itself is, and unless we can say what literary criticism is we shall not really be able to say what is wrong with it or what it ought to be doing. We shall not even be able to speak of literary criticism as being in a state of crisis, any more than we can speak of anything being in a state of crisis without knowing what the natural course, or the normal function, of that thing actually is.

What, then, is literature? There are quite a number of definitions, from Carlyle's 'the thought of thinking Souls' and Godwin's 'the grand line of demarcation between the human and the animal kingdoms' to Stevenson's 'the shadow of good talk' and Pound's 'language charged with meaning'.[248] In between, chronologically speaking, we have Mackail's 'language put to the best purpose, used at its utmost power and with the greatest skill, and recorded that it may not pass away, evaporate, and be forgotten,'[249] while more than 1,500 years before any of these we have Lu Ji's more poetic statement, the concluding section of which reads:

> of literature
> Lies in its conveyance of every truth.
> It expands the horizon to make space infinite,
> And serves as a bridge that spans a myriad years.

It maps all roads and paths for posterity,
And mirrors the images of worthy ancients,
That the tottering Edifices of the sage kings of antiquity may be reared again,
And their admonishing voices, wind-borne since of yore, may resume full expression.
No regions are too remote but it pervades,
No truth too subtle to be woven into its vast web.
Like mist and rain, it permeates and nourishes,
And manifests all the powers of transformation in which gods and spirits share.
Virtue it makes endure and radiate on brass and stone,
And resound in an eternal stream of melodies ever renewed on pipes and strings.[250]

Put together, and as it were conflated, these definitions and descriptions give us at least the beginnings of an answer to the question, 'What is literature?' They enable us to see that literature consists of words, that is, words as committed to writing, and that these words are organized in such a way as to give rise to feelings of pleasure and delight in the reader or listener. Moreover, notwithstanding some rather loose talk about chimpanzees and typewriters and the collected works of Shakespeare, words come to be organized in this particular way not by accident but as a result of the creative activity of the person we rather ambiguously designate 'the writer', that is, the poet, novelist, dramatist, or essayist. In organizing words in such a way as to give rise to feelings of pleasure and delight the creative writer does four things. He conveys information, he gives expression to his individual sensibility or his individual experience of life, he communicates his personal sense of values, and he brings about a modification in the being of his audience, a modification that may be either superficial or profound, temporary or permanent. A working definition of literature would therefore be 'that it is a pleasurable organization of words that conveys information and, at the same time, gives expression to the writer's sensibility, communicates his sense of values, and modifies the being of his audience.'

This definition could of course be worked out in greater detail. It would be possible, for instance, to bring out the fact that the writer's sensibility finds expression by way of a process of imaginative crystallization, as it has been called. But the definition as it stands is sufficiently detailed for our present purpose, which is simply to make it possible for us to say what literary criticism is by giving a tolerably adequate idea of the particular phenomenon that constitutes the object of literary criticism, namely, literature in all its forms. With the help of this definition we can see that literary criticism is in fact concerned with a number of things. To begin with, literary criticism is concerned with words, though with words not in isolation but in their contextual reality. It is concerned with their meaning, down to the very finest shades, with their origin and history, and with the different ways in which they have been used, as well as being concerned with their tone quality, their weight, and their texture. We can also see that literary criticism is concerned with the feelings of pleasure and delight which arise when these words are organized in a particular way, that is, in a particular sequence. It is concerned with the principles which make such an organization of words possible, with the exact nature of the pleasure and delight itself, and with the various methods by which that pleasure and delight is produced. We can see, moreover, that literary criticism is concerned with the kind of information conveyed by a particular pleasurable organization of words, regardless of the actual nature of that information or the particular branch of knowledge to which it belongs. We can see that literary criticism is concerned with the individual sensibility or individual experience of life that finds expression in and through that same pleasurable organization of words. We can see that it is concerned with the values communicated, as well as concerned with the effect which the pleasurable organization of words produces on the reader or listener and the way in which that effect is produced.

Thus a great deal is demanded of literary criticism, or rather, a great deal is demanded of the literary critic – for it is probably better to speak in concrete rather than in abstract terms. The literary critic must be 'well nurtured in his mother tongue'[251] and have at least a nodding acquaintance with linguistics. He must be a person of great emotional sensitivity, with an enormous capacity for the enjoyment of literature in all its forms, for unless he actually enjoys the poems, novels, dramas, and essays with which, as critic, he is concerned, all the scholarship and intellectual acumen in the world will avail him nothing and he will be a literary critic only in name. The literary critic must also be possessed of a wide general knowledge of the arts and sciences, especially of social, political, and economic history, and of a considerable degree of psychological penetration. What is more, he must be familiar with the fundamental questions of philosophy and religion and be sufficiently mature, both intellectually and spiritually, to appreciate the supreme values communicated by the best and greatest literature.

From all this it is obvious that it is not easy to be a literary critic and that literary critics are, in fact, less common than it is sometimes thought. Here, as elsewhere, many are called but few are chosen. It is also obvious why Dryden, Johnson, Coleridge, and Arnold are generally considered to be our greatest literary critics. Above all, perhaps, it is obvious, in the light of what is demanded of the literary critic, that the terms 'literary criticism' and 'literary critic', with their unfortunate suggestion of mere fault-finding, are singularly inappropriate. As Dryden complained 300 years ago,

> they wholly mistake the nature of criticism who think its business is principally to find fault. Criticism, as it was first instituted by Aristotle, was meant a standard of judging well; the chiefest part of which is, to observe those excellencies which should delight a reasonable reader.[252]

The mistake thus magisterially corrected arises, no doubt, from the fact of our using one and the same word for both 'the act or an instance of making an unfavourable or severe judgement, comment, etc.' and 'the analysis or evaluation' – nothing is said about the enjoyment – 'of a work of art, literature, etc.' The usage is by no means universal. In the Indian literary tradition the literary critic, as we call him, is designated the *rasika* or 'man of *rasa*'. The word *rasa* originally meant sap, juice, essence, flavour, taste. In literary criticism it is used in a metaphorical sense and means the 'taste' or 'flavour' that is essential to the enjoyment of literature and which in fact constitutes literature's very essence. The *rasika* or man of taste (also known as the *sahṛdaya* or 'man of soul') is the one who tastes, that is, who appreciates or enjoys, the unique and indescribable flavour of a work of literary art. This taste of his is not a matter of aesthetic judgement (as when we speak of good taste and bad taste), but rather one of aesthetic experience, so that the best equivalent for *rasa* is probably 'aesthetic experience' and the best equivalent for *rasika* 'the man of aesthetic experience'.

According to a leading modern authority, *rasa* or aesthetic experience, *aucitya* or propriety, and *dhvani* or significance, form the three great contributions of Sanskrit *alaṃkāra-śāstra* or poetics, *rasa* being the very soul (*ātman*) of poetry and drama.[253] Such being the case it is not surprising that *rasa* should have been the subject of intense discussion throughout practically the entire history of Indian literary criticism, from its beginnings in the fifth or sixth century CE down very nearly to modern times. One of the principal topics discussed was that of the number of *rasa*s, for though *rasa* as such was fundamentally one, different names were given to it according to its evolving conditions. These names, or these *rasas*, together with the consequent plurality and difference, were held to be ultimately unreal; or they were at best *like* parts or aspects of a whole – the whole that was the ineffably blissful *rasa* itself. Metaphysics apart, however, *rasa* was ordinarily spoken of in the plural rather than in the singular, the number of *rasas* being usually given as eight, though some authorities admitted nine or even ten. The eight orthodox *rasas*, as they are sometimes called, are love (*śṛṅgāra*), valour or heroism (*vīra*), disgust (*bībhatsa*), wrath or fury (*raudra*), mirth (*hāsya*), terror (*bhayānaka*), pathos or compassion (*karuṇā*), and wonder (*adbhuta*), and the two unorthodox ones tranquillity or contentment (*śānta*) and parental fondness (*vātsalya*). Twenty-five or thirty additional *rasas* are also mentioned, while according to some theorists *rasas* are in fact innumerable. Be that as it may, the mere enumeration of the eight *rasas*, whether in English or in Sanskrit, serves to give us no idea of their real nature. It is therefore fortunate that the Indian poet and dramatist Michael Madhusudan Datta (1824–1873) should have written sonnets on the four *rasas* of pathos, valour, love, and wrath, and still more fortunate that these sonnets should have been reproduced in the first issue (November 1987) of *Words International*. The third sonnet, 'Pathos', not only communicates something of the 'aesthetic experience' of that name but also connects pathos with poetry.

> graceful woman by a stream,
> Grave and sorrowful as the autumn moon
> When it fears eclipse. All alone she sat;
> Her face was wet with softly flowing tears.
> One by one they slid from her eyes like pearls,
> Fell on the surface of the stream, and there,

> Floating, turned into full-bloomed lotus flowers –
> Golden lotus, moist with nectar for bees
> To suck, rich with scent for the breeze to waft.
> Bemused, I looked around uneasily.
> The land was empty; a divine voice spoke:
> 'That stream is poetry; that woman's name
> Is Pathos, queen of rasas. Blessed is he
> Who can, through meditation, conquer her.'[254]

It should be noted that in this poem Michael Madhusudan does not describe pathos directly (a *rasa* cannot in fact be described) but rather paints a word picture which, of its own accord, evokes this particular aesthetic experience for the aesthetically educated reader or listener. It should also be noted that like the other *rasas* pathos is not an emotion, though like them it has a dominant emotion as its basis. If we want to apply the word emotion to *rasa* at all then we shall have to do it by terming the latter 'art emotion', as some modern authorities have in fact done. This raises the interesting and important question of the difference between emotion and art emotion, that is, between emotion and *rasa*.

The nature of the difference between the two is very clearly illustrated in the scene of a play within a play in Kṣemīśvara's *Naiṣadhānanda*, Act IV. As A. K. Warder relates,

> Nala, incognito, is sitting with Ṛtuparṇa in the audience seeing a play about the terrible experiences of Damayantī, his wife. Ṛtuparṇa has an aesthetic experience, but Nala instead reacts emotionally, though Ṛtuparṇa keeps reminding him that it is a play and is puzzled at his strange excitement.[255]

Here we cannot but be reminded of another play within a play, that is, the famous one in *Hamlet*, Act III, Scene ii, when the guilty Claudius, 'frighted with false fire', reacts emotionally rather than aesthetically to the play that is being performed before him. Whether in medieval India or Renaissance England, the subject matter of the drama is human life in all its aspects, and the drama depicts human life through the medium of the characters participating in the action of the play. These characters are personated by the actors, and according to classical Indian dramatic theory (with which Indian literary criticism in fact begins) the actors represent the emotions (*bhāvas*) of the characters they personate by representing the causes and effects of these emotions as expressed in bodily movements, speeches, etc. Thus the characters represented are not, in fact, present on the stage at all, neither are their emotions present, for the actors do not experience the emotions they represent but only act them. The characters in a play are present only in the imagination of the audience, and it is the imagined emotions of these characters which are the object of the aesthetic experience. This does not mean that the aesthetic experience is not a matter of perception but only of inference and that we infer the emotions of the characters from perceiving their effects represented. On the contrary, the aesthetic experience is immediate, not indirect. It is not a matter of ordinary perception, however, but rather of a special kind of perception – the perception produced by art. In the words of Abhinavagupta, as paraphrased by Warder,

> *Aesthetic experience* is not perception as in everyday life; it is detached, pure, not involved, does not arouse our everyday concerns but takes us away from them. It is universal or completely objective, not particular or subjective. Thus it does not arouse the emotions of the audience but is a detached perception of the emotions of others.[256]

Moreover, the fact that it is the *imagined* emotions of the characters in the play which are the object of the aesthetic experience means, in effect, that the difference between *rasa* and the experience of *rasa* is purely notional. The perception of *rasa* is inseparable from its existence; or, in other words, *rasa* is identical with the experience of itself.

If all this makes *rasa* sound rather mystical the fact is hardly surprising, for it is obvious that between aesthetic experience on the one hand and religious or mystical experience on the other there are definite analogies. These analogies did not escape the notice of the numerous authors and commentators who contributed to the development of Indian literary criticism. Bhaṭṭa Nāyaka speaks of the experience of *rasa* as a process of disinterested contemplation akin to the contemplation of the Absolute, while according to Abhinavagupta aesthetic experience is non-individual and transcends space, time, and particular circumstances. In it the individual forgets himself, thereby attaining the highest happiness. Many other examples could be adduced.

Nonetheless, though the connection between aesthetic experience and mystical experience was widely recognized there was never any question of subordinating literary criticism to religion. In India literary criticism was an autonomous, independent discipline, and it did not depend on religion or on any other extraneous authority. As Warder points out:

> The critics in fact held a variety of religious and philosophical opinions, which did not prevent them from contributing to the common field of criticism and developing each other's views on the basis of the principles of criticism itself. Bhāmaha was a Buddhist; his commentator Udbhaṭa appears from Jaina references to have been a Lokāyatika; Kuntaka who developed Bhāmaha's theory further was a Kāśmīra Śaiva. All this seems to have no bearing on their work as critics.... The principles of literary criticism in the main tradition are derived from literature itself, from what authors do and what readers enjoy.[257]

There are thus significant resemblances between Indian literary criticism and Western literary criticism. In Western literary criticism, too, the analogies between aesthetic experience and religious or mystical experience have not escaped the notice of the critics, particularly those associated with the Romantic movement, such as (in England) Coleridge, Hazlitt, and De Quincey. Like its Indian counterpart, moreover, Western literary criticism has never been subordinated to religion – except, perhaps, during the Middle Ages, when the function of criticism, like that of literature itself, was severely restricted. Western literary criticism too, therefore, has been a (largely) autonomous, independent discipline, its principles, like those of Indian literary criticism, being 'derived from literature itself, from what authors do and what readers enjoy', or at least were so derived until comparatively recently. But if there are significant resemblances between Indian literary criticism and Western literary criticism there are, at the same time, no less significant differences. Only two of these differences need be mentioned in the present connection. One of them is the fact that the Western tradition of literary criticism is much less continuous than the Indian tradition, and much less progressive. The other is the fact that although Western literary criticism continues to be autonomous and independent there has been a marked change in its relation to religion, at least in principle, so that it does not suffice to say of it – as it may suffice to say of Indian literary criticism – simply that it is not subordinated to religion.

The reason for this change is that there has been a change, here in the West, in the relation of literature itself to religion. Due to a variety of causes – causes into which I cannot enter now, but with which you will no doubt be familiar – in the course of the last 300 or more years religion has ceased to be the sole, or even the supreme, bearer of values. For an increasing number of people, indeed, religion has ceased to be a bearer of values at all, with the result that – to cut a long story short – some of the more sensitive and discriminating among them have, in effect, come to regard literature as the principal bearer of values for the modern world. In other words literature and its sister arts are now performing, for a sizeable section of the population, a function that used to be performed by religion. The church has been replaced by the art gallery and the concert hall, the Bible by Shakespeare – except, of course, so far as the Bible is read not 'as literature' but as the inspired and inerrant Word of God. Literature, in particular, is able to take the place of religion in this way because it is a bearer of values in its own right, so to speak, independently of religion, so that in performing the function of religion it is, in reality, only performing its own function. Indeed, the fact that literature has been obliged, in recent times, to perform what was thought to be the function of religion has served to illuminate literature's own real nature. Literature is no longer regarded merely as a source of information or entertainment but, instead, as a separate and independent means of access to reality.

It is because literature is seen in this way that there has been a change in the relation of literature to religion and, therefore, a change in the relation of literary criticism to religion, so that it no longer suffices to say of Western literary criticism, at least, simply that it is not subordinated to religion. As I have already pointed out, literary criticism is no more than criticism of literature, and the fact that literature has been obliged, in recent times, to perform the function of religion, and that this has served to illuminate literature's own nature as a bearer of values, must be taken into account by any literary criticism deserving of the name. Indeed, such criticism will have to take into account the analogies between aesthetic experience and religious or mystical experience, for example, to a far greater extent that was possible at the time of the Romantic movement. It will have to recognize that there is an area where literature and religion actually overlap and it will have to investigate the nature of the area. So far, no literary critic has done this to any appreciable extent, except for one neglected and virtually forgotten figure (forgotten, that is, as a critic) about whom I would like to say a few words. Before doing this, however, I want to go back to the Indian tradition of literary criticism and see what it has to say about its own subject matter. We have already seen that in that tradition the literary critic, as we call him, is designated the *rasika* or man of taste, the man who appreciates or enjoys the flavour of a work of literary art, and it may be worth our while to see how what we call literature is designated.

The relevant Sanskrit words here are *kāvya*, *sāhitya*, and *vāṅmaya*. The last of these means simply 'consisting of, or relevant to, speech (*vāk*)' and therefore is not of much help to us. *Sāhitya* means 'combination' or 'alliance', the combination or alliance in question being – according to the traditional authorities – that of expression (*śabda*, literally 'word') and meaning (*artha*). 'Expression and meaning combined' has, in fact, been the standard definition of *kāvya* from the seventh or eighth century onward, though Bhāmaha, the author of the definition, qualifies it by the statement that both expression and meaning are endowed with beauty (*alaṃkāra*, literally 'ornament'), beauty itself being defined as figurative or indirect (*vakra*, literally 'crooked' or 'curved'). This figurativeness and indirectness (*vakratā*) is an important feature of *kāvya*, particularly in view of the part that effective utterance plays in the production of *rasa*. Beauty of expression includes the choice of grammatical as distinct from ungrammatical expressions, while beauty of meaning includes the various figures of speech, starting with metaphor, but is further extended to cover the literary application of epistemology and logic, much as we might speak of a solution to a problem in mathematics as elegant. All the traditionally accepted figures of speech, in fact, are beautiful, and according to Bhāmaha this beauty in literature is a kind of deviation from ordinary, everyday expressions, being an added expressiveness created by the genius of the author.

> Literature follows a 'curved' route, so to say, instead of the shortest line, uses indirect expressions, takes in additional meanings, as it were a wider prospect of the country traversed. Thus the characteristic of all beauties of literature, of all accepted *alaṃkāra*s, is their crookedness or curvedness, *vakratā*.[258]

From this it is clear that *kāvya* designates only a small part of what we call literature, for as Warder points out the English language has no word for 'literature' in the precise sense of literature as an art, and it is just literature in this sense that *kāvya* designates. Western scholars have in fact tended to render the term *kāvya* as 'poetry', or even as 'ornate poetry', not to speak of 'court poetry'. This has given rise, however, to a certain amount of misunderstanding. *Kāvya* is not ornate quite in the sense that is implied by the English term, neither does the fact that it was cultivated, more or less exclusively, at the courts of Indian princes, really tell us very much about its actual nature. Above all, *kāvya* is not poetry as distinct from prose but poetry as distinct from metrical composition. As Sushil Kumar De comments:

> The doctrine that prose is the opposite, not of poetry but of verse, which began to be realized rather late in European critical theories, was very early admitted without question by Sanskrit authors with whom metre does not play the same part as it does in European poetry; for in India from the earliest time, it was usual to put down even the driest teachings in a metrical form.[259]

Enlarging upon this theme in a footnote, the same authority declares:

> One need not emphasize the point that Sanskrit theorists define poetry so as to include any literary work of the imagination in its scope, and absolutely refuse to make of rhyming or versing an essential. This tradition is so well established that the question is nowhere discussed and never doubted. Thus, the theorists include under the heading of poetry romances like *Kādambarī* or *Harṣacarita* which are written for the most part in prose. Vāmana even quotes a dictum which says that prose is the touchstone of the poets...'

Vāmana seems to have flourished around 800 CE, that is, about a century after Bhāmaha and two centuries before Abhinavagupta, and the meaning of the dictum which De refers to him as quoting may become clearer if it is paraphrased as follows: 'The real poet is the one who is able to write poetry in prose.' Thus while on the one hand *kāvya* designates less than what we call literature, on the other hand it includes more than what we usually think of as poetry. In other words, *kāvya* is art literature or, as we are more accustomed to say, creative literature or imaginative literature in the widest sense (which does not mean in the loosest sense), and it is this art literature that forms the subject matter of Indian literary criticism and is enjoyed by the *rasika*.

Perhaps the best way of getting an idea of what constitutes *kāvya* is to draw up a select list of those works of English literature which could be regarded as designated by the term. Obviously the list would have to include *The Faerie Queene*, *Macbeth*, and *Paradise Lost*, as well as Smart's 'Song to David', Gray's 'Elegy Written in a Country Churchyard', Keats's Odes, Tennyson's 'The Lotos-Eaters', Poe's 'To Helen', Fitzgerald's *Rubáiyát of Omar Khayyám*, and Rossetti's *The House of Life*. But it would also have to include Milton's *Areopagitica*, Sir Thomas Browne's *Hydriotaphia* or *Urn Burial*, De Quincey's 'The English Mail Coach', Coleridge's marginal glosses to 'The Rime of the Ancient Mariner' (as well as the 'Rime' itself, of course), Melville's *Moby Dick*, Pater's *Studies in the History of the Renaissance*, Hudson's *Green Mansions*, Wilde's *Poems in Prose*, Synge's *Deirdre of the Sorrows*, and Lawrence's *St Mawr*. All this – and much more besides – is *kāvya* or art literature, and it is this 'English *kāvya*', therefore, that we must concentrate on if we want to know what kind of material Indian literary criticism is concerned with and what it is like to be a *rasika* or man of taste.

But it is time I left *kāvya* and the Indian tradition of literary criticism and said my promised few words about the neglected and virtually forgotten figure to whom I referred a few minutes ago – the figure who, alone among the critics of his time, investigated to any appreciable extent the area where religion and literature overlap. The figure in question is John Middleton Murry (1889–1957). As my reference to him implied, though Murry may have been forgotten as a literary critic he is not completely forgotten. In some ways we remember him very well. We remember him as the friend of D. H. Lawrence, as the husband of Katherine Mansfield, and as the opponent – so far as theories of literature went – of T. S. Eliot. In particular, perhaps, we remember him as the man who somehow let Lawrence down very badly, even actually betrayed him, thus bearing out the truth of Murry's own words when he wrote, apropos of the relationship between Godwin and Shelley:

> There are few harder fates for the man of some genius than to be intimately associated with a man of more. He is remembered, but in such a way that it seems better to be forgotten.[260]

In short, Murry as a person has had a bad press, and this fact has helped obscure the importance of his contribution to English literature and, indeed, to English life. At any rate, there has been no biography since F. A. Lea's 'official biography' of 1959 and only two or three short critical studies, the most substantial of them by an American scholar. To make matters worse, all Murry's books are now out of print in England, as are Richard Ree's 1960 and 1970 volumes of selections from his enormous output, while second-hand copies of *Style* and *Keats and Shakespeare* are less easy to come by than they were ten or fifteen years ago.

Nevertheless, it seems the tide has begun to turn. Now that he has been dead for more than thirty years it seems that the friend of D. H. Lawrence and the husband of Katherine Mansfield is coming into his own at last. Two years ago there appeared *Beloved Quixote*, Katherine Middleton Murry's deeply moving memoir of her father, and the fact that four or five of his best known works are currently available in American reprint (at vastly inflated prices) suggests that on the other side of the Atlantic, at least, a process of reappraisal is already in progress. If the tide has indeed begun to turn, and if Murry is indeed coming into his own, it is an occasion for rejoicing, and we must hope that there will be a process of reappraisal on this side of the Atlantic too. Looking back in 1960 on the years following the First World War, Herbert Read observed of him that, at his best, he was 'the most stimulating "creative critic"' of his time, and in the same year another reviewer applauded

> his insight into literature as a composite appeal to the reader's entire nature, which helped reawaken confidence in poetry and fiction, as a medium for the intelligence of the age at a time of dejection and uncertainty.[261]

It is difficult to believe that a critic of whom such things could be said has no significance for us today. Not that he should overlook the phrase with which Read is careful to qualify his praise: it is Murry *at his best* who is the most stimulating 'creative critic' of his time. But neither should we overlook the epithet with which Read characterizes Murry as a critic. As Ernest G. Griffin, the American scholar already referred to, points out:

> The epithet 'creative' which Read applies to Murry is much abused nowadays, but it is useful in distinguishing his criticism from that which is found more commonly in academic circles. Murry's criticism was of a kind which led to a wider creative atmosphere for writers and to wider literary appreciation rather than to the academy. His tastes in later life demonstrated this difference: on the one hand, he had little sympathy with the scholarly critics loosely termed 'the new critics', and, on the other, he was excited to discover the work of J. D. Salinger. In fact, the combination of a moral concern with society and a personal, frequently mystical, enquiry into religious values, which one finds in Salinger and other modern American writers, was just that which was basic to Murry's own work.[262]

Murry's own epithet for himself as a critic was not 'creative' but 'emotional'. Writing to Katherine Mansfield in 1919 he told her:

> I can't treat art as a clever game, and I am (to myself anyhow) always notoriously weakest in the examination of the technical side of a work. My test is extremely simple. If a work awakens a profound response in me, then I sit up and try to find out what it is that is working on me. In other words I am an absolutely emotional critic. What may seem intellectual is only my method of explaining the nature of the emotion.[263]

It was because he was an emotional critic that Murry was able to perform what he saw as the critic's primary function. The task of the critic was to discover and work from the 'creative centre' of the writer with whom he was concerned. The greater the writer, the more mystical would the apprehension of that creative centre be, since the greatest artistic perceptions were those moments of 'immediate apprehension of the unity of the world' in which the basic paradox of life was resolved. In characterizing himself as an emotional critic Murry does not, however, have in mind the usual meaning of the word emotion and its derivatives.

For him emotion is not merely an immediate feeling but a 'mode of experience' based on a subtle interplay and development of original emotions with which, as the development becomes more complex, there grows a progressively acute understanding of the human situation in general.

At the beginning of his 1919 lecture on 'The Nature of Poetry' there is a passage in which Murry gives an impressionistic account of how, as an emotional critic, he approaches the task of criticism. After speaking of the 'curious exaltation that comes to a critic as he begins to disengage – as he believes – the central, golden thread of a poet's being', and quoting the 'small wise sentence' of Anatole France to the effect that criticism is the confession of the adventures of a man's soul among books, he continues:

> Whether it is that I have some special liability to such adventures, or that my mind is such that the adventures I do have take a peculiarly exciting form – I cannot say; but the fact is that there are moments when criticism of a particular kind, the only kind I care for, utterly absorbs me. I feel that I am touching a mystery. There is a wall, as it were, of dense, warm darkness before me – a darkness which is secretly alive and thrilling to the sense. This, I believe, is the reflection in myself of the darkness which broods over the poet's creative mind. It forms slowly and gradually gathers while I read his work. The sense of mystery deepens; but the quality of the mystery becomes more plain. There is a moment when, as though unconsciously and out of my control, the deeper rhythm of a poet's work, the rise and fall of the great moods which determined what he was and what he wrote, enter into me also. I feel his presence; I am obedient to it, and it seems to me as though the breathing of my spirit is at one with his.[264]

Murry is conscious that these are 'vague words', but though claiming to have none better to offer he does, in fact, devote the next few pages of his lecture to explaining, and enlarging upon, his approach in somewhat more analytical terms. From the way in which he does this it is clear that for Murry literary criticism is a very serious matter and that, therefore, literature is a very serious matter too. Referring to the fact that it is not in literature only but in all things that 'the directest and truest apprehension we have is a sudden communication, a sudden communion rather, between mystery and mystery,' he speaks of 'the universe of life of which literature is the symbol and the flower'.[265] It is evident that these last words, casually as they appear to have dropped from Murry's pen, are deserving of careful study. In what sense is literature the symbol and the flower of the universe of life, and what is the precise point of the distinction between literature as the symbol of that universe and literature as its flower? It is also evident that in speaking of literature in this way Murry has, in fact, given us yet another definition of the subject matter of literary criticism. Not only is literature 'the thought of thinking Souls', 'the shadow of good talk', and 'language charged with meaning' and so on. Literature is also the symbol and the flower of the universe of life.

Thus we have come full circle. We have come back to the point from which we set out nearly an hour ago, that is, the point at which I raised the question, 'What is literature?' Since then we have seen the beginnings of an answer to that question, and having seen the beginnings of an answer to it, in the form of a working definition of literature, we have been able to achieve at least some insight into the nature of literary criticism, East and West, as well as some insight into what is demanded of the literary critic. We are therefore now in a position to say what would, in principle, constitute a crisis in literary criticism. Literary criticism would be in a state of crisis if it had a false, or an inadequate, idea of literature and, consequently, a false or an inadequate idea of its own function. Whether literary criticism in England and America is currently in a state of crisis *in this sense* I do not really know, even though I strongly suspect that there is, in fact, something wrong with it at present. But if literary criticism is in crisis, or even if it is just in a mess, or if it is in a crisis because it is in a mess, then the fundamental reason for its being in such a state can only be that it has a false, or an inadequate, idea of literature and, consequently, a false or an inadequate idea of its own relation to literature. What literary criticism therefore ought above all to be doing, if in fact it is in crisis, is trying to achieve a truer and more adequate idea of literature and literary criticism, such as I believe is reflected, albeit fragmentarily, in what I have been saying to you on these subjects in my capacity as an outsider. How literary criticism will achieve such an idea of literature and literary criticism I do not know. Perhaps a dictum of John Middleton Murry's will provide a clue. 'The true literary critic,' he says, 'must have a humanistic philosophy. His inquiries must be modulated, subject to an intimate, organic governance, by an ideal of the good life.'[266] But even if Murry's words do not provide a clue, and even if literary criticism is unable, at this juncture, to achieve a truer and more adequate idea of literature, there are still a number of things it ought to be doing, and I shall conclude with a few words on some of the more important of these things. In speaking of them I shall not be observing any particular order.

Firstly, literary criticism ought to be concerning itself with actual concrete works of literature (that is, works of 'art literature'), and it ought to be concerning itself with them *as literature*. This is so obvious and so elementary a point that had I not come across two rather shocking examples of the way in which literary criticism does *not* concern itself with concrete works of literature I should hardly have dared to make it. In a recent article on 'T. S. Eliot, Robert Lowell and the New Critics' the poet and lecturer Philip Hobsbaum, having referred to 'scholars who wrote their doctoral theses on Lowell and devoted their lives thereafter to the study of his work' continues:

> Beyond their purview, a further school of critics has arisen which shows less and less interest in literature. Not the nascent poetry of our own time, but marginal works of the past ... are the hostages of these other critics, and the works under discussion are not so much texts as source-material for clashes among the ideologies.[267]

This is bad enough, but there is worse to come. In a still more recent article on John Buchan, the critic and editor David Daniell tells the painful story of how Buchan came to be labelled anti-Semitic.

> Gertrude Himmelfarb, an American historian of English life, wrote from New York in the September 1960 number of *Encounter* an article about Buchan later reprinted, with changes, in her 1968 book, *Victorian Minds* – which began this particular myth. There she propounded a racist Buchan who was grossly anti-Semitic. Most of her evidence was made up: her portrait was grossly untrue. 'Buchan's Jewish villains', her invention, do not exist. She showed that she had read virtually no Buchan at all, and what she

> had, she had taken so carelessly that she thought Greenmantle was a woman. Yet her piece had been enormously influential, and traces of it are everywhere. Buchan, she announced – with no evidence – was the fictional 'perpetrator' of the 'Jewish-capitalist-communist-conspiracies.' It seems difficult to get over to a large part of the public that this is a lie.[268]

Obvious and elementary though the point may be, it therefore becomes necessary to insist that literary criticism ought to be concerning itself with actual concrete works of literature, and concerning itself with them *as literature*, and that the literary critic should at the very least have read the poems or the novels or the plays with which he – or she – is purportedly dealing.

Secondly, literary criticism ought to be enjoying the works of literature with which it is concerned and which form its particular subject matter. It is not enough that the literary critic should have enjoyed *Paradise Lost* or *Middlemarch* or *Julius Caesar* twenty years ago, when he was 'reading English' – assuming that, unlike the girl in Robert Graves' anecdote, he did in fact enjoy them then. He must enjoy them here and now, when he is writing about them, and something of that enjoyment must find expression in his criticism. By enjoyment I do not, however, mean the pseudo-aesthetic self-indulgence that Tennyson, in 'The Palace of Art', satirizes in the figure of the 'glorious Devil, large in heart and brain, That did love Beauty only'.[269] By enjoyment I mean the self-forgetful delight that comes when one surrenders to a work of literature and allows oneself to experience it with one's whole being, emotional and intellectual, sensitive and intuitive.

Thirdly, literary criticism ought to be getting out of the universities, or at least trying not to confine itself to them. In other words literary criticism ought to be emancipating itself from the constraints that our current system of higher education tends inevitably to impose on any creative activity. It ought to be transforming itself from a profession into a vocation.

Fourthly, literary criticism ought to be widening its horizon and getting to know the traditions of literary criticism that have developed in India, in the Far East, and in the Islamic world.

Fifthly, literary criticism ought to be re-evaluating our literary heritage. As John Middleton Murry wrote in 1920:

> The function of true criticism is to establish a definite hierarchy among the great artists of the past, as well as to test the production of the present; by the combination of these activities it asserts the organic unity of all art.[270]

In fulfilling this function and establishing the hierarchy of which Murry speaks literary criticism must have the courage of its aesthetic convictions and not hesitate to put down the mighty from their seats and exalt the humble and the meek. Among the mighty I would include James Joyce, Virginia Woolf, Ezra Pound, and (probably) T. S. Eliot, all of whom I believe to be overrated, and among the humble and the meek Cowley, Thompson (author of *The Seasons*), Johnson, Crabbe, Scott, Patmore, Rossetti, Gissing, and Wyndham Lewis, all of whom I believe to be underrated.

Sixthly, and lastly, literary criticism ought to be pointing us in the direction of literature, even as literature itself points us in the direction of life.

BUDDHISM AND WILLIAM BLAKE

Buddhism is a universal teaching. It speaks to all men. It speaks to them, moreover, not as belonging to any particular social group, e.g. clan, tribe, caste, race, nation, but as individual human beings. What it tells each one of them is that he can grow – that he can grow from manhood into Buddhahood, or from unenlightened humanity into Enlightened humanity. It also tells him how he can do this. When Buddhism speaks to men in this way it of course has to speak to them in a language which they can understand. This means much more than speaking to them in their own vernacular. It means communicating with them through the medium of their own ideas, their own culture. Since Buddhism originated in ancient India it at first had to speak – the Buddha had to speak – the language of ancient Indian culture. In fact it had to speak the language of two cultures, the Shramanic and the Brahmanic. Later, when Buddhism spread outside India, it had to speak the language of other cultures, in particular those of South-east Asia, China, Japan, and Tibet. (Sometimes, when the indigenous 'linguistic' resources were inadequate, it had to take Indian culture along with it, but that is another story.) Since Buddhism did not spread beyond Asia, all the cultures with which it came into contact, and through which it had to communicate, were Asian cultures. Although it is in reality a universal teaching, when identified with its medium of communication Buddhism tends to appear as a phenomenon of the cultural history of the East. It tends to appear as an Eastern religion.

During the last century Buddhism has begun to spread beyond Asia. It has begun to make contact with Western culture. As yet, however, it has not really begun to communicate through the medium of that culture. Western Buddhists, and those interested in Buddhism, therefore have to study it in a foreign language, as it were, i.e. through the medium of one or another Asian culture. The situation is made more difficult by the fact that what Asian Buddhist teachers bring to the West is, only too often, not so much Buddhism as the cultural forms with which, for them, it is associated, even identified. Buddhism will not really spread in the West until it speaks the language of Western culture. This will take time. One of the ways in which we can hasten the process is by bringing Buddhism into contact with those Western poets, thinkers, and mystics in whose life or work, or both, there is a reflection, however faint, of the supra-historical splendours of the principial Dharma and who, therefore, already communicate to us something of the spirit of Buddhism in the language of Western culture. One of the greatest of these winged spirits is the English poet, prophet, and visionary William Blake.

Blake was born in London on 28 November 1757, and died there on 12 August 1827. His life thus coincided with one of the most momentous periods in English – indeed in modern Western – history. As a young man he saw and welcomed the American and French Revolutions, while in middle life he was witness to the tremendous upheavals of the Napoleonic wars. He also lived through the Industrial Revolution, with all the changes that this brought about in the social, economic, and political life of the nation. Although he lived in such eventful times, Blake's outward life at least was uneventful. He attended a drawing school for a few years (the only formal education he received), and when he was 15 his father, a hosier, apprenticed him to an engraver, with whom he spent the customary seven years learning his trade. Thereafter Blake supported himself by his own labour, but since the skill of the engraver was less in demand than previously he had often to fight a losing battle with poverty and want – a battle that ended only with his death. In 1782 he married the daughter of a market gardener, and though childless the union was a happy one. From 1782 to 1827 only two events occurred to interrupt the even tenor of Blake's existence in a succession of London lodgings and his work as engraver, poet, painter, and printer of his own illuminated books. The first of these was when, at the invitation of his would-be patron William Hayley, he and his wife left London for Felpham, a village on the coast of West Sussex, where they lived – not very happily – for three years (1801–1803). The second occurred shortly after this period of exile when, as a result of an incident with a drunken soldier which had taken place the previous summer, at Felpham, Blake was accused of seditious libel and tried for the capital crime of high treason. Apart from these two events, both of which made a deep impression on him, the history of the greater part of Blake's life is the history of his spiritual realizations and his creative work.

This truer history begins quite early, for Blake's extraordinary qualities quickly revealed themselves. When only 4 years old he saw God looking in at the window, which set him screaming, and thereafter visionary experiences of this sort were not uncommon. Indeed, they became part of his ordinary waking life. His literary and artistic development was no less rapid. It has been said of him that he 'became an artist at the age of 10, and a poet at the age of 12'. More remarkable still, his tastes and preferences were very decided, and he showed striking independence of judgement. As he wrote long afterwards, 'I saw and knew immediately the difference between Raffaelle and Rubens'.[271] This was not a difference that was apparent to everybody at the time, but neither then nor in later life did Blake ever hesitate to differ from – or to denounce – even the most respected authorities. Both as a man and as an artist he thought and felt and spoke for himself, without fear and without favour. Independence and originality were in fact among his most outstanding characteristics, together with sturdy self-confidence, honesty, openness, and extreme vehemence of expression. But much as his independence and originality contributed to the ultimate greatness of his achievement, they tended to isolate him from his contemporaries. Some people thought him mad. Although he is generally included among the older generation of the Romantic poets, along with Wordsworth, Coleridge, and Southey, and his life and work accounted part of the Romantic movement, his personal contact with them was of the slightest, and they knew hardly anything of his work. Southey, indeed, was among those who thought him mad. Yet despite isolation, and even neglect, Blake's life was a happy one, and towards the end of it he had the satisfaction of gathering around him a small group of young artists who loved and venerated him. When death came he was ready. 'His countenance became fair, his eyes brightened, and he burst out into singing of the things he saw in heaven.'[272]

Being so much an individual himself, it was only natural that Blake should uphold the importance of the general principle of individuality. Indeed, he regarded it as the indispensable basis of true morality and true religion. For him the individual was sacred and inviolable. He therefore believed that it was the duty of each man to be himself, to develop his own potentialities to the utmost, and to allow others to do likewise. 'The Worship of God,' he wrote in one of his finest passages, 'is honouring his gifts in other men; & loving the greatest men best, each according to his Genius: which is the Holy Ghost in man'.[273] Blake meant this quite literally: for him God is man, and there is no other God. In another passage he insists that vice is not so much giving expression to one's own energies as hindering the energies of others. Man cannot develop his potentialities unless he is free. The corollary of the principle of individuality is the principle of liberty. As a young man Blake was a revolutionary, and he therefore saw liberty in primarily social and political terms, as freedom from the tyranny of kings and priests. Later his ideas changed, or rather they developed as he developed, and he saw it first psychologically, as the liberation of the instinctual and emotional energies from the bondage of reason, and then as the liberation of the whole man from the internal divisions into which he had fallen, including the division between reason and emotion. True liberty was to exercise 'the Divine Arts of Imagination'. It was to expand one's consciousness, exploring 'inward into the Worlds of Thought'. It was to enter, or rather re-enter, Eternity.

Blake's enlarged conception of liberty corresponds to an enlarged conception of man. Man is not twofold but fourfold, consisting of the body and its instincts, reason, the emotions, and imagination. This obviously anticipates Jung's four basic functions of sensation, thought, feeling, and intuition. There is also some resemblance to the first four of the five spiritual faculties of Buddhist tradition, i.e. to (in matching order) vigour (*vīrya*), wisdom (*prajñā*), faith and devotion (*śraddhā*), and concentration (*samādhi*), although the fact that these are accompanied by a fifth spiritual faculty, that of mindfulness (*smṛti*), which balances faith and wisdom, and vigour and concentration, means that all four are raised to a higher level and enabled to work together for the attainment of Enlightenment. For Blake man is fourfold both in his divided and in his undivided state. In his fallen and divided state the body and its instincts are present as his Shadow, by which Blake meant suppressed desires, the emotions as his (fallen) Emanation, or split-off feminine counterpart, while reason is present as his Spectre, which is also the self-centred Selfhood with which the fallen man now identifies himself. Imagination, or his Humanity, is absent, or rather is in abeyance, sunk 'in deadly sleep'. Within the context of this enlarged conception of man the individual develops his potentialities when his Humanity awakes. When his Humanity awakes, i.e. when he identifies himself with his Imagination, he can enter his Shadow, absorb his Emanation, and cast out (and also love) his Spectre.

In man's unfallen and undivided state, or in Eternity, the four basic functions appear in their 'archetypal' forms as what Blake calls the four Zoas. These are Tharmas, 'the mildest son of heaven', the Zoa of sense; Urizen, the Prince of Light, the Zoa of reason; Luvah, the Prince of Love, the Zoa of the emotions; and Urthona, 'the keeper of the gates of heaven', the Zoa of Imagination. There is thus a correspondence, in the hermetic sense, not only between the four basic functions and the four Zoas, but also between Shadow, (fallen) Emanation, Spectre, and sleeping Humanity and the four Zoas, in other words between the fallen and divided and the unfallen and undivided states of the four basic functions. This is not unlike the general correspondence, in the Mahāyāna and Vajrayāna forms of Buddhism, between *saṃsāra* and Nirvāṇa, *kleśa* (defilement), and *bodhi* (Enlightenment), or, more specifically, between the five poisons of delusion, hatred, pride, craving, and jealousy, and the mandala of the five Jinas or five Buddhas, i.e. (in matching order), Vairocana, Akṣobhya, Ratnasambhava, Amitābha, and Amoghasiddhi. There is, however, one important difference. In Buddhism there is no doctrine concerning the absolute beginning of things, which is said to be imperceptible. *Saṃsāra* does not originate from Nirvāṇa; *bodhi* never becomes the *kleśas*. In Blake's system the four Zoas divide one from another and fall from Eternity into time, from Truth into error. They fall in anticlockwise order. Tharmas, whose compass point is west, enters time first, followed by Urizen (south), Luvah (east), and Urthona (north). The story of how the Zoas fell, and what terrible conflicts took place between them and their Emanations, as well as the story of how they were all delivered and restored to unity, constitutes Blake's great myth. It is this myth which, in various stages of development, forms the subject matter of the major prophetic books, especially the second longest of them, the central but unfinished *Vala*, or *The Four Zoas*.

The correspondence between psychic functions and Zoas, and poisons and Buddhas, is not the only one. Both Blake and Vajrayāna Buddhism see the whole of existence as one vast and complex system of correspondences. Both use the hermetic principle, as it may be termed, as a principle of order, as a means of organizing the more prominent features of our experience into a beautiful and meaningful pattern, i.e. into a mandala, and in this way achieve integration. Both Blake and Vajrayāna Buddhism are therefore concerned to establish sets of correlations, some of them natural and obvious, others apparently quite arbitrary. Blake correlates the four Zoas not only with the four basic psychic functions, but also with various other sets of four, such as the four points of the compass, the four worlds, the four occupations, the four metals, the four continents, the four arts, the four quarters of the British Isles, the four cities, and the four senses. Thus Tharmas, the Zoa of sense, is associated with the western direction, the world of generation, the occupation of shepherd, the metal brass, the continent of America, the art of painting, Ireland, the city of York, and the tongue or sense of taste. Some of the correlations are quite elaborate (though not without minor discrepancies), such as those between the counties of Great Britain and the Sons of Israel, and the counties of England and the Sons of Albion. Blake's system of correspondences is most fully worked out in Jerusalem, the Emanation of the Giant Albion, the longest of the prophetic books, and the last. In much the same way Vajrayāna Buddhism correlates the five Jinas or five Buddhas not only with the five poisons but with the five wisdoms (*jñānas*), the five colours, the five directions, the five elements, the five *mudrās* or hand-gestures, the five emblems, the five vehicles or mounts, and the five aggregates (*skandhas*). (The Vajrayāna deals in pentads rather than tetrads inasmuch as the central Buddha Vairocana and his absolute wisdom represent the unity of the other four – though according to an early Buddhist Tantric tradition 'everything goes in fours'.) Thus the Buddha Akṣobhya, the Imperturbable, is associated with the mirror-like wisdom, the colour blue, the eastern direction, the element water, the earth-touching mudra, the emblem of the vajra or mystic thunderbolt, the elephant vehicle, and the aggregate of form (*rūpa*). There are, of course, many other sets of correlations. Both Blake and Vajrayāna Buddhism see a correspondence between the order in which the four Zoas, or the four Buddhas (i.e. the five Buddhas minus Vairocana, the Buddha of the centre) are distributed round the four quarters of the mandala and the successive stages by which the individual develops his potentialities. Beginning with Tharmas in the west, the four Zoas enter into time in anticlockwise order, which is the order in which their corresponding psychic functions develop in the individual. In Buddhism, of course, there is no original cosmic fall, but when the four Buddhas, beginning with Amoghasiddhi in the north, are enumerated in anticlockwise order this corresponds to the order in which, upon the occurrence of the profound spiritual experience of turning about (*parāvṛtti*), the five sense consciousnesses, the mind consciousness, the soiled mind consciousness, and the (relative) store consciousness, are transformed into the corresponding four Buddha wisdoms.[274] It also corresponds to the clockwise order in which the five Buddhas appear to the consciousness of the deceased person in *The Tibetan Book of the Dead* (where, so far as the individual is concerned, a 'fall' may indeed occur), as well as to the order in which they are depicted as constituent parts of the visualized seed syllable *hūṃ* in the yoga of the long *hūṃ*.[275]

Blake's emphasis on the importance of individuality connects not only with his conception of man and his system of correspondences but also with his deep insight into the true nature of the individual. Man is in reality not a natural but a spiritual being, and his essence is eternal. Nature has, indeed, no existence apart from man, and like man is fundamentally spiritual, being simply 'a portion of soul [i.e. the emotions] discerned by the five senses, the chief inlets of soul in this age'. Nature appears as a separate entity from man only after the fall, when the individual's senses are turned inside out, so that he perceives what is internal as external, and when, forgetting his true existence, he passes through various states or worlds. These states are quite different from the individual who passes through them, and it is important that the two should be distinguished. States can change, and be annihilated, but individuals cannot. States may be judged and condemned, but individuals can only be forgiven. This is Blake's great doctrine of the forgiveness of sins, and since the forgiveness of sins is mutual it is the basis of the brotherhood of man. The way in which fallen man passes, like a traveller, through various states or worlds, is not unlike the way in which, according to Buddhist tradition, the ever-changing stream of consciousness wanders as a result of spiritual ignorance (*avidyā*) from one to another of the five (or six) realms of conditioned existence, appearing now as a god, now as an animal, and now as a man, and so on, through a whole series of lives until, with the cessation of craving and the attainment of Nirvāṇa, the process of compulsory rebirth comes to an end. In keeping with its refusal to recognize a causal nexus between phenomenal existence and the Absolute, Buddhism does not, of course, speak of a fallen Buddha who wanders through the five (or six) realms of conditioned existence for a while and then gains, or regains, Enlightenment. Yet there is a parallel between Blake and Buddhism at least so far as the origin of the states or worlds is concerned. According to Blake the states are created by the imagination, or by Jesus (for him it amounts to the same thing), as a means of defining the errors into which man has fallen and thus delivering him from them. In Buddhism, at least in its Tibetan form, Shinje, the Lord of the Dead, who judges people after their death and assigns them a place in the other world according with their deeds, is in reality a form of Avalokiteśvara, the Bodhisattva of Compassion.

The fact that the states are created by the imagination makes it clear that, as Blake insists, 'The Imagination is not a State: it is the Human Existence itself....'[276] Since the imagination is also identified with Jesus, and since Jesus is God, the true man is not only the imagination, or poetic genius, but also God. Blake in fact explicitly equates God and man. 'Thou art a Man, God is no more, / Thy own humanity learn to adore....'[277] This does not mean that man in his fallen state, or man as a purely animal and rational being, can be set up in the place formerly occupied by God, as so often happens in the case of secular humanism. It means that instead of submitting to the arbitrary commands of an angry God who dwells high above him in an external heaven, man should develop his own imagination, his own divine humanity, and become what, in the depths of his being, he truly is. Blake's humanism is a spiritual humanism, and as such is akin to the transcendental humanism of Buddhism, which acknowledges no form of existence higher than a Buddha or perfectly Enlightened human being. Blake not only equates God and man but also, with equal explicitness, rejects deism. His position is, in fact, not just non-deistic but even, in effect, non-theistic, and so to that extent not really Christian, at least not in the traditional sense of that term. His name for the 'angry God' is Nobodaddy (i.e. 'nobody's daddy'), and he identifies him with the jealous God of the Old Testament, with Satan the Accuser, and with the fallen Urizen.

It is this false God, the God of this world, that is worshipped by the worldly. Blake's position here is broadly that of Gnosticism. He also rejects the religion of this God, which is that of punishment for sin, as well as the dogmas of the Virgin Birth, the Vicarious Atonement, a personal Devil, and an everlasting Hell. He rejects, in fact, the whole structure of orthodox Christian belief, and although he considers himself a Christian his version of Christianity – if it can be called that – is not only different from, but diametrically opposed to, the more popular 'Urizenic' version. Blake is fully aware of this opposition. In a well-known couplet he declares, 'The vision of Christ that thou dost see, / Is my vision's greatest enemy.'[278] At times he seems to reject not just orthodox Christianity but religion itself, as when he speaks of Jesus sending his seventy-two disciples 'against religion and government'. One modern commentator in fact says that Blake often used 'religion' as a smear word, and it is true that at his best and most characteristic he speaks in terms of artistic inspiration rather than in terms of religious belief. Even when he does use the language of belief he uses it in his own way, i.e. not literally and dogmatically but metaphorically and symbolically. According to him this is in fact the right way to use it, for all religion is 'decayed poetry'[279] and to understand it poetically is to understand it as it was originally meant to be understood. Then as now, it is the poetic genius, the man of imagination, who is the truly religious man.

A whole century before Buddhism was really known in the West Blake offers us the unique example of a non-theistic imaginative vision of rare intensity and integrity. That he could do this was due in the first place to his own extraordinary creative powers – powers which manifested early, and of which he remained in unimpaired possession to the end of his days, he being faithful to them, and they being faithful to him. It was also due to the fact that in addition to the Bible and the major English poets Chaucer, Spenser, Shakespeare, and Milton (and, of course, the works of Michelangelo and the monuments in Westminster Abbey) Blake was able to draw inspiration – indeed, to derive certain elements of his own system – from the 'alternative tradition' of Agrippa and Paracelsus, Boehme and Swedenborg. He was also indebted to some of his more unorthodox contemporaries, such as the freethinker and radical Thomas Paine, the Swiss poet and theologian Gaspar Lavater, Thomas Taylor the Platonist, and the mythologogue William Stukeley.

But important though all these were for his development, Blake's combative and fiery genius probably owed as much to his spiritual enemies as to his spiritual friends, for it was largely in opposition to their mistaken beliefs that he formulated his own system. The most distinguished and influential of these enemies – the enemies of Blake's 'Divine Vision' – were Bacon, Newton, and Locke, whose mechanistic science, mechanistic natural philosophy, and mechanistic psychology left no room for imaginative truth or spiritual values. In setting himself in opposition to them – a David against three Goliaths – Blake set himself against the master current of the age, and in this lies the true measure of his greatness. Indeed, through his life and his creative work Blake accomplishes in his own person what he calls a Last Judgement, which is not a condemnation of sinners to everlasting hell-fire but a final casting out of error from the bosom of the Eternal Man or the imagination. What Blake therefore offers us is not only a non-theistic imaginative vision – not only something of the spirit of Buddhism in the language of Western culture – but an example of the kind of radical revaluation of Western religion and culture that Buddhism, in the person of the Western Buddhist, may soon be called upon to undertake.

URTHONA INTERVIEWS

Urthona, a 'journal of Buddhism and the arts', taking its name from William Blake's Zoa or archetypal spirit of the creative imagination, was founded in 1992 by Dharmachari Ratnagarbha (then Ambrose Gilson). Over the years Sangharakshita was interviewed for the magazine several times; those interviews are reproduced here.

SANGHARAKSHITA IN CONVERSATION WITH AMBROSE GILSON AND ANANDA

Urthona nos. 4 and 5, Autumn 1995

In this wide-ranging conversation Sangharakshita covers many topics of interest to art lovers and practitioners. Dharmachari Ananda introduces the interview:

I was keen to hear Bhante's responses to the questions on art we had sent him a few weeks ago. However, on the way to Bethnal Green Station I was thinking, 'Am I really prepared for this? Am I just wasting his valuable time? Am I really going to hear what he has to say, really take it on board, let my life be re-formed by the meeting? How much will I actually take in? Will I forget to ask him the most crucial question of all, the one that's been secretly nudging my left shoulder for the past three months? And will I go away inspired or daunted, steady or shaking?'

As we rattled up the escalator Ambrose confided to me that he was feeling pretty nervous too. Would he be able to get the question out when it came to it? I tried to remember how I'd felt twenty years ago when I first met Bhante in the seedy basement of the Sakura shop in Monmouth Street, Covent Garden. I think I so much wanted to see him as a great guru in those days that any stray comment he happened to make reverberated in my mind like the voice of the Wizard of Oz, shimmering with endless levels of significance.

Gradually over the years I've come to realize he is something much greater than a guru – a fully-lived human being who enjoys honest and energetic communication with his many friends. Our meeting took place in Bhante's small flat adjoining the London Buddhist Centre, on a very warm afternoon in June. It was no surprise to find piles of books overflowing from the burdened shelves onto the floor. They all looked as though they were in the process of being read, although Bhante admitted he hadn't got around to reading many of them, saying he preferred to wait until he was in the mood, and had sufficient space to get into them. I sympathized. We were slightly concerned that we wouldn't get through all the questions in the time available, but true to form, in the event Bhante found plenty of time to address them all. As a final comment before we began recording, he observed that he would prefer to talk ad lib, rather than editing himself on the fly, as it were. He would leave it up to us to produce a faithful 'final cut'. I very much hope we have succeeded in doing that.

DISCIPLINE AND SOLITARY LABOUR

AMBROSE: Recently you have stressed a whole-hearted engagement with life as a necessary condition for the arising of transcendental awareness. In this context quite a bit has been said about right livelihood as a suitable field for this wholehearted engagement. Do you see the practice of an artistic skill as an equally suitable arena of engagement, for those with that kind of vocation? I wonder if the fact that most artistic disciplines involve many hours of solitary labour, rather than work in a team, presents a disadvantage in this respect?

SANGHARAKSHITA: As far as I remember I haven't ever spoken of 'a wholehearted engagement with life', and I would regard that expression as being a bit vague, not to say woolly. But I have recently spoken at some length about whole-hearted engagement with team-based right livelihood as a means and an opportunity for the arising of Insight. I certainly do see a parallel, to some extent at least, between that and engagement in artistic endeavour.

One of the connections between the two is discipline, without which you can't be involved in any of the arts. I see the arts themselves as disciplines in the strict sense, disciplines involving wholehearted engagement, even commitment, as well as concentration, unification of resources, and so on – and, as you say, many hours of solitary labour. I recently read a biography of Paul Scott, the author of the *Raj Quartet*.[280] The fact that he was working on those four novels isolated him from his wife and children to an extent that caused severe strain on the marriage, and even break-up for a while. At times both he and his wife seemed to be trembling on the verge of insanity; but his work, the finishing of the *Quartet*, seemed to demand that isolation.

Another very striking example is to be found in Simon Heffer's recently published biography of Thomas Carlyle.[281] Especially after his move to London, when he became the 'sage of Chelsea' – a solitary sage – Carlyle isolated himself to an incredible degree, and this imposed a terrific nervous strain on his wife. Carlyle only became aware of this after her death, when he read her diaries, and when he realized the strain she had been under, he was very remorseful. He even left his social life to his wife; she used to entertain his visitors, while he would remain upstairs in his study. Eventually he had a cork-lined room in which he did his writing! It does seem that for him it was a case of solitary labour for hours, days, weeks, months, and even years. It took him seven years to complete his biography of Frederick the Great, and meanwhile his poor wife had to suffer.

Talking of cork-lined rooms makes me think of Proust, who also isolated himself. And Balzac was in the habit of working at night and dosing himself with coffee to keep himself awake. So yes, most artistic disciplines very definitely involve many hours of solitary labour, and from the point of view of work in a team, that is a definite disadvantage. But for some writers and artists such labour is the necessary means of the artistic production.

AMBROSE: Yes. People who are drawn to an artistic discipline generally seem to feel that they must do it, and that it's not really an alternative for them to give it up for what might appear to be a healthier situation, working in a team.

SANGHARAKSHITA: It isn't that they don't regret the pain inflicted on those who are near and dear to them. Very often they regret the sacrifice of their social life, but they feel that there is no alternative. This isolation is the only way in which they can get on with their creative work, whether it's writing or painting or whatever. Among painters one could cite the example of Michelangelo, working up there on the ceiling of the Sistine Chapel. If you paint portraits at least you have the company of your model. But the writer does seem to be a somewhat solitary creature in many cases, though there are some examples of more gregarious writers who were able to write in the midst of the family. The family did not necessarily share in what they were doing, but they carried on with their work in the midst of family life. Sir Walter Scott seems to have been able to do that, and Jane Austen, it seems, had to do it. She didn't have a room of her own in which to write and she did at least as well as Virginia Woolf – indeed, I would say, very much better.

AMBROSE: And some have chosen to work at the café table, of course.

SANGHARAKSHITA: Yes, for some the solitary café table in the corner.

COLLECTIVE ARTS ACTIVITIES

AMBROSE: In the light of this tendency to isolation, perhaps our writers and painters need to put much more effort into developing the other-regarding aspects of their work – for example, attending or running workshops, discussing their work with others, perhaps even setting up studios where artists may work together. Do you see these things as important?

SANGHARAKSHITA: Personally I do not. Having always been a solitary writer myself (when I do write), I don't see such collective activities as being at all important so far as the actual production of works of art is concerned. As for the other-regarding aspects of the work of writers and painters, surely it consists in the fact that they are, even if only implicitly, addressing an audience. They have an audience in mind – maybe not in a very specific or concrete sense, but they are not writing in a complete vacuum. They are not just expressing themselves; they are communicating to a quite definite audience, or sometimes even to humanity in general. That is the other-regarding aspect of the artist's work.

I have personally always felt that running workshops and discussing one's work with others, even setting up studios with other artists, has got very little, if anything, to do with creative activity. It may be convenient to share a studio with others, but I don't see that the sharing of facilities has anything to do with the creative work itself. As for discussing one's work with others, my impression is that most real artists and writers are quite reluctant to discuss their work – indeed, would rather discuss anything other than their work. Running workshops may perhaps help others, but I don't think it has anything to do with creative activity. I see it as something quite separate. So from the point of view of the production of works of art, whether in literary or visual form, I don't see all these allegedly other-regarding aspects as at all important.

AMBROSE: There is the aspect of understanding the context in which you are producing the work of art, the way in which you are trying to move towards creating a new culture with other Buddhist artists. Surely one could clarify that through discussion with others?

SANGHARAKSHITA: Well, perhaps, but I think it would only help one to produce works of art indirectly. In any case, I don't think it can be a question of consciously deciding to produce a Buddhist work of art. If you are a Buddhist, something of Buddhism will manifest in your work of art, though it may not be recognized or identified as such. In the West, of course, Buddhists are in a minority, which means that Buddhist artists and writers are in a minority. We have only the very beginnings of a Buddhist culture, and this puts us in a different position from someone producing a work of art within a thriving culture. If you are immersed in a culture in that way, if it is in the air around you, you don't have to discuss anything with anybody. But if it is helpful, say, to the Buddhist writer to clarify with other Buddhist writers what it means to be a Buddhist writer, that is only because of the accident of the fact that we don't live in a Buddhist society. It has nothing do with the requirements of the artistic process.

AMBROSE: In the FWBO a good deal of effort has been put into shared arts projects – for example the two arts centres, and the arts retreats run at several of retreat centres. There seem to be three main strands of activity: (1) workshops which help people to hone their skills in an artistic discipline, for example writing workshops; (2) workshops (often on retreats) where the emphasis is not so much on technical skill as on using artistic media to explore the imagination, in particular Buddhist symbols, for example the 'Game of Death' retreat held a few years ago at Padmaloka; and (3) workshops designed to educate one about the work of a particular artist or artistic movement, for example a talk on Dante at the London Buddhist Arts Centre. Which of these do you think is the most important? Have we got the balance about right?

SANGHARAKSHITA: I think all three are useful. Workshops that help people to develop their skills in an artistic discipline, like writing groups, are useful, though probably only to the extent that they concentrate on basics. I am very sceptical about writing groups. I think a lot of people who attend them need help with simple things like sentence structure and appreciation of the meaning of words, or even just spelling. I think one has to start on this basic level, not encouraging people to be creative when perhaps they just do not have that capacity, but might be able to produce some decent work if at least they honed their skills in a more down-to-earth sense.

Workshops where the emphasis is not so much on technical skill as on using artistic media to explore the imagination, and in particular Buddhist symbols, can be helpful in a mildly therapeutic way, if you see what I mean. I don't see them as having any value from a purely artistic point of view. The working artist can dispense with them – indeed, for him they will be a waste of time – but for, as it were, ordinary people, for non-artists, they can have a definite value in provoking the imagination.

And then thirdly, workshops focusing on the work of a particular artist or artistic movement – yes, these are useful too. If I remember rightly, the Croydon Arts Centre did specialize in this way, and they did have some very good programmes and speakers, but overall the emphasis was on passive appreciation – just listening, just learning – not on doing anything.[282] I think it was useful, but useful within certain limits. It was one-sided. But having said that, I certainly do think that such workshops are of value.

If an arts centre is doing all these three things – helping people to develop their skills, exploring the imagination, and educating people about the arts – that is a quite valid programme. I do not see it, though, as turning out artists, or even as helping artists very much. I see it more as a general cultural activity which has its uses from the general cultural point of view.

THE DANGERS OF DABBLING

AMBROSE: With all these workshops, do we run a risk of encouraging people to distract themselves by dabbling in all sorts of different areas of artistic expression? I wonder if in general we need to spend less time on self-expression and more time studying the great masters of the past, to clarify what we really want to achieve with our art.

SANGHARAKSHITA: Yes, there is certainly an over-emphasis on self-expression, not just within the FWBO but in the world of the arts as a whole. I could encapsulate my thinking by saying that one has to have a self before there is any question of expressing it. For many people, more time spent studying the great masters of the past would in fact be more useful. And yes, I do think there is a danger that if we have lots and lots of arts workshops of various kinds we may encourage people to distract themselves by dabbling.

Dabbling is a great danger nowadays not just within the FWBO or with regard to FWBO centres but more generally. People dabble in a bit of poetry or they dabble in a bit of watercolour painting or they dabble in a bit of creative writing. This is quite counter to the basic seriousness, commitment, and whole-hearted engagement that any of the arts demands. It might be all right to dabble a bit in different media if you are not quite sure which one you want to take up, but I suspect the person who has a real artistic urge will find his or her appropriate outlet or medium without any such dabbling or experimentation. The painter will know that he wants to be a painter; the writer will know that he wants to write – maybe from a very early age. If you find yourself wondering 'Now, how shall I express my creativity? Shall I take up pottery, or oil-painting, or portraiture, or the guitar?' I'd say the chances are that you are not really a very creative person. You may just be looking for an extra social accomplishment, like the young ladies in the Victorian era who would play the piano a bit and do some watercolours, and thereby increase their chances of marriage.

AMBROSE: Do you see any way of avoiding this tendency, or reducing the risk of it?

SANGHARAKSHITA: Well, it's a free country. What can you do? But in our own arts centres, broadly speaking, we can encourage a greater seriousness in people's approach to the arts. The arts are not to be messed around with. They should be an aspect of our serious approach to life, our serious approach to the Dharma. By serious, of course, I don't mean heavy, I mean involved and whole-hearted.

ANANDA: I wonder if you have any feelings about the effect of the media upon this dabbling consciousness. Take watching television. When you watch television, you don't have to put a lot of effort into understanding what is going on. I think that learning and, even further, creativity, comes as a result of individual effort to grapple with a particular idea. There is no grappling involved in television watching; it is very passive.

SANGHARAKSHITA: That is true. I certainly do not depreciate television as a medium – I think it is a very good one – but I'm not so sure that it is very well used. Studies have been done which show that children who spend a lot of time watching television tend to be less creative in their schoolwork, more passive generally, and less healthy, simply because the fact that they spend so many hours a day sitting in front of the television means that they are not out playing, or exercising or interacting. One could even say that however instructive and enlightening (for the sake of argument) television programmes may be, if one gets into the habit of watching too many of them, one adopts a passive attitude that is not very helpful to one as an individual, and especially not helpful if one is trying to produce anything in the nature of a work of art.

ART AS REBELLION

ANANDA: I would like to bring in the idea of art as rebellion – that is, art as an activity or expression which challenges accepted ideas or value, as opposed to making us feel safe and comfortable by affirming the values we are familiar with. I am thinking of Damien Hirst's sheep in formaldehyde and the notorious pile of bricks.[283]

SANGHARAKSHITA: I think it is quite dangerous for the artist to think of himself as a rebel. In fact, more often than not, artists do not think of themselves as rebels. (When I say 'artist', of course I mean writers as well.) Some writers and painters who have produced something new have been surprised by the reaction they received, because they did not start writing or painting with the idea of breaking conventions. They just wrote or they just painted; they just tried to embody their own particular vision. Sometimes, as I said, they have been quite surprised that people did not take to it or appreciate it. I think that art as rebellion is almost a contradiction in terms. In the context of literary history or the history of art it may be seen as a rebellion, but I don't think the artist ever consciously sets out to be a rebel.

AMBROSE: I suspect Damien Hirst has a very self-conscious and superficial view of rebellion.

SANGHARAKSHITA: Yes. The point has often been made that great artists have not been understood in their own lifetime. That may be true in some cases, though it is often exaggerated. Some great artists, poets, writers, musicians, were greatly appreciated in their own lifetime. Mozart, Haydn, Bach, Handel, Walter Scott, Jane Austen, the Brontës, and Dickens were all very well appreciated in their lifetime. And some artists have been appreciated less since their death.

AMBROSE: What about Blake?

SANGHARAKSHITA: It isn't that Blake was not appreciated so much as that he was not known. But yes, there have been instances where great writers and artists have not been appreciated. I'm afraid, though, that this has tended to be generalized as 'great artists are not appreciated in their lifetime' and then turned round the other way; 'If you are not appreciated in your lifetime, you must be a great artist.' That is logically flawed, obviously.

A similar thing happens with the idea that if you are a great artist, you have to break the rules. That does sometimes happen. Mozart apparently broke the rules of harmonics by introducing dissonances into his music. But then people think, 'Ah! If you break the rules, you are a great artist,' and they set about breaking rules in a rather self-conscious way, as though that would make them great artists and enable them to create works of art. I think Damien Hirst and Andy Warhol come in this category. I can't take them seriously at all. I have not seen the sheep but I've seen photographs of it, and I'm afraid I can't take it seriously. I think such artists have got lost.

DO SHOCK TACTICS WORK?

ANANDA: But if it is the case that an aspect of the Dharma is to make us more aware of reality, or to make us perceive the world in a new way, what do you think about works which attempt to shock us into this new way of seeing by trying to make us question the basis of our existing values? In other words, does 'art as rebellion' through the presentation of something conventionally thought of as ugly or distasteful have any place in your vision of a spiritual art, an art which transforms our sense of values?

SANGHARAKSHITA: I suppose the short answer is no, not really; but I'll just make a few comments. Yes, it is an aspect of the Dharma to make us more aware of Reality. In fact, you can say that it is the principal function of the Dharma. But what is Reality, and what does it mean to perceive the world in a new way? In the Buddhist context it is to perceive the world from the standpoint of absolute reality. I don't think you achieve that by just playing around with technicalities on the artistic level, by just self-consciously trying to do things in a different way. If you do that, you remain on the same level, or even sink beneath it. For instance, you might compare Hirst's *Away from the Flock* with a Gainsborough landscape. Well, I'd say that a Gainsborough landscape challenges us much more than a sheep in formaldehyde.

AMBROSE: How does Gainsborough challenge us?

SANGHARAKSHITA: In the sense that he sees nature, sees that particular landscape, in a way that perhaps you have not seen it. If you studied that painting, you would start to share something of Gainsborough's vision, and realize that he sees things differently from you, that he has a deeper vision. But the sheep in formaldehyde is just different; it is just not what you expected on quite a mundane level. I don't think it's a revelation of, or points to, Reality in a deeper sense, in the way that what I would regard as a real work of art does. Hirst is just out to shock, or perhaps not even that, maybe just playing around, doing something different. Again, I can't take it seriously Do you see what I mean?

ANANDA: But I imagine that Hirst would say that by shocking people you are actually waking them up....

SANGHARAKSHITA: By shocking them? You can shock people in many ways, but that has nothing to do with a spiritual waking up. You merely shock them.

ANANDA: But don't you make them question the things that they took for granted, like the idea of beauty? What is conventional beauty? Is it a lovely landscape or a sunset or flowers or something like that? Putting a dead sheep in an art gallery...

SANGHARAKSHITA: Rembrandt did the same thing, but he did it as an artist; there is the painting of the flayed ox, but he didn't put an ox in formaldehyde! You see? I think people like Damien Hirst just play around with ideas; it's all very interesting and amusing, but I don't think it has any deeper significance. I'm not even sure about the *Flayed Ox*. This raises larger questions about the religion of art. I don't know if you've read my essay *Criticism East and West*?

AMBROSE: Yes.

SANGHARAKSHITA: Do you remember that I referred to Indian poetics there, and discussed the difference between aesthetic experience and emotional experience? Say, for example, in the course of a play one character is about to stab another. If someone in the audience jumps up and tries to prevent the actor from striking the fatal blow, what does that mean?

AMBROSE: He is taking it literally.

SANGHARAKSHITA: Yes, so in art there is a sort of distance; this is the difference between a work of art and a chunk of nature. You are, as it were, distanced from the work of art in a way that you are not distanced from nature, so you don't react to what is happening (if anything is happening) in the work of art as you would if that same thing were happening in reality. This is the objection to pornography; it is the intrusion of the sexual element into, say, a piece of writing in such a way that you are forced to respond to it not as part of the writing but as though it was actually happening. (This, of course, applies especially to films.) Your reaction is non-artistic.

AMBROSE: I'm reminded of that film *The Unbearable Lightness of Being*, which does have a lot of explicit sexual scenes but doesn't provoke a pornographic response because of the way they are filmed. They are shot with this tremendous emotional tension, and you feel very strongly what is going on in the characters' minds.

SANGHARAKSHITA: A few days ago I saw the film *Rob Roy*, and I felt that a couple of the sex scenes were prolonged. The prolongation was not in the least essential to the story; in fact, the sex scene itself was not really essential, but you could have overlooked that if it had been much shorter. When it goes on and on, with all the pawing and so on, you think 'Just get on with the story!' Clearly the director has deviated from his aesthetic intentions for the time being. A sexual element in a work of art that provokes a non-artistic reaction is pornography. In the same way, if the picture of the flayed ox evokes a response of disgust and horror to such an extent that you cannot appreciate it as a work of art; well, to that extent it ceases to be a work of art. I think it would be quite difficult for a sensitive person, perhaps especially a vegetarian, to see Rembrandt's *Flayed Ox* as a work of art. So, to come back to the sheep, there is no distancing. It is just a sheep in formaldehyde, and to that extent it cannot be a work of art. Incidentally, this whole question of distance is gone into quite thoroughly from another point of view in Schiller's *Letters on the Aesthetic Education of Man*.[284]

STRUGGLE IN THE CITY OF ART

ANANDA: Blake said 'everything that lives is holy'. He also said that the artist achieves his work by continual conflict and struggle in the city of Golgonooza, the creative furnace. How do you see this struggle manifesting in the life of a Buddhist artist?

SANGHARAKSHITA: I assume it manifests more or less as it manifests in the life of any artist. I do not see that there can be art without struggle; at the very least there is the struggle with your medium, which is a big enough struggle if you take your artistic work seriously.

Then there is the struggle to embody your ideas; there is the struggle to find out within yourself what your ideals, and your feelings, actually are. Sometimes you may not be very clear about that; you may discover what you really believe only in the process of writing and rewriting repeatedly. So I think the fact that the artist is a Buddhist does not exempt him from that struggle; it may modify it in some ways or turn it in a particular direction but I think that to the extent that he resolves his struggle he probably resolves his art too. One can look at the work of an artist who has produced a lot of work as the resolution of a whole series of struggles, or sometimes even the resolution of the same struggle from different points of view. Some writers seem to have one basic problem or conflict which they are dealing with all the time; in the case of Dickens it was his miserable childhood – that seems to feature very strongly in his work. So I certainly would not see the Buddhist artist as exempt from conflict and struggle; it could be that the Buddhist artist is able to meditate, and to have periods of refreshment on retreat, but I think he would still have to struggle with his creative work. I do not see any easy opt out, even for the Buddhist artist.

ANANDA: I agree. I think that the fact that one is a Buddhist really just intensifies that conflict, it certainly does not remove it.

Sangharakshita: It might refine it, but you would not essentially change the need for struggle. On the other hand, that conflict is not necessarily tragic or disastrous. Blake no doubt experienced great conflict, but he was a very happy man. I think one can enjoy the creative struggle, there is no doubt about that. One might even say that one can get out of the creative struggle, with one's medium, with oneself and so on, an enjoyment that one perhaps does not get in any other way.

ARTISTIC FRIENDSHIPS

AMBROSE: Do you have a favourite example of an artistic friendship, a friendship in which two or more individuals really sparked each other off and brought something into being that neither could have produced on their own?

SANGHARAKSHITA: I've thought about this quite a lot, but I haven't been able to come up with an example of the kind of mutually creative artistic friendship that you describe, although there is a bit of an exception which I'll mention in a minute. A good example of artistic friendship in general is that between Goethe and Schiller, especially as manifested in their correspondence. But I think the importance of that friendship for each of them consisted in the fact that the other was, you could say, his equal. It's usually said that Goethe was greater than Schiller but perhaps one shouldn't emphasize that too much. They were both very great men. Goethe was in communication with no one else of the artistic rank of Schiller, and likewise Schiller was in contact with no one else of the rank of Goethe.

So Goethe and Schiller certainly sparked each other off. But I don't think we can say that either brought into existence as a result of the friendship something that would not otherwise have been created. It's as though they were a bit like two knives sharpening each other. The contact between them made Goethe more like Goethe, and Schiller more like Schiller. Their friendship enabled each of them to understand himself better, perhaps, and do his own work more effectively, but it didn't result in any joint work that neither of them could have produced individually.

Of course there are such things as joint works. In drama we have the example of Beaumont and Fletcher, who produced a number of plays between them. They each produced independent work as well, but probably neither could have produced on their own the plays that they wrote in collaboration. There's a tradition that one of them wrote the tragic bits and the other the comic bits.[285] In the case of light opera, Gilbert and Sullivan were collaborators. But that's rather different from working on one and the same work of art, different from two painters painting a picture, because there's a division of labour: Sullivan wrote the music and Gilbert wrote the libretto.

ANANDA: I suspect that Ambrose wasn't thinking of that kind of collaboration, but of the possibility of an artist producing better work as a result of his contact with another artist.

AMBROSE: Yes. For example, perhaps Coleridge couldn't have written *The Rime of the Ancient Mariner* if he hadn't been inspired by meeting Wordsworth.

SANGHARAKSHITA: Well, it certainly wasn't a joint product, although Wordsworth is credited with a couple of stanzas, including the one containing the lines 'Thou art long and lank and brown / As is the ribbed sea-sand'.

Of course, nowadays some feminist critics are fond of maintaining that the wives of great writers had a larger share in their work than has been generally admitted, but that's probably quite impossible to tell, unless you happen to come across large chunks of manuscript in the wife's handwriting – and even then it might have been dictated. We know, for example, that Tolstoy's wife copied out the whole of *War and Peace* in different versions seven times, but no one has ever suggested that she actually wrote part of it.

So I don't think there's any example of collaboration so close that a joint work was produced. This suggests that artistic activity, like all higher cultural activity, is essentially an individual pursuit, though not without reference to a potential audience, a reference which makes it individual but not really isolated.

NEOPLATONISM

AMBROSE: I'm very intrigued by your avowed interest in Neoplatonism, which I gather you have studied in some depth. Could you say a bit more about what first attracted you to it, and which texts have particularly inspired you?

SANGHARAKSHITA: I can't remember what first attracted me to Neoplatonism, although I can remember my first contact with it. When I was in my teens, before I went to India, I acquired a copy of Thomas Taylor's translation of selected *Enneads* of Plotinus,[286] and that was my first and only contact with Neoplatonism until I came back to Britain in the sixties. As to which texts have particularly inspired me, I would single out those of Plotinus. His *Enneads* – well, many of them at least, the not-so-technical ones – are inspiring. Proclus, I think, is inspiring only in very small doses, and the same goes for the other Neoplatonic writers.

AMBROSE: Neoplatonism is, I gather, a scholarly term for the tradition which developed the mystical side of Plato's thought. Does this tradition stand in a similar relation to Plato to that in which Buddhism stands to the Buddha? In other words, was Plato's insight the main spiritual impulse of Neoplatonism, or is there not really a lineage which can be traced back to Plato in that way?

SANGHARAKSHITA: Neoplatonism didn't develop just the mystical side of Plato's thought; it also developed the rational, dialectical side. I think that the combination of the mystical and the rational is one of the things that attracted me to Neoplatonism, and in particular to Plotinus. Someone once said, writing about Buddhism, that the Theravāda is rationalism tinged with mysticism, and the Mahāyāna is mysticism tinged with rationalism. I think in Plotinus you get a fairly good balance between the two, as in fact I think you do in Plato though not always in the same work. One of the things I find interesting in Plotinus is that he often explores a question as far as he possibly can rationally and dialectically, and then, when he is at the end of his rational and dialectical resources, he takes a great mystical leap. But he doesn't take that leap prematurely; he exhausts his rational and dialectical resources first.

As to whether the Neoplatonic tradition stands in the kind of relation to Plato that Buddhism does to the Buddha, I would say that it doesn't quite, because Plotinus is indebted not only to Plato, but also to Aristotle, to quite a considerable extent. There are important strands in Plotinus' thought which go back to Aristotle, if only by way of correction and adaptation. He is also considered by scholars to include Stoic elements. He is not eclectic – he certainly has a system of his own – but he incorporates considerable elements from the Aristotelean tradition and from the Stoic tradition, even though the predominant influence is that of Plato, both on the mystical side and on the rational side.

I think one could say that Plato's insight was the main spiritual impulse behind Plotinus. But although there was a kind of Platonic lineage, it went through different stages of development, and one of those stages, the stage known as the Academy, the sceptical Academy, wasn't really anything very much like the Neoplatonism of Plotinus at all. So there wasn't a continuous tradition in that sense, even though there was a Platonic school located for hundreds of years in Athens itself, in the Academy. The Academy's own thinking underwent quite a series of changes, and Plotinus' thinking was not in that 'lineage'. One might say that Plotinus went much more directly back to the dialogues themselves, as well as to the works of Aristotle. There were also what are called the Middle Platonists, some of whom influenced Plotinus' thought, as some of their works were commented on within Plotinus' circle.

Plotinus seems not to have given lectures; he held study and discussion groups in the course of which people would bring up difficulties and ask for clarification of obscurities in his thinking, and then he wrote the *Enneads* on the basis of those discussions.

AMBROSE: But presumably he had a living teacher.

SANGHARAKSHITA: Yes. According to the accounts his teacher was Ammonius Saccas, but we don't know what he taught because it was an oral tradition, and he didn't write anything down. But the guess of scholars is that Ammonius Saccas functioned very much in the way that Plotinus did. He got his disciples to read out texts, maybe a passage from Plato or Aristotle, or perhaps from one of the Middle Platonists, and he just commented on it verbally. And it seems that Plotinus functioned mainly in that way too, except that he did write these philosophical essays, the *Enneads*, on the basis of some of the things he said in these discussions.

ANANDA: There's a fascinating parallel with the FWBO there.

SANGHARAKSHITA: Yes.

IS THE GOAL OBJECTIVE?

AMBROSE: One of the things I find attractive about Neoplatonism in general, and the thought of Plotinus in particular, is that although he makes it clear that the goal cannot be defined in words, he is not afraid to use positive terms such as 'the Good' and 'the One' to point to it. Personally I find such modes of expression more helpful than more neutral terms such as 'Reality' or even 'the Transcendental'. To think that I am heading for an ideal realm of goodness, unity, and harmony stirs my spiritual energies. However, as Dhardo Rimpoche makes very clear in his *Buddhism in Tibet*, Nirvāṇa is 'not an objective reality into which men enter and rest'.[287] Does this mean that it is better to avoid terms such as 'the One', which suggest an objective realm or being? After all, Buddhism seems not to have spared its criticism when it encountered similar conceptions in the Hindu tradition.

SANGHARAKSHITA: Well of course there are several traditions within Buddhism itself. In the Pāli canon there are passages which do suggest that the Buddha thought of the Unconditioned, or at least spoke of it, as an objective reality. He says in the *Udāna* that 'There is, monks, that sphere where there is neither this not that (and so on). If there was not that sphere no liberation from this *saṃsāra* (the conditioned world) would be possible.'[288] So yes, it does seem that the Buddha himself did speak, sometimes at least, in those terms. We can't really avoid speaking in that way. We just have to beware of excessive literalism.

In the *Ariyapariyesenā Sutta*, the Buddha says that when he was a bodhisattva, he went from the conditioned to the conditioned, but then thought, well, why not try to go from the conditioned to the Unconditioned?[289] He does seem to speak there of the Unconditioned, the *asaṃskṛta*, as an objectively existing reality. Perhaps our mind, and certainly our speech, is so constituted that we can't really do otherwise.

The mere fact that something is the object of your statement in a grammatical sense gives it a certain quasi-metaphysical objectivity. We say 'I go for refuge to the Buddha', not 'to the idea of the Buddha', which implies that the Buddha does exist objectively in some sense. One could say that that objectivity is at least as certain as our subjectivity. So long as we are trapped within that subject–object duality, we cannot but think in terms of subjects and objects, and even of spiritual realities as being in some sense objectively existing realities 'out there'. If one tries to avoid that, except when making a fine philosophical point, one lends oneself to all sorts of confusion.

AMBROSE: I suppose in Plotinus we have the additional element that he uses very positive terms such as 'the Good' and 'the Beautiful'.

SANGHARAKSHITA: I suspect that this is a rather subjective matter. I think some people would find 'the Good' or 'the One' very abstract, while they might be really sparked off by terms like 'Reality' or 'the Transcendental'. In a sense it doesn't matter what we call it. This is why in Buddhism we find a whole plethora of different terms, positive and negative, symbolic and paradoxical, from which to take our pick.

AMBROSE: It would seem from Plato's *Symposium* that a crucial point on the path is that point at which we move from the contemplation of physical beauty to the beauty of the virtues we see in others, and thence to the beauty of knowledge. It strikes me that those artistic works which help us to see the qualities of humanity on a broad scale are particularly helpful in this respect. I mean the kind of works of art which shows us 'real people' – imperfect, but with noble qualities shining through – Rembrandt springs to mind here. Would you agree that this is the case?

SANGHARAKSHITA: Well, to begin with we need to make sure that the phrase 'real people' is very firmly in quotation marks. I don't feel too happy about the way in which some people talk about 'real people' as though you could distinguish between 'real' people and those who are not real. Usually it's people like taxi drivers and bus conductors and charwomen who are considered to be real, while everybody else isn't, which is really ridiculous.

But I think I see what you're getting at, and yes, some Rembrandts do exemplify it, especially his etchings. I suppose it could be helpful to see these noble qualities 'shining through', as you put it, but I can't think of anybody other than Rembrandt who achieves this.

AMBROSE: It seems to me that there are many novelists who bring this quality out. Dickens, for example, springs to mind.

SANGHARAKSHITA: Real people, imperfect but with noble qualities shining through – yes, there are examples in Dickens. For instance, there's Sir Leicester Dedlock in *Bleak House*. He's a real dried-up old aristocrat, with all the limitations of his class, but when it comes to the point when he discovers that his wife has betrayed him, his reaction is really quite noble, despite his limitations, and it does shine through. Yes, he's quite a good example.

AMBROSE: You can perhaps see this in a more concentrated way in art than in life, because all our friends and associates are imperfect, and it's not often that we get the chance to see their noble qualities coming through very obviously like that.

SANGHARAKSHITA: There may be some characters in Shakespeare this applies to – Hamlet perhaps. Doesn't Horatio say 'Now cracks a noble heart'? There are certain noble qualities in Hamlet, although he is rather exasperating in some ways. I think one could probably find more examples in literature than in painting – apart, perhaps, from portraits.

AMBROSE: I recently saw Sean O'Casey's play, *The Plough and the Stars*. O'Casey tries to show what happens when some people who live in a tenement block are caught in the conflict at the beginning of the Irish rebellion. It was quite striking to see how these people who spent all their time bickering were brought together, and became much more focused. And some of them became quite noble in an ordinary way. Someone dives through the crossfire to organize a funeral. Things like that come across quite genuinely in the play.

SANGHARAKSHITA: Well, that is an ability coming out under very extraordinary conditions – though it does happen, obviously.

NOBLE PATHOS

AMBROSE: Are there any other artists or writers to whom you have particularly responded for this quality of noble pathos?

SANGHARAKSHITA: It occurs to me that the great writer in whom this quality of noble pathos is especially prominent is Homer. The particular example that comes to mind is the death of Odysseus's dog, Argos. The old dog has waited twenty years for his master to come back, and when Odysseus finally does come back the dog just recognizes his master and dies. I think the one translation which does justice to this episode is Pope's verse translation. Although Pope is considered in some ways to be a rather artificial writer, he often translates Homer with great feeling, within his particular idiom, and he translates this episode especially well. It is quite touching – he does communicate that noble pathos.

I think there are also one or two examples in Dr Johnson, for instance in his *Life of Swift*.[299] Do you know the story of Swift and Stella? He married her secretly and wouldn't acknowledge her as his wife, so Dr Johnson comments on this.

> Whilst she was at her own disposal [that is, when she was still unmarried] he did not consider his possession as secure. Resentment, ambition or caprice might separate them. He was therefore resolved to make sure, doubly sure, and to appropriate her by a private marriage, to which he had annexed the expectation of all the pleasures of perfect friendship, without the uneasiness of conjugal restraint. But with this state poor Stella was not satisfied. She never was treated as a wife, and to the world she had the appearance of a mistress. She lived sullenly on, in hope that in time he would own and receive her, but the time did not come for the change of his manners, and deprivation of mind made her tell him when he offered to acknowledge her that it was too late. She then gave up herself to sorrowful resentment, and died under the tyranny of him, by whom she was in the highest degree loved and honoured.

He loved and honoured her, but that was how he treated her. There's something similar in the life of Ruskin, in the relationship between Ruskin and his father. When his father died Ruskin wrote to a friend,

> You are one that have had losses. But you never have had, nor with all your medical experience have you ever probably seen, the loss of a father who would have sacrificed his life for his son, and yet forced his son to sacrifice his life to him, and sacrifice it in vain. It is an exquisite piece of tragedy altogether.

So there's noble pathos in both of those, arising out of the fact that two very noble and well-meaning people, on the one hand Swift, and on the other Ruskin's father, treated, in Swift's case his mistress-cum-wife and in Ruskin's father's case his own son, someone whom they loved, in such a destructive way. They loved them but they couldn't help destroying them. There's a sort of noble pathos in that. Neither of them were bad people, but the one they loved had to suffer.

TRANSFORMING EXPERIENCES

AMBROSE: You have said that there is a kind of beauty which not only expresses an artist's sensibility, but also communicates a profound set of values with sufficient force that one's life can be transformed by those values, transformed by the artist's vision of what is truly meaningful. Can you recall one or two of your own experiences of this kind of 'shattering beauty'?

SANGHARAKSHITA: Yes, I think I can, though one can't really be quite sure, because one can't measure the extent of these influences. I'll mention a couple of very early ones and then a much later one. One very early experience of mine was when I read Rimbaud's *The Drunken Boat*. I think it's called *Le Bateau ivre*, I read it in an English translation by Norman Cameron. It struck me very forcibly. I'm not quite sure why – perhaps it was the sequence of images and the swift treatment of the theme, and its vividness and directness. Two poems that I read even earlier had a similar effect: Shelley's *Adonais* and Dryden's *Alexander's Feast*.

A much later experience was seeing El Greco's painting *The Burial of Count Orgaz*. I read somewhere recently that *The Burial of Count Orgaz* communicates a vision of existence in the same way that Dante's *Divine Comedy* does, and I think the comment is justified. The painting impressed me very deeply when I saw it in Toledo a few years ago, and I wrote an essay trying to say what it was that the artist was communicating.[291] I saw a Neoplatonic element in it. I remember seeing a reproduction of this painting years and years ago, before I went to India, and it struck me then, although I had no understanding of it and no knowledge of El Greco, except a little bit from something that Aldous Huxley had written. If ever you go to Spain, if ever you go to Toledo, don't miss this extraordinary painting.

EXPERIMENTS AND VALUES

Urthona no. 14. In June 2000 Shantigarbha spoke to Sangharakshita at his home in Birmingham. In this interview he talks about the arts in the twentieth century, how the arts communicate values, and his new collection of poetry.

SHANTIGARBHA: The twentieth century was a time of great experimentation in art and culture. Which experiments do you think succeeded, and why?

SANGHARAKSHITA: I looked up this word 'experiment' in the dictionary. It says, 'An attempt at something new or different. An effort to be original.' Personally, I'm not in favour of an effort to be original, and I wonder why somebody should want to be original. That's not to say that I'm against originality, by any means. If as a writer, painter, poet, or whatever, you really do your best, you will be original. You don't have to strain after originality. And you certainly don't become a good writer or artist simply by being different, by being original, by doing something which hasn't been done before.

But yes, it's true that the twentieth century was a time of great change and experimentation in art and culture. There are so many changes, so many experiments, that it's very difficult to know where to start. And how does one judge success? We're not so interested in commercial success. But an experiment *could* be regarded as successful if it results in the production of a genuine work of art. It could also be successful if it shows other artists or writers how to do things in a new way. It would have a sort of historical importance.

So, taking some examples from my area of interest, firstly there's poetic drama. In the nineteenth century, there were many attempts to resuscitate poetic drama – some of them completely successful. Then, near the middle of the twentieth century, there was another attempt. Christopher Fry and T. S. Eliot did succeed in producing some good work, especially perhaps Eliot's *Murder in the Cathedral* and *The Cocktail Party*. But the experiment was not successful in that it did not spark off a revival in poetic drama in English literature.

Then there's biography. It has been pointed out that the present age is, from a literary point of view, an age of biography. It's not an age of great fiction, broadly speaking, but it is an age of great biographies. I think some of the biographies have been very successful. One thinks of Richard Holmes in this connection, and Richard Ellmann, who wrote the biography of Oscar Wilde.[292]

But the real area of change and experimentation in arts in the twentieth century was film. It's obvious that a lot of creative energy has gone into film. Some very good films have been made, some in black and white and some in colour. I'm sure that a lot of creative energy that in previous centuries would have gone into painting or sculpture or perhaps even literature, in the last century went into film. Film is probably the major new genre in the field of the arts.

SHANTIGARBHA: Which experiments do you think failed?

SANGHARAKSHITA: I think Ginsberg and the Beats represent an experiment that failed. I don't think Ginsberg can be regarded as a great poet. I think it's fairly doubtful whether he can be regarded as a good poet. There are a few good poems, but I think he represents a cul-de-sac. I don't think anybody has followed in his footsteps in any really productive sort of way. So yes, he's interesting, but I regard his work as an experiment that failed.

SHANTIGARBHA: Could you say which elements of his approach were responsible for its failure?

SANGHARAKSHITA: It lacks discipline. Compare him with Walt Whitman – there's only a very superficial similarity between Walt Whitman's poetry and Ginsberg's. Whitman has a wonderful sensitivity to language and to rhythm, but Ginsberg just doesn't have that. So yes, Ginsberg's experiment with language and new poetic forms is interesting, but I don't think it is successful. From a strictly poetic point of view he's of very minor interest, however important he may have been from a social and more broadly cultural point of view.[293]

SHANTIGARBHA: The twentieth century saw a widespread loss of faith in humanity. Events such as the Holocaust and the threat of nuclear annihilation were said to make art and the arts irrelevant. Would you comment on this?

SANGHARAKSHITA: That's a very broad statement. I would say it should at least be limited to Europe and America. The most one could say is that the twentieth century perhaps saw a loss in our former rather naive belief, on the part of many people, in the essential goodness of human beings. I think that naive belief suffered a severe shock, from which we haven't recovered, and from which perhaps we shouldn't recover.

Back in the Middle Ages people believed in original sin – orthodox Christians still do. But from the eighteenth century, the period of the Enlightenment, partly as a result of the influence of Rousseau, we began to think that human beings were fundamentally good, that they only became evil as a result of wrong social institutions. I think that sort of naive Rousseauistic view of human nature has been dissipated.[294] I think we have a more balanced view, that human beings are capable of very great and very noble achievements. But they are also capable of behaving in a way that we can only describe as inhuman, and on a large scale.

I certainly don't think that the Holocaust and the threat of nuclear annihilation make art and the arts irrelevant. I might even go as far as to say that it makes them, at least in the traditional sense, more relevant than ever. I see the arts as the bearers of values – in Buddhistic terms – and I think that values are more essential than ever.

SHANTIGARBHA: The process of abstraction was a significant feature in twentieth-century art, particularly in the visual arts, in an attempt to 'go beyond form'. Why do you regard some form of representation, rather than abstraction, as necessary to communicate values in the arts?

SANGHARAKSHITA: I'm not sure that the visual arts can communicate values *purely* by visual means. For instance you could say that religious paintings communicate values, but do they do it by purely visual means? If you go to any art gallery in the Western world, you will find that a very large proportion of paintings illustrate episodes from the Old Testament, the New Testament, the gospels, and so on, and you'll find a lot of paintings which illustrate classical mythology. But do they communicate values by purely visual means? I'm very doubtful about that.

I've seen this with regard to friends of mine, when we go to art galleries. Since they don't know their Bible or Greek and Roman mythology, they are bewildered, even depressed, because nothing is communicated, no *values* are communicated. Religious paintings seem able to communicate values only by using a non-visual language which is already familiar to the person looking at the painting. If you see a painting of the Virgin Mary and baby Jesus, you can admire it as painting of a mother and child, but unless you are a Christian, or know about Christianity, you will not think that this is the virgin mother of God, and this is baby Jesus incarnated for the salvation of the world. The Christian message, Christian values, will not come across to you.

So it's not just a question of abstraction not being able to communicate values. I don't think that the visual arts as such communicate values independently of explicit or implied literary reference.

SHANTIGARBHA: Do you think music can communicate spiritual truths or values?

SANGHARAKSHITA: Well, obviously I don't – at least not unaided! And sometimes of course music does call for aid to words. For example, Beethoven's Ninth Symphony....

SHANTIGARBHA: The setting of Schiller's *Ode to Joy*...

SANGHARAKSHITA: It's as though he wasn't fully able to express what he wanted to express just by means of music. Then we have the example of Wagner and what he called the 'complete artwork'.[295] Apart from the overtures to his operas, he composed very little purely instrumental music. It's as though he is saying that music by itself cannot communicate values.

I looked up the word 'values' in the dictionary. Values are defined as 'the moral principles and beliefs or accepted standards of a person or social group'. To communicate them one needs ideas, one needs concepts and therefore language. I don't think they can be communicated by purely visual or auditory means. If the visual arts or music want to communicate values, they have to call for aid to literary or quasi-literary sources or associations.

SHANTIGARBHA: Modernism seemed to be one of the most significant movements of the century. T. S. Eliot saw it as a last-ditch attempt to protect high culture against commercialism and kitsch, by making it intentionally more difficult. Do you agree? Did it succeed?

SANGHARAKSHITA: I'm not sure, because there are many Modernist writers, artists, etc., and I just don't know whether that was why they intentionally made high culture difficult. Certainly, I know that T. S. Eliot believed that contemporary poetry had to be difficult, had to be complex, because modern life was complex.[296] I wouldn't necessarily agree with that, but I know that this was his view. Nonetheless, it is clear that much of the high culture of Modernism was difficult – Eliot himself is a good example.

Of course Modernism wasn't able to stem the tide of commercialism and kitsch. They are so predominant nowadays it's arguable that high culture just isn't possible any longer. It's possible that bad money has driven good money out, if you see what I mean. But I don't really know enough about what is happening in contemporary art to be able to say.

SHANTIGARBHA: Is it more difficult for people to distinguish between high culture and commercialism or kitsch?

SANGHARAKSHITA: Their prevalence has made it difficult for people to distinguish. Their taste has been blunted. They can't tell the difference any longer between good art and bad art, or what is art and what is just not art.

SHANTIGARBHA: Do you have any favourites among the century's painters – for instance Monet, Cézanne, or Matisse?

SANGHARAKSHITA: There are some twentieth-century painters whose work I definitely like, or at least I like some of their work. But they are not favourites in the sense that I go back to them again and again. I like Klee's and Kandinsky's work. The year before last, when I was in Munich, I saw an enormous amount of Kandinsky's work, and I was really quite impressed. Then, someone very different, Otto Dix. And of course George Grosz, the German impressionist. I like Magritte – remember the big Magritte exhibition at the Tate, years and years ago. I like Joan Miró's work. So yes, there are some twentieth-century painters whose works I like. In the field of sculpture, I like some of Jacob Epstein's work, especially his portrait busts. I was very impressed by those years and years ago.

SHANTIGARBHA: And poets?

SANGHARAKSHITA: Despite Eliot's view about Modernism, there were some good poets who were not Modernist in the sense of being difficult. I won't say that they were great poets, but they were good poets who wrote some good poetry. I would especially mention Philip Larkin in this connection. I think that his poetry is very good indeed.

If you look back to the earlier part of the century, there's the later Yeats. Without being a modernist, he is as good or great a poet as Eliot himself. Then we have Betjeman, who in defiance of Modernism wrote poetry which was very good and accessible, not difficult, but technically very accomplished. And there was Robert Graves, and I would say Robert Bridges, who in metrical terms was quite experimental, with quantitive measures. And of course Gerard Manley Hopkins – because the twentieth century was when he was published. We mustn't forget him. He was rather more difficult – not so accessible as some of the others.

And of course there was another poet I like quite a lot, who was certainly not Modernist, who was popular and twentieth-century – Walter de la Mare. He produced some very fine poetry. I would also include D. H. Lawrence as a poet. So we have here a whole galaxy of good poets, who were good despite not being Modernist. However, it's very doubtful whether any of them, with the possible exception of Yeats and Eliot himself, could be regarded as great poets.

SHANTIGARBHA: What about novelists?

SANGHARAKSHITA: I haven't read many twentieth-century novels. I've read mainly D. H. Lawrence, Thomas Mann, and Hermann Hesse. I know Mann is classified as one of the great novelists. I am not sure on what grounds, but I've certainly enjoyed his work. As regards D. H. Lawrence, my maturer judgement would be that I appreciate the best of his novellas better than his major novels. I think they are more successful as works of art. In the case of the novels, he wasn't attempting to write a novel in the ordinary sense. He thought of his novels as thought-adventures, and perhaps they are that. So perhaps they are a different genre, but they don't succeed as novels in the more 'classical' sense – as of course Thomas Mann's do. Not that one can really compare the two. I've enjoyed E. M. Forster and....

SHANTIGARBHA: Malcolm Lowry's *Under the Volcano*?

SANGHARAKSHITA: Yes, I've enjoyed that. More recently I've enjoyed Truman Capote, Carson McCullers, and Nathanael West. I've enjoyed Ivan Klíma, the contemporary Czech novelist, very much. But I don't read much contemporary fiction. There's an enormous amount of it, and the reviews, even when they are favourable, put me off!

SHANTIGARBHA: Your new collection of poems, *The Call of the Forest*, appears to be something of a departure.[297] It is by turns humorous, provocative, and preoccupied with death. What prompted this departure?

SANGHARAKSHITA: I can only say, in a sense, that nothing prompted it. I didn't set out to write a little collection of poems that would be rather different. All my poems come spontaneously – I don't think about them beforehand. Usually, when I'm quiet or on my own or sometimes in the middle of the night a verse comes to me or a line comes to me, and a poem grows out of that. But I don't think beforehand, I want to write about this or I want to write about that. It isn't as though I consciously decided to put together a collection of a certain kind. I've simply put together all the poems that came to me in this way during the five years following the publication of my *Complete Poems.* And it's just that they happen to be rather different. But that's not the result of any design or intention. Why I wrote this or that poem, I don't know. It wasn't a conscious departure. Most of them haven't been read at a poetry reading. Perhaps three or four, 'The Call of the Forest', 'White Tara', and 'The Dance of Death'. But the others, no one has heard.

SHANTIGARBHA: You seem to use a number of voices....

SANGHARAKSHITA: Yes, an appropriate persona. Take the poem 'Revenge'. I'm speaking in the voice of somebody else, I'm not advocating murder, personally.

SHANTIGARBHA: That was a curious poem. Was there a situation which prompted it?

SANGHARAKSHITA: I remember it very clearly. I went for a walk in our little park. It was autumn time. I was looking at some trees and their red leaves. The sun was shining through the leaves, and I thought, that looks just like blood. The poem grew out of that, just as I was walking around.[298]

THE FACE OF SUPREME BEAUTY

Kathleen Raine and Sangharakshita in conversation

Urthona no. 17. Kathleen Raine, one of the foremost scholars of Blake in modern times, has been, throughout her long life, a defender of the arts as a 'channel to higher worlds'. Her vision of the life of the Imagination has many parallels with the ideas of Sangharakshita, especially as expressed in his book The Religion of Art. *Here we publish the highlights of a conversation between Kathleen Raine and Sangharakshita that took place in front of an audience at the Independent Arts Centre in Croydon in 1988.*

KATHLEEN RAINE: It fills me with joy to enter a room filled with seekers for truth. I'm not a Buddhist, I'm too old to be anything. I've been a seeker for many years myself, and the older one grows the more mysterious the whole thing becomes, but there is no doubt that Buddhism is a way of supreme beauty and truth, and its values are beyond criticism by any standards. It is perhaps the final and greatest of the religions. I haven't reached that point yet, I'm much too fond of this life. I'm afraid to renounce it, I find this world wonderful. As Tagore said about this world, 'I have found it unsurpassable.' When we started the review, *Temenos*, in 1980 we affirmed that literature and the arts existed as vehicles for a vision of higher worlds, and this was a view that seemed to be dropping into a void.... But now one comes here or to other groups, Buddhist, Sufi, and so on, and one finds a tremendous turn of the tide going on because people cannot live by bread alone; it isn't that they wouldn't like to, but it is impossible and therefore the soul searches for its proper food. I have read your book, Sangharakshita. I think basically it is a book about these questions....

SANGHARAKSHITA: I was very interested to hear you speaking of Buddhism as a way of supreme beauty because that's not the way that many people have come to think about Buddhism. Some of them, in both the East and the West, think of Buddhism as something rather grim and rather terrible – ascetic and life denying. They don't see that Buddhism in fact is a way of supreme beauty. It's a way that leads to the cultivation and experience of states of mind which are supremely beautiful. So I think this is a very appropriate way of describing Buddhism, though not the usual one. And I remember in this connection that years ago when I was in South India, I went along to a lecture which was given by Rukmini Devi Arundale, who was a famous exponent of Indian classical dance. She gave a talk under a banyan tree on 'Buddhism and Beauty', which impressed me very deeply because up to that time (I was only about 22 or 23), I hadn't myself thought of Buddhism so much in terms of beauty. But this is one of the things I have tried to say in *The Religion of Art*: that there is no incompatibility between Buddhism and beauty, between the purely spiritual approach and the aesthetic approach to life or to reality, inasmuch as that aesthetic approach consists above all in a mediation of higher spiritual values.

KATHLEEN RAINE: Beauty is the mark of the truth of the spiritual state. Speaking of India, I can describe to you my encounter with Buddhism in India. I had been in Varanasi (it was my first visit to India), and I thought I was prepared for anything, but I wasn't! I'd thought of the idols, the gods and goddesses in India, as works of art and that was all right. Instead of that one found in one temple after another an absolutely naked confrontation with effigies of Kali with her black face and her tongue. A curtain would be drawn and you would see a blood-red, terrifying image of Shiva. They were awe-inspiring, they were powerful, but they were not beautiful. You know Varanasi, I'm sure, and they are not beautiful, are they?

SANGHARAKSHITA: In a sense they are not, but they have a definite appeal. I'd say that they were sublime rather than beautiful.

KATHLEEN RAINE: Then we went to Sarnath, which is the birthplace of Buddhism, where the Lord Buddha preached his first sermon, and found a wonderful museum of effigies of the Buddha, which are surely some of the most beautiful icons of our humanity that have ever been produced in the world. They transcend nearly all the effigies of Jesus Christ, which are highly individualized depictions, usually of human torture and suffering. Occasionally in the Greek Church you get these superb Pantokrators, which are Christ the King, but there is no uniformity, you cannot say the face of Jesus Christ is this or that; whereas when I went to Ajanta and Ellora (ancient Buddhist cave monasteries, in India) I saw many depictions of the supreme beauty of human spiritual reality in these effigies of the Buddha. They always speak the same language, however simple they are, whether they're carved in wood or stone, whether they are in Cambodia or in the Musée Guimet or the Far East; what Buddhism says is in the face of the Buddha, is it not?

SANGHARAKSHITA: One does find that the face of the Buddha speaks to people who've never even heard of Buddhism, people who aren't especially interested in any spiritual path. I remember my own experience at Ajanta many years ago, when I saw the fresco of the famous Ajanta Buddha. I don't know if you happened to see that?

KATHLEEN RAINE: Yes.

SANGHARAKSHITA: It's Padmapāṇi, a three-quarter-length figure looking down in compassion on the world and holding a blue lotus. And it seemed to me at the time, and I think even reproductions do capture this to some extent, that it was really possible to express, in terms of a human face and a human smile, transcendental compassion, as we say in the Buddhist tradition.

KATHLEEN RAINE: No words would express these things. This is the supreme icon of the higher humanity.... This is art at its highest value. These wonderful Buddha figures are communicating spiritual content through form, and that is what all art should be – this channel, this vehicle, this embodiment.

SANGHARAKSHITA: Yes, and beyond the Buddha's smile there is only silence....

KATHLEEN RAINE: But to return to this theme of the religion of art, I have been a Blake scholar for many years, and Blake was the first so far as I know to speak of 'Jesus the Imagination', in other words he was using the name of Jesus when the Indians would use the word 'Self' and as a Buddhist what would you call it, the Buddha nature?

SANGHARAKSHITA: You could say Buddha nature, the Zen people often say Buddha nature.

KATHLEEN RAINE: It is that which is within us all. It is human existence itself in Blake's terms, and he identifies this with Jesus. He said Jesus and his disciples are all artists, meaning that the human imagination, the true Self within us, naturally expresses itself in this way.... May I read you what Blake said?

SANGHARAKSHITA: Please do.

KATHLEEN RAINE: It is perhaps the basic text of what you write of as the 'religion of art' in the true sense. (It has a false sense as well, the art dealers make a religion of art.) So this is what he wrote quite late in his life:

> A Poet, a Painter, a Musician, an Architect; the Man or Woman who is not one of these is not a Christian. You must leave Fathers and Mothers & Houses and Lands if they stand in the way of Art. The Eternal Body of Man is The Imagination, that is God himself, The Divine Body, It manifests itself in his Works of Art (In Eternity All is Vision). Prayer is the Study of Art. Fasting &c All relate to Art. Praise is the Practice of Art.... Jesus & his Apostles & Disciples were all Artists. The Old & New Testaments are the Great Code of Art. Science is the Tree of Death. Art is the Tree of Life. The Whole Business of Man Is The Arts & All Things Common. Christianity is Art.

SANGHARAKSHITA: Where does this come from?

KATHLEEN RAINE: This is the comment on the Laocoon. He did a drawing of Michelangelo's Laocoon statue and he wrote this all round it.[299] This is what I think is the foundation of the religion of art, regarding the arts not as a sort of decoration but as fundamental expressions. What would you say about that?

SANGHARAKSHITA: I would agree with that very much. In the introductory essay of *The Religion of Art,* I do make the point that the Buddha himself, in a sense, was a poet, which is not how Buddhists usually think of the Buddha.[300] But the Buddha often spoke and taught in verse. Whether it was very good poetry it is difficult to say. One would need to read it in the original. Sometimes it is really quite good and many of his disciples were poets. I don't know whether you're aware that in the Buddhist Pāli scriptures, there are two books which are collections of poems, songs by the Buddha's male and female disciples. There's the *Theragāthā*, the songs or poems of the elder monks, and the *Therīgāthā,* the poems of the elder nuns; poems written 2,500 years ago by some of the direct disciples of the Buddha himself. And at least one of them ends with the woman poet concerned gaining Enlightenment. The end of the poem was the end of her spiritual quest....

KATHLEEN RAINE: I would define poetry as the natural language of the soul, which tends to be rhythmic, because the higher one goes in the level of consciousness, the more rhythmic it becomes, and of course prophetic, supreme poetry is the language of the spirit. Yeats talked about this in his wonderful passage about Byzantium as the perfect city. He said:

> I invented an almost infallible church, a poetic tradition of stories and of personages and of emotions inseparable from their first expression, passed on from generation to generation by poets and painters with some help from philosophers and theologians. I wished for a world where I could discover this tradition perpetually and not in pictures and in poems only but in tales round the chimney piece and in the hangings that kept out the draught.... Whatever I can imagine those mouths speaking may be

> the nearest I can go to truth. When I listened they seemed always to speak of one thing only. They, their loves, every incident of their lives, were steeped in the supernatural.[301]

It is out of the human consciousness itself these forms emerge.

SANGHARAKSHITA: It is from the deeper or higher levels of human consciousness. I have said sometimes in the past that if I was forbidden to speak of Buddhism in Buddhist terms, I think I could manage to speak of it in Christian terms in the sense that I know there are certain verses in the New Testament that I could make use of to express what I myself actually think and feel.

KATHLEEN RAINE: I'm sure.

SANGHARAKSHITA: But I must also say that there are some verses which I would have to just put aside. And of course I do greatly admire many of the Christian mystics. I'm not so much thinking of Blake, who tends to transcend these categories, but I must say that I have some favourite Christian mystics. I particularly like, and you might be surprised to hear this, Catherine of Siena. I rather admire that lady, I must say.

KATHLEEN RAINE: I've never read her. I don't like Christian mystics!

SANGHARAKSHITA: I'm glad we've found something to disagree about!

KATHLEEN RAINE: Well, I always turn for fresh air to the Far East. I turn for fresh air to the *Bhagavad Gītā* or to the *Upanishads* or the *Rāmāyaṇa*. I don't know the Buddhist scriptures so well, but I'm sure one will find the same, that there is this pure air. Would you not say that all religions were cultural in a sense, and that the supreme truth transcends any religious cultural tradition?

SANGHARAKSHITA: It does, of course, but what does this mean in practical, down-to-earth terms? There is a whole series of Buddhist *sūtras* called the Perfection of Wisdom, and especially the *Heart Sūtra*, which is the heart of the Perfection of Wisdom. In it all dualities are reduced to *sunyata,* which is the one absolute, except you can't even call it absolute, because if we say it's absolute, that means it isn't relative, and this absolute is neither absolute nor relative, nor, as we say in Buddhism, both or neither. So once again we end up with silence, perhaps a little prematurely. But to return to the Christian mystics, I must say within Christianity itself I find myself in the deepest sympathy with the Orthodox Eastern tradition, that is to say the Russian or Greek orthodox tradition. I find that in some ways very congenial.

KATHLEEN RAINE: And they have this beautiful icon of the risen Christ, the timeless, spiritual Christ, rather than this continual dwelling on the mortal body on the cross which is the icon of the Western Church and very terrible it is.

SANGHARAKSHITA: They also have the icon of Sophia, the female wisdom, red in colour and with red wings. I find this a very attractive and rather mysterious figure....

KATHLEEN RAINE: The symbols of any religion though, surely emerge according to the imagination of that particular culture, and Western Christianity has thrown up the cross and the mangled body which always seemed to me to evoke a certain sadomasochistic response.

SANGHARAKSHITA: Yes, I've really noticed this when I have visited art galleries in Italy and traced the development of Christian art from its very early beginnings. With Byzantine art and with the mosaics of Ravenna and San Marco in Venice you get a different world, and as you come down the centuries it just gets bloodier and bloodier....

KATHLEEN RAINE: Curiously enough, I had this experience in Washington DC, at the Mellon Gallery. I'd never really thought of Christianity in those terms, but as I wandered through the pictures, I thought that all those wounds, sadism and masochism, the delight in cruelty and suffering, were terrible. And then I went across the road to the Freer Gallery, which is a very beautiful Oriental museum, and one went between two, are they called *yakṣas*, guardian demons?

SANGHARAKSHITA: Yes, *yakṣas*. They are kindly demons.

KATHLEEN RAINE: Oh very, full of energy and wickedness! You walked through between the *yakṣas* and you were in a world of serene beauty. It is mainly Buddhist art, sculptures, vases, pots, jars, paintings. It isn't as if there wasn't bloodshed and cruelty and wickedness in China or Indonesia or anywhere else in the world, but Buddhism sees it as necessary to free the spiritual essence from all that mangled flesh....

SANGHARAKSHITA: The obsession with wounds seems to start with the Renaissance.

KATHLEEN RAINE: Yes. It is when individual human selfhood and its experiences in this world comes to take precedence over the spiritual reality, which you still get in Ravenna and in other places, even up to Giotto, but not much after.

SANGHARAKSHITA: I remember my first visit to Italy was in 1966, and rather to my surprise, my greatest aesthetic experience, if one can call it that, was in connection with the mosaics, especially of Ravenna.[302] I thought even the best of Renaissance paintings in certain respects could not touch those mosaics.

I'm afraid we don't have very many great or even good artists in the field of Buddhism. We have standard, conventional Buddhist art, but much of that seems to lack genuine inspiration, in the sense of real contact on the part of the artist with a higher level of being. The artist is just reproducing the traditional formulas....

KATHLEEN RAINE: Of course Jung says this is the age of 'interiorizing' symbols. I don't think there will in the future be great poets in the sense in which there were in my childhood or my middle age, or great art in the old sense. We're not going to look for our message in contemplating however beautiful an effigy of the Buddha. One is going to look for it within. Which is very much what I felt in Ajanta – I expect you know some of the caves I mean. They are like the nave of a medieval Christian church, and there are carvings of events from the Buddha's life.

SANGHARAKSHITA: And columns carved out of rock, very squat and solid.

KATHLEEN RAINE: And then at the end through, as it were, the chancel arch, you will have either a stupa or an image of the Lord Buddha, and as you go in it is like going into your own soul and finding there written an image of the Self, the Self with a capital S in the Hindu or Jungian sense. It does communicate that inwardness of the image. Christianity is always stressing the historicity whereas Buddhism stresses the interiority.

SANGHARAKSHITA: That's a very interesting thought. It reminds me very much of a set of third-century Buddhist cave temples or cave monasteries at a place called Bhaja near Pune. The FWBO has a meditation centre just within a few hundred yards of those caves. I remember when I was there last, looking from the veranda of the meditation centre up towards the cave temples, and in the evening when the sun shines from the west the last beams of the sun penetrate right into the depths of that cave temple and shine directly onto the stupa at the far end. And it becomes, as it were, golden as the depths are being lit up....

KATHLEEN RAINE: This is the depths, this is the depths of the soul, this is the heart....

SANGHARAKSHITA: Lit up, you could say, by the supernal sun.... I wrote some time ago, way back in the fifties, that it's much better to worship a tree than not to worship anything, just to be a scientist. Much better to worship a tree or to be an animist. It was in an essay called 'In Defence of Animism'. But I'm afraid no one would publish it and it's been lost. Sometimes you read books about Buddhism, especially Burmese Buddhism, where they remark how terrible it is that the Burmese have mixed up beautiful pure spiritual Buddhism with animism. But I think it is a thoroughly good thing. I'm all in favour of animism. I wish we had more of it in Buddhism.... More sacred wells, holy stones....

KATHLEEN RAINE: Well, in India, practically anything you stumble over may be sacred. An anthill may have marigold leaves on it because it is a sacred anthill to the goddess, and the rivers are sacred. And what else could a tree be but sacred? I was looking recently at the way trees are clipped and cropped in England and thinking how in India you will see a temple with an ancient tree coming through the temple wall, breaking down the wall. Well, why is this? Because the tree is sacred, the wall is something you can make; so when the tree gets too big you take away the wall, you don't lop the tree.

SANGHARAKSHITA: If this had been India, we would be sitting here wearing marigold garlands.

KATHLEEN RAINE: That would be nice.... May I read you a poem?

SANGHARAKSHITA: Oh, please do.

KATHLEEN RAINE: It's called 'Memory of Sarnath':

> It was the face, they say, of the Enlightened One,
> Recalled his first disciples, unconvinced
> By words, whose countenance
> Blissful as life and calm as death, tells all
> And nothing to generations of our kind.
> Carved in wood, or stone, or cast in bronze,
> Silver or gold, great civilisations have adorned
> With all the treasure of the soul
> That plenitude of emptiness, that known unknown,
> The unknown known all know and are. That prince
> Who fled by night his palaces and gardens,
> Fathomed our mystery, whose only scripture is a smile
> All read, and know its doctrine to be true:
> Being itself, unbounded as the stars.

SANGHARAKSHITA: Thank you.

A LIFE LIVED IN POETRY

Urthona no. 29. Vidyadevi wrote the following article on the basis of four conversations she had with Sangharakshita about his favourite poetry.

In Sangharakshita's memoirs, woven through the story of his Dharma life is another, equally colourful strand: his life as a lover of poetry. If his discovery of Buddhism as a teenager seems precocious, poetry came in search of him even younger, when at the age of 6 or 7 he met his first metaphor with 'a shock of delight'. A little later on, *Paradise Lost* gave him 'the greatest poetic experience of my life', and as a teenager, the intensely fused sensuousness and mysticism breathed by Dante Gabriel Rossetti's poems 'went to my head like some subtle and dangerous perfume', Housman's 'Loveliest of trees' 'seemed almost the last word in consummate beauty of expression', and as he read Donne and Herrick, 'An unusually felicitous line went through me like a spear.'[303]

Shock, vision, delight, sublimity, profundity, awakening echoes, danger, a spear. It is hardly surprising that when, a few years later, he found himself, now teaching the Dharma in the Himalayan town of Kalimpong, still in poetry's thrall. In a poem written in 1949, he described himself as 'Perplexed between the East and West',[304] and in his memoirs he confesses that 'I had not yet succeeded in integrating the East as represented by Buddhism with the West, as represented by English (and European) literature, and in particular by English poetry.... My spiritual life seemed to derive nourishment from both streams of inspiration.'[305] And intriguingly, 'sometimes it happened that when I thought I enjoyed a poem, I really responded to a religious teaching, and when I thought I responded to a religious teaching, I in fact enjoyed a poem.'[306] A rapprochement was reached when, while helping some Nepali students prepare for their English examinations,

> suddenly I realized *I was teaching the students Buddhism.* It was not that I had forgotten about the poem I was supposed to be explaining, and had unconsciously slipped into teaching Buddhism instead. In explaining the poem I was teaching Buddhism. This could only mean that at a certain level of experience poetry and the Dharma were the same thing. There was a sense in which Beauty *was* Truth, and Truth Beauty, and even if this was *not* all that I needed to know on earth it had at least become clear to me that my interest in poetry was not incompatible with the spiritual life, as I had sometimes felt, or had been made to feel, but that the two things were complementary aspects of the same process of higher human development.[307]

In the sixty years since then, many of Sangharakshita's Dharma students have been intrigued by this aspect of him. The notion that 'at a certain level of experience poetry and the Dharma are the same thing' is music to some people's ears, but others are made anxious, incredulous, or even indignant by the thought that somehow they might be required to drum up an enthusiasm for Shelley or Christina Rossetti as an aspect of their Dharma life. This was in my mind when I met Sangharakshita to discuss a proposed anthology of his favourite poems. These days, failing eyesight prevents him from reading – 'And I don't very often ask people to read poetry to me, because I know the experience will be rather excruciating' – so his list of choices (which was long, and kept growing as we talked) included *memorable* favourites, many of whose verses he has by heart (and that's the right phrase).

Some of his choices reflect his nationality and the period he grew up in, but also a particular slant on that period: Kipling, Masefield, de la Mare, and Hardy rather than T. S. Eliot or the poems of the First World War. ('Well, war isn't a favourite subject of mine.') The sea is a theme in many ('Perhaps that's not surprising. Some people say that the sea figures in the imagination of all English people') – from the long, withdrawing roar of Arnold's *Dover Beach* to the fierce old mother of Walt Whitman's *Sea Drift* and the silent sea and emerald ice of the *Rime of the Ancient Mariner*.

The number of narrative poems and ballads in the list is striking. What's the appeal? 'I think it's the simplicity and directness, and the closeness to everyday speech, and also the touch of the archaic. I still remember the nursery rhymes of my childhood; some of them are beautiful poetry, and they make simple direct statements. Some nonsense verse is very good too. It's difficult to be a modern poet in English – the rich heritage is burdensome, and you can't compete with it – but ballads such as *The Twa Corbies*, *Clark Sanders*, and *Sir Patrick Spens* take us back to the roots of poetry, and a sense of genuineness and authenticity. Milton spoke of poetry as being simple, sensuous, and passionate.[308] That's what appeals to me. Keats, for example, was a very sensuous poet. He gives you a very strong feeling of how things are actually experienced.'

I was struck by his unabashed preference for simplicity and directness, even that of nursery rhymes, over complexity or attempts to deal with abstract themes. There was also the question of whether poems can, or 'should', carry 'teaching'. Can poetry and the Dharma be 'the same thing' at the simple level of a moral message? I was reminded of the passage in the Mahāyāna *White Lotus Sūtra* when the Buddha, in response to the doubts of those present, decides to tell a story, remarking that 'intelligent people, through a parable, reach understanding'.[309] Is there a parallel?

'Yes. George Herbert wrote, "A verse may find him who a sermon flies."[310] The effect of a poem is not its moral, exactly, but a resonance. The rhyme and metre give a poem a certain inevitability. When the rhyme is completed, that's how it is, that's how it should be. There's a satisfaction in that. That's what gives metric poetry its special impact. It has a mantra-like effect: the sound reinforces the message. Think of Gray's *Elegy*, for example:

'The boast of heraldry, the pomp of power,
And all that beauty, all that wealth e'er gave,
Awaits alike th'inevitable hour.
The paths of glory lead but to the grave.'[311]

Poems 'clearly in accordance with the Dharma' include Kipling's *If*, whose twin impostors of triumph and disaster are 'clearly a reference to how one should respond to the worldly winds', and even the *Rime of the Ancient Mariner*, whose strange phantasmagoria end in a simple homily ('He prayeth well who loveth well / Both man and bird and beast') and a 'sadder and wiser' listener. But I felt almost a reproof in Sangharakshita's resistance to my pressing for poetry to reach moral conclusions: 'I don't feel any necessity for finding morals in poems I happen to like. Sometimes I just enjoy immersing myself in the mood of the poem – in Tennyson's *Lotos-Eaters*, for example, the rhythm and the versification and the pictures it paints. Likewise, in *The Lady of Shallott* I'm not sure there's any message conveyed; it's a series of wonderfully vivid pictures. Poetry isn't a guide in the way the Dharma is. Poems don't tell you what to do, though they may inspire you, and I think some of them have reinforced a particular direction in my life. A good friend of mine said years ago, 'That which we love, we adorn'. If you love the truth, you'll want to adorn it, and that's what some of the poets do. But the best poetry is not just decorative; it tells you something about life. Take the *Rubáiyát of Omar Khayyám*; some of the verses do express my real sentiments – for instance:

'One Moment in Annihilation's Waste,
One Moment of the Well of Life to taste.
The Stars are setting and the Caravan
Starts for the Dawn of Nothing – oh, make Haste!'[312]

Listening to the loving recital of loved cadences, I thought the reproof I had felt was that of a lover defending his beloved. As we talked he quoted lines of simple beauty and purity from Blake's *Book of Thel*, Dryden's *The Hind and the Panther*, and love poems like Byron's *She walks in beauty*. What is *not* on the list is also instructive. Nothing written in the last seventy years: perhaps partly because beauty is what Sangharakshita seeks above all in reading poetry?

'Yes – nowadays artists and poets don't seem to think very much in terms of beauty. The pre-Raphaelites set out to create it, and Oscar Wilde spoke about the House Beautiful,[313] but now, to find spiritual values in works of art, we usually have to go back to the past.'

I wondered about the other qualities of poetry that move us. Cannot 'the poetry be in the pity', as Wilfred Owen wrote?

'Well, Thomas Aquinas' definition of beauty is 'that which when seen, delights'.[314] It's beauty that delights. There are poems that excite our pity, but pity is not compassion. It is those poems that give us the sort of experience that Shelley's skylark gives us that are beautiful in the highest sense of the term.'

Can appreciating beauty constitute a spiritual path in itself, or is there something missing? If it's possible to be a practitioner of what Sangharakshita has called 'the religion of art', what are its practices, and does it have an ethical dimension?

'The religion of art doesn't explicitly include the ethical element, but the enjoyment of beauty makes you happy, and a happy person is much more likely to behave ethically than an unhappy one. From a practical point of view, I would say that to practise the religion of art, you should make your living space beautiful, and consider how you dress, your surroundings, and even the crockery you use – though you have to be careful that it doesn't just become aestheticism; it has to go deeper than that. In *Either/Or* Kierkegaard sees an ultimate duality between the aesthetic and the ethical.[315] I think there is that duality, and sometimes the two pull in different directions. If you're working on your novel or your poem, or your painting, you may sacrifice worldly prospects for the sake of your art, and your family may suffer. So there can be a genuine clash.'

But the desire is to transcend oneself?

'Yes. Kierkegaard would probably say that you can transcend yourself through the arts but it doesn't last, and perhaps the Dharma would agree with that. It's only when your character is fortified by ethics and other spiritual practices that you can sustain that more selfless attitude. I'm reminded of Philip Kapleau, who was a stenographer at the Nuremberg trials. When he found out that people who had committed the most horrible crimes were at the same time able to enjoy Beethoven and Bach, that made him feel that – to put it in Kierkegaard's language – aesthetics were not enough. That was one of his reasons for taking up Zen.[316] Perhaps in an ideal world poetry would be enough, but in our present-day world you need a more solid prop if you're to lead a spiritual life than just the occasional enjoyment of the arts. But for those who are practising the Dharma, the arts in the best sense of the term can be very helpful. And for a lot of people it is the arts that are the bearers of values, not organised religion.'

Can a Buddhist appreciate Christian poets, or does religion get in the way? 'I can enjoy *Paradise Lost*, my favourite long poem, despite the religious content, in the same way that I enjoy the *Iliad* or the *Aeneid*. The more personal kind of Christian poetry I don't find attractive at all. I can appreciate some of Gerard Manley Hopkins' poems, but in a religious sense they're alien to me. My own spiritual life, generally speaking, has not been angst-ridden – perhaps it should have been a bit more like that, but it hasn't been, so I can't empathize very easily with angst-ridden poems, and perhaps my list of favourites reflects my optimistic nature. I do like Hopkins' *Starlight*, but I don't like it when he writes a wonderful poem and then brings Jesus in at the end, as though he feels he has to make a forcible connection with what he believes theologically.' But there's also the church as metaphor: in Matthew Arnold's *The Forsaken Merman* it represents 'spiritual possibility, the escape from what neo-Platonists would call the sea of materiality', while in *Dover Beach* the receding tide is the modern retreat from religion to the refuge of personal relationships – 'a diminishing, I would say'. Popular theism – and the desire for utopian bliss – is satirized in the form of Rupert Brooke's *Heaven*:

Unfading moths, immortal flies,
And the worm that never dies.
And in that Heaven of all their wish,
There shall be no more land, say fish.[317]

Beyond fishful thinking, where does real transcendence lie? There are few 'personal poems' on the list, the kind treasured as touchstones, or fragments that we shore against our ruins, showing a glimmer of a different dimension to the selves we know and the world we live in day to day, but allowing us the security of that self, that world. Sangharakshita seems more drawn to poetry that takes us imaginatively into other lives, other realms of existence, poems in which we do not simply find 'our own resemblance', in the language of Andrew Marvell's 'The Garden', but 'Far other worlds, and other seas'. And singing through all the songs and stories are the endless refrains of impermanence and eternity, 'the note of eternal sadness', like the melody played by the bodhisattva to arouse the gods from their lotus-eating dream in the Tibetan wheel of life. In *Tam O'Shanter* Burns 'makes a philosophic point, but very beautifully':

But pleasures are like poppies spread:
You seize the flower, its bloom is shed;
Or like the snow fall on the river,
A moment white – then melts forever.[318]

These poems are not all full of fading flowers, though. Oscar Wilde's *Ballad of Reading Gaol* demonstrates a harsher side of life and death:

The Governor was strong upon
  The Regulations Act:
The Doctor said that Death was but
  A scientific fact:
And twice a day the Chaplain called,
  And left a little tract.[319]

There's Stevie Smith's *Not waving but drowning*, which 'expresses a true situation – Thoreau's "lives of quiet desperation"'.[320] And there's Dylan Thomas's great cry, *Do not go gentle into that good night* – 'not just the dying of life, but the dying away of a greater understanding, maybe, in society'. But most often evanescence is mingled with beauty. Many of the poems are autumnal: Keats' *Ode to Autumn*, Yeats's *Wild Swans at Coole*, Lawrence's *Ship of Death*: 'The apples falling like great drops of dew/ To bruise themselves and exit from themselves.'

The song of Shelley's skylark blends with that of Thomas Hardy's darkling thrush: 'The *Skylark* is clearly about the archetype of the poet. Shelley has been for me a source of great inspiration, that Neoplatonic element of upward aspiration, and I think his poems are among the greatest treasures of English literature. Not that he has always appealed to me as a person; his political idealism didn't exclude a certain blindness where individual human beings were concerned. Another of my very favourite poems is Thomas Hardy's *Darkling Thrush*. The thrush is 'gaunt and battered and frail' – it could hardly be more different from Shelley's skylark – but it's singing; that note of optimism again.'

The human predicament is seen in its broadest terms in Pope's *Essay on Man*, whose most famous lines, 'sometimes dismissed as facile, seem to me a wonderful expression of the contradictory nature of human beings':

Know then thyself, presume not God to scan;
The proper study of Mankind is Man.
Plac'd on this isthmus of a middle state,
A being darkly wise, and rudely great:
With too much knowledge for the Sceptic side,
With too much weakness for the Stoic's pride.[321]

But many of the poems rejoice in the merits of human beings, from Samuel Johnson's *On the death of Mr Robert Levet* to Stephen Spender's *I think continually of those who were truly great.* Among the falling leaves and the twilight birdsong, there's the sense of human potential, 'soul'. In Shelley's *The Sensitive Plant*, the lady represents the soul of the garden, which 'seems Neoplatonic, the soul informing matter, especially the human individual – as in Keats's "vale of Soul-making"'.[322]

Reflecting on all this – and there was much more than there's room for here – I'm reminded of an episode in another Mahāyāna *sūtra*, the *Vimalakīrti-nirdeśa*, in which a distant world is revealed where the Buddha teaches the Dharma 'only by means of perfumes'. This subtle and beautiful world is contrasted with our own, in which, because of our 'wild and uncivilized nature', teachings have to be much more blunt: 'This should be done and that should not be done.... This is the right path and that is the wrong path' and so forth.[323] It seems clear why this came to mind. At a certain level of experience poetry and the Dharma may be 'the same thing', and we may delight to live our Dharma life part of the time in the subtle, transcendent realm of poetic beauty, but – because 'poems don't tell you what to do' – as Dharma practitioners we will need also to spend plenty of time with our feet on the ground of ethics, meditation, and wisdom.

For Sangharakshita the poetry he loves is suffused with the Dharma, just as his Dharma teaching is suffused with poetry (as I know from many years of tracing his quotations in the course of my editorial work). But the key word here is not really poetry but love. Something Sangharakshita has said many times in many ways is that if our Dharma practice is to be effective, if we are to 'transform a purely intellectual recognition of the rightness of something into an ardent desire to achieve it', we have to find an emotional connection. For some of us that may be Shelley, or indeed the work of a poet of whom Sangharakshita takes a dimmer view (some of my own favourites got short shrift in our conversation, I have to admit); or poetry may leave you cold and it's an entirely different aspect of truth or beauty that captures your heart. The important thing is surely that we should feel the 'shock of delight' first experienced by Sangharakshita when he met a metaphor eighty years ago. He is clearly still delighted.

Late Writings

INTRODUCTION

MADHYAMALOKA REFLECTIONS

Madhyamaloka ('the middle realm') was the name Sangharakshita gave to the house in Moseley, Birmingham where he lived for sixteen years, from the spring of 1997, when he was 71 years old, to the spring of 2013, when he moved to Adhisthana in the Herefordshire countryside. In her introduction to *A Moseley Miscellany*, Kalyanaprabha wrote:

> Standing back and surveying those sixteen years that Sangharakshita lived at Madhyamaloka, they seem to fall into three more or less distinct phases or, you might say, chapters. The first, 1997–2000, sees the Madhyamaloka community coming together and the College of Public Preceptors, with its Council, establishing itself. During this time Sangharakshita was active on many fronts, continuing to visit Buddhist centres both in the UK and abroad, giving talks, conducting seminars, meeting people; and engaging in literary work including writing his memoirs, completing his translation of the *Dhammapada*, composing book reviews for the *Times Higher Education Supplement*, and so on. He read extensively and kept up his cultural interests, visiting art galleries and occasionally the theatre.
>
> And then, in August 2000, on an occasion marking his seventy-fifth birthday, at a gathering of Order members in a hall at Aston

University in central Birmingham, Sangharakshita handed on what he considered to be the last of his responsibilities – at least, the last of those responsibilities that could be handed on: he handed on the Headship of the Order. To whom did he hand it on? He handed it on to the eight members of the Preceptors College jointly.

No doubt he had plans – to do some of those things which his duties had not left him time for before. He was now free to come and go, to spend time at Madhyamaloka or time away. His programme for the spring of 2001 included a visit to Belgium and a ten-day tour in Germany. But such freedom was not to continue very long. Less than a year after handing on the Headship, unexpectedly and dramatically, as he recounts in these pages, his vision deteriorated and suddenly he could no longer read or write.

Despite this major setback, undaunted, it seems, in the face of this adversity, he gradually found ways to continue his literary and other work. Once more he was visiting centres and giving talks such as those given in June 2002 at the London and Manchester Buddhist Centres on creativity in relation to art, meditation, friendship, and institutions. In September he visited Buddhafield in Devon, and attended the opening of the new Sheffield Buddhist Centre. A few months previously, in May that year, he ventured into *terra incognita*, spending ten very happy days in Krakow for the launch of the Polish translation of *A Survey of Buddhism*.

But life had not yet finished dealing out a series of heavy blows. In October 2002 Sangharakshita began experiencing the extreme insomnia that was to lead him into 'a season in hell', an experience about which he writes so movingly here. (Yet even that dreadful season brought some compensations in the form of dreams and visions of other, one could say heavenly, worlds. And perhaps an even greater compensation was the blessing of friendship, also an essential part of that time.) But there was more to endure. Some months after the insomnia had set in, 'the good ship FWBO' hit stormy seas and there was unrest among some of its passengers and crew. About that, too, we can read something in these pages, taken from the logbook of the captain. And still there was more to be endured. In the summer of 2004, Sangharakshita suffered a heart attack and was detained in hospital for a week. I recall cycling over from Moseley one hot day to visit him, one of several visitors who came and sat beside their friend and teacher for a short time. Perhaps we all wondered what was going to happen now....

Within a single lifetime one can discern cycles that mirror the great cycle of birth, death, and rebirth – and sometimes dramatically so. There came to Sangharakshita in due course a new lease of life. Sleep returned, and though his energies were not all they had been before his insomnia and the heart attack, nevertheless he once more enjoyed reasonably good health for one of his age. And so the third period begins, the longest one, from perhaps 2005 or 2006. It sees Sangharakshita mostly at home at Madhyamaloka, though for a few years he was still making some trips away. I was living in Berlin when he visited in 2008 and gave a talk at the centre there, the Buddhistisches Tor. He spoke to a full house on the 'Six Distinctive Emphases' of the FWBO, a theme he spoke on at several centres during this period. In 2010 he and Paramartha went searching for traces of his Suffolk ancestors. (You can read about what happened in 'Looking Back'.) People continued to come and see him at Madhyamaloka, and he continued with his wide correspondence and some substantial literary work: *Living Ethically* and *Living Wisely*, books based on teachings he had first given during a seminar on Nāgārjuna's *Precious Garland* in 1976, were put together at this time and published in 2009 and 2013 respectively. Between 2009 and 2012, through intensive discussions, chiefly with Subhuti (the first chair of the College of Public Preceptors), he issued a series of papers, written by Subhuti and carefully checked by him, papers that laid down as clearly as possible some of the basic principles, the key ideas, the common practices and so on, on which the Triratna Order and movement, now and into the future, was to be based.

So in this third period, too, there was much significant and creative output; and though he could no longer read, he kept up his interests in culture and in the wider world through audio books and the radio – 'Mr Wireless' – as reflected in several of the poems of this period. Yet most characteristic of this time, I think, is a contemplative mood. I think of Sangharakshita as I sometimes caught sight of him from a window in the main house, taking his morning walk round the garden (which by now had been beautifully landscaped by Sanghadeva and planted with flowers and shrubs). I see him as he passes the great cedar tree, moves slowly through the ivy archway, past the lavender beds and along the holly hedge before coming up along the other side of the lawn towards the pond and the miniature box-hedge knot gardens. Or again, I see him before my mind's eye in his room, the 'room with a view' – a view over the garden – a room in which he spent so many hours, seated in his red armchair with its white-lace-edged antimacassar, there in the very modest space that served as his and Paramartha's sitting and dining room, the walls to the left lined with books, on the right a bookcase on which stood Buddhist images. He is looking towards the door on which hangs a picture of the Egyptian god Thoth and sitting, just sitting quietly, until there comes a gentle knock.

I used to be one of those who gave that gentle knock. In the summer of 2010 I began working with Sangharakshita as his – I suppose one could call it 'literary assistant' – and I well remember leaving my little flat (I lived in an attic over the garage of another house on Chantry Road), making my way past the front gardens and the large old houses with their curious architectures, and turning into the drive of Madhyamaloka; going through the main house and then along the little passage that connected it with the granny flat. Pausing to take off my shoes, I would tiptoe upstairs, past the Buddha rupa where the stairs turned a corner (occasionally incense was burning) and along the landing on whose walls hung a photograph of a statue of Anagarika Dharmapala, and pictures of Thomas Carlyle and John Ruskin. 'Come in!' would ring out in answer to my knock. And in I would go, take up my seat opposite, and after a few personal exchanges work would begin.

It was a seat in which many others also sat – indeed, many readers of this volume will have sat there, coming to see their teacher – seeking clarification or blessing or reassurance or simply contact; or occasionally wanting to argue or complain.

So this is the context, the world, beautifully evoked by Kalyanaprabha, in which this miscellany arose. Its poems and book reviews now appear elsewhere in the *Complete Works* (the poems in vol. 25, pages 430 to

452, the reviews in vol. 8), but while the pieces included in this volume are certainly reflective, hence the new title, *Madhyamaloka Reflections: Excerpts from A Moseley Miscellany*, they are also quite various – indeed, still a miscellany. Kalyanaprabha introduces them:

> In 'My First Eight Years', his 'mosaic of memories' written in 2010, Sangharakshita recounts some of his own childhood memories with something of the child's simplicity and directness so that one finds oneself transported to the South London of the 1920s and 30s; and into the child's mind – a child whose experiences were, I think, exceptionally vivid. These recollections supplement those recounted in 'Giants and Dragons', the first chapter of his memoir *The Rainbow Road*.
>
> Next we have eight 'Reveries and Reminiscences', composed when the author was 85 and 86. A reverie is said to be a composition suggestive of a dream-like or musing state. In such a state thoughts and images, memories and ideas, arise and lead on to others by way of association. To engage in reverie might be said to be an old man's occupation. But if that old man has spent a whole life in the Dharma, what then? Here, we find out. Each reverie begins with a memory, a thought, or an idea: 'Above the mantelpiece of my study...'; 'Every language is unique ...'; or 'How big is God?' – a question he had pondered as a boy. Having posed the question, we are led on to consider how 'big' and 'great' are sometimes not distinguished, the one coming to stand for the other, and so to the Bamiyan Buddhas that were blasted by the Taliban. From there it is a short step to a consideration of what Sangharakshita calls 'principled vandalism' and iconoclasm. Having taken his reader to London's National Gallery and the Brighton Pavilion for further examples of such vandalism, and with a brief glimpse of two men jumping on Tracey Emin's *Bed* in the Tate Modern, we are brought with a wonderfully unexpected U-turn of thought from the negatively destructive to the positive, and so to the world of Madhyamaka Buddhism. In a single short piece we find memory, observation, critical comment, art, and Dharmic exposition all present.
>
> But these eight pieces are not just *Reveries*; they are also *Reminiscences* and, particularly in the first three, we are able

to read Sangharakshita's own account of notable times in his own life and in the life of the movement he founded; and the development of a notable friendship.

Thirdly, comes 'Looking Back', which tells the rather extraordinary story of how Sangharakshita came across the Lingwood Family Papers on the very first day of his search for his paternal ancestors. Based on what he discovered in those papers, he writes about the lives of some of those great and great-great etc. grandparents, his Suffolk forebears, and concludes with some reflections.

And fourthly, an appreciation. Ayya Khema became a good friend of Sangharakshita towards the end of her life after they both attended the European Buddhist Union Congress in Berlin in 1992, to which they had been invited as Western Buddhist teachers. His personal tribute to her was published – in German translation – in the *Gedenkschrift* (commemorative volume) brought out after her death in 1997. It appears for the first time here in the original English.

ADHISTHANA WRITINGS

This second collection of late writings is linked to the first in several ways by its opening piece, 'A Reverie-cum-Reminiscence in the Form of a Letter to Paramartha'. At the beginning of this, we see Sangharakshita and his faithful friend and companion Paramartha making the move (in February 2013) from Madhyamaloka to their new home, which Sangharakshita named 'Adhisthana', 'place of blessings'. And it ends with the launch of *A Moseley Miscellany*, on the occasion of Sangharakshita's ninetieth birthday, marked by Kalyanaprabha's beautiful words and the memorable appearance of a rainbow after a tremendous downpour.

The 36 pieces that follow were written (or rather dictated, for Sangharakshita could no longer see to write) between 2015 and 2018. They are here arranged according to theme, which has meant slightly changing the order in which they were written, and cover a remarkably wide range of themes and styles: dreams and stories, accounts of people and events of long ago, musings on what might have been, never before recorded reflections on Dharma themes, thoughts inspired by current reading on many subjects, including fiction, science, and Islam, and all kinds of matters of life and death, good and evil. Regular readers of Sangharakshita will recognize familiar inspirations – friendship, forgiveness, beauty – all cast in a new light, reflected on afresh – and will also find him considering and expressing entirely new subjects. The last piece was finished just over two weeks before his death on 30 October 2018. Taken together, the collection gives many insights into the mind and heart of Sangharakshita as he reflected and reminisced at the end of a long life, and also considered new ideas, ever curious and thoughtful about the world in which he found himself, right up to the moment of his leaving it.

Vidyadevi
Herefordshire
February 2022

With many thanks to Kalyanaprabha for permission to quote from her introduction to A Moseley Miscellany.

MADHYAMALOKA REFLECTIONS: EXCERPTS FROM *A MOSELEY MISCELLANY*

I: MY FIRST EIGHT YEARS: A MOSAIC OF MEMORIES

NEIGHBOURS AND EARLY FRIENDS

Our nearest neighbours were the Hartnells, who lived in the flat below ours. There was old Mrs Hartnell, her son Fred, and Fred's wife Florrie. There was also Roy, a ginger-haired dog of medium size and no particular breed who was very much a member of the family. Roy liked to lie on the tiled area before the flat's twin front doors. My sister and I had played with him since our earliest years, for he was a good-tempered old dog and never minded how much we tugged at his collar or fondled his soft, velvety-brown ears. He was also a dog of regular habits. At 4 o'clock every afternoon he would go padding up the road to Marsden's Dairy, which was on the corner, only five or six doors away, whence he would return carrying in his mouth a bar of Nestlé's Milk Chocolate. This he would deposit at the feet of Mrs Hartnell, who would remove the wrapper for him and tell him he was a good boy. On Friday she would go to the dairy herself and settle the week's bill on Roy's behalf. Mrs Hartnell was indeed a kind old lady. The horse who drew the milk float got his daily lump of sugar as regularly as Roy got his bar of chocolate. Our family photograph album contained a snapshot of the horse with his forelegs up on the pavement taking the sugar from Mrs Hartnell's outstretched hand.

I remember her very well. Auntie Hartnell, as my sister and I called her, was a widow, and always wore black. (I remember being told that old Mr Hartnell was ill, but I have no recollection of his funeral.) Of medium height, she was slightly built, had a yellowish complexion, brown eyes, and a head covered with small dark curls. She was certainly very kind to Joan and me. When she made a fruit trifle, for example, there would always be a portion for us, which she would bring up to us in two cut-glass tumblers. She was also concerned that we should not be upset or frightened, so that when, one sultry July afternoon, there exploded overhead the mother of all thunderstorms with continual loud rumblings and crashes of thunder and repeated brilliant flashes of lightning, she insisted that we be brought down to what she seemed to think was the greater security of her kitchen, where she distracted us with tea and biscuits until the storm was over.

Uncle Fred was fairly tall, and rather thin. He had a pale, bony face, and thinning hair brushed straight back. He was a bespoke tailor, and I sometimes wandered down to see him at work in the Hartnell kitchen, slipping through the communicating door in the hallway, which was usually left unbolted. More often than not, I found him sitting cross-legged on the kitchen table, which was set lengthwise against the room's only window for the sake of the light. I do not remember him ever talking to me, but he sometimes gave me a piece of tailor's chalk to play with. My father knew him quite well, for they had grown up together, and gone to the same school, the turquoise cupolas of which could be seen from our front gate. (It was to this same school that I started going, unwillingly, when I was four years old.) My father thought Fred Hartnell a milksop, averring that when he was a boy his mother mollycoddled him to such an extent that in the morning she used to sit on the toilet seat to warm it for him before he got up. He also told me that as a young man Fred had been quite a dandy. When he went out he wore pin-stripe trousers, a black tailcoat, and spats, and sported a top hat, on account of which he had been nicknamed the Duke of Selincourt, Selincourt being the name of the street in which we lived. Thus attired he had courted and won his wife Florrie, though how and where was not known, having apparently led her to believe that he had money in the bank and a house of his own. It was, therefore, a cruel disappointment to her when she discovered, after the wedding, that he lived with his parents in a rented ground floor flat in Tooting, and that this was her new home. The marriage was not a happy one. There were frequent quarrels, which from time to time were so violent, and so loud, that my father had to go downstairs, taking advantage of the communicating door, and try to calm things down.

While I have vivid mental pictures of old Mrs Hartnell and Fred, I have no such picture of Florrie Hartnell. I do, however, remember her as being dark-haired and olive-complexioned, which in later years suggested to me that she may have been of Italian, or partly Italian, descent. Despite her unhappiness, she was kind to my sister and me, so that it is all the more unfortunate that she should have been the unwitting cause of the most unpleasant experience of my early childhood. Playing one day in the porch, I chose to press my cheek against the wall between the two front doors, at the same time spreading out my arms, as though in an embrace, until my fingers touched the doors, both of which were half open. Auntie Florrie was at home at the time, and happening to notice that the front door had been left open she closed it, thereby trapping my hand between the door-jamb and the hinged side of the door. On hearing my shrieks of agony, she opened the door to see what was the matter, thus freeing my hand, the third finger of which was crushed and bleeding. The upshot was that for the next two weeks or more Auntie Florrie came upstairs every morning to change the dressing on my injured finger, sitting with me at the kitchen table to do so. I well remember the sessions. First I immersed my finger in a tumbler of hot water so as to loosen the old dressing prior to its removal. This was the most painful part of the proceedings and took a long time. Eventually, however, it was over, and the finger could be examined for signs of improvement and given a fresh dressing, after which I would be free to go and play.

The Harveys lived a couple of doors away, in the direction of the school. There were four of them. The one we saw the most was Mrs Harvey, who was at home all day and could often be seen in their tiny back garden or leaning from their upstairs back window as she hung out her washing. She was a tall, well-built woman, who wore gold-rimmed spectacles, and whose smooth, ginger hair was pulled back into a bun. Mr Harvey was jovial and portly, and wore a gold watch-chain across his capacious stomach. A printer by trade, he was generally to be seen only at weekends. The couple had two teenage sons. As they were much older than us, Joan and I had little or no contact with them, and I do not even remember their names. As the grandest family in the street, the Harveys commanded a lot of respect. They did not own a car (nor did anyone in the street, or even in the neighbourhood), but the family enjoyed regular outings in a chauffeur-driven hired car, on which occasions the children of the neighbourhood would gather round the car and watch their departure with great interest.

The Harveys were not only the grandest family in the street. They were also probably the most literary. At least they took in the popular weekly, *Everybody's*, and when they had finished with it they passed it on to us. I do not remember if my parents read it but I certainly did. I particularly enjoyed the short accounts of striking events in the lives of famous people. These were written in what I later came to recognize as a journalistic style. Thus it was that a French king's discarded mistress 'scrawled on a sheet of scented parchment,' rather than the more straightforward, 'wrote on a piece of paper,' etc. The Harveys had also taken in, week by week, the successive parts, sixty-one in all, of Harmsworth's *Children's Encyclopaedia*. When they learned that I had been diagnosed as having valvular disease of the heart, they very generously gave me the entire set. For this kind act they have my undying gratitude. For the next two years and more the *Children's Encyclopaedia* was my constant companion, turning what might otherwise have been a period of gloomy imprisonment into a time of enrichment and enjoyment, and opening up for me all the treasures of the human spirit.[324]

At a gate midway between the Hartnells' flat and Marsden's Dairy, there often stood, immobile, a stout, middle-aged woman in a pinafore. She never spoke to anyone, and so far as I remember no one ever spoke to her. It was as though she was waiting for someone who never came. This was Mrs Hoare. Joan and I were very conscious of her presence at the gate, for one side of her face was entirely covered by a reddish-brown birth mark. Rather unkindly, we called her 'fishpaste-face', for the birthmark was of the same colour as the fishpaste we had for Sunday afternoon tea, along with watercress, celery, and winkles.

The neighbour who was on the most intimate terms with us, in a sense, was red-faced Thomas Whitehead. He was close to us on two counts. Not only was he my godfather, he was also a close friend of my grandmother, and the two old people used to go on outings together. Being a little pitcher, and having a little pitcher's proverbially long ears, I knew that Uncle Tom had asked my grandmother to marry him, promising that if she did so he would make me his heir. She had no difficulty resisting this temptation. She had buried two husbands, she told him bluntly, and she had no wish to bury a third. Uncle Tom therefore remained a bachelor. He lived on the other side of the road, almost directly opposite us. He lived with his niece Barbara, a small, thin woman with lank brown hair, a long red face, and a long red nose who always looked as though she had been crying. I often visited him in his room, the attraction being not so much Uncle Tom himself but the stuffed fox with a pigeon in its mouth which occupied a glass case against the wall. I longed to possess this wonder, for the collecting instinct was already strong in me, and I believe my godfather had promised that the fox should be mine one day.

Uncle Tom often came to see us, being very much part of the family, especially at Christmas and on birthdays. On my own birthday he would seat me on his knee, tell me to hold out my hand, then slowly count into my palm as many half crowns as he felt disposed to give me. My father always paid this birthday money into the Post Office savings account he had opened for me soon after I was born, as he did any money I was given when I was young. Forty years later, when I returned to England after an absence of twenty years in the East, I withdrew all the money. By then it amounted to a tidy sum, for my father had had the interest made up at the end of each year, and Uncle Tom's money went towards financing my 1966 travels in Italy and Greece. By then my godfather was long dead. He died when I was 5 or 6 and I disgraced myself in the eyes of the family by demanding, when I was told of his death, 'Shall I get the fox now?'

For the first four years of my life my playmates were Joan, who was fifteen months younger than me, and a lively little girl of my own age called Frances who lived next door to Marsden's Dairy. Later, my friends were boys of my own age who were in the same class as me at school or who lived in the same street. My principal friends at this time were Gerald Inkpen and Robbie Rudd. Gerald lived in the next street, and I was often at his house. His mother and mine were friends, so that whenever my mother went to see Mrs Inkpen, who was a Rechabite,[325] I would go too, a circumstance which must have facilitated the development of my friendship with Gerald. He was taller than me, though no older, and we swapped cigarette cards and comics, roamed the streets together, and played with each other's lead soldiers and Meccano sets. Robbie Rudd lived in a ground floor flat at the end of the block, as an American would say. His father was a policeman, and he had a much older sister called Ivy. My mother and his mother were *not* friends. Littler pitcher that I was, I knew that Mrs Rudd had run away with another man, returning to her husband three weeks later rather worse for wear, and the other women who lived in the street tended to avoid her. Robbie said nothing to me about this, of course. He was a dark-haired boy of my own age, reserved rather than shy, and fond of reading. Since he lived so near, I saw more of him than I did of Gerald, so that his parents and sister were used to seeing me around. On entering their kitchen one day I saw four or five black kittens crawling about on the floor. I had not seen kittens before, and the sight of the helpless little creatures gave rise to an emotion I could not then have described. It was compounded of surprise, delight, curiosity, and pity. I have always loved animals. During the four years before, and the four years after, my confinement to bed, I had a variety of pets. They included two guinea pigs, a pair of green budgerigars, two white mice (soon there were forty of them), and half a dozen lizards caught on Wimbledon Common. Later I had a frog, and a toad who liked to have his neck scratched.

When my two years of confinement to bed were at length over, and I was able to lead a more or less normal life, I discovered that Gerald and Robbie were no longer around. Robbie's parents had moved to a council house in another part of Tooting, and what had happened to Gerald I never learned. I therefore had to make new friends. This was not easy, as I was not allowed to run, or even to walk fast, and therefore could not join in sports or games. A few friends I did make, however, mostly among my classmates. There was Leonard Westward, who was better dressed than most of the other boys, Alec Havell, who had a hare lip, Owen Wheeler, who liked to run round the playground with outstretched arms pretending to be an aeroplane, Freddie Timmins, whose father was the local chimney sweep, Douglas Nicholas, who was a cry-baby, and whom I once rescued from a group of boys who were bullying him, and ginger-haired Raymond Parratt, who collected American postage stamps. I too collected postage stamps, but not American ones, and I wondered why anyone would want to collect the stamps of a country as uninteresting as America. I favoured the more exotic varieties, such as the orange-and-purple, high denomination stamps, with the king-emperor's head in the middle, that came affixed to the parcels received by the family from Uncle Dick, my mother's youngest brother, who was stationed in India.

In 1936 I moved with my parents and my sister to a council house in the same part of Tooting where Robbie now lived. It was not long before we resumed our friendship, which lasted until, in the second year of the War, I was evacuated to North Devon.

IN THE CLASSROOM

Mrs Davis was my teacher when I was in the top class of the Selincourt Road Infant School. She was stout, grey-haired, and motherly, and like the other teachers she wore a housecoat to protect her dress from the clouds of chalk dust that flew from the blackboard whenever it was wiped clean. Her housecoat had a pattern of brown leaves and yellow flowers, and I have a mental picture of her in it as she sat at her desk in front of the class trying to thread a needle. Her eyes bulged as she focused her gaze on the eye of the needle and the tip of the thread, and I could see that the whites of her eyes were yellow.

The upper half of the classroom door was glassed in like a window, while across the lower half of the window there hung a short curtain. One day Mrs Davis painted this curtain with broad vertical stripes of all the colours of the rainbow, as it seemed. This gave a touch of brightness and gaiety to the rather drab classroom, as no doubt she had intended.

I did not learn very much while I was in Mrs Davis's class. I have vague recollections of white cards printed with such sentences as 'the cat sat on the mat', of our chanting the multiplication tables in unison, of scripture lessons, and of our teacher reading to us some of the Enid Blyton stories, none of which I remember, a fact that suggests I did not find them very interesting. One autumn afternoon she wrote on the blackboard the lines:

> Please to remember the fifth of November,
> Gunpowder, treason and plot.

She did not tell us anything about Guy Fawkes, or about the nature of the famous plot, but she did want to know if anyone could read the words 'remember' and 'November', pointing to them with her ruler as she put the question. I was the only one who could do so, for some of the other children were still struggling with 'the cat sat on the mat', whereas I had no difficulty with words, and by this time was reading such classic children's books as *Black Beauty, The Water Babies*, and *The Swiss Family Robinson.*

We had no formal singing lessons, but in the course of the term Mrs Davis taught us a few songs. One song touched me deeply, but it was not the simple tune that affected me so much as the words. The song was a lullaby, sung by a mother to her baby, and the second verse ran:

> Sleep and rest, sleep and rest,
> Father will come to thee soon;
> Rest, rest, on mother's breast,
> Father will come to thee soon;
> Father will come to his babe in the nest,
> Silver sails all out of the West
> Under the silver moon.[326]

When we came to the words 'silver sails all out of the West' I experienced a thrill of intense delight, and there flashed upon my inner eye a vision of bright silver sails. What was more, those silver sails came not from a particular point of the compass but from somewhere beyond all geography. This was one of my earliest experiences of the magic of poetry, as well as of my capacity to match its images with vivid mental pictures of my own.

Although there were both boys and girls in Mrs Davis's class, I do not remember any of the boys. On the other hand I do remember two of the girls. Indeed, I remember them extremely well. Daphne Taylor was an ash blonde with green eyes, white skin, and a slightly prominent nose. Sometimes we shared the same desk, and on one memorable occasion we simultaneously bent down, as if searching for a fallen pencil, and under cover of the desk kissed each other on the lips. Daphne's lips were deliciously soft, and meeting them with my own was definitely a sensuous, even sensual experience, though not at all sexual. I liked Daphne, but I was much fonder of her friend Gladys Gown, who was as shy as Daphne was forward. Whether I knew it then or not I was in love with Gladys. A little taller than Daphne, and quite slim, she had straight fair hair, blue eyes, and a small nose and small mouth. I thought of her constantly, so much so that at night, in bed, I used to pretend that my big teddy bear was Gladys and would hug him for a few minutes before going to sleep. I called this ritual 'Gladys's love'.

Shortly after moving from the top class of the Infant School to the bottom class of the Junior School, and from the care of Mrs Davis to that of Miss Browne, I came down first with scarlet fever, then with chickenpox, and spent three weeks in hospital. When my mother came to take me home one of the nurses told her that my pulse was unusually fast and that I should be taken to see a doctor without delay. The result was that I was found to be suffering from valvular disease of the heart and my parents were told that I must be put to bed and kept absolutely quiet, this being the standard treatment at the time for my condition. For the next two years, therefore, I was confined to bed, seeing no one except my parents. This was followed by six months in a wheelchair. I was then deemed well enough to go back to school. I had not forgotten Gladys, and looked forward to seeing her again with great eagerness. I went back to Miss Browne's class, which was the Junior School's top class, but Gladys was not there. When I did see her I received a shock. She wore a navy-blue beret and a short black coat, and was not only taller than before but so thin as to be positively skinny. What was worse, in their black stockings her thin legs looked like the black hairy legs of a spider (not that I disliked spiders). I fell as quickly out of love as I had fallen *in* love three years earlier. It was one of the biggest disappointments of my young life.

OUTINGS

We were up 'in the gods' together. There were six of us: my mother, Joan and I, and my mother's friend Margaret and her two children – Rita, who was the same age as me, and Mavis, who was the same age as Joan. We were up there with our bottles of lemonade and our buns. It was Christmas time, we were at the Wimbledon Hippodrome, and I was seeing my first pantomime. From where I sat I had a clear view of the stage far below. The pantomime was 'Shock-headed Peter', a character of whom I had not heard before. I do not remember what the story was, but I well remember the small figure of the pantomime's eponymous hero. He wore a black jacket with a belt, and black breeches, and he had an enormous shock of white hair. On the stage there was also a well. As I watched, Peter jumped into the bucket that hung above the well and *disappeared from sight*. I was overwhelmed by feelings of indescribable horror and dread. It was as though Peter had descended into unfathomable Tartarean depths and was lost forever. I expect he reappeared later on in the pantomime, but of this I have no recollection. For me his disappearance must have been absolute, and the feeling of horror and dread must have persisted for some time. I do, however, remember the pantomime's principal boy singing 'Whistling in the Dark', a song which evoked in me an eerie feeling of loneliness and desolation.

Christmas was also the time when Joan and I visited one of the big department stores in Tooting Bec, or Balham, or Brixton, to meet Santa Claus. It was always our mother who took us, for our father detested shops and shopping. Dazzled by the myriad lights and deafened by the noise we would push our way through the milling crowds to where Santa Claus sat or stood at the entrance to his magic grotto, his sack of presents beside him. He was dressed from head to foot in red, and his abundant white beard reached down to his waist. In return for our sixpences he dipped into his sack and gave Joan a pink package and me a blue one and we were allowed to enter the grotto, where we saw not only more lights but all manner of wonders, from Santa's sleigh and his two reindeer (were they real?), to huge Christmas trees hung with tinsel and silver bells and topped with a glittering star or no less glittering fairy. On reaching home we would open the presents Santa Claus had given us. One Christmas Joan's contained a small celluloid doll, mine a tin whistle.

Although our father never took us to see Santa Claus, he certainly took us out – particularly me. One grey Saturday afternoon he took me to see a football match. We went with Uncle Jack, my mother's brother, who was a staunch Fulham supporter. The match was at White City, a name that conjured up a vivid mental image for me. Though for much of the time I sat perched on my father's right shoulder, which I was still small enough to be able to do, I could see little or nothing of the game, with the result that I did not enjoy the outing. Moreover, there was a drizzle of rain, and I felt cold and wet. I must have expressed my dissatisfaction to my father afterwards, for he did not take me to a football match again. My first football match was therefore also my last.

A black ditch, and across the ditch a wooden plank. My father and I had to walk over the plank in order to get to Figge's Marsh and to the fair that was in progress there. It was a new experience for me, and as we wandered in and out of the good-natured holiday crowd, I with my hand firmly in my father's, I took in eagerly the unfamiliar sights and sounds. Roundabouts whirled to the music of the mechanical organ, the riders of the brightly-painted wooden animals screaming with laughter; swingboats carried people high into the air. We passed coconut shies and shooting galleries, passed purveyors of bright pink candyfloss and vendors of balloons. I was particularly attracted by the stalls where, for a single penny, one could win a big box of chocolates. These stalls were circular in shape, the proprietor standing in the middle, entirely surrounded by his counter. On the counter there was laid out a tempting array of large and small boxes of chocolates. From behind a barrier one tossed a penny on to the counter, aiming for one of the boxes of chocolates. If your penny landed on the box and stayed there, it was yours. With pennies supplied by my father I made several attempts to win one of the boxes, but even if it hit the box I had chosen it bounced or rolled off it onto the counter. As we turned away from the stall, my father and I, a man walked past carrying an enormous teddy bear he had won. Some people were luckier than others, it seemed.

The fair at Figge's Marsh was a new and exciting experience for me, and it is not surprising that I should have vivid memories of it, but I have an equally vivid memory of an experience of a very different kind, albeit one still connected with the fair. My father and I happened to pass by a small tent, and seeing that the front was open we looked in. Seated at a small table were two midgets, a man and a woman. Though fully grown, they were no bigger than I was then at five or six. They were folding leaflets, working steadily and silently. Neither of them looked up at us or showed any sign of being aware of our presence. They just carried on folding the leaflets. The sight was infinitely touching, and the image of the two midgets at their task haunted me for a long, long time.

... I was inside the Big Top. I do not remember how I got there, or who took me there, but I was inside the Big Top, eyes fixed on the arena below, oblivious to everything else. White horses trotted round the arena at the command of a man wearing a top hat and carrying a long whip; an elephant did ponderous tricks; red-nosed clowns in white made me laugh at their antics. But best of all were the Japanese acrobats. They ran nimbly up and down the high wire, a parasol helping them to keep their balance. From time to time one of them let out a tremendous shout in a language I did not understand. Another pretended to be about to fall off the wire but recovered himself in the nick of time with miraculous agility. Yet another ran up to the top of the wire then slid all the way down to the bottom holding his parasol triumphantly aloft as he did so. It was a glorious time I had, inside the Big Top that day.

Like other London children, Joan and I were taken to see the animals in London Zoo. This was a family outing, in that it was both our parents who took us to the famous institution. We saw the Chimpanzees' Tea Party, had a ride on the back of an elephant with our father while our mother watched anxiously from below, and saw a polar bear stand on its hind legs to receive a stream of condensed milk which someone on the terrace above poured into its open mouth. These and a hundred other sights I shared not only with Joan and my parents but also with tens of thousands of other visitors to the zoo. Three of those sights made a stronger impression on me, perhaps, than they did on other people. The macaw is a gorgeous bird, but there was not just one of them. There were a dozen or more in a row, all on their individual perches, all preening themselves in the sunlight. It was the most brilliant display of colour I had ever seen. But if the gorgeous macaws impinged on my sense of sight, the occupants of the Big Cat House impinged less on my sight than on my sense of smell. It was not that I paid no attention to the lions, tigers, and leopards, as that I was much less conscious of what they looked like than of how they smelt. Their combined stench was indeed overwhelming, and not easily forgotten. There was also Monkey Hill. It was surrounded by a moat and a parapet and inhabited by two or three dozen monkeys, all of the same species. The monkeys were always on the move. They ran up and down the hill, darted in and out of its caves, chased one another, and even sometimes fought. One monkey did not move about much. It was a female, and she sat there clasping a baby monkey in her thin arms. It did not take me long to realize that the baby was dead, had perhaps been dead for some time, and that the mother was refusing to part with the body. It was a pathetic sight, and must have moved me deeply, for forty years later, when I had long forgotten it, and when I was in a distant place and in a strange situation, the image of the mother monkey clasping her dead baby suddenly surfaced, as I have related elsewhere.[327]

Another family outing was the day trip we took from London Bridge to Clacton-on-Sea on a steamship of the Eagle Line. I spent much of the voyage leaning on the rail watching the Thames slowly widen as we moved downstream. It was the first time I had been on the water. On our arrival at Clacton-on-Sea I saw that the beach was jam-packed with people, which I suppose was the reason why we did not go there. At least I have no recollection of our going. All I remember is that we spent some time in the town, then boarded the ship for the return journey. When my grandmother gave me a model yacht on my seventh birthday I named it White Eagle, this being the name of the steamship that had taken us to Clacton-on-Sea. The yacht had adjustable sails and a polished wooden deck, and my father used to take me to Clapham Common so that I could sail it on the pond there. Once a dog swam out to it, seized it in its jaws, and returned with it to the shore. The yacht bore the mark of the dog's teeth on its deck for the rest of its days.

Not all my childhood outings were as exhilarating as my visits to the circus or the zoo. There were also outings of a quieter character. Most of them were with my father, who in those days was often out of work. I liked being with my father, for he always talked to me, and told me things. Several times he took me with him to the employment exchange (as I think it was) at Tooting Bec. There he always saw the same person. Her name was Mrs Cheeseman, and she always gave me a chocolate drop. There were also trips to Mitcham Common, where I fished for sticklebacks in the pond, and occasionally to the more distant Raynes Park. When he was in work he sometimes took me to his workplace on Saturday mornings, from where we would go somewhere in the afternoon. Once he took me to Bennett's Yard, which was somewhere in the City. We climbed up a wooden outside staircase into a kind of loft where four or five men were at work. They must have been carpenters, for I remember that the floor was ankle-deep in wood shavings. Another time he was working at Dean's Yard, Westminster, and one Saturday afternoon we visited the Abbey. I do not remember the monuments, but I well remember seeing the very lifelike funeral effigy of Queen Elizabeth. I was no stranger to Good Queen Bess for I had already come across her in a story book, where she was depicted seated in a chair and wearing the familiar farthingale and ruff. My father bought me a picture postcard of her effigy, and I added it to my postcard collection. She has always been my favourite historical character. Another Saturday afternoon found us at the Natural History and Science Museums in South Kensington. I was tremendously impressed by the 100-foot long replica of a Diplodocus skeleton and by Leonardo da Vinci's winged flying-machines. We also saw the stuffed animals. Among them was the famous War Office Cat, an exceptionally large tabby. As a very small child he had ridden on its back, my father told me, for his father had worked in the War Office, and his mother had sometimes taken him there. I cannot vouch for the truth of what he said about his riding the War Office Cat, for my father was an inveterate teller of tall stories, which he always told with a perfectly straight face. When Joan and I were quite small, he once told us that when he first met our mother she was so thin that she could get through a keyhole. Naturally we believed him and spent the next half hour carefully studying the keyhole of the kitchen door and trying to work out how our mother had managed to get through.

SHOPS AND SHOPPING

My earliest memories of shopping are connected with my mother. We are walking along the street together, and she is carrying a shopping basket. Every few yards, as it seems to me, my mother meets someone she knows, and the two women stop to talk. They talk, and talk, and talk, and soon I am tugging at my mother's hand and saying impatiently, 'Oh, come *on*, Mum!' until finally she detaches herself and we continue our progress until she meets someone else or we enter a shop. It was one of the mysteries of my boyhood why women talked so much.

I remember some of the shops we entered by their smell. In one there was the cool, fresh smell of cheese and butter, in another the fusty smell of cloth, and in yet another the sickening smell of blood. This last was the smell that pervaded the butcher's shop, and so much did I dislike it that I insisted on waiting for her outside whenever my mother shopped there. There were also visits to Tooting Market. It was a covered market, with stalls on either side of a central aisle. One of the stalls sold rabbit meat, and skinned and unskinned rabbits hung upside down from hooks. Only later did I realize that there was a connection between them and the rabbit stew we occasionally had for lunch. One morning we learned that there had been a fire at Tooting Market and that much of it had been destroyed. The next time I went there with my mother only the first few stalls were open for business. The rest of the market was a tangle of charred and blackened beams.

My mother did not always take me with her when she went shopping. Sometimes she left me in the flat on my own, with the admonition that I was not to answer the door if anyone knocked or rang the bell. As soon as she was gone I would crawl under the kitchen table, for the tablecloth hung down on all four sides, thus making a tent in which I could hide. As I could not yet read, I amused myself by scribbling with crayons on the unpolished underside of the table. More often than not there would be no unexpected callers, but if the silence of the flat did happen to be suddenly broken by a knock or a ring, I would sit frozen with terror, imagining that someone or some*thing* horrible had managed to open the front door and was slowly creeping up the stairs. If the knock or the ring was not repeated I would gradually relax and the pounding of my heart would slow down. Only when I heard the front door open and my mother's familiar step on the stairs did I crawl out of my hiding place and sit on the floor, as if I had been there all the time. I never told my mother about the terror I had felt, probably because I did not have the words with which to describe my feelings.

Though my father disliked shops and shopping, there was at least one shop to which he did not mind going. This was the little toyshop in Tooting Bec, to which he took me from time to time. When quite young I had been given a wooden fort, complete with brightly-painted lead soldiers, but I was not particularly fond of soldiers and did little to add to their number. On the other hand, I was hardly less fond of lead animals than I was of their flesh and blood originals, and was always wanting to add to my collection. Hence the visits to the little shop in Tooting Bec with my father. By the time I was seven or eight I had a sizeable collection of lead animals of various kinds. My favourites among the wild animals were a giraffe, a kangaroo, and an elephant. The elephant came complete with a howdah, which could be placed on its back, and on which six tiny human figures could sit, three on each side – just like their real life counterparts at the Zoo. I also had a whole farmyard of domesticated animals, including a pig, piglets, a sheep, a bull, and a duck and ducklings. Sometimes I made a farmyard for these animals, with cardboard painted green for grass and a piece of mirror for a pond. I would then amuse myself arranging and rearranging them within the imaginary fences of the little farmyard until I was satisfied – or until the table had to be cleared for a meal.

Once I was taken shopping by my grandmother. Nana, as my sister and I called her, often came to see us on a Saturday afternoon, after she had been to Wandsworth Cemetery and placed fresh flowers on the grave of her second husband and their only daughter, who had died very young. It was in the course of one of these visits that she took me shopping with her. My sister wanted to have a black doll. She already had a white doll, called Muriel, but she very much wanted a black doll too and Nana had promised to buy her one. We did not have to go very far or search for long. At the entrance to one of the shops in Mitcham Road there was a large basket full of dolls of various kinds. Among the dolls there were several black ones, and one of these Nana bought. It cost her a shilling. Joan was delighted with the new doll, whom she christened Topsy. Thereafter she spent many happy hours playing with her two dolls, dressing and undressing them, putting them to bed when they were ill, and giving them medicine, and scolding them when they were naughty. In short, she loved both her dolls dearly and treated them equally without the least help from any Commission for Racial Equality.

There were two shops in the neighbourhood with which I was particularly well acquainted. One was the dairy at the top end of the street; the other the sweetshop that was just round the corner opposite the dairy. I was familiar with the dairy because my mother sometimes sent me there for an extra pint of milk, and old Mrs Marsden, who was usually behind the counter, knew me as well as I knew her. One day she gave me a pair of Oxo spectacles. They were an advertising gimmick on behalf of the well-known beverage, but I did not know this, and wore them proudly until they fell apart. At the dairy I naturally encountered other customers. One of them was a very old woman dressed from head to foot in rusty black. She had a yellow face and yellow, claw-like hands, and she emitted a horrible smell. I never learned who she was or where she came from and probably thought it better not to ask. The sweetshop was an Aladdin's Cave of multicoloured confectionery. Besides chocolate bars and other more expensive items, there were sherbet dabs, liquorice sticks, jelly babies, and scores of other sweets the names of which I have forgotten. The pleasure was not just in buying but in choosing, and I spent a lot of time deciding what I wanted. In those days, when there were two ha'pennies to a penny, or four farthings, one could get quite a lot of sweets for a penny, and like other boys I wanted to get as many sweets for my money as I could.

Everyone has two parents, four grandparents, and eight great-grandparents, but not everyone is brought up knowing them all. Apart from my parents, I knew only my father's mother and *her* mother, all the rest having died before I was born. I was my grandmother's first grandchild, and I was very much part of her life, as she was part of mine. In the family photo album there is a picture of her standing in the porch of her house in Southfields and holding me in her arms. I am still wearing long clothes, and she is smiling at me.

As a small child I sometimes stayed for a few days with Nana and Auntie Noni, Nana's unmarried daughter, who lived with her. A little bed was made up for me on the floor in the corner of the big downstairs bedroom they shared. When I was older I shared a bed with Uncle Charles, my father's much younger half-brother, who still lived at home, and who had a room upstairs. In the morning I watched him exercising with a pair of chest expanders, and once he gave me a blue and white school tie.

Nana lived not far from Wimbledon Park, and whenever I stayed with her she and Auntie Noni took me to feed the ducks who lived in the pond there. On the way we passed the local tennis courts, the entrance to which was flanked by enormous clumps of tall African grass, and where people in white could usually be seen playing. In the background, high up on the embankment, the red carriages of the District Line trains sped back and forth, their wheels going *clickety-click, clickety-click* as they passed. Among the ducks swimming on the pond, there floated a pair of swans, probably the first I ever saw.

It was Nana and Auntie Noni who took me on my first journey by train. I was then 3 or 4 years old. Our destination was Besthorpe, the Norfolk village where Nana had been born and where my father had spent several years of his childhood. At Attleborough we alighted and soon the three of us were walking along the road to Besthorpe. While Nana and Auntie Noni chatted, I ran on ahead, darting from one side of the road to the other excitedly plucking flowers from the hedgerows. We had not gone very far when from the opposite direction there came an old countryman on a bicycle, a sack of potatoes over one shoulder. Just then I happened to spot some flowers growing in the hedgerow opposite, and at once darted eagerly towards them. Unfortunately I did not look both ways first, as I had often been told I must do before crossing the road, and ran smack into the bicycle and its rider. The old countryman lost his balance and fell off his bicycle, and the sack burst open, spilling potatoes all over the road. As for me, I was knocked unconscious, and had to be carried to Besthorpe and my great-grandmother's cottage.

I did not know all this at the time, of course. I came to know it later because my father was fond of relating how he had seen Nana, Auntie Noni, and me off at Liverpool Street station, and how after the train's departure he had heaved a sigh of relief, thinking that whatever mischief I might get up to in the Norfolk countryside I was at least in no danger of being run over, as I certainly was in London owing to my habit of running out into the road without looking first to see if it was safe to do so. Evidently he had underestimated my capacity for getting into mischief, he would ruefully observe, after which he would recount the details of the accident as he had heard them from Nana and Auntie Noni.

The first thing I can remember after regaining consciousness was being given a boiled egg for my tea. The reason why I remember this is that the egg had two yolks, and as I had never seen such an egg before, I thought it a wonderful thing.

In an upstairs room, probably the one in which I stayed, there hung an enormous crinoline. By some coincidence, I was given a children's book to look at in which ladies were depicted wearing just such crinolines over a pair of long frilly pantaloons. In an adjacent room lay Auntie Fanny, who was probably one of Nana's sisters. She was an invalid, I was told, and bed-ridden. The room was darkened, and all I could make out was a thin white face and the white bedclothes.

One morning I was taken to see Aunt Luke, who lived in the nearby row of almshouses. Whose aunt she was I do not know, but she was very old, said how pale I was, and gave me a glass of elderberry wine.

My only other recollection of my first visit to Nana's ancestral village, was of being told that I should on no account go near the well. This well was situated at the end of a lane behind the cottage, and apparently it was assumed that if I was allowed to go near it, I would somehow manage to fall in.

I have no recollection of my great-grandmother, but I remember my mother speaking of her, some years later, as a little woman and as 'a dear old soul', and no doubt the description would have held good at the time of my visit. She died not long afterwards, and my father travelled to Besthorpe for the funeral. He was very fond of his grandmother, and in after years I more than once heard him say that if ever he became rich he would put a headstone on her grave.

One of the things I looked forward to on my visits to Southfields was the Camp Coffee which Nana put into my hot milk. It was a mixture of coffee and chicory, which we did not have at home, and I was particularly fond of the taste of this famous beverage. A label on one side of the bottle depicted a kilted soldier seated in front of his tent as his turbaned Indian bearer brought him his Camp Coffee on a tray. I also looked forward to seeing Uncle Leonard, one of my father's Lingwood cousins, whose shoe repair shop was just round the corner from where Nana lived. The first time I went there it was with Nana, who wanted to have some shoes re-soled, but thereafter I went on my own. I always found Uncle Leonard working at his bench in the shop. He was about the same age as my father, had a lot of untidy brown hair, was invariably unshaven, and had a pair of very bright eyes. He always treated me in a very friendly fashion, and I never visited him without his giving me a few coppers from the till. Under the counter would often be a litter of puppies, for Uncle Leonard bred Sealyhams, and I looked forward to seeing the puppies too. Sometimes I went through into the living quarters behind the shop to see stout and hospitable Auntie Louie and the three boys, the youngest of whom was about my own age, and sometimes I stayed for a meal.

I do not know if Nana had a Norfolk accent, but her voice had a lilt, and she certainly always said *shootin'* instead of 'shooting', and *Tootin'* instead of 'Tooting'. Though she had spent the greater part of her life in London, she was a countrywoman at heart. Once I was in the kitchen with her, Auntie Noni, and my mother when a mouse ran across the room. Auntie Noni and my mother screamed, jumped onto chairs, and lifted up their skirts; but Nana, like a true countrywoman, seized a poker, chased the mouse, cornered it at the bottom of a cupboard, and killed it.

Both Nana and Auntie Noni believed that my sister and I were growing up rather spoilt, and since both were outspoken by nature they did not hesitate to tell my father so. But all he would ever say in response to this criticism was, 'Let them enjoy themselves. They are only young once.'

On the horizon, close together, there are two reddish-brown cones. They gradually grow larger, then disappear behind the rooftops.... Then I am in a large room. There are squares of glass on the walls of the room, and behind the glass something is moving. It looks like a spider.... I am lying on my back in another, much smaller room. I am lying in a kind of cradle, and faces are looking down at me.

These are among my very earliest memories. The facts behind the memories are that I was lying back in my pram, looking out on the world, that my mother was taking me to the post-natal centre at St George's Hospital, Tooting, and that the reddish-brown cones were the cowls on the hospital's chimneys. The large room was probably the waiting room, and the squares of glass were either pictures or aquaria, but I have no idea what the 'spider' behind the glass may have been. In the smaller room I was evidently being weighed, and the faces looking down at me must have been the faces of the doctors or nurses. Walking beside my mother, and also pushing a pram with an infant in it, there would have been her friend Margaret, whose daughter Rita was almost exactly the same age as I was. The two women may well have met for the first time at the post-natal centre. Auntie Margaret, as I called her, lived in Bickersteth Road, which lay at the end of Selincourt Road, and formed a T-junction with it. I remember once being at Margaret's house when Margaret was suckling her baby, which probably was not Rita, but her second daughter, Mavis. I thought the big, brown dug was rather an ugly sight. I must have already forgotten my own breast-feeding days!

There were other things I had forgotten by this time, but about which I heard later from my parents, usually from my father. Several of the experiences I had forgotten were painful ones. There was my vaccination by our GP, Dr Bradlaugh, when I was a baby. Even if my parents had not told me about the vaccination, there on my upper left arm were the four tell-tale scars, each the size of a fingerprint, which testified to the fact until I was well into my teens. Then there was the time when I burned my left foot by touching a hot flat iron. I was then a baby, and was sitting on the kitchen table while my mother was ironing clothes. When she went into the scullery to get more clothes for ironing I crawled towards the flat iron, which she had stood up on the table, and happened to touch it with my foot. My piercing screams brought her hurrying back to the kitchen to see what was the matter. What happened next I do not know. What I do know is that for many years I had a small scar on my foot. Above all, there was the unremembered time when my parents, Joan, and I all went down with the flu. It must have been in 1927 or 1928, when Joan was still a baby. The four of us lay helpless in the big front bedroom together. Dr Bradlaugh came every day, and my father gave him the key to the front door, as neither he nor my mother had the strength to go downstairs and let him in when he called. Old Mrs Hartnell, who lived in the flat below, came and cooked for us, though I suspect none of us had much appetite.

Not long after we had all recovered from the flu my father was away for three weeks. He had been sent to a convalescent home for ex-servicemen in St Leonards, near Hastings, for the injuries he sustained during the War had left him without the full use of his right arm and right hand. I do not remember missing him while he was away, but I must have missed him greatly, especially at bedtime, as he always came to my room and talked to me for a while before I went to sleep. Though I have no recollection of his going away, I well remember his return. This was due partly to the fact that he had a present for me from a relative called Aunt Dick, of whom I had not heard before, and of whom I never heard again. She lived in Hastings, and was probably my father's cousin or aunt. Her present to me was a toy telephone, which gave me many hours of innocent pleasure. I derived no less pleasure from my father's account of life at the convalescent home. Afternoon tea was served out in the garden, and I particularly enjoyed his description of the birds that came to the table and pecked fearlessly about his and the other men's feet. There were not only the ubiquitous sparrows, but robins and blue tits, as well as finches of various kinds and colours. So graphically did my father describe the birds that in my mind's eye I had a vivid picture of them as they hopped on his table and fluttered round his feet in all their diverse colours.

Though I have only one actual recollection of experiencing pain myself (when my finger was caught in the Hartnells' front door), I have several memories of my mother suffering pain. Like many other working-class women she had bad teeth, and when she was about thirty she had them all out and replaced by false teeth (c.f. the pub scene in T.S. Eliot's *The Waste Land*, first published in 1922). On her return from the hospital she told my father what had happened, and little pitcher that I was I could not but overhear what she said. While under the anaesthetic she could hear someone screaming in the distance and realized that it was she herself who was doing the screaming. The nurse had scolded her when she came round, saying, 'Oh Mrs Lingwood, you *did* make a fuss!' The removal of the teeth made a great difference to my mother's appearance. Without them, she looked like an old woman, as she did afterwards whenever she took her false teeth out, which it was her custom to do at night. There was also the occasion when my mother treated herself to a 'permanent wave', and as a result experienced severe headaches for several days. The flat, regular waves of the perm made her face look thinner and younger, but it did not improve her looks. My mother was never beautiful, or even very pretty, but old or young, pretty or not pretty, I loved her and could not bear even to think of her being hurt.

Fortunately for us both, only once during my early childhood did I actually see her hurt. Our back stairs were quite steep, and my mother was down them and up them twenty times a day. One day she lost her footing on the way down and fell headlong to the bottom. Though she was not injured, she was badly shaken and could not help crying. The sight of her flushed, tear-stained face affected me deeply and remained a painful memory for a long time afterwards.

There was another accident in the family around this time. One morning the door bell rang and my mother went downstairs to see who was there, and I trailed along after her. On opening the front door she found herself face to face with a member of the St John's Ambulance Brigade, across whose outstretched arms there lay a small body so completely swathed in bandages as to look like an Egyptian mummy. My mother let out a shriek, and without waiting for explanations turned and dashed up the stairs calling loudly for my father, who then happened to be at home. The 'mummy' was my sister Joan. She was not dead, only injured. It transpired that she had been playing outside with her friend Frances, a lively, adventurous little girl of about my age, and that Joan had been knocked down by a car as the two of them were crossing the main road, a thing which Joan, at least, was strictly forbidden to do. Frances was not hurt, but Joan sustained a few cuts and bruises, and for the next three weeks was confined to bed.

When I was six years old I underwent two minor operations. The first took place in hospital, the second at home. One was for the removal of my tonsils, the other for the lancing of a large swelling that had developed in my groin. About an experience I had at the hospital, and of how it aroused in me a sense of injustice (and therefore of justice), I have written elsewhere.[328]

The operation I had at home took place in my bedroom. While Dr Bradlaugh conferred with my parents in the kitchen, the anaesthetist was with me in my bedroom making his preparations. Inquisitive as ever, I wanted to know the name of the liquid with which he was soaking a wad of cotton wool. In fact I wanted to smell the liquid, but this he would not allow me to do. I soon found out what it smelt like! Afterwards I was told that when the time came for the anaesthetic mask to be placed over my face, I fought like a tiger and that it took the combined strength of Dr Bradlaugh, the anaesthetist, and my father, to hold me down. When the operation was over, and there stood beside my bed a basin half full of a yellow liquid, I complained vigorously. If I had been allowed to smell the liquid when I wanted to, I said, there would not have been all that fuss!

As a child, I knew that I had once had both measles and whooping cough, but I did not remember having them, probably because I was very young at the time. But I certainly remember having scarlet fever. I had it when I was eight, and I remember it mainly because it was the first of a series of events which, culminating in my being confined to bed for two years, affected the whole subsequent course of my life. Those two years draw a thick black line between my early childhood, on the one hand, and on the other my later childhood and my adolescence.

II: REVERIES AND REMINISCENCES

A ROOM WITH A VIEW

I shall soon be leaving Moseley, the quiet, leafy Birmingham suburb where I have lived for the last fourteen years, and I wonder what memories of my present residence I shall carry with me to my new home in the countryside and how long those memories will persist.[329] I shall certainly remember the garden, with its trees and shrubs, the flights of stone steps down to the lawn, the perimeter path round which I walked every morning, and the pond into which a small boy jumped thinking that the green algae with which it was covered was grass. The sounds of the place, too, I shall remember. I shall remember the hum of bees in the azaleas, the patter of rain on the roof of my study, and the dull drone of the low-flying passenger aircraft on its way to Birmingham Airport. Above all, I think, I shall remember the tremulous cry of the owls that lived in the neighbouring trees and called to one another in the late evening. I would remember the cry of the owls because my memories of the last two places in which I lived are inseparable from memories of the sound of birds. When I lived in Norfolk, on the outskirts of a village, I used to hear the sound of the wild geese flying overhead.[330] They flew very low, so low that I could distinctly hear the regular beating of their wings. I also used to hear the cuckoo. As in the old rhyme, he came in April, sang all day in May, in June changed his tune, prepared to fly in July, had to go in August, and in September was only a memory – until the following spring. When I lived in East London, as I did later on, I used to wake up every morning in summer to the sound of a blackbird's full-throated song.[331] He sang from the top of a neighbouring chimney pot, and he sang for an hour or more, after which he flew away, no doubt to go in search of his breakfast. I would have liked to celebrate the blackbird as magnificently as Shelley had celebrated the skylark but this was a feat far beyond my limited poetic powers, and all I could produce was the following verse:

> *Trill trill trill* goes the blackbird
> At the cold blue edge of day,
> *Trill trill trill* goes Apollo's bird
> From the chimney pot across the way.

This became the first verse of 'Birds and Their Gods', a series of six verses in each of which I describe a particular bird, its song, and the figure in Western mythology with which it is associated.[332]

The poem was written some time in 1992. During the last fourteen years I have written very little poetry, and I shall probably carry with me into my new home memories of only two of them, 'The Pilgrim' and 'Love and Duty'.[333] I shall carry them with me because I know them by heart, and I know them by heart not because I made an effort to memorize them but because they came spontaneously from somewhere deep in my psyche and have remained with me ever since. With me will go, also, all those poems and fragments of poems that I have memorized in the course of my life or which have clung to me almost in spite of myself, from 'Old King Cole' to 'Lycidas', and from 'Onward, Christian Soldiers' to 'Sister Helen'.[334] With them would be at least one line by a poet I 'discovered' only in the 1990s, though his name was familiar to me long before that. I was then corresponding regularly with an elderly Belgian Buddhist, a teacher of Zen, who was in the habit of sending me the typescripts of the talks he gave to members of his Zen group. The talks were interesting, and I enjoyed reading them. In the course of one of them he quoted the line 'Death is no different whined at than withstood'. It was a thunderbolt of a line and it struck me to the heart both as a Buddhist and as a lover of poetry. The line was by Philip Larkin, and came from his poem 'Aubade'. I was therefore soon deep in Larkin's *Collected Poems* and delighting in his highly individual style, which I found to be characterized by conciseness, lack of sentimentality, and a kind of controlled lyricism. His view of human existence was rather bleak, but I found it stimulating rather than depressing, and I found myself wanting to know about the man behind the poetry. I therefore read first Andrew Motion's biography of the poet,[335] then Larkin's famous – or infamous – *Selected Letters*, and finally his *Required Writing: Miscellaneous Pieces 1955–1982*.

Though I have written few poems during the last fourteen years, and will probably carry only two of them with me in my heart to my new home in the countryside, during the same period I wrote three books, besides editing – and to some extent revising – four seminars I had given some years earlier. I say I wrote the three books, but the fact is that I had to dictate them. I had to dictate them, for my eyesight had suddenly deteriorated. The trouble started when I was on a reunion retreat at Il Convento, the half-ruined monastery in Tuscany where, surrounded as we were by olive gardens and arbutus woods, I had led, for many a blue-roofed Italian summer, ordination retreats for men of several different nationalities.[336] One day I woke up to find my vision strangely distorted, and that I could neither read nor write. This did not disturb me unduly, as for the past week my eyes had been sore due to what I took to be eye-strain and they would, I thought, recover if I gave them a little rest from my constant reading and writing. My vision remained distorted, however, and it became obvious that it was time I saw a doctor. Someone therefore drove me to Grosseto, and to the town's new health centre. This was an imposing place, all white marble and huge, gilt-framed mirrors, and before long I was being seen by a young man in a white coat who may or may not have been a doctor. I told him what had happened, whereupon he wrote it all down, asked me a few questions, examined my eyes, and finally ushered me into the presence of a large, elderly man who may or may not have been a consultant. This gentleman read what the young man had written, grunted, wrote out a prescription for pills, assured me that my vision would be back to normal within ten days, and charged me the equivalent of sixty pounds for the consultation.

Though I took the pills as directed there was no improvement in my vision, and it became obvious that despite my reluctance to leave the retreat I ought to return to England without delay and seek further medical advice. A few days later, therefore, I was back in Birmingham and my eyes were being examined and my vision tested by a cheerful, friendly ophthalmologist who stank of tobacco. Things were serious, he told me. I had 'wet' macular degeneration in both eyes (the 'wet' is the more rapidly developing form of the disease) and I ought to have seen him weeks ago. When I showed him the pills I had been taking he snorted contemptuously and tossed them into the wastepaper basket, saying 'they use a lot of these things in Europe'. But all was not lost. He would arrange for me to see a colleague of his, he said, and a week later I had my first appointment with her. There followed half a dozen sessions of laser treatment, a cataract operation on my right eye, a series of monthly Lucentis injections into my left eye, and a series of regular vision tests every few months that has continued down to the present day. Neither the laser treatment nor the Lucentis injections resulted in an improvement in my vision, but they prevented any further deterioration, and without them I would probably have become more than half blind by this time. The cataract operation, on the other hand, resulted in a marked change in my perception of colour. I saw the colour blue much more vividly than before. As I wandered round the garden, two days after the operation, the giant delphiniums, in particular, seemed almost to assault me with the intensity of their blueness, and I thought of D. H. Lawrence's blue gentians and their blazing torches of blueness.[337] Colour has always been important to me, which is why I love artists as different as Titian, Miró, and the Pre-Raphaelites,[338] as well as precious and semi-precious stones and birds like the peacock and macaw. People are also important to me, but that is quite another matter, and I shall return to it later.

The three books I dictated, either wholly or in part, are *Moving Against the Stream* (2003), *From Genesis to the Diamond Sūtra* (2005), and *Precious Teachers* (2007). I worked on each of these books with a definite purpose in mind. In the case of *Moving Against the Stream*, only the last ten chapters of which were dictated, I sought to give a complete account of the events that led not only to my decision to return to England from India as I had promised, but also to the realization that a new Buddhist movement was needed in the world. 'Do you know what this means?' I asked the friend who was with me at the time I received a certain letter. 'It means a new Buddhist movement!' The letter in question was signed by one of the directors of the English Sangha Trust, under whose auspices I had been teaching in London, and in it he informed me, on behalf of the Trust, that they were dissatisfied with me and did not want me back. That was by no means all. He went on to suggest, in the blandest manner, that I should issue a statement saying that I had decided not to return to England after all, as I had changed my mind. But I had *promised* my friends and supporters that I would return to England, and I had *not* changed my mind, and I was deeply shocked that the representative of a Buddhist organization, writing to a Buddhist teacher, should suggest that he should not only break a promise but publicly lie about the reason for his doing so.[339] I also sought, in *Moving Against the Stream*, to give an account of my relationship with Terry Delamare, the friend who had been with me in India when I received the Trust's letter. In the epilogue to the book I tell the story of the last two years of Terry's life, a story of increasing depression that culminated in him taking his own life. He was my closest friend, and I felt his loss keenly.

Whereas *Moving Against the Stream* is wholly autobiographical, *From Genesis to the Diamond Sūtra* is only partly so. The reason for this is that I wrote the book with a double purpose in mind. In the first place I wanted to describe how one Western Buddhist saw Christianity, especially in its Roman Catholic form, the form that for centuries had dominated the civilization and culture of Western Europe. In the second place, I wanted to make open acknowledgement of the nature of my sexual orientation, which I had not done in writing before. The two came together in my criticism of the Roman Catholic Church's attitude towards heresy and homosexuality, its attitude towards the latter case still being very much a live issue. *From Genesis to the Diamond Sūtra* is thus a very personal book. Probably it is the most personal of all the books I have written. Though the process of dictating it was irksome and laborious, working on it gave me a deep satisfaction. I equally enjoyed giving expression to my rejection of the central doctrine of mainstream Christianity and expressing my admiration for some of the masterpieces of Christian art. Unfortunately, like a much more distinguished predecessor *From Genesis to the Diamond Sūtra* fell stillborn from the press.[340] Indeed, it was lucky to fall from the press at all. The people at Windhorse Publications did not like the book and published it, as I thought, only grudgingly.

Precious Teachers is almost wholly autobiographical, covering as it does my last seven years in Kalimpong, a small town in the foothills of the eastern Himalayas. If I wrote *From Genesis to the Diamond Sūtra* as the result of an inner urge, then I wrote *Precious Teachers* largely in response to requests from disciples and friends that I should write something about my eight main spiritual teachers, six of whom were from Tibet, while one was from India, and one from China. They were remarkable men. Besides being well versed in the traditions to which they belonged, they were men of deep spirituality, and I benefited greatly from their teaching and from the example they offered, in their different ways, of a life lived in accordance with the Dharma. Wherever I go I shall carry with me the memory of their great kindness to me and to all who came within the magic circle of their influence. Like visions of a divinized humanity, they soared above the horizon of our petty earthly concerns.

Precious Teachers was the latest (and it probably will be the last) of a whole series of autobiographical works, a series which began with *The Rainbow Road* and included *Facing Mount Kanchenjunga* (1991) and *In the Sign of the Golden Wheel* (1996), as well as *Travel Letters* (1985), and *Through Buddhist Eyes* (2000). Although I call these works autobiographies, each of them covers only a certain period in my life, not the whole of it, and in the past I have spoken of them as memoirs rather than as autobiographies. Thus I have written no autobiography, and the 'memoirs' are just that. Their subject is my life at a particular period, as seen through my own eyes. They do not criticize, or evaluate, or compare; neither do they seek to contextualize my life with regard to the cultural and political happenings of the time. But whatever one may call them, I enjoyed writing *The Rainbow Road* and its successors. I enjoyed writing about my immediate surroundings, about my day-to-day activities, and about the various experiences that had befallen me. I enjoyed writing about the products of nature and about the creations of man. Above all, I enjoyed writing about people – the people with whom I had lived and worked, whom I had met in the course of my travels, and with whom I had enjoyed relationships of one kind or another. My descriptions of some of these people, such as the irascible Buddharakshita,[341] or the exigent French nun,[342] could have come from the pages of a novel.

Indeed, the relationship between the two genres seems to be closer than I had supposed. In *Experience*, Martin Amis speaks of 'higher autobiography',[343] by which he appears to mean something better than the ghost-written memoirs of a popular footballer or film star. He also suggests that autobiography is in process of replacing the novel as the dominant literary genre. This struck a chord. In the course of my life I had written *one* novel and *seven* volumes of autobiography, and it occurred to me that I might be an example of the general trend from novel to autobiography of which Martin Amis speaks. I wrote my novel when I was seventeen, after reading D. H. Lawrence's *The Rainbow*, an experience which I later described as being an emotional revelation. The typescript of the novel has long since disappeared, and I remember very little about it. There are two main characters, the young music master at a girls' school (I forget what name I gave him) and Bertha Aldobrandini, his sixteen-year-old pupil, who is of partly Italian descent. They fall in love, Bertha becomes pregnant and has a miscarriage, and the lovers move to Cornwall, my descriptions of which are based on my recollections of Devon. There is also a rather high-flown description of the interior of a Victorian Gothic railway station and a discussion of the art of El Greco, whose paintings I knew only from reproductions in a book by Sacheverell Sitwell.[344] The characters of Bertha and the young music master were not based on people I knew, neither did they have any literary progenitors. I created them, and I still have a strong sense of what they were like. The music master was tall, slim, and dark ('a pillar of darkness', as Lawrence might have said), whereas Bertha was of middle height, plump, and dark. He was serious, even melancholy, while she was carefree and impulsive. She may have been from Venus, but he was certainly not from Mars but Saturn. I had not intended that there should be a neat complementarity between the two main characters of my novel: it simply emerged as I wrote, and may have reflected a division within my own psyche. How good or how bad my novel was I cannot say. It would certainly have needed a lot of revision before it could be published, and Lawrence's influence on my style could not have been a good one. When I returned to *The Rainbow* some years ago, I found it unreadable. Nonetheless my admiration for Lawrence remained undiminished. Over the years I have read everything he wrote, and regard him as the outstanding creative force of his generation. The last time I was in the United States I spent a few days in hot, arid New Mexico, where I visited the isolated ranch where Lawrence had lived and worked, and saw the little chapel in which his ashes are enshrined.[345]

TERRA INCOGNITA

Every language is unique, and for this reason a completely faithful translation from one language into another is hardly possible. To translate is to betray. This is especially the case with regard to poetry, in which language reaches the highest point of its development, and I have more than once noticed how a poem in one language can be translated into another language in half a dozen different ways. The best translations are not translations at all, in the literal sense of the term, but re-creations of the 'meaning' of the original in accordance with the genius of the language into which it is translated, a process of which Fitzgerald's rendition of the *Rubáiyát of Omar Khayyám* is probably the best example,[346] closely followed by some of Rossetti's translations from the Early Italian poets.[347] It would be too much to expect that poems of mine that have been translated into other languages should be re-creations of this kind, faithful though they might be in many ways to their English originals. Indeed, in one of the sixty-odd poems that have been translated into French (*Poèmes*, 2009)[348] there is one that perfectly illustrates the difficulty, even the impossibility, of translation from one language into another, particularly in the case of poetry. The line is 'Life is King', which also serves as the title of the poem, but the rules of French grammar do not permit a faithful translation. One has to say 'La Vie est Reine' (Life is *Queen*), which completely distorts my meaning. Similar difficulties arise in connection with the translation of a novel or other prose work of imagination from one language into another, but here there are probably more ways of getting round such difficulties than there are in the case of a lyric or other short poem, in which so much often hangs on so little. In the course of the last thirty or more years my books have been translated into some twenty European and Asian languages, and since I am far from being a polyglot I have been obliged to rely on the competence of my translators and the judgement of those who commissioned their work. At the same time I was always available for consultation and in this way I became more aware of the distinctive character, even the genius, of the particular language into which I was being translated. It has been said that to learn a new language is to acquire a new soul,[349] and perhaps one can acquire a little of that soul, or at least get a glimpse of it, on the strength of a very modest knowledge of the language in question. I remember that my old friend Lama Anagarika Govinda, who was equally at home in German and English, once told me that in his opinion my newly published book *A Survey of Buddhism* (1957), would translate well into German, indeed would read better in German than in English, by which I understood him to mean that the two languages had very similar souls. Despite Lama Govinda's prognostications, the *Survey* has not yet been translated into German in its entirety.[350] Complete translations of the *Survey* have however appeared in two other languages, Spanish and Polish,[351] and I have had the satisfaction of knowing that what many regarded as my foundational work on Buddhism was now accessible to a wider circle of readers.

I have travelled in Spain with a friend,[352] have spent months together in a secluded valley high in the mountains near Alicante,[353] and on the shelves of my cottage there I have a small collection of books on Spain and its people. Even before my first visit to Spain, which took place in 1986, I had some knowledge of the country's history, and was acquainted with the literature and art of what has been called the golden age of Spain. Of Poland and its people I knew, until fairly recently, almost nothing. I knew that the Second World War had started with Germany's invasion of Poland in 1939, and that thousands of 'free Poles' had fought on the side of Britain – and that was about all. In 1945 Poland disappeared behind the Iron Curtain, and it was only with the emergence of Solidarity in 1980 that I again became aware that there was a country called Poland and that it was part of Central Europe.[354] Thus for many years Poland hardly existed for me, or existed as a *terra incognita* which it was unlikely I should ever visit. Then ten years ago, in 2001, there came from the heart of this *terra incognita* a letter informing me that *A Survey of Buddhism* had been translated into Polish and inviting me to visit Kraków and launch the publication of the book. The result was that in May 2002 I spent ten days in Kraków, the ancient capital of Poland, having flown there from Gatwick with two of my Polish friends. Those ten days in Kraków were the most delightful I had spent for a long time. In retrospect they were all the more delightful in that they preceded the upheavals and tribulations of 2003, my *annus horribilis*. I did not keep a diary while I was in Kraków, and I cannot recall all the things my friends and I did there in the order in which we did them. Not that this matters very much. As I now look back on the events of those ten days, they have 'the glory and the freshness of a dream'[355] and, as often is the case with dreams, it is difficult for me to remember what came first, what last, and what between. Certain experiences touched me deeply, simple though they were, and after returning to England I wrote three Kraków poems, as I called them.[356] In the first poem I am having breakfast on the balcony of the first floor apartment where I am staying. Sparrows are flying in and out of the eaves, chirruping loudly. There are a lot of them, and they make quite a noise, but I do not mind. I am glad to have the company of the little brown birds, for it is a long time since I saw so many of them together, the sparrow population of England having declined steeply in recent years. While having breakfast I watch the men working in the fields below. It is early morning, and spring has come to the Polish countryside (our apartment is in a house outside Kraków), and soon the sky will be a cloudless blue, as it would be for all ten days of my visit, except for a sudden heavy downpour late one afternoon. In the second poem it is evening, and I am sitting outside one of the restaurants in the great square of Kraków, said to be the second largest square in Europe. With me are the two Polish friends who flew with me from Gatwick, as well as six or seven other friends, mostly Polish, who have come from London, Brighton, and Paris. Some are staying with me at the apartment, others at hotels in the city. They are all here in Kraków for the launch of the Polish translation of *A Survey of Buddhism*. I drink tea, join in the conversation from time to time, and watch the passers-by. The young men are tall, and bear themselves well, as though they had spent time in the army. Nearby, there is a group of gypsy musicians, and I listen to them. Their ancestors came from India, many centuries ago, and the weird, wild music makes me think of the many years I spent in that country, eating its food, and sharing its culture. The third poem was addressed to my interpreter, Michal Balik. He was one of those staying with me at the apartment, and without him it would not have been possible for me to visit Kraków.[357]

Between breakfast on the balcony in the morning and the evening cup of tea in the great square there was always much to see and much to do. There were occasions when all the members of our party kept together, and others when they split into little groups to explore different parts of the city or pursue particular interests. One of the things we did as a party was to attend a performance of a piano concerto by Chopin (I forget which one) given by a young Polish pianist at the Philharmonic Hall. It was a very bad performance; but the audience was in a forgiving mood, and applauded warmly. After all, they seemed to be saying, the pianist was a Pole, he was performing the music of Chopin, their national composer, and young talent ought to be encouraged. To this the young man responded by performing a short piece by Chopin by way of an encore. This time he played brilliantly and was rewarded with an outburst of spontaneous applause. After the concert those who had cameras took photographs of the rest of us as we stood in a row outside the Philharmonic Hall.

I carried out my personal exploration of Kraków in the company of Michal and a few others. Much of the exploration took place within the old city, which was agreeably located within a circular park. If the park was the ring, then the stone in the ring was Wawel Castle, the seat of the old Polish kings, and it was only at this point that the circular park was interrupted. One morning Michal and I and a few others made our way up the steep, winding ramp that led to the Castle entrance, passing on our way the official residence of the archbishop of Kraków. Inside, the principal object of interest was the beautiful three-storeyed courtyard in Renaissance style. Open to the blue sky, and filled with sunshine, it had been built by, or for, an Italian princess who was married to the king. It was this princess who brought with her from Italy a painting that is the City Art Gallery's greatest treasure: Leonardo da Vinci's 'Portrait of a Lady with an Ermine'. This was a favourite painting of mine, and I was overjoyed at having the opportunity of spending some time in front of it. Besides the Renaissance courtyard, we saw underneath the Castle, on the river, the cave from which the legendary Kraków dragon had terrorized the people of the surrounding countryside. One could not be long in Kraków before hearing of this celebrated monster. Indeed, at the airport I had been presented with a small statue of the dragon by my Polish publisher. The people of Kraków in fact seem rather proud of their dragon, especially now that it was dead and could not do any harm. According to one account it had been killed by a shoemaker's apprentice known as 'Little Twine' who had stuffed a dead sheep with gunpowder and left it outside the dragon's cave. The dragon naturally ate the sheep, but when the gunpowder reached its fiery entrails (for the dragon was a fire-breathing one) it exploded, blowing the unfortunate creature to pieces.

In the course of my travels in Italy, Germany, and Spain I had always been keen to visit their churches, mainly for the sake of seeing their art treasures; but in Kraków I felt no such inclination, even though the city was full of churches and monasteries and was the ecclesiastical capital of Poland. Even the cathedral was left unvisited. I did, however, see the inside of the Franciscan Church, which was situated not far from the great square. This was because Michal wanted to show me a beautiful mural in Art Nouveau style painted by a Kraków artist in the early twentieth century.[358] Though the friars had commissioned the mural, when they saw what the artist had done they were horrified and wanted to withdraw from the project. It was too bright and colourful for a church, they said. Nevertheless, in the end they had been obliged to accept the work. There were also big stained-glass windows by the same artist, one of which showed God the Father creating the world. Since the church was poorly lit, and I was partially sighted, I could hardly see the mural, though I could see the reds, blues, and yellows of the stained-glass windows. Though the cathedral might be unvisited, it could hardly be ignored, for it was an imposing structure and dominated part of the great square. Neither was it possible for one to ignore the bugle call which sounded from a window at the top of the cathedral tower. The first time I heard it Michal and I were sitting in the sunshine outside a café in the great square, and I looked up to see where the sound came from. It was the Kraków bugle-call signal, Michal told me, and it was played every day on the hour by a member of the fire brigade, as well as being played live on Polish radio every day at 12pm in full. It dated back to the Middle Ages, when it announced the opening and closing of the city gates. The bugler also sounded the alarm whenever he saw an outbreak of fire or an enemy army approaching the city.

The Kraków bugle call was a long one, not unlike the Last Post, but it ended abruptly. This was said to commemorate the bugler who was shot through the throat by a Tatar archer when the Mongols besieged the city in 1241. The Mongol armies were then penetrating deep into Europe and the Middle East. Four centuries later, Eastern and Central Europe were threatened by the forces of the Ottoman Empire, and it was a Polish king, John Sobieski, who played a leading part in turning back the tide of advancing Islam.[359] The name of John Sobieski came up in the course of a conversation I had with Czarek Wozniak, the publisher of the Polish *Survey*. He wanted to know how many famous Poles I had heard of, apart from Chopin and the Pope. I could think of only three: Paderewski, the pianist-president, Górecki, whose 'Symphony of Sad Songs' was then very popular in England, and John Sobieski. I failed to mention Copernicus, the famous astronomer, and Czarek reminded me that he, too, was a Pole, despite his name.[360]

My publisher was a cultured man who lectured on philosophy and had written a book on Heidegger. He was also a member of a Dzogchen group and in his capacity as a publisher he had brought out a number of books on Buddhism. Having read *A Survey of Buddhism* he had not only commissioned a translation but had invited me to come to Kraków to launch the book in its new garb and in that connection he had arranged for me to give three lectures. The first lecture was on 'Buddhism and Art', a favourite topic of mine, and I gave it at the Manggha Japanese Centre, a modern building overlooking the river. The subject of the second lecture was my own life and work as a Western Buddhist and the founder of a new Buddhist movement, and it was followed by a documentary film showing the various activities of that movement in different parts of the world. This time the venue was a gallery of modern art. The third and last lecture was on 'The Tension between the Academic and the Practical Approaches to Buddhism', the venue being the religious studies department of the Jagiellonian University, one of the oldest universities in Europe. All three lectures were fairly well attended, which was not the case with the formal launch of the Polish *Survey*, which took place at the Empik bookshop, next to the cathedral. Since I did not speak Polish, I had to use an interpreter, and for all three lectures my interpreter was Michal. I could not have had a better interpreter. He was fluent and confident, and only once or twice was momentarily at a loss for a word, and it was evident that he was communicating the spirit as well as the letter of what I had to say. Several members of our party commented that we seemed to be in complete harmony with each other, as though we were of one heart and one mind. In a way this was surprising, considering how different we were in age, in temperament, and in personal history. Moreover, we had not known each other for very long, nor had we spent much time together. I had first met Michal a year or two earlier in Berlin. We met at a conference organized by the German Buddhist Union. He could not attend the talk I was about to give, as he had to go and cook a meal for me at the flat where I was staying with a German friend.

Our next meeting also took place in Berlin, at a club where I was giving a short series of talks.[361] This time he was accompanied by four or five friends from Frankfurt University where he was then studying. In 2000 he came to England and joined Friends Organic, a team-based right livelihood business based in Bethnal Green, East London.[362] He also moved into a residential men's community. In late January or early February he came to see me in Moseley, and we went for a walk in Cannon Hill Park. He was then about to leave for Poland, where his mother was ill in hospital. She died in March. During the months that followed Michal continued to work at Friends Organic and live in a men's community. He also liaised with Czarek Wozniak regarding the publication of the Polish *Survey* and the arrangements for my visit to Kraków. Finally, he organized a meeting of the friends, mostly expatriate Poles, who were interested in being with me in Kraków for the launch. The meeting was held at the London Buddhist Centre and was attended by eight or nine people, including me. The result was that early in May we were all in Kraków, and Michal was staying with me at the rented apartment, translating my lectures, and accompanying me wherever I wanted to go. In the course of one of our explorations we came across a tablet commemorating the Katyn Massacre. It was a reminder that terrible things had happened during the War, and that Auschwitz was only sixty miles away.[363] Horrors of a very different kind were to be found nearer home – architectural ones. An acquaintance of Michal's had invited our party to eat at the pizza restaurant he had recently opened in Nowa Huta, a sort of satellite town that the Communist government had built in an effort to lure the inhabitants of Kraków from their ancient city, away from the influence of its 'uncooperative' civic authorities. They had even built a church there! On our arrival at

Nowa Huta, which was more like a sleazy suburb of Kraków than a separate town, I saw row upon featureless row of multistorey apartment blocks, all grey and dingy, and separated by what seemed to be waste ground. As for the new restaurant, the food was remarkable for quantity rather than quality, and I soon realized that we had been invited not as guests but as customers and would have to pay for our meal. The host-proprietor nonetheless sat and ate with us. He was more than half drunk, and had evidently been reading books on Zen Buddhism, for he kept firing 'Zen-like' questions at me from the opposite end of the table. I amused myself by responding in similar fashion, often monosyllabically and forcibly, which puzzled and confused him, so that in the end he subsided into silence. After the meal it was a relief to feel the cool night air and look up at the stars.

Another exploration took Michal and me to the Arcade, a huge building situated almost in the middle of the great square. On our entering at one end, I saw that for its entire length it was lined on either side with brightly lit shops. We were there because we would soon be leaving Kraków and I wanted to take back with me a few presents for friends. I could not have come to a better place. The shops specialized in traditional Polish handicrafts, of which there was an amazing variety on display on open counters or under glass. I bought an amber egg for Paramartha, with whom I had travelled in Spain and elsewhere; an onyx chess set for Prasannasiddhi, with whom I had travelled in Italy and elsewhere; and little painted wooden boxes and T-shirts for various other friends. On my last day in Kraków the members of our little party met for a farewell meal at an Indian vegetarian restaurant where Michal and I ate more than once in the course of our stay. I ordered a *masala dosai*, which was one of my favourite Indian dishes; but no sooner was it set before me, and I had raised the first morsel to my lips, than I experienced an utter revulsion to the very idea of food and started retching violently. So violent was the retching that I thought I was about to vomit and made a dash for the toilet. The intense revulsion I felt was probably akin to the kind of insight known to Buddhists as 'the perception of the loathsomeness of food'.[364] Be that as it might, I soon recovered, the uneaten *masala dosai* was distributed among our friends, and a few hours later, with Michal and another friend, I was flying back to England, ten wonderful days in Kraków now behind me.

A SEASON IN HELL[365]

The liner had left port a few days before. She was a new ship, though some of her timbers had been salvaged from an ancient craft that had come to the end of its seafaring days. On board there were more than a thousand passengers. The majority of the passengers were middle-aged, but there were old people and young people too, and a few children. Manning the liner there was a crew of thirty, headed by the captain, an experienced officer who had been associated with the ship since the laying down of its keel. Besides having a strong sense of duty, he loved his beautiful ship, with its clean lines; he loved his well-trained crew, and he loved his passengers and was concerned for their safety and comfort. During the voyage the passengers occupied themselves in various ways. Some of them spent much of their time in the ship's gym, others sat on deck watching the rising and falling of the waves, while a few simply counted the hours to the next meal and slept a lot. As might have been expected, disagreement sometimes broke out among the passengers, and occasionally these were so serious that the captain had to intervene personally to restore peace and harmony. Thus life went on more or less smoothly from day to day. The sky was generally clear, the sea generally calm. Only once did the ship encounter a storm, when it pitched and rolled dreadfully and a number of passengers were seasick.

One morning some of the passengers noticed that the captain was not on the bridge as usual. They thought nothing of it, however, and life on the ship went on much as before. But another morning came, and yet another, and still the captain was not seen on the bridge. Nor was that all. Other figures appeared on the bridge from time to time. First it was one of the ship's officers, then a small group of crew members, all talking loudly and apparently disagreeing with one another. But still there was no sign of the captain, and before long a rumour went round the ship that he was seriously ill and was confined to his cabin. This was later confirmed and the passengers were informed that the captain was seeing no one except his personal steward. By this time it was clear that the ship was no longer steaming straight ahead but was veering now to the right, now to the left, in a highly erratic and even dangerous manner. Some of the passengers welcomed the change. They were tired of always travelling in the same direction, they said. Most of the passengers wished the captain well, and hoped he would soon be better; but a minority criticized him, saying that he was not properly qualified, that he wore his cap at the wrong angle, and so on. A few were of the opinion that the passengers should take over the ship and elect their captain. A few others declared that they had never trusted the captain, and they wished they were travelling on another liner. As if in answer to their wish a vessel suddenly appeared out of the early morning mist. So many passengers rushed to get a better view that the ship listed dangerously and the crew had to remonstrate with them. The strange ship flew a variety of flags, and from bow to stern was so swathed in colourful bunting that it was difficult to make out its outline or even whether it actually was a ship. The passengers who wished they were travelling in another liner at once lowered one of the lifeboats, rowed themselves over to the strange ship, and were welcomed on board. A few of the other ship's passengers then jumped into the now empty lifeboat, rowed back to the ship it came from, climbed up over the side, and joined the passengers. All this time the captain remained in his cabin, cared for by his personal steward and, occasionally, by a couple of crew members. It was rumoured that he was very ill, even dying, though no one knew what was the cause of his illness. Some thought it was a bug he had picked up in the tropics, others that it was bad karma catching up with him. But the captain did not die, and eventually appeared on the bridge again, though less frequently than before, and looking paler and thinner. The liner was set on its old direct course, the crew was reorganized, the passengers reassured. Having seen to this, the captain then sat down in his cabin and wrote his report.

The liner in the parable is the good ship FWBO (since refurbished, and renamed Triratna Buddhist Order and Community), and the captain is the present writer. Given this key, even those who were not around in 2003 will have little difficulty interpreting the parable and understanding something of what happened to me and to the FWBO in that year. They should, however, bear in mind that not every detail of the parable corresponds to something that actually happened, while not everything that happened to me in 2003 has its parabolic counterpart.

From the beginning of May 2002, when I returned from Kraków, to the beginning of January 2003, when the events shadowed forth in the parable began, I continued to lead quite an active life, despite my age.[366] After my return from Kraków I spent the rest of May first at Madhyamaloka, dictating the epilogue to *Moving Against the Stream*, then at Guhyaloka, the men's retreat centre in Spain, where I dedicated the stupa that had been built to enshrine a portion of the ashes of Dhardo Rimpoche.[367] Guhyaloka was a favourite place of mine. Over the years I had spent many a month in the high valley in the mountains, usually in the summer, drinking in the silence and inhaling the pine-scented air. Later on in the year I spent time at Padmaloka, another favourite place, where I lived in the eighties, besides visiting Sheffield, where I 'cut the ribbon' at the opening of the new Sheffield Buddhist Centre, and London, where I lived in the nineties. Despite being busy in these and other ways, I kept in touch with Michal, who was still living and working in East London. Both he and I were keen to develop the friendship that had sprung up between us in Kraków, and which was to be such an important part of both of our lives in the years ahead. When I was in London, staying in my old flat above the London Buddhist Centre, we spent as much time together as we could, and one evening I had dinner with him and the other members of the Amritakula community.[368]

In August Michal came to see me. It was my 77th birthday, and he gave me a silver spoon with a bear handle. I was much moved by the gift, especially as the spoon had been given to Michal by his brother, and soon afterwards I wrote a poem entitled 'The Silver Spoon'.[369] One of my friends thought the poem sentimental, but it was a true expression of my feeling for Michal. It was at about this time, I think, that Michal started coming up to Madhyamaloka every other weekend in order to study with me. But black clouds were already gathering on the horizon, and a storm was brewing. In October I had to pull out of a study retreat I was leading at Madhyamaloka, as owing to insomnia I was too tired to continue. As I wrote at the time to Padmadaka at Padmaloka, I was 'half dead from sleeplessness'.[370] In all the years that I had lectured and led retreats and seminars, this was the first time I had been forced to let people down in this way, and I was much mortified. But insomnia was only part of the problem. Writing to Vidyadevi[371] in Herefordshire a few weeks later, I confided, 'At the moment I am enjoying a relative respite from my sleeplessness but the underlying problem is still there and will no doubt shortly be confronting me again. It is a combination of high blood pressure, insomnia, and palpitation, which appear to reinforce one another and between them to create a cycle which is difficult to break through.' The underlying problem was indeed still there and a week later I was writing to the same friend that I had 'experienced a few ups and downs with my health, including an alarm on Christmas Eve that took me to the primary care unit of Selly Oak Hospital for a consultation, and I am not sure what the future holds'. The alarm in question was the sudden acceleration of my pulse rate to a dangerously high level, and for this the doctor at the primary care centre prescribed beta blockers, which together with other prescription drugs I am still taking ten years later. Though my pulse rate had been stabilized, at least for the time being, as regards my insomnia there were still ups and downs. In fact there were now more downs than ups, and I was fast moving into a period of chronic sleep deprivation that would last for a year or more. Michal was aware of these developments, and at the beginning of January 2003 he moved into Madhyamaloka. I had already asked him, some time in the autumn, if he would like to keep me company and study with me, and he was thinking about it. The reason he did not say yes immediately was that he quite liked his life in London, where he attended classes at the London Buddhist Centre, and where he had a girlfriend, and in any case he was debating whether to spend half the week in London and half at Madhyamaloka. Before he could make up his mind, however, my insomnia became much worse, and I told him that I needed him. He hesitated no longer, and moved to Madhyamaloka as soon as he could leave Friends Organic.

By this time I had been living at Madhyamaloka for six years. Paramartha[372] and I had moved there straight after returning from a seven-month tour of the United States, Australia, and New Zealand, in the course of which we had visited all the FWBO centres in those countries.[373] Though I did not then know it, this was the last time I, at least, would travel outside Europe. The house to which we moved was a large, late Victorian property, and it stood halfway down a winding, tree-lined street of properties of a similar size and similar design. The house had a garage, and above the garage there was a flat consisting of three small rooms, together with a kitchen and a bathroom. There was also a small guest-room downstairs. During our absence abroad the flat had been thoroughly renovated, not to say redesigned, and it was into this flat that Paramartha and I moved. My books, manuscripts, archives, and images had been brought from Padmaloka, so that for the first time for many years I had them all under the same roof as myself. I did not have Paramartha's company for long. Three or four months after our arrival at Madhyamaloka he went to live with his girlfriend in Beaconsfield. We remained in regular contact until he rejoined me in 2008. In the meantime I turned his room into a private office, where I kept my dozens of box files and my scores of ring binders on improvised shelving. Despite Paramartha's departure I was not alone. Next door to me, occupying the four-storey Victorian house, was the Madhyamaloka men's community, the members of which were senior members of the Western Buddhist Order. I had brought them together at Madhyamaloka in the hope that as a result of living and working in harmony under one roof for a few years they would be better prepared for the time when I handed on to them, and to their counterpart in the women's community nearby, the leadership of the new Buddhist movement I had founded. My hope was fulfilled only to a limited extent, but that is another story, a story that does not belong here. My insomnia was naturally a cause of much concern to the community, as it was to many friends both far and near, and they were greatly relieved when Michal arrived and moved into Paramartha's old room, the box files and ring binders having been distributed round the rest of the flat and a bed installed in their place.

I had started trying some of the traditional remedies for insomnia towards the end of 2002, and I carried on taking them well into the following year. First I tried camomile tea, drinking a cup of it before I went to bed, and sometimes getting up to make a second cup in the course of the night. Next I tried valerian tea, which disagreed with me, so I experimented with some of the Bach flower remedies, which reminded me of Bishop Berkeley's belief in the efficacy of tar-water, and seemed to be based on a similar understanding of the natural world, the world of trees and flowers.[374] Lastly, I tried drinking brandy and hot water last thing at night. Dr Johnson had extolled brandy as the drink of heroes;[375] but I could not have been much of a hero, for I found both the smell and the taste repugnant, and soon stopped taking it. With the exception of valerian, all these remedies had a slightly relaxing effect, but they made not the least difference so far as the insomnia was concerned. In the end, I went to see my doctor, whom I was already seeing in connection with my high blood pressure and palpitation. She prescribed Temazepam, a popular sleeping pill, which at best gave me a couple of hours of something that was not really sleep, and which I took much longer than I should have done. At the suggestion of a doctor friend, I also started taking acupuncture treatment. Eight years later I am still taking it, and from the same practitioner, Rosi Roper, now a good friend. The first time she saw me, Rosi afterwards related, my face was green. As a result of the insomnia, which by then amounted to chronic sleep deprivation, I was extremely debilitated, had very little energy, and was on the verge of collapse.

Though I have spoken of 2003 as my *annus horribilis*, the latter did not exactly correspond with the calendar year. The period of my chronic insomnia in fact lasted for more than a year, and though I know roughly when it began I find it difficult to say when it ended. During the whole of this period I carried on more or less as usual, except that early in 2003 I told Subhuti, Sona, Mahamati,[376] and the rest of the community, that I did not want to hear anything of a disturbing or controversial nature, with the result that for about a year I did not know about the upheaval that was going on within the community and within the FWBO.[377] I dictated letters to Khemavira, my secretary, who was a member of the community, worked on *Living with Awareness*[378] with Cittapala, also a member of the community, continued to have laser treatment at the hands of Miss Tsaloumas, my consultant ophthalmologist, walked in the garden, and went through a number of Buddhist texts with Michal. I did all this while living, at the same time, in a kind of hell, the hell of chronic insomnia. The insomnia was cumulative in its effect. Tiredness was piled on tiredness, suffering on suffering, torture on torture. I more than once declared, to whoever would listen, that prolonged insomnia was in fact torture, and that I could well understand how a prisoner who had been deprived of sleep for four or five days might well be prepared to confess to anything, sign anything, in order to end the torture and get some sleep. Even when, on a 'good' night, I had three or four hours sleep, I did not have it *en bloc*, so to speak, but in anything up to eight or nine bits, each separated from the other by a period of wakefulness. Thus the clouds were very black, but they had, from time to time, a lining not of silver but of gold.

That lining was made up of the dreams and visions that came to me during my *annus horribilis*, whenever I was able to enjoy a little sleep. In the earlier part of that period I used to find myself sitting in the midst of a group of monks. Sometimes the group was yellow-robed, sometimes red-robed, but it was always either the one or the other. The monks I saw in my dreams were not monks I had known in real life, but I always knew the monks very well, in those dreams of mine, and I felt quite at home with them. I did not always find myself with the other monks in the same kind of place. Sometimes it was a temple, sometimes the forecourt of a monastery cut out of the rock. In front of us there would be a shrine, and we were all chanting. I do not know in what tongue of men or angels we chanted, but there was a sense of our worshipping the Buddha and chanting his praises. Reflecting on these dreams, I concluded that they were not just a reminiscence of my days as a monk, even though such reminiscences may have provided those dreams with their 'language'. What the dreams really expressed, I believe, was the upward thrust of my being, a thrust which showed itself in my lifelong devotion to the Buddha and his teaching, in my enjoyment of poetry, music, and the visual arts, and in my love of noble friendship.

These 'monastic' dreams were succeeded but not entirely eclipsed by dreams in which I saw glittering displays of precious stones, mostly diamonds. Some displays took the shape of many-petalled flowers, others that of necklaces and tiaras, and yet others that of complex geometrical designs. All these displays were constantly changing, so that they were more like clouds than solid objects. There were also occasions when I saw diamonds strewn across a dark background like stars across the midnight sky. Once I found myself walking down a broad tunnel that led into the depths of the earth. The tunnel was not dark but filled with a soft golden radiance, while the walls of the tunnel were lined at every turn with diamonds which flashed and glittered.

My dreams also assumed a variety of architectural forms. Many times did I find myself, for example, alone in a dark, empty, cathedral-like structure which I seemed, in successive dreams, to take over. Once there was carried into the vast building, in a little procession, the dead body of an ecclesiastical dignitary of some kind. The atmosphere of these dreams was one of solemnity and awe. At other times I was walking in the mountains, amid the most beautiful scenery, each turn of the road revealing a prospect more glorious than the last. Far below me there was a river, while away in the distance, on the horizon, was a strip of dark blue that was the sea. In more than one dream did I make my way down from the mountain to the scattering of sunlit, white villas lying at their foot, walk through them to the beach and the sea, or up and down the promenade, mingling with the holiday crowd. These 'mountaineering' dreams were accompanied by feelings of expansion, exhilaration, and joy. In another dream I found myself not beside the sea but high above it, looking down on a small white cruise liner far below. There was nothing but the blue sky above, nothing but the blue sky all around. I think I intended to drop straight down onto the deck of the liner, but before I could do so the dream ended and I awoke. Most of my dreams during this period were not so much dreams as visions, but there were a few in which I heard music. On one or two occasions the music came from a hall, outside which I was standing, and once it simply came from above. It was not orchestral music, but the music of a thousand human voices. The music from above, in particular, was of an indescribable beauty and sublimity, far surpassing any music I had ever heard, and it threw me into an ecstasy. What was strange, it progressed, but at the same time it stood still. Paradoxically it was static music. It united time and eternity. At the time I did not know Thomas Tallis's *Spem in Alium*,[379] but when I did happen to hear it, years later, I was at once reminded of the heavenly music I had heard in my dream, of which it seemed a distant echo.

I was about halfway through my *annus horribilis*, in which dreams went some way towards redressing the imbalance between pain and pleasure in my life, when there occurred an incident that gave everyone cause for concern. Michal and I often spent the morning in Cannon Hill Park, where after walking round the bigger of its two ponds we would settle down in the courtyard in front of the tea house over a cup of tea and get on with Dharma study. After finishing Sogyal's *The Tibetan Book of Living and Dying*,[380] on which we had made a start during my visits to London, we passed on to select portions of the

Pāli scriptures and, I think, some of my own writings. The road from Madhyamaloka to Cannon Hill Park was partly downhill, which meant that on the way back it was partly uphill. One day I took the acclivity more quickly than I should have done, and arrived at the top hot and a little out of breath; there was a cold wind blowing. Ten or fifteen minutes later, when Michal and I were back at the flat, I suddenly felt sick and dizzy. Michal sat me down on a chair, and I fainted. The next thing I knew was that two burly paramedics were bending over me, and administering oxygen, Michal having telephoned for an ambulance. I was chairlifted down the stairs and taken by ambulance to Selly Oak Hospital, where I was given a number of tests and told that I had suffered neither a heart attack nor a stroke and that there was nothing wrong with me. Nonetheless, during the time that I was unconscious my pulse had been barely discernible for three or four minutes, and Michal and other friends urged me to have a proper health check. After all, I was now 77! I therefore went to see my doctor, who gave me a referral to Dr Sandler, a 'general specialist'. After giving me a thorough physical examination he gave me referrals in his turn, first to a radiologist, then to a psychiatrist. The radiologist looked at my heart and other internal organs (I looked with him), while the psychiatrist, with whom I had an interesting conversation, assured me that Freudian psychoanalysis was out of date, having been superseded by cognitive behavioural therapy, which was much more effective. The next time I saw Dr Sandler his opening words to me were that he had only good news for me. As I wrote to Paramartha the following week, 'he went on to say that my heart was quite sound organically and was functioning well, as were my other internal organs, and I therefore had no cause for concern. In fact he said that I was in robust physical health and that there was no reason why I should not be good for another ten or fifteen years.' This was good news indeed, especially as my sleep seemed to be gradually improving and my energy returning, though there were frequent blips and though the end of my period of chronic sleep deprivation was not yet in sight. The improvement was due principally to the acupuncture treatment I was receiving from Rosi, whom I now saw only once a week, instead of twice a week as before. More than once, when I was not well enough to go to her for treatment, she came and treated me at the flat, and I well remember the skill with which she manoeuvred herself round my bed on her knees so that she did not risk straining her back by having to bend over me. But although it certainly did seem that acupuncture worked, I had no idea how it worked. In particular, I was not sure whether it worked, in my case, by attacking the insomnia directly, or whether it worked by building up my energy so that I was better able to tolerate the insomnia.

Be that as it might, I soon noticed that the improvement in my sleep was being accompanied by a change in the nature of my dreams, which were now less visionary and more mundane. Not that the more visionary dreams entirely disappeared, especially those in which I was surrounded by magnificent mountain scenery, which I continued to have for some time. In these more mundane dreams I often found myself walking through darkening streets, occasionally going into a shop, usually a second-hand bookshop. Before long I would happen to meet two or three friends (friends in the dream, not in real life), and together we would go to a café or a tea shop, where I would have a cup of tea and a cake. Strange to relate, I never consumed more than a cup of tea and a cake, even though the food and drink of the dream seemed to stand for food, and I was as hungry for sleep as a starving man is for food. In the early days of my acupuncture treatment with Rosi I had once dreamed of a fierce black bull, a bull that I was trying to stop escaping into another field. Rosi thought the bull represented my natural energy, of which the insomnia had deprived me and which I was now trying to 'capture' or regain. Much later on, when I was beginning to get a little more sleep, I started having dreams of very young animals, usually puppies or kittens. Both puppies and kittens were very playful, and sometimes I played with them. Rosi saw these dreams as a sign that my energies were returning, and I was inclined to agree with her. They were like the green shoots which show that spring is on its way. But although I might not have survived without Michal's unfailing care and support and the regular sessions of acupuncture with Rosi, there were other friends who in various ways also helped me to get through my *annus horribilis*. One of these was Saraha, a member of the Madhyamaloka community,[381] who on many an afternoon sat and meditated beside me as I had my siesta, in the hope that the positive atmosphere thus created would help me to sleep. It *did* seem to help! On two or three occasions I was suddenly plunged into a deep sleep that lasted for twenty or thirty minutes, from which I woke feeling refreshed. Another friend who helped me was Mahamati.[382] Once, when I was getting even less sleep than usual, and Michal was in London visiting his girlfriend, Jenny, and other friends, he remained at my bedside all night, holding my hand and talking to me in a way that made the time pass more quickly. Other members of the community must have helped me from time to time, but it is Saraha and Mahamati whom I remember in this regard. 'Get well' cards came from friends both old and new, and around the time of my 78th birthday there arrived at Madhyamaloka hundreds of birthday cards, some of them very large and colourful and signed by scores of people. There was also a small group of friends who helped me in a special way, and to whom I am particularly grateful. These were Bodhaniya in Birmingham, Karunamati in East London, Kularatna in Stroud, and Santacitta in Brighton – four doctor friends, whom I felt free to telephone for information and advice, since my own GP was not easily available. There were times when I telephoned at an unreasonable hour, but they never minded, and were invariably sympathetic and helpful. So far as I remember, I needed to consult them not about the insomnia but about the alarming vagaries of my blood pressure and my pulse.

In October 2003 I left Birmingham for the first time in more than a year. For the first time in many months I was separated from my usual environment and all my customary supports, except for Michal and the cocktail of prescription drugs I was now having to swallow every day. The cottage Michal had found for us was situated in the depths of rural Shropshire. Completely isolated, with no sign of other human habitation in any direction, it was surrounded on all sides by hills, including the Stiperstones, which legend associated with the Devil. During our three days at the comfortable, well-appointed cottage we did not do very much. We went for walks (I now had to use a walking stick), talked, and took photographs, and in the evening sat back with legs stretched out towards the warmth of a blazing fire, which Michal kept well supplied with logs. So far as I remember, we did not do any study. My most vivid recollection of the place, and of the time we spent there, is of its intense silence. At night, when I stepped outside to look up at the sky, there was not a sound to be heard – not even the bark of a dog. All was utter stillness and silence.

It was also in October that I issued a report on my *annus horribilis*, which I termed 'the most difficult year of my life'.[383] In the report I traced the rise and progress of my insomnia, acknowledged how much I had been helped by acupuncture treatment, and insisted that any attempt to diagnose the cause or causes of my insomnia was purely speculative and that nobody, myself included, really knew why it had been visited upon me. I also confided that the sleep deprivation had made me even more sensitive than usual, so that I had 'shed many more tears than usual, sometimes to relieve tension and sometimes because I was touched by hearing of some noble or inspiring action or experience'. Some of these actions and experiences belonged to well-known figures of the past; others to men and women of our own day. What touched me most often, however, and most often brought tears to my eyes, was seeing how day in and day out, week after week, in small matters and in great, Michal (later to become Nityabandhu) regularly put my needs before his own. It therefore was not surprising that in these circumstances the friendship between us should have deepened.[384]

I concluded my report with the hope that I would eventually be able to return to something like normal health for one of my age.

THOTH, HERMES, AND SANATKUMĀRA

Above the mantelpiece of my study in East London, long ago, there hung a reproduction of Holman Hunt's *The Scapegoat*.[385] It hung there for quite a few years. Visitors sometimes looked askance at the evil-eyed goat who was the subject of the painting, evidently wondering how it had come to occupy the place of honour in the study of a Buddhist writer and teacher. There was a reason for its being there. I had always liked and admired the Pre-Raphaelites,[386] of whom Holman Hunt was one, and *The Scapegoat* (of which there are two versions) is one of his finest works. I also wrote two poems entitled, respectively, 'Scapegoat' and 'The Scapegoat',[387] the second poem being a sonnet in which I describe the version of the painting in which the goat is white-haired and there is a background of dayglow yellow sky and a line of mauve-pink hills. Both poems were written a few years before I hung Holman Hunt's painting on my study wall, and several of my friends speculated that my fascination with the subject was due to my having been made a scapegoat by the then British Buddhist establishment. Yet although I had indeed been cast out by that body, I did not feel in the least like a scapegoat and was quite happy to live in the wilderness, where instead of dying like the poor goat, as my critics had expected, I became the founder of a new Buddhist movement. However, scapegoat or not, my mood must have changed, for eventually Holman Hunt's *The Scapegoat* was taken down and replaced by Turner's *The Bridge of Sighs, Ducal Palace and Custom-House, Venice*.[388] I had paid my first visit to Venice thirty-three years earlier, in 1966,[389] and Turner's well-known painting, where the pink and white façade of the Doge's Palazzo gleamed from across the olive green water and the pink and white finger of the Campanile points into the blue Italian sky, reminded me of the days I had spent in the great and glorious city, which for centuries was Europe's gateway to the mysterious East.

In 1997 I moved from East London into a different city and a different flat.[390] My study in the new flat had no mantelpiece, and there was very little wall space, two walls being lined with bookshelves, while a third was taken up by a picture window. Any picture I favoured had to be hung or pinned on the inside of the door, so that seated at the opposite side of the room in my red armchair, with the picture window behind me, I could have it directly in view. Over the years many a picture had taken its turn on the door, as my mood or interest dictated, but there is one picture that has lasted longer than any other and which, for the last five or six years, has confronted my gaze whenever I looked across the room. It is a small picture of the Egyptian god Thoth, the ibis-headed inventor of writing, author of the sacred texts, and patron of the arts and sciences. He wears a short kilt, the whiteness of which contrasts strongly with the reddish brown of his body. He is depicted in profile; his left hand holds up a tablet, his right a brush or stylus, as if in readiness to take down a message from the gods. He is the very embodiment of Ancient Egypt, with its pyramids, its temples, and its priestly lore. I came across that Egypt, as I came across so many other things, in the pages of the *Children's Encyclopaedia*. I marvelled at the strange yet comprehensible art, the colours which were still fresh after more than 3,000 years, at the bewigged men in their still white garments, and at the beds of tall papyrus reeds from which there protruded the mild head of a cow. Above all, I marvelled at the colossal temples, which seemed built not for men but for giants. Nor, indeed, had they been built for men but for the gods, whose houses they were, from which through the semi-divine pharaohs and priests they ruled, dynasty after dynasty, over a humble, happy, and hard-working people who, if they had honoured the gods and lived rightly, could look forward to an even happier life hereafter. In many ways it was an attractive picture.

It was a picture that formed the backdrop of Joan Grant's evocation of Ancient Egypt in *Winged Pharaoh*,[391] which was the first book I borrowed when, after three years of invalidism, I rejoined the children's section of the Tooting Public Library. A *winged* was an *initiated* pharaoh, and according to the author the pyramids of Egypt were not tombs, as was commonly believed, but places of initiation, in whose central chamber a pharaoh underwent, alone, the spiritual trials that would transform him from a human being into a semi-divine personage. What was more wonderful still, Joan Grant claimed that *Winged Pharaoh* was a work not of imagination but of recollection, that she had once lived in Ancient Egypt, and that she was simply recording what she remembered of her life in that particular existence. I cannot remember how literally I took that claim, but I could have offered little resistance to the idea of reincarnation, which from then on came to be entwined with my thinking. Even so, the effect that *Winged Pharaoh* had on me was less philosophical than literary, for not long afterwards I started writing a short story set in Ancient Egypt. The story began, and perhaps ended, with a detailed description of a lotus pond. (I am by nature fond of detail.) The pond was situated in the garden of a white marble palace or temple surrounded by cypresses, and it was here beneath an eternally blue sky that the hero of my story lived. Unlike the author of *Winged Pharaoh* I had no memories of a previous life in Ancient Egypt on which to draw, but it was not difficult for me to imagine – or to dream – that I had lived beside the Nile in the days when Stonehenge was new or perhaps not yet built. Probably I would have been a priest, shaven-headed and clad in stiff white garments, and had spent my life in the service of one or other of the gods, whether Ra, or Thoth, or Ptah, or the dead and resurrected Osiris; and perhaps, when I was old, I would have spent the cool of the evening in the temple garden, beside the lotus pond, and perhaps, when the moon rose, the young priest would come and ask me about my life, and I would say, 'I was born into a baker's family, and as a boy I used to take a basket of fresh loaves to the temple every morning. The pillars and walls of the temple were decorated with pictures of men and beasts, and with strange signs. I was fascinated by the pictures, and used to stop and look at them. One of the priests noticed this, and one day he asked me if I would like to know the meaning of the pictures. I said I would, so a few days later, with the consent of my parents, I entered the temple as a novice. For the next few years I swept the temple floor, served the priests, learned how to arrange the tray of offerings to the gods, and eventually learned to read the sacred texts. Soon afterwards I became a priest, and from that time onward I spent my days performing the sacred rituals, studying the sacred texts, and exploring the mysteries of our religion. Now I am old. I have passed on what I know to the younger priests. Soon I shall die. My body will be embalmed, Thoth will conduct me to the Hall of Truth, my heart will be weighed, and I trust I shall be found worthy to enjoy the company of the blessed gods for all eternity.' No, it was not difficult for me to imagine all this, and I could almost hear the sound of the old priest's voice as he told the story of his life to his young auditor. Nor did I find it difficult to imagine myself living in Ancient Egypt centuries later, during the time of the Ptolemies and the Roman occupation.[392] Then, too, I would probably have been a priest, and perhaps, when a visitor asked me about myself, I would say, 'All my life I have lived here in Hermopolis,[393] serving the great god Thoth, whom the Greeks call Hermes. In my younger days we had few Greek visitors. Now there are many. They are a young upstart people. They think they know everything. But a few of them have begun to realize that we, the priests of old Egypt, far surpass them in wisdom, and that they have much to learn from us.'

Thoth and Hermes each possessed a number of different attributes and functions, and since they possessed some of these in common it was not difficult for the Greeks to see in Thoth an Egyptian version of their own god Hermes. Both Thoth and Hermes were originally moon gods, we are told, for the moon has no light of its own and simply reflects the light of the sun. Thus Thoth is called 'ray of Ra', the Egyptian sun god. Similarly, when Hermes, the divine messenger, delivers a message from Zeus, the words he speaks are not his own but 'reflect' the words of Zeus, as when he tells the nymph Calypso, in the *Odyssey*, that she is to allow Odysseus to leave her island, where she has detained him the last seven years.[394] Thoth and Hermes have two important functions in common. Both are communicators or messengers, and both are psychopomps, guides or conductors of the souls of the dead from this world to the next. Thoth is the scribe of the gods, as well as being the inventor of writing and author of the *Book of the Dead*[395] and other sacred texts, so that it is not difficult for us to see him as the revealer or communicator of divine wisdom to mankind. Hermes, similarly, communicates the will of Zeus to the lesser gods and to mortal men. Both Thoth and Hermes are channels of communication between heaven and earth, the divine and the human, even the Transcendental and the mundane. Moreover, just as Thoth conducts the deceased person to the Hall of Justice, in the same way Hermes drives the ghosts down to the River Styx. As Virgil says of Hermes in the *Aeneid* (Dryden's translation):

> But first he grasps within his awful hand
> The mark of sovereign power, his magic wand;
> With this he draws the ghosts from hollow graves,
> With this he drives them down the Stygian waves;
> With this he seals in sleep the wakeful sight;
> And eyes, though closed in death, restores to light.[396]

I had first learned about Hermes and the other Greek gods, as I had learned about the gods of Ancient Egypt, from the lavishly illustrated pages of the *Children's Encyclopaedia*. Later I became better acquainted with them through the *Iliad* and the *Odyssey*. From then onwards they were no less real to me than were the characters in a play by Shakespeare or a novel by Dickens. In a way they were more real, for the greatest of them had, considered as archetypes, a numinous quality that characters in a novel and the drama did not possess. At the same time they all had a distinct individuality that was evident in everything they said and did. Reading the *Iliad*, in particular, in Chapman's translation,[397] I found Hera and Pallas Athena at least as believable as Agamemnon and Achilles, and I followed debates among the gods with the same eagerness that I followed the skirmishes between the Greeks and the Trojans. I sided with the Greeks, though I was sorry for the Trojans, for I was well acquainted with the events that led to the armies of the Greeks being encamped before the walls of Troy. The story began with a secret. The secret concerned Thetis, one of the sea nymphs, and was to the effect that she was destined to bear a son who would be greater than his father. Now Zeus wanted to marry Thetis, but when he learned the secret he changed his mind and Thetis was married to Peleus, a mortal. All the Olympian gods took part in the wedding feast, in the course of which a golden apple was thrown onto the festive board. It was thrown by Atë, or Discord, and it was inscribed 'For the Fairest'. Hera, Pallas Athena, and Aphrodite each laid claim to the apple, and in the end Zeus decided that the case should be judged by Paris, one of the sons of Priam, the King of Troy. Each of the three goddesses showed herself naked to

Paris and at the same time offered him a bribe. Hera offered him power, and Pallas Athena knowledge, but Aphrodite offered him the love of the most beautiful woman in the world. It was therefore to Aphrodite that Paris awarded the golden apple. The most beautiful woman in the world happened to be Helen, the wife of Menelaus, the brother of Agamemnon, King of Argos. Paris therefore sailed for Argos, in the Peloponnese, with Aphrodite's help abducted Helen and sailed away with her, and Helen of Argos became Helen of Troy. Soon Agamemnon and Menelaus had gathered an army and a fleet and set off in pursuit of the fugitives. Thus began the Trojan War, in which Hera and Pallas Athena sided with the Greeks, and Aphrodite and Ares with the Trojans, and which resulted in the utter destruction of Troy and the death or enslavement of her people. The real subject of the *Iliad*, however, is not the Trojan War but the 'wrath of Achilles', the son of Peleus and Thetis, who was the handsomest of the Greeks and their greatest warrior – the baneful wrath that 'imposed infinite sorrows on the Greeks and many brave souls loosed from breasts heroic',[398] due to Achilles' quarrel with Agamemnon. But that is another story.

Not many years after I first 'heard Chapman speak out loud and bold'[399] I paid my first visit to the British Museum and, in particular, to the galleries of Greek and Egyptian antiquities. Almost the first thing I noticed was that the gods of Greece and the gods of Ancient Egypt were represented in very different ways. With few exceptions, the former were represented in human form, whereas the latter were theriomorphic, having human bodies but the heads of animals, including reptiles and birds. There were male divinities with the head of a ram or a hawk and female divinities with the head of a hippopotamus or a cow. Whether because of the skill of the sculptor or for some other reason, these hybrid deities were artistically and spiritually credible, and I did not find it difficult to imagine them being objects of worship. I was especially fascinated by the figure of the lioness-headed goddess Sekhmet, the personification of the hot wind that blows in from the desert bringing with it clouds of dust. There were several representations of her in the museum's collection, all hewn from black stone and all of full human size. The finest of these showed her seated, upright, as though on a chair. Dignified and composed she sat there, her hands on her knees, and her leonine face had what I thought was a grandmotherly look. By contrast, the gods in the adjacent Greek and Roman galleries were represented in human form, indeed in *idealized* human form. Hermes, the divine messenger and intermediary between gods and men, was represented as a beautiful young man, naked except for his winged sandals and winged hat, and carrying the caduceus, a rod round which two snakes were twined, one male and one female. The image of the divinely beautiful, slightly androgynous young man is not confined to Ancient Greece or to the figure of Hermes. In the Christian art of the Middle Ages and the Renaissance angels are often represented as beautiful young men, albeit decently clad in flowing robes and equipped with a pair of multicoloured wings. In this connection it is noteworthy that when, in *Paradise Lost*, Milton describes the archangel Raphael, whom God has sent to warn Adam and Eve to be on their guard against Satan, who has just escaped from hell, he can think of no one better with whom to compare the beautiful archangel than Hermes, the son of the mountain nymph Maia and Zeus.

> Like Maia's son he stood,
> And shook his plumes, that heavenly fragrance filled
> The circuit wide.[400]

In Christianity the angels have no feminine equivalent, though the Virgin Mary may be seen as an equivalent to some extent. She is invariably depicted fully clothed, so that her youthful beauty has to be expressed, even concentrated, entirely in her face. In the Buddhist art of the East the beautiful young man appears in the form of the Mahāyāna bodhisattva, the wise and compassionate being who, in the popular imagination, gives up his own salvation in order to work for the salvation of others. He is depicted neither naked nor fully clothed but wearing the armlets and jewelled headdress of an Indian prince. There are also the *devas* and *brahmas* of pre-Mahāyāna Buddhist cosmology who when they appear to human beings do so in the form of a beautiful young man radiating brilliant light in all directions.

The story goes that Govinda, the learned brahmin, has heard that anyone who remains in solitude for the four months of the rainy season and cultivates the absorption in universal compassion, sees Brahmā face to face and converses with him. Having so heard he decides to practise that discipline, and informs the king, his brahmin students, and his wives accordingly, and has a new rest house built to the east of the city. There he wholeheartedly cultivates the absorption in universal compassion for the four months of the rainy season, pervading each of the four quarters in turn with thoughts of compassion for suffering living beings. Despite all his efforts, however, at the end of the fourth month Govinda does not see Brahmā, nor does he converse with him, and he experiences anguish and distress. Becoming aware of Govinda's thoughts, Brahmā Sanatkumāra, the Eternal Youth, vanishes from his own heaven and appears before Govinda in the form of a beautiful young man radiating brilliant light in all directions. Govinda is struck with fear and trembling at the sight, so that his hair stands on end, and he exclaims, 'O Glorious vision, tell me who you are.' To which the vision replies, 'in the highest heaven I am known as Brahmā Sanatkumāra, the Eternal Youth. Know me as such.' Govinda asks his divine visitor what offerings he requires, and Sanatkumāra replies that he takes the offerings as already given, and says that Govinda should ask him for whatever he desires, whether it pertains to this world or the next. After reflecting Govinda puts a question that will be not only for his own benefit but for the benefit of others. He wants to know what mortals have to do in order to reach the deathless world of Brahmā. Sanatkumāra's reply goes to the heart of the matter:

He among men, O Brahmin, who eschews
All claims of 'me' and 'mine'; he in whom thought
Rises in lonely calm, compassion-filled,
Aloof from 'stench', from lust exempt and free –
Established thus, and training thus, I say,
Can mortals reach the deathless Brahmā world.

Govinda then says that he understands, in detail, what Sanatkumāra has told him. The one thing he does not understand is what he means by 'stench'. Sanatkumāra therefore goes on to explain what he meant, giving a long list of negative mental states, from anger and lying down to dullness and delusion, all of which prevent a man from reaching the world of Brahmā. Govinda realizes that these negative mental states are not to be overcome if one lives the household life and resolves to go forth as a homeless wanderer, a decision that Sanatkumāra approves.

It seems that the story of the brahmin Govinda and the Brahmā Sanatkumāra was a popular one among the early Buddhists, and several versions of it have survived in various Buddhist scriptures. My own telling of the story is a free adaptation of the *Mahāgovinda Sutta* (*Dīgha Nikāya* 19), as translated by Rhys Davids and by Walshe, though in the case of the story's central event, the exchange between Govinda and Sanatkumāra regarding the way to the deathless world of Brahmā, I have produced a composite version of the work of the two translators.[401] The fact that the story of Govinda and Sanatkumāra was popular with the early Buddhists, and indeed came to be incorporated in a text regarded as *buddhavacana* or 'word of the Buddha', suggests that it is worthy of serious attention. To begin with, it would appear that the deathless Brahmā world (*amatambrahmalokaṃ*) of which both Govinda and Sanatkumāra speak, is none other than the 'Deathless State' (*amatapadaṃ*) of the *Dhammapada*[402] and other Pāli texts, the Deathless State being synonymous with Nirvāṇa. Sanatkumāra is thus a hypostasis of this deathless world or deathless state, as his name, the *Eternal* Youth, clearly suggests. Moreover, when Govinda asks Sanatkumāra how a man may reach the immortal (or deathless) world he is using much the same language as the Buddha uses in the *Ariyapariyesana Sutta* (*Majjhima Nikāya* 26) when, speaking of his early struggles, prior to his attainment of supreme Enlightenment, he relates how, having formerly sought that which was subject to birth and death he decided to seek what was *not* subject to birth and death.[403] The brahmin Govinda is in fact Everyman. When he asks Sanatkumāra how mortals can reach the immortal world of Brahmā he is humanity becoming aware of its contingent nature and aspiring to go beyond all contingency. At the beginning of the story Govinda has political power, social position, and domestic happiness, but he wants to find out for himself if, as he has heard, one who practises the meditation on universal compassion for the four months of the rainy season really does, at the end of that period, see Brahmā and converse with him. Govinda practises the discipline faithfully, but despite all his efforts Brahmā does not appear and he is overwhelmed by anguish. Here two points are worthy of comment. Govinda practises the meditation on universal compassion, but not universal love. However, it is universal loving kindness (*mettā*) itself that becomes universal compassion (*karuṇā*) when confronted by the suffering of living beings. Secondly, and more importantly, Sanatkumāra appears to Govinda not because he has completed the discipline but in response to his anguish, for his anguish reveals how deep and how sincere was his longing to see Brahmā and converse with him. An intense feeling of spiritual failure, or remorse for unethical behaviour, or of one's own utter contingency – all may serve to precipitate a spiritual experience, or even a liberating insight.

In my view the story of Govinda and Sanatkumāra is an example of what may be called pre-Buddhist Buddhism. After his attainment of Supreme Enlightenment the Buddha had no alternative, at first, but to communicate his radical message through the medium of the existing religious language. He was obliged to put his new wine into the old bottles. Later he devised a religious and philosophical language of his own, and for a while the two 'languages', the old and the new, appear to have existed side by side within his community. Later still, however, when the Buddha's new wine was increasingly being stored in bottles of his own design, the old bottles came to be regarded as containing the old brahminical brew. Thus when the compilers of the *Majjhima Nikāya* came to include the story of Govinda and Sanatkumāra in their collection a sequel was added in which the Buddha is represented as declaring not only that he himself was Govinda in a former life, but that the path he had then taught, the path to union with Brahmā, did *not* lead to Nirvāṇa: it led only to rebirth in the Brahmā world, that is, to the Brahmā world in the sense of a heaven within the sphere of mundane existence. Here for 'former life' we must surely understand – reading between the lines – 'early stage in the Buddha's teaching career'. Elsewhere in the *Mahāgovinda Sutta* Sanatkumāra assumes the form of a minor divinity called Pañcasikha or Five-Crest,[404] and with this we pass from early Buddhism to the Mahāyāna, in which the 'archetypal' bodhisattva Mañjughoṣa or Mañjuśrī is depicted wearing on his head a wreath of five blue lotuses. Like Hermes, he appears in the form of a beautiful young man, radiating light, and indeed his full name is Mañjuśrī-kumārabhūta, or Mañjuśrī – 'who became a youth'. Like Thoth, he is the patron of the arts and sciences and is associated with writing. One of my own precious teachers, the incomparable Jamyang Khyentse Chökyi Lodrö, was widely revered as a manifestation of Mañjughoṣa, and it was from him that I received initiation into the *sādhana* of Mañjughoṣa, whom I have come to regard as a hypostasis of the Buddha's transcendental wisdom.[405]

THE BIG AND THE GREAT: VANDALISM AND ICONOCLASM

'How big is God?' This was a question that perplexed me when I was a child and I thought about it from time to time. I had probably been told about the greatness of God at Sunday school, and thinking that 'great' meant 'big' I tried hard to imagine how big he was. From the way this greatness was described I concluded that God was not only very big but that he possessed, moreover, a giant human form. I therefore tried to imagine an enormously big foot, no doubt thinking that with this as a starting point I could work my way up to an idea of just how big God really was. The foot I imagined was a hundred miles long from heel to toe, and in my mind's eye I saw it stretching from where I stood into the far distance. To visualize a foot of such enormous dimensions was difficult enough, but when I tried to visualize the leg to which that foot belonged I failed entirely. I could not get even as far as God's ankle. Most human beings tend to identify great with big, so that it is not surprising that as a child I should have tried to work out how big was God. This very natural tendency finds expression in the field of the visual arts. In Michelangelo's *Last Judgement*[406] his Hercules-like Christ is of superhuman dimensions, while colossal images of the Buddha are to be found throughout the East. I think in particular of the twin Standing Buddhas of Bamiyan in central Afghanistan, both of which were carved out of the side of the cliff in the sixth century CE. One was 180 feet high, the other 121 feet. For 1,500 years they looked out over the fields of the peaceful Bamiyan Valley. They looked out over them until March 2001, when on the orders of Mullah

Mohammed Omar, the Taliban leader, they were blown up with dynamite, the government having declared the two Buddhas to be 'idols'.

The destruction of the Buddhas was widely condemned, though it should not have come as a surprise to anyone familiar with the history of Islam. It was no coincidence that the second name of the mullah who ordered the destruction should be Omar, that being also the name of the Muslim general who was responsible for the burning of the great Library of Alexandria, with its 700,000 volumes, in 640 CE. There were commentators who characterized the Taliban's action as pure vandalism, or vandalism for the sake of vandalism. But I do not think it was that. There are in fact two kinds of vandalism: pure vandalism, such as the wanton vandalism of boys defacing a poster or Napoleon's soldiers using the Sphinx for target practice, and what may be termed *principled vandalism*, or vandalism which is the practical corollary of a philosophical or theological principle. The Taliban's vandalism was of the second kind. They demolished the Twin Buddhas because they saw them as idols and because they hated idolatry as the greatest of sins. When I first heard that the Bamiyan Buddhas had been reduced to a heap of rubble I felt shocked and dismayed, both as a Buddhist and as a lover of art. At the same time, I reminded myself that images, and the worship of images (if indeed it is the image itself that is being worshipped), had not always been part of Buddhism. Was it not well known that for at least two centuries after his *parinirvāṇa* the Buddha's presence was indicated by such symbols as a tree, a wheel, and a pair of footprints? Indeed, it is not difficult to imagine a Buddhism that is without images, and therefore without image-worship, and even without religious art of any kind, and a Buddhism of this stripped-down kind may well exist somewhere in the Buddhist world. What I, for one, cannot imagine is a Buddhism that did not include among its spiritual practices puja or worship, in the sense of the inward and outward expression of a heartfelt devotion to the Buddha, whether as represented by a material image, a painting, or a mental image. I also reminded myself that what I have called principled vandalism was by no means unknown in England and other countries to which the Reformation had spread. In the seventeenth century, under Oliver Cromwell,[407] English Puritans destroyed an enormous quantity of religious art on the grounds that statues and paintings of Christ and the saints were idols and that their worship constituted idolatry. Even today there are Protestants for whom the Roman Catholic Church, which continues to worship what Milton in a celebrated sonnet derisively calls 'stocks and stones',[408] is idolatrous and hence not truly Christian. The Eastern Orthodox Church, after a good deal of internal conflict, decided to allow the worship of two-dimensional paintings (commonly known as 'icons') but not that of their three-dimensional counterparts.

Principled vandalism is fuelled by hate, an emotion which in Buddhism is regarded as a highly unskilful mental state. When its object is a material image it may be termed iconophobia. Iconophobia had its origins in Ancient Judaism, from which it passed to some forms of Christianity and to Islam. It appears in conjunction with monotheism, but seems to be unknown to polytheism and pantheism. Perhaps the most characteristic feature of iconophobia is its conviction of its own absolute rightness, a conviction that enables it to override all other considerations. The Taliban soldiers who dynamited the Twin Buddhas of Bamiyan did not care that they were hurting the religious feelings of millions of Buddhists throughout the world. They may even have been glad to hurt them, for in their eyes were not the Buddhists idolators and therefore deserving of punishment and even death? Neither did the Taliban soldiers care that in demolishing the Buddhas they were destroying *works of art*, or, at the very least, works of archaeological importance that were part of the cultural heritage of the people of Afghanistan and of mankind. For the Taliban, the need to destroy idols trumped all other values.

Principled vandalism also has its more secular forms. Besides being responsible for a great deal of human suffering, Communist China's 'Cultural Revolution' of 1966–1969 saw the wholesale destruction of works of art of every kind. Acts of principled vandalism may be committed not only by governments but also by individuals, whether as a form of political protest or as a means of drawing attention to a personal grievance. I remember Leonardo da Vinci's drawing of the Virgin Mary and St Anne, in the National Gallery. The painting was fired at with a sawn-off shotgun, splinters from the shattered protective glass piercing the painting. (The damage was afterwards invisibly mended.)[409] A few years later a student set fire to the Music Room at the Brighton Pavilion, destroying the ornate, gilded interior almost entirely. The cost of restoration ran to tens of thousands of pounds, but so far as I remember the culprit was not even fined.[410] In my view such principled – or rather unprincipled – vandalism should be treated as a crime, and punished regardless of the merits of the cause for whose sake it was committed. I am aware, however, that it would be difficult to arrive at a legally satisfactory definition of vandalism, and still more difficult to decide how an object the destruction of which constitutes vandalism is to be defined. Were the two visitors to Tate Britain who jumped up and down on Tracey Emin's unmade *Bed*, thus disturbing its carefully arranged disarray, guilty of vandalism?[411] Or was Lady Churchill guilty of it when, after her husband's death, she destroyed a portrait of the former prime minister by Graham Sutherland that others thought a masterpiece, but which she detested?[412]

In his *Novum Organum* Francis Bacon speaks of the idols of the tribe, the idols of the cave, the idols of the market place, and the idols of the theatre, which represent the false ideas that prevail in the four principal areas of human life and activity.[413] Thus the word 'idol' can not only be used literally, as referring to figures of wood, stone, or metal considered to be objects of worship; it can also be used metaphorically, as when it refers to ideas, as in the *Novum Organum*, or to a book, a nation, or a person. But where there are idols there will be iconoclasts, or breakers of idols, regardless of whether the idols in question be of the literal or the metaphorical variety. And behind the iconoclasm fuelling it, there will be at least a degree of iconophobia. This means that iconoclasm is of various kinds according to the nature of the object against which it happens to be directed. In apophatic theology or mysticism, for example, whatever concept that can possibly be predicated of God, the Absolute, or Ultimate Reality, however abstract or rarefied it may be, is rejected as inadequate. Similarly, in the *animitta* or 'signless' *samādhi*, which is achieved through deep contemplative insight into the transitoriness of conditioned existence, the Buddhist meditator realizes that the Unconditioned is altogether beyond words. This apophatic trend within Buddhist thought and spiritual practice finds its fullest expression in the Prajñāpāramitā or Perfection of Wisdom scriptures, the best known of which is the *Heart Sūtra*, in which the most cherished doctrinal categories of Buddhism, from the five *skandhas* or 'heaps' to Nirvāṇa, are one by one negated. The *Heart Sūtra* might therefore be described as the manifesto of transcendental iconoclasm. As Buddhaghosa observed long ago, 'As on the unwholesome plane hatred does not cling, does not stick to its object, so wisdom on the wholesome plane. As hate seeks for faults, even though they do not exist, so wisdom seeks for the faults that do exist. As hate leads to the rejection of beings, so wisdom to that of all conditioned things'.[414] The radically iconoclastic nature of wisdom is symbolized in the Vajrayāna by the figure of the wrathful Vajrapāṇi. Dark blue in colour, and surrounded by flames, he holds in his right hand the vajra with which he annihilates all mental constructions. Perhaps Nietzsche's 'philosophizing with a hammer' may be seen as a distant reflection of Vajrapāṇi's vajra.[415]

But let me return to the Twin Buddhas of Bamiyan. Many years ago I saw, in a book or magazine, a photograph of them as they loomed up out of their cliff, the pleats of their robes accentuating their extreme verticality. At their foot was a scattering of black dots that I took to be human beings but so tiny that I was unable to tell whether they were local people, or travellers, or Buddhist pilgrims. Whatever they were, they were utterly dwarfed by the figures of the two Buddhas. Had they been pilgrims, they would have had an overwhelming sense of the spiritual greatness of Vairocana and Śākyamuni (as the two Buddhas are said to have been called); for although bigness and greatness are not synonymous, it is certainly possible for the former to suggest, or symbolize, or shadow forth the latter, so that I was not entirely on the wrong track when, as a child, I tried to ascertain how big was God. I was not on the wrong track because I had, even at that age, an obscure sense of something not merely greater than me but immeasurably *higher* in the scale of existence. This sense has always been strong in me, and as I grew up it became increasingly focused on the person of the human, historical Śākyamuni, the Buddha or Enlightened One. Between the Buddha and the ordinary, unenlightened human being there is an immense gulf. The Buddha attained Nirvāṇa, a state utterly free from greed, hatred, and delusion. The ordinary, unenlightened human being is dominated by these three 'poisons', which in depictions of the wheel of life are represented by a cock, a snake, and a pig. This is not to say that human beings are not potentially enlightened, or that they may not from time to time give evidence of generosity, compassion, and wisdom, but the path to the actualization of that potential has to pass through many steps and stages. Scratching the surface of one's being with a little meditation will not be sufficient to reveal the Buddha within. If one thinks one is near Enlightenment, one is far from it; and if one thinks one is far from it, one is near.

I began writing these pages around the tenth anniversary of 9/11, the day when hijacked passenger aircraft were deliberately flown into the twin towers of the World Trade Center in New York and into one wing of the Pentagon, the US government's military complex in Washington DC.[416] I do not remember precisely where I was when I first heard of the attack, or what I was doing at the time, but I must have been in my study and heard about it on the radio not long after it took place. Being partially sighted I neither saw what had happened on television nor read about it in the newspapers; but so graphic were the radio reports of the atrocity that I could see it all in my mind's eye. I could see the twin towers, see the hijacked aircraft approaching their target, see one of the towers blazing, see scores of people jumping, some of them hand in hand, to their deaths hundreds of feet below. The picture of all those bodies falling through space, as in a Magritte painting, haunts me still.[417] Some years after the attack I wrote a poem on 9/11. More than 3,000 people had lost their lives on that fateful day; but I did not write about this, for it was a subject beyond poetry – beyond any poetry that I could write, at least.

> Proudly they stood, those towers, a monument
> To money, and the power that money brings.
> But hate was stronger. Now they lie in dust,
> And impotent hands a mighty nation wrings.

On second thoughts, I decided that the inversion in the last line was clumsy, and therefore changed the line to 'And a mighty nation wrings its impotent hands', albeit at the cost of two hypermetric syllables. Thus from being a rhymed quatrain the poem became four lines of blank verse. But if the terrorists were motivated by hatred, those who had built the World Trade Center were surely motivated by greed and worshipped what Francis Bacon called the 'idols of the market place'. These idols are of two kinds, the first of them being words which are names of things that do not exist. Some years ago I had a long discussion with a friend who had co-authored a book on money, and the conclusion to which we came was that there was no such thing as money: money did not exist.[418] At the same time, although money does not really exist those who possess or control this non-existing thing have tremendous power, as we have been reminded by the economic events of the last few years. However, this is not a suitable topic for a reverie or reminiscence, at least not at present.[419]

MY FIVE LITERARY HEROES

In the beginning there were the gods. Later there came the heroes, who were part god and part man. The Babylonian *Epic of Gilgamesh* (third millennium BCE) says of its eponymous hero,

> When the gods created Gilgamesh they gave him a perfect body. Shamash the glorious sun endowed him with beauty, Adad the god of the storm endowed him with courage, the great gods made his beauty perfect, surpassing all others, terrifying like a great wild bull. Two thirds they made him god and one third man.[420]

The Greeks were not so exact. They were content to say of their heroes that they were part human and part divine, since they were either the offspring of a god by a mortal woman or of a goddess by a mortal man. Heracles (or Hercules) was the son of Zeus, the king of the gods, by Alcmene, with whom he had contrived to sleep by assuming the form of her husband Amphitryon. Alone among the heroes, after his death Heracles was taken up into heaven and received into the company of the gods. Zeus was also the father of Perseus, the slayer of Medusa the Gorgon, by princess Danaë, upon whom he descended in a shower of gold, after her father had shut her up in a brazen tower on being told that she would give birth to a son who would supplant him. Achilles, whose 'baneful wrath' brought infinite sorrows on the Greek forces besieging Troy, was the son of the sea goddess Thetis by Peleus, a mortal man. When he was born his mother dipped him in the black waters of the river Styx, one of the rivers of the Underworld, which made him invulnerable – except for the heel by which she had held him. It was by an arrow through this heel that he was eventually slain, which is why we still speak of a person's weak spot as his 'Achilles' heel'. Although only Achilles was vulnerable in this kind of way, the other heroes were not without their weak spots, any more than are their modern secular counterparts. Aeneas, the eponymous hero of the *Aeneid*, who was the son of Venus (or Aphrodite) by the Trojan prince Anchises, had to be reminded of his duty as the founder of the future Roman Empire.[421] All these names and stories were familiar to me almost from my earliest days, along with the narratives of the Old Testament and the parables of the New. Besides the *Children's Encyclopaedia*, my only sources of information were Charles Kingsley's *The Heroes*[422] and a little book entitled *The Story of the Iliad,...*[423] yet Hercules and the other heroes were very alive for me and it was not difficult for me to believe in their historical existence. Or rather, the question of their historical existence did not arise for me at that time.

Years later I read Thomas Carlyle's *On Heroes and Hero Worship*. According to Carlyle, world history is at bottom the history of great men. It is the story of heroes, as well as of hero-worship and the heroic in human affairs. Great men were indeed 'the modellers, patterns, and in a wide sense creators of whatsoever the general mass of men contrived to do or to attain.'[424] Heroism could manifest itself in any field of human ability, and Carlyle describes the different forms taken by the hero in different phases of human history. There are six such forms. The hero can appear as Divinity, as Prophet, as Poet, as Priest, as Man of Letters, and as King. One of Carlyle's heroes was one of my heroes too. This was Samuel Johnson, who along with Rousseau and Burns was for Carlyle an example of the Hero as Man of Letters.[425] Samuel Johnson was one of my literary heroes, not one of my spiritual heroes, though in his case, at least, there was a degree of overlap between the two.

There are five men of letters who, throughout my life, have been my literary heroes. It was not simply that I admired the writings of these men – and I admired them immensely. Their lives and their personalities were also of great interest to me, and it was this combination that made them my literary heroes. Over the years I not only bought and read their works but read books about them by their friends, their admirers, and their critics. Thus I came to be the owner of a small library of books about each of them. From time to time I would immerse myself in one or another of these libraries, in this way renewing my acquaintance with this or that literary hero and deepening my understanding of his life and work. I was so fortunate as to meet with all five heroes quite early in life, so that I have now had the benefit of their companionship for more than seventy years. I met Dr Johnson, as I have always called him, before I met any of the others. I met him at the Tooting Public Library, when I borrowed, two at a time, the six volumes of his *Lives of the Poets*, edited by Birkbeck Hill.[426] What led me to him I do not know, though the *Children's Encyclopaedia* may have had something to do with it. Months later, when living in Barnstaple, I was able to borrow from the local public library most volumes of an early edition of *The Works of Samuel Johnson,* LL.D., and during a visit to Ilfracombe I obtained for a shilling a second-hand copy of Boswell's *Life of Johnson*. By the time I was fifteen I was an ardent Johnsonian and have remained one down to the present day, when a portrait of the great lexicographer looks down at me from the wall of my study. I greatly admired the precision of my hero's language and loved the beautiful literary style of *The Rambler* and its successors.[427] I also admired his poetry, especially the long, sombre *The Vanity of Human Wishes*,[428] and the much shorter, tender and pathetic *On the Death of Dr Robert Levet*.[429] The theme of the long poem is the inconstancy of such objects of human ambitions as wealth, political power, literary fame, and military glory, a theme the poet illustrates by graphic descriptions of the dramatic rise and fall of men like Cardinal Wolsey[430] and Charles XII of Sweden. I found the lines describing the fall of the latter particularly moving, and I soon knew them by heart.

> His Fall was destin'd to a barren Strand,
> A petty Fortress, and a dubious Hand;
> He left the Name, at which the World grew pale
> To point a Moral, or adorn a Tale.

I particularly relished the cumulative effect of the adjectives in the first two lines. Towards the end of the poem, when he has sufficiently enlarged upon his theme, the poet abruptly asks a question:

Where then shall Hope and Fear their Objects find?
Must dull Suspense corrupt the stagnant Mind?
Shall helpless Man, in Ignorance sedate,
Roll darkling down the Torrent of his fate?[431]

It is a good question, for it is an existential question, and one which every reflecting human being must ask himself at some time. Johnson proceeds to answer his own question, and with this the poem concludes. His answer is the traditional Christian one. Man must trust in God; for God in his infinite wisdom knows what is best for us, and we must accept his decisions. Though I was far from sharing my hero's religious beliefs, I could appreciate the sincerity with which he held them, besides appreciating the language in which he gave expression to them. A practising Christian as well as a believing one, he examined his conscience at regular intervals, and bitterly reproached himself for his shortcomings. One shortcoming, which perhaps was his 'weak spot', was Sloth, one of the Seven Deadly Sins. But though he was a Christian he was not a happy one. Melancholic by nature, and with a Calvinistic streak in his sober Anglicanism, he tormented himself with the thought that he was damned and would suffer in hell everlastingly. It pained me to think that so good and great a man should be afflicted in this way, and when I came to the end of Boswell's biography I was relieved to find that Johnson's life had ended peacefully.[432] Dr Johnson was a good man, as well as a great one. Compassionate and truly philanthropic, he was the sworn foe of cant and humbug, a moralist in the best sense of the term, and a passionate believer in the importance of friendship.[433] Throughout my life he has been to me much more than just a literary hero.

William Blake, my next literary hero, was born in 1757, and the first twenty-seven years of his life overlapped with the last twenty-seven of Dr Johnson's. Whereas Johnson was conservative in politics and religion, Blake was decidedly radical in both. Although the two men lived in the same city they moved in different social circles – indeed inhabited different worlds. My first acquaintance with Blake and his work was through Swinburne's *William Blake: A Critical Essay*, published in 1868 and available to me per courtesy of the Tooting Public Library, an institution to which I shall be ever grateful.[434] In this pioneer study

Swinburne quotes extensively from Blake's literary output, from the early lyrics to the last of the so-called Prophetic Books, thus giving me an idea of his extraordinary originality as both a poet and as a thinker. As I realized later, Blake was quite aware that he was original, but he did not seek to be original. He was 'original' because he was true to his own experience and his own spiritual vision. At that time I was greatly struck by *The Marriage of Heaven and Hell,* a short work which includes what Blake called 'The Proverbs of Hell'.[435] I was fascinated by its bizarre imagery and by its bold reversal of conventional values, a reversal that reminded me of certain of the old Gnostics and which seemed to anticipate Friedrich Nietzsche. I know how impressed I was by *The Marriage of Heaven and Hell*, for I remember copying out the whole work, or as much of it as Swinburne gives, into one of my notebooks. I also greatly enjoyed some of Blake's shorter poems, especially the beautiful *Thel*, a minor Prophetic Book, and the much earlier 'To the Muses', a youthful lament for the disappearance of true poetry. Later, I became acquainted with Blake's graphic output, for he was that *rara avis*, a poet who is as much a painter (or a painter who is as much a poet as one might also say), the only other example known to me being that of Dante Gabriel Rossetti, who was born a year after Blake died, and who was to acquire important Blake manuscripts. I was particularly fond of Blake's illustrations to the Book of Job, my favourite book of the Bible. In fact I came to own an edition of the authorized version of the Book of Job in which the text was printed as poetry, and which was illustrated, moreover, by Blake's sublime engravings. I spent many a happy hour poring over the precious volume, which I lost in the summer of 1943 when our house was destroyed by a German V-1 or 'flying bomb'.[436]

In the years – or decades – which followed my love for Blake steadily grew, and I had the satisfaction of seeing him become a popular figure with the poets and writers of the Beat Generation on both sides of the Atlantic, but especially with Allen Ginsberg. When Ginsberg came to see me in 1979, in London, he chanted one of Blake's poems for my benefit, chanting in a hoarse, unmusical voice to the accompaniment of his finger cymbals.[437] I was then still struggling to understand Blake's major Prophetic books, *The Four Zoas*, *Jerusalem*, and *Milton*.[438] In these extraordinary works, written in a kind of loose hexameter, scores of strange, non-human beings with outlandish names act and interact with one another in ways that run the whole gamut of human emotions. At intervals, there are descriptive passages of astonishing beauty, as well as spiritual insights such as are hardly to be met with elsewhere in English poetry. In *Milton*, the eponymous hero of the poem declares:

> I go to Eternal Death! The Nations still
> Follow after the detestable Gods of Priam, in pomp
> Of warlike Selfhood, contradicting and blaspheming....
>
> I will go down to self-annihilation and Eternal Death;
> Lest the Last Judgement come and find me unannihilate,
> And I be seiz'd and giv'n into the hands of my own Selfhood.[439]

Blake's bodily death took place in 1827, when he was 69. He died happily, even joyfully, singing songs of his own composition, and leaving to the world a rich spiritual legacy. The complex myth he created in the Prophetic Books is not really part of that legacy, for a myth is the creation of a whole people, not of any individual, however gifted. Perhaps the most valuable and influential part of his legacy is his emphasis on the importance of the imagination. It is not just a human faculty but the man himself, in the deepest and truest sense, and without it there can be no true art and no true religion. It is the Divine Vision or Divine Humanity, in which all things have their existence.

In his insistence on the importance of the imagination Blake resembles Samuel Taylor Coleridge, my third literary hero, who was the first to distinguish between fancy and imagination. For me there is no first meeting with Coleridge that I can remember. It is as though I have always known him, or at least have always known *The Rime of the Ancient Mariner, Christabel*, and *Kubla Khan*.[440] *The Rime of the Ancient Mariner*, especially, has always formed a part of my imaginative landscape. I delighted in its subtle rhythms, its vivid and precise images, its nightmarish apparitions, its glimpses of heavenly beauty. Underlying all this there are the deeper, darker themes of sin and guilt. With his crossbow the Mariner has shot a friendly albatross, as a result of which the body of the innocent bird is hung round his neck instead of a cross as a sign of his guilt. It is only when he marvels at the beauty of the water-snakes and blesses them that a 'spring of love' gushes from his heart, whereupon his burden falls from his neck and sinks 'like lead into the sea'. Love and guilt were important themes in Coleridge's life and in his work. Though he craved for love, he did not always find it. His marriage was not a happy one (unlike Blake's), and he was desperately in love with Wordsworth's sister-in-law, whom he was hardly ever able to meet. He also felt guilty on account of his failings as a husband and a father and his failure to fulfil his brilliant early promise. These feelings of being unloved and a failure were among the factors contributing to that fatal dependence on opium for which he is best known to the general public. Now although *The Rime of the Ancient Mariner* has always been part of my imaginative landscape, Coleridge's prose writings have not. My first acquaintance with them was when I read his *Biographia Literaria* in the Everyman edition.[441] I read it while living in the foothills of the eastern Himalayas, and it at once became one of my favourite books. Whereas Blake speaks of the imagination in a bewildering number of ways (though his general drift is clear), Coleridge attempts a formal definition which owes much to the German idealist philosopher Friedrich Schelling.[442] In chapter 13 of the *Biographia*, after delays and hesitations, Coleridge at last says:

> The Imagination then I consider either as primary, or secondary. The primary Imagination I hold to be the living power and prime agent of all human perception, and as a repetition in the finite mind of the eternal act of creation in the infinite I AM. The secondary Imagination I consider as an echo of the former, co-existing with the conscious will, yet still as identical with the primary in the kind of its agency, and differing only in degree, and in the mode of its operation. It dissolves, diffuses, dissipates, in order to recreate: or where this process is rendered impossible, yet still at all events it struggles to idealize and to unify.[443]

Coleridge's account of the imagination has given rise to a lot of discussion, a discussion that continues down to the present day.

Between the death of Coleridge in 1834 and the birth of Oscar Wilde, my fourth literary hero, there is a gap of twenty years.[444] The Industrial Revolution was at its height, and both Wilde and D. H. Lawrence, my fifth literary hero, were in their different ways out of sympathy with the age in which they lived. Wilde was an aesthete, a lover of beauty, and a leading representative of that cult of 'Art for Art's sake' of which the high priest was Walter Pater.[445] As such Wilde is akin to Tennyson's 'glorious Devil, large in heart and brain, That did love beauty only', and who eventually tires of his solitary, selfish enjoyment of the arts and seeks to purge his guilt through renunciation.[446] For several years I have had on my shelves the three stout volumes of the beautiful Folio edition of Wilde's complete works, and looking into them I can see that at one time or another I have read – or seen on stage – almost everything he wrote. It so happened that of all Wilde's writings I first read the early poems and some of the fairytales, and I read them in the green pocket volumes of the uniform edition. While the poems may not be among the jewels in the crown of English literature, they are of interest as revealing both Wilde's innate Hellenism and his taste for the cultural trappings of Roman Catholicism. Among the shorter poems I particularly liked 'Requiescat', which shares its title with a similar poem by Matthew Arnold,[447] and 'The Harlot's House', with its concluding image of the dawn creeping down the long, silent street 'like a frightened girl'.[448] My favourite among the longer poems was 'The Sphinx'. I greatly admired its clever internal rhymes, its exotic imagery, and its rich vocabulary.

Next there came *An Ideal Husband*,[449] which I saw in a war-time production, and *The Picture of Dorian Gray*.[450] I have always regarded the latter as a highly moral work, illustrating as it does the truth that conduct affects character, and that a morally ugly life creates a morally ugly soul and vice versa. Wilde nonetheless prefaces *The Picture of Dorian Gray* with a series of aphorisms some of which appear to subvert morality. Among them are 'All art is quite useless' and the no less provocative 'There is no such thing as a moral or an immoral book. Books are well written, or badly written. That is all.' In all Wilde's work there is, in fact, an element of 'reversal of values' that makes him, in this respect at least, a link between Blake and Nietzsche. Later in life I read and re-read Wilde's essays, especially *The Soul of Man under Socialism* (a very Wildean Socialism), *The Importance of Masks*, and *The Decay of Lying*.[451] They were of importance to me at a time when I was giving such lectures as 'The Individual, the Group, and the Spiritual Community',[452] and coining aphorisms like 'Better a live sinner than a dead saint', 'One should not waste time helping the weak. Nowadays it is the strong who need help', and 'I am much worse than people think I am, and also much better.' Around this time I also read Wilde's *De Profundis*, an incomplete edition of which I had read in my teens without being able to understand what it was all about. It is a long, bitter, and recriminatory letter to Lord Alfred Douglas, his lover, and he wrote it while in prison serving a two-year sentence, with hard labour, for what was then the crime of homosexuality.[453]

In 1895, the year of Wilde's trial, David Herbert Lawrence was ten years old. He died in 1930 at the age of 44. Though his life was a comparatively short one it was packed with creative activity in a variety of genres. Besides the famous novels, from *The White Peacock* to the three versions of *Lady Chatterley's Lover*,[454] there poured from him a stream of short stories, novellas, essays and articles, plays, travelogues, critical studies, book reviews, and letters, not to mention colourful paintings. In the latter part of his life Lawrence was a great traveller, despite his poor health moving from country to country and eventually travelling round the world. He wanted not only to get away from England, which he both loved and hated, but hoped to find, or found, a community of like-minded people dedicated to fostering new shoots of life within themselves. His nomadic lifestyle did not interfere with his writing, and often provided him with fresh material. He seems never to have suffered from writer's block, and provided he had paper and pen (or pencil) he could settle down and write wherever he found himself. One of the places in which he found himself was Taos, in New Mexico, and it was in Taos that I first met Lawrence, so to speak. The book that brought us together was Mabel Dodge Luhan's *Lorenzo in Taos*[455] (borrowed, inevitably, from the Tooting Public Library). It was not the best introduction to Lawrence the man, any more than *The Rainbow* was the best introduction to Lawrence's own writings. But be that as it may, as I have testified elsewhere, *The Rainbow* struck me with the force of an emotional revelation, and I at once started work on a novel of my own.[456] I completed it in the autumn of 1943, shortly before receiving my call-up papers. Thereafter I returned to books by Lawrence, as well as about him, whenever I had an opportunity, especially in the 1970s and 1980s, when I read or reread everything he had written. Among the novels, *Kangaroo* and *The Plumed Serpent* in particular chimed with me, as did *The Woman Who Rode Away* and *The Man Who Died* among the short stories, while 'The Ship of Death' has long been one of my favourite poems.[457] I always enjoyed Lawrence's lively and sensitive style, whatever the genre in which he wrote. If it could be said of Oliver Goldsmith that he touched nothing that he did not adorn,[458] it could be said of Lawrence that he touched nothing that he did not bring to life.

I am conscious that I have not done justice to the genius of my five literary heroes. I have not even done justice to my feeling for them or to the influence they have had upon me. I would have liked to write a full-length study on each of them, but other activities, perhaps more important ones, have left no room for this. All I have been able to do in this connection is to write a poem in which I briefly describe each of the major works of Dr Johnson,[459] an article on 'Buddhism and William Blake',[460] and a book review on a biography of Lawrence entitled 'D. H. Lawrence and the Spiritual Community'.[461] I am also aware that my literary heroes are all men and that I do not have a single literary heroine. This certainly does not mean that I do not admire and enjoy the poetry of Christina Rossetti or the novels of Jane Austen, the Brontë sisters, Mrs Gaskell, and George Eliot. It only means that they are not literary heroes in the sense in which I am using the term. I do, however, have three heroines of another kind. The first of these is Elizabeth I (1533–1603), celebrated by the poets of her time as 'Gloriana' and the 'Faerie Queen', who has always been my favourite historical character. The second is Florence Nightingale (1820–1910), the legendary 'Lady with the Lamp', the founder of nursing as a profession, whose biography by Cecil Woodham-Smith I read in my twenties.[462] The third is Edith Cavell (1865–1915), who was matron, or head nurse, at a hospital in occupied Belgium during the First World War. She secretly helped wounded Allied soldiers to escape, and for this she was court-martialled by the Germans and executed by firing squad. There is a statue of her in the heart of London, opposite the entrance to the National Portrait Gallery. On the base of the statue are words which, while they may not have been her last, were certainly among her last: 'Patriotism is not enough. I must have no hatred or bitterness towards anyone.' Edith Cavell was eventually buried in the grounds of Norwich Cathedral, and I remember being taken to see her grave as a boy.

THE LANGUAGE OF SCENTS

On returning from church on Sunday mornings I would go straight to the kitchen, where I would usually find my mother putting the finishing touches to the Sunday lunch. More often than not, there would be a batch of cakes fresh from the oven. Sometimes it was rock cakes, sometimes coconut pyramids. When it was rock cakes my mother would burn two or three of them, for I was particularly fond of the taste of burnt cake, a predilection which continues down to the present day. I was also fond of the smell of coal, and from time to time I would open the door of the coal bunker, put my head inside, and stand inhaling the dusty fragrance with deep breaths. Another favourite smell was that of roasting coffee beans. As we did not have coffee at home, I experienced this pleasure only when I happened to pass a certain shop in the Tooting Bec High Street. My nostrils would respond to the rich, warm aroma long before I came abreast of the shop, in whose window a coffee mill would be perpetually grinding the roasted beans. I was then 12 or 13. Even now, though I am not a coffee drinker, I can enjoy the smell of freshly ground coffee. Whether suddenly caught in a crowded restaurant, or slowly inhaled after sharing a meal with coffee drinking friends, that unique aroma can give rise to all kinds of associations, just as the scent of the famous madeleine was responsible for Proust's 'remembrance of things past'.[465] More often than not, I would float on cloud upon cloud of recollection to South India, where I spent 1947 and 1948, and where I used to hear just before dawn the *clunk clunk* of stone on stone as the housewife pounded roasted beans for the morning coffee.

During much of my time there I stayed at the haunted ashram in Muvattupuzha with my Bengali friend Buddharakshita (then known as Satyapriya), whom I had first met in Singapore, with whom I had teamed up in Calcutta, and with whom I had 'gone forth' from home into the homeless life in Kasauli in 1947. Buddharakshita had many sterling qualities, but as readers of *The Rainbow Road* will know he was possessed of a vile temper, or rather there were times when a vile temper possessed him.[464] This demon of ungovernable rage would possess him whenever he thought – often mistakenly – that he was being slighted, or looked down on, or treated as an inferior. His fury would then know no bounds and might even lead to an act of violence, an act of which he would afterwards feel deeply ashamed and for which he would apologize profusely. Over the years I have often wondered why my old friend was cursed with such a temper, and what it was that made him so quick to take offence. Perhaps there was a clue in the way he had been brought up. I knew that he came from a Brahmin family, and that even as a very small child he had been – according to his own gleeful admission – unruly and disobedient in the extreme. I also knew that as a boy he had been highly competitive, for he had more than once regaled me with stories of how he had always come first at this or that sport or taken the lead in this or that activity. Evidently the young Buddharakshita, like the Buddharakshita I knew, always had to be on top. Thus when he went to see his family in rural Bengal after being ordained as a *bhikkhu* in Ceylon (now Sri Lanka) he had given them an ultimatum. Either all his elder brothers and his mother (his father was long dead) must bow down before him in the traditional Buddhist manner or they would never see him again. They had all bowed down, he told me triumphantly. I was not surprised to hear this. It had so happened that I had been ordained as a *bhikkhu* before him, which meant that according to monastic custom he was junior to me and therefore had to bow down before me.[465] When we met for the first time after our respective ordinations, however, he told me, with an embarrassed laugh, that he would not be bowing down before me as we were friends. I said nothing, but I knew quite well that if he had been the senior his attitude would have been very different.

But the smell of coffee – to return to my original theme – was not the only smell for which I remembered South India. There was also the smell of coconut oil. The housewife cooked with coconut oil, young men drenched their hair in it just as I had once plastered mine with Brylcreem, and it filled the lamps in the temples and in homes that were without electricity. From coffee-drinking South India the clouds of recollection carry me to *cha*-drinking North India. There the cooking medium was not coconut oil but mustard oil. This was certainly the case in crowded, insanitary Calcutta, to which in the 1950s and 1960s I was a fairly regular visitor. As darkness fell, smoke arose from innumerable cooking fires, and the air would be filled with the acrid smell of mustard oil as the Calcutta housewife fried not only vegetables but fish, of which the Bengalis were passionately fond. Not that all the smells of North India were unpleasant. In the foothills of the eastern Himalayas, 300 miles north of Calcutta, was the little town of Kalimpong, where I lived for fourteen years. There I became familiar with the fresh, purifying smell of the juniper, masses of which were burned by the town's Tibetan Buddhists in connection with their religious observances. Juniper also entered into the composition of Tibetan incense, along with a variety of Himalayan herbs. I liked to burn a stick of Tibetan incense in the morning and a stick of the much sweeter Indian incense in the evening. The effect of the one was stimulating, I found; that of the other, calming. In Kalimpong I also became familiar with the seductive fragrance of the gardenia. I had no gardenias in my own garden, but on the day of the Vaiśākha full moon, when I celebrated the anniversary of the Buddha's attainment of supreme perfect Enlightenment, Princess Irene of Greece, who lived further up the hillside, would send down to me a huge wicker basket filled to the brim with the velvety white blossoms for the decorating of the shrine-room.[466] Not that I was always in Kalimpong, which was perhaps more my headquarters than my home. During the winter months I usually travelled in the plains, criss-crossing the northern and central parts of India by train, bus, and bullock cart. The clouds of recollection now bring to me the intensely sweet perfume of a tiny red rose. I first inhaled this perfume in Rajasthan, when I saw small baskets of the flowers being offered at the shrine of a *pir* or Muslim saint. Later I breathed in the same perfume in Maharashtra, where Buddhist friends would offer me a posy of the little red flowers when I gave a lecture or officiated at a ceremony.

The clouds of recollection also bring to me, from that time, the scent of the thin sticks of incense that burned in the houses I visited, or to which I was invited for lunch. Sometimes the scent was that of white sandalwood, delicate and purifying; but more often it was the strong, sickly sweetness of the cheaper kind of incense, which owed its sweetness to chemicals rather than herbs. The lighting of a stick of incense was one of the ways in which the Indian householder traditionally received an honoured guest. On his arrival the guest would be given water with which to wash his feet, then water to drink, and a garland of sweet-smelling flowers would be placed round his neck. He would then be conducted to the seat of honour, an oil lamp lit and a stick of incense burned to drive away the flies and mosquitoes. Finally, the guest would be served a meal, after which he would be sprinkled with rosewater and entertained with song and instrumental music by the daughters of the house, all dressed in their best. In the Mahāyāna these simple acts of hospitality were transformed into a set of seven (or eight) ritual offerings to the Buddha, the guest of all guests, who appears to us as it were from another dimension – the dimension of the Transcendental. On Tibetan Buddhist shrines these offerings are represented by a row of small bowls. Normally the bowls are filled with water, the water being changed each day. On special occasions one bowl is replaced by a lighted lamp, another filled with scented water, the remaining three (or four) being filled with rice. The bowls of rice are topped, respectively, by a flower, a stick of incense, a ripe fruit, and a pair of finger cymbals, though when there are seven bowls the cymbals are placed beside the last bowl. Incense of one kind or another has in fact been used in religious worship since the earliest times, and by faiths widely separated in time and space. It was certainly used by the ancient Egyptians. According to Plutarch, in the temples of Egypt frankincense was burned in the morning, myrrh at noon, and *kifr* (also spelled *kyphir*), a compound of various herbs and resins, in the evening. Moreover, certain gods were associated with specific types of incense. For example, Hathor, who was the goddess of Love as well as of War, was strongly associated with myrrh.[467] The ancient Greeks, too, associated certain gods with specific types of incense. Thus in the 'Orphic' hymns the chanting of the hymn to Zeus is to be accompanied by 'the fumigation from borax' (Thomas Taylor's translation), that to Hermes by 'the fumigation from frankincense', and that to the Muses by 'the fumigation from myrrh'. To the modern ear the word 'fumigation' is suggestive of the sickroom and the beehive, but to the Egyptians and Greeks, and the other peoples of antiquity, it meant something very different. It meant the cleansing and purifying not just of the atmosphere we breathe but the 'psychic' atmosphere in which we live as spiritual beings. If *this* atmosphere is sufficiently pure the gods would be more likely to come near and the worshipper be more likely to feel their presence. The burning of incense was thus an essential part of religious worship.

In 1964 I returned to England, where for the next five or six years I lived in London. The smells that the clouds of recollection now bring to me from this juncture are not of the pleasantest kind. The predominant smell is that of petrol, a smell occasionally overpowered by the stronger smell of frying fish and chips. I did not then reacquaint myself with the smells of English flowers, though I had arrived at the height of summer and the little front gardens were bright with flowers of every hue. Later, when I once more had a shrine, my nostrils were again pleasantly tickled by the smell of incense, usually of the Indian sandalwood variety. Later still, when I was living on Highgate West Hill, not far from where the much diminished Coleridge had spent his last days,[468] I used to hold what I called incense-burning parties. By this time I was familiar with many different types of incense. There was the sweet Indian incense of both the inferior and superior kind. It came in thin black sticks, which sometimes were so flexible that they would bend. This was the first kind of incense I ever bought. When I was about eleven or twelve years old I bought a few sticks of it (at a penny a stick) from a little shop in Brighton, along with a small glass Buddha of Japanese manufacture. Then there was Tibetan incense. This, too, came in sticks, though the sticks were not only reddish brown in colour but longer and thicker than their Indian counterparts. Wherever they had been made, whether in a monastery in Tibet or at a Tibetan refugee settlement in India, when lit they gave off the same healthful, invigorating scent as the incense I was accustomed to use in Kalimpong. Chinese incense was less interesting than either the Indian or the Tibetan variety. The sticks came in bright red packets, and were sand-coloured, and they gave off a smell rather like that of burning sawdust. Chinese incense was in fact of an austere, 'Confucian' character, and unlike its Indian cousin it made no concessions to sensuous enjoyment. Thai incense, too, had a woody smell, but the smell was mixed with a touch of sweetness. The sticks in which it came were remarkable in that each of them broadened at the top end into an inverted cone. Finally, there was Japanese incense, which came in short thin sticks of different colours and had a fragrance like that of women's face powder, so that it was redolent more of the boudoir than the shrine. If Tibetan incense was masculine, then Japanese incense was decidedly feminine. Thus we had many types of incense with which to experiment at our incense-burning parties. These gatherings started at about seven in the evening and generally went on until midnight. The eight or nine people who came to them were friends I had made since my arrival in England a few years earlier. They were all young people, nearly half of them being students at a well-known art school. Sessions began with the burning of a single type of incense, and we all sat around inhaling the aroma and chatting quietly. At the very centre of things was blonde, beautiful Louie in her long green dress who officiated as priestess, so to speak, and who remained in contact with me much longer than any other member of the group.[469] Every now and then a different type of incense was burned, so that smoke mingled with smoke and scent with scent. At one time we burned different types of incense together, at another we burned them in a certain order, in each case noting the particular way in which we were affected. As the evening progressed, the atmosphere in the room changed, there would be a kind of quiver in the air, and we would feel less and less inclined to talk. Whether because of the order in which the different types of incense had been burned, or because of the cumulative effect of the various odours of the various aromas we had inhaled, by the end of the evening we would find ourselves in a state of altered consciousness that was both individual and collective. In the hippy jargon of those days we were 'stoned'.

It was at about this time that I had my first experience of LSD. I have written elsewhere about the second time I took it,[470] and perhaps the time has now come for me to record the little that I remember of that first occasion. I took LSD together with my young American friend and flatmate Carter, whom I had befriended when he was in deep disgrace with some of my other friends.[471] He had taken LSD some seven or eight times, but the trips had all been bad ones, and he was convinced that if he and I dropped 'acid' together he would at last have a good trip. I agreed that we should do this, whereupon he obtained from a contact in California (by post!) a few tablets of what was guaranteed, he said, to be one hundred percent pure LSD. The trip lasted for about twelve hours. I had intended to record the effects of the LSD as it took hold, but this proved not to be feasible. All I could write was 'feel as though little fish were nibbling at my brain', followed by the single word 'laughter'. I was, in fact, laughing uncontrollably, and the laughter was releasing huge quantities of energy. After that, there were only squiggles on the paper. The entire trip is virtually a blank to me. All that I could remember of it, even immediately afterwards, was of my being present at the dawn of creation. 'First light on first water' were the words that came to me, accompanied by the visual image of a vast expanse of water upon which a light was shining. The experience was not a spiritual one, strictly speaking, but neither was it psychological in the narrow sense of the term. Perhaps it is best described as 'cosmic'. Whatever it was that had happened during those twelve hours, I was well satisfied with my first experience of LSD, though it left me feeling physically and mentally tired. Carter, for his part, was greatly relieved at having had a good trip, even though nothing remarkable had happened.

It was about this time, too, that Carter and I were in the habit of smoking cannabis in a secluded corner of Parliament Hill Fields, which lay only a stone's throw from my flat on the way to Kenwood House.[472] It was high summer, and we lay on our backs in the long grass feeling the warmth of the sun on our bodies. The cannabis gave me a delightful, floating sensation. I was floating through the air, floating with the white clouds – floating, floating. At the same time, strange to say, I had the feeling that I was not moving at all! Though I smoked a good deal of cannabis that summer, I was in no danger of getting hooked, and when Carter returned to his native California I gave up the habit for good and have not been tempted since.

Years later, when even Louie was no longer in touch with me, I took to burning frankincense and myrrh, as well as *kifr* allegedly made in accordance with a recipe that had been found in an ancient Egyptian papyrus. I obtained them by post from an agency which catered for the ritual needs of witches and warlocks, together with a supply of the thick charcoal discs on which they could be safely burned. The odours of the frankincense and the myrrh, though not the *kifr*, were much stronger and more distinctive than those of the different incenses that had been burned at my incense-burning parties. Each odour communicated something. It had a *meaning*. That is to say there is an olfactory language of smells and scents, just as there is a visual language of form and colour and an aural language of sound. Dogs, for example, understand this olfactory language, at least on their own level of intelligence, while human beings are acquainted with it only to a very limited extent. We can distinguish between different perfumes, we can recognize the food in front of us by its smell, and we can tell whether another person is sick or well, and what kind of emotional state they are in, by their body odour; but that is about all. Evidently we have a lot to learn in this area. In any case, even if we succeed in developing a sense of smell as keen as that of a dog, that is still a long way from our being able to understand the meaning of scents, as distinct from understanding the associations to which they give rise. The *Vimalakīrti-nirdeśa*, an important Mahāyāna scripture, appears to envisage the possibility of human beings being able to do this. It speaks of a world in which everything is made of fragrances and in which Fragrance-Accumulated, the Buddha of that land, communicates the Dharma by means of fragrance. As a bodhisattva from that land tells Vimalakīrti, the eponymous hero of the scripture,

> The Thus Come One in our land does not employ words in his exposition. He just uses various fragrances to induce heavenly and human beings to undertake the observance of the precepts.[473]

Another important work, *The Awakening of Faith in the Mahāyāna*, uses the image of perfume and what it terms 'perfuming' to elucidate a serious problem. This problem arises out of the fact that the leading of the spiritual life involves, by its very nature, the positing of a dichotomy between *saṃsāra* and Nirvāṇa, the conditioned and the Unconditioned. How, then, shall a mortal attain the Immortal State, or a conditioned being achieve the Unconditioned? That is the question. According to *The Awakening of Faith in the Mahāyāna*, just as our worldly clothes have no scent of their own but can acquire one, so our worldly, saṃsāric mind is perfumed by Suchness (a Mahāyāna term for the Unconditioned), and it is because they are perfumed by Suchness that sentient beings, though defiled by greed, hatred, and delusion, are able to aspire to the attainment of Enlightenment.[474] In other words, the dichotomy is not absolute, but can be transcended.

AND ON HIS DULCIMER HE PLAYED

I have sometimes been asked if I had any regrets as I looked back over my life. To this I usually replied that I wished I had learned to play a musical instrument, either the harpsichord or the organ, or perhaps the sitar. Reflecting on this recently I realized that my usual reply to the question of whether I had any regrets was misleading, implying as it did that I had never learned to play as much as a tin whistle. The fact is that I *did* once play an instrument. When I was eight or nine, and confined to bed with alleged heart disease, I was given a shiny black dulcimer, with a hole in the middle and wires that could be tightened by turning a screw, and on this dulcimer, like the Abyssinian maid in *Kubla Khan*, I played, picking out tunes – or at least sequences of notes – with a little hammer. This could not have been my first experience of music. I have vague recollections of sitting on the floor near my mother as she played the piano. All her brothers and sisters played the piano and they may well have learned to play on this very instrument, for it was the old family piano which on the death of her father had passed to Auntie Kate,[475] my mother's eldest sister, and from her to my mother. She did not have it for long. When I was four or five it disappeared, most likely passing into the keeping of Uncle Jack, my mother's youngest brother but one, who lived not far from us.

Looking back at what I have just written, it occurs to me that the dulcimer was not the only musical instrument on which I learned to play. There was, in fact, another instrument, on which I learned to play very early in life, on which I have played regularly ever since, and which only recently has begun to show signs of wear and tear. This instrument is my own voice. I do not remember my mother ever singing to me, or teaching me any songs; but what I did not learn at home I certainly learned at what was then called Infant School, which I started attending (at first very unwillingly) when I was 4. There, together with the other children of my own age, I learned to sing a number of songs, of varying quality as to both words and music. These included 'Sweet and Low', which was a setting of a poem by Tennyson,[476] the rather mawkish 'Away in a Manger', which was really a hymn,[477] and a song from which we learned how the violet acquired its name and which involves angels. It consisted of only four lines, and ran:

She came one day from a sky of blue,
And angels found her beneath the dew.
They said, 'Little one, your eyes are wet,'
And so they called her Violet.

I could not understand why the angels had called her Violet because her eyes were wet rather than because she came from a sky of blue. However, as a child I was a quite fond of this song, and used to give solo performances of it, until my voice broke, at family gatherings. When I came to the word 'Violet', it was my custom to end the word on as high a note as I could manage, which usually earned me a round of indulgent applause. It was also at Infant School, I think, that I first sang 'O God, our help in ages past'. I certainly have vivid memories of singing it at Junior School, which I started attending after the conclusion of my long period of confinement to bed and wheelchair. The famous old hymn was usually sung at morning assembly, as well as on special occasions such as Empire Day, and the sound of three hundred or more youthful voices raised in the mournful, dirge-like tune that, for me, is inseparable from the words, rings still in my ears. Not that I ever forgot the words of the hymn, especially the solemn ones that remind us of the fleeting, dreamlike nature of human life.

Time, like an ever-rolling stream,
Bears all its sons away;
They fly, forgotten, as a dream
Dies at the opening day.[478]

Far from my forgetting them, the words remained deeply imprinted on my consciousness, there to blend, years later, with the *Diamond Sūtra*'s teaching of the transitoriness of all conditioned things. I was still in Junior School when it put on a performance of *The Pirates of Penzance*, all the parts being taken by the children themselves.[479] I was cast as a pirate and with my fellow pirates sang 'Let's vary piracy-ee with a little burglary' to a catchy tune that was to remain with me for the rest of my life. All the tunes were catchy, and none more so than 'Poor Wandering One', the lovely aria sung at one of the high points of the action by Mabel, the opera's noble heroine. In Senior School, to which I was promoted when I was twelve or thirteen, we had a proper music teacher. He should rightly have been called our *singing* teacher, for there was no question of any of us being taught to play a musical instrument. Not that he did not give us the beginning of a musical education. Tall and portly, Mr Scheu had a pale face and black hair parted down the middle. He was German, a convinced Nazi, and an excellent teacher, who threw himself into his work with an energy and enthusiasm that succeeded in arousing the interest of even the dullest and most backward members of the class. Besides greatly improving our singing, he taught us a wide variety of songs, from traditional English ballads and rounds to Handel arias. He also prepared us for our first orchestral concert, which took place at the Methodist Central Hall, Tooting Broadway, in front of an audience of children drawn from all the schools in the district. The principal item on the programme was Mendelssohn's overture *The Hebrides*,[480] and in the course of the weeks preceding the concert Mr Scheu took us through the piece almost bar by bar, playing as much of it as he could on the piano, and telling us what to look out for on the day. Although this was my first *live* orchestral concert, I had certainly heard orchestral music before. My father possessed a small collection of gramophone records, prominent among which was Gershwin's *Rhapsody in Blue*.[481] I was very fond of this work, which I had nicknamed 'The Aeroplane', from the way in which the solo clarinet soared up into the sky, as it were.

By the time the Central Hall concert took place there had been a major change in the external circumstances of my life. The family had moved from the upstairs flat where I had been obliged to spend so much time in bed to a semi-detached council house on the other side of Tooting. We now had a very much bigger garden, an indoor toilet, a proper bath, and constant hot water. The change meant that I had a longer walk to school, which I did not mind. It also meant that I could join the local unit of the Boys' Brigade, which for the next four years was to play an important part in my life.[482] On Sunday mornings we gathered for an hour of prayer, hymn-singing, and exhortation by the unit's 'captain'. Our favourite hymn was a suitably martial one.

Onward Christian soldiers
Marching as to war,
With the cross of Jesus
Going on before....
Hell's foundations tremble
At the shout of praise.
Brothers, lift your voices,
Loud your anthems raise!

We indeed lifted our voices with a will, which it was all the more easy for us to do inasmuch as the tune to which these rousing words were sung was a march, with a steady beat, like that of a victorious army.[483] But there was one change that affected me even more deeply, and for much longer, than my joining the Boys' Brigade. This was the fact that the family now had a wireless set. Before long I was spending as many evenings as I could on my own in the sitting room, listening to the wireless. Though I enjoyed the popular songs of the day (or at least some of them), I 'listened in' only to classical music, which meant that I was a devotee of the Third Programme, as I think it was called. For me at that time classical music meant orchestral music, and orchestral music meant either overtures (Beethoven, Mozart, Weber) or symphonies (Beethoven, Mozart, Haydn). My favourite composer was Beethoven. I was passionately fond of *all* his symphonies (except the Ninth, which I do not remember hearing at that time), as well as of the *Egmont* and *Coriolanus* overtures and *Leonora* no. 3. They thrilled and excited me, rousing my emotions to fever pitch, and carrying me out of myself on a wave of ecstasy that seemed to touch the heavens. Mozart was hardly less of a favourite than Beethoven, though he affected me differently. Of his symphonies, it was the last three, especially no. 39 in E-flat, that gave me the most intense pleasure, a pleasure that was so intense as to be almost painful. Haydn's works were played less frequently than those of Beethoven or Mozart, I think, but I always enjoyed them, and came to love the 'Hen' and the 'Clock' symphonies. In the course of my months and years of 'listening in' I noticed that as well as the staple symphonies and overtures there were certain works that were played again and again. They included Bach's *Brandenburg Concerto* no. 3 (it was always no. 3), Debussy's *Prélude à l'après – midi d'un faune*, Delius's *On Hearing the First Cuckoo in Spring* (it was played all the year round), and Sinding's *Rustle of Spring*, which I must have heard a dozen times then, but have not heard since.[484]

In the middle of 1940 I was evacuated to Devonshire, the Second World War having started the previous year with Hitler's invasion of Poland. This naturally brought my musical evenings to an abrupt end. On my return to London the following year, however, I at once restarted them and they continued to be an important part of my life for the next two years and more. But although I was as passionately fond of music as ever, music now had serious rivals for my time, my energy, and my emotional investment. The most dangerous of these rivals, at least until I discovered Buddhism and realized I was a Buddhist, was poetry, of which I was hardly less fond than I was of music, and which I had been writing for a number of years. Sometimes the two passions clashed, sometimes they cooperated, as when I put into the mouth of Beethoven a blank verse monologue in which he expostulated with Goethe for what he considered his servility to princes,[485] and also when I wrote a series of stanzas modelled on Baudelaire's *Les Phares*.[486] Whereas Baudelaire had written about the great painters, I wrote about the great composers. The poem has not survived, but fragments of it still linger in my memory. The stanza on Beethoven began, perhaps predictably, 'Beethoven, blast of hurricane and storm', and I assume I must have gone on to mention his more tender side. 'Bach, endless time where echoes cease to be' and 'Lost in the gulf of that immensity/ Wherein he adumbrates the source of things' are all I can remember of the stanza devoted to Bach. The grandiloquent nature of the language suggests that when I wrote it I had in mind the *Toccata and Fugue in D minor*, my first encounter with which was probably the greatest single musical experience of my life.[487] The stanza devoted to Mozart, unlike the stanzas on any of the other great composers, has survived in my memory complete. It ran:

Mozart, an elegant despairing mien,
Poised like a skater in the evening shade
That trembling falls on some rococo queen
Sighing in palaces of purest jade.

Strictly speaking, this is nonsense. At the same time, it does give an idea of the kind of impression Mozart's music made on me at that time. It was *elegant*, and it was *poised*, in that it had perfect balance and control. It was also *rococo*, by which I meant that it was light and airy, without the least trace of dullness or heaviness. *Queen* and *palaces* suggested refinement and aristocracy, as did *jade*, though it was an aristocracy not of birth but of the mind. As for *despairing, evening shade*, and *sighing*, they reflected my feeling that running through much of Mozart's music there was a vein of melancholy. My characterization of Mozart in this stanza, written when I was sixteen or seventeen, is probably rather one-sided, but it shows how carefully I listened to him and the other great composers. In 1943, when I was eighteen, I was conscripted, and once again my musical evenings came to an abrupt end, as did many other things that were important to me. Only twice in the course of the next four years did I have an opportunity of imbibing a few drops of what Byron once called 'the brandy of the damned'.[488] The first time this happened I was in India, to which the Signals unit to which I belonged had been sent a year after my conscription. Having spent the evening in Delhi, I was walking the last few hundred yards back to camp through the darkness, the stars brilliant overhead, when there came to me from somewhere in the distance, through the stillness and silence of the night, the familiar sound of the slow movement from Mozart's *Eine Kleine Nachtmusik*. It was a magical moment. The second time it happened I was in Singapore, to which my unit had been posted shortly after VJ Day,[489] and it happened when I saw Walt Disney's *Fantasia*. Once again I heard old favourites like Bach's *Toccata and Fugue in D Minor*, Beethoven's *Pastoral Symphony*, and Schubert's *Ave Maria*, only this time I heard them as orchestrated by Leopold Stokowski and as illustrated, in the case of the three compositions I have mentioned, by Disney's undulating railway track, dancing centaurettes, and upward-soaring Gothic arches.[490]

Early in 1947 I left Singapore for India, where for the next seventeen years I was occupied with the study, practice, and realization of the

Dharma, at first as a freelance wandering ascetic, then as an ordained Buddhist monk. In 1964 I returned to England and took up residence at the Hampstead Buddhist Vihara, where I lived for the next two years. I held meditation classes at the Vihara, and gave lectures there and at other venues. One of these lectures was on 'Buddhism and the Problem of Death', and at the end of it I was approached by a tall, well-dressed young man who said he wanted to tell me something. Thereafter he came regularly to my lectures, visited me at the Vihara, and started giving me lifts to my engagements in and around London in his VW. The young man's name was Terry Delamare, and it was in this way that there developed between us what was to be one of the most important friendships of my life. Terry had a flat near the Vihara, and soon I was spending time with him there. Besides talking (we had a lot to say to each other), we listened to records on Terry's record player. We had much the same musical tastes, our favourite records being those of the Mozart and Haydn symphonies and of Elgar's *Enigma Variations*, all of which we played over and over again. Unfortunately, Terry had long been the victim of chronic depression, and although he accompanied me on my 1966–7 'farewell' visit to India the change of scene gave him no relief from his suffering, as we had hoped it would. He killed himself on 14 April 1969, four years after our first meeting, as I have related in *Moving Against the Stream*. Shortly before Terry's death I had started a new Buddhist movement in London, so that for the next few decades I had little time for the enjoyment of music. Not that music was entirely banished from my life, or that I had lost the capacity to enjoy it. Indeed, as our new Buddhist movement spread I was often away on tour, which meant that I was sometimes able to attend operas and concerts in cities other than my native London. Thus over the years I saw an *avant garde* production of Handel's *Giulio Cesare* in Düsseldorf,[491] heard a brilliant performance of Vivaldi's *The Four Seasons* in Prague, and heard a suitably solid performance of Brahms' *German Requiem* in Berlin. In more recent years, when I have done little or no travelling, CDs and Radio 3 have made it possible for me to explore the whole heritage of Western music, from Thomas Tallis and Palestrina to Prokoviev and Philip Glass. This exploration has enabled me to deepen my appreciation of old favourites like Bach, Beethoven, and Mozart, as well as to discover new favourites, like Sibelius and Richard Strauss. One of Strauss's shorter works has in fact come to have a special significance for me. This work is his *Four Last Songs*, especially the fourth song, 'Sunset'. I am now at the sunset of my life, and friends have asked me what kind of funeral I would like to have. Though I have no strong preference in this connection, I would like music to have a part in my obsequies. I would like Jeremiah Clarke's *Trumpet Voluntary* (version with kettledrum) to be played at my cremation or burial and Strauss's 'Sunset', preferably as sung in German by Elisabeth Schwarzkopf, to be played at whatever memorial service is held afterwards. If my consciousness is hovering round, I shall certainly listen.[492]

III: LOOKING BACK

THE SEARCH

One bright, sunny morning in the middle of June 2010, Paramartha and I left Madhyamaloka for Ipswich, with Paramartha at the wheel. Our journey had a double objective. We were to visit the Ipswich Buddhist Centre,[493] where I was to give a talk, as well as meet members of the local sangha, and we were to search for traces of my Lingwood ancestors, who we knew came from that part of Suffolk. On the way we visited Bury St Edmunds, a place I had not seen before, where we spent a couple of hours looking round the cathedral, and where we had lunch in the cathedral refectory. From Bury we drove straight to Ipswich, and soon we were being warmly greeted by Swadipa and Carol, with whom we were to stay.[494] In the evening, after I had rested, Ḥarshaprabha, an old friend of ours, took us out to a quiet Italian restaurant for dinner.[495] After the meal he drove us round the town, of which we had not seen much during our visit the previous year. We saw the marina, where I was astonished by the enormous number of dinghies and other boats, the docks, and an early Norman Foster building – a controversial one, according to Harshaprabha.[496] We also saw, on a house in the old part of the town, a plaque that informed us that the house opposite was the birthplace of the great Cardinal Wolsey, Ipswich's most famous son.[497]

After breakfast the following day Paramartha and I set out for Felixstowe, which before the war was a popular holiday resort. The reason for our going there was that I very much wanted to see the sea, a pleasure I had not had for some time. As the product of an island race I was very conscious of the sea, and as all my ancestors on the spear side were from Suffolk I was particularly conscious of the North Sea. Indeed, since I first encountered it in my teens in Kate Freiligrath Kroeker's translation, Heine's cycle 'The North Sea' has been one of my favourite longer poems.[498] Be that as it may, there we were on the deserted beach that morning, Paramartha and I. Except for the wind, it was a perfect June day. The sun was bright, the sky without a cloud. I walked down the sand to within a few feet of the white surf, and stood there looking out over the rollers to the distant horizon, where the Prussian blue of the sea met the eggshell blue of the sky.

From Felixstowe we drove to Battisford. Thanks to the Internet, Paramartha had discovered that my great-grandfather Edward Lingwood was born in Battisford in 1828, and in the absence of other clues we had decided that it was in Battisford that we would begin our search for traces of my Lingwood ancestors. The village was rather scattered, and we had to drive round for a while before finding the lane that led to the parish church. It was built of flints, like so many Suffolk churches, had a quaint belfry-like structure at one end instead of the more usual round tower, and was dedicated to St Mary. Finding the door unlocked, we entered and spent the next fifteen or twenty minutes looking round the church's well-lit interior. There was a memorial tablet on one of the walls, and there were red heraldic shields in two of the windows, but these did not relate to any member of the Lingwood family, though it was more than likely that my great-grandfather was baptized in the ancient stone font. We therefore continued our search in the graveyard. It was overgrown with grass and weeds, and the graves were not in neat rows, as in a modern municipal cemetery, but scattered, as if whenever a new grave was needed the sexton simply dug it wherever there was an unoccupied space. Moreover, the ground was very uneven, so that I had to tread carefully. This meant that soon Paramartha was not only ahead of me but out of sight round the other side of the building. I paused, and stood in the hot sun surveying the scene. Before long Paramartha was back. He had found something, he said quietly with a broad smile. I followed him as quickly as I could to the back of the church. Close to the wall there was a grave with a small double headstone. The inscriptions on all the other headstones we had seen were illegible, as the soft sandstone had weathered over the years, but the inscription on the double headstone could be read quite easily, probably because the grave was protected by the wall. Two children were buried there. One was Arthur, who was born in 1841 and died the same year, aged only a few months; the other was Elizabeth, who was born in 1840 and died in 1849. They were the children of Edward and Sarah Lingwood, the headstone said, which meant that they were my great-grandfather's brother and sister.

We left Battisford well pleased with the start we had made. It was more than we had dared hope for from the first day of our search. We had not driven for more than half a mile along the road out of the village, a road bordered on both sides by trees in the full glory of their summer leafage, when Paramartha suddenly slowed down, then stopped. He had seen on the other side of the road, at the entrance to a driveway, a sign that said 'St John's' and the name had jogged his memory. He had come across it while researching my ancestry on the Internet! We therefore parked just inside the driveway, and Paramartha strode up to the house to make enquiries. Minutes later he was talking to whoever it was had come to the door in response to his knock. As he afterwards told me, he had apologized to the lady for disturbing her but explained that he had with him an old gentleman whose family may have had a connection with the house. Naturally she wanted to know the family's name. When he said it was Lingwood she told him that the family had indeed once occupied the house and that she had a box of papers relating to its history. Paramartha hurried back to me with the news, whereupon I walked with him up the driveway and introduced myself to the lady to whom he had spoken, who by this time had emerged from the house. Soon the three of us were seated on chairs under the trees. Her name was Pat Knoch, the woman told us. She was eighty, had lived at the house for some years and it was called St John's because the Knights of St John had occupied the site until the time of the Dissolution of the Monasteries under Henry VIII.[499] The Knights had planted the holm oak under which I was sitting. Having given us this information and more besides, she went back into the house to fetch what she called her Lingwood box. Paramartha and I 'looked at each other with a wild surmise'.[500] Was providence, or our good karma, about to vouchsafe us the miracle of a breakthrough in our search for traces of my ancestors? When at last the box came we were not disappointed. A cursory inspection showed that it contained wills, personal letters, photographs, obituaries, and other items of interest. A treasure had fallen into our hands. It had fallen into them by accident, or rather by virtue of a whole series of accidents. Had we not been driving along that particular road that morning Paramartha would not have spotted the sign that said 'St John's'. Had his memory not been jogged by the sign we would not have stopped, and he would not have gone up to the house to make enquiries. Had Pat Knoch not been at home at the time, we would not have known of the existence of the Lingwood box. Finally, had Pat Knoch not been of a generous, trusting disposition she would not have allowed us to take away the precious box and photocopy its contents. Indeed, it was clear that she shared in our joy, and was glad to have been of assistance to us in our search.

Paramartha and I had been so absorbed in our fresh discovery that we had forgotten about lunch, and it was only when we were on the road again that we realized we had not yet eaten. Swadipa had recommended the Red Lion, this being the only vegetarian pub in Suffolk, perhaps in all England. As it was situated a little off the beaten track we experienced some difficulty finding it, and eventually we had to pull into the side of the road and phone Swadipa for directions. Though it was mid-week we found the place full, which suggested that vegetarianism had made some headway in Suffolk. We secured a table in a quiet corner, some distance from the bar, and while waiting for our meal dipped into the Lingwood box, which we of course had not left in the car. After the meal, which was a reasonably good one, we drove straight back to Ipswich. I went to my room and rested, as in the evening I would be giving a talk at the Ipswich Buddhist Centre. Paramartha went and had the entire contents of the Lingwood box photocopied. The result was 200 pages of material.[501]

I had opened the new Ipswich Buddhist Centre the previous year, and this time I had been asked to bless the centre's newly completed chapter room.[502] This I did by chanting a few Pāli verses, after which I shared with my closely packed auditors some of my recent reflections. First, though, I spoke of Paramartha's and my search for traces of my Lingwood ancestors and of the remarkable discovery we had made that very day. That search would probably bring us back to Ipswich again, and thus my ties with the local sangha would be further strengthened. I then adverted to the events of the past year, and in particular to the change from 'Western' to 'Triratna' in the nomenclature of our Order.[503] This enabled me to speak on the subject of the Three Jewels, i.e. on the Buddha or Perfectly Enlightened One, the Dharma or body of truths taught by the Buddha, and the Sangha or spiritual community of those practising the Dharma. Usually, I said, the three were enumerated in this order, which was the chronological one, as it were, the Dharma having originated from the Buddha, and the Sangha from the Dharma. But the order could be reversed. There was no Sangha without the Dharma, and no Dharma without the Buddha. It was the Dharma that made the Sangha. Without the united practice of the Dharma by its members the Sangha was no more than an ecclesiastical institution or a social club. I then spoke about the Buddha. It was important that we knew about the life of Śākyamuni, the historical Buddha, for it was ultimately on him that we depended for what knowledge of the Dharma we possessed. The most reliable source of information about that life was the Pāli scriptures. Besides providing us with the earliest account of his teaching, those scriptures tell us a good deal about his personal appearance, his way of life, his manner of teaching, his relations with his disciples, and with a wide variety of other people, from princes to peasants, and from ascetics to well-to-do farmers. We can also get a sense of the Buddha's living presence by going on pilgrimage to the places where he was born, where he gained perfect Enlightenment, where he gave his first teaching, and where he passed into *parinirvāṇa*. This, or something like it, was what I said that evening, though at somewhat greater length. I also answered a few questions.

On our second and last whole day in Suffolk it was dull and overcast. But Paramartha and I did not allow our spirits to be dampened, and after breakfast we left for the village of Barking where my great-great-great-grandfather Edward Lingwood of Eye was buried. He was buried in the parish church of St Mary. His grave was an altar grave, that is to say it was situated immediately in front of the altar. I sat in the car, and Paramartha went to investigate. On his return he reported that the area in front of the altar was carpeted and he had been unable to see whether or not there was a grave underneath. We therefore drove to Battisford, where Paramartha gave back the Lingwood box to Pat Knoch and thanked her for allowing us to photocopy the contents.

Before he left she insisted on his taking photographs of the Victorian flush toilet and of the Maltese cross above the door, the well-known badge of the Knights of St John. The Lingwood box having been returned to its owner as promised, Paramartha and I were soon on our way to Eye, some thirty miles to the north. When we were a few miles from our destination we happened to see a cemetery by the roadside, and as the gates stood wide open we drove in. Just inside the entrance, on the right, there was a small chapel, and beyond it several acres of old graves. While Paramartha went in search of inscriptions I stayed near the car and studied a row of new graves on the left of the path, some of them with bunches of fresh flowers on them. They were all close together, and had small white headstones of what may have been marble. Some graves, I noticed, were very small, so that I wondered if they might hold not a dead body but only a handful of ashes. Paramartha returned from his search to say that he had not found anything of interest. Here, as elsewhere, the headstones were of sandstone, which meant that any inscriptions on them soon became illegible. We therefore resumed our journey north.

Eye was not a village but a town. It dated back to the end of the eleventh century, when William the Conqueror granted the lordship of Eye to William Malet, who built a castle and established a market. Before long there was a flourishing town on the spot. Towards the end of the fourteenth century the church of St Peter and St Paul was built, and it was enlarged a hundred years later, when the hundred-and-one foot tower was added. Both church and tower were built of knapped flints which, glittering in the dull morning light, contrasted well with the dressed stone that had also been used. The building was, in fact, a fine specimen of East Anglian medieval architecture, and testified to the wealth of the town in the middle ages. The interior was no less impressive than the exterior. It had a nave with two side aisles, a high, arched wooden roof, and a wooden rood screen that connected the end pair of pillars. Paramartha and I were not the only visitors and we wandered round looking at the memorials to departed worthies, at the carved woodwork, at the richly coloured and gilded panels depicting various kings and saints, including (as I later discovered) the martyred King Edmund and St Edward the Confessor, and at the very gothic cover of the stone font. There was no sign of the Lingwood name anywhere, and soon we were out of the town and on our way to Brome.

The door of the parish church of St Mary, Brome, was open, but as the sky was still overcast it was dark inside. Paramartha groped his way round the nave to a light switch but the single electric bulb gave only a feeble light and I could see very little. Nonetheless, I managed to make my way to the Cornwallis family tombs, on the other side of which Paramartha was moving about. There must have been four or five tombs all crowded together to the left of the altar. In the gloom it was difficult for me to make out their shadowy forms but I passed my hand over the bare head of the recumbent figure on the tomb nearest, then over the gable peak headdress of the recumbent figure by his side, a headdress that told me that the couple had lived in the early Tudor period. The stone was cold to the touch. I thought of a passage in 'The Eve of St Agnes', in which Keats describes the ancient beadsman and the castle chapel:

> The sculptur'd dead, on each side, seem to freeze,
> Emprison'd in black, purgatorial rails:
> Knights, ladies, praying in dumb orat'ries,
> He passeth by; and his weak spirit fails
> To think how they may ache in icy hoods and mails.[504]

The sky had now cleared, and after the darkness and cold of the church it was pleasant to wander among the crumbling headstones in the warm sunshine, looking for inscriptions that were legible. As usual, Paramartha took the lead in the search, forging ahead, and moving rapidly from one headstone to another. After fifteen or twenty minutes he motioned me to follow him to the back of the church. Side by side, their headstones against the cobbled back wall of the church, there were five coffin-shaped tomb graves. The inscriptions were all quite legible. The graves were those of my great-great-great-great-grandfather Thomas Lingwood of Brome, his wife, and three of their sons. It was very quiet there behind the church. I stood regarding the five graves for a few minutes, then turned away and slowly walked back to the car with Paramartha. The day's search had ended in an important discovery, and it was time for us to leave Brome for Ipswich, the dead for the living, and the past for the world of the twenty-first century.

We were in a mood of quiet satisfaction as we drove back to Ipswich, eating the sandwiches Carol had made for us on the way, and not talking very much. On reaching the town we did not drive straight to Swadipa's and Carol's hospitable home. Instead, we drove through Gainsborough Road, for it was in a house in this road that my great-grandfather Edward

Lingwood of Battisford had spent the last years of his life and we wanted to see what it looked like. As far as we could judge, the houses were all late Victorian, but not having an address we could not tell in which of the houses, if in any, my great-grandfather had lived. In the afternoon, after resting for a couple of hours, I had tea with Srivandana at her flat. Our last evening in Ipswich passed quietly. After dinner with Swadipa and Carol, I spent the rest of the evening in my room, reflecting, while Paramartha had a long talk with Swadipa downstairs.

The following morning was a morning of farewells. Paramartha and I thanked Swadipa and Carol warmly for their hospitality. They assured us that we were welcome to come and stay with them next year and continue our search, which was by no means finished. Torrential rain lashed us on the way back to Birmingham, and we arrived at Madhyamaloka in time for lunch. For me, at least, our three days in Suffolk had been a holiday. I greatly enjoyed driving through the beautiful Suffolk countryside, spending more time in the open air than usual, exploring the old parish churches and viewing the long unvisited North Sea. I was also glad to have had a little more contact with the Ipswich sangha. Perhaps Paramartha and I would return next year, and continue our search for traces of my Lingwood ancestors.

THE ANCESTORS

It was the year 1528. King Henry VIII had been on the throne for nineteen years, the great Cardinal Wolsey was still Lord Chancellor of England, and in Rushmere St Michael in the county of Suffolk, on 2 August in that year, Robert Lynghoode was making his will. Very likely he was dying, perhaps of the plague, for it is clear from the terms of the will that his six children are all under age, besides which his wife Joan is pregnant with a seventh child, and that he is concerned for their future welfare. After declaring that he is 'in good mind and whole remembrance' he leaves his soul to God Almighty and Our Lady and all the holy company in heaven (for England is still Catholic) and his body to be buried in the church of Saint Michael of Rushmere. Perhaps his conscience was troubling him, for his first bequest is to the high altar of Rushmere church 'for my tithes forgotten'. There are also bequests to the high altars of three other churches in the locality and a bequest to Rushmere church for repairs. His principal bequests are to his children

Nicholas, Elizabeth, Margery, Laurence, Thomas, Robert, together with the unborn child, to each of whom he leaves five marks sterling, a cow, and a quantity of barley. Should one of his children die before reaching the age of twenty, the five marks is to go to an honest priest to say mass for the testator and his friends in Rushmere church. Should two of them die, an honest secular priest is to have ten marks to say mass for a whole year. Should more than two children die before reaching the age of twenty the money is to go to their mother. Relatives and friends are not forgotten. To his brother Steven Lynghoode he bequeaths one of his black cattle at Waldsdyke, and to Ellen Gyldorne, who may be a servant, a measure of barley. Finally, Robert Lynghoode of Rushmere leaves all his remaining goods to his wife Joan, whom he makes his executrix. He directs her to deliver all his children's money to Sr Thomas Bedingfeld and Sr Laurence Mayewe for them to hold for the benefit of the children until such time as they should require it.

The will is witnessed by Sr Thomas Bedingfeld, Sr Robert Clarke, and John Leslyn.

Sir Thomas Bedingfeld of Oxburgh belonged to an East Anglian family well known to historians of the Tudor period. He was High Sheriff of Norfolk and Suffolk in 1522 and died in 1538 after making a nuncupative will in which he left everything to his wife Alice, daughter of William London, Mayor of Norwich. His brother Sir Edmund Bedingfeld (1479/80–1553) was knighted in 1523 for demonstrating bravery in the French wars and eventually inherited from his brother Robert Bedingfeld the great estate of Oxburgh Hall, Kings Lynn, Norfolk. Following Henry VIII's divorce he was entrusted with the care of Katherine of Aragon at Kimbolton Castle. It was the father of the brothers, Sir Edmund Bedingfeld (1443–1496) who built Oxburgh Hall where Henry VII and his queen once stayed. Oxburgh Hall is now a National Trust property. Sir Henry Bedingfeld (1509–1583) of Oxburgh, the son of Thomas Bedingfeld and nephew of the younger Sir Edmund Bedingfeld, had the care of the Princess Elizabeth (the future queen Elizabeth I) when on the orders of Queen Mary she was transferred from the Tower of London to Woodstock in Oxfordshire.

It should be noted that Sir Thomas Bedingfeld is both entrusted with the children's money until they are of age *and* a witness to Robert Lynghoode's will, whereas Sir Laurence Mayewe is only entrusted with the children's money and Sir Robert Clarke and John Leslyn are only witnesses to the will. This suggests that Robert Lynghoode had a closer connection with Sir Thomas Bedingfeld than with the three other men, which indeed is not unlikely. Sir Thomas's father originally came from Bedingfeld, which is situated in the same part of Suffolk that my Lingwood ancestors came from, so the two families may well have known each other for several generations.

Robert Lynghoode's will was of great interest to me. It told me quite a lot about my ancestor. He was married to a woman named Joan, had at least six children, and died at a comparatively early age. He was quite well-to-do, being in a position to leave money, a cow, and a quantity of barley to each of his children, as if to set them up in life as soon as they came of age. His wife was left the residue of his estate, which no doubt meant a house and land and the means of providing for herself and the children until they grew up and could fend for themselves. The bequest to his brother suggests that he had land in Waldsdyke as well as in Rushmere. That he made bequests to so many churches does not necessarily mean that Robert Lynghoode was especially pious. Probably it was no more than what a person of good standing in the community was expected to do in those days. More significant is the fact that he expressed a wish to be buried in Rushmere church, i.e. not in the graveyard like ordinary folk, and apparently took it for granted that his wish would be respected.

Besides his will, there were two other sources of information about Robert Lynghoode of Rushmere. One is a genealogy included in the Lingwood family papers (LFP); the other, the Suffolk Subsidy Returns for 1524. In the genealogy Robert Lynghoode is styled constable, a term that in this connection means an officer who, under a High Sheriff, is responsible for the maintenance of law and order, probably within a certain area. It is not clear whether Robert Lynghoode served under Sir Thomas Bedingfeld or under some other occupant or occupants of the post of High Sheriff of Norfolk and Suffolk. The subsidy of 1524 was granted by parliament to Henry VIII to finance the war in France. It was a graduated tax, spread over four years. In the first two years land and houses paid one shilling for each pound of their yearly value. Those who had moveable goods valued at £20 and upwards paid one shilling for each pound. According to the Suffolk Subsidy Returns of 1524 Robert Lynghoode paid, or was assessed at, the sum of £16.8s.0d – it is not clear which it was. In either case he must have been quite well to do, as indeed is evident from the terms of his will.

Robert Lynghoode of Rushmere thus emerges from the early Tudor records as a substantial Suffolk yeoman, a man of some position in his community, a responsible father and husband, a good Catholic, and with contacts – even friends – among the gentry of East Anglia. On the whole it is a not unattractive picture.

Nicholas Lingwood of Badingham, yeoman, Robert Lynghoode's eldest son, farmed at Badingham, had four sons and three daughters by his wife Margery, and according to the Suffolk Subsidy Returns of 1568 he paid, or was assessed at, the sum of £10. He died in 1591, his wife in 1563.

Next in line is John Lingwood of Dennington, yeoman, Nicholas Lingwood's eldest son, who was born in 1548 and died in 1597. He married (1) Margaret Connold of Laxfield and (2) Mary. He had five sons and a daughter. One of the sons bore the unusual name of Wulfran.

John Lingwood of Swaffing, yeoman, John Lingwood's eldest son, was born in 1575, married Mary, and by her had three sons and three daughters, plus an unnamed child.

The record for Thomas Lingwood of Hynten St Blythburg, yeoman, who was born in 1600, is sparse. All that is known of him is that, unusually for the philoprogenitive Lingwoods, he had only one child, a son.

This son, Thomas Lingwood of Badingham I, yeoman, did a little better than his father in the generative department. He had two sons, and died in 1683.

Thomas Lingwood of Badingham II, yeoman, the elder of Thomas Lingwood I's two sons, married Annis Aldous, and died in 1698, leaving two sons and four daughters.

Thomas Lingwood of Brome I, gentleman, the elder of Thomas Lingwood of Badingham II's two sons, was born in 1688, died in 1748, and was buried in the graveyard of Brome parish church. His wife was Mary Peake of Wickenham Skeith, who was born in 1695 and died in 1763. They had one son, though the records may be incorrect and there may have been other children. Thomas Lingwood of Brome was the first of my Lingwood ancestors to be styled gentleman. All his ascendants, from his father to Thomas Lingwood of Badingham up to and including Robert Lynghoode of Rushmere, are styled yeoman. It is an interesting example of upward social mobility.

Thomas Lingwood of Brome II, gentleman, was born in 1736 and died in 1815, leaving a will. Like his father, he was buried in the graveyard of Brome parish church. He married Mary Lathbury, who was born in 1735 and died in 1802. They had twelve sons and three daughters.

It was the coffin-shaped tomb graves of Thomas and Mary Lingwood and three of their children that Paramartha and I found behind the back wall of the parish church of St Mary, Brome, when we visited Suffolk in June 2010.

The last will and testament of Thomas Lingwood of Brome II is dated 1809, which means that he made it seven years before his death, the witnesses being Mary Kelly, Richard Kelly, and J. Bellman. The will is prolix, repetitive, and entirely devoid of punctuation, and must have been drawn up by a lawyer. After a simple invocation of the Deity (for England has long been Protestant), the testator appoints three of his sons as his executors. They are Thomas Lathbury Lingwood, Peter Lathbury Lingwood, and Decimus Lathbury Lingwood, and the three names occur again and again throughout the will like a kind of refrain. He gives them 'all and every my messuages, farms, lands, tenements and hereditaments and all other my real estate whatsoever situate, lying, and being in, Brome, aforesaid, and Thrandeston in the said County, or in any other Town, Parish, or place near or adjoining thereto as are freehold or charter hold... (punctuation added).' He then proceeds to make sundry bequests, the gist of which is as follows:

1. The interest from a sum of £1,500 in consolidated bank annuities is to continue to be paid annually to Robert Page and Mary Page (Thomas's daughter) and is to be paid for the rest of their natural lives.
2. He bequeathes to his granddaughter Mary Page (daughter of the above) the sum of £100, to be paid on her attaining her 21st birthday.
3. He also asks his executors to set up from the moneys from his estate a fund to pay annuity of £10 to Mr Thomas Bond, yeoman, of Starson, in the county of Norfolk.
4. A similar fund to be set up to pay annuity of £10 to Ann Pretty (who lives with him).
5. Lastly, he directs that the residue of the monies from the sale of his real and personal estates be divided and shared alike amongst his children, namely, Thomas Lathbury Lingwood, Peter Lathbury

Lingwood, Joseph Lathbury Lingwood, Charlotte Edmonds (his daughter), Edward Lingwood, Decimus Lingwood, and Benjamin Lingwood.

In 1811 Thomas Lingwood of Brome added a codicil to his will in his own hand. The codicil was witnessed by Ann Pretty. In it he bequeaths £500 each to his granddaughters Mary and Charlotte Page, the amounts to be paid to them within six months of their attaining the age of twenty-one. The genuineness of the codicil may have been questioned, for in 1815 Edward Lingwood of Eye, Thomas's eldest son, confirmed that the codicil was indeed in his father's handwriting.

The will and its codicil do not really tell us much about Thomas Lingwood of Brome. They tell us what he owned, which evidently was quite a lot, but they tell us nothing about the man himself. He may have left generous bequests to his two granddaughters because he was particularly fond of them, but on the other hand he may have done so just because that was what was expected of a wealthy grandfather. Our only other source of information about him comes from an item in the *Norfolk Chronicle* of 22 June 1782, which reports on the General Meeting of the 'Diss Association for apprehending and prosecuting Horse-Stealers'. At this meeting 'the Gentlemen residing in or near the said Hundred, associated for prosecuting Horse-Stealers, held the fifth Day of this Instant June in the King's Head at Diss, the Treasurer's Accounts for the last Year were settled, and it was agreed that Mr Benjamin Fincham of Diss, aforesaid, should be continued Treasurer for the Year ensuing, and that the Articles of this Association should remain in full Force, and that the Reward of Ten Guineas, together with all reasonable Charges, be continued to be paid by the Treasurer to any Person or Persons who shall apprehend, and prosecute to Conviction, the Stealers of any Horse, Mare, or Gelding, from any of the undermentioned Subscribers.' Among the undermentioned subscribers is Thomas Lingwood of Brome, which suggests that he would have shared, to an extent at least, the interests and opinions of the other landowners and gentlemen farmers of East Anglia.

Thomas's sons must have been no less prosperous than he was. One of them, Thomas Lathbury Lingwood, could afford to give his only son a university education. This son was Robert Maulkin Lingwood, born in 1813. A Cambridge graduate (B.A. 1836, M.A. 1840), he was a botanist and entomologist, was in the Channel Islands and in Ireland with the distinguished C. C. Babington (a correspondent of Charles Darwin), discovered and named various plants, and was a member of a number of scientific bodies. He was High Sheriff of Herefordshire in 1848, and in 1860 he became Deputy Lord Lieutenant of the county. Robert Maulkin Lingwood married his first cousin Elizabeth Lingwood, daughter of Benjamin Lingwood, but they had no issue. He died in 1887, at Lystone House, Llanwarne.

While he was at Cambridge Robert Maulkin Lingwood applied to the College of Arms for a grant of arms. In 1835, since he was able to 'prove his pedigree' to their satisfaction, the application was accepted. The grant was made not to Robert Maulkin himself, but to his grandfather Thomas Lingwood of Brome, and to all the latter's male descendants. Among the LFP there is a sketch of the armorial bearings of the family, together with the motto *crede deo*. In traditional heraldic terms the arms are: azure a saltire, engrailed, erminoise, between fleurs-de-lis, or crest: a talbot's head, erminoised erased, and ear sable with mural crown gules.

Edward Lingwood of Eye and Needham Market, the eldest son of Thomas Lingwood of Brome II, was born in 1770 and died in 1849, and was buried in front of the altar of Barking parish church. He married Hannah Ward, who was born in 1766 and died in 1798, at the age of 32. They had two children, Edward and Hannah. It was his altar grave that Paramartha was unable to see as the area in front of the altar was covered by a carpet.

Edward Lingwood of Battisford, the only son of Edward Lingwood of Eye and Needham Market, was born circa 1797 and baptized 12 June 1797 at Eye. In 1827 he married Sarah Haywood, and they had eleven sons and three daughters. He died in 1864, after living in retirement at The Elms, Stowmarket, and was buried in the graveyard of Battisford parish church, of which he had been 'Perpetual Churchwarden'. According to the Census of 1851, Edward Lingwood of Battisford, then aged 53, lived at St John's, farmed 400 acres, and employed sixteen men and eight boys. There lived at home with him seven children, including Edward, his eldest son, as well as two male and two female lodgers.

St John's – or The Manor House, as it was also known – was the large, tree-surrounded house Paramartha and I had come across on the first day of our search for traces of my Lingwood ancestors. It was where we met Pat Knoch, its present occupier and owner or custodian of the Lingwood box, from whom we learned that the property had once been occupied by members of the Lingwood family. Though we could see that the house was old, despite its relatively modern frontage, at the time we had no idea how old it really was or how long and varied was its history. That history began with the mention of Battisford Manor in the Domesday Book where it is described as a farm. According to a note in the LFP, 'a priory was founded on the spot in the time of Herbert Losinga, bishop of Norwich, by Radulfus Fitzbrian and Emma, his wife. It was dedicated to St Leonard and endowed by them with lands and tithes'. More information is to be found in the English Heritage (grade II) listing. After describing St John's as it exists today, in great detail, it goes on to say, 'The house is built upon the moated site of the Preceptory of the Knights Hospitallers founded here in circa 1154 and dissolved in 1540'. In the reign of Elizabeth I the property was owned by Sir Thomas Gresham, Lord of the Battisford and St John's Manors, and the founder of the Royal Exchange. Dame Anne, Sir Thomas's wife, rebuilt the house in 1570, and in the course of the rebuilding 'many rafters were reused from a large open hall of late C13 or early C14'.

Sarah Lingwood was born in 1803 and died in 1879. She appears to have been an educated, intelligent, and pious woman, and came from a prosperous and well-connected family. Her brother Edward Haywood was Bar-at-law of the Inner Temple. He married Christine Annette Campbell of Brighton, daughter of the late Daniel Campbell, cousin to the Duke of Northumberland and to Lord Carbery. In the LFP there are typewritten copies of two letters from Sarah to her and Edward's third son, Henry Lingwood, then seventeen and living first at Wickham Market, Suffolk, and afterwards at Crabtree, near Plymouth, Devonshire.

The first letter is headed Battisford and dated 19 September 1848. Sarah was writing because his brothers were all fully employed. His father was busy carting barley, which suggests that the harvest was well under way. There followed news of various members of the family. Tom had that day gone to Woolpit bullock fair instead of his father, who did not like to leave home. They had been surprised to see Horace, who came with a friend to see the balloon at Stowe, probably one of the hot-air balloons popular at the time. They had heard of a situation for James at Yarmouth, but his father had not yet decided. Mr Page had taken great pains to make enquiries. Sarah probably had an ear for music, for she commented that Mr Cooper, who married Henry's sister Sarah, played the flute beautifully. His sister had come with him, and Sarah had found her a most pleasing amiable person and quite liked her. She and Sarah junior had gone for a ride to Brice and would spend the next day with Sarah senior's mother. Other news was that Mr Moores and Mr Wood had been at St John's shooting, which probably means shooting pheasants; that her brother and his wife had been at Bosmere, but had not come to St John's; that Mr Edmonds had left ten shillings for him, which he was not to spend on 'those hateful things', cigars. He had not given so much to his sister Sarah, who was a 'most extraordinary woman for her age'. What made her daughter so extraordinary Sarah did not say. Finally, she had admonished him, her dear boy, to walk in the strait path, for 'he that walketh uprightly walketh safely'.[505] That God might abundantly bless him in this life and save him for ever was, she assured him, the very frequent prayer of his mother.

Sarah Lingwood's second letter to her son Henry, now eighteen and working in a mill in or near Plymouth, bears no date but is marked 'To be posted Battisford, Saturday evening.' The envelope is stamped 'Ipswich 1 July 1849' and 'Plymouth 3 July 1849.' She writes:

> My dear Henry,
> I was truly glad to receive your interesting letter for which I was looking most anxiously – fearing perhaps mine had not reached you – I wish my dear boy you had not so many hours to work without rest, and rejoice at your determination to do your best and when we are in the path of duty, we may hope and expect God's blessing on our honest endeavours – nevertheless nothing would give us more pleasure than to find you were promoted to some place in the Mill, where you had less to do. I am thankful you do not omit to go to church – I am glad you like Plympton church, because I conclude you can go there in all weathers, and it is not good to roam from church to church, if we know where to go to hear God's word rightly preached.
>
> I should like much to see the glorious view of the ocean at Plymouth and am thankful that every opportunity you have of taking a walk, that you can command such lovely views.

I was very pleased with the green plant, I think I have found it out – it is so fleshy, that probably it will not dry well, but Sarah will be glad to have whole specimens of what you find, but a blossom pleases me much. Sarah went to Burstal on Wednesday and is to return to-night. James is gone to the train to meet her. James came home last Monday – he is rather taller but not stouter I think; he is full of spirits – he seems to like his occupation much and is improved in manner. He received your letter and will answer it he says when he goes home, which he is to do next Thursday – he has his meals alone at the back of the shop, to be in waiting when called.

Sarah half expects Mr. C. C. next week to go with her to the Flower Show at Ipswich; the children being all at home I should prefer his visit another time. My Brother & his wife are still in Dublin staying with Mrs Putland – Mrs H. is of '*immense consequence*' so my Brother says. I should like to see the Slate quarry – is not Plymouth Dock cut out of slate? When the flints are ground what coloured earthenware is it used for? *White?*

I think I heard from Horace just after I wrote to you; he seems very comfortable and contented and I hope will continue so – he wrote quite a long letter. – I was afraid he would miss the *gun*.

We have two large hay and stover stacks got up very well –

Mr. & Mrs. R. Lingwood have been on a trip to the Lakes.

Your father has given up all thoughts of hiring Roydon Hall which I am glad of – Edward and Thos. are very anxious to go to the Norwich Show. Thos. has been ailing and taking medicine every day since you left – I hope however this illness has been for his good in some respects and I have no longer any cause for uneasiness: you understand this.

There are 4 young peafowls, they are very pretty, and are kept in the partridge coop by the walnut tree. The peahen hatched 5 chickens but soon walked them to death. Sarah has 12 Ducks hatched.

I have had a very bad face-ache all the week, but it is much better. Do you get any Beer, as I read whiskey cider is the usual drink? I am sure you will smile at my odd mixture of subjects – (you write where instead of were very often in your letters).

Sarah is just returned and left all friends well at Burstal. She went to the Ipswich Museum and to some gardens at Bramford. She had a long ride on 'Jack' she is very much obliged for the plant – I must bid you good night with my kind love and best wishes –

Your most affectionate
Mother

A mixture of topics indeed! Henry may well have smiled reading his mother's letter. As she does in the first letter, Sarah shows herself to be solicitous for both the material and spiritual welfare of her son, and perhaps even more for the latter than the former. Though thankful that he still goes to church, she appears not to be concerned what kind of church he attends, whether Anglican or Nonconformist. Her principal concern is that he should be able to hear God's word rightly preached. In this she is firmly Protestant, even Evangelical. Yet though she is pious, Sarah is not parochial. She has a strong desire to see the ocean, which she has either not seen or saw a long time ago, and she wonders if Plymouth Dock was not cut out of slate, and would like to know of what colour was the earthenware made from ground flints. Horizons were expanding in remote, rural, Suffolk. People went on trips to the Lake District, Ipswich had its own museum, and the fact that someone had gone to meet a train could be mentioned without comment.

The walnut tree mentioned by Sarah in her letter, beside which was the partridge coop where she kept her peafowl chicks, was no longer to be seen at St John's. It had been blown down in a storm during her time at the house, Pat Knoch told Paramartha and me. Neither were there any peacocks there, as there may have been when Sarah lived in the old house. I had no difficulty imagining them strutting haughtily about the place, displaying their magnificent plumage and bringing a touch of oriental splendour to the sober English countryside.

Thomas Lingwood, the second son of Edward and Sarah Lingwood, was born in Battisford in 1832, but spent the greater part of his life at Shrub House, Brockford. He evidently inherited the strong religious feelings of his mother. According to an obituary in the LFP, he was for much of his life devoted to mission work, holding Sunday services in the old oak beamed house at Brockford, fitting up the barn as a mission hall when numbers increased, and erecting a gospel hall on his land at Brockford six years before his death. We have no clue as to the precise nature of his religious views. Probably he was an evangelically-inclined protestant and, like his mother, believed that thirteen people should be able to 'hear the word of God rightly preached'. He may also have been dissatisfied with the lukewarm ministrations of the local Anglican clergy.

But Thomas Lingwood's interests were not exclusively religious. He was a lover and breeder of horses, a subject on which his advice was frequently sought, and for sixty years he never failed to appear at the Woodbridge Horse Fair. He was an active member of several local charities, and a keen horticulturist whose garden was greatly admired for its wealth of old-fashioned flowers, including a fine display of roses. He died in 1915, at the age of 83. A large number of people attended his funeral, which was held in the Gospel Hall, from which his oak coffin was taken to Wetheringsett Cemetery on the shoulders of tenants from his estate. He never married. In his will he provided for the upkeep of the Gospel Hall, and for the disposal of his books on religion. He also left generous legacies to his numerous nephews and nieces, as well as to his housekeeper and various friends.

In the LFP there is a photograph of Thomas Lingwood, and beside it a photograph of his twin sister Sarah Lingwood Cooper. He has a broad forehead, deep set eyes, and full lips similar to those of my father. His expression is one of strength and kindness, and he wears a kind of bow-tie. Sarah is seated, and reads a newspaper. Behind her is a fireplace and a clock the hands of which point to 1.55. Her face is thin, her nose aquiline, and she wears on her head a small cap. Both brother and sister are in their fifties, even their sixties.

James Grace Lingwood, the fourth son of Edward and Sarah Lingwood, was born in 1832. His second name was that of one of his three godparents, a Mr Grace. A note to a genealogical tree in the LFP describes him as an artist, but we do not know if he ever went to art school or practised as an artist professionally. From Sarah's letters to his brother Henry we know that as a young man he worked in a shop in Yarmouth and seemed happy there. He never married, and died in 1863, aged 30. Behind the bare facts there may well be a story of blasted hopes and unfulfilled aspirations.

Two of Edward's and Sarah's sons emigrated to Canada. They were Septimus Robert (known as Robert), their seventh son, born in 1835, and William Herbert, their eleventh son, born in 1845. Robert went first, when he was in his early twenties, and William followed later. Both brothers married in Canada, and founded, in Robert's case at least, a branch of the Lingwood family in that country. Initially, Robert leased a farm in Nichol township, but the venture was not a success. He then became a director of a company drilling for oil, and with his brother William went into the brewing and canning business.

One of the most interesting aspects of the lives of the two brothers in Canada is their membership of the Fergus Company, a militia organized for defence against the Fenian Raids of 1865–6.[506] Once the Fergus Company was ordered to go to Sarnia.[507] They went by wagon to Guelph, where they were joined by the Elora Company and took the train to Sarnia. There was no confrontation with the Fenians. On another occasion the Fergus Company went to Niagara, where they were in a skirmish with the Fenians under General O'Neill.[508] The Fenians were repulsed. According to family tradition, Robert was wounded in the hand during the fighting, the wound festered, and it had to be amputated. Later he moved from Fergus to Guelph, where he died of TB in 1875, leaving four sons, four daughters, and a handwritten will.[509] Edith Wilson, who put together the Lingwood box, was his granddaughter. In the LFP there is a photograph of Captain Robert Lingwood in his militia uniform. William Herbert Lingwood returned to England in about 1900, and after enduring much hardship eventually settled in Stowmarket, where he died, blind, in 1924, leaving one child, a daughter, then living in the United States.

Edward Lingwood of Ashfield, the eldest son of Edward Lingwood of Battisford and his wife Sarah, stayed at home and made his contribution to the history of the Lingwood family, including the line that ends with the present writer. He was born in 1828, and educated at Eye Grammar School. In his late twenties he married Catherine Sophia Sheldrake (known as Kate), the daughter of Edward Sheldrake of Ixworth Priory. They had fourteen children, at least four of whom died in infancy. The census of 1861 records Edward Lingwood as farming 232 acres in Ashfield, Suffolk, and employing thirteen men and five boys. He was then 32. Subsequent censuses show him as living, successively, in Wetheringsett-cum-Brockford, Thwaite, Bramford, and St Margaret (Ipswich), all in Suffolk. An obituary in the LFP gives a summary of his career:

> He started farming at the age of 20, at Ashfield; and in later years he acted as agent for Lord Thurlow. For some time he was a well-known follower of the Essex and Suffolk Foxhounds, his favourite meet being at Hintlesham Park gates. About fifty years ago he was a member of the Needham Market Bowling Club, and he would ride a dozen miles in order to participate in his favourite game. He was for a long period a member of the Stowmarket Farmers' Club, and was one who read papers in various districts on sheep breeding. The noted flock of the later Mr Henry Lingwood was developed from sheep drawn from the deceased gentleman's flock when he relinquished farming twenty-five years ago. During his long period of activity Mr Lingwood represented parishes in which he resided on the Stowmarket or Hartismere Boards of Guardians; in politics he was a staunch Conservative, for considerable periods he held the position of churchwarden or overseer. He was an ardent collector of birds' eggs, and had a wonderful knowledge of bird-life in general, travelling long distances to hear and see rare specimens. Up to the date of his death he could quote the Latin name for almost any English bird.

Edward Lingwood spent the last years of his life in retirement at his residence in Gainsborough Road, Ipswich, where he died in 1909, his wife Kate having died earlier that year. They were survived by six sons and two daughters.

In the LFP there are two three-quarter-length photographs of Edward Lingwood of Ashfield and his wife Kate. Both are seated beside a table. He looks to his left, she to her right. Edward has the same broad forehead and deep-set eyes as his brother Thomas, as well as the same full lips, but he is bearded and his expression is sad, even tragic. Between his hands he holds an open book or magazine. Kate has a thin, pale face, and about her lips there is a hint of a smile. Her smooth dark hair is parted in the middle and surmounted by a small cap. She has a full skirt and full sleeves, and appears to be reading. On the table at her elbow there is a row of books.

One of those books could have been *Prayer and Praise at Eventide*, a copy of which, inscribed to him in her own hand, Kate gave to her son Philip Francis Lingwood, my grandfather. I found this book at the bottom of a cupboard when I was a child and read the inscription.

In the house at that time there were only two other articles that had belonged to my grandfather, a silver-mounted amber cane and a wooden dispatch case, and all that I really knew about him was that he had died young. Even now I know very little more than that. There are two reasons for this. The first is that the Lingwood box contained no information about him, the compiler being more concerned with the fortunes of the descendants of Septimus Robert Lingwood in Canada. The second is that he died when my father was three years old, so that the latter had no personal recollections of him to pass on to me.

Philip Francis Lingwood, the seventh son of Edward Lingwood of Ashfield and his wife Kate, was born in 1873 at Occold, Suffolk. At some point he came to London, where in 1896 he married Anna Ellen Butters, born 1872, the daughter of Walter Butters, a farm labourer, of Besthorpe, Norfolk, and his wife Caroline.[510] They had two children, Philip Edward Lingwood, born at Woolwich, Kent (now part of Greater London) in 1899, and Helen Frances Lingwood, born in 1902. He died in 1902, at Charlton, London. Anna Ellen lived until 1952, having remarried after the death of Philip Francis, and had two more children.

As a child I knew that my grandfather had died young, but I also knew, from what I heard – or overheard – from my elders, that there was a mystery about his death, or at least something unexplained. One version was that he had caught a chill after going for a swim and had died of pneumonia. Another version of the story was that he had picked up a deadly infection from certain diplomatic papers that had arrived from the Far East, papers he had handled in the course of his duties at the War Office. If there was any truth in this account, the papers may well have been kept for a while in the wooden dispatch case, which had soon passed into my possession, along with the silver-mounted amber cane. The case was lined with green beige and it could be locked. On its polished back a crest was picked out in gold. The crest was in the form of a shield, on the shield there was a horizontal bar, and on the bar a row of three balls. I do not know if the crest was my grandfather's or that of a previous owner of the case. It also seems that my grandfather had a fine copperplate handwriting, on account of which he was given the task of making out the commissions that went to the queen for signature. However, hearsay is not evidence, as a libel lawyer once reminded me, and I cannot vouch for the truth of all the things I heard – or overheard – as a child.

Though she had a framed photograph of my grandfather hanging in her kitchen, not far from a similar one of her deceased second husband, I can remember my grandmother speaking of him only once. This was when I was 14 or 15. My mother and I were alone with her one day, and my mother, who was like a daughter to her, happened to remark that over the years her memories of her first husband must have gradually faded. 'Oh no!' my grandmother at once exclaimed, a joyous expression lighting up her face. 'It's all as fresh as if it were yesterday!'

Philip Edward Lingwood, who was born in 1899 and was the only son of Philip Francis Lingwood and his wife Anna, married in 1920 Catherine Florence Margaret Ketskemety (known as Florrie to her brothers and sisters and Kit to her husband and his relations). They had two children, Dennis Philip Edward, who was born in 1925, and Joan Doreen, who was born in 1926 and died in 2001, leaving a husband Edward Turner (known as Eddie), and four children, John, Maria, David, and Kamala (known as Kay). Philip and Florrie/Kit were divorced in 1946 and both remarried, the former once, the latter twice. Philip Edward died in 1971, and Florrie/Kit in 1990, after being twice widowed.

Philip Edward, my father, grew up in Besthorpe, Norfolk, and in Tooting, South London. After leaving school he worked for, or was apprenticed to, a jeweller, along with several other boys. The boys all 'lived in', and my father more than once told me, when I was a child, how he and the other boys used to play tricks on the jeweller's elderly housekeeper. When the First World War began he was fifteen, and it was not long before he enlisted, giving a false age. He served in the trenches, was badly wounded, was invalided back to England, and while recovering in St Benedict's Hospital, Tooting, met my mother, who was working there as a VAD.[511] Later he trained as a French polisher at the Lord Roberts Workshops.[512]

Had Philip Francis Lingwood, his father, not died young, my father probably would have had a very different life. He certainly would not have grown up in Tooting, and though he may have enlisted he almost certainly would not have met my mother, so that, had I been born at all, I would have been born to a different mother and with a different genetic inheritance. In a word, I would not have been quite me, and would have had a different kind of life.

But speculation is a waste of time. I have had the life I have had, and it has been a life very different from that of any of my Lingwood biological ancestors or, for that matter, from the life of any of my Ketskemety ancestors. I have never married, and at 85 I am unlikely to do so, and I therefore will have no biological descendants. I will, I trust, have many spiritual descendants, in the form of the members of the Triratna Buddhist Order. In other words, my spiritual descendants will be all those who, whether in Suffolk, in England, or in any other part of the world, go for Refuge to the Three Jewels, and who study, practise, and communicate the Buddhadhamma as taught by me in the course of sixty and more years.

REFLECTIONS

The discovery of the Lingwood box was important for me. Before it, I had known of my paternal Lingwood ancestry only that my grandfather was from a good Suffolk family and had died young. Now I knew a good deal more than that. Thanks to the contents of that box, I was suddenly swept back over four centuries of English history, over a dozen generations of Lingwoods, to the reign of Henry VIII and to Robert Lynghoode of Rushmere, the first of my known Lingwood ancestors. I was in a position similar to that of one who, having been adopted at an early age and brought up by adoptive parents, one day discovers that he has real parents and is a member of a real, biological family. The difference between us was that his discovery related to the present, whereas mine related to the past.

To discover one's true parents is to learn something about oneself, and to discover a whole series of previously unknown ancestors is to learn even more, and to learn it with greater certainty. The basic fact about my Lingwood ancestors was that they were farmers. Generation after generation they had ploughed, sowed, harvested, and gathered into barns. Farming was therefore in my blood, along with other ingredients, and it was natural that when, in a foreign country, I acquired a stone cottage and four acres of hillside land, I should have cultivated those four acres as a matter of course. During the seven years that I lived at the cottage I grew maize and buckwheat, cared for my hundred orange trees, and saw to it that there were vegetables for the table and flowers for the shrine.[513] There were good practical reasons for my doing this, but I did not do it only for these reasons. I also did it because engaging with the soil gave me a deep inner satisfaction. It was the kind of satisfaction that Edward Lingwood of Battisford must have experienced when carting barley a hundred years earlier.

Ancestry is far from being merely biological. It is also cultural and religious, and the different ancestries can overlap, the biological with the cultural, the cultural with the religious. Probably the most important part of our cultural heritage is language, through which so much of our knowledge and experience is mediated. In my own case, I inherited from my Lingwood ancestors not only some of my genes but the language in which I think, speak, and write. From my Ketskemety ancestry I inherited it only to a limited extent, for until two generations ago that side of my family spoke not English but Hungarian, of which I know hardly a word. Not that this really mattered. I grew up speaking, as my native tongue, one of the world's great languages, through which I had immediate access to one of the world's great literatures. I have always been thankful that I speak the language that Shakespeare and Milton spoke and have been able to enjoy their works in the original, as well as the works of so many other poets, dramatists, novelists, historians, philosophers, and essayists who have contributed to the creation of the glory that is English literature. Nor is that all. Much has been translated into English from other languages, both ancient and modern, Eastern and Western, to the cultural enrichment of the English-speaking world. Among the works translated have been the Buddhist scriptures. Had none of them been translated it would not have been possible for me, as a boy of sixteen or seventeen, to discover the Dharma.

Proper names are an integral part of any language. As I look back over the line of my paternal ancestors I see four Thomas Lingwoods, three Edwards, two Johns, two Philips, one Robert, and one Nicholas – but no Dennis. There was no Dennis until 1925 when I was born and baptized Dennis Philip Edward at the parish church of St Nicholas, Tooting. The person responsible for this innovation in the matter of names was my aunt Helen, my father's sister, who was also my godmother. 'Dennis' must have been a name she particularly liked; but I have never liked it, and would much rather have been called Edward, or even Philip. I was not the only one who disliked the first of my baptismal names, my dislike being shared by at least one other person. This was old, red-faced Thomas Whitehead (known to the family as Uncle Tom), my bluff, hearty godfather.[514] As a small child I often heard him declare, as I sat perched on his knee, 'He's not Dennis. He's little Phil.' Whether my two godparents had argued the point over the baptismal font at my Christening I never knew. Years later I was to undergo more than one change of name. From Dennis I became first Dharmapriya, then (for a few hours) Dharmarakshita, after that Sangharakshita, and finally Urgyen Sangharakshita.[515]

The change from Dennis to Dharmapriya and its successors was much more than a simple change of name. It marked a change of religion on my part. Dennis and the two other names I was given at the font were my baptismal names. They bore witness to the fact that I had undergone the rite of admission into the Christian church. The change from Dennis to Dharmapriya was therefore an event of singular moment. It was a change from being a member of the Christian church to being a member of the Buddhist sangha, from being a Christian, albeit a very nominal one, to being a believing and practising Buddhist. At the same time, this did not mean that I ceased to appreciate and enjoy Christian art, though I appreciated it aesthetically, without giving intellectual assent to its doctrinal content. Even when I was a small boy, and had as yet no definite religious ideas, whether Christian or non-Christian, I was unaccountably drawn to old churches. Visiting them, and photographing them with my box camera, was one of the highlights of my summer holidays at Shoreham-by-Sea with my parents and my sister.[516] It was therefore only natural that I should have felt at home in the parish churches of Suffolk, where so many of my Lingwood ancestors were baptized, were married, where they sang hymns and heard sermons, and where, finally, they were buried.

There followed from this, inevitably, the thought of impermanence and death as the fundamental reality of the human condition. I cannot claim, however, that my search for traces of my Lingwood ancestors, or the discoveries I made about them, gave me any fresh or original insights into that reality, though they reinforced, and underlined, the insights I already had. My discoveries did, however, give me a more vivid sense of how one generation succeeds another, and of how important it is that within the span of human life allotted to us we take full advantage of our spiritual opportunities, especially if we are so fortunate as to be able to study and practise the Dharma.

Though I have biological ancestors I certainly will not leave behind me any biological descendants; but perhaps, in years to come, there will be spiritual descendants of mine who will, one day, search for traces of me in Tooting and Kalimpong, Hampstead and Moseley, and elsewhere. I wonder what they will discover.

IV: AYYA KHEMA: A PERSONAL TRIBUTE

Many of those who knew Ayya Khema in recent years will have known her as their beloved teacher, and most of the tributes appearing in this present volume will probably be from their pens. Others, however, will have known her simply as a very dear friend and fellow Dharma-farer, and one of these may be permitted to add his own flower to the wreath with which her memory is rightly being honoured.

Ayya Khema and I came to know each other in the autumn of 1992, in the course of the European Buddhist Union's biennial congress, which was held that year in Berlin and in which we both participated as speakers.[517] It was not quite our first meeting. We had met once before, some ten or twelve years earlier, when Ayya Khema came to see me in London not long after her ordination as a nun. Nothing came of that meeting, and perhaps nothing would have come of our meetings in Berlin had it not been for the panel discussion in which I took part on the last morning of the congress. During the discussion I happened to say something that it seems impressed her, as I discovered when with the other speakers we were entertained to lunch at Hakuin's.[518] Ayya Khema, who was seated at another table, had to leave early. As she left she came over to me and without preamble said, 'People say I am a bold woman, but I would not have had the courage to say what you said this morning.' Not being aware that I had said anything particularly courageous, I was puzzled by her words. Later the mystery was cleared up by one of her disciples, who told my companion what it was she had been referring to.

Apart from the fact that she was reputed to be a bold woman, Ayya Khema's cryptic remark told me three things about her. In the first place, it told me that she respected courage. Secondly, it told me that she was direct in her dealings with people, and did not hesitate to tell them frankly what she thought of their proceedings. Thirdly, it told me that on certain issues we were of one mind, for my supposed act of courage had consisted in my publicly dissenting, *pace* a popular fellow panellist, from a view with which she, also, happened to disagree.[519]

It was therefore not surprising that after the congress we should have remained in touch, and that whenever she came to England, which she did every year, we should have arranged to meet. In London she always stayed at the Zen Centre with Venerable Myokyo-ni (Dr Irmgard Schlögl),[520] whom I had known for many years, and when we met there her hostess would join us for afternoon tea. Ayya Khema, I noticed, on such occasions did not hesitate to partake of a biscuit or a piece of cake. Though a strict observer of the Vinaya in all essentials she was no formalist, and was critical of Western *bhikkhus* who believed that they could eat chunks of cheese and bars of chocolate in the afternoon without technically breaking the 'no solid food after midday' rule. 'It's very bad for their stomachs,' she would say disapprovingly. For her, spirituality and common sense were not incompatible.

At one of our meetings she apologized for having been a little confused when I had telephoned the previous day. She had been deep in an Agatha Christie detective novel, she explained, and it had taken her a minute or two to realize who was speaking and what the call was about. Ayya Khema was in fact an Agatha Christie fan, a fact that showed there was a human side to her character, and that she was not quite such an austere figure as one might have thought. I was *not* a fan of the famous Queen of the Detective Novel and had never read any of her books, but I was at least able to tell my Dharma-sister that I had met her once or twice during the War.[521]

As we saw each other only once a year, Ayya Khema and I kept in touch principally by means of letters. I quickly discovered that she was an excellent correspondent, who rarely kept me waiting for more than a week or two before replying to my latest budget of news and views. As she wrote in one of her earlier letters, 'It is my habit to answer all letters almost immediately, as otherwise I would not be able to cope with them.' Believers in astrology might attribute her methodical ways to the fact that she was a Virgoan, her birthday falling the day before my own. Personally, I like to think that her fidelity as a correspondent was due to the fact that she believed, with Dr Johnson, that one should keep one's friendships *in constant repair.*[522] She was a good correspondent because she was a good friend.

In the course of the letters that passed between us we touched on a variety of topics. Apart from keeping each other informed about our movements and activities (we both travelled a good deal), and about the progress of our respective organizations, we discussed questions relating to the teaching of the Dharma in the West as well as more personal matters. Writing on 16 January 1993, Ayya Khema expressed her concern that a leading Buddhist teacher seemed to steer away from the truth of *dukkha* and make statements which seemed to contradict the Buddha's teaching in a fundamental way. One such statement was that you should 'embrace your rage', on which Ayya Khema tersely commented, 'Embracing means loving and drawing near. To my mind that is nonsense, but the way to purification is: Recognition, no blame, change.' This was very much my own opinion and paralleled what I had repeatedly said in connection with the popular New Age belief that one should 'accept oneself'.[523] Another well-known teacher had maintained that 'Enlightened Beings could still have cravings.' With this proposition, too, we both disagreed, if by an Enlightened Being one meant an *arhant*, as the teacher in question apparently did.

In the same letter, dated 28 August 1993, in which she had written about the second of these aberrations, Ayya Khema observed,

> 'I don't think it is surprising, if we have strange outcrops of the Dhamma in our times. We are not living in a spiritual age and the majority of Europeans have lost their connection with their own religious background, whereas Americans have probably never had such a connection. To superimpose a totally strange culture and utterly different social mores on people in the name of spirituality (or religion) seems to me a psychological disaster. An example is the assumption … that everyone will meet peaceful and wrathful deities after death. I would assume that a devout Catholic would encounter Jesus or the Virgin Mary, whereas practising Jews might have visions of Moses or such like. Not to speak of Theravādins who might encounter a vision of Buddha, or

> Ānanda or whatever. Peaceful and wrathful deities are not exactly part of a Central European mental culture. The same applies to the inordinate importance given to Japanese eating habits (chopsticks) and cultural implements in some of the Zen courses.

Once again, these were very much my own sentiments.

Ayya Khema belonged to a German Jewish family that had emigrated as a result of Nazi persecution. Writing to her about the VE Day commemoration in Britain[524] I therefore commented that for people of Jewish origin the occasion was no doubt one of special poignancy, adding, 'Like many others I still cannot understand how a civilized people like the Germans, who through their philosophy, music, and literature have made such an important contribution to world culture, could have produced the monster of Nazism.' To this she replied on 11 May 1995, with sadness for the past but also hope for the future,

> When the Nazis were persecuting the Jews here in Germany, my father said the same thing you wrote in your letter, namely that he could not believe that a civilized people like the Germans, who had produced Bach, Beethoven, Schubert, Wagner, Goethe, Schiller, Lessing, Kleist, Kant, etc., etc., could go along with an uneducated man like Hitler. But eventually he had to believe it and emigrate to China, where he died in a Japanese prisoner-of-war camp, five days before the end of the war. I fully agree that only the Dhamma will and can bring true peace and am directing all my efforts and energy to propagate this, which especially here in Germany finds many willing ears.

Thanks to Ayya Khema, there are now many more such willing ears – both in Germany and elsewhere – than there might otherwise have been.

In her teaching Ayya Khema dwelt more on practice and personal experience than on theory and speculation, and it was therefore not surprising that in her letter of 29 November 1994, she should have written, 'My whole emphasis has been on the *suttas*, although I did study the Vinaya for some years…' In similar vein, on 11 May 1995, she wrote that she considered the work of producing a new German version of the *Majjhima Nikāya* to be more important than translating the Abhidhamma. She also believed in the value of spiritual friendship, and in the same letter agreed with me that it was lacking among the Western Theravādin Sangha. Not that Ayya Khema always agreed with me, or I with her. This was far from being the case. But she possessed the rare virtue of being able to disagree without rancour, so that differences of opinion between us on such controversial topics as the nature of tolerance and the relation between Buddhism and Christianity were never allowed to disturb our friendship even slightly. She indeed was a remarkably fair-minded, balanced, and rational person.

The last letter I received from Ayya Khema was written in her own hand on 1 October 1997 – a month and a day before her death. In it she wrote, 'My health is not really improving, rather the contrary. I am trying in all ways to safeguard the teaching, so that my death will not be too disruptive.' It was typical of her that even at such a time she should think not of herself but of the teaching to which she had dedicated the last twenty years of her life, as well as of those who relied on her spiritual leadership. Though she now has gone the way we all must go, she lives on in her books, in the Order she founded only a week before her death, and in the memories of all who came in contact with her. While those who knew her as their beloved teacher will surely miss her supportive and inspiring presence, one who knew her as a very dear friend and fellow Dharma-farer will miss her friendship – and her letters – no less. May she attain Nibbāna!

This tribute was originally published in German translation in 'Grenzenloses Sein: Gedenkschrift für Ayya Khema', Jhana-Verlag, 1998.

ADHISTHANA WRITINGS

I
A REVERIE-CUM-REMINISCENCE IN THE FORM OF A LETTER TO PARAMARTHA

Dear Paramartha,

You left last Thursday, and that night I had a dream. I dreamed about my Auntie Kate. She was my mother's elder sister, and when I was very young I often stayed with her in the rather dark upstairs flat in Fulham where she lived with Uncle Dan.[525] She was extremely fond of me even though I was very naughty, pulling out her long hairpins when she had her afternoon nap or even tying her to the back of her chair. Far from minding she would only laugh at my tricks. She was indeed extremely fond of me, and I was extremely fond of her. The dream was quite a short one. I was in my mother's room, waiting for the arrival of Auntie Kate. The room was small and comfortably furnished, like a small nest, and there were colourful rugs on the floor. It was not like any room that my mother had actually ever occupied. In the dream, as in many other dreams, I was of no particular age, and I was not doing anything. I was simply waiting for the arrival of Auntie Kate and listening for her step on the stairs. I eventually heard it, the door opened, and in walked Auntie Kate. She was no bigger than a very small child, and I had to go down on the floor so that we could embrace each other. It was an intensely emotional occasion for both of us. I then woke up. The dream was fled, but my heart was still filled with love for Auntie Kate.

You will agree that it was a strange dream, and I cannot think what might have occasioned it. Though I have dreamt of my mother a number of times, this was the first time I had dreamed of Auntie

Kate. And why did she appear in the dream as a small child? The only connection I can make between the dream and a recent happening in my waking life is one that concerned Mallika, though admittedly it is a rather tenuous one. I had recently been told that 85-year-old Mallika was planning to move from Bethnal Green to Aberdeen in order to be near her youngest daughter, even though the move would mean leaving behind all her sangha friends, some of whom had been helping her for years.[526] The words that came to my mind when I heard of this were, 'the leaves return to the tree'. In other words, when we suspect that we may not have much longer to live we often feel a strong urge to return to our place of origin. Mallika was of Scottish origin and perhaps it is not surprising that she should want to go back to Scotland and be near her daughter. My own place of origin was South London, I having been born in Stockwell and brought up in Tooting. Though I am unaware of any urge to go and spend my last days in South London, in recent years I have often dreamt of standing and waiting for the Tooting Broadway bus or Underground train. Sometimes it would arrive, sometimes not, and I would be left waiting. I have also dreamt that I was sitting in the Tooting Broadway bus and looking out of the window as I waited for the bus to arrive at its destination, where I got out and started walking towards my old home. In some dreams that home would be associated with my mother. In one such dream I was walking home with her and on the way we stopped at a pub, where she had a meal before we continued on our way. In a more recent dream I was with a group of friends and I was anxious because I had promised my mother to be back by eight o'clock and it was now nine-thirty. I would have to get a taxi, I said. Whereupon you stepped forward, saying, 'Don't worry, I'll drive you to your mother's place.' On this occasion, as so often in real life, you were there when I needed you.

I certainly needed you towards the end of 2012. I was to move from Madhyamaloka, where I had lived for sixteen years, to my new home at Adhisthana; from a Birmingham suburb to the Herefordshire countryside. At the time I was quite ill. I was suffering from insomnia, which Temazepam sleeping tablets did little to relieve. Indeed, they made me feel worse. Moreover a doctor at the local surgery whom I had not seen before had prescribed a very high dose of Mirtazapine and this I was taking regularly with the Temazepam and my other medication. Thus during the last two weeks of February I was not at all in good shape. Yet the move still had to be made. In fact I felt that it had to be made as soon as possible. I had the strong conviction, whether rational or irrational I know not, that otherwise I could die before getting to Adhisthana, and I wanted desperately to get there and spend my last days within its peaceful shades.[527] A great deal of packing had to be done, and done quickly. Ill as I was I helped Vidyaruchi pack the images and books from my study.[528] You, almost single-handedly, packed everything else that was in the flat and in the treasury next door. This included crockery, kitchen utensils, clothes, books, pictures, box files, thangkas, and more than ninety *rūpas* of various kinds. You worked like a Trojan, if that is not too hackneyed an expression, or even like a demon, but the term would be incompatible with what one of your friends calls your 'angelic disposition'. Eventually, everything was packed, and at 11.30 a.m. on Sunday, 24 February 2013, we set off for Adhisthana. You were at the wheel, tired but determined. With us in the car was Vidyaruchi, while Ashvajit followed in his own vehicle. We had not gone very far when I started feeling nauseous, and we had to stop for a few minutes. As we joined the motorway you warned me that it would not be possible for you to drive as slowly as I might have wished. An hour and a half later we had reached our destination and were being welcomed by the Adhisthana team.

Two and a half years have passed since that day. The rest of 2013 proved to be a difficult time for me. Adhisthana was still a building site, with noisy heavy machinery operating each day of the week until August, when Adhisthana had its official opening. I was still very ill, with only very small improvements in my condition from month to month. Fortunately, my new GP reduced my Mirtazapine from the highest to the lowest dose, which seemed to help. I continued to suffer from insomnia, and I often felt – and looked – exhausted. I also suffered from night sweats, which were often so heavy that I had to change my pyjamas and even my bedding in the course of the night. My first months in my new home were thus neither very peaceful nor very happy. Nonetheless, I saw visitors from time to time and kept up with my correspondence as best I could. Dictating letters, especially letters to old friends, was one of my few sources of pleasure. It provided me with an outlet for creativity, albeit a limited one, and the more creative I could be the better I felt. My principal source of pleasure was the evenings in study and discussion I spent with a close friend. This friend, as you know, was you. You were not always at Adhisthana. There were times when your professional work took you to London and other parts of England, but wherever you were you kept in touch with me and made sure that I was being looked after. I sometimes think that without you I would not have come through 2013 even as well as I did. Nothing was too much trouble for you, even when it meant sacrificing your own comfort and convenience. As I came to realize, there were times when you sacrificed even your health and well-being for my sake. More than once I tried to expostulate with you on this account, but you were always emphatic that there was no question of any sacrifice. You did what you did of your own free will and you would not have chosen to be in any other situation. Yet I know that 2013 was a difficult year for you, as it was for me. Even so, you never complained.

By the end of the year my health had improved sufficiently for you to be able spend a month in New Zealand with your mother, leaving me in the hands of Buddhadasa (who had arrived in April), of Suvajra (who had finally arrived in November), and of Ashvajit who had become my secretary in succession to Vidyaruchi.[529] On your return at the end of January 2014, it did not take us long to get back into the previous year's routine. Indeed I had not departed from it very much while you were away. One of the things I had most missed during your absence, apart from your actual presence, was our evening study and discussion. This we did, as before, on those days when you were 'at home', though I cannot remember when we started. What I do remember is that having enjoyed a dip into Neoplatonism we immersed ourselves first in the *Saṃdhinirmocana Sūtra,* then in the much longer *Śūraṅgamasamādhi Sūtra.*[530] As we soon discovered, if we had not known it before, the two *sūtras* are very different in character, and breathe as it were different atmospheres. The *Saṃdhinirmocana Sūtra* is of a more philosophical nature, while the *Śūraṅgamasamādhi Sūtra* is more mythical, though in their different ways both point to the transcendental dimension of existence. While the first called for more discussion, as well as for note taking, on your part, the second demanded a more imaginative response. Though I had long wanted to study the *Śūraṅgamasamādhi Sūtra,* I did not at first take to it, and it was only after we had spent two or three evenings on it that I began to feel at all at home in its radiant world. It was a world inhabited by Buddhas and bodhisattvas, by gods and goddesses of various kinds, and towards the end of the *sūtra* there appears the cunning and malignant figure of Māra, the Evil One. As the weeks and months of study and discussion went by I felt that I was not merely a spectator of this world but living in it and breathing its unique atmosphere. Moreover, the *sūtra* came to be increasingly dominated by the figure of the great and glorious Mañjuśrī, the Bodhisattva of Wisdom, who appears as a supremely beautiful youth clad in princely garments and holding to his heart the scripture of Perfect Wisdom. With this figure I was already familiar, through my practice of the *Mañjughoṣa Stuti Sādhana*, but the *Śūraṅgamasamādhi Sūtra* gave me a much more vivid awareness of his presence and of his true nature. He was the veritable embodiment of the *dharma-niyama* and to be worshipped and meditated upon as such. Whether I shared this insight with you at the time I cannot remember. Thus the *Śūraṅgamasamādhi Sūtra* became a permanent part of my spiritual life, as I believe it did yours.

Thus far had my recollections led me when I reminded myself that although my short-term memory was reliable as regards events, it was less reliable as regards the chronology of those events. I therefore decided that I had better consult you about the sequence of our studies, as I knew you had kept a diary at the time. I could not consult you face to face, as you are now in New Zealand, having left Adhisthana a few days before I started writing this letter to you. I therefore had to consult you by telephone last night. This morning came a message with the desired information. According to your diary, we studied the two *sūtras* not in 2014, as I had supposed, but during the last four months of 2013. The discrepancy does not affect my recollection of the two *sūtras* themselves, especially that of the *Śūraṅgamasamādhi Sūtra*. The world of this *sūtra* is as much beyond time as it is beyond space, and while I was in it I too was beyond time. Strictly speaking, I should not even be locating my experience of the *sūtra* in the past. As I have already said, it remains a permanent part of my spiritual life.

Although we may not have studied the two *sūtras* in 2014, we did study other things on the evenings when you were 'at home', or at least, we engaged in discussion. Sometimes the discussion was very personal, and went very deep. During the same year my health continued to improve, especially after I stopped taking Zopiclone sleeping tablets, and it has continued to improve this year. By the end of May you were able to take me away on holiday. We spent six days in north Somerset. This was the farthest I had been away from Adhisthana since my arrival there nearly two years earlier, and at first I was concerned that I might not be able to make the journey. But my fears proved to be unfounded. I enjoyed the journey and enjoyed the holiday itself.

The bungalow we had taken was rather isolated and very quiet, and in the course of our stay we went out on only three of the six days we were there. Our first expedition was to Burnham-on-Sea and the coast, for you will remember that I very much wanted to see the sea, which I had not seen since we were in Felixstowe five years earlier. I did see the thin, dark blue line of the sea in the distance, but there was a strong wind blowing, and we stayed on the promenade only long enough for you to push me for a few dozen yards in the wheelchair we had brought with us. You did some shopping and we had a drink in a café in the smart little town. While I had not seen Burnham-on-Sea before, Glastonbury was a place with which we were both familiar. We did not attempt to climb the Tor but from below gazed up at the tower that crowns its summit, and a sociable fellow pilgrim was kind enough to take a photograph of us with the Tor and its tower in the background. This photo, together with a couple of others, you later put on my Facebook page. We also spent some time in the historic little town, where we explored the second-hand bookshops and had a drink in a rambling old café with rough wooden tables and benches. While you were getting our drinks, I became aware that sitting at the next table there was a group of young people and that from them there drifted towards me an aroma with which I had been familiar in the sixties and seventies. Our last expedition was to Cheddar Gorge, which I had not seen before but which you had visited with Jinaraja. I had not realized that it was so big or so impressive, and as we drove through it I gazed up at the rocky cliffs on either side with feelings of wonder and awe. Having driven through the whole length of the gorge, which was much longer than I had expected, we turned round and drove back through it to the little town from which Cheddar Gorge takes its name. Here we could find not a single empty parking space and in any case there was no disabled parking. We therefore drove on, and after a few miles were so fortunate as to come upon a wayside tea-house.

All three outings took place in the morning. We left the bungalow soon after breakfast and returned in time for lunch, which tended to be a late one. During our stay you cooked not only all our lunches, dinners, and breakfasts but also did all the washing up, laundering, and hoovering, doing everything with your usual smoothness and efficiency. Our afternoons and evenings, and the whole day when we did not go anywhere, we spent quietly at the bungalow. When planning our holiday we had talked of the study we would do and the discussions we would have, but so far as I remember we had only one session of study and there was little discussion between us. In fact we talked very little. Our study was concerned, I think, with the *Saṃdhinirmocana Sūtra*, which we had been studying during the previous two months for the second time. I was particularly struck by the fact that according to the *sūtra* the Buddha's teaching was a *miśra dharma*, or a mixed, or mingled, or integrated *dharma*, drawing as it did upon the teachings of all three *yānas*, these being the *yānas* of the *śrāvaka*, the *pratyekabuddha*, and the bodhisattva. As I had quickly perceived, Triratna teaches a *miśra dharma*, drawing as it does not only on these three *yānas* but drawing on, and integrating, teachings from all the major forms of Buddhism. When not cooking or cleaning, you spent much of your time reading and meditating or sitting outside in the sun, which I also did once or twice. I did virtually nothing apart from eating and sleeping. I felt no need to talk, or even to think. There seemed to be between us and all around us a great ocean of silence in which we were both content to live, move, and have our being. Later on, when we had returned to Adhisthana, you in fact remarked that it had been more like a retreat than a holiday.

June and July and the first three weeks of August passed quickly, and soon our holiday was a beautiful dream. Nor was it long before you were back at work, travelling to London and other places, while I returned to seeing visitors and dealing with correspondence. Adhisthana was then a hive of activity. Besides servicing the different retreats that were going on there, the resident sangha was busy making arrangements to celebrate my ninetieth birthday with a series of special events. Neither of us had much to do with these arrangements, though we could not help knowing what was going on. Whenever you were at home we continued spending our evenings in study and discussion. This time we started going through the papers that Subhuti had produced on the basis of his discussions with me five or six years ago. We had gone through three papers, and were going through a fourth, when you received the news that your mother was seriously ill. For a couple of days you were quite perplexed, not knowing what to do. You wanted to be with me on my birthday, but you also wanted to do the best you could for your mother. In the end it was decided that you should leave for New Zealand immediately. You left Adhisthana on Thursday, 20 August, having booked a flight that would leave Heathrow the following day. To an observer our parting might have seemed a very matter of fact affair, but each knew what the other felt and there was no need for words.

Three days later, on Sunday 23 August, you were in Christchurch from whence you sent me your first letter. It was a clear, crisp day, you wrote, with the mountains covered with snow. From Christchurch you flew to Invercargill where you found your mother in good spirits, all things considered. It was not long before you realized, however, that you might have to remain in New Zealand for quite a long time. Whether the time be long or short, your absence will surely be felt by those of whose lives you are an important part. Deji will feel it, as will the depleted Annexe Team, which now consists of Buddhadasa, Suvajra, and Sthanashraddha, my new secretary,[531] assisted from time to time by Mahamati and Yashodeva. I, too, will feel your absence, of course. How much I will feel it, you only will know.

Two days after your departure, when you were still in the air, Adhisthana saw the launching of my new book, *A Moseley Miscellany*. It was not clear whether or not I would be attending the event, but in the end I did attend it, and was deeply touched by the reception I received from the 400 Order members who had gathered in the marquee. In the evening, after dinner, I wrote an account of the launch while it was fresh in my memory, and this account I now insert in the present letter.

> Buddhadasa, Suvajra, and I left the Annexe for the big marquee a few minutes before five. As we did so, there were loud rumbles of thunder and the rain fell very heavily. We drove through 'tent city', which I had not seen before, and up to the back entrance of the marquee, where I was received by Yashodeva and Lokeshvara. Once inside I took my seat on my mother's chair (transported to the marquee for the occasion) with Parami on my right and Buddhadasa on my left. All this time, everyone was chanting the Śākyamuni mantra. Parami then said a few words, after which Subhuti very capably introduced Kalyanaprabha at some length.[532] While he was speaking the rain poured down heavily, so that he had to raise his voice above the uproar despite having the help of

> the microphone. Kalyanaprabha herself then spoke. She spoke very beautifully, and fortunately the rain stopped just as she began. Her voice was loud and clear, and she gave a résumé of the contents of *A Moseley Miscellany*. I was then given a large birthday cake and presented with a beautifully bound birthday card from the thousand and more Order members who had contributed to the £110,000 for the *Complete Works* and for translations.[533] This was the signal for everyone to sing 'Happy Birthday'. Buddhadasa, Suvajra, and I then returned to the Annexe, by which time the skies had cleared. The whole event had lasted for about 45 minutes. I was told that as I entered the marquee many people, both men and women, were in tears. One thing I forgot to mention was that after I had taken my seat I was garlanded by a young Dharmacharini with a flower garland that she and Sanghamani had made. Suvajra now tells me that several Order members who were outside the marquee while Subhuti was introducing Kalyanaprabha saw a rainbow over the Annexe!

My ninetieth birthday came four days after the book launch and I spent it quietly. Not much was happening at Adhisthana, and after lunch Suvajra drove me round to the Library, where Saddhanandi and Danasamudra gave me a guided tour of the *Nine Decades* exhibition that had been set up there[534]. Fortunately you were able to see the exhibition shortly before you left, so I shall not attempt to describe it. Suffice it to say that it showed both imagination and professionalism on the part of those who set it up and that it would have graced any museum. So far as I remember, the idea for the exhibition came either from you or was the outcome of a discussion between you and Saddhanandi. During the months preceding my birthday Saddhanandi and I met up every few weeks, or even every few days, depending on circumstances. We dealt with one decade at a time. Saddhanandi would describe the three objects representing the decade, then ask me about them and about my life at that time. She was an excellent interviewer, putting questions that enabled me to express myself fully and freely. By the time we reached the ninth decade we had produced what proved to be a highly popular overview of my life, and a friendship had sprung up between us.

I have now come to the end of this odd 'Reverie-cum-Reminiscence' of mine, cast in the form of a letter to you, and I must admit that I do not know how to proceed. Perhaps a reverie or a reminiscence simply goes on and on till it peters out and I think the time has now come for me to say *finis*. I have enjoyed writing it even if I've not always written about enjoyable things, and I hope that you will enjoy reading it.

Yours with much love, as ever, Bhante

2

MEMORIES OF PEOPLE PAST

Old Mr Boutell · The Young Philip Lingwood · Some Bombay Friends · Encounters on the Underground · Remembering Alaya · The Young Florence Ketskemety · My Uncle Leonard · A Brace of Uncles

OLD MR BOUTELL

I never met my father's stepfather but he was an important influence on me in my early life. He had been in the merchant navy and it was he who had brought back from China and other countries the curios that so fascinated me whenever I visited my grandmother.[535] A large photograph of him hung on the wall in her kitchen, opposite a smaller photograph of my own grandfather. He had a smooth round face with a heavy moustache, and his eyes looked out on the world with a calm, clear gaze. I do not know when the photograph was taken but he must have been about thirty at the time. Neither do I know when he married my grandmother or when he died. There were two children of the marriage, a girl and a boy. There was Dorothy who died before I was born, and Charles, who was ten years younger than my father and whom I knew quite well. My father always spoke of him either as 'Dad' or as 'the Old Man' and my mother used to refer to him as 'Old Mr Boutell'. He could be violent, and it seems that when he was really angry the only person who dared stand up to him was my mother. More than once did her intervention save Charles from a beating and it was therefore not surprising that he should always have been quite fond of her.

There were times when Old Mr Boutell was drunk. Not that he liked to drink alone. He liked to drink in the company of his male friends. Every two or three weeks the big front room of the flat would be the scene of a rather rowdy party. Crates upon crates of beer would arrive beforehand, my father once told me, and on some nights there might be as many as twenty or thirty revellers. There would be a lot of talking and laughing, shouting and singing. At such times my grandmother would keep out of the way. One of the revellers was Harry Lauder, the Scottish entertainer, who lived nearby, and who may well have entertained the company with a rendering of his well known *I Love a Lassie*.[536] Where the money came from I do not know.

Old Mr Boutell had no regular occupation, and he spent the whole day at home. His hobby was breeding prize bulldogs. When a pup was old enough he would tease it with a piece of rag until it became angry and clamped its teeth on the offending object, whereupon he would whirl the pup round and round in the air. If it kept hold of the rag it was a good bulldog and he would rear it. He must have hated cats as much as he loved bulldogs. Whenever one strayed into the small back garden he would catch it and kill it, burying the body at the foot of a grapevine that he was trying to grow in a corner of the garden.

Besides the curios he had collected, the Old Man possessed a formidable array of live shells of various kinds, one of which exploded when he was handling it, blowing off a thumb. After his death, my grandmother directed my father to get rid of these dangerous toys. Very gingerly he packed them in a suitcase and took them to the nearest police station, but the police refused to have anything to do with them. Chuck them into the nearest pond they told him. The suitcase must have rotted away long ago, but it is not unlikely that the shells are still lying at the bottom of a pond on Tooting Bec Common.

My grandmother got rid of a lot of other things as well. She herself once told me that soon after her husband's death she had thrown away all the grass skirts with which the walls of the front staircase were decorated. She was tired of having to dust them every day, she declared. She also got rid of some of the other curios. One of the ways in which she did this, to my great delight, was to give them to me, sometimes as a birthday or Christmas present. In this way I came into the possession of a pair of opium pipes with jade mouthpieces, a chopstick set, and a thunderbolt. He had acquired the thunderbolt, the Old Man had once told my father, when he was in South Africa. During a thunderstorm he had taken shelter in a bungalow with a corrugated iron roof and the thunderbolt had pierced through the roof and buried itself deep in the earth not far from his feet. He had dug it up, and it proved to be two inches in diameter and quite heavy.

Many of the curios he had collected were of Chinese provenance and in this connection, too, the Old Man had a story to tell. He was in Peking (this must have been around the turn of the century), and had acquired a number of ornate jugs, basins, and other vessels, all of solid gold. These he had packed in a strong wooden box and sent home by sea, but the box never arrived at its destination. Had it arrived, he had once told my father, he would have been a very rich man.

THE YOUNG PHILIP LINGWOOD

When I was very young my great pleasure was to spend time with my father. One of the reasons I liked spending time with him was that he used to talk to me telling me the names of flowers and trees and the stars, for although he lived and worked in the city he was at heart a countryman. He did not talk much about himself or about his own early life, though he may well have told me much that I have forgotten. His father having died when he was a few years old, his mother had sent him to live with his grandmother in Besthorpe, a village near Attleborough in Norfolk, where she herself had been born and brought up. There my father attended the village school. I remember once seeing a group photo of the children of the school, perhaps two or three dozen in number, seated in rows in front of the school building. Boys and girls alike, they all wore white pinafores. In the middle of one of the rows sat the small figure of my father. I cannot remember whether I was able to recognize him or whether my father pointed him out to me. My father was very fond of his grandmother, and must have lived with her and her blind husband for much of his childhood. He more than once told me how he went scrumping with the village boys and how they used to be chased by the farmers whose fruit they stole.

How old my father was when his mother brought him back to London, to live with her and his younger sister and, later, with his stepfather, I do not know. She must have been living at 23 Sellincourt Road, Tooting, where I was to spend my own childhood, for I know that my father attended the Sellincourt Road School. He had little or nothing to say about his schooldays, except that he used to fight with other boys. Like them, he must have left school at 14 and started looking for work.

It would appear that he was soon working for a jeweller. Whether he had been apprenticed in the traditional way, or was simply an employee, was never clear to me. The only reason I think he may have been apprenticed is that he 'lived in' and that with him there were other boys, whether apprentices or not. They were mischievous boys and played tricks on the establishment's elderly housekeeper. One of their tricks, my father once told me, was to catch cockroaches and string them at eye level across the passage where the short-sighted woman would, to her horror, bump into them. My father remembered the jeweller quite fondly, for he seems to have been a favourite of his. From time to time he would give him semi-precious stones, including several garnets, all of which in time came into my possession.

Then came the war, and it was not long before my father enlisted. 'Mum,' he told his mother, 'I've joined up.' She was not a woman of many words. 'Well,' she said, 'it's your decision, and you will have to live with it.' In what year my father enlisted I do not know, but at the time he could not have been more than sixteen or seventeen. Like many other young men at that time, he had given a false age and the authorities were naturally disinclined to question his word. I remember seeing a photograph taken of him shortly after he enlisted. The face that looked out from under the peak of the big army hat had an expression of shyness and self-consciousness, though at the same time it was evident that young Philip Lingwood was not devoid of self-assurance. Soon he was in France and living in the mud and blood of the trenches with other young men, hearing the dull thud of the heavy artillery of both sides and the screaming of shells overhead. Fragments from one of these shells hit him, and when he regained consciousness he was lying in a field hospital tent with a badly damaged and very painful right arm and hand. My memory next finds him an inmate of St Benedict's Hospital, Tooting, and wearing, like the other inmates, the light blue suit and red tie of the convalescent soldier. As a young man he had a hot temper, and he once told me that while at St Benedict's he had fought with another soldier, despite his injured arm, and had been pulled off him by one of the nurses in a way he found excruciatingly painful. His only other anecdote from this period of his life related to my mother. She was then a member of the Voluntary Aid Detachment (VAD) and her work sometimes took her to the hospital, which is how she and my father met. They used to go out together and sometimes, when he had stayed out after hours, she would help him climb back over the wall. From St Benedict's my father went to the Lord Roberts Workshops by which time he must have been discharged from the army. At the Lord Roberts Workshops, where disabled ex-servicemen were taught a trade, he opted for French polishing, and soon was able to earn a living. One day he said to his mother, 'Mum, I am going to get married.'

'Well,' she said laconically, in words she had once used before, 'It's your decision, and you will have to live with it.'

SOME BOMBAY FRIENDS

They ran down the slope holding hands, laughing like happy children. The scene was the garden of The Residence, Gangtok, where they were staying as guests of Apa Pant, the political officer with whom I also sometimes stayed. It was my first sight of Maurice and Hilla. We soon became acquainted, and they invited me to visit them at their Bombay home the next time I was in the city. The time must have been the mid-1950s.

Maurice Frydman was Polish, had spent some time in a Jesuit seminary, had come to India before the war, and for some years had worked as a civil engineer in Aundh, the smallest of the princely states. The ruler of the state was known as the Chief of Aundh and in Maurice's time the chief minister happened to be Apa Pant, the ruler's son. The two men had become friends and they had kept up their friendship after Independence, which was how Maurice and Hilla came to be staying with Apa Pant in Gangtok. Maurice was a very small man, with a big head of the long, dolichocephalic type, and he had one shoulder higher than the other. He always wore a white Indian shirt, over white pyjama pants, both garments being of khadi or hand-loomed cloth, for in matters economic Maurice was a staunch Gandhian. The costume was completed by a shoulder bag, in which he carried his spectacles and various papers, and by a pair of large black army boots. His white hair was close-cropped, his light blue eyes had the innocence of a child, while his thin face generally wore a mildly beatific smile. At the time of our first meeting he must have been in his mid-sixties. Hilla Petit was a Parsi by birth. She was rather taller than Maurice, and wore her grey hair bobbed in European style. She was probably older than Maurice and I never knew how they had originally met.

Maurice and Hilla lived in Bombay, in the exclusive Malabar Hill district. Whenever I was in Bombay I used to visit them at their ground floor flat on the Nepean Sea Road. In the living room there was much old-fashioned black teak furniture, which evidently had once graced a much bigger room. I particularly remember an elaborately carved settee some ten or twelve feet in length which could have comfortably accommodated seven or eight persons. From the centre of the ceiling there was suspended a huge crystal chandelier, which hung so low that a moderately tall person had to take care not to pass beneath it. The dining room was dark. If I happened to visit them in the morning, Hilla would press me, very warmly, to stay for lunch, which I often did. Lunch was a strange meal for Hilla liked everything to be passed through a blender, so that it all had the same consistency. With us at table there would be Hilla's adopted daughter, then 12 or 13 years old. Hilla doted on her, but Maurice had doubts about the wisdom of a middle-class, childless woman taking over the daughter of her servants, and in effect alienating her socially and culturally from her parents, who in this case were Goanese Catholics, as were many servants in Bombay. Despite his doubts, Maurice accepted the situation and liked to joke that theirs was what he called a synthetic family, rather than one made in the natural way.

Once I stayed on so long after lunch that both Maurice and Hilla pressed me to stay the night, which in the end I did. Maurice insisted on giving up his room to me, saying he would sleep on the floor in Hilla's room. His room was quite small and on three of its walls there hung huge framed portraits of Gandhi, Ramana Maharshi, and Krishnamurti. So large were they that they dominated the room, which contained little more than a mattress and a few books. These three were Maurice's heroes. Gandhi had been assassinated in 1948, Ramana Maharshi had died peacefully in 1950, but Krishnamurti was still alive, as I was soon to be reminded. On going to see my two friends one morning I found them in a state of suppressed excitement. Krishna-ji was in Bombay, they hastened to tell me, and he would be giving a few talks. On no account should I miss hearing him. They had some influence with the organizers of the talks, they added, and they would make sure I had a good seat. I was touched by their eagerness that I should hear Krishnamurti, and gladly accepted their offer. The name of Krishnamurti was well known to me. I had read some of his talks, and knew something of his history. As a boy he had been 'discovered' by the theosophist Charles Leadbeater, had been educated in England, and had been promoted by Leadbeater and Annie Besant as the new World Teacher, the Maitreya of the Buddhists, and the Messiah of the Christians, and a cult had developed around him. Krishnamurti had eventually broken free of the theosophists, dramatically rejecting the claims they had made on his behalf, claims which it seems he had once accepted. Since then he had travelled the world denouncing every form of religious faith and had, paradoxically, again become the centre of a cult! It was therefore not surprising that I should have wanted to see Krishnamurti in the flesh, and hear him speak.

Maurice and Hilla having been as good as their word, I had a seat near the side of the platform. There were about three hundred people in the hall, representing the cultural elite of Bombay. They sat on chairs rather than on the floor in the traditional manner and there was an expectant hush in the air. When Krishnamurti entered I observed him closely. He was tall and thin, with long grey hair, and he was dressed in a kind of white robe. His face was deeply lined, and his expression, I thought, was one of intense suffering. He reminded me of a fallen archangel. He spoke in English, with a public-school accent. The gist of his talk was that the Unconditioned was to be found in the conditioned, though how it was to be found he did not say. As I knew from the talks I had read, he did not believe there was such a way. The path to reality was a pathless path, nor did it lead anyone anywhere. The talk was not all on this high level. At one point Krishnamurti exclaimed in tones of withering scorn, 'There you all are, rotting beneath your *Bhagavad Gītās*!' A sigh of satisfaction passed through the audience. This was what they wanted. This was what they had come to hear. They were like a Christian congregation responding with deep satisfaction to the denunciations of the hellfire preacher who told them they were all damned. After the talk there were questions from the audience. 'Sir, we have been following you and listening to you for forty years,' said a woman of western appearance, her voice quivering with emotion, 'but we have not got anywhere.'

I do not remember what Krishnamurti said in reply. What I do remember is that a number of people turned towards the woman with expressions of irritation and annoyance. How could she be so obtuse, they seemed to be saying. After the meeting Maurice and Hilla were eager to know what I thought of Krishnamurti's talk. I had enjoyed it very much, I said, as indeed I had. Whereupon they offered to make arrangements for me to hear the rest of his talks, evidently assuming that having once had a taste of him I could not but want more. I declined the offer. Krishnamurti believed that one should not try to repeat an experience, I reminded them, and I had no intention of trying to repeat the experience I had been vouchsafed that evening. I also asked Maurice about his hero's condemnation of the study of the *Bhagavad Gītā* and other scriptures. If it was wrong to study them, why did he allow his talks to be published in book form? Krishna-ji's books, Maurice retorted, were not books but slices of experience. This by no means satisfied me. If his books were slices of experience, I wanted to know, were not the *Bhagavad Gītā* and other scriptures also slices of experience?

Maurice had three heroes, but Hilla seemingly had only one, as I discovered when she showed me her room one day. Inside the door, to the right, there was a kind of sideboard on which stood, all in silver frames, twenty or more photographs of Krishnamurti at different stages of his life. A stick of incense was burning. There were other differences between the two friends. Hilla sometimes liked to talk, but she could not be described as talkative, whereas Maurice could be extremely talkative. He was very fond of giving advice, regardless of whether or not it was wanted. He gave it good-naturedly and seemed not to mind if it was not taken. I was a particular object of his solicitude. He appeared to think that I was young and inexperienced, and needed the guidance of those who were older and wiser. He was especially concerned to advise me on my work among the ex-Untouchables, as they were then called, who in 1956 had converted to Buddhism under the leadership of Dr Ambedkar. He gave me advice on this subject whenever we met, as well as sometimes advising me in writing. Not that Maurice ever wrote letters. He wrote only postcards. His handwriting was so big that on a postcard there was room only for a couple of short sentences and his signature. His advice was often too general to be useful, but once he said something that made a deep impression on me. 'Sangharakshita,' he once said, taking me by the arm, 'you are wasting your time teaching these people about Buddhism. They do not need a Buddha. What they need is a Manu.' As I knew, Manu was the legendary Indian Lawgiver, whose code governed every aspect of Hindu social life from the cradle to the grave, and I could not but acknowledge that there was truth in Maurice's words. More than once had I found, on meeting a group of newly converted Buddhists, that they did not ask about Buddhist philosophy, or about meditation, or even about ethics. Their first question was invariably, 'Now that we are Buddhists, how are we to perform the marriage ceremony?'[537]

Although many of the new Buddhists were illiterate, especially in the rural areas, there had sprung up, even before 1956, a small educated elite. To this elite belonged Professor Shewalay. I do not remember how we first met, but it must have been in or near the Siddharth College of Arts and Science in Bombay, where he taught. He had brought with him in his tiffin box a little wad of chapattis, and it being lunchtime he offered me one. I took the chapatti and we continued our conversation. Afterwards he told me how impressed he had been by the matter of fact way that I had taken the chapatti. He came from an ex-Untouchable community, he explained, and although untouchability had been outlawed in India there were many caste Hindus who would not accept food from his hands or even touch him. The fact that I had accepted a chapatti from him meant that we were friends. He was a small man, even smaller than Maurice, and unlike Maurice he wore a Western-style jacket and trousers, complete with collar and tie, and he had a mop of black hair. His eyes were unusually bright and his thin face at times wore a sweet smile. His voice was rather loud for such a small man, and his laugh was unpleasantly raucous. Even in ordinary conversation he tended to hold forth emphatically, as though he was lecturing a class of rather dull students. As I soon discovered, Shewalay was a very ambitious man. His ambition was to create a Buddhist university. In his own mind, indeed, the university already existed. He would say such things as, 'The university will be closed next week', or, 'Pāli classes will be held at the university at eight o'clock every evening', and so it stood before him in all the glory of bricks and mortar. Pāli classes were indeed held, but they were held in a room at Siddharth College and they were taken by Shewalay himself. Though his subject was history, Pāli grammar was his passion. Unfortunately, my friend was not a good communicator. All he did was drill the thirty or more new Buddhists who came to his classes in declensions and conjugations. 'I *love* teaching Pāli grammar', he told me enthusiastically, his eyes shining. But the students had come not for declensions and conjugations but for the Dhamma, and gradually they stopped coming.

It was around this time that I got to know Muriel Payne OBE. I was introduced to her by Maurice, who had known her for many years. She was a tall, well-built woman of about 50, with well groomed white hair, and she wore a simple blue dress. Her manner was dignified but friendly, and her face wore a pleasant smile. She was an educationist and had been awarded her OBE for her work in the field of Indian education. She was also a trained nurse, and during the war she had lived with Krishnamurti for six months and nursed him through a mental breakdown. In the course of her work with schools in different parts of India she had noticed that there was no real communication between teachers and pupils, just as I had noticed that there was none between Shewalay and his Pāli students, and that it was largely owing to this lack of communication that educational standards were so low. She had also noticed that there was little communication between the teachers themselves or even between some husbands and wives. In order to remedy this appalling situation she had devised what she called 'communication exercises'. Though she was no writer she had written a book with the title *Creative Education*, in which the exercises were described.

I was fascinated by all this, for the exercises helped one to become more aware of the person with whom one was communicating, and mindfulness or awareness was an important Buddhist virtue. So fascinated was I that one day I told Miss Payne, as she was always called, that if she would agree to teach the exercises to a group of people, I would undertake to find both the people and a venue for the course. The result was that for three or four successive evenings she taught the 'communication exercises' to me and about twenty other people, all friends of mine, including Professor Shewalay. I found the exercises not only useful in developing awareness but also exhilarating, and I have since taught them to others. Shewalay, not surprisingly, found the very idea of communication difficult to grasp, and insisted on arguing with Miss Payne instead of doing the exercises. She must have thought of him as being the embodiment of all that was worst in the Indian educational system. Miss Payne had other tricks up her sleeve, so to speak. Happening to notice that there was a slight squint in one of my eyes she asked if I would like her to 'run a process' on me, to which I readily agreed. She then told me to think of an eye, which I did. Could I see the eye? Yes. What was the expression of the eye? 'Oh, it is very angry,' I exclaimed. Next she asked me if I knew where I was, whereupon everything changed. I was a baby and lying on my mother's lap, my mother herself being seated on a low nursing chair. My father's sister, who was also my godmother, was looking down at my mother with an expression of anger that seemed to include me. I think the squint that Miss Payne had noticed disappeared, though it may return at times of stress.

I never met Miss Payne again, and never heard what became of her after I had left India in 1964. Shewalay had told me that one day he would follow in the footsteps of the Buddha quite literally. He would marry, would have a son, and then go forth from home into homelessness, and, as I learned a few years later, this he had actually done. He had married a prostitute (on principle), had had a son, and had been ordained as a *bhikkhu*, under the name of Sivalibodhi. After his ordination he had continued to live with his mother, his wife, and his son, supporting them out of his salary as a professor at the Siddharth College of Arts and Science. Whether he went to work each morning wearing his yellow robe I never knew. Knowing my old friend as I did, I think that he probably did just that.

ENCOUNTERS ON THE UNDERGROUND

I was born and brought up in South London, and it was therefore not long before I became acquainted with the extensive network that is the London Underground system. I made my first journey on the Tube, as it was popularly called, when I was six, and I made it in the company of my father. Most likely we were on our way to one of the South Kensington museums. My predominant impression, as we sat in the rapidly moving carriage, was one of stifling heat, and noise so loud that we could hardly hear each other speak. Thereafter I was to make regular use of the Underground both before my departure for India in 1944, and after my return in 1964. It was in the early years of this latter period that

I had my four encounters. Two of them took place on the Northern Line and two on the Central Line.

It was eleven o'clock at night, and I was travelling on the Northern Line, heading for north-west London where I was then living. I must have been leading a meditation class or giving a lecture and had stayed on afterwards talking with friends until quite late. My mind still being preoccupied with our discussion, I did not at first take much notice of the person sitting opposite. Eventually I looked at him, or rather, I realized that he was looking at me. He was wearing cherry-coloured corduroy trousers and a buttercup-yellow shirt open at the throat. I judged him to be seventeen or eighteen and his beautiful face was lit up with a smile. He was not only looking at me but looking at me with what could only be called love. In fact he seemed to be in love with me. I did not know what to think, especially as the angelic young man was evidently in a state of sexual arousal. Who was he? What did he want with me? Should I speak to him, or should I wait for him to make the first move? Such were the thoughts that passed through my mind. How long we sat gazing at each other, he with that look of adoration in his eyes, I do not know. It could not have been for more than five minutes for by this time I had reached my destination and had no choice but to alight.

The young man did not move. Over the years I have often reflected on the encounter. Had the young man taken LSD, in which case would he have looked at whoever came and sat opposite him with the same love with which he had looked at me? Alternatively, perhaps our paths had crossed in this way because we were meant to be friends and companions and I should not have allowed my habitual cautiousness to prevent me from asking him to go home with me regardless of what some of my friends might think. Whatever I should or should not have done, the vision of the beautiful young man in the cherry-red corduroy trousers and buttercup-yellow shirt remains with me to this day.

My second encounter took place on the Central Line. At the time I was living at Sukhavati, above the FWBO's centre in Bethnal Green, and every few months I would have a little holiday, taking the Tube from Bethnal Green to Tottenham Court Road, from whence I would explore the bookshops of Charing Cross Road. On one such occasion I was caught up in the morning rush, and found myself hemmed in by commuters. To my right was the back of a woman. She had a bag slung over her shoulder and the mouth of the bag was half open. Facing me and the woman's back stood a well-dressed man in his thirties. We had not been long on our way before he slid his hand into the woman's bag. I looked at him and slowly shook my head as if to say 'you shouldn't be doing that, you know'. The man smiled and withdrew his hand from the bag. A few minutes later the train stopped, the doors opened, and several people including the pickpocket got out, and the woman and I continued on our way with rather more elbow room than before. Reflecting on the incident afterwards, I concluded that the well-dressed man was a professional pickpocket, taking systematic advantage of the cramped conditions that prevailed on the Underground during the morning and evening rush hours.

My next encounter also took place on the Central Line when I was returning from Tottenham Court Road to Bethnal Green. I was sitting at the end of the carriage. Opposite me, but a little nearer to the exit, there sat an elderly couple. The woman had a small closed basket on her lap, from which a faint mewing could be heard. From the other end of the carriage there came towards us a strange figure. He was tall and raw-boned and his filthy, tightly fitting clothes clung to him like a second skin. His long hair was unkempt, and his expression was fierce and scowling. As he came he sang in a loud raucous voice accompanying himself with strident strummings on his guitar. As he neared the old couple the gentleman asked him, very politely, not to sing and play so loudly. They had a kitten in their basket, and the noise was frightening it. The man snarled a peremptory refusal and went on singing and playing more loudly than ever. Some people gave him money, others did not. I was one of those who did not give him anything. It was not that I disapproved of buskers, even though busking was illegal, but I was disgusted by his behaviour towards the old couple and their kitten. Far from disapproving of buskers, I would generally give them a few coins. At Tottenham Court Road station near the exit from the southbound platform there was a corner in which a busker would be playing. More often than not he or she was an out of work classical musician, and as one stepped off the escalator one would hear in the distance the sound of a violin or a flute playing a beautiful Bach melody.

From out of work musicians to out of work actors is only a short step, and I am reminded of an encounter, if such it may be called, that took place not on the Underground but in a café. The café was the As

You like It, which was situated next door to Sakura, the Buddhist shop, in Monmouth Street, in whose basement the FWBO's first meditation classes were held. After a class, my friend Terry and I would sometimes adjourn to As You Like It, where I would have a cup of tea and he his evening meal. Barrie, the owner of the café, was a very thin, very camp man of about 35. He spent much of his time talking on the phone, for As You Like It doubled as a kind of theatrical agency, and there were usually two or three good-looking young actors lounging about. Just inside the entrance there invariably sat a very elderly woman. She was dressed entirely in black, and her black hat made her yellowish features look almost cadaverous. She never spoke to anyone, except for a word to Barrie or to the young actor who brought her meal. It was always a big meal, and probably her one square meal of the day, and I noticed that Barrie never charged her for it. With her she had a large handbag, stuffed full of newspaper cuttings, and when not eating she would take out some of these and study them closely. I never saw her arrive, and I never saw her leave. She seemed to be a permanent fixture of the place.

My last encounter took place on the Northern Line, as I was travelling down to Tottenham Court Road. There were not many people in the carriage and looking along the gangway to the left I saw a man standing with his back towards me in front of the closed doors of the carriage. Of medium height and sturdily built, he wore a dark suit and was bare headed. He was obviously waiting for the next stop. The instant I set eyes on him I said to myself, 'That's not a human being, that's a little devil,' and I decided to keep him under observation. This I could do for only a few minutes, for the train soon came to a halt and the doors slid back. As they did so, the man turned round and very deliberately thumbed his nose at me. He then skipped onto the platform and ran laughing to the exit. It was as though he was saying, 'You haven't caught me yet.'

REMEMBERING ALAYA

In my bedroom in the Urgyen Annexe there hangs a framed print of Dr Johnson, one of my five literary heroes. The print was a birthday present from Alaya.[538] I do not remember which birthday this was, but I do remember Alaya giving me the print at the Norwich Buddhist Centre in All Saint's Green, which I was then visiting. Alaya had framed the print himself, for he was a carpenter and had been a member of the team that created Sukhavati, our centre in Bethnal Green.[539] Though I did not have many meetings with Alaya over the years, three of them stand out. The first was when we attended a retreat held at Court Lodge, the home of Subhuti's parents. I particularly remember his mass of ginger hair, which made a pleasing contrast with his dead-white skin. Our second meeting took place when I visited him when he was living as a member of a kind of hippy commune. I used to go past the commune, which was situated not far from the road, whenever I drove from London to Padmaloka. It stood opposite a pub called, I think, the Angel (connoisseurs of Norfolk pubs will correct me if I am wrong). I remember Alaya proudly showing me the communal earth closet, where he said he often enjoyed friendly chats with other members of the commune. Our last meeting took place in Norwich, at his home, when I spent a pleasant evening with him, his wife, Ratnamala, and their son, Sam. He had long been suffering from epilepsy but was at that time in a reasonable state of health. Subsequent bulletins about his health made it clear that his condition was deteriorating and I was not surprised when I heard that he was in hospital. His death at 55 came as rather a shock, and my heart goes out to Ratnamala and Sam. He was a friendly person, fun-loving but serious, and he was concerned to keep up his connections with the Order. His practice was the Green Tārā *sādhana*, which I remember giving him. May she protect him on his way!

THE YOUNG FLORENCE KETSKEMETY

My mother's earliest memory was of being in a perambulator with her younger brother, Jack, and being pushed round Battersea Park by her eldest sister, Kate, who had brought her up, her mother having died when she was very young. Jack was connected with another early memory. On Sundays straight after Sunday school the brother and sister had to go and pay their respects to their aunts, Faith, Hope, and Charity, who were unmarried and lived together. All three dressed in black, with buttons right up to the throat, but although they looked very severe, they always treated their little visitors kindly. After they had made their little bobs to each of the aunts in turn, a rather formal conversation would ensue, and Florence and Jack would each be given a glass of lemonade. As soon as they were out of the house, the two children would scamper down the street, laughing and shouting, glad that the constraints of the visit were over. My mother never spoke about her schooldays, but she did tell me how she used to help her Hungarian grandfather in his grocery shop in Vauxhall Bridge Road. Though he had lived in England for much of his life, her grandfather's command of English was far from perfect, and my mother had picked up from him a few words of Hungarian. The shop being situated in a working-class district, many of its customers were quite poor. Mothers would send their children to buy a ha'p'orth of pickles and she remembered giving them the pickles in a paper cone. Her father was a clarinettist and had been in the army. She was his youngest daughter, and very much his favourite. He used to call her his little fairy, she once told my sister and me, and from the way she said it, it was clear she had been very fond of her father. He had once taken her with him when he had a professional engagement in France. The Channel crossing may very well have been a rough one for my mother more than once spoke of her fear of the sea. 'You won't catch me going on the water,' she would say. After their father's death the brothers and sisters would gather on Saturday night at the family home, where some of them still lived, for a fish supper. George, the eldest brother, would preside, asking each of them in turn, 'Haddock or kipper?'

At the time of her father's death the young Florence Ketskemety may already have been living not in Fulham, where she grew up, but in Merton, with her sister Kate and Kate's husband, Dan. He was a tall, well-built Irishman with a loud voice and a crude sense of humour. At parties he would put three fingers up the chimney into the soot, then make three black stripes on the sleeves of the girls' white silk blouses, despite their protests. He called this 'making them sergeants'. He was also not above trying to take liberties with his young sister-in-law. Once he went so far that she threatened to tell Kate if he persisted. 'He was not a nice man,' she commented many years later when telling me about the incident. After leaving school, Florrie, as she was called, worked in a laundry. 'That's why I've got strong arms,' she once told me years later, not without a touch of pride. She also practised regularly with the India clubs, and was fond of playing diabolo. My father once told me and my sister, Joan, that when our mother was a girl she could throw the 'devil' up in the air in one street and then run round the block and catch it as it came down in the next street. Joan and I were then both quite young and could not always tell if our father was serious or pulling our leg.

When Florrie was sixteen the First World War began, and it was not long before she left the laundry to work as a waitress in the restaurant of the Army and Navy Stores in Victoria Street, where her elder brother Bert was manager of the catering department. At the time waitresses were a novelty, but the waiters having all joined up, their places had to be filled up somehow. One day Florrie had a terrifying experience. She still lived with Kate and Dan in Merton, and was on her way home from work when she became aware of the silver shape of a Zeppelin high in the air above her, going in the same direction as herself. On coming to a crossroads she turned left and the Zeppelin too turned left. Convinced that the silver monster was following her, she took to her heels and ran all the way home. Nearly seven hundred Londoners were killed by bombs dropped from Zeppelins, and nearly two thousand were seriously injured, so Florrie had good reason to be frightened. Florrie's elder brother Tom was in the army as was her younger brother Jack. Tom was better suited to military life than his more sensitive brother and it was not long before Jack deserted, taking refuge in the family home in Fulham. Looking out of the window one day, Tom saw in the street below two policemen who were looking for Jack and called out to them, 'Come and get the bugger! He's here!' His sisters shrieked and did their best to drag Tom away from the window. What happened next I never learned. What I did learn, years later, was that Tom had died as a prisoner-of-war in Silesia and that after the war Jack had suffered a nervous breakdown.

As a young woman, my mother naturally had interests outside the family and her workplace. She once told me that there was a young man whose eye she seemed to have caught. He was in the army and was a regular visitor at Kate and Dan's place, where he used to entertain them all by playing on the piano. This was the family piano on which all the brothers and sisters had practised and which had passed into Kate's keeping on the death of their father. I remember that piano very well, for from Kate it had eventually passed to my mother, and I remember her playing on it occasionally when I was quite small as I sat on the floor near her feet. Besides working as a waitress, the young Florrie was an active member of the VAD (Voluntary Aid Detachment). A photo in my possession shows her wearing her VAD uniform. It was probably taken in a studio for she stands with her right hand resting lightly on the back of a chair and her right foot slightly advanced. She wears a trench coat belted at the waist, together with dark stockings and sensible shoes. The face beneath the dark beret is rather thin with a big nose, and she looks straight ahead. The impression I get as I look at the photo is of a young woman of some strength of character. Part of her work as a member of the VAD consisted in visiting wounded soldiers who were convalescing. One of the hospitals within her area was St Benedict's in Tooting, and it was there that she met my father, who was recovering from shrapnel wounds to his right arm. Neither of them ever spoke of their first meeting, or of their courtship, but a day came when the young Florence Ketskemety could display on the third finger of her left hand a diamond ring.

MY UNCLE LEONARD

Uncle Leonard was the only uncle I had from my father's side of the family. One of his father's brothers had been the first husband of my grandmother, who was still 'Aunt Anna' to him. My grandmother, now widowed for the second time, lived in Elborough Street, Southfields, and Uncle Leonard lived round the corner in Replingham Road. Whenever I stayed with Nana, as I called my grandmother, I would go and pay a visit to Uncle Leonard, whom I always found working at the bench in his shoe repair shop, a cigarette in the corner of his mouth and sometimes unshaven. He was always glad to see me, and when I left he would give me a few coppers from the till. Besides having his shoe repair business, Uncle Leonard bred Sealyham Terriers. They lived under the counter in the shop and if I was lucky there would be puppies to see. After talking with Uncle Leonard and playing with the dogs I would wander into the living quarters behind the shop to say hello to Auntie Louie.

All this was before I was 8 years old, and before I was confined to bed with valvular disease of the heart. As I look back I can still see in my mind's eye Uncle Leonard's kindly smiling face, and it occurs to me that as a young man he must have been quite handsome. It also strikes me that there was a strong resemblance between him and my father and that the resemblance was not only facial but extended to their characters. Both were good-natured, generous, unambitious men, who were devoted to simple pursuits, in my father's case his garden and in Uncle Leonard's his Sealyhams. Although Uncle Leonard was about the same age as my father, as far as I know he had not fought in the First World War as my father had done. The eldest of his three sons did, however, fight in the Second World War and was awarded the Military Cross. I never met either him or the next eldest brother, but I did know John, the youngest of the three, who used to visit me when I was staying with Nana after my convalescence. I remember a photograph of the two of us. I am sitting in my wheelchair in Nana's porch and John, who was of about my own age, is standing beside me. He is still in short trousers and already beginning to look like his father.

Soon after my return to England in 1964, a friend drove me through Elborough Street and into Replingham Road. Nana's house, with its white porch and well-kept front garden, was still there, but Nana was not, having died some years earlier, and when we turned into Replingham Road, I scanned it for Uncle Leonard's shoe repair shop in vain. The name of Lingwood was no longer to be seen.

A BRACE OF UNCLES

Uncle Dan and Uncle Charlie were my uncles by marriage, each of them having married one of my mother's sisters. Uncle Dan was Irish, and on marrying him, Auntie Kate, who was my mother's eldest sister, had converted to Catholicism, which she took more seriously than he seemed to do. I remember him as a tall, well-built man, with a loud voice and a red face, part of which was disfigured by a kind of carbuncle. He always dressed in black, down to his very boots, which were big, black, and shiny, as if to proclaim his proletarian status, he being the only man in the family who wore boots instead of shoes. For similar reasons, no doubt, he wore a flat workman's cap.

Uncle Charlie, who had married my mother's sister Jessie, was of medium height, and always wore a three-piece brown suit, with brown shoes and a collar and tie, and of course a trilby. His face was pink rather than red, and it had none of Uncle Dan's corrugations. Uncle Dan worked as a stoker at Lotts Road Power Station in Fulham, and he was an active member of his Union. I never saw him when I stayed with Auntie Kate, for he would be on the night shift, and I remember her making up his bottle of cold tea, as well as laying out his dress clothes when he had a Union meeting. Uncle Charlie was in the butchery line of business, and he and Auntie Jessie lived in Chiswick above the butcher's shop of which he was manager. I never knew the details, but

I gathered that Uncle Charlie had once got into serious trouble for levying an unauthorized tax on the contents of the till. This did not surprise me, as he was a betting man and may well have been losing money on the gee-gees.[540]

It was only at Christmas and the New Year that I saw both uncles at the same time, when with their two wives they visited my parents at our Tooting home. The three men would talk politics, which my father otherwise hardly ever did, though he was a supporter of the Labour Party, or at least always voted for it. (His mother, being a property owner, always voted Conservative.) Much to the disgust of my mother and her sisters, Uncle Dan had a lavatorial sense of humour, which their protests could not always silence. Decades later, when the name of Uncle Dan happened to come up between us, my mother remarked with some feeling: 'He was not a nice man.'

3
ALTERNATIVE LIVES

Colin Wilson Revisited · What Might Have Been · The Young Man in the Hut · Alternative Lives · Living with Carter · Four Visitors

COLIN WILSON REVISITED

Colin Wilson's *The Outsider* was published in 1956, and a few years later a friend of mine lent me the book with the comment that I would find it interesting. This friend considered himself to be very much an Outsider, as he had more than once told me, and the consciousness that he was an Outsider deeply rankled with him, making him feel bitter and resentful.

That was fifty or more years ago. Though I found the book interesting, I did not follow up the idea of the Outsider until some years later, when I was concerned with the nature of the difference between the individual and the group member, and between the group and the spiritual community.[541] Neither was I then concerned with the question of whether or not I was myself an Outsider in Colin Wilson's sense of the term. As I look back over my life it appears to me that even if I did not think of myself as an Outsider there were times when I was seen as one by others, at least in certain respects. For the first few years of my life the question of whether or not I was an Outsider did not arise. Indeed, it could not arise for I was born into a family of which I was a fully accepted member from the beginning. I belonged to it, and took the fact of my belonging to it for granted. This happy state of affairs came to an end, to an extent, when at the age of 10 or 11 I went back to school after an absence of two or more years. I was absent because I had been confined first to bed and then to a wheelchair, and I was confined to them because I had been diagnosed as suffering from valvular disease of the heart. Even when I was back at school I was not allowed to play games or take part in PT, or even to walk fast, much less still to run. I was not allowed to stand during morning assembly, for it was thought that if I stood for too long it would put a strain on my heart. A classmate was therefore deputed to follow me into the hall carrying a chair, and on this chair I would sit during the hymns, prayers, and announcements. I sat on it even when the rest of the assembly sat on the floor, which made me a very conspicuous figure. In this way I came to be considered different from the other boys and perhaps even as something of an Outsider.

Being an Outsider, if such I was in those days, was not without its advantages. Because I could not run around in the playground with the other boys I stayed in the classroom during breaks and read. Sometimes I had a companion. This was a boy of my own age called Douglas Nicholas. He was fair-haired and green-eyed, with a yellowish complexion, and though he was quite a big boy he was very timid and was known as a cry baby. Since he was afraid of being set upon he did not go out into the playground during breaks and thus sometimes came and sat by me. Though he was timid, he had a vicious streak in his character and liked to pinch me in the leg quite hard so that I was not fond of his company. On leaving school one afternoon I found that Douglas Nicholas was being pinned against a wall by a group of eight or nine boys. They were punching, poking, and pushing him and he was blubbering. Without thinking I pushed my way through the boys, seized Douglas by the hand, and to jeers and catcalls led him away to safety, which meant taking him halfway home, though his home was in a different direction from mine. The incident made me realize that being an Outsider gave me a certain immunity, even a certain status, so that I was able to do things that I could not otherwise have done.

A few years later there came the war, and with the war there came the great evacuation of school children from London to places of safety in the countryside, for it was expected that London would be bombed by the Luftwaffe. The bombing did not come at once, but it did come later, when in 1940 the Luftwaffe rained bombs on London for fifty-seven nights in succession, killing 20,000 people and destroying much of the city, including sixteen Wren churches. I had been evacuated a few months earlier, travelling with my suitcase and my gas-mask to distant Devonshire in the company of several dozen classmates. At first I was made welcome, but in my second billet the landlady conceived an aversion to me eventually referring to me as a ''vacuee' in tones that suggested that for her an evacuee was among the lowest forms of human life.[542] To her I was an Outsider, not only because I was an evacuee but because I spoke with a different accent and had interests that were beyond her ken. My younger sister, Joan, had a more positive experience of evacuation. She had been evacuated the previous year to Sussex, being billeted with a farmer and his wife not far from Chichester. When she had been with them for a couple of months my mother and I paid her a visit. Mr and Mrs Ayling were both in their late thirties. They were childless, and it was soon evident that they treated Joan as their own daughter. Mrs Ayling was like any other housewife, but in his corduroy britches and leather gaiters Mr Ayling was the very picture of a farmer. I do not remember how long the visit lasted, but we stayed long enough to accompany Joan and Mr Ayling to a livestock auction, Mr Ayling having a cow he wanted to sell. It fetched only £2 and I shall not easily forget the look of disappointment, almost of anguish, that passed over his bronzed, handsome face. Back at the farm my mother chatted with the Aylings, while Joan snuggled up to Mr Ayling, and I picked up a book that was lying around. It bore the title *My Life in Time*, and it had been written by Mr Ayling's aunt. As its title suggested, the authoress had a life outside time as well as in it, and I soon discovered that the work was of the occult or 'mystical' type, such as were soon to become known to me through the writings of Madame Blavatsky.

This was not the first time that I had picked up and read a book while visiting with my mother. Not long before our visit to the farm she had taken me to see Auntie Jessie, one of her elder sisters, who lived in a downstairs flat in Chiswick. The visit probably occupied the greater part of the day, for the two sisters had a lot to say to each other, and it was not long before I started looking around for something to read. There was nothing lying around, but in my aunt's living room there was a glass-fronted bookcase and in the bookcase I could see several rows of books. Soon I had taken out three of the books – E. W. Hornung's

Raffles, and Marie Corelli's *The Mighty Atom* and *Jane* – and by the time my mother and I had said goodbye to Auntie Jessie I had read all three. Raffles, the eponymous hero of the novel, is a gentleman crook and the book seemed to be an attempt to make crime look glamorous. Marie Corelli's books were shorter and much more moral. Indeed, I remember them as being full of moral indignation. In *The Mighty Atom* the indignation is directed against those wicked people who thought that children should be brought up without being given any religious instruction. Here the eponymous hero is a dear little boy who hangs himself with his beautiful silk sash because he wants to find out whether or not there is a God. In *Jane* her indignation is directed against the frivolous, loose-living upper classes. The eponymous heroine inherits a fortune and decides to see what fashionable society is like. She buys a big house in London, entertains the highest aristocracy, including royalty, and one evening has the satisfaction of ordering everyone to leave her house at once. Young as I was, I well understood that in the person of her heroine, Marie Corelli was pronouncing the verdict of the virtuous middle-class on the doings of their profligate social superiors. Marie Corelli was a bad writer, according to the critics, but she was highly readable, which is probably why I remember those books to this day.

As my behaviour on these visits suggests, I was in the habit of picking up and reading any book that I found lying around. Whether young or old, at home or abroad, one of the first things I would do on finding myself in a new place was to see what books were there for me to read during my visit. One of the most memorable of such finds took place more than sixty years ago. I was in South India with a friend. We were wandering ascetics, having gone forth from home into the homeless life as the Buddha had done many centuries earlier. We had no identity papers, no possessions other than the *gerua*-dyed robes we wore and, in my case, a copy of the *Dhammapada*. We went barefoot, walking from place to place and relying for our food on the generosity of the people through whose villages we passed. We were Outsiders. We were in the world, but not of it, at least so far as externals went. We were celibate, had no family, and no worldly occupation. The occasion I am recalling finds my friend and me, footsore and weary, approaching an unpretentious building, being warmly welcomed, given food, and finally being settled in a bungalow nearby. We were in Anandashram, the abode of Swami Ramdas, and we stayed there for six weeks.[543]

We spent much of our time in meditation, but every now and then we went to the Bhajan Hall where we listened to the devotional songs and talked with Swami Ramdas. It was not long before we discovered that the ashram possessed a library, or rather a small, very miscellaneous collection of religious books. Among them, to my surprise and delight, was Suzuki's translation of *The Awakening of Faith in the Mahāyāna*. I had seen a version of it before, but I had not read it, and I therefore proceeded to copy it out into my rather fat notebook. This notebook I still have, and together with twenty-six other items it formed part of the *Nine Decades* exhibition that was held in connection with my ninetieth birthday celebrations.

From Anandashram my friend and I travelled to the ashram of the celebrated Ramana Maharshi. We stayed there for six weeks, occupying a cave at the foot of Mount Arunachala, the mountain of light. Every few days we would pay a visit to the ashram in order to have *darshan* of the Maharshi. One night I had a vision of Amitābha, the red Buddha, the Buddha of the West.[544] I took the vision to mean that having spent two years as a freelance wandering ascetic I should now seek ordination as a *bhikkhu*. Not long afterwards, therefore, my friend and I were given the lower or *sāmaṇera* ordination by a senior Burmese monk, and more than a year later, my friend having left for Ceylon, I received the higher or *bhikkhu* ordination from a sangha consisting of monks from Burma, Ceylon, India, and Nepal. The Buddha had reminded his *bhikkhu* disciples that upon entering the sangha they left behind them their former names and social identities and henceforth were reckoned simply as Sons of the Buddha, but I soon found that in modern times this was not always the case. A Sinhalese monk, for example, was often Sinhalese first and a *bhikkhu* afterwards. Moreover, many monks were keenly interested in politics, even to the extent of supporting one political party rather than another, and some years later this involvement of monks in politics culminated in a Prime Minister of Ceylon being assassinated by a Sinhalese *bhikkhu*. Far from being Outsiders, as the Buddha and his *bhikkhu* disciples were, such political monks were as much Insiders as were the laity.

But it is time I went into reverse and reconnected with the war years. Since I suffered from valvular disease of the heart, and was still supposed not to run or even to walk quickly, I had assumed that I was quite unfit for military service. At my Medical Board, however, I was classed as B2, while the cardiologist to whom I was referred, at my request, told me that there was nothing wrong with my heart. Thus, from being an Outsider who could not even run quickly I was transformed, overnight, into an Insider who, with two or three dozen other men, was drilled, went on route marches, and learned to handle a variety of lethal weapons. In *The Rainbow Road* the chapter in which I describe my early days in the army is headed 'The Misfit'. In a sense we were all misfits, having been plunged into the army from various walks of life and at various ages from 18 to 45. Though I did not realize it at the time we were comparatively lucky. We were lucky because on the strength of our knowledge of Morse code we had been posted to a semi-secret unit of the Royal Corps of Signals, and had to undergo only the most basic military training. Even so, after four or five months it became evident that the authorities wanted to get us off military training and into full-time technical training as quickly as possible. No more drill, no more guard duty, and no more route marches, and we were given as many weekend passes as we wanted!

In this more civilized atmosphere tensions relaxed, and we were able to take up the thread of interests that we had had to drop on entering the army. In my own case I had more time for walks in the countryside and for reading and writing poetry. Nor was this all. Living at close quarters with other men, especially those of my own age, I became more aware than ever that I was an Outsider. I was not an Outsider because I loved the poetry of Robert Herrick, or was exhilarated by Nietzsche's *Thus Spake Zarathustra*, or even because I regarded myself as a Buddhist. I was an Outsider for deeper and darker reasons. I was an Outsider because I was sexually attracted to men, not to women, and I had been aware of this since the age of 14.

In subsequent years, thanks to my wide reading, I had become aware that there were, and always had been, men like me, among them being some of the brightest names in poetry, literature, music, and the visual arts. By the time I entered the army, therefore, I knew just where I stood, sexually speaking. I also knew what the majority of people thought of sexuality such as mine. Homosexuality was unnatural. It was wicked, sinful, and perverse and a homosexual was a moral leper. This was not the worst. In my own country, as in other civilized countries, any kind of homosexual activity was a criminal offence, and there were countries in which it was punishable by death. It therefore behoved me to be very careful what I did or said, or even how I looked at other men. This was not without its consequences for my emotional life. Keeping my feelings to myself became a habit, especially when those feelings were very strong and directed to another man. Many years were to pass before I was able to give expression to such feelings even to a limited extent.

Though it was on account of my particular type of sexuality that I was an Outsider, one could be an Outsider for all sorts of other reasons, as Colin Wilson made clear. One could be an Outsider for reasons that were political, or religious, or cultural, or commercial, or purely social. Whatever the reason, there were advantages as well as disadvantages to being an Outsider, as I had discovered when at school. One advantage was that as an Outsider one had a sharper sense of separation from the group to which one belonged. It gave one a heightened awareness of one's individuality and, therefore, of the possibility of a development that went beyond group values to the higher values of philosophy, religion, and the arts. Another advantage was that as an Outsider one was unusually sensitive to subliminal signals coming from other people. In certain situations, the ability to read those signals might be a matter of life or death. A political dissident living under a totalitarian regime, or a homosexual living in a country where homosexuality was a criminal or even capital offence, needed to be constantly on the alert. Like some animals he would have to sleep with one eye open. Any talk of the advantages of being an Outsider is likely to have a hollow sound in the ears of one who is himself suffering from being an Outsider. Such suffering is of two kinds, external and internal. The former includes ostracism, torture, imprisonment, and death. The latter occurs when the Outsider introjects the values of the group and condemns himself because the group condemns him. If the Outsider is homosexual he will feel shame and guilt on account of his sexuality. He may even try to deny it. In extreme cases he may take his own life. As George V famously said, 'I thought men like that shot themselves.'[545]

Again I must go into reverse and reconnect with my time in India as a Buddhist monk. In 1956, 400,000 men and women renounced Hinduism and embraced Buddhism under the leadership of Dr Bhimrao Ambedkar. I was then living in Kalimpong, a small town in the foothills of the eastern Himalayas, and it was not long before I became involved in the movement of mass conversion that had been thus inaugurated. The converts were ex-Untouchables. They were Outsiders in that they were outside the Hindu caste system and were systematically treated in a humiliating and degrading manner by the caste Hindu majority. I met Dr Ambedkar several times, and after his untimely death spent much of my time travelling among the new Buddhists and teaching them the fundamentals of the Dhamma. This I did for seven or eight years, in this way winning their confidence so that even after my departure for England in 1964 they did not forget me. Some of my non-Buddhist friends wondered how I could have so much influence with the new Buddhists. I was not an Indian. I was British, and as such an Outsider, a mere *mleccha* or barbarian. To this I replied that I was indeed an Outsider, not only because I was not a citizen of India but because I was a Buddhist monk, there being very few *bhikkhus* in India at that time. It was because I was an Outsider that the new Buddhists trusted me. Like them, I was outside the Hindu caste system. We were Outsiders together.

In 1962 I was invited by the English Sangha Trust to spend six months in England. As I wanted to finish the book on which I was working, and had moreover undertaken a nine-month tour among the new Buddhists, it was not until 1964 that I was able to leave India. At that time there were two Buddhist organizations in London, both of them quite small. There was the Buddhist Society of London and there was the English Sangha Association, the trustees of which had invited me to make the visit. Membership of the Buddhist Society was open to all. One did not even have to be a Buddhist to be a member, or a practising Buddhist if one happened to be Buddhist at all. Membership of the English Sangha Association, on the other hand, was open only to those who wanted to see a branch of the Buddhist monastic order established in England and who were committed to its support when established. The Buddhist Society, which had originally been the Buddhist Lodge of the Theosophical Society, functioned as a common platform for different forms of Buddhism, though the dominant form was a Zen deriving mainly from the writings of D. T. Suzuki. Committed as it was to the establishment of an indigenous monastic order, the English Sangha Association naturally favoured Theravāda Buddhism. As I soon discovered, the four or five hundred English Buddhists were more or less evenly divided between the Society and the Association, though a handful belonged to both. Though I was based at the Hampstead Buddhist Vihara, which belonged to the English Sangha Trust, I gave lectures and led meditation classes for the members of both the Association and the

Society. In this way I sought to bring the two Buddhist organizations together. This did not please everybody, and eventually I saw that a new form of Buddhism was needed in England, perhaps in the West. As was not the case with the Society, all the members of this new form of Buddhism would be committed Buddhists, though unlike the Association they would not be committed to any one form of Buddhism. Two years later, after I had paid a brief farewell visit to India, this new Buddhist movement came into existence in London as the Friends of the Western Sangha. Yet it did not emerge fully formed all at once, like Pallas Athena from the head of Zeus. It was not a blueprint but a seed, and like a seed it needed time for its development.

This development has now been going on for forty-eight years and it will continue to develop and expand after my death. To begin with I gave all the talks, led all the meditation classes and country retreats, and conducted all the ordinations within the Triratna Buddhist Order, as the Western Buddhist Order eventually became. Soon the seed was quite a tree, a tree with several big branches, a number of twigs and innumerable leaves. So many twigs and leaves were there that sometimes it became difficult for people to see the structure of the tree. I therefore started speaking in terms of the six distinctive emphases of the Triratna Buddhist Order and Community and gave more than one talk on them. This is not the place for me to summarize those talks.[546] I do, however, remember an interesting coincidence. The Triratna Buddhist Community was founded in 1967, membership being open to all, including homosexuals. It so happened that it was the same year, 1967, that homosexual acts between consenting adult men in private were decriminalized in England and Wales. A homosexual was no longer a complete Outsider, at least officially. When I started speaking in terms of the six distinctive emphases of Triratna, senior members of the Order were already running most Triratna activities, and before many years had passed they were running them all.

At the time of writing I am living at Adhisthana. It is autumn, the poet's 'season of mists and mellow fruitfulness', and there have been mists enough and much mellow fruitfulness in the form of the loads of apples that have been carted away from the neighbouring orchards. Though I have visitors, it is a long time since I paid any visits, and a long time, therefore, since I have had the experience of picking up a book that happened to be lying around and reading it on the spot. This does not mean that from time to time I do not come across a book of which I have never heard but on which I am willing to spend a few hours. I am a member of Calibre Audio and of the Royal National Institute for the Blind, both of which supply talking books to blind and partially-sighted people. When I joined those organizations I asked for works on religion and on philosophy, but since hardly any works on these subjects were available I changed to biography and classic fiction. Thus it was that I came to be listening to novels by Anthony Trollope, and finding in two of them characters that were reminiscent of Colin Wilson's concept of the Outsider. Ferdinand Lopez, in *The Prime Minister*, is definitely an Outsider, being of Portuguese descent, probably Jewish, and not a gentleman in the English sense of the term. Having neither profession nor a regular income he speculates on the commodity market and the reader is not surprised that eventually his speculations fail and he takes his own life. Dr Thorne, the eponymous hero of the novel of the same name, is an Outsider in the eyes of other doctors, for he is his own apothecary. His niece Mary, who lives with him, is an Outsider of another kind, for she happens to be illegitimate. When Mary unexpectedly inherits a fortune the titled lady who has treated Mary with great cruelty and done her best to keep her away from her son is now happy to welcome her as a daughter-in-law despite her illegitimacy. Thus from being an Outsider Mary, overnight, becomes an Insider, a not unusual development where money is concerned.[547]

Whether listening to Trollope or any other novelists I listen in the living room of the Urgyen Annexe where I have now lived for more than two and a half years with Paramartha. I usually listen sitting in a comfortable armchair that belonged to my mother and which I inherited when she died twenty-five years ago. All around me are mementos and memorabilia of my long and eventful life. There are paintings and photographs, images and artefacts, gifts from groups and gifts from individuals. Among the last are things that Paramartha has given me over the years. They include a wall plate from Morocco, a silver statuette of Milarepa, and a replica of an ancient Greek vase depicting Hercules. As I look at them or handle them I think of my friend and remember the times we have spent together, whether on retreat at Guhyaloka, or travelling, or studying the Dharma together in the conservatory here at the Annexe. As I write these words Paramartha is in New Zealand, looking after his mother who has cancer. He left Adhisthana more than two months ago, and does not know how long he will be away. We exchange emails every week and talk on the phone. I have been sending him my recent writings, and I will send this one too, as soon as I have a title for it.

WHAT MIGHT HAVE BEEN

'What do you want to be when you grow up?' I used to be asked when I was 13 or 14. Sometimes it would be 'What do you want to do when you grow up?' Although I remember being asked these questions I cannot remember who asked them. I never thought about what I would be or do when I left school and went out into the world. What I did think about was what I wanted to do at the time. I wanted to write, especially to write poetry, and I wanted to draw and paint, as well as to read as much as I could about literature and the arts. At the time of which I am speaking I spent more time painting than writing. I liked to paint pictures of historical figures such as Henry VIII and Queen Elizabeth, Catherine de' Medici and Marie Antoinette. I particularly liked painting pictures of women, for depicting their long, flowing draperies, with all their folds and creases, gave me a keen aesthetic pleasure. It also meant that I did not have to depict their bodies, especially their legs, which at this time was beyond my skill. The fact that I was spending much of my free time painting could hardly escape the notice of those around me, especially my parents and my sister and other members of the family. It was well known that Dennis painted and that he was perhaps going to be an artist when he grew up. There was even some talk about the possibility of my going to art school. It was not my ambition to be an artist. I just wanted to paint and draw. Although it was well known that Dennis painted, it was not so well known that he also wrote poetry. Indeed it was known only to the girl next door, a girl of my own age to whom I showed my first poems. 'They are very good,' she said. Despite this appreciation, I did not show her any more of my poems, nor did I show them to anyone else. It was as though writing, unlike painting, was something personal and private and it was some time before I showed anyone else anything that I had written. This does not mean that I wrote only for myself. I wrote for an audience, or at least for a potential one, but that audience did not include anyone around me. Eventually, when I was 17, it came to include Claire Cameron, editor of the *Middle Way*, who published not only a few of my poems but also my first articles on Buddhism.[548] I was 18 when these appeared.

By this time Britain had been at war with Nazi Germany for four years. During those years I had been evacuated, had worked for a year in a coal merchant's office, and for two years had been a clerical assistant in the LCC's Public Health Department at County Hall. Now I was conscripted into the army. I had not expected to be conscripted. I had assumed that with my long history of valvular disease of the heart I would be considered unfit for military service. This proved not to be the case and I have sometimes wondered how my life would have developed if I had not been conscripted at 18, had not experienced life in the army, had not been posted to India, had not become a Buddhist monk, had not written *A Survey of Buddhism*, and had not become the disciple of Tibetan lamas, all of which followed from the simple fact of having been found fit for military service. Thus the fact that I had been found fit for military service had led to my having for the next twenty years a life very different from what I would otherwise have had.

But what would that other life have been like? Where would I have lived? What would I have done? I would not have lived at home, for I had no home, my parents having separated a year or so earlier. Perhaps I would have lived with my grandmother, occupying the room that Uncle Charles had occupied before his marriage. Probably I would have continued to be a clerical assistant at County Hall, though I would not have known how long my job would last. I was no more than a temporary clerical assistant, having been recruited during the war, and would probably have been replaced sooner or later by someone returning from having served his country in the armed forces. In some respects, therefore, my life would have been an uncertain one, even a precarious one. Not that it would have been uncertain in all respects. I would have kept on writing whatever the circumstances. I would have continued to write for the *Middle Way* and would have kept up my friendships with Clare Cameron and Arnold Price, the translator of the *Diamond Sūtra*. I would have attended lectures and meditation classes at the Buddhist Society's rooms above a tea shop in Great Russell Street, as I had been doing for some time, and I am sure that before long I would have been giving lectures there myself. I might even have succeeded Clare Cameron as editor of the *Middle Way*.

Not that all my activities would have revolved around the Buddhist Society. I would have sent off articles and poems to the editors of literary magazines, some of whom might have paid their contributors. Very likely I would have joined the PEN Club[549] and met other writers, and I would certainly have continued to patronize the theatre and cinema, as well as to frequent museums and art galleries. Within ten or twelve years of my rejection by the army I would, I think, have published a slim volume of poems, have collected my Buddhist articles into a book, and have produced a substantial work on Buddhism. It would not have been *A Survey of Buddhism*, of course, but it would have been very much like it, for whether in England or in India, my understanding of the Buddha's Dharma would have developed along similar lines. Even if that crowning work had not been well received I would surely have written more books and would have planned to write even more. The truth is that throughout my life there have always been books that I planned to write but which, for one reason or another, I never got round to writing.

Thus during those ten or twelve years I may well have had a moderately successful career as a writer, at least as a writer of books and articles on Buddhism. But what would my emotional and spiritual life have been like? Some of it would have found expression in my poetry, but there would have been much going on that would have found no expression at all. This would have been especially the case with my sexual feelings, which, being a young man's feelings, would have been very strong. What, then, would I have done? I find it difficult to say. Perhaps I would have acted upon those feelings, perhaps not. In any case I would have been faced by a serious problem for my sexual feelings were directed towards other men and in England acting upon such feelings was a criminal offence punishable by imprisonment. Had I simply repressed my feelings I might not have fallen foul of the law, but my whole sexual and emotional life would have been stultified. On the other hand, had I ventured to act upon them, even to a limited extent, I would have had to do so furtively, even secretly, with the consciousness that I was not only breaking the law but leading a double life. I would have been always anxious, afraid of being found out, and unable to be fully open even with those with whom I broke the law. But perhaps eventually I would have become careless, would have knowingly taken risks, or would have trusted the wrong person, with the result that one day I would have been caught and exposed, thus disgracing my family, alienating my friends, and losing whatever standing I then had in the world. Like others in the same position I would have had to decide between two alternatives: suicide or prison. But here my imagination falters and I return with relief from the possible fate of my hypothetical self to the subject of my unwritten books.

Some of these unwritten books were to have formed part of a series called 'The Heritage of Buddhism'. There were to have been five volumes in all, but only *The Three Jewels* and *The Eternal Legacy*, the first and second volumes in the series, were actually written. Both were written in Kalimpong in the foothills of the eastern Himalayas where I was living at the time. Volume 4, on 'Meditation in the Three Yānas', and volume 5 on 'Forms and Functions of Buddhist Art' were never written. Of the 'Patterns of Development in Buddhism', the third volume in the series, I was able to write only the first three sections, also written in Kalimpong. All these volumes – the written, the unwritten, and the partly written – were the result of my having been invited to contribute the articles on Buddhism to the *Oriya Encyclopaedia*, one of the fourteen regional language encyclopaedias then being sponsored by the Government of India. I was more than happy to write the articles, and set to work on them immediately, putting aside *The Rainbow Road*, on which I had been working for some time. I wrote in the morning after breakfast and carried on until lunchtime. If I grew stiff, or if I came up against a doctrinal or a literary difficulty, I left my desk and walked up and down the veranda until the difficulty had been resolved. Within two years I had written, despite interruptions, up to 100,000 words – far more than the 14,000 for which I had been asked. Partly because my subject was Buddhism, and partly because the act of writing was so pleasurable, I enjoyed writing them and was sorry when I had to stop. The reason for my having to stop was that I had been invited to write the article on Buddhism for the new edition of the OUP's *The Legacy of India*[550] and the article was needed at once. By the time I had written this article it was 1964 and high time I fulfilled my promise to the English Sangha Trust, namely, that I would spend six months in England. I was never able resume my work on the articles for the *Oriya Encyclopaedia* and 'The Heritage of Buddhism' therefore remains incomplete. *The Three*

Jewels was eventually published by Rider in 1967 and *The Eternal Legacy* by Tharpa in 1985.

One of my favourite unwritten books was planned but unwritten not in the foothills of the eastern Himalayas but amid the flat landscape of Norfolk. I was then living at Padmaloka, a men's community on the outskirts of the village of Surlingham, some seven miles from Norwich. During my time there I naturally developed an interest in the area, especially as I was living only twenty miles from the village of Besthorpe, near Attleborough, where my paternal grandmother had been born and where my father had spent much of his childhood. Norfolk is one of the bigger English counties and in the Middle Ages Norwich was second in importance only to London as is testified by its forty-odd churches, including its twelfth-century cathedral. Where there is history there will be heroes and heroines, and as I thought about the ones who belonged to Norfolk, either by birth or domicile, five names not only stood out for me but seemed to form a constellation. These five I came to think of as my Five Norfolk Worthies, and before long I was planning a book about them. The five were Julian of Norwich, Sir Thomas Browne, Thomas Paine, Lord Nelson, and Edith Cavell. There was to be a chapter on each of them and these chapters would make a small book. Though the plan was clear enough in my mind, and though I liked thinking about my five worthies, my life at Padmaloka was a busy one and I was unable to write even a word about any of them. *Five Norfolk Worthies* thus became one of my unwritten books.

Though I never wrote about my five Norfolk worthies I did not forget them, and they continued to haunt the fringes of my consciousness. In the case of Julian of Norwich (1342–1416) I was able, during my stay at Padmaloka, to visit the cell where she had spent the greater part of her life. The cell was built up against the wall of the Church of St Julian in Norwich and it had two windows, one opening into the church, so that Julian could hear mass, the other opening onto the street, so that she could communicate with the people who came to see her. I saw the place at the invitation of a friend who belonged to a meditation group that met there regularly and once invited me to join them. Seven or eight people were gathered there, including my friend. I do not know what kind of meditation they practised, but the atmosphere was very peaceful and I enjoyed my visit. Years later I learned that the original cell had been destroyed by a German bomb and that the one I had seen was a reconstruction. I had heard of Julian of Norwich long before my time at Padmaloka and had read a popular edition of her book, *Revelations of Divine Love*. In this, the first English book to be written by a woman, Julian not only describes her sixteen visions of Jesus Christ but also comments on them at some length, as though she was trying to understand their meaning. Had I written my chapter on her I would no doubt have read this work again and may well have compared it with the writings of other Christian mystics. I may also have thought it necessary to discuss the question of whether the mystical experience was entirely subjective or whether the mystic really did encounter a higher transpersonal reality.

Like Julian, Sir Thomas Browne (1605–1682) had a close connection with Norwich, but there the resemblance between them ends. She was an anchoress and a mystic, he a doctor, a scholar, an antiquarian, and a busy professional man. Above all he was the author of *Religio Medici*, a work remarkable for its beautiful, baroque style. I came across it when I was 14 and was so fascinated by its style that I strove to imitate it in an essay of my own. So far as I remember, Sir Thomas Browne was the only writer whose style I ever wanted to imitate. Had my chapter about him been written, I would have discussed the question of literary style in detail and no doubt would have had something to say about the immense variety of English prose styles. Sir Thomas Browne lived through the Civil War, in which he took the Royalist side, for which he was knighted by Charles II when the king visited Norwich after the Restoration. He lies buried in the Church of St Peter Mancroft in Norwich.

Julian of Norwich is known mainly to students of mysticism, and Sir Thomas Browne is known mainly to lovers of English literature, but Thomas Paine (1737–1809) is much more widely known. He was involved in both the American and the French Revolutions and his book *The Rights of Man* is a classic of political literature. I do not find him a sympathetic character and had I written about him I would probably have said little about his life and much more about the whole question of 'rights'. As long ago as 1951 I wrote an article on 'Rights and Duties' in which I argued that the two were, in fact, not only complementary but inseparable, and that the emphasis should be on duties rather than rights. As I then put it,

> But just as, in the case of a walking-stick, although its two ends are inseparable, so that one is unthinkable without the other, nevertheless it is the handle of the stick that must be grasped, not the tip, so in human relationships it is duties that must be performed, rather than rights demanded, even though the two in fact are inseparable so that the one necessarily follows from the other.[551]

Since I wrote those rather uncompromising lines there has been in many parts of the world, including Britain, a disturbing change. Rights and duties are no longer seen as being inseparable and complementary. Rights are separated from duties, so that duties come to be neglected, and social and political discourse is dominated by the concept of rights. Rights are of many kinds and the number seems to be constantly on the increase. There can also be a conflict between different rights, as when the mother's right to do what she pleases with her own body conflicts with the right of the foetus to live. The confusion that has been generated by the one-sided emphasis on rights can be resolved by a greater emphasis on duties. The Buddha spoke of duties, not of rights. According to him duties are complementary: parents have duties towards their children, and children have duties towards their parents, and so on through the whole gamut of human relationships.[552] Members of a Buddhist community will therefore think in terms of duties rather than rights, and act accordingly. They will take hold of the right end of the stick. In Thomas Paine's time, in both England and France, the emphasis was on duties rather than rights, especially where the common people were concerned. It is therefore understandable that throughout his career Thomas Paine should have preached the gospel of human rights. His statue stands in the marketplace of Thetford where he was born.

Lord Nelson (1758–1805) belongs not just to history but to legend. Perhaps he belongs more to legend than to history, at least in the collective memory of his fellow countrymen. The principal facts of his life were known to me from an early age, but it was the legend that appealed to me, and had I written about Nelson it was probably on the legend that I would have dwelt. I would perhaps have begun by emphasizing the fact that his was an extremely attractive personality, and that as an admiral he was as popular with his subordinates as he was unpopular with some of his superiors in the service. He did not hesitate to disobey orders, as when he put his telescope to his blind eye when he did not wish to see a signal with whose orders he disagreed. His relationship with Lady Hamilton, whom he met in the romantic setting of Naples, is very much part of the legend. He is as much the Hero as Lover as he is the Hero as Victor, and although the legend speaks of one great love, the victories were many. Nelson's greatest victory was at Trafalgar when he destroyed Napoleon's Franco-Spanish fleet and established Britain's naval supremacy. The victory cost him his life. He was struck down by a bullet from a marksman stationed in the rigging of a French ship and died in the arms of his faithful Hardy. His last words were, 'Thank God I have done my duty.' Trafalgar Square and Nelson's Column were familiar sights from my boyhood, serving to remind me of the man and his legend. Had I written about him, I think I would have had something to say about his connection with the sea. The land for which he gave his life is an island, as the BBC's shipping forecast reminds us every Saturday evening.[553] One is never more than seventy miles from the sea and it has been said that the sea is in an Englishman's blood. I have not spent much time at sea and sometimes wish I could have spent more, especially as I have happy memories of short trips by ferry. One of these was from Harwich to Götheburg. It was a brilliantly sunny day and the sea, calm as a lake, reflected the cloudless cerulean sky. Another trip took me from Brindisi to Igoumenitsa. As I have written elsewhere,

> It was a fine, clear morning, the sea could not have been more calm, and we were sailing between the mainland and some four or five small, widely separated islands. Despite the muffled hum of the ship's engines, and the occasional muffled shout coming from the swimming pool, there was a breathless hush in the air, and as I gazed out over the dark blue waters it was as though time stood still, as though nothing had changed, and that I was seeing what Homer – had he not been blind – might have seen three thousand years ago.[554]

Edith Cavell (born 1865) was executed by a German firing squad on 12 October 1915. Her crime was that she had helped Allied prisoners of-war and others to escape from occupied Belgium to Holland. I have often wondered what were the feelings of those young German soldiers as they shot a defenceless woman. They were, of course, obeying orders, and had they done otherwise out of pity for their victim they would in all likelihood have been court-martialed themselves and been shot by a firing squad of their own comrades. Edith Cavell was born in the village of Swardeston, where her father was vicar, and had her schooling in nearby Norwich. After five years as a governess, she trained as a nurse and worked in hospitals in different parts of England, including London. In 1907 she became matron of a newly established nursing school in Brussels and a pioneer of modern nursing in Belgium. When Germany occupied Belgium, Edith Cavell's clinic and nursing school were taken over by the Red Cross and she continued working as a nurse. This brought her into contact with wounded Allied soldiers and it was for helping many of these escape that she was sentenced to death by the German military. Her last words were, 'Patriotism is not enough. I must have no hatred or bitterness towards anyone.' These words are inscribed on the pedestal of her statue in St Martins, near Trafalgar Square. I have often passed that statue and have wondered how many of the tourists and other passers-by know her story. Had I written about her, I would have had quite a lot to say about those famous last words, which reminds me of *Dhammapada* 5: 'Not by hatred (*vera*) are hatreds (*verāni*) pacified. They are pacified by love (*avera*).' The remains of Edith Cavell were finally buried in the grounds of Norwich Cathedral.

As I think of my Five Norfolk Worthies, and try to imagine what I might have written about them, I regret that the book of which they were to be the subject should be one of my unwritten books. Other books that were planned but not written included one on the relationship between Neoplatonism and Buddhism. Neoplatonism has fascinated me since my teens, when I dipped into the *Enneads* and read Dean Inge's *The Philosophy of Plotinus*, to both of which I returned years later. Indeed, I have a small library of works on Neoplatonism and related subjects. At the centre of my book there would probably have been a comparison between the three hypostases of Neoplatonism and the three *svabhāvas* of Yogācāra Buddhism.[555] I also very much wanted to write a biography of the Buddha. Not that I planned it in any detail but from time to time I thought about it quite a lot. In particular I wanted to bring together the historical Buddha and the legendary or archetypal Buddha in such a way that the reader would see and feel them as the mundane and transcendental aspects of a single undivided personality. My approach would have been both philosophical and devotional.

Another unwritten book was my autobiography. Friends might protest that I have in fact already written my autobiography, and written it not in one volume, but many, but this is to confuse memoirs and autobiography. As the word itself suggests, memoirs are what one remembers of one's life as one looks back on it. Some events and experiences will be remembered more clearly than others, and some may not be remembered at all. Thus in memoirs there will inevitably be gaps. Moreover, one may misremember certain events and experiences and one's account of them may differ widely from that of others who were present at the time and who have different memories. An autobiography, on the other hand, is an *auto*-biography. It is an account of one's life by oneself written in the first person, and it draws not only on one's own memories, but on letters, diaries, and other documents. It also contextualizes one's life with regard to other people and to the public events of one's time. In my own case, for example, I have described in my memoirs my arrival in India in 1944 without reference to the political situation that existed there at the time. In my autobiography, had I written it, I would have given an account of that situation and perhaps of my own reaction to it. Be that as it may, I mourned my unwritten autobiography as I mourned all my unwritten books. It is too late in life for me to think of writing any of them now and they must remain unwritten for ever.

Though my autobiography must remain unwritten, I can at least look back over my life and reflect upon its vicissitudes. I can reflect on the establishing of a new Buddhist movement in London, on my work among the ex-Untouchable Buddhists of India, on the founding of the Triyana Vardhana Vihara in Kalimpong, on my ordination as a *bhikkhu*, on my life as a freelance wandering ascetic, on my life in the army, and so on back to the time when, as a teenager, all I wanted to do was to write, especially to write poetry, as well as to draw and paint, and to read widely. I did not want to be or do anything when I grew up, nor have I wanted to be or do anything since.

THE YOUNG MAN IN THE HUT

On my reaching the years of puberty some of my female relations started teasing me about the sort of woman I would marry when I grew up. One of my mother's sisters, in particular, used to speculate in this way when we met. 'You will marry a short, fat little woman,' she would tell me, 'with short, fat little legs.' I have no idea why my aunt was so sure that I would marry a short and fat woman rather than a tall and thin one. At that time of life I had no thought of marrying anyone of whatever size and shape, and I may have told my aunt as much. Strange to say, even when I was very young I used to tell people I would never marry, even though I did not know what marriage meant.

Many years later I was reminded of my aunt's prediction when I read about the so-called Palaeolithic Venus. This was the name given by archaeologists to the 150 or more female figurines of various sizes that have been discovered in many parts of the world. Most of them belong to the period 24,000–19,000 BCE. The typical Palaeolithic Venus was short and fat. She had exaggeratedly large hips, breasts and vulva, but her head was small and featureless and her legs tapered downwards. Opinions differ as to the significance of these figurines. According to some archaeologists they were amulets, while others believe that their significance was religious and that they had a place in ritual. Whatever the truth may be, it is evident that for the men (and perhaps for the women) who fashioned them women were essentially producers of children. The figurines were fertility symbols, and fertility was important in ensuring the survival of the group.

Hundreds of centuries passed. By the time of the Italian Renaissance woman was still seen as being essentially the producer of children, but there had been changes. Her primary and secondary sexual characteristics were now less exaggerated. Her body had grown a head, so to speak, and her face wore an expression. The Venus depicted in Botticelli's *Birth of Venus* is very different from her Palaeolithic ancestress. I first encountered the famous painting in the pages of the *Children's Encyclopaedia*, and years later I had the privilege of seeing the original in the Uffizi Gallery in Florence. It was a dark December evening and the gallery was almost deserted, so that I was able to sit in front of the painting for as long as I wished. The goddess is standing on a huge shell, and her pearl-white body is naked. To the left two wind-gods with distended cheeks are blowing her towards her island home. With her right hand she covers her right breast while with her left she covers her vulva with the end of her blonde tresses. Her expression is one of wonder and delight. She is delighted to have escaped from the depths, delighted to look out on the world with its calm sea and tranquil sky. On the right a handmaid hastens forward holding a rich garment with which she is about to clothe the goddess. On the far right, just behind the handmaid, rise three leafy trees.

Besides depicting Venus and other pagan deities, Botticelli also painted the Virgin Mary, and although her features are sometimes those of the goddess, again there are changes. Whereas his Venus is naked, save for the half-concealed breasts and vulva, in his *Madonna of the Magnificat* the Virgin is completely draped. Here woman is not only emancipated from her sexuality but is seen as the embodiment of ideal beauty. Her expression, though, is very different from that of the goddess of the *Birth of Venus*. The latter is one of wonder and delight, whereas that of the Virgin Mary in the *Madonna of the Magnificat* is expressive of submission to the will of God. Perhaps it was only Leonardo da Vinci who, among the artists of his day, was able to depict woman, in the person of the Virgin Mary, as a spiritual being. He does this in the *Virgin of the Rocks*, as well in his drawing of *The Virgin with St Anne*, both of which can be seen in the National Gallery in London. But Mary is Mother as well as Virgin, and in the works of Velázquez, Murillo, and El Greco, a century later, she breaks free of her child, so to speak, and is depicted in her own right. She is now a goddess as much as Venus ever was and her name is the Immaculate Conception. I painted her as such when I was 13 or 14, depicting her standing on a crescent moon and wearing a white inner robe and a blue outer one. She has long black hair and her arms are crossed on her breasts. Above her head and to her left and right are small red roses. These were my own additions to the traditional depictions of her.[556] Years later I noticed that in the *Birth of Venus* a few small red roses fall through the air.

Where there is a Palaeolithic Venus one might have expected to find a Palaeolithic Apollo. So far as I know, he has not been found and may never have existed. Something more interesting has been found. Three thousand years before Botticelli, sculptors in Ancient Greece created the Kouros, the so-called Archaic Apollo. The typical Kouros is a standing naked youth with broad shoulders and narrow hips and evident musculature. His arms hang down at his side and his face wears the famous archaic smile. He provides the pattern for an ideal of male beauty that culminates in the gods and athletes of the classical period, such as the *Apollo Belvedere* in the Vatican and the *Discobolos* in

Athens. That model may be said to have persisted down to the present day. A man with narrow shoulders and broad hips would be regarded as unnatural, as would a woman with broad shoulders and narrow hips. The breadth of a man's shoulders and the narrowness of his hips may, of course, be greatly exaggerated so as to make him look more masculine. An example of this is the Phantom in the American comic strip. Similarly, the size of a woman's breasts and hips may be greatly exaggerated too, so as to make her look more feminine in the sense of being sexually more attractive, as in the notorious 'Page 3 Girl'.[557] For the ancient Greeks the male body was more beautiful than the female body, because of the greater harmony that existed between its different parts and because of its less obvious connection to its biological function. The genitals were never emphasized in the depiction of gods and athletes, though the satyrs, the companions of Dionysus, were sometimes endowed with enormous phalluses. For the Greeks beauty was not merely physical, but also mental. One might go as far as to say that their ideal was not just a healthy mind in a healthy body[558] but a beautiful mind in a beautiful (male) body.

Not everyone will agree that the male body is more beautiful than the female body, and the idea will come as a surprise to many men and most women. The reason for this is that beauty is commonly identified with sexual attractiveness, and men find women beautiful because they find them sexually attractive. This is not to say that women have no share in beauty, but their beauty is in their face rather than in their body. If men have more beautiful bodies than women, women have more beautiful faces than men. But faces, whether of men or women, have expression, and the expression will depend on the person's mental and emotional state. The effect of a face that is formally beautiful can be entirely spoiled if its expression is one of hatred, or contempt, or greed. Conversely even a homely face is beautiful when it has an expression of sympathy, or understanding, or content.

A striking example of the latter came within my experience many years ago, as I have related in *The Rainbow Road*. I was staying with a friend at Ramana Maharshi's ashram in South India. Happening to explore the area to the west of the ashram we came upon a wattle and daub gate and beyond it a tiny mud-walled hut, thatched with palm leaves. Opening the gate and crossing the tiny cow-dunged courtyard we quietly opened the door of the hut.

> Inside was a single small room, completely bare, and inside the room, almost directly facing us, there sat, meditating, the most beautiful young man I had ever seen. Slim and fair-complexioned he sat there, with closed eyes, beautiful not only on account of his perfectly proportioned body, naked save for a small cloth but, even more so, on account of the beatific smile that irradiated his face. He was quite oblivious to our presence. Unable to take our eyes off him, we stood there for several minutes. Then, having closed the door behind us even more gently than we had opened it, we slowly made our way back to the ashram.[559]

The expression on the young man's face must have stayed with me, for some weeks later it resulted in the poem, 'The Face of Silence', in which I changed the setting of my experience but not its nature. The last three verses were as follows:

> O'er his still features breathed a calm
> I had not seen before.
> It drew me as some maiden's charm
> A lover to her door.
>
> The light he saw I could not see,
> And yet it seemed to glow
> Upon his face more beauteously
> Than sunlight on the snow.
>
> At last I turned away, and blessed
> The womb that gave him birth,
> Knowing that there in truth was rest
> And peace for those on earth.[560]

I have described the young man in the hut as beautiful even though in modern times men are hardly ever described as such. At most they are 'handsome' or 'good-looking'. This is not to say that there are no exceptions. In the course of the last few months I have listened to talking books of some of Anthony Trollope's so-called political novels, and was surprised to find that he does not hesitate to describe some of his male characters as beautiful, and even to insist on the fact. One young man is actually compared to Apollo, and it was probably the *Apollo Belvedere* that Trollope had in mind.[561] I have also come across an article by the journalist and author Jilly Cooper in which she interviews two footballers, one of whom was George Best, and candidly admits she was surprised to see how beautiful they were. Trollope and Jilly Cooper were speaking of physical beauty, but the young man in the hut was not only physically beautiful but spiritually beautiful, and he was spiritually beautiful on account of his expression. This does not mean that there are only two kinds of beauty, the physical and the spiritual. Beauty is of many kinds, and it has many degrees, for there is a hierarchy of beauty, just as there is a hierarchy of being and a hierarchy of knowledge. Plotinus gives us a glimpse of this hierarchy in his tractate 'On Beauty' in the *Enneads*:

> Beauty is mostly in sight, but it is to be found too in things we hear, in combinations of words and also in music, and in all music [not only in songs]; for tunes and rhythms are certainly beautiful: and for those who are advancing upwards from sense-perception ways of life and actions and characters and intellectual activities are beautiful, and there is the beauty of virtue. If there is any beauty prior to these, it itself will reveal it.[562]

But what *is* beauty? There are numerous definitions, but I have always liked that of St Thomas Aquinas, according to whom beauty is that which, when seen (or heard), delights, and that in which we take pleasure, or which we enjoy, or in which we delight, we will love.[563] Thus there is a connection between beauty and love, the latter being our natural response to the former, and just as there are different degrees of beauty there will be different degrees of love. Where there is physical beauty, heavenly beauty, and spiritual beauty there will be, corresponding to these, earthly love, heavenly love, and spiritual love. Having seen heavenly beauty we may well look down upon earthly beauty, and so on, and there is a story in the Buddhist scriptures that illustrates this point. A young man named Sundarananda, or Handsome Nanda, is in love with a beautiful śākyan maiden with long hair. The Buddha happens to come for alms, and his bowl having been filled he hands it to Sundarananda and tells him to follow him back to the vihara. This the young man does rather unwillingly, all the time looking back over his shoulder to the maiden he has left behind. On their arrival at the vihara the Buddha directs Śāriputra and Mahāmaudgalyāyana to ordain Nanda and the young man suffers himself to be made a monk. Though now a monk, he is unable to forget the śākyan maiden and finds it impossible to meditate. Knowing this, the Buddha by his magic power takes Sundarananda up to a higher, heavenly world and shows him the nymphs who live there. The nymphs are of extraordinary beauty, and on seeing them Sundarananda exclaims that in comparison with them the śākyan maiden is no better than a she-monkey with her nose and ears cut off. Back on earth he redoubles his efforts for the Buddha has assured him that if he meditates with sufficient intensity he will attain to that higher, heavenly world and there see the beautiful nymphs again. The other monks ridicule him for having such a lowly objective, and feeling shamed and humiliated he redirects his efforts and attains Nirvāṇa. In the story Sundarananda ungallantly declares that in comparison with the heavenly nymphs his former love is no better than a she-monkey with her nose and ears cut off.[564] This is not to suggest that she has no beauty at all, for there are degrees of beauty. That the higher beauty is higher does not mean that the lower beauty is not beautiful, much less still that it is ugly. Another story in the Buddhist scriptures makes this clear. The Buddha tells the ascetic Bhaggava that, contrary to what some people say of him, he does not say that when one reaches up to the liberation called the beautiful one sees the whole universe as ugly; what he does say is that when one reaches up to the liberation called the beautiful one knows indeed what beauty is.[565]

From the beautiful young man in the hut I passed on to my poem 'The Face of Silence', to the appreciation of male beauty by two very different writers, to Plotinus and the *Enneads*, to beauty and love, and so to the story of Sundarananda and to the liberation called the beautiful. I now want to return to the young man in the hut. In particular I want to say something about his beatific smile. He was oblivious of my presence and that of my friend, and his eyes were closed. He was therefore not smiling on account of anything he saw with his physical eyes, but because of what he saw with his inner vision. Perhaps he saw one of the heavenly nymphs, or the god Shiva, or perhaps he contemplated the impersonal Absolute of the Advaita Vedānta. Whatever he saw, he evidently delighted in it, and since he delighted in it he would have loved it. The degree of that love would have corresponded to the degree of the beauty he saw and since he was oblivious to the outer world it may be assumed that the beauty he saw, and the love which that beauty inspired, were not of the earthly kind. The principal difference between earthly love and heavenly love is that the former wishes to acquire, possess, and dominate its object and is associated with jealousy, as well as with fear and hatred of possible rivals. Heavenly love, on the other hand, experiences these emotions in a subtle form. Only spiritual or supersensible love is entirely free from them. It is not possible for one to experience earthly love at the same time that one experiences heavenly or spiritual love. One may enjoy earthly beauty at the same time that one experiences heavenly or spiritual beauty, but one will enjoy it on its own level, so to speak, and will not make it an object of attachment, whether gross or subtle. William Blake says much the same thing in his poem 'Eternity':

> He who binds to himself a joy
> Does the wingèd life destroy;
> He who kisses the joy as it flies
> Lives in eternity's sunrise.[566]

The face of the young man in the hut was radiant with a beatific smile, a smile that was expressive of his experience of inner bliss. But what of features cast in bronze or carved in stone? Are *these* capable of communicating that experience? Over the centuries Buddhist artists have sought to depict the Buddha in such a way as to give the worshipper an idea of his spiritual greatness, their object nothing less than to depict perfect Enlightenment in a human form. Few have succeeded in doing this, even to a small extent, but their works are nonetheless among the masterpieces of world art. But what of the sculptors and painters themselves? Were they in touch, at least to an extent, with the spiritual experience that they were trying to express in their depiction of the Buddha? It is difficult to say. We do know that a Tibetan thangka painter should ideally meditate on the Buddha or bodhisattva he is painting and repeat their mantra as he works. Similarly, in the Eastern Orthodox Church the icon painter is exhorted to fast and pray. Besides Buddhas and bodhisattvas, Buddhist artists have depicted the *arhants* or those who, by following the teachings of the Buddha, have attained Nirvāṇa. But not all these artists seek to represent, in the person of the *arhant*, Nirvāṇa in a human form. In Chinese Buddhist art, *arhants* are often depicted in a way that could be said to caricature them. Most are old, and some have crooked limbs and bulging eyes, while others are grimacing. Despite their common spiritual attainment the *arhants* all have very individual characters, the artist seems to be telling us. In contrast to the *arhants*, all of whom are monks, the great bodhisattvas such as Avalokiteśvara and Mañjuśrī are beautiful young men wearing the garments and jewels of an Indian prince. Their expression is one of compassion, as in the unique wall painting of Padmapāṇi at Ajanta in central India. In Sino-Japanese Buddhism, Avalokiteśvara undergoes a transformation. From a beautiful young man he becomes a beautiful female figure known as Guanyin. She wears a long white robe, her head is covered, and her expression is one of motherly kindness. In the West she is popularly known as the Goddess of Mercy and her likeness to the Madonna has often been remarked on. Perhaps the most extraordinary of Avalokiteśvara's transformations is the one in which he becomes the eleven-headed, thousand-armed Mahākāruṇika, or Greatly Compassionate One. The compassion of the bodhisattva looks in every direction and he helps suffering sentient beings in every conceivable way. In the early days of the FWBO, now the Triratna Buddhist Community, I happened to be reading, or writing about, the myth in which Avalokiteśvara becomes the Greatly Compassionate One. As he contemplates the sufferings of sentient beings he is overwhelmed by compassion. So intense is the compassion his head splits into a thousand pieces. When I reached this point in the story I was very deeply affected. I started sobbing uncontrollably. In between my sobs I kept crying out to the friend who was with me, 'His head split into a thousand pieces! His head split into a thousand pieces!' This sobbing and crying out must have lasted for up to half an hour. I am not a person who sheds tears easily, and the experience has not been repeated, though the impression it made on me persists.

In these pages I have covered quite a lot of ground, but despite my aunt's prediction at no point did I discover in myself a predilection for short, fat little women with short, fat little legs.

ALTERNATIVE LIVES

In the summer of 1967 I moved with my friend Terry Delamare into a flat in Highgate West Hill. Though I did not know it at the time, it was to be my home for the next three years. 'Our new home', as I wrote many years later in an unpublished article,

> was situated on the second floor of a Victorian terraced house; it consisted of two rooms and a kitchen, and from the back windows there was a view of Hampstead Heath. The landlady was a small, grey-haired woman of 70 who informed us, when we called in response to her advertisement in the *New Statesman*, that her name was Joy and that she was blind. That she was blind, or very nearly so, was evident from the condition of the hallway, the stairs and passages, and the vacant flat on the second floor, all of which were badly in need of redecoration. Landladies being a suspicious breed, Terry and I naturally had to give some account of ourselves. I do not remember if we told Joy that I was a Buddhist monk, but we certainly told her that I was a writer and that Terry was studying philosophy. No sooner was the word writer pronounced than the withered old face lit up with an expression of surprise and delight. A writer! Many of her friends had been writers, Joy assured us, and she liked to have writers as her tenants. In the days before the war a group of literary people who called themselves the Leopards had met at her house every week, and on one memorable occasion they had received a visit from Aldous Huxley. By this time Joy had led us into her sitting room on the ground floor, the art nouveau furnishings of which had a shabby, dusty look. Here we paid our first month's rent and it was agreed that we should move into the flat as soon as we had decorated the two principal rooms.[567]

The decorating took Terry only two days and within the week we were installed in our new abode. At the time there were only two other tenants, a room on the first floor being occupied by a buck-toothed woman in her thirties and the attic by a young man in his early twenties. Joy had expressed the hope that the four of us would have coffee with her in her sitting room at eleven o'clock every Thursday morning and engage in intelligent discussion about books as the Leopards had once done. Terry and I would not have minded doing this, but the other tenants declined the invitation. They had full-time jobs, they said, a fact that Joy seemed to have overlooked.

Neither Terry nor I encouraged visitors. In recent months much had happened to us and we needed time for reflection. I also had lectures to prepare, while Terry was still suffering from depression and did not feel like meeting people. Though we gave our new address only to a few close friends, our whereabouts could not be kept altogether secret and before long people came knocking at the big, black front door of the house.

One of my most colourful visitors was my old friend and enemy Jinaratana Thera, whom Terry and I had last seen in Calcutta a few months earlier, when we were packing up my books and Buddhist artefacts for dispatch to the UK, and who was almost the last person I had expected to see in London.[568] His robe was bright yellow and his bald pate shone with scented oil. He was on a world tour, he told me in his usual abrupt manner, and the Sinhalese monks in West London with whom he was staying had given him my address. In the India of those days no self-respecting guru could afford not to have a world tour, a tour that would win him more disciples and enhance his reputation, and Jinaratana had more than once told me that as soon as he had saved up 25,000 rupees he would have a world tour of his own. Now here he was in London and his next stop would be Washington DC where there were Sinhalese monks and a small Theravāda centre. He asked me what I was doing, though more as a matter of course than because he was really interested. I told him that I had started a meditation centre in central London and was giving lectures in different parts of the town. He stayed no more than half an hour and I think I gave him tea.

Whereas Jinaratana had been known to me for many years, another colourful visitor seemed to come from nowhere. I do not remember her name, or how she came to know of my existence. She was Burmese, wore the traditional sarong and little jacket, and her thick black hair was so short as to be almost cropped. My earliest recollection of her is of her coming up the stairs holding a large bowl of trifle, and this may well have been our first contact. Thereafter she came quite a number of times, always bringing with her a trifle or a cake or some other comestible. Once or twice she was accompanied by a lanky Englishman of her own age, which I judged to be about 35. He was interested in Zen, he told me, but otherwise he was silent. The lady herself was not interested in Zen. She invariably wanted to talk about pain and suffering and seemed to be confused between Buddhism and Christianity. Was she,

I wondered, a 'born Buddhist' who had been educated in a Christian institution? Whatever her background, it was evident that she had an emotional investment in pain and suffering, and we had some intense discussions around the subject. On one of her visits she looked at the books in my bookcase and pulled out one of them. The title of the book was *The Theology of the Pain of God* and I was not altogether surprised when she asked if she could borrow it. I had read the book or had at least dipped into it. It was written by a Japanese Christian and so far as I remember it attempted to show that Japan was not the aggressor in the Second World War but the victim, for it was on Japan that the first atom bomb had been dropped. Japan had suffered as Christ had suffered on the cross, and her sufferings had a sacrificial quality that redeemed not only Japan but the world.[569] The author seemed to have forgotten, or at least had disregarded, Japan's invasion of Manchuria, the Nanking atrocities, the attack on Pearl Harbor, the enslavement of the Korean 'comfort women', and the brutal treatment of Allied prisoners of war. Unlike Germany, which did its best to atone for its Nazi past, Japan seemed disinclined to admit that it had done anything wrong, and it was not until 1998 that the Prime Minister of Japan wrote an open apology for his country's wartime past. Even so, he did not use '*shazai*', the key Japanese term for sorrow. As early as 1971, however, Emperor Hirohito who had been Japan's head of state during the war, made a state visit to Britain at the invitation of the government. Like many others, I thought that he should never have been invited. No doubt relations with Japan had to be normalized, but Hirohito was an old man and it would have been more seemly if the government had waited for his death and invited his successor.

Another colourful visitor was Jiyu Roshi, though she was colourful only metaphorically, not literally. She was shaven headed and wore a voluminous black robe that made her look bigger and fatter than she really was. I had corresponded with her in my Kalimpong days. She was then plain Peggy Kennett and a member of the Buddhist Society in London, of which I had once been a member myself. I am not sure why she wrote to me, for she wrote only to tell me that she would be travelling to Japan, where she hoped to train in the Zen tradition. Her next letter was not from Japan but from Malaysia, and I gathered that she had been unexpectedly ordained there, though the nature of the ordination was by no means clear. Eventually I heard that she had arrived in Japan and been accepted into a Zen monastery. Now, having spent seven or eight years training in Zen, she was back in the UK and staying at Sarum House in Purley, Surrey, where there was a little FWBO community. I knew that she was coming since the proprietor of Sakura, the Japanese shop in whose basement I held my meditation classes, had been in correspondence with her. Emile was an aficionado of Zen, and he had urged Jiyu to settle in London and teach there instead of carrying on to the United States as was her plan. He had received a very strange reply. She could not possibly teach in London, she had told him. She had enemies there, and it would be dangerous for her to do so. In one of her aerogrammes she even wrote that she might be assassinated, and reading it I formed the distinct impression that she was suffering from paranoia. The supposed enemies, of course, were from the Buddhist Society where Zen was taught, though of a kind different from Jiyu's. I was therefore interested to meet her and invited her to have lunch with me at the flat. She came accompanied by her shaven-headed, black-robed attendant and a casually dressed young American, and from the beginning she was very much on her dignity as a roshi. I therefore decided to behave informally, which I did all the more easily as I was not wearing my robes. While I was serving up the meal, and while we were all eating, Jiyu and her attendant talked to each other in what I thought was a very artificial and stilted manner. They talked about various conflicts that were going on within their own tradition back in Japan, at the same time nodding gravely at each other. They spoke slowly and deliberately, as though repeating words they had learned by heart, and I realized there was more in all this than met the eye. After the meal I asked Jiyu if it was true that she had decided to settle in the United States. She replied in the affirmative, adding that she would be establishing herself at a place called Mount Shasta, in California. I then asked her if she knew what the word *śāstā* meant in Sanskrit? It was a long time since she had done her Sanskrit, she replied rather haughtily, and I could see that I had offended her. I had certainly not intended to expose her ignorance of Sanskrit but only to point out the appropriateness of the name 'Shasta' for what she planned to establish there. It meant 'teacher', I explained, as in 'the teacher of gods and men', which was one of the titles of the Buddha.[570]

After Jiyu's departure with her entourage I reflected on the visit as I washed the dishes. Later on I heard that some of the members of the

Sarum House community had noticed that Jiyu's personal attendant was always hungry. At mealtimes, feeling sorry for him, they plied him with second and third helpings, but he was never satisfied. After a few days someone ventured to ask Jiyu if anything was wrong. Was he ill or undernourished, they wanted to know, and Jiyu was obliged to explain that he had been mirroring. They all overate, she declared, and her attendant was simply mirroring their behaviour in order to shame them out of it. So *that* was what the strange dialogue between Jiyu and her personal attendant had been all about! They had been mirroring, but what they had been mirroring and for whose benefit, I never knew. The famous mirroring technique seemed not to work in the West, from which I concluded that what worked in one culture could not easily be transplanted into a culture of a very different kind.

Like the Burmese lady, Kati seemed to come from nowhere. She was tall and dark-haired, with a slightly swarthy complexion, and although only 16 she was of an independent nature. I do not remember how we met, for she came neither to my meditation classes nor to my lectures. As I search my memory, I see in my mind's eye the saloon bar of the Prince of Wales in Highgate, where I used to go on a Saturday night when I was not away on retreat. I am sitting at the bar with my first or second vodka and lime and I am alone. At the other side of the room there sits a good-looking young man and he is accompanied by several women. Kati enters and joins the group, but as soon as she sees me her face lights up with pleasure and she darts across the room and joins me at the bar. She is wearing her school uniform. We talk for a while, after which she goes back to the young man and his women.

I know the story. The young man is married to one of the women, but his current girlfriend is also there, as well as his previous girlfriend. Though good-looking, he has a weak character and is very much under the thumb of his women. Kati is not in love with him as far as I know, but during the week she goes to see him in the evening and if his wife is away she spends the night with him. Otherwise, she comes and stays with me at the flat. By this time Terry has left me to live with his girlfriend Mafalda, and I have joined the two single beds together to make a double bed, and Kati shares this bed with me. There is no question of sex, and nor is she very affectionate, but she likes me and we have become friends. She lives in Hampstead with her mother, who is a pianist I have heard on the radio, and it is too late for her to go home. The little rendezvous went on for five or six months, coming to an abrupt end when I moved from Highgate West Hill to Muswell Hill and ceased to frequent the Prince of Wales on Saturday night.

I cannot remember whether it was Dr Cooper who wanted to see me about Terry or whether it was I who wanted to see him about my friend. Whichever it was, we communicated through Terry, who was seeing Cooper once a month and who was keen that I should meet the controversial psychiatrist. Once or twice he had turned up at the appointed time only to find Cooper too much under the influence of drink to be able to give him a consultation. His bill came at the end of the month as usual though, and I gathered that this was all part of the treatment. At Cooper's suggestion we met at the Round House in Chalk Farm, where he was attending a session of the Congress of Dialectics of Liberation. We would have half an hour together after the session ended. I arrived on time but the session was still in progress. It was not only still in progress but had run over time and the last speaker was still on her feet. She was a Swedish feminist and was shrieking rather than speaking about the outrages and humiliations to which women were subject all over the world. On and on she went, shrieking and weeping, until one of the organizers went up to her and took away the microphone. By this time it was long past the time for our meeting and Cooper had another appointment. He therefore invited me to have lunch with him, and a few days later I was sitting opposite him in a crowded and noisy restaurant in Soho. So noisy was it that no serious conversation was possible and I therefore invited Cooper to have lunch with me at the flat. He did not come alone but with his girlfriend, whom I had not met before. She was a rather ordinary looking woman of about 35. Cooper himself was overweight and balding and I judged him (wrongly) to be some years older than me. He was at that time perhaps at the height of his career and he and his more famous colleague, R. D. Laing, were names to conjure with in the world of the alternative community. Terry had told me much about him. He had founded the famous *Villa 21* for the treatment of young schizophrenics and Terry had spent some time there after the breakup of his marriage, Cooper having diagnosed him as schizophrenic. Cooper had his own ideas about the genesis of schizophrenia and how it was to be treated, and had developed what he called anti-psychiatry in opposition to orthodox psychiatry and its methods. So far as I remember, we did not discuss his theories and did not even talk about Terry very much. What I do remember is that in the course of the lunch I formed a very definite impression of Cooper as a man. He seemed to me to be like a big white mushroom, a mushroom that was thoroughly rotten within. I was not surprised when I learned some years later that he had died of chronic alcoholism at the age of 55.

In the course of my first year under Joy's roof the young man in the attic came to see me several times. His name was David and he had been born and brought up in Whitechapel. He was small in stature, fair-haired, and he always dressed entirely in white. As I soon discovered, he was fond of metaphysical discussion, and tended to tie himself in knots that I could not unravel. I was therefore not sorry when he stopped visiting me. After he had visited me two or three times I thought I ought to pay him a return visit, so went up and knocked on his door. There being no response I pushed open the door, only to close it as quickly and quietly as I could. During the few seconds that it had been open I had caught a glimpse of two naked white bodies chasing each other round the room, one of them belonging to a girl who had been attending my retreats in the Surrey countryside. How the two had met I never knew, as David did not come either to my meditation classes or to my public lectures.

The attic did not remain long unoccupied after David's departure, his place being taken by a Nigerian student. I hardly ever saw him, for he kept to his room and seemed to spend all his time preparing for his examinations. One afternoon I answered the doorbell to find a neatly dressed young woman standing on the doorstep. She asked if the student lived there, mentioning his name. I replied that he did, and invited her to go straight up the stairs to the attic. Thereafter she came once a week, always on the same day, at the same time, and each time it was I who answered the door when she rang, for Joy was almost as deaf as she was blind and often did not hear the bell. One afternoon, as it happened, she did hear the bell when the young woman rang and answered it herself. What passed between the two women I never knew, but Joy had somehow managed to discover that the young woman had not come to take dictation, as I had assumed, but for a very different purpose, and she had lost no time in confronting the student with her discovery. What do you think he said, she asked me shortly afterwards, still agitated and indignant. He said it was his bodily need. His bodily need indeed! She had given him a month's notice on the spot. She was not going to have *that* sort of thing going on in *her* house. I felt sorry for the poor student and hoped that his next landlady would be more tolerant.

A few days before I moved to Muswell Hill, Joy told me, with evident satisfaction, that a young married couple would be moving into the basement flat. They would be decorating it at their own expense, she added, and they had told her that they would regard it as a privilege to live there. A privilege to live there! This was the sort of thing Joy liked to hear, as it bolstered up her idea that her house was still a sort of cultural centre. I could forgive her this little weakness, as I knew that she needed not only more tenants but ones on whom she could depend. In the course of the last three years she had more than once been ill in bed and unable to move and I had done her weekly shopping for her along with my own. The young couple would be no less helpful, I hoped. Perhaps they would even join her for coffee at eleven o'clock every Thursday morning.

LIVING WITH CARTER

In the early days of the FWBO I was living on my own in a second floor flat on Highgate West Hill, in north London. Two or three times a week I would go down to Sakura, our centre in Monmouth Street, either to lead a meditation class in the basement shrine and meditation room or to attend a council meeting. Usually I walked down to Camden Town, took the Tube from there down to Tottenham Court Road, and then walked along Shaftesbury Avenue to Monmouth Street, halfway down which Sakura was situated. One fine summer evening in 1968 I arrived there to find a cluster of people waiting for me, some in the shop and others on the pavement outside. One of them was a shabbily dressed young man who seemed to be the object of general disapproval. Clearly something was wrong. The proprietor of Sakura told me what had happened. A young American had turned up the previous evening, and as he had nowhere to stay, he, Upaya (Emile Boin), had allowed him to spend the night in the shrine and meditation room downstairs. The young traveller had fallen asleep while reading by the light of a candle, something had caught fire, and soon the whole place was ablaze. Fortunately he had managed to grope his way through the smoke to the narrow winding stairs and had emerged into the shop.

He had had no time to dress and therefore emerged naked, and the clothes he was now wearing were some of Upaya's old working clothes. Clearly there could be no class that evening, and for many evenings to come, and slowly the people who had gathered there went their several ways. What was to be done with the young American? No one wanted to accommodate him, and he could hardly occupy the shrine and meditation room a second night, it having been gutted by the fire and much of it black with soot. I was not particularly keen to accommodate him myself, but I felt sorry for him, so I took him back with me to my flat.

Over a drink and a snack Carter, as the young American was called, told me a little about himself. Like millions of other young Americans of his generation he had heeded the call of Timothy Leary to drop out, tune in, and turn on. He had left his comfortable middle-class home in California, had experimented with LSD and other psychedelic drugs, and for the last few weeks he had been hitching his way around Europe. He had been I think in Norway and had spent a few days there in prison, apparently on account of drugs. Now he was in London and with me. By this time we were in my bedroom and it was time to sleep. 'Shall I make you up a bed on the floor, or will you sleep with me?' I asked. 'I'll sleep with you', was Carter's prompt reply. I slipped into bed and he soon followed but not before he had divested himself of Upaya's paint-stained cast-offs. It was as though a beautiful butterfly had emerged from its chrysalis. Six feet or more in height, and twenty-one years old, he had tousled, sun-bleached hair and blue eyes, and his well-proportioned body seemed made of gold rather than flesh. The words that came to me were, 'the gift of the gods'. I had been kind to Carter and perhaps my kindness was being rewarded. As soon as he was in bed, he snuggled up to me and I put my arm round him, saying 'Is it all right?' 'Yeah, sure, sure', he replied putting his arm around me, and although I could not see his face I knew that he was grinning. Within minutes we were being swept up on a wave of sexual ecstasy such as I, at least, had not experienced before. How long we remained on it I do not know, but when it subsided I was left feeling deeply satisfied and went straight to sleep. That wave was to sweep us away more than once during the months that followed and I shall remain ever grateful to Carter for the part he played in my initiation into the world of erotic bliss.

It was several weeks before the Triratna shrine and meditation room was again fit for purpose, but it took Carter only a matter of days to acquire some new clothes. His sartorial taste was by no means the same as mine. Among his purchases was a pair of what he called his 'bermudas'. I had never before seen or heard of this garment, which was too short for trousers and too long for shorts. Carter's culinary tastes were also very different from mine. He was fond of peanut butter and jam sandwiches, whereas I had discovered peanut butter only after my return to England. He also used expressions that were new to me, such as 'nitty-gritty', and he was fond of music that was not always to my liking. Like other west coast hippies he had dipped into Zen, but he was not seriously interested in either meditation or Buddhism, and during his stay with me he hardly ever accompanied me to my classes or lectures. Although he had turned up at Sakura, he was not really part of the FWBO. His relationship was with me. If he had any spiritual practice at all it consisted in having dropped out, and trying to tune into something beyond ordinary experience with the help of drugs. Besides acquiring new clothes, Carter soon found a way to supply himself with cannabis, of which he was a regular user. I had not tried it, though some of my friends were devotees of the weed; but it was not long before Carter persuaded me to share a joint with him. During the time that he was with me I must have smoked it every day. Our favourite place was Hampstead Heath, which lay immediately behind my flat and could be seen from the kitchen window. A corner of the Heath was covered with long grass, and there we would lie, flat on our backs in the sunshine and gazing up at the blue sky. Often I had the sensation that I was floating, as though on a magic carpet.

One afternoon, as we lay there, Carter confided to me that he had taken LSD not once but eight times and that every trip had been a bad one. If he could have a trip with me, he said, he was sure he would have a good one at last. Despite initial reservations, I eventually agreed, and Carter went about making the necessary preparations, including choosing records for us to listen to during the trip. Rather than writing a second time about the trip I shall quote what I wrote when I was a little nearer to the experience than I am now.

> The trip lasted for about twelve hours. I had intended to record the effects of the LSD as it took hold, but this proved not to be

> feasible. All I could write was 'feel as though little fish were nibbling at my brain', followed by the single word 'laughter'. I was, in fact, laughing uncontrollably, and the laughter was releasing huge quantities of energy. After that, there were only squiggles on the paper. The entire trip is virtually a blank to me. All that I could remember of it, even immediately afterwards, was of my being present at the dawn of creation. 'First light on first water' were the words that came to me, accompanied by the visual image of a vast expanse of water upon which light was shining.[571]

Carter did not have a good trip, but he was relieved not to have had a bad one, and for this he was grateful.

The two summers that Carter was with me, 1968 and 1969, were both fine English summers, and both provided the setting of events that were significant to me: my holiday in the New Forest, and my visit to Glastonbury. Joy Baines, my landlady, owned a caravan in the New Forest and she agreed to rent it to me for a week. Ananda would be staying with us in the caravan, which was quite a small one, and Mike (Abhaya) would be paying us a day visit at some point.[572] A couple of days before our departure Carter asked me if we could add a young woman called Samantha to our little party. He felt very sorry for her, he explained. She was being badly treated by her mother and elder sister and needed a break. I could not but agree as I could see that Carter was genuinely concerned for her. She could spend the previous night with me at the flat, he suggested, and he would spend the night with a friend nearby. He did not say who this friend was, and in retrospect I do not know whether it was a male friend or whether he had at last found a girlfriend. A few weeks after moving in with me he had complained that I did not go out and about with him very often, but spent much of my time at my desk. This was true, as I had letters to answer and lectures to prepare. I therefore told Carter that he should find a girlfriend, and that she would probably go out and about with him as much as he wanted. He objected that he did not know how to get a girlfriend, and I had the impression that his experience of women was limited and that he was not altogether at ease with them. All you have to do, I insisted, is to go to parties, and sooner or later you will find someone you like and who likes you. He must have followed my advice, for he did in the end find a girlfriend. Her name was Andrea and she was to play a decisive part in both our lives.

Samantha turned out to be about twenty and she had long amber-coloured hair, violet eyes, and milk-white skin. After Carter had left, she seated herself on the edge of my bed without saying anything. When she did speak, it was in a tone almost of defiance. 'Either I sleep in all my clothes', she said, 'or I take everything off.' 'Do as you please', I responded, as I got into bed, 'I don't mind either way.' She seemed to consider this, then, very slowly she took off her clothes and climbed into bed with her back towards me. I did not know what Carter had told her about me, but she seemed to expect that we would have sex. I had not had sex with a woman before and I wanted to find out what it was like. But before I could do so, I heard, clear as a bell, an angelic voice. The voice said, 'Don't', so I didn't, for soft and gentle though the voice was it was utterly compelling and could not possibly be disobeyed. I have often wondered where that angelic voice came from and why it should have intervened when it did. Since then I have not had the slightest inclination to have sex with a woman, even to find out what it was like. For me women have always been friends, not sex partners.

Joy's caravan was on the edge of a piece of woodland and Carter, Samantha, and I reached it after a long walk uphill. Ananda arrived soon afterwards from another direction. It was a wonderful day, with a sky of unclouded blue. We enjoyed the warmth of the sun and the little breezes that fanned our cheeks from time to time. We enjoyed the size of the trees and of the tall purple foxgloves that grew among the fern. We enjoyed one another's company. We enjoyed watching the famous New Forest ponies which, unafraid of man but a little shy, grazed not far away. Mike came up from Bournemouth as promised. Thus for a day I enjoyed the company of two of my closest friends and for a while, at least, Samantha seemed to be drawn into our little circle. All this and much more is reflected in some of the poems that I wrote that summer.[573] It was a time of light and colour, harmony and peace. From time to time Carter and I wandered off on our own to get some exercise, and in the course of one of these excursions we came upon a magnificent oak, which, as the inscription informed us, marked the spot where William Rufus died, slain by an arrow from an unknown hand. On another occasion we returned to find Ananda sitting with just a towel round his waist. I do not remember what Samantha was wearing, if indeed she was wearing anything at all, and I had the impression Ananda had just warded off an attack on his virginity.

A few days after my return to Highgate West Hill I received a visit from a troubled young man. He had been Samantha's boyfriend, he told me, and she had given him and others syphilis, for which he was receiving treatment. He had urged her to get treatment, but had met with denial and defiance, and his purpose in coming to see me was to ask me to intervene. This I did as soon as I could, but whether she did seek treatment or not I do not know, and I never saw her again.

My 1969 visit to Glastonbury was not planned in the way that the visit to the New Forest had been. It just happened, as one might say, and it involved not just Carter and me but quite a number of other people. So far as I remember, it grew out of one of the Buddhist festivals that the FWBO was celebrating at Aryatara. There was a bonfire in the garden and perhaps fireworks, though I may be confusing that year's celebrations with those of another year. Be that as it may, a dozen or so people stayed on after the rest had gone home. Among these were the three members of the English Mystical School of Painting and their respective girlfriends, all of whom I had got to know after seeing their end of year exhibition at Goldsmith's College of Art. They were not so much members of the FWBO as personal friends who attended some of my lectures and visited me at the flat. There was a xylophone in the shrine-room and one of them started playing it. It was an improvization that went on and on, hour after hour until some of us went into a sort of trance or fell asleep. In the morning we set out for Glastonbury, though how we reached the decision to go there I do not know. Soon we were on the road. As we crossed London Bridge we saw thousands, perhaps tens of thousands, of tightly packed people streaming towards the City. 'Where are all those people going?' asked Carter, his eyes goggling. 'They are going to work', I explained. 'To work!' my friend exclaimed in tones of mingled shock, horror, and disgust that people should be going to work on such a fine summer's day as this. They should all be on the beach. But of course this was not California. Before long we were heading west and I noticed that the big van in which we were travelling was being joined by other, smaller vans, and that we were all picking up hitchhikers. It was as though a wind was carrying us all in the same direction, towards Glastonbury.

My long poem *On Glastonbury Tor* was written shortly after this visit, and I do not propose to describe for the second time, in prose, how we made the ascent of the Tor or what happened when we reached the top. The poem is the definitive account. I want simply to make the point that the events described in the poem did actually happen. I really did see, with my physical eyes, the three UFOs that suddenly appeared in the evening sky. They were UFOs in the literal sense of the term, being unidentified, at least by me; they flew, and they were objects in the sense that I saw them with my physical eyes, as did many others including some nightwatchmen, as was reported in the newspapers. Similarly, I actually did see a dark shape enter into the young man and speak from or through him words in a language that was unknown to me. In the poem I do not reproduce the actual words but only give an impression of their sound, which was harsh and guttural. The young man was a Canadian who was known to Carter but whom I had not met. The poem ends with the Tor expanding in all directions and soaring aloft. It was an image of Vairocana's Tower, which contains in a state of mutual interpenetration everything that exists. All this I actually experienced, though whether the experience was mundane or transcendental, or something in between, I cannot say. *On Glastonbury Tor* was not only one of my longer poems, but written in a style quite different from my usual one. It was not deliberately experimental but the style seems to be the natural expression of what I experienced. Indeed, the poem itself was an expression of much that was happening in the 1960s, especially among the younger generation.[574]

By this time Carter had his girlfriend in the person of Andrea and I had met her once or twice. She was of medium height, had long fair hair, and was thin rather than slim. Her face was quite pale and drawn, probably because she ate little and was on drugs. Whether she was estranged from her upper-middle-class family in the way that Samantha was I never knew, though I gathered that her grandfather was a dignitary in the Church of England. At times she seemed small, pathetic, and waif-like and I imagine that this was one of the things that had drawn kind-hearted Carter to her, for as the poet says, 'Pity melts the mind to love'.[575] Andrea had an upstairs room in a house not far from where I lived, so that it was easy for Carter to come and go between us. Sometimes he spent the night with me, sometimes with Andrea. Although he had originally wanted a girlfriend who would go out and about with him, Andrea must have been a disappointment in this respect. She spent most of her time in her room smoking, so if Carter wanted to go out with someone he sometimes had to fall back on me. I would call on him at Andrea's place where more often than not I found both of them in bed despite the lateness of the hour. After the three of us had chatted for a while, Carter would dress and we would go out together. On one of my visits I found that Carter had covered a large sheet of paper with doodles executed in pencils or crayons of various colours. The effect was bright and positive and I thought it reflected the state of Carter's mind at the time. He was happy. He was happy because he had Andrea and he had me. On one of the rare occasions when the three of us went for a walk on Hampstead Heath together he put an arm round each of us and declared that it was the happiest time of his life, for he had with him the two people whom he loved best in the world.

This idyllic state of affairs did not last. As the weeks went by, I noticed that, in Carter's case, just as pity had melted into love so love had developed into infatuation. With Andrea there was a similar transition. In her case, infatuation had developed into possessiveness and jealousy. Two of my memories at the time illustrate what was going on. We had booked seats for a play at the Aldwych and we were making our way to the Tube station. We walked together, but every ten or fifteen yards Carter and Andrea would stop for prolonged smooching, as though they could hardly get enough of each other. This delayed our arrival at the theatre, where we found we had the wrong tickets. The scene of my other memory was the Highgate West Hill flat. Carter had come to see me with Andrea. He came upstairs as usual, but she remained obstinately down in the hallway so that Carter could spend only a few minutes with me, as no doubt was her intention. On leaving me, Carter put his arms round me and gave me a big hug and I noticed that he had an erection. He noticed it too, and we both laughed. Carter eventually realized that all was not well as regards Andrea's attitude to me. I was quite happy that he should sleep with Andrea, but Andrea was not happy that he should sleep with me or see very much of me. One day Carter suggested that the three of us should spend a week together on holiday. Though he did not say so, I knew that he hoped that this would bind the three of us more closely together and help Andrea develop a more positive attitude towards me. I was sceptical, and told Carter that I did not think his scheme would work. I could see that Andrea was implacable in her dislike of me and that we would never be friends. Nonetheless, I allowed Carter to persuade me and agreed to take part in the experiment.

Mike was willing to lend us his car for a week. He had moved from Bournemouth to Millbrook in Cornwall, and it was therefore to Millbrook that we travelled to pick up the car. Behind the wheel Carter was a very different person. The carefree hippy changed into a competent young American who had been driving all his life. We had no plan as to where we would go on our holiday and I left it to Carter to decide the route. Our first stop was in Laugharne. I had visited the little town the previous winter with Rick, one of the English Mystical painters, and we had visited Dylan Thomas's grave in the churchyard and seen the famous boathouse.[576] I was not just sightseeing, but looking for a country centre for the FWBO. We found only one that might have been suitable, but at £4,000 it was beyond our means. The owner was an elderly woman and Rick and I spent some time talking with her in her kitchen. She seemed to have an animus against marriage. 'Don't you get married,' she told Rick. 'First they marry you for your beauty, then they throw you away. So don't marry.' It was as though she was addressing a young woman rather than a young man. Neither Carter nor Andrea was interested in Dylan Thomas and we spent our time in Laugharne driving up and down the broad, flat sands where Sir Malcolm Campbell had broken the land speed record with his Blue Bird.[577] At one point Carter handed over the wheel to me and I drove round in circles for a while greatly enjoying myself. It was the only part of our holiday that I really enjoyed. The following day found us at Glastonbury Tor. Carter wanted to show Andrea the place, and we spent the night in the grim old tower.

The only other part of our holiday that I remember was finding myself in Bath. In particular, I remember the three of us being in a small park. Carter and I felt like stretching our legs for a while. Andrea wanted to sit down and we left her sitting in a little arbour. When we returned fifteen or twenty minutes later Andrea was nowhere to be seen and Carter panicked. We at once set about searching the neighbouring streets, he frantic with anxiety and I scarcely less worried. Eventually we found her more or less by accident. She was sullen and silent and would not say where she had been or what she had been doing. It seemed to me that she was playing on Carter's fear of losing her. If she was, it worked. For the next day or two he would not allow her out of his sight and the situation became rather strained. In the end I told Carter that the holiday was not proving a success and that we should separate, and to this he unwillingly agreed. There was an emotional parting and even Andrea seemed a little moved. He would return the car to Mike at the end of the week, then take the train back to London and me.

I never saw him again.

From friends of friends I learned that he had sent home for his best suit and that shortly afterwards he had married Andrea and taken her back to America with him. Before leaving he sent me a message. It was scribbled on a postcard with various coloured pencils and it read, 'I know I am hurting you. Give me two years, and I will be back.' I was indeed hurt. Carter had been an important part of my life for just over a year, and it took me a long time to recover from the loss. Recover I did, though, and I was soon finding consolation elsewhere.

Two years later I had news of Andrea. She had been attacked while alone on the beach one night and had returned to England. She had been injured, but how badly I did not hear.

Many years later I was in San Francisco, and one day I found myself in the centre of the city being driven through heavy traffic. Suddenly, I saw a shabby figure, clad in black, standing between the streams of traffic, panhandling. He was in profile, and I knew that profile. It was surely Carter! There was no time to check whether I was right. The traffic moved on and me with it, and in an instant the black-clad figure was out of sight. I have never been sure whether or not the figure I had glimpsed was really the Carter whom I had known and loved.

FOUR VISITORS

'You didn't expect to see me,' said the angel, seating himself on the arm of my chair. I knew it was an angel because I had seen paintings of them, and there was Milton's wonderful description of the Archangel Raphael in *Paradise Lost*.[578] Like them, my celestial visitor was young and beautiful with aureoled golden hair and a pair of iridescent wings and was clad in a loosely flowing robe of dazzling whiteness.

'No, I was not expecting you,' I replied. 'After all, I am a Buddhist, not a Christian. If I had been expecting anyone, it would have been a bodhisattva.'

'You used to be quite fond of me and my brethren,' responded the angel. 'You may not have been aware of it, but we used to visit you from time to time, and though you could not see us you used to draw pictures of us.'

'That was a long time ago,' I protested. 'I could not have been more than 13 or 14, and since then I have been more concerned with bodhisattvas than with angels.'

'That may well be so,' was the beautiful being's response, 'but has it not occurred to you that your bodhisattvas may have been angels in disguise? May not one of us have been your own guardian angel, watching over you and protecting you from harm?'

'I was never conscious of the presence of any such being,' I said, 'though some Buddhists have the idea of a *puṇya devatā*, which I suppose is a little bit like the Christian guardian angel.'

'Have you forgotten you once heard a warning voice? And did you not describe it as an angelic voice?'

'I remember it very well,' I admitted, 'and I remember thinking how strange it was that I should have described that voice as angelic rather than describing it in Buddhist terms.'

'Well, now you know. It was the voice of your guardian angel.'

'But I heard that voice only once in my whole life, and it spoke no more than one word. Surely my guardian angel, if I have one, should have been more active than that?'

'Your guardian angel takes on many forms, even Buddhist ones, and in the course of your life he has helped and protected you more often than you knew. You have been in quite a few tight corners, and you have always thought that it was your good luck or your good karma that extricated you from them. In fact, it was your guardian angel, working behind the scenes, who did so every time.'

'But why should my guardian angel – if he exists – have intervened on that particular occasion? Surely there must have been a reason for his doing so?'

'There indeed was a reason, and a very good one. He saw that you were about to do something that was not in the line of your natural development, and he wanted to stop you. Had he not done so, the consequences could have been quite serious, not only for you but for a lot of other people.'

'What other people?'

'I mean people whose line of natural development was the same as yours and who were attracted to the Dharma but were not made welcome in other Buddhist groups. You are the founder of an order and a movement in which people of that nature were made welcome and who could not only practise the Dharma but be open about who they were.'

At this point there came from somewhere to my left the sound of a once-known voice. 'Excuse me, gentlemen,' said the voice, 'but I couldn't help overhearing your conversation. We have met once or twice before,' the voice continued suavely, addressing me, 'but perhaps you have forgotten your old friend.'

'I have not forgotten you,' I retorted. 'You are Māra the Evil One, and you are not my friend and never will be. On our first meeting you tried to convince me that there existed nothing except matter, and I gave you a proper reply.'

'Yes, you did,' sighed Māra. 'You are always ready with a reply. That is one of your little weaknesses. But I haven't come to chop logic with you. This is just a friendly visit. I want to tell you something.'

'What might that be?' I enquired, even though I knew that Māra could not possibly wish me any good.

'I want to tell you that things are getting worse, or rather that they are getting better, and that you ought to consider your position.'

'What do you mean?'

'You are aware that I once swore "Evil, be thou my Good."[579] Since then I have done what you call evil and what I call good.'

'Yes, I know, and you are still doing what I call evil and you call good.'

'Indeed I am,' said Māra complacently. 'Just tune into Radio 4 and hear what is going on all over this world of yours. Nothing but violence in one form or another. Dip into social media and what will you find? Nothing but hatred spreading from mind to mind like a poisonous fog. All this is my work, operating through my chosen human agents. But that is nothing. Think of what happened in your twentieth century. Two world wars. Nazism and Communism. Hundreds of millions of people enslaved, tortured, killed, and imprisoned, and all this at the hands of their fellow countrymen and their own government or party. Your twentieth Christian century was productive of more human suffering than all the previous centuries of human history put together. This is why I told you that things are getting better, which from your point of view means that they are getting worse. I liked the way you stood up to me at that first meeting. I thought you had the making of a really good devil, and that is why I have come to see you.'

At that moment, a tiny red rose fell through the air and landed on Māra's chest, and I noticed that he turned pale. 'Forgive me, gentlemen,' he stammered, 'but I must leave you. Someone is about to arrive whom I am anxious not to meet. We had a little difference of opinion some time ago and I do not want to have to disagree with a lady again. As you know, "the Prince of Darkness is a gentleman".' With these words Māra disappeared.

'Who is this lady?' I asked the angel. 'And why is Māra so afraid of her?'

'She has many names,' responded the angel, smiling, 'but we call her the Queen of the Angels. She and Māra, as you call him, indeed did have a little difference of opinion a long time ago. It ended when one of her roses gave him a nasty bruise that kept him out of action for quite a while. There is more in those little red roses than one might think.'

These words were hardly out of his mouth when I felt something land on my chest just opposite my heart. It was a little red rose, and at its touch I felt a sensation of ineffable bliss pervade my entire being. I closed my eyes to experience it the better, and when I opened them again I saw standing before me a tall figure. She wore a pure white under-robe and over it a mantle of deepest blue. She had long black hair and her arms were crossed on her breast.

'It is a long time since you thought of me,' she said, in a low, sweet voice, 'but I have not forgotten you. You were only 12 or 13 years old and you painted me just as you see me now. You copied paintings of me that you had seen but you added a touch of your own: three red roses, one to each side of me and one above my head. Do you remember?'[580]

'I do,' I said, 'but I cannot remember why I added those three red roses. I just gave them to you. For me you will always be not so much the Queen of the Angels as the Lady of the Three Red Roses.'

'But what about the Lady of the White Roses?' came another low sweet voice. And I saw that another tall, stately figure had appeared beside the first. She was clad in a milk-white robe, one corner of which was modestly draped over her chignon. In one hand she held a flask from which she dispensed ambrosia, while in the other she held a bunch of white roses.

'It's the Goddess of Mercy,' whispered the angel to me, 'whom you Buddhists call Guanyin. She is one of the many forms in which the Lady of the Three Red Roses appears to Buddhists.'

Though the angel had whispered, the second lady heard what he had said. 'No, young angel,' she said mildly. 'Your Lady of the Three Red Roses is one of the many forms in which I appear to Christians.'

'No, you are one of the forms in which I appear,' said the other lady politely.

'This happens whenever they meet,' said the angel, smiling, 'but it always comes right in the end.' As if to confirm his words, the two figures moved towards each other as though they were about to embrace, but instead, each melted into the other, so that Guanyin wore the red roses and the Queen of the Angels carried the white. The united figures then dissolved into a brilliant white light, tinged with pink and blue, which was soon lost in the deep blue of the sky.

The angel and I were now alone and I saw that his iridescent wings had begun to quiver, as though he was preparing for flight. 'Tell me,' I said, 'before you go. Which of those two ladies was only one of the forms of the other lady?'

'I don't really know,' he replied. 'I am only an angel. To get an answer to that, you would have to go right up to the top of the celestial hierarchy, to the cherubim, who are filled with wisdom, and the seraphim, who are on fire with love.'

'Just one more question before you go,' I begged, for I could see that his wings were now half spread.

'Just one,' he agreed, 'but no more.'

'This is my question,' I said, hoping that I was not being too personal. 'Are angels masculine or are they feminine?'

'They are neither. They are spiritually androgynous, though they generally appear as beautiful young men with iridescent wings like mine.'

'And you? Was it you who said 'Don't' to me at that critical moment? Are you my guardian angel?' But he had already disappeared, and I was once more alone.

4
LIFE AND DEATH, GOOD AND EVIL

On the Edge of the Etheric · Some Reflections on the Gārava Sutta *· The Good Friend, the False Friend, and the Spiritual Friend · A Complex Personality: A Note · Evil in Myth and in Human Experience · Blake and the Gates of Paradise ·* News from Nowhere *– and from India · Evil Revisited – and Good · Disparities*

ON THE EDGE OF THE ETHERIC

He was tall and well built, with long back hair, and he wore buckskin leggings. The upper part of his reddish-brown body was bare. He reminded me of the Red Indians about whom I had read in boys' weekly magazines when I was quite young, but he was not a Red Indian. He was an *asura* or anti-god, a denizen of one of the six realms depicted in the wheel of life. We met in 1962 or thereabouts, when I was on a visit to Bombay. The two of us would have to fight, he told me. We would have to fight with rapiers, and whichever of us drew blood from the other would be the winner. He fought very well, but so did I, and eventually I succeeded in drawing a thin red line diagonally across his chest with the point of my rapier. 'You have won,' he told me, 'and I shall have to give you something. In a few days' time you will be in danger from fire and I will give you something that will protect you from it.' He then gave me the seed syllable *raṃ*, which I knew to be the seed syllable of the element of fire, whereupon he disappeared and I returned to my normal consciousness. It was not a dream, nor a vision. It was as though I had been with him in his own realm, the realm of the *asuras*.

Two or three days later I happened to be giving a lecture on Buddhism. This was nothing new, as I gave lectures whenever I was in Bombay. What was new was the fact that on this occasion I was giving it in a building recently acquired by my friend Dinshaw Mehta, the founder of the Society of Servants of God.[581] He had acquired it for the activities of the Society and my lecture was part of the inaugural festivities. I was giving my lecture in a room on one of the upper floors, and there were between thirty and forty people present. Dinshaw presided, and sat next to me on the platform. I had been speaking for perhaps half an hour when I saw, out of the corner of my eye, someone enter the room and quietly hand my friend a slip of paper. The latter glanced at the paper, then quietly left the room. As I was well into my lecture I paid scant attention to what was going on and continued speaking. Twenty or more minutes later Dinshaw returned as quietly as he had left, resuming his seat beside me, and it was not long before my lecture came to an end. He afterwards told me what had happened. A room nearby had been turned into a meditation room, candles had been left burning there, and curtains had caught fire. He had been summoned and with the help of two other people he had been able to put out the blaze. It was most fortunate, he added, that I had been holding people's attention with my lecture. Had they known that a room was on fire only a few yards away they could have panicked and in the stampede for the exit people could have been injured or even trampled to death. I said nothing to my friend about the *asura* or about what he had given me.

It took me only an hour to get from London to Brighton by train, and in the 1960s I used to visit the Brighton Buddhist Society every month. There was a meditation class, and from time to time I would give a talk on Buddhism in a hired room above a tea shop. The meditation class was held at the home of an elderly married couple, the Wraggs. Usually I returned to London the same evening, but on more than one occasion I stayed overnight at the Wraggs, occupying their comfortable guest room on the ground floor, next to the shrine-room in which the meditation classes were held. In this way I got to know Carl and Violet quite well and even came to regard them as friends. They had been Spiritualists for many years, becoming interested in Buddhism quite late in life. As a bookcase in the guest room testified, they had read widely in the fields of comparative religion and mysticism, and I was in the habit of dipping into one of their books before going to bed. I particularly remember dipping into the *Sephar Zohar* or 'Book of Splendour', the fundamental text of the Kabbalah in five volumes, which I had not seen before. One day I heard that Violet had died, and I went down to Brighton for the funeral. Carl showed no sign of distress. For him, Violet was not dead, and when his two sons-in-law turned up in black he told them to go home and change into ordinary clothes. The funeral was almost a merry affair and we must have scandalized the solemn-faced undertaker's men with our lightheartedness.

On my next monthly visit to the Brighton Buddhist Society I stayed with Carl who was living alone, so to speak, on the upper floor of the house. He greeted me warmly, sat me down in the sitting room in my usual chair, and went off to prepare tea. I had not sat there for more than a few minutes when Violet entered the room and seated herself opposite me, as she usually did. We then talked for a while, as we always did, and she then left me. When Carl returned with the tea I told him that I had just seen Violet. 'Oh yes,' he replied, 'she's always around.' I have more than once told friends about my experience of seeing Violet and talking with her when, in the ordinary sense of the word, she was dead. Each time I have emphasized, as strongly as I could, that it was not Violet's ghost that I had seen and talked with. It was Violet herself.

'Would you mind taking over from me for a while?' Terry asked me, putting his hand over the mouthpiece of the telephone. He had been on the phone for more than three hours, talking to a friend and trying to persuade him not to take his own life. On my agreeing to take over, Terry spoke again to the friend. He was with a Buddhist monk, he told him, and he was sure the monk could help him. Would he like to speak to the monk? The friend agreed to do so, and I took the phone from Terry. I already knew the man's history. His girlfriend had left him and he felt that as he could not live without her he had no alternative but to take his own life. I must have spoken to him for about two hours, after which Terry took over from me and spoke to his friend again for an hour or more. By this time it was one o'clock in the morning and it seemed that between us, Terry and I had succeeded in persuading him not to take his own life. Terry therefore went home and I went to bed.

At five o'clock the man's mother phoned to say that her son had just died by suicide. I was not really surprised. While talking to him I had the distinct impression that I was talking not to a human being but to a demon, a demon who had taken possession of Terry's friend and driven him to take his own life. I knew that should one allow oneself to be overwhelmed by a violent negative emotion such as craving, or hatred, or fear, one could eventually lay oneself open to possession by a negative psychic entity. In the case of Terry's friend he had been overwhelmed by grief for the loss of his girlfriend and felt he could not live without her. An 'evil' non-human entity had taken charge of him and he had taken his own life.

Broom House Farm was located just within what may once have been a forest and was now a vast conifer plantation. It was conveniently near Thetford in Norfolk and in the early 1970s I used to run retreats there for a dozen or more people. One of these retreats was an ordination retreat, the ordination ceremony being held in the loft of the small barn that stood next to the farmhouse. I also once spent a few days at the farmhouse with a companion. One evening we happened to be sitting in the living room, he on one side of the fireplace, in which a log fire was burning, and I on the other. Suddenly my companion exclaimed, 'What's wrong? You look as though you're being attacked.' I replied, 'Yes, that is what I feel, I feel as though I'm being attacked.' The attack was not physical but psychical, as though I was being attacked by invisible non-human entities. The attack did not last very long. I realized that I had in my hand and had just been reading some literature that a friend had sent me from Findhorn, an intentional community in north-east Scotland, and that this literature contained references to what it called *devas*. Clearly, these were the non-human entities that were attacking me. I threw the literature into the fire, whereupon the attack ceased. In a sense I had brought it upon myself. The friend in question had been to see me before his departure for Findhorn and I had asked him to send me some of its literature.

The following morning I had much to think about during my solitary walk along one of the broad, straight tracks that ran through the plantation. Why had the *devas* attacked me? Had I done anything to offend them? Such were my thoughts as the track took me further and further into the plantation. There was no sign of animal or bird life, and it was eerily quiet. I became aware that the trees were very angry.

They were angry because they were all close together and forced to grow upwards to where they had a small crown of greenery which alone ever saw the light. Perhaps it was the tree spirits that were angry rather than the trees themselves, and perhaps the tree spirits were related to the Findhorn *devas*, though why the latter had attacked me that evening at Broom House Farm I never knew.

One Christmas in the late 1960s, finding myself alone in the Highgate flat, I decided to spend the holiday reading *The Lord of the Rings*, the three volumes of which a friend had just lent me. I read the first volume on Christmas Eve, the second on Christmas Day, and the third on Boxing Day, and thus for a while found myself living in the mythic world of the elves and the ents, of Sauron and Gandalf, the hobbits Frodo and Sam, Shelob and Gollum, and the other creations of the writer's fertile imagination. *The Lord of the Rings* and its cast of characters, both good and evil, soon became part of the counter-culture of the times and no one in the FWBO thought it strange that one of its country retreat centres should be called Rivendell, that being the name of the home of Elrond, one of the elves. The mythic Rivendell was hidden in a deep valley whereas the FWBO Rivendell was located in the flat Sussex countryside. In the 1980s I held there a ten-day ordination retreat for women, occupying a separate wing of the building. Though I led the meditation and gave talks, I still had enough time to write a chapter of *Ambedkar and Buddhism*, the book on which I was working at the time. One night I woke up at two o'clock in the morning and realized that there was somebody else in the room. As it was dark I could not see anything but I felt that quite near me there was a cold sinister presence that sent shivers up my spine. I recited a mantra and the presence slowly withdrew. It visited me on at least two more nights. I said nothing to the women about my nocturnal visitor, as I did not want to alarm them or spoil the atmosphere of the retreat. Later on I learned that years ago a woman had taken her own life in the house, it being then the rectory of the neighbouring church.

It was Tuesday, 30 January 1990. Paramartha and I were having breakfast in our flat above the London Buddhist Centre when I suddenly *knew* that I had to see my mother that very day. She was then in hospital in Southend-on-Sea and I had seen her only a few days before, and on leaving had promised to see her again in two weeks' time. But now I had to see her that very day. Paramartha did not question my intuition, and we set out for Southend-on-Sea as soon as we could. Having arrived in the town before visiting hours, and wanting to get some exercise, we walked along the front in the direction of Leigh-on-Sea. The sky was overcast, a cold wind was blowing, and although it was midday one would have thought that it was already four o'clock.

On arriving at the hospital we went straight to the ward where I thought I would find my mother, on the way passing through a room in which there were four beds. The bed in the corner was empty and the thought struck me that that bed might have been occupied by my mother. The ward sister of whom I enquired where I would find Mrs Wiltshire wanted to know who I was and I said, 'I'm her son.' For a moment or two she was silent, then she said, 'I am sorry to have to tell you that your mother died at two o'clock this morning.' I was stunned by the unexpected news, but all I said was, 'Is it possible to see her?' The ward sister said she would find out, then ushered us into a waiting room, gave us tea, and left. We talked a little about what had happened and I was glad that Paramartha was with me. An hour later the ward sister returned. 'You can see her now', she said, whereupon we were taken through a series of rooms to the mortuary chapel. My mother's body lay covered with a white sheet except for her head, behind which was the altar. She looked very dead. Though there were the same sunken eyes, now closed, the same large, prominent nose, and the same small mouth, they looked as though were carved in wood and had never been made of flesh. Paramartha seated himself on the other side of the body while I seated myself on this side so that we faced each other across it. I took my *mālā* from my pocket and Paramartha, with a little smile, took out his. We then chanted the Vajrasattva mantra in unison for about half an hour. All this time we were aware that a foot or more above my mother's chest there was an area within which there was some kind of electrical or psychic vibration. We left the chapel quietly, closing the door behind us, and soon we were out of the hospital and on our way back to London.

There were three unusual things about our experience. While having breakfast that morning I had known that I had to go and see my mother that day. There were only two previous occasions in my life when I had been visited by a similar experience, both of them connected with the death of someone I knew. Then, I had never before taken my *mālā* with me when I went out and neither had Paramartha, yet before we left the flat we had both slipped a *mālā* into our pocket without knowing that the other had done so. No wonder Paramartha had given me that little conspiratorial smile as he took his own *mālā* from his pocket. Finally, there was the strange phenomenon of the area above my mother's chest in which there was some kind of electrical or psychic vibration. Did this mean that my mother was not really as dead as she seemed to be? If what the ward sister had told me was correct, when we saw my mother she must have been dead for a little over twelve hours. But I knew that according to some Buddhist traditions it took rather longer than that for the consciousness to sever its connection with the body.

The sound of the voice did not wake me up, for I was already awake, listening to the faint sound of traffic on the Aslacton Road. It was a soft, warm, friendly voice, and it was quite near. 'Hello Bhante-ji,' the voice said. It was an Indian voice, as I knew from the intonation. And though it was dark in the bedroom and I could not see anything, I knew that there was someone with me. One of my Indian Buddhist friends must have died, I thought, and had come to pay me a final visit. The sound from the Aslacton Road grew fainter, and soon I was fast asleep.

SOME REFLECTIONS ON THE *GĀRAVA SUTTA*

One is never too old to learn. It is only relatively late in my Dharma life that I have become more aware of or have focused on the *Gārava Sutta* of the Pāli canon.[582] I knew of its existence before, but it started having a significance for me that it had not had before. What struck me was that the Buddha was giving the hearer a glimpse of the workings of the Buddha-mind. But who was the original hearer? According to tradition, it was Ānanda, the Buddha's companion in the last years of his life. But now the 'hearer' is the person who reads or hears this section of the *Saṃyutta Nikāya*, whether in Pāli or in a translation. Hearing those words myself, and doing my best to absorb them, it occurs to me that we need to reflect deeply on them in order to bring out, as best we can, their full significance. On the surface, they are easy enough to understand. The Buddha says, 'What if I were to dwell in dependence on this very Dharma to which I have fully awakened, honouring and respecting it?'

But what is that Dharma? It is surely not the sum total of the Buddha's teachings, for it would be absurd to think of him as honouring and respecting something of which he himself was the source. Before saying more about the Dharma to which the Buddha had awoken, I want to say something about his honouring and respecting that Dharma.

In a preceding section of the *sutta* the Buddha declares unequivocally that it is painful to live without honouring and respecting anyone, from which it follows that he himself needed to live in such a manner. To modern, egalitarian, 'politically correct' ears the first part of this statement will seem incredible. Are we not all equal, so that there is no question of having to look up to anyone? Moreover, no one is more spiritually developed than anyone else. They are just *differently* developed. In the Buddha's teaching, however, there are steps and stages such as the eight stages, both mundane and transcendental, of the Noble Eightfold Path, the six *pāramitās*, and so on, and there are individuals who are on these steps or at these stages, so as to form a hierarchy of levels and of practitioners. According to the Buddha it is actually painful not 'to live honouring and respecting' someone, and this, too, will sound incredible to modern ears. They will deny that they feel any such discomfort, protesting that they can live quite happily without honouring and respecting anyone. If they honour or respect anyone at all, it will be the politicians or media celebrities of the day, but this will not be the kind of honour and respect of which the Buddha speaks, any more than the politicians and celebrities in question will be truly worthy of such honour and respect. The word *gārava* has a richer connotation than is suggested by the English words used to translate it. It includes such emotions as admiration, wonder, and delight in the fact that there exist, or existed, others superior to oneself in creative ability or spiritual attainment. It is akin to such terms as *vandanā* or salutation and *pūjā* or worship, all of these acts being expressive of positive emotion. To live without looking up to anyone represents an impoverishment of one's emotional life and, indeed, an impairment of one's very humanity.

I have never found it difficult to look up. As a boy I looked up to such heroes as Alfred the Great, Robin Hood, and Sir Walter Raleigh, as well as to the gods and heroes of Ancient Greece and Scandinavia. Later on, I was to enjoy Carlyle's *On Heroes, Hero-Worship and the Heroic in History*, though not all his heroes were mine.[583] In my teens I discovered the painters, sculptors, and architects of the Italian

Renaissance, some of whom seemed to tower above ordinary humanity. I also discovered the great poets and playwrights of my own country, as well as its great prose writers of both sexes. To all of these I looked up with admiration, wonder, and delight, rejoicing that such individuals had lived and worked among us and that the products of their genius were still available to us. It was in my teens, too, that I extended my horizon beyond Europe to take in the wise men of Asia, and especially the Buddha, whom I came to see not just as a historical figure but as the embodiment of ultimate reality. I came to look up not only to the Buddha and to his Dharma and his Enlightened disciples, but also to those religious geniuses who in India, China, and Tibet had helped to bring out the significance of certain aspects of his teaching. Nearer home, I looked up to and still look up to my personal teachers, honouring and respecting them as best I can in my own life and teaching. I look up to Jagdish Kashyap, who taught me Pāli and Abhidharma. I look up to Chattrul Sangye Dorje, who gave me the Green Tārā initiation. I look up to Kachu Rimpoche, who gave me the Padmasambhava *sādhana*. I look up to Jamyang Khyentse Rimpoche, who initiated me into the *sādhanas* of Mañjughoṣa, Avalokiteśvara, Vajrapāṇi, and Green Tārā. I look up to Dudjom Rimpoche, who initiated me into the Vajrasattva *sādhana*. I look up to Dhardo Rimpoche, who initiated me into the White Tārā *sādhana* and gave me the bodhisattva precepts. I look up to Dilgo Khyentse Rimpoche, who introduced me to Jambhala, to the Amitābha *phowa*, and to Kurukullā.[584] I look up to Yogi Chen, who shared with me the treasures of Vajrayāna and Chan. I look up to all these compassionate teachers, whose influence has entered into my life and has through me entered into the life of the Triratna Buddhist Order. To them do I look up with devotion and endless gratitude.

The fact that I find it easy to look up, especially to my spiritual teachers, does not mean that I am able to do this simply because I am of the devotional rather than of the intellectual type. One's personal type has little to do with it. The capacity to look up to something or someone higher than oneself is inherent in human nature and reaches across religions and cultures. In his or her spiritual life the Buddhist seeks to balance faith and wisdom, meditation and vigour, all with the help of the central faculty of mindfulness or awareness. On certain important occasions, whether in one's individual life or in the life of a whole community, there may be a special outpouring of devotion and gratitude towards a certain person or persons. In the Triratna Buddhist Order this may occur in connection with one's private and public preceptors at the time of ordination. I have witnessed it on a much larger scale in the case of the attitude of the new Buddhists of India, who feel an unbounded devotion to Dr Ambedkar, who led them from bondage to freedom, from darkness to light, and from despair to hope. Any attempt to minimize the importance of devotion in the spiritual life, or to limit it to a particular personality type, is a betrayal of the Buddha's teaching and does less than justice to human nature.

In the *Gārava Sutta* the Buddha declares that it is painful to live without honouring and respecting anyone. He also says that he cannot see, among the Brahmins and ascetics of his time, anyone who is superior to himself and whom, therefore, he can live honouring and respecting. This too will sound incredible to modern ears, though not necessarily for the same reasons. Some will maintain that the Buddha's statement displays arrogance, while according to others the Buddha could not be superior because it is their own teacher or prophet or saviour who is superior to all others, along with his gospel or revelation. Comparisons between the different religions of the world are inevitable. At the same time the fact that each religion claims not only that it is true but that it is in exclusive possession of the truth makes comparison difficult, even impossible, for there is no common standard of comparison on which all are agreed. Each religion lives in a self-contained world of its own. To describe one religion in the terms of another is to do it an injustice. Religions are mutually incommensurable. Any scholarly or objective comparison of one religion with another by someone standing as it were outside them all cannot but misrepresent them. The same is true of any attempt to describe individual religions in those terms.

Where does this leave the individual Buddhist? In the case of an Eastern Buddhist there is no problem. He or she lives within the self-contained world of their own form of Buddhism. For the Western Buddhist, however, there is a problem. A Western Buddhist can, of course, join a branch of an Eastern Buddhist Sangha, but this may involve an alienation from his or her own culture, with subsequent psychological problems. It may involve trying to be a Thai Buddhist or a Japanese Buddhist rather than a practitioner of the Dharma, especially if the religion adopted is tainted with what I have called religio-nationalism. What Western Buddhists need is a self-contained

Buddhist world of their own that is faithful to the Dharma and at the same time draws for inspiration on the best of Western culture, whether that of Ancient Greece, the Italian Renaissance, or the Romantic movement. I believe that the Triratna Buddhist Order can be the model for such a self-contained 'Western' Buddhist world, extending as it does from Europe to India, Australasia, and the Americas.

To believe that one is in exclusive possession of the truth can cause one to see others as heretics or unbelievers. It can lead one to persecute, torture, and even kill such people in the name of one's god or one's religion. Such an attitude is foreign to the spirit of Buddhism. A true Buddhist of whatever provenance, though firmly believing in the truth of the Dharma, will behave with courtesy and goodwill towards those of another faith. This will not always be easy, for one's natural assertiveness and competitiveness may well smuggle themselves into one's adherence to the Dharma. Thus one hears of Japanese warrior monks doing battle with one another or Sinhalese monks exhorting soldiers to kill Hindu Tamils. Many years ago during my early days in India I often told people in my lectures that Buddhism was a religion of peace and that no blood had ever been shed in its name. Now I would be ashamed to make such a claim, for my words would be belied by what is going on in many parts of the Buddhist world. One cannot but lament that in some quarters Buddhism should have degenerated to such an extent, though it is of course Buddhists who have degenerated, not their religion. *Corruptio optimi pessima* (The corruption of the best is the worst). Or, as the poet has it, 'Lilies that fester smell far worse than weeds'.[585]

The Buddha certainly believed that he was in possession of the truth, though in his case 'possession' would not have meant what it means to ordinary, unenlightened mortals. He spoke of having wondered whether he should dwell depending on that Dharma to which he had fully awoken, thus giving us an insight into what I have called the workings of the Buddha-mind. But what is that Dharma? If it is not the sum total of the Buddha's verbal teachings, then what is it? We should not assume that because the Buddha has spoken of it, and about his living in accordance with it, that we really do understand what he is talking about. To my mind, the Buddha is speaking about what it is that makes a Buddha a Buddha, whatever that may be. In other words, he is implying that we live in a universe of such a nature that, provided certain moral and spiritual conditions have been met, it is possible for a human being to attain

Buddhahood. It is probably no accident that although he speaks of that Dharma and that his attainment of his Buddhahood was dependent on the fact of its existence, he does not describe or define it. In the course of Buddhist history that Dharma has been spoken of in various ways, but to the unenlightened mind it remains a mystery. This is of more than theoretical interest; there are practical consequences. It is not that there is an *x* by virtue of which the Buddha becomes an awakened one and lives in dependence on that *x*, honouring and revering it. What the Buddha is doing is giving us an example at the very highest level of how one should live. Like other Buddhists, members of the Triratna Buddhist Order should look up. We should look up to the Buddha, to our spiritual teachers, and to all those who, in the words of one of the finest poems of the twentieth century, were truly great.

> Born of the sun, they travelled a short while toward the sun
> And left the vivid air signed with their honour.[586]

THE GOOD FRIEND, THE FALSE FRIEND, AND THE SPIRITUAL FRIEND

According to the *Upaḍḍha Sutta*, there was a time when the Buddha was staying in the territory of the Śākyans, the tribe to which he belonged by birth, and Ānanda was living in seclusion nearby. While in seclusion Ānanda reflected that the successful practice of asceticism depended on the cultivation of two factors: spiritual friendship (*kalyāṇa mitratā*) and manly vigour (*vīrya*). Having thus reflected, Ānanda went to see the Buddha, and after saluting him told the Buddha what he had thought, namely, that spiritual friendship was half of the holy life (*brahmacarya*). The Buddha flatly disagreed. Spiritual friendship, companionship, or comradeship was not half of the holy life, he told Ānanda. It was the whole of it! He then proceeded to explain that when a monk (*bhikkhu*) had a spiritual friend it was to be expected that he would develop and cultivate the Noble Eightfold Path. He further explained how the Eightfold Path was to be cultivated, the Eightfold Path of Perfect Vision, Perfect Emotion, Perfect Speech, Perfect Action, Perfect Means of Livelihood, Perfect Effort, Perfect Awareness, and Perfect *Samādhi*.[587]

In denying Ānanda's idea that there was a manly striving separate from spiritual friendship, the Buddha was in fact denying that there was any such thing as a purely individual spiritual life. Man was a social being, and this applied as much to his spiritual life as to his worldly life. In the oft quoted words of the poet-preacher John Donne, 'No man is an island entire of itself.'[588] From the moment of birth to the moment of death the individual human being, like other animals, is able to survive only because he or she belongs to a group and is dependent on it in all sorts of ways, from the most basic to the most refined. We depend upon other human beings for our education, for the food we eat, and for the amenities we enjoy. We depend upon them for our ideas and for the institutions and social structures that make the development of friendship possible. These structures exist on various levels and make possible friendships on various levels. In the Pāli scriptures there is the more worldly friendship of the *Sigālovāda Sutta* and the more spiritual friendship of the *Upaḍḍha Sutta* of which the Buddha speaks to Ānanda. These may be distinguished, in English, as good friendship and spiritual friendship, the Pāli word *mittatā* being used in both senses.

At another time the Buddha was staying at the Bamboo Grove in Rajagaha. Here he met Sigala, a young Brahmin, and explained to him how good friendship is one of the six basic relationships of human life, the others being the relations to parents, to teachers, to wife and child, to workers and servants, and to Brahmins and ascetics. There is an important difference between good friendship and the five other kinds of relationship. In the latter the relationship in each case is between those who are unequal, whereas the relationship between friends is one of equality. Friendship is thus an area of freedom. With a friend one does not have to act a part, or be guarded, or conceal what one really thinks. One can say to a friend what one cannot say to one's wife, or one's parents, or one's employers. There are five ways, the Buddha told Sigāla, in which a man should be of service to his friends: by giving gifts, by speaking kindly, by looking after their welfare, by treating them like himself, and by keeping his word to them. The friends, for their part, reciprocate by looking after him when he is inattentive, by looking after his property when he is inattentive, by being a refuge when he is afraid, by not deserting him when he is in trouble, and by showing concern for his children.

The false friend is described no less graphically. He is a great talker, a flatterer, a spendthrift, one who takes everything and wants a lot for very little, one who does his duty to you out of fear, who seeks his own ends, who talks of past and future favours, but in the present pleads his inability due to some misfortune. What is worse, he assents to bad actions and dissents from good ones, he praises you to your face and disparages you behind your back. He is your companion when you indulge in strong drink, when you haunt the streets at untimely hours, when you frequent places of entertainment, and when you indulge in gambling.

The good friend, the Buddha further told Sigāla, is loyal in various ways. Among other things, he is a helper, he is the same in happy and unhappy times, he points out what is good for you, he is sympathetic, in business he lets you have twice what you ask for, he tells you his secrets and keeps yours, he does not let you down in misfortune, he would even sacrifice his life for you, he keeps you from wrongdoing, and he points out the path to heaven.[589] Thus the good friend does a lot for you. He will even sacrifice his life for you, even show you the path to heaven; but that is all he can do. Only the spiritual friend can help you to go further, beyond the worlds of the *devas* and the *brahmās*, beyond all that is conditioned, to Nirvāṇa. For, as the Buddha told Ānanda, if a man had a spiritual friend it was to be expected that he would develop and cultivate the Perfect Eightfold Path. Thus it could be seen that spiritual friendship is the whole of the holy life. With him for spiritual friend, beings subject to birth are freed from birth; beings subject to ageing are freed from ageing; beings subject to death are freed from death; beings subject to sorrow, lamentation, pain, displeasure, and despair are freed from sorrow, lamentation, pain, displeasure, and despair. Thus the Buddha was the original spiritual friend. He was the spiritual friend of Ānanda and Mahākassapa, Sāriputta and Moggallāna, and they in their turn were the spiritual friends of their own disciples and so on down to the present day.

Not all Buddhists have as vivid a sense of the Buddha as spiritual friend as their predecessors had. Such a sense is an important element in the Buddhist spiritual life and one that can be cultivated. Before describing some of the ways in which this may be done I want to touch on the meaning of the term *brahmacariya*. It would seem that the 'holy life' has come to be accepted as the translation of *brahmacariya*, and so far I have followed this usage. The term 'holy' has, however, Judaeo-Christian connotations and little or nothing to do with Buddhism. I would therefore prefer to render *brahmacariya* as the 'divine life', which is theologically more neutral. In Buddhist and pre-Buddhist parlance, Brahmā is a divine being higher in rank than human beings and *brahmacariya* thus means following after Brahmā or in other words following a way of life that is conducive to spiritual liberation. In the Pāli scriptures we come across Brahmā, the ruler of ten thousand worlds, and the radiant *brahmās* who are occupants of the various levels beyond the levels of the *devas*. All are disciples of the Buddha, who is represented as visiting them on occasion and being visited by them. Thus following the Perfect/Noble Eightfold Path and being a *brahmacārin* are practically synonymous. *Brahmacariya* can also mean chastity or celibacy, so that a *brahmacārin* is one who is celibate, though this is a more limited usage of the term.

One way in which the modern Buddhist can develop a more vivid sense of Śākyamuni, the historical Buddha, as their spiritual friend, is by reading the Pāli scriptures, in which there are passages descriptive of many of the events of his long life. We learn how he left home, how he practised extreme asceticism to no avail, how he gained supreme Enlightenment while meditating under the *bodhi* tree, how he gained his first five disciples, and how he spent the rest of his life wandering from place to place teaching all kinds of people the way to liberation that he had discovered. One should read such passages slowly and mindfully, imagining oneself to be actually present at the event described and being affected by it. In this way, one can feel the future Buddha's exhilaration as he leaves home, his utter determination as he practises extreme asceticism, his sense of selfless triumph as he gains supreme Enlightenment, and his joy as he shares the fruits of his attainment with other beings, whether rich or poor, high or low, happy or unhappy, Brahmins or ascetics, doers of good or evildoers. There are also passages dealing with incidents of a less dramatic character, as when the Buddha and Ānanda nurse a sick monk who has been neglected by his companions[590] or when he advises Soṇa to practise in a balanced way, being neither too taut or too slack, as when one plays a stringed instrument.[591] Some of these events have been illustrated by artists both ancient and modern, the latter often being more representational than iconic. I particularly remember Nandalal Bose's *Buddha as Ascetic*.[592] This does not relate to the Buddha's period of extreme asceticism but to his old age. He wears a simple robe, carries a small bowl, and he is standing just outside the door of a hut. His scant hair is white and his expression is one of resignation. Whether or not it was because I myself was old when I first encountered this painting, it touched me deeply. I felt that the Buddha could have indeed looked like that during the last years of his life, and I could imagine myself walking with him just as Ānanda had done centuries ago.

We can also read biographies of the Buddha. One of the most popular of these is *The Light of Asia* by Sir Edwin Arnold. It was first published in 1879 and is still in print, having been translated into many languages and illustrated by many artists. Written in fluent blank verse, the story of Śākyamuni's life has been put into the mouth of an imaginary devotee. One of the reasons for the book's popularity is the fact that Arnold is able to draw on his own experience of the sights and sounds of India, in some respects not so very different from what they were in the Buddha's day.[593] This brings the biography to life in a very special way, so that one can read it and reflect on it in the same spirit that one reads and reflects on the biographical passages in the Pāli scriptures. Another popular biography is the *Lalitavistara*, a Mahāyāna work that tells the story of the Buddha's life from a docetic point of view in which he only appears to pass through the different stages of his earthly existence, being in a sense already Enlightened.[594] Some years ago a friend read the work to me and I could not but be caught up in the current of intense devotion that runs through the work. For the author, the Buddha is always 'that pure being', regardless of what he happens to be doing.

One can also develop a sense of the Buddha's presence and of his being our spiritual friend by reciting the traditional formula by which he is described in the Pāli scriptures and elsewhere. He is indeed the Richly Endowed One (*iti'piso bhagavā*), the Foe-Destroyer (*arahaṁ*), the Perfectly Enlightened One (*sammā-saṃbuddho*), Fully Endowed with Knowledge and Conduct (*vijjācaraṇasaṃpanno*), The Well-Gone One (*sugato*), Knower of the Worlds (*lokavidū*), Unsurpassed Charioteer of Men to be Tamed (*anuttaro purisadammasārathi*), Teacher of Gods and Men (*satthā devamanussānaṁ*). Thus he is the Richly Endowed Enlightened One (*buddho bhagavā ti*). This formula one repeats like a mantra, at the same time reflecting on the meaning of each of the Buddha's epithets.[595] Alternatively, one may recite the Śākyamuni mantra *oṃ muni muni mahāmuni śākyamuni svāhā*, which by referring to the Buddha as Śākyamuni connects him with the tribe into which he was born and thus with the fact of his historicity. Going a step further, one may visualize him as the central figure of a *sādhana*, but this will have to be the subject of another paper.

While working on the above, I was listening to Vera Brittain's *Testament of Friendship*,[596] in which she describes the friendship between herself and the writer Winifred Holtby, whose novels *Mandoa, Mandoa!* and *Poor Caroline* I had enjoyed some time previously. At the beginning of her work Vera raises the question of whether there can be friendship between women in the same way as there is friendship between men. This question she answers very much in the affirmative, and in her sprawling and very lengthy memoir she gives ample evidence of how Winifred was a good friend to her and she a good friend to Winifred. Both women exemplify the Buddha's idea of what a good friend should be. Winifred is in fact a good friend to quite a large number of people, from struggling writers to black South Africans stranded in London. Neither Winifred nor Vera seem to have had any false friends, with the possible exception of Winifred's unreliable lover, who pops in and out of the narrative from time to time, usually at long intervals. Winifred died in 1935, at the age of 37. At that time there was little or no Buddhism in England, but had she lived as long as her friend, who died in 1970, she might well have encountered it. Indeed, it is pleasant to think that she might have encountered the young FWBO and to come to see the Buddha as spiritual friend.

A COMPLEX PERSONALITY: A NOTE

In the personal statement that I issued on 30 December 2016 I said, among other things (1) that Triratna sometimes bore the marks not of the Dharma but of my own particular personality and (2) that that personality was a complex one. These words have been the subject of much discussion within the Order and in some quarters they have been seriously misunderstood. The fact that I spoke of Triratna sometimes bearing the marks not of the Dharma but of my own particular personality has been taken to mean that those marks were always negative. Far from this being the case, I believe that those marks were almost entirely positive, as will be seen if we take a look at some of the strands that go to make up the complexity to which I refer.

I do not know if phrenologists still exist, but I am confident that if one of them was to examine the bones of my skull he would say that I had an especially large bump of veneration. In other words, he would say that I had a natural tendency to look up to and to revere what was above me in any way, whether in human life or thought or culture. This bump of veneration developed at an early age, and may indeed be congenital. The fact that I had a natural tendency to look up to and to revere what was above me meant that I had an affinity with Buddhism inasmuch as the path taught by the Buddha led to higher and ever higher states of being and consciousness. In a sense, I was a born Buddhist.

This strand of my personality is closely connected with another strand, that of my being drawn much more to the arts than to science. It is not surprising that the majority of Order members should resemble me in this respect. In the Order we have writers of every kind, from poets to playwrights, besides painters, sculptors, and musicians. One of the six distinctive features of the Triratna is that it encourages the appreciation and practice of the arts as an aid to the spiritual life. This is not to say that an interest in science is discouraged. I have more than once expressed a wish that we had in the Order more people who were drawn to science, a knowledge or understanding of which can be for some people an aid to the spiritual life. In recent years I have been greatly struck by the vistas opened up by recent advances in the exploration of the universe in which we live, from the infinitely small to the infinitely great. These vistas cannot but induce a sense of wonder and awe in anyone with a little imagination.

Closely connected with my natural affinity with Buddhism is my preference to think in terms of what is to be cultivated, such as equanimity and compassion, rather than what is to be rooted out, such as greed and delusion. This is not to say that there is nothing in us that needs to be rooted out, but my natural tendency is to emphasize the positive aspects of spiritual life, an emphasis which most people find helpful. There is also a practical side to my nature. As friends both old and new have remarked, I am a good organizer, which is probably the reason why we have an order rather than an organization of a looser structure. I am also cosmopolitan, and have always delighted in meeting people of different nationalities, cultures, and religions. It is therefore hardly surprising that the Order should be an international one and bear this mark of my personality. Neither is it surprising that one of the distinctive features of Triratna is that it is open to all, irrespective of nationality, gender, race, social position, or sexual orientation.

Thus my nature is a complex one. I have a natural affinity with Buddhism, prefer the positive to the negative, am drawn to the arts rather than to science, am a good organizer, and am cosmopolitan. Moreover, friends have always been important to me, and recognizing the spiritual significance of friendship to the spiritual life is another of the distinctive features of Triratna. The nature of this friendship is still a matter of discussion in Triratna, and I suspect that it will be a long time before the last word on the subject will have been spoken. Meanwhile, personal experience has shown me that it is better to keep one's sexual relations and one's spiritual friendships separate.

One would have thought that this was quite enough complexity for one person, but there are still more strands to be teased out, some less obvious than others. The first of these is that I am by nature conservative. I have always loved what is old, whether old churches, old books, or old manners and customs. Being conservative, I do not welcome change, especially sudden change, which tends to make me socially and politically a gradualist. Nonetheless, this natural conservatism has not prevented me from being what has been called 'a new voice in the Buddhist tradition' or from founding a new Buddhist movement. As befits a conservative, I am a collector of what used to be called curios and are now called collectibles. As a boy I collected cigarette cards, postage stamps, and old coins, while later in life I have collected Buddhist artefacts and semi-precious stones, many of them being given to me by friends. 'Collecting', being akin to acquisitiveness, is hardly a Buddhist virtue, and I have sometimes had to curb this tendency of mine. I am also critical, especially of wrong views, which makes me a critic of 'scientific Buddhism', of mindfulness without the Dharma, of 'Buddhism without beliefs', and of so-called 'secular Buddhism'.

I need hardly say that I am also a writer. Indeed, I have sometimes found it difficult to say whether I was a Buddhist who writes or a writer who was a Buddhist. Be that as it may, I have always enjoyed the process of writing, down to the feel of the pen in my hand and the pressure of the nib on the paper. As such, the act of writing was almost a sensuous experience. Whether writing about the Dharma or the arts, I have always sought to give expression to what I genuinely thought and felt. This has often meant asking myself what I really thought and what I really felt and then finding the exactly appropriate word or phrase. It has also meant going carefully through what I have written and doing my best to eliminate hackneyed similes and clumsily constructed sentences. This has always been the case, even though my literary style has changed considerably over the years, from the youthful eloquence of the *Survey* and other early writings to the more succinct style of *The Three Jewels*. There is also the straightforward narrative style of the many volumes of memoirs, as well as the rather magisterial style of some of the book reviews.

The American poet and activist Allen Ginsberg once told me that he was surprised that someone so radical in his Buddhism as I was should write such traditional poetry.[597] He was only partly right. Much of my poetry, especially my early poetry, is indeed traditional, but more than a handful of later poems are experimental. By this I do not mean that I experimented deliberately, but that what might appear to be experimental was the natural expression of what I was trying to say. Probably the most notable example of this more 'experimental' style is the long poem 'On Glastonbury Tor', written shortly after my first visit to that ancient site of pagan and Christian pilgrimage. In it I run words together, for example, as though I was writing in Anglo-Saxon or German rather than in modern English. Whether traditional or not, my poetry could be described as 'occasional' in the sense that each poem expresses what I was thinking or feeling at the time. Some of the poems are about the Buddha, some about the natural world, and some about places and people. Written as they were over seven decades, the poems between them add up to a sort of autobiography, in some cases including insights that are not to be found in my prose memoirs.

On the whole, I have written for a comparatively small audience consisting mainly of Western and Western-educated Buddhists and lovers of poetry and the fine arts. Only rarely have I ventured into the arena of public debate. One such occasion was when I gave a public lecture on 'Buddhism, World Peace, and Nuclear War'.[598] Another was when I spoke on 'Buddhism and Blasphemy', in which I put forward the idea of what I called 'therapeutic blasphemy'.[599] Both lectures were published as booklets and a passage from the latter was quoted in Parliament in the course of a debate.[600] Though I have rarely intervened in a public debate I am not in principle opposed to doing so, either as a Buddhist or as a writer. It has been a question of what, in the circumstances, was the best use of my time and energy. It could be argued that a Buddhist teacher, especially a monk, should not become involved in worldly affairs in this way (perhaps I thought so myself at one time), but there is no doubt that a writer, both as a writer and a citizen, should be so involved. In modern times there have been a number of writers who, in the interest of truth and justice, have dared to criticize an oppressive or tyrannous regime, sometimes paying for their temerity with their lives. Now that I have retired from active participation in the work of Triratna, I may feel like involving myself in matters of public debate. Some of my friends may consider this a better way of using my time and energy than writing about my complex personality, which may seem rather self-indulgent.

EVIL IN MYTH AND IN HUMAN EXPERIENCE

In the Tibetan wheel of life, between the human realm and the realm of the *pretas* or hungry ghosts, there lies the world of the gods and the *asuras*. They are fighting for possession of the Wish-fulfilling Tree, which grants all desires. In some modern versions of the wheel the *asuras* are depicted as being equipped with rifles. Yet the gods and *asuras* were not always at war. According to an ancient Indian myth, they once cooperated on an enterprise of cosmic significance – nothing less than the churning of the Great Ocean of Milk. Taking Mount Sumeru for their churning stick and the cosmic serpent for their churning rope, they pulled and pulled, the *asuras* holding the cosmic serpent's head and pulling one way, the gods holding its tail and pulling the other way. Thus did they churn the Ocean of Milk. After a while, there rose like butter to the surface a series of treasures of various kinds, including the goddess of wealth, a pot of nectar, the cow of plenty, and various gems. Both the gods and the *asuras* were delighted with these and other treasures they had churned up. But their delight was short-lived. Suddenly there rose to the surface the pot of poison, a poison so powerful that it was capable of destroying everything, and at the sight of it the gods and the *asuras* alike recoiled in fear and horror.

Avalokiteśvara, the Bodhisattva of Compassion, was then in attendance on the Buddha Amitābha in the latter's Pure Land, Sukhāvatī. On happening to look down to the lower realm of the gods and *asuras*, he saw the pot of poison that had been churned up and the fear and horror that this had aroused. Instantly he descended, caught up the pot, and drank the poison it contained to the last drop. Such was the virulence of the poison that his throat turned blue, on which account he came to be known as Nīlakaṇṭha or Bluethroat. (In the Hindu version of the myth it is the great god Shiva who drinks the poison and whose throat turns blue.)

Exchanging the language of myth for the language of human experience, we may say that the poison drunk by Avalokiteśvara stands for the suffering that results from evil, whether natural or moral. Natural evil is what we experience from the fact of our having a human body with a nervous system, a body that is subject to old age, disease, and death, as well as to such collective ills as earthquakes, volcanic eruptions, hurricanes, floods, epidemics, forest fires, and tsunamis. Some of these calamities used to be called acts of God in that no human agency was responsible for them. Moral evil consists of those actions of body, speech, and mind committed by the individual under the influence of the three poisons of greed, hatred, and delusion. Sooner or later the fruits of those actions will be experienced in the form of suffering, whether in the present lifetime or in a future one. In terms of the Four Noble Truths, there will be freedom from suffering only when there is freedom from craving as a result of following the Noble Eightfold Path (in both its mundane and transcendental stages). The Buddha once compared moral evil, or the defilements, to a stain on a pure white cloth.[601] The stain is indeed a stain, but it need not be permanent. It can be removed by washing the cloth in water. Washing the cloth represents our efforts to purify the mind by means of ethics, meditation, and wisdom. It is no accident that in a famous verse of the *Dhammapada*, abstention from all evil (*pāpa*) is followed by undertaking what is skilful (*kusala*), and by the complete purification (*sacittapariyodapanaṃ*) of one's mind.

Before the process of purification can begin, however, one has to recognize the fact that the mind is 'stained' and that one has acted in an unskilful (*akuśala*) way. In a word, we have to confess the evil that we have done (*pāpa deśanā*). Confession of the unskilful actions that one has committed has been an important part of the Buddhist spiritual life from the beginning. Monks or nuns who had acted unskilfully confessed to their spiritual superiors or to one another. The practice gradually fell into desuetude, and by the time I was ordained as a *bhikkhu* it had degenerated into a purely formal ritual that was to be got over as quickly as possible. Readers of my memoirs will remember how disappointed I was the first time I took part in a 'confession' of this kind.[602] When I founded the FWBO/Triratna, I was therefore determined that members of the Order should take the practice of confession seriously. Thus, confession has become an integral part of every chapter of the Order. Meetings of the chapter are held, ideally once a week, and the warmth and intimacy of the meeting makes it easier for the individual member to confess any unskilful behaviour and to receive help from their fellow members. Moreover, Order members, Mitras, and friends regularly take part in the collective recitation of what has become known as the 'Sevenfold Puja', the fourth part of which is devoted to the confession of evil. In the Bennett translation of verses from the *Bodhicaryāvatāra*, as arranged by me for liturgical purposes, we say:

> The evil that I have heaped up
> Through my ignorance and foolishness –
> Evil in the world of everyday experience,
> As well as evil in understanding and intelligence –
> All that I acknowledge to the Protectors.[603]

Here we confess not to our fellow Buddhists but to the Buddha, having conjured up an image of him in our minds. It is as though we owe the Buddha an apology, so to speak, for having failed to live up to the teaching he has so generously given. Continuing, we say:

> Standing before them
> With hands raised in reverence,
> And terrified of suffering,
> I pay salutations again and again.

In other words, the confession takes place within an overall context of devotion in which we not only stand face to face with the Buddha but also recognize the immense gulf that exists between the Buddha and ourselves. We are also keenly aware of the fact that our unskilful actions will lead to suffering. But though we stand before the Buddha, he is not a judge (that is the work of karma, or rather *karma-vipāka*), and we therefore conclude with the words:

> May the Leaders receive this kindly,
> Just as it is, with its many faults!
> What is not good, O Protectors,
> I shall not do again.

We are thereby assured that the Buddha will accept our confession and we promise him not to do evil again.

Important, even essential, though confession is, it is not the whole of the spiritual life. In the Sevenfold Puja, therefore, just as confession is preceded by Going for Refuge, so it is followed by rejoicing in merit. There is a change of mood, as it were, from remorse to jubilation, and we say:

> I rejoice with delight
> In the good done by all beings,
> Through which they obtain rest
> With the end of suffering.
> May those who have suffered be happy!

Before rejoicing in the good done by others, we have to recognize that what they have done is good. We have to be free from carping criticism, competitiveness, and jealousy. Moreover, we have positively to delight in the good that they have done. In particular, we rejoice in all manner of spiritual attainments, up to and including that of Buddhahood itself. We should also rejoice, in my view, in humanity's achievements in the fields of literature, the arts, and music, the enjoyment of which can raise us to spiritual heights, as can the contemplation of the beauty of the natural world, which human beings have done so much to destroy.

The good in which we take delight here in the fifth section of the Sevenfold Puja is moral good, and moral good is productive of merit (Pāli *puñña*, Sanskrit *puṇya*). In the popular Buddhism of the East, the accumulation of merit is a major preoccupation of the serious-minded Buddhist, for it is the merit that has been accumulated by one's skilful actions of body, speech, and mind that will ensure a good rebirth in this world or in a higher heavenly world. Certain good actions are regarded as particularly meritorious. These include releasing birds and fish from captivity, offering food to monks, and building temples and stupas. Such actions can indeed be performed with a pure intention, but only too often they are a simple 'going through the motions' for the sake of social prestige. This is not to underestimate the importance of accumulating merit for all Buddhists, Eastern or Western. The merit generated by the regular performance of acts of generosity, by the observance of the precepts of morality, and by the practice of concentration-meditation, is the indispensable foundation for the development of the wisdom or insight that leads to liberation.

The traditional teaching of the four Māras is one that does justice to both the mythic and the human aspects of evil. The four Māras are Māra the son of a god (*devaputta-māra*), the Māra of death (*maccu-māra*), the Māra of the defilements (*kilesa-māra*), and the Māra of conditioned existence (*khandha-māra*).[604] The first of these is also known as Māra the Evil One (Māra Pāpiyān). He is the Māra who, according to the Pāli scriptures, constantly dogs the Buddha, seeking to find entrance into him and miserably failing. He also troubles the Buddha's disciples in various ways, and has even been known to appear to Buddhist practitioners in modern times.

The Māra of death is part of natural evil because unless we are in extreme pain or are utterly disillusioned with life, we do not want to die. I have been close to death more than once in my life, the last time being nearly a year ago when I was in hospital with pneumonia, the old man's friend. One night, when it was completely dark, I felt that I was very close to death. Strange to say, it was a comfortable feeling, as though death was lying down beside me in a companionable sort of way. At the same time, I knew that I was not going to die just then. Whether I shall have that comfortable feeling when I actually die, I do not know.

The Māra of the defilements is the equivalent to moral evil. Traditionally these defilements are greed, hatred, and delusion, which at the hub of the wheel of life are depicted by a rooster, a snake, and a pig, each of them holding in its mouth or beak the tail of the one in front. Alternatively, moral evil is represented by the formula of the five poisons of craving (Pāli *taṇhā*, Sanskrit *tṛṣṇā*), hatred (Pāli *dosa*, Sanskrit *dveṣa*), delusion (*moha*), conceit (*māna*), and envy (Sanskrit *īrṣyā*). They are rightly termed poisons, for whether in their gross or their subtle form, they affect our mental and spiritual health. For these poisons, whether three or five in number, the Buddha's teaching is the medicine, for which reason he is often described as the Great Physician.

In Buddhist thought a distinction is made between that which is conditioned (*saṅkhata*) and that which is unconditioned (*asaṅkhata*), and the Buddhist life consists, in the simplest terms, in making the transition from the one to the other. This does not mean that Buddhism is a metaphysical dualism any more than that it is a metaphysical monism. The Māra of conditioned existence is all that which is marked by suffering (*dukkha*), impermanence (*anicca*), and insubstantiality (*anattā*). He is the grim figure that holds the wheel of life in his grasp. Beyond the wheel of life, standing on a little cloud, a saffron-robed Buddha points out the Way.

BLAKE AND THE GATES OF PARADISE

For the last few days the word forgiveness has been hovering about in my mind. As it hovers it is joined by such sentences as 'The cut worm forgives the plow' and 'Drive your cart and your plow over the bones of the dead', both of which are from 'The Proverbs of Hell' in William Blake's *The Marriage of Heaven and Hell*.[605] In my mind's eye, the word forgiveness is written in a cursive, flowing hand against a background of white clouds and rainbows.

For Blake the plough has a very positive significance. It stands not just for the cultivation of the earth, important as that is, but for the cultivation of the soul. The ploughshare digs deep, reaching down into the rich, accumulated humus. There the worm lives, and the plough cannot help cutting it in two. But the worm forgives the plough, for it knows that the work of the plough is necessary to human wellbeing, even to human existence. The worm does not think of itself or its own life. It is content to be part of a wider productive and creative endeavour. If you cannot paint, you can at least grind the artist's colours for him. If you cannot write, you can at least type the author's manuscript for him. For Blake the humble worm has a positive significance, and he surely loved the worm no less than he loved the plough.

The worm is a living being and it feels pain when cut by the plough. The bones of the dead feel no such pain, however rudely you drive your cart and your plough over them. Eventually they will crumble and become part of the soil, and we should have no compunction about driving over them. The bones are the remains of animals and human beings that were once alive. They are the remains of dead cultures, dead civilizations, and dead religions and Blake exhorts us to drive our cart and plough over them for they are dead and we are alive, and the living should not be sacrificed to the dead. This makes Blake a revolutionary. He was a revolutionary in politics, in religion, and in morals. He was a revolutionary because he was an idealist, and wanted to build Jerusalem in England's green and pleasant land.

When I was a child, one of the first things I learnt by heart was the Lord's Prayer. At that time I did not think about its meaning, but in later years I reflected on it, especially on the fact that in the prayer we asked for forgiveness on the grounds that we had already forgiven those who had trespassed against us. I find it interesting that we have, it seems, to forgive others their trespasses against us before we can ask for forgiveness for our trespasses against them. Only too often nowadays people want to be forgiven before they forgive. Blake goes much further than this. In a famous verse he speaks of a 'Mutual Forgiveness of each vice', and declares that 'such are the Gates of Paradise'.[606] We have all been guilty of indulging in this or that vice, great or small, and we all have to forgive those who have trespassed against us before asking for forgiveness for ourselves.

Alexander Pope (1688–1744) was a very different kind of poet from Blake (1757–1827), but he too had something to say on the subject of forgiveness. In an oft quoted line, he says, 'To err is human, to forgive divine.' Here he lifts the whole subject of forgiveness onto a higher level, from the ethical to the spiritual. When we forgive another who has trespassed against us we become ourselves divine, at least for the time being. Pope speaks of human error rather than of vice, but the meaning is much the same. We all commit errors, and those errors only too often bring us into conflict with other human beings. But if we suffer as a result of someone else's error, instead of reacting with anger, we should do our best to forgive.

What Blake, the Lord's Prayer, and Pope are all, in essence, saying is that true forgiveness is unconditional. There should be no question of our laying down terms and conditions, such as that we will forgive the person their trespasses against us only if he or she repent and apologize for what they have done. Otherwise our so-called forgiveness is no more than a sort of bargaining. The granting of forgiveness is a free act of the true individual, and it has nothing to do with the reactive mind.

When I was in hospital last year, and close to death, I not only confessed my unskilful actions but asked for the forgiveness of those I had harmed. Reflecting on this recently, I realized that I had been wrong to ask for forgiveness. It was enough that I had confessed and that I had also forgiven all those who had offended me. My confession covered a wide field, as my unskilfulness had done, from being disrespectful to my father as a teenager to some of my sexual activity with Order members and Mitras.

There is a *sutta* in the Pāli scriptures in which the Buddha describes himself as ploughing. It is sowing time and he has come to the place where the wealthy brahmin Kasībhāradvāja is ploughing with a team of oxen, and he stands to one side with his begging-bowl for alms. On seeing this, the brahmin tells the Buddha that he, Kasībhāradvāja, ploughs and sows, and then eats, adding that the Buddha should do likewise, for brahmins do not love homeless, wandering ascetics who live on others. To this the Buddha replies that he too ploughs and sows and having ploughed and sown, he eats. Kasībhāradvāja is taken aback and tells the Buddha, perhaps sarcastically, that he does not see the Buddha ploughing and would like to know what sort of ploughing he does. The Buddha thereupon explains:

> Faith is the seed, practice the rain,
> And wisdom is my yoke and plow.
> Modesty's the pole, mind the strap,
> Mindfulness my plowshare and goad.
>
> Body and speech are guarded well,
> And food and drink have been restrained.
> Truthfulness I use for weeding,
> And gentleness urges me on.
>
> Effort is my beast of burden,
> Pulling me onward to safety.
> On it goes without returning,
> Where, having gone, one does not grieve.
>
> This is how I plow my plowing —
> The crop it yields is deathlessness!
> And when one has plowed this plowing,
> One is released from all suffering.[607]

Deeply moved by these words, Kasībhāradvāja throws himself at the Buddha's feet and goes for Refuge to him, as well as to his teaching and his community. Afterwards he becomes a monk and eventually attains liberation. Faith (*saddhā*) is one of the five spiritual faculties (*indriyas*) and the first of the positive 'links' (*nidānas*), and it is therefore not surprising that in his response to Kasībhāradvāja, the Buddha should speak of it first. Without seed there is no crop, and without faith there is no true spiritual life. From the golden germ of faith there spring all spiritual flowers and fruits, including the sweetly scented flowers of confession and forgiveness. Like each of the other *indriyas*, faith has the support of the other four. Having the support of wisdom (*paññā*), it is clear-sighted, not blind. Having the support of energy (*viriya*), it is active, not passive. Having the support of mindfulness (*sati*) it does not get distracted. Having the support of concentration (*samādhi*) it has both depth and focus.

Over the years I have often turned to Blake for inspiration, and have found some of his utterances as very much in accordance with the Dharma. In particular, I have found what he says on the subject of forgiveness helpful both to the individual and to the spiritual community. What he says about mutual forgiveness could hardly be more suitable as a motto for a spiritual community like Triratna. If we could all forgive one another our trespasses, it would bring us nearer to the realization of Blake's Jerusalem or, in Buddhist terms, to the creation of a Pure Land on earth.

NEWS FROM NOWHERE – AND FROM INDIA

William Morris was one of the great Victorians. Born in 1834 and dying in 1896, the greater part of his life was passed during the reign of Queen Victoria. At the same time, he was not in the least Victorian in his attitudes. By his own admission, he hated the world in which he lived, and Victorian England, industrialized and philistine, was in the forefront of that world. In *News from Nowhere*, his utopian novel, he compares the England of his day with the socialist England of the future, when privilege and inequality would be swept away in the fires of revolution.

Morris was a socialist but it is difficult to say what kind of socialist he was. He was equally critical of state socialism on the one hand and anarchism on the other. Nor was he a Fabian. He was also critical of the intentional community which, like the monasteries of the Middle Ages, separated itself from the wider society and had as little to do with it as possible. The FWBO/Triratna has been described as an intentional community but it is certainly not one in Morris's pejorative use of the term. Whether or not the monasteries of the Middle Ages separated themselves from the wider society, Triratna certainly does not. Through its urban centres, its country retreat centres, and its team-based right livelihood businesses, it seeks to make the Buddha's teaching available to as many people as possible. As I went through *News from Nowhere* recently, I was not only struck by what Morris says about work but also reminded of what I had said about livelihood in *Vision and Transformation* and elsewhere.[608] It should do no harm to other living beings, nor should it be boring or repetitive or injure one physically or mentally. Morris goes much further than this. In his ideal society everybody works, both men and women, and they enjoy their work and it does not take up the whole of their time. Unpleasant or dirty work that cannot be done by machines is shared among them.

For Morris, work is a human need, and if the inhabitants of his ideal society are afraid of anything, they are afraid of there being a shortage of work – not because they are afraid of starving, as they would have been in the England of Morris's day, but because they would not be realizing their full potential. In Morris's ideal society, some men and women work with their hands, producing beautiful objects for everyday use, and we are reminded not only of Morris's critique of the economy of 'planned obsolescence' but also that he was associated with the Arts and Crafts movement of the late nineteenth century.[609]

In *News from Nowhere* Morris paints an attractive picture of the England of the future. People are healthy and happy. They wear simple, colourful clothes, and live in attractive houses surrounded by gardens. Children are free to move from one social group to another, for Morris does not believe in the nuclear family, and everybody is friends with everybody else, addressing one another as either 'neighbour' or 'friend'. There is no army and no police force, and any differences are settled by friendly discussion. Yet Morris is no facile optimist regarding human nature, admitting that even in an ideal society sexual jealousy may lead to homicide.

The picture that Morris paints is indeed an attractive one. But how does the transition from the old unequal and unjust society of Morris's day to his happy, socialist England take place? It takes place neither gradually nor peacefully. It takes place as the result of a revolution, and that revolution involves violence and bloodshed, for Morris believed that, human nature being what it is, a non-violent revolution is not possible. He puts his account of that revolution into the mouth of Hammond, an old man who lives in what remains of the British Museum and is interested in history. Hammond, who is imagined to be living two centuries after Morris's own time, describes the revolution which he says took place in 1952 in response to a question from Guest, a man from Morris's day, who has somehow found his way into the England of the future. Guest has already questioned others about this strange new society, so different from that from which he has come, and this is the most important of his questions. Hammond's lengthy account of the revolution is the most powerfully written part of *News from Nowhere*, and one feels that Morris's heart is very much in what he writes. He believes in revolution and he believes that revolution must be violent.

But must it? The answer comes not from Morris in England but from Dr Ambedkar in India. On 14 October 1956 (four years after Morris's imaginary revolution) Ambedkar took the Three Refuges and Five Precepts from a Buddhist monk, thereby fulfilling his vow that though he had been born a Hindu he would not die one. Having become a Buddhist, he at once administered the Refuges and Precepts to some half a million of his followers, who had flocked to Nagpur, central India, at his call. In this way were they too converted from Hinduism to Buddhism. Thus began what was to become known as the Dhamma Revolution. It was an entirely non-violent revolution, and one that by the end of the decade had touched, and transformed, the lives of millions all over India.

Bhimrao Ramji Ambedkar (1891–1956) grew up in a society dominated by the system of hereditary caste, and he and his community were at the very bottom of the heap. Untouchables, as the Dalits were then called, lived in separate quarters outside the village, often in unhygienic conditions, and were subject to a wide variety of restrictions and prohibitions. Despised and exploited by members of the higher castes, they did the dirtiest and most demeaning work: typical occupations being the removal of dead cows and the disposal of human excrement. There was no question, of course, of marriage between a Dalit and a caste Hindu, and social contact was minimal. The young Ambedkar was a brilliant student and with the help of a liberal minded maharaja he became a highly educated man, devoting himself not to his personal advancement but to the uplift of his people. Realizing that there was no hope for them as long as they remained within the Hindu fold, he decided that they would have to change their religion – a radical and revolutionary step. For years he studied and compared the different religions, rejecting the Communist option, for he believed that religion was the basis of society. Though he admired the Jesuits for their educational work, Christianity was after all a foreign religion with no roots in Indian culture. The same was true of Islam, with the additional consideration that if his people converted to Islam it would seriously upset the demographic basis of India and could well lead to conflict and violence. He therefore opted for Buddhism, which was of Indian origin and not in conflict with modern knowledge. Though Liberty, Equality, and Fraternity were Ambedkar's ideals, and though he often spoke of them, he always insisted that he had taken them not from the French Revolution but from the teachings of his master the Buddha.

After Ambedkar's untimely death, I spent much of my time travelling from one group of converts to another, teaching them the Dhamma and encouraging them in its practice. The biggest of such groups were in Nagpur, Bombay, and Poona, each of which I visited a number of times and where I made a number of friends, with some of whom I remained in contact even after I returned to England in 1964. I had not forgotten them and they had certainly not forgotten me. Years later, Order members visiting India made contact with some of these friends, and this eventually led to the formation of a wing of the Order in India.

News from Nowhere is still read, and there is much that we can learn from it. Morris has an honoured place in the history of English socialism. But those who would bring about radical social change without violence will turn for a model not to Morris but to Ambedkar and his Dhamma Revolution.[610]

EVIL REVISITED – AND GOOD

'The roaring of lions, the howling of wolves, the raging of the stormy sea, and the destructive sword, are portions of eternity too great for the eye of man.' Thus William Blake in *The Marriage of Heaven and Hell*.[611] To Blake's examples one might add the crash of the tsunami as it hits land, the crack of thunder, and the havoc wrought by volcanoes and earthquakes. All these are manifestations of non-human energy, of the tremendous power of nature. All are forms of natural evil, in that they may be causes of pain and suffering to human beings. What of Blake's destructive sword? In one sense it belongs to nature, for the materials of which it is made are of natural origin. It is destructive only in the hands of man, who has made the sword.

Man, the individual man, is himself an embodiment of energy. He embodies it in more highly developed forms than the lion or the wolf, and like them enjoys using his energy and expressing it. He too roars and howls. We may call this expression 'human culture'. Not only does man enjoy expressing his energy, he can enjoy seeing the expression of energy by the natural world. He can delight in the storm, for he can feel in it an energy akin to the energy of which he is an embodiment. Similarly, he can enjoy the sight of a forest fire, when the golden flames shoot up hundreds of feet into the air, even though he can, at the same time, feel sorry for those who lose their homes or even their lives in the conflagration.

He can even delight in killing other human beings and in seeing them killed. Worse still, he can enjoy inflicting pain and suffering. He can enjoy torturing them, using his more developed intelligence to devise more sophisticated forms of torture, from the rack and the iron maiden to waterboarding and prolonged solitary confinement. In all this he is guilty of committing moral evil. The mind and emotions can also be made to suffer unbearably, as when a child is tortured in front of his parents, or a friend in front of a friend. This is perhaps the worst form of human suffering, from which it follows that delight in inflicting such suffering is the worst form of moral evil.

But moral evil does not exist in a vacuum. It is something done by human beings to other human beings, as well as to animals. It is an individual human being like ourselves who is cruel, malicious, and sadistic, whether in act or in speech. He or she can actually enjoy inflicting pain and suffering. But why is this? Why does one human being delight in inflicting pain on another human being? To some it has seemed that the answer to this question lies at the bottom of a very black hole. In the case of a small boy who torments small creatures, it is due to a lack of empathy which normally he develops as he grows up and is socialized. Adult human beings may give reasons for their behaviour, which they do not necessarily see as being evil. Some may believe that they are acting in the interest of their religion, as when heretics are burned at the stake or tortured to death. Others see it as necessary for the maintenance of the existing social and political order.

According to Nietzsche's Zarathustra, 'Man is the cruellest animal.'[612] This does not mean that every human being commits actions of conscious, deliberate cruelty, but the potential for doing so, and even for delighting in so doing, is in us all. Usually we do not like to think of ourselves in this way. We like to think that we are basically good and kind, and incapable of doing anything really evil. At the same time we do not find it difficult to see the evil in others, or even to project onto others the evil that is in ourselves. Thus it is possible for us to demonize the enemy or the opponent, whether in war or any other situation of conflict or disagreement. To 'demonize' means to see the other person as a demon, that is, to see them not as another human being but as a devil. This can be done not only by the individual but by whole societies, especially those of a religious or quasi-religious nature. Thus the terms heresy, sorcery, witchcraft, and sexual perversion come to be conflated.

A boy is able to torture small creatures because he is bigger and stronger than them. He, in his turn, may be made to suffer by a bigger and stronger boy, and the latter may suffer painful chastisement at the hands of an adult who has authority over him. In all these cases there is a disparity of power, whether real or perceived, and it is this disparity that makes it possible for one person to torture another, as well as to delight in so doing. There is a similar disparity of power between employer and employee, which is why in a democracy employees band together in trade unions in order to reduce the disparity, even though it cannot be abolished completely. Beyond both employer and employee is the government, whether democratic or totalitarian in structure. In the latter case, the imbalance of power is extreme, or even absolute, with the government possessing virtually all the power and individual citizens hardly any or none at all. In these circumstances the government, through its various agencies, can do whatever it likes with the individual. It can imprison him or her, it can determine what kind of work they do, how and where they live, and it can physically and mentally torture them without any possibility of appeal. Such a government can persecute, even massacre, whole communities of its own subjects, as did Stalin in Russia, Mao Zedong in China, Pol Pot in Cambodia, and Robert Mugabe in Zimbabwe. Hitler's systematic extermination of six million or more European Jews had a complex background, involving as it did religious, ethnic, and pseudo-scientific factors.

Disparity of power makes it possible for the stronger to oppress and abuse the weaker and even to torture them and to delight in torturing them. Thus there is an immense amount of suffering in the world, suffering that is due not to natural power but to human agency. So much suffering is there, indeed, that some have thought that moral evil was not just a part of human nature but that there existed a principle of evil outside humanity. Beside this principle, however, there was a principle of good, and human beings were urged to fight on its side. Be that as it may, the disparity in power does also make it possible for the stronger to help the weaker, and to delight in helping them, whether materially or in other ways. For many Buddhists this spirit of unbounded altruism is embodied in the figure of Avalokiteśvara, the Bodhisattva of Compassion. Avalokiteśvara has many forms, in one of which he appears with eleven heads and a thousand arms and hands. Some serious-minded Buddhists, whether within Triratna or outside it, aspire to be a hand of Avalokiteśvara, or even a finger.

In the course of the transmission of the Dharma from India to China, Avalokiteśvara underwent a change of sex, becoming Guanyin, known in the West as the goddess of mercy. She is clad in a milk-white robe, one corner of which is modestly draped over her chignon, and her face wears an expression of maternal concern. Sometimes she is depicted sitting on a rock, for compassion is based upon wisdom and is not separate from it.

Here we are not so far from Blake as one might have thought. 'The most sublime act is to set another before you', he says in *The Marriage of Heaven and Hell*. It is of this 'sublime act', performed constantly and in an infinite variety of circumstances, of which Avalokiteśvara/ Guanyin is the radiant embodiment.

The figure of the sex-changing Avalokiteśvara may be of particular interest to those people who are making or who have made the difficult journey from one gender to the other.

DISPARITIES

'You cruel little devil!' shouted our neighbour over the wire netting that separated her back garden from ours. The reason for her wrath was that I had just 'shot' a cat with my water pistol. It was not that I wanted to hurt the cat, but only to stop it scratching up my father's bulbs, and in any case, a few drops of water would do it no harm. Recollecting this incident years later, it occurred to me that the good woman was right in assuming that only a devil would wish to inflict suffering. I had certainly no wish to hurt the cat, whether because of instinct or education, but I did have the ability to hurt it. I could have thrown a stone at it or, if I had met it in the street, I could have given it a kick or pulled its tail. I could have done any of these things because I was stronger than the cat, just as the cat was stronger than the mouse. In other words, there was between me and the cat an imbalance of power. Such an imbalance is found both within the natural world and throughout human society. The state has more power than the individual citizen, the millionaire more than the pauper, the employer more than the employee, the teacher more than the student, the master (or mistress) more than the slave, and the parent more than the child. The last is especially the case when the child is a baby. The balance of power between them is then virtually absolute. The parent can beat the child, starve it, confine it, abuse it sexually or emotionally. All this the parents can do, unless they live in a country in which there is a law against such behaviour, and even where there is such a law it may well be broken. During the last few decades there have come to light horrifying stories of parental cruelty, as well as of abuse of children by other adults, including in institutions meant for their protection. Some years ago there was even a case in which two small boys tortured and killed an even smaller boy.

Whatever the form parental abuse may take, it will almost certainly have a traumatic effect on the development of the child, so that as adults they may be still struggling to deal with the psychological problems to which the abuse has given rise. In some cases the damage may be irreparable, even with the help of a whole army of therapists and psychoanalysts, and in the end the unfortunate sufferer may feel that the only solution is suicide.

But why should any parent torture their own child? Why should one human being, indeed, want to inflict pain on another? In some cases, it may be that they themselves have suffered at the hands of their parents or other adults. They may also be unduly influenced by one false ideology or another, perhaps even against their own better instincts. Be that as it may, there is only one other imbalance of power that parallels the imbalance between the parent and the child, especially when the child is an infant. This is the imbalance that exists between master and slave, whether sanctioned by law, as in Ancient Rome or pre-Abolition America, or with the sanction of society. The slave, no more than the infant, has no will of his own, and his owner may do with him as he will.

To the extent that one human being deliberately inflicts pain on another, or on an animal, he or she is evil. They are under the influence, so to speak, of the Māra of Defilement (*kleśa māra*), as they are when they are acting under the influence of intense craving, hatred, or delusion. They have become, at least for the time being, a devil. If they are often possessed in this way, or if such possession becomes habitual, they will become a devil in human form, and on death they may be reborn in one of the lower heavens as a Māra Son of a God (*devaputra māra*). So far as I know, only once in my life have I encountered a devil in human form, as I have related elsewhere.[613] Fortunately such devils are extremely rare, though occasionally we may see a person working himself or herself up into a state of such intense craving, hatred, or delusion that they are in danger of allowing themselves to be possessed by *kleśa māra*.

Most people are subject to one or other of the *kleśas* from time to time, and an angry mood or a feeling of frustrated craving may last for quite a while, sometimes for days or weeks together. At the same time, the intervals between these states may be filled with experiences of love, joy, and peace. This will be especially the case when one deliberately cultivates such emotions through the regular practice of meditations like the *mettā bhāvanā* or respiration-mindfulness (*ānāpānasati*). It is amazing, however, how quickly a positive mental state may be followed by a negative one, and vice versa. It is a practice in itself to observe how fickle the mind is and how easily it is distracted. The more the mind is filled with skilful mental states the more the individual is transformed into an angel, so to speak, or into a *brahmacārin* or *brahma*-farer in the sense of one who has their being in a higher plane of existence and who at the time of death will already be on that plane, so that there is little or no sense of transition, apart from the fact that the physical body is no longer there. Violent negative emotion will distort the features and may even lead to bodily convulsions, and conversely strong positive emotion will transfigure the features, however ordinary, and make one attractive to others.

Exercise of power is pleasurable. One can enjoy the feeling of strength that one experiences in playing a game of tennis, one can enjoy influencing an audience through one's oratory, and one can enjoy the mental capacity that enables one to solve a crossword puzzle. More importantly, one can use whatever power one possesses either negatively or unskilfully, on the one hand, or positively and skilfully on the other. One can harm other living beings or help them. In the case of a child the parents may treat it in the horrifying ways I have described or bring it up in such a way that it grows into a happy and healthy member of society with no childhood traumas to resolve. Education is thus of extreme importance. For the Buddhist parent it is not so much a question of teaching a child Buddhist doctrines as of bringing it up in a loving, peaceful, and supportive atmosphere. Not that there should not be a degree of moral guidance, if only by example.

There is an imbalance of power not only between the parent and the child but also between a younger and a much older person. The disparity can sometimes be very great, as when the older person is bed-ridden or suffering from dementia. In such cases, the older person is at the mercy of the younger generation, and he or she may be badly treated by members of their own family or by workers in care homes. Stories have come to light that parallel the horrifying behaviour of parents towards their own offspring.

The 'cruel little devil' is now an old man of 92, and although I am neither bedridden nor suffering from dementia there is still a disparity of power between me and the people with whom I live. In practice this disparity works to my advantage, one might say, as my carers now do for me many of the things that I no longer have the strength to do myself. They do them willingly, even joyfully, which has helped to make the last year or more one of the happiest periods of my life. Nor am I alone in this respect. One hears of sick or aged members of the Triratna Buddhist Order being cared for by fellow community members or friends in the same way. Indeed, not a few have been lovingly cared for, month after month, even year after year, up to the time of death. It would seem that my talk, 'A Case of Dysentery',[614] has been taken to heart by members of the Triratna Buddhist Order and become an integral part of the way we do things.

5
THE ARCHETYPAL REALM

Hints to a Hypothetical Artist · Green Tārā and the Fourth Lakṣaṇa · The Bodhisattvas Are Also Necessary · Rainbows in the Sky · A Passage to America · Dreams Old and New I · *Dreams Old and New* II

HINTS TO A HYPOTHETICAL ARTIST

William Blake (1757–1827) is one of my literary heroes, and I was therefore pleased when a seminar on his life and work was held at Adhisthana under the title 'Energy is Eternal Delight'.[615] The retreat was accompanied by an exhibition of Blake's illustrations to the *Book of Job*, organised by Satyalila.[616] There was also a reproduction of his engraving 'Death's Door', which shows an old man wearing shepherd's garments and with a lantern in his hand about to enter the darkness of a crypt. I greatly enjoyed being wheelchaired round the exhibition by Paramartha, who explained to me the illustrations from the *Book of Job*, some of which I remembered quite well and could almost see in my mind's eye. We had entered the library atrium in which the exhibition was held by the front door, and we left by the back door, which leads into the grassy area in which paths have been laid down by Sanghadeva,[617] who is planning further developments in the shape of flower beds and a water garden. Paramartha pushed me along these paths, pointing out as he did so the spot where I am sooner or later to be buried,[618] so that I felt that I was standing, like Blake's old man, at my own 'death's door'. There was nothing morbid about this. It was a fine summer morning and I was out in the open, enjoying the fresh air and the sight of the adjacent fields.

Blake was not only a great artist but a great poet, a very rare combination, especially at his level of achievement. The only other example of this combination of which I am aware is Dante Gabriel Rossetti (1830–1894), another of my literary heroes.[619] I was familiar with Rossetti's work well before I was aware of Blake's. In the passage that led from my room to my parent's bedroom there was a small reproduction of 'Dante's Dream', one of Rossetti's major works, the original of which I was to see in the Walker Art Gallery, Liverpool, many years later. I remember sitting in front of it with a friend, while another friend filmed me as I talked about the work. One night Dante had dreamed that Beatrice, the unattainable object of his youthful passion, was dying, and the painting depicts his dream. Clad in his customary black, the tall figure of Dante stands looking at the dying, half-risen Beatrice, who is garmented in white, with golden hair hanging down. Two handmaidens in raiment of soft green hold a canopy over her. An angel dressed in red, with red wings, holds Dante's hand and leans down to Beatrice, his lips almost touching hers, as if love could bring her back to life.

Dante was the subject not only of Rossetti's art but also of his poetry, especially of his long poem 'Dante in Verona'. The subject of the poem is Dante's years of exile in Verona, and Rossetti prefaced it with a quotation from *The Divine Comedy*. Though born and bred in Florence, the internal politics of his native city forced Dante into exile, and the lines quoted by Rossetti express all the bitterness of his soul:

> Yea, thou shalt learn how salt his food who fares
> Upon another's bread, – how steep his path
> Who treadeth up and down another's stairs.[620]

It is the cry of exiles everywhere and at all times, including our own.

I have visited both Verona and Ravenna, with its umbrella pines, where Dante died and where he is buried. The city is also associated with Shelley and Byron, two other exiles, though they were exiles for social rather than political reasons. Their stay in Ravenna and their evening rides together along the seashore are commemorated in Shelley's long poem 'Julian and Maddalo: A Conversation'. In the poem Julian stands for Shelley and Maddalo is Byron, and we are given a vivid portrait of the relationship between the two poets, so different from each other in character and personality, as they ride and talk together in the fading light.[621]

Rossetti naturally had a closer connection with Dante than did Blake. He was himself of Italian descent, though born and brought up in London, where he became one of the founder members of the Pre-Raphaelite Brotherhood, a group of English painters, poets, and critics who rebelled not only against the Mannerism that succeeded Michelangelo and Raphael but also against the materialism and philistinism of the age. Blake, too, was a rebel in his own way and aspired to build Jerusalem 'In England's green and pleasant Land'. This was an aspiration that was shared by some of the later Pre-Raphaelites, especially by William Morris, who was an active socialist and author of *News from Nowhere*, a Utopian vision of a future socialist England. Though much less close to Dante than was Rossetti, Blake towards the end of his life produced a series of illustrations to *The Divine Comedy*. It is interesting to note that the manuscript of some of Blake's poems came into Rossetti's hands and has become known as 'The Rossetti Manuscript'.[622] Rossetti appears to have appreciated Blake's poetry, different as it was from his own, for he was a man of catholic tastes. He was also the first to appreciate Fitzgerald's *Rubáiyát of Omar Khayyám*, copies of which he gave to his friends.

The poetry and art of both Rossetti and Blake were an essential part of the world of my imagination in my early teen years. These were the years in which I wrote my first poems and devoted much of my spare time to drawing and painting. It then seemed to my elders that I was more likely to become an artist than a writer. These were also the days when I attended the Sellingcourt Road Senior School and was a pupil of Mr Smoker. On the walls of Mr Smoker's classroom there hung three pictures, all of which I remember and can see in my mind's eye as I write. There was a painting called 'Napoleon on Board the Bellerophon', in which the ex-emperor is seen standing on the deck of the ship. He is being taken into exile and is gazing at the receding shores of France. At some distance behind him there is a small group of English officers, one of whom is surveying Napoleon with an expression of mingled curiosity and satisfaction.[623] On the other side of the door hung 'The Golden Stairs', by the Pre-Raphaelite painter Edward Burne-Jones. It showed a number of beautiful young women, all clad in white and with fair hair, making their way down a spiral staircase.[624] At the back of the classroom there was a print of William Caxton in his Westminster workshop, showing his printing press to Edward IV and his queen.[625] I do not know whether Mr Smoker had chosen the pictures or whether they had been supplied by the LCC's education department. Whatever it may have been, they were part of my regular environment for a year or more, and it is not surprising that I should remember them.

Though I wrote poetry and drew and painted various figures, both historical and imaginary, there was no crossover between the two. I neither illustrated my poems nor wrote poems about what I had painted. It is only very recently that I have seen the possibility of illustrating something I have written, whether poetry or prose. I am thinking in particular of my story 'Four Visitors',[626] which I think lends itself to illustration, especially as there are five figures in it. If I possessed the requisite talent, I would have tried to do the illustrations myself, but since this is not possible I would appeal to those of my friends who are artists to carry out the work in my stead. In order to help them, I would like to make a few suggestions.

The figure of the Virgin Mary, clad in her traditional white and blue, should be in the middle of the picture. On her left, clad entirely in white, there should stand the figure of Guanyin. Since I have not described the latter in much detail, the artist should feel free to depict the figure in his or her own way, provided only that it is recognizably the Buddhist bodhisattva. I would also like the two figures to be depicted at the point at which they start merging. Below the two ladies there should come the decidedly masculine figure of Māra. When I wrote about him in 'Four Visitors' I did not see him as the rather ineffective Māra of the Pāli scriptures. I saw him as the much more dangerous Māra of the *Śūraṅgamasamādhi Sūtra*,[627] which I studied some time ago with Paramartha. Māra is bulky and brown in colour and he occupies more than twice the space occupied by the two ladies. His expression is one of extreme cunning. I sit to Māra's left and should be depicted sitting in my armchair with my back to the viewer, so that only the back of my head is visible. The Angel sits on the right arm of my chair and should be depicted just as I described him – young and beautiful and with multicoloured wings. Thus I am between Māra and the Angel and our three heads are in alignment, so that Māra speaks into my left ear and the Angel into my right. Red roses should naturally feature, and I leave the artist free to place them wherever he or she thinks fit. Above the two ladies is the blue sky, perhaps studded with stars. At the bottom of the picture I suggest that the artist should depict the Adhisthana skyline, including the library where I saw the Blake exhibition with which this article starts.

GREEN TĀRĀ AND THE FOURTH *LAKṢAṆA*

Jamyang Khyentse Rimpoche was an old man at the time, and did not have much longer to live, but on 24 October 1957, despite failing health, he initiated me into the *Mañjughoṣa Stuti Sādhana*. As his name indicated, he was an embodiment of Mañjughoṣa (Jamyang), the Bodhisattva of Transcendental Wisdom, and friends had urged me to ask him to initiate me into the *sādhana* of the bodhisattva. It would be a source of great blessing to me and my disciples, they assured me. I accordingly made the request, which the guru granted. He would not only give me the *sādhana* of Mañjughoṣa, he told me, but also the *sādhanas* of Avalokiteśvara, Vajrapāṇi, and Green Tārā. I have described the initiation in *Precious Teachers* and I do not propose to repeat what I said there.[628]

That was sixty years ago, and for many years the *Mañjughoṣa Stuti Sādhana* was my main spiritual practice, together with the *sādhana* of Green Tārā which I had received earlier from Chattrul Sangye Dorje. For a short while I practised the Avalokiteśvara *sādhana* that I had received from Jamyang Khyentse Rimpoche, though I must confess that for one reason or another I never got around to practising the Vajrapāṇi *sādhana*. Recently a *Mañjughoṣa stuti sādhana* retreat led by Subhuti, Mahamati, Sanghadevi, and Paramabandhu was held at Adhisthana, and I was delighted that what I had received from Jamyang Khyentse Rimpoche was being passed on within the Triratna Buddhist Order. Fifty or more people took part in the retreat, some of whom had received the *sadhana* from me and had been practising it regularly for many years. Similar retreats devoted to the *sādhanas* of Avalokiteśvara and Green Tārā have also been held at Adhisthana, and I very much hope that retreats of this kind will continue to be held here.

After my initiation by Jamyang Khyentse Rimpoche a friend procured for me a copy of the four *sādhanas* I had received from him, and I perceived that the four formed a set. I also saw that the four bodhisattvas were in a relationship of 'correspondence' (in the hermetic sense) with the *lakṣaṇas*, the *samādhis*, and the *vimokṣas*. Concentrating on the insubstantiality of things, one enters into the *śūnyatā samādhi* and 'sees' the bodhisattva Mañjughoṣa. He is golden yellow in colour and wears the jewels and silks of a prince. Concentrating on the unsatisfactoriness of things, one enters into the wishless (*apraṇihita*) *samādhi* and 'sees' the figure of Avalokiteśvara, pure white in colour. Concentrating on the impermanence of things, one enters into the signless (*animitta*) *samādhi* and 'sees' Vajrapāṇi . He is dark blue in colour, like indigo or lapis lazuli. Concentrating on the repulsiveness of conditioned things, one enters into the *samādhi* of pure beauty, and 'sees' Green Tārā, who has the colour of emeralds or jade. All four bodhisattvas are young and beautiful and radiate light. Meeting them, one, in a sense, meets the Buddha, for they are all embodiments of this or that aspect of the Buddha's Enlightened nature.

The connection between a particular bodhisattva and a particular *samādhi* is not arbitrary. As I have said, they are in correspondence. In other words, the Unconditioned is to be found or encountered in the depths of the conditioned. In Mañjughoṣa's *śūnyatā samādhi*, what is true of the individual becomes through wisdom true of all things. In Avalokiteśvara's wishless *samādhi*, there is no will of one's own, no preferences, one simply responds with compassion to the needs of others, especially those who are in distress. That compassion may be likened to a perfect sphere, which the lightest touch can set rolling in any direction. In Vajrapāṇi's signless *samādhi*, there are no ideas or concepts, all of which have been eliminated by the power of insight. In Green Tārā's *samādhi* of pure beauty, the perception of the repulsive (*aśubha*) has been transformed into the perception of pure beauty.

The *samādhis* are also known as doors of liberation (*vimokṣa-mukhas*), for it is through them that one passes to the liberation that is Enlightenment. They thus mark the passage from the conditioned to the Unconditioned, although just where the one ends and the other begins it is difficult to say. The door is a universal symbol, marking as it does the passing from a lower to a higher state of existence. Thus William Blake speaks of the golden string which, when wound into a ball, 'will lead you in at Heaven's gate, Built in Jerusalem's wall'.[629] Using Blake's language, we may say that the *samādhis* are the golden string of which he speaks, while the winding of the string into a ball represents the spiritual discipline that eventually takes one to the end of the conditioned and the beginning of the Unconditioned.

Though I have spoken of four *samādhis* or *vimokṣas*, Buddhist tradition speaks of only three. There are, however, reasons for reckoning the *samādhis* as four in number, not the least of which is that Jamyang Khyentse Rimpoche seemed to put the Green Tārā *sādhana* on the same level as the three other *sādhanas*, the four in fact forming a set. Another reason is that besides *duḥkha*, *anitya* (Pāli *anicca*), and *anātman* (Pāli *anattā*), there is a fourth *lakṣaṇa* i.e. the ugly or repulsive (*aśubha*). Moreover, there is the reflection on the ten stages in the decomposition of a body, a standard Buddhist practice which not only helps free one from the attachment to the body but also opens one up to the perception of the pure or beautiful (*śubha*).[630] This opening up may go through several stages, as we learn from the well-known story of Nanda and the heavenly nymphs. After seeing the divine beauty of the heavenly nymphs Nanda compares his earthly beloved to a monkey with ears and nose cut off. Not that his beloved is really ugly but only that she is less beautiful than the heavenly nymphs.[631] Thus there are degrees of beauty from the sensuous to the spiritual, and from the spiritual to the Transcendental.

Historically speaking, Buddhism has not developed a spiritual path in which the goal is envisaged in terms of ideal beauty and the path in terms of increasing love for that beauty. There is no reason, however, why such a path should not be developed within the general framework of Buddhist practice, especially as we have models for such an approach within the Western spiritual tradition. The *locus classicus* of such an approach is to be found in the *Symposium* of Plato (427–347 BCE), one of the most sublime works of Western literature. In this celebrated dialogue, known to me since my teens, Socrates represents himself as being instructed in the art of love by Diotima. In her instruction, the object of love is beauty, both human and divine.[632] A similar approach is to be found in the writings of Plotinus (204/5–270 CE). In his tractate 'On Beauty', he says:

> Beauty is mostly in sight, but it is to be found too in things we hear, in combinations of words and also in music, and in all music [not only in songs]; for tunes and rhythms are certainly beautiful: and for those who are advancing upwards from sense perception,

> ways of life and actions and characters and intellectual activities are beautiful, and there is beauty of virtue. If there is any beauty prior to these, it itself will reveal it.[633]

Over the centuries poets and mystics have been inspired by Plato and Plotinus and their influence can be seen in some forms of Christian and Islamic mysticism. It would be surprising therefore if that influence was not to extend, sooner or later, to Western Buddhism. Indeed, such an influence is already being felt in some quarters. As I wrote in 1950:

> It is not love that seeks to bind
> Two bodies in a fierce embrace;
> Nor love, true love, that dreams to find,
> The highest beauty in a face.
>
> Love soars beyond the scathe of hands,
> Outstrips a face, and is employed
> Where it both sees and understands
> A Beauty without form and void.[634]

THE BODHISATTVAS ARE ALSO NECESSARY

I have told this story before, but never mind, I will tell it again. It was told me by my teacher, the venerable Jagdish Kashyap, and it was about himself. Born into a Hindu family in Bihar, he had converted to Buddhism and had been ordained as a *bhikkhu* in Sri Lanka. Though a scholar in Sanskrit and Pāli, he was a gentle, unassuming man who did not mind telling a story against himself. Soon after his ordination he was invited to Penang by a group of Chinese Buddhists, he once told me. They were excellent hosts, looking after his every need and showing him around their temples, in which there were images of both Buddhas and bodhisattvas. Being a Theravādin, Kashyap-ji related, he had saluted the Buddhas but he had not saluted the bodhisattvas. The following day he was served a lunch consisting only of rice, which had surprised him a little, and this happened for a few more days. Eventually, without actually complaining, he drew his hosts' attention to the fact, saying, 'No doubt rice is the main thing, but the vegetables are also necessary.' 'Yes,' agreed his hosts, 'that is very true. Similarly, the Buddha is the main thing, but the bodhisattvas are also necessary.' 'Thereafter,' concluded Kashyap-ji, with a smile, 'I was careful to salute the bodhisattvas as well as the Buddhas.' The fact that Kashyap-ji, as a Theravādin, did not salute the bodhisattvas did not mean that the bodhisattva, in the Pāli form of *bodhisatta*, was not known to the Theravādin tradition. In the tradition, however, *bodhisatta* referred to Gotama up to the time of his attainment of supreme, perfect Enlightenment, though it was also applied to him in his many previous lives. The bodhisattvas of Chinese Buddhism, as well as the bodhisattvas of the Mahāyāna generally, are purely ideal figures and have no historical existence. As I have written elsewhere, they are represented as beautiful young princes.

> Gem-studded tiaras sparkle on their brows, while their nobly proportioned limbs are clad in light diaphanous garments of coloured silk. They wear gold bracelets and strings of jewels, and round their necks hang garlands of fragrant flowers.[635]

In recent years there has been a good deal of discussion among Buddhist academics about the historical origin of the bodhisattva ideal. Originally it was thought that it arose among the Buddhist laity, who were looking for a simpler and easier way of practising the Buddha's teaching. More recently, however, it has been claimed that the ideal arose among a group of more serious practitioners who lived near stupas containing body relics of the Buddha. To my mind, the two positions are not contradictory. The bodhisattva ideal has, in fact, a double aspect, neither of which precludes the other. On the one hand we have those who actually try to live the life of the bodhisattva and practise the *pāramitās* or perfections for the benefit of all beings, while on the other there are those who worship the bodhisattvas in the hope of obtaining worldly blessings. In the Theravāda, broadly speaking, neither monks nor lay people worship the Buddha for the sake of worldly benefits, and in the absence of bodhisattvas such as those found in the Mahāyāna, the Theravāda laity have tended to appeal for help to a variety of lesser divinities. In Sri Lanka for instance they worship the Hindu god Vishnu, who is in fact seen as a follower of the Buddha and a protector of his Dhamma. Similarly, Burmese Buddhists worship the Nats, the spirits of wood and water, which is not seen as incompatible with the practice of Buddhism.

In the Mahāyāna the number of bodhisattvas is incalculable, but in the course of centuries certain bodhisattvas assumed a more and more individual character. By some they were worshipped as embodiments of the ideal, while others depended upon them for worldly benefits.

Once I too, like Kashyap-ji, was invited by a group of Chinese Buddhists to visit Penang, whence I visited Buddhists in other parts of Malaysia. Once I found myself spending the night at an Avalokiteśvara temple run by a community of nuns. In the morning I saw that women were arriving with offerings and I asked one of the nuns what they wanted from the bodhisattva. 'They want babies,' she replied. This was not the kind of thing I associated with the practice of the Avalokiteśvara *sādhana* that had been given to me by Jamyang Khyentse Rimpoche. Neither was it associated with any of the other *sādhanas* that I had received, beginning with the Green Tārā *sādhana*, which had been given me by Chattrul Sangye Dorje, the first of my Tibetan teachers.

Well do I remember receiving that *sādhana* and what the receiving of it meant to me at the time, now sixty years ago. I was then 32, had been a monk for nine years and since even before that time I had been practising the Mindfulness of Breathing and the *mettā bhāvanā*. I practised them according to the Theravādin tradition, so that by accepting the Green Tārā initiation from Chattrul Sangye Dorje I had passed from the practice of the Theravāda to the practice of the Mahāyāna and even the Vajrayāna. Not that I had left the Theravāda behind or that I was unfamiliar with the teachings of the Mahāyāna. I had, however, reached something of an impasse in my personal spiritual development. For some time I had been preoccupied with the question of 'getting beyond the ego', and had even written an article on the subject,[636] but how could the ego go about getting beyond the ego? That was the question. As it happened, I had, at around this time, become acquainted with Dinshaw Mehta, a Parsee mystic who believed that while he was in a state of trance, he received a direct guidance from God. 'Guidance' was the keynote of his teaching. There were three kinds of guidance, he told me. There was guidance received direct from God in a state of trance, such as he himself experienced, and there was guidance received from the person guided by God, which was the guidance received by his disciples from him. There was also what he called 'guidance by circumstances'. I had no desire to be 'guided' by Dinshaw Mehta, much as he would have liked to guide me, but I could see that he had a point.[637] One could get beyond the ego only with the help of something or someone that was itself beyond the ego. What was that something? Perhaps it was one's *iṣṭa devatā* or *yidam*.

When I met Chattrul Sangye Dorje I therefore asked him to tell me who my *iṣṭa devatā* was, for his very presence had inspired me with confidence. He thereupon told me that my *yidam* was Green Tārā, adding that she had been the *yidam* of many of the great pandits of India and Tibet. One of these, as I knew, was Atiśa (980–1054 CE). On his being invited to Tibet he had consulted Tārā, who told him that if he accepted the invitation his life would be shortened by several years but that his visit would be of great benefit to the Dharma. He therefore accepted the invitation, and became the founder of the Kadam school of Tibetan Buddhism.

It was at about this time, too, that I came to see that the act of Going for Refuge to the Buddha, Dharma, and Sangha was central to the Buddhist life. It was what made one a Buddhist and it was naturally followed by the practice of five, or eight, or ten moral precepts. This was the path that underlay all forms of Buddhism, whether Theravāda or Mahāyāna. It was a path of self-effort and self-development, in which one relied on self-power to attain liberation from suffering. It should also be noted that although each precept is observed by the individual for his or her own benefit, each has an other-referential or even altruistic dimension. Observing the first precept, one abstains from injuring other living beings and especially from killing them. This refers, in my view, not only to the killing of other human beings but to the killing of animals, whether for sport or food. The precept could also refer more generally to the protection and preservation of all forms of life and even cover concerns of an environmentalist nature. Observing the second precept, one abstains not only from stealing but from taking from others what has not been freely given. This implies abstaining from all sorts of economic exploitation. Observing the third precept, one behaves mindfully and sensitively in one's sexual relations. Neither does one traffic in sex. Observing the fourth precept, one abstains from false, harsh, useless, and slanderous speech, and neither does one sponsor misleading advertising or help to spread fake news. Observing the fifth precept, one abstains from drinks and drugs that cloud the mind and from dealing in any of them, including so-called recreational drugs, whether indulged in on one's own or with others. Besides the outward observance, there is the inner attitude. One therefore also abstains from covetousness and hatred, as well as from wrong views. Thus there is an altruistic dimension to the whole path of self-effort and self-development, from the act of Going for Refuge onwards. This aspect finds its fullest expression in the bodhisattva ideal, which I see as the altruistic dimension of the act of Going for Refuge.

I cannot claim that Tārā ever spoke to me in the way that she spoke to Atiśa, but doing her *sādhana* must have made me kinder and more considerate than I naturally was. Be that as it may, there were certainly times when I felt that a higher power was acting through me. This usually happened when I was communicating the Dharma. The words that came from my lips were not really mine and I listened to them as though someone else was speaking. In later years there was a certain amount of discussion in the Order about the nature of this supra-personal force, as it was sometimes called; and as far as I know, the discussion continues.

RAINBOWS IN THE SKY

> My heart leaps up when I behold
> A rainbow in the sky:
> So was it when my life began;
> So is it now I am a man;
> So be it when I shall grow old,
> Or let me die!

So wrote William Wordsworth in 1802. More than two hundred years later my heart, too, leaps up when I see a rainbow, as does the heart of anyone who is capable of responding to the beauties of the natural world, and especially to its various colours. Indeed, rainbows have marked some of the most important events of my life, which is why I gave the first volume of my memoirs the title *The Rainbow Road from Tooting Broadway to Kalimpong*. I must admit, though, that I saw my first rainbows not in the sky but in two works of art. One of these was Millais's *The Blind Girl*, and the other was one of the two versions of Holman Hunt's *The Scapegoat*, both of which have been familiar to me since my childhood. I saw my next rainbow in the film *Fantasia*, which I had the opportunity of seeing in Singapore towards the end of the war. In this pioneering film, Walt Disney blended animated imagery with well-known pieces of classical music. I remember in particular the images that accompanied Beethoven's *Pastoral Symphony*. The storm is over, the sky clears, and across the screen there shoots the goddess Iris, trailing behind her a brilliant rainbow.

Many years later, when I took up the practice of the Green Tārā *sādhana*, I remembered Iris and her rainbow as I visualized the offering goddesses emerging from the crown of my head and making offerings to the bodhisattvas in the sky. There were seven such goddesses, each of whom trailed a rainbow behind her as she rose into the air holding her offering. Pleased with the offerings, the bodhisattvas sent down blessings. The offering goddesses and their rainbows were not always easy to imagine, and I was glad to be able to see a real rainbow from time to time to refresh my memory. They were of varying degrees of proximity and brilliance. The most memorable in this respect was a rainbow I saw in Auckland in 1997. Auckland is a city well known for its variable weather. Standing in front of the men's community one afternoon after a passing shower, I saw the biggest and brightest rainbow I had ever seen. It rose majestically from immediately behind the houses on the other side of the road, its arc seeming to enclose half the sky. The colours of its unusually broad bands were particularly vivid and looked both solid and diaphanous.

Big and bright as was the rainbow I saw in Auckland, this was not the rainbow after which my first volume of memoirs was named. It was named after a whole series of rainbows I had encountered more than fifty years earlier. I was then staying in a hill station in east Punjab and it was there that I decided to go forth from the world as a homeless wanderer as the Buddha and his disciples had done. With me was my friend Satyapriya, whom I had met in Singapore. On the morning of 18 August 1947, therefore, we changed our civilian clothes for the traditional saffron of the ascetic and set out on foot for the plains. In the words of *The Rainbow Road*:

> As we left Kausali it was raining, but as in the course of our descent we emerged from the clouds into the bright sunshine below, we saw arching the road, at intervals of a few dozen yards, not only a single but double and triple rainbows. Every time we turned a bend we found more rainbows waiting for us. We passed

> through them as though through the multicoloured arcades of some celestial palace. Against the background of bright sunshine, jewel-like glittering raindrops, and hills of the freshest and most vivid green, this plethora of delicate seven-hued bows seemed like the epiphany of another world.[638]

Thus the rainbow became for me a symbol of the spiritual path, the track of which I have followed, in one way or another, all my life.

The symbolism of the rainbow, and of its individual colours, of course varies from culture to culture and religion to religion. Green, for example, is the colour of Islam, and I remember that the little village mosques I passed in the course of my visit to Malaysia were all painted bright green. Similarly, I have seen Muslim fakirs who wore green in much the same way that the Hindu sadhus wear saffron. When *The Rainbow Road* came to be translated into Spanish, I was told that the title would have to be changed, because the rainbow, in the United States and elsewhere, was the symbol of the gay rights movement. I was able to verify this when I visited San Francisco. One day a friend took me for a walk from the Mission district, where I was staying, through the Castro, and I saw scores of small rainbow flags fluttering from windows and balconies. The flags indicated, so my friend explained, that a gay household lived there. Gaily they fluttered in the sunshine, those little flags, and it was good that they should do so. The gay rights movement had made some progress in the USA though in other parts of the world homosexuals were being persecuted and even killed. I had not aligned myself with the gay rights movement, but I sympathized with its aims and in my own way had done my best to promote them. When I founded the FWBO in 1967 I made it clear that it was open to all, irrespective of gender, race, nationality, and sexual orientation, and I rejoiced that in that same year consensual sex between adult men was decriminalized in the UK. Much as I sympathized with the gay rights movement, however, I was far from identifying the rainbow with any socio-political movement. For me the rainbow symbolized not just the spiritual path but spirituality itself, especially when that spirituality reflected or was touched by something even higher. Thus, in the Buddhist art of Tibet rainbows emanate from saints and yogis as well as from stupas. Some highly spiritual beings, indeed, are made entirely of rainbows.

This is especially the case with Padmasambhava, who is known as the Rainbow-Bodied One. Padmasambhava came into my life the first time I visited the Tamang Buddhist Gompa in Darjeeling. This must have been in the early 1950s, shortly after I settled in Kalimpong. But great as was the impression made on me by the lifelike image in the gompa, it was not until October 1962 that my relationship with the Precious Guru was ritually confirmed, when I received in Kalimpong the Padmasambhava initiation from Kachu Rinpoche, the abbot of Pema Yangtse Gompa in western Sikkim. In the course of the two-day initiation he explained to me how I was to meditate on Padmasambhava and gave me the name of Urgyen, this being the Tibetan form of Uḍḍiyāna, a part of north-west India associated with the early life of the Great Guru. Kachu Rinpoche also explained how I was to do the Going for Refuge and Prostration Practice with Padmasambhava as the object of refuge.[639] This practice I did regularly until my departure to the UK in 1964, by which time I had done it a total of 20,000 times – not a lot by Tibetan Buddhist standards. After the founding of the FWBO in 1967 I taught the practice to a number of Order members, some of whom have in turn taught it to others. Thus, Padmasambhava has been present in the life of the Order from the very beginning and he continues to be in it and part of it to the present day.

Recently I have been pained and surprised to learn that some Order members believe that Padmasambhava has been sidelined, and this some of them connect with a narrowing of the movement, and in particular, with my remark about the re-founding of the Order.[640] On the contrary, Padmasambhava is still very much alive in my own life and in the life of the Order, and his day is still widely celebrated at our centres. His image stands on my shrine, together with the four-armed Avalokiteśvara and the photo of Jamyang Khyentse Rimpoche, at whose behest Kachu Rimpoche gave me the Padmasambahava initiation. As for the alleged narrowing, when I spoke of a re-founding of the Order, what I had in mind was a reaffirmation of the principles and ideals for which we stand and for which we have stood from the beginning. If one can speak of a re-founding at all it can only be in the sense of making the original foundation stronger.

Shortly after my return to the UK, I gave a talk at the invitation of the then Brighton Buddhist Society. What I spoke about I no longer remember, but it must have been one or another aspect of the Dharma. After the talk an elderly woman approached me. She had seen a strange figure standing behind me while I spoke, she said, and she wanted to know who the figure was. I naturally asked her to describe the figure. He was wearing a kind of red cloak, she said, and a strangely shaped hat. What was more, he was neither Chinese nor Indian but something in between. From what the woman told me, it was evident that the figure that she had seen standing behind me was none other than the one I had seen in the Tamang Buddhist Gompa in Darjeeling all those years before. Since I visited Brighton regularly, Violet, as she was called, became a friend and a few years later I was able to see her and chat with her after her death, as I have related in detail elsewhere.[641]

The last rainbow of significance in my life appeared on my ninetieth birthday, which was celebrated at Adhisthana and throughout the movement. In the afternoon I was driven from the Annexe where I lived to the marquee in which four hundred or more Order members were waiting to receive me. It was raining heavily at the time, and there was a deep rumble of thunder. I was later told that at that time a rainbow of particular brightness had appeared over Adhisthana, including the Annexe. I did not see the rainbow myself as I was inside the marquee listening to the speeches, but even hearing about it made my heart leap up.

A PASSAGE TO AMERICA

It was my first visit to the United States. In previous years I had made several long-distance flights, but this was the first time I had crossed the Atlantic. The reason for my journey was that I had been invited by the philosophy department of Berkeley College, a residential college at Yale University, to give a series of lectures on Buddhist philosophy. Although I had no academic qualifications, I had been invited on the recommendation of two very distinguished scholars, Dr Edward Conze and Professor F. N. Findlay, both of whom thought highly of *A Survey of Buddhism*, which had been published some years earlier. Thus it was that one day in the winter of 1969–70, I found myself bidding goodbye to London (Heathrow) and heading for New York (Kennedy).

I remember little of the five or six hour flight. In some respects it was like a dream, or even a nightmare. I had a window seat in the right-hand aisle from which I had a view of the information screen which flickered and danced with the vibrations of the aircraft. From time to time we encountered an air pocket, suddenly dropping hundreds of feet before regaining height. On these occasions my heart seemed to come up into my mouth and for a few seconds I felt that I would go on falling for ever. Each time it happened I felt a little more disoriented and did not know quite where I was, and whether I was sitting or falling. Moreover, the information screen seemed to be talking to me and even sending me messages. 'Calvary,' it flashed, which I took to be an ill omen for my journey. 'Calvary,' it repeated. 'Death. Death. Death.' I was heading for Calvary, not New York. I was heading for death. In ordinary parlance, a Calvary is a period of intense mental suffering, but this was not the Calvary of which the information screen spoke. It was speaking of the Agony in the Garden, the night that Jesus spent, alone, before being crucified. He knew he was going to die a hideous death, and prayed that the cup might pass from him. As I sat with my eyes on the screen, I recalled disjointedly the words of the Gospel account, as well as recalling paintings of the Agony in the Garden that I had seen – in particular, a small one by El Greco in the National Gallery. Jesus kneels on a kind of promontory while his disciples sleep below, and an angel bends down from heaven and offers him a kind of chalice.[642] As every Christian knows, Jesus drained the cup, thereby signifying his acceptance of God's will for him, and the next day he was crucified on a hill outside Jerusalem.

Crucifixion was a common form of execution among the Romans of the time. Jesus was not crucified alone, but between two thieves. The victim's hands would be nailed to the arms of the cross and his feet nailed to the upright with a single nail. He would die of asphyxiation, or exhaustion. It was a painful and ignominious death, and over the centuries Christian artists have depicted the sufferings of Jesus on the cross in increasingly realistic detail. It is some years since I saw the Isenheim Altarpiece, but its horrifying depiction of the crucified Jesus still haunts me.[643] Jesus was put to death in the reign of the Emperor Tiberius, when Roman civilization was at its height, and cultured Romans who enjoyed the poetry of Virgil, Ovid, and Horace would have seen nothing shocking in the crucifixion of common criminals. Nor would they have been shocked by the fact that a generation or two earlier six thousand survivors of the revolt of the slaves under Spartacus had been crucified by a victorious Roman general, the crosses with their ghastly burden lining the Appian Way from Rome to Capua. I had not read Howard Fast's novel *Spartacus* nor seen the film that was based on it, but somehow the fate of the former gladiator and his followers had made a strong impression on me, and as I sat there in the aircraft the crucified slaves passed before my inner vision in wave after wave. Suddenly I was jolted back to the present reality by the grinding sound of the lowering of the undercarriage and by the bump by which it was immediately succeeded as the aircraft hit the runway. Once more the information screen flashed. 'Calgary! Calgary!' it said.

I still do not know why I kept seeing 'Calvary' instead of 'Calgary'. Was it a case of hallucination? But if it was, why should I have hallucinated just then, and why should the hallucination have taken the form it did? There were several elements to it, and, hallucination or not, they must all have had some significance for me, perhaps on a level deeper than that of my conscious mind. For one thing, I was on my own and was not sure how I would get on at Berkeley College away from all my friends. Then there was Calvary and Christianity. Calvary and the Crucifixion were part of the Christian myth, as to me the story was. I was a Buddhist, not a Christian, and did not take the myth literally. Why, then, did it play such a prominent part in my hallucination, or whatever it was that I experienced? There was also Tiberius and the Roman Empire and the fact that culture was not incompatible with cruelty; there was Spartacus and the 6,000 crucified slaves lining the Appian Way, as well as the horrors of the Isenheim Altarpiece. Where did it all come from? What did it all mean?

Despite my earlier misgivings, I got on well at Berkeley College. It was my first experience of university life, as well as my last, and I quite enjoyed the experience. I joined an intercollege poetry reading group, ate my first pizza, travelled up to Cape Cod to see a total solar eclipse, visited the Mongolian lama Geshe Wangyal, and of course lectured my dozen or so students on Buddhist philosophy, basing myself on *A Survey of Buddhism*. I also led a weekly meditation class, which was attended by about eighty people. It was held in the dining hall of the college under the watchful eye of Bishop Berkeley, whose portrait hung there. In later years I visited the United States a number of times, accompanied by a friend or two, but I never saw Yale again, though Berkeley College and the friends I had made there remained a pleasant memory. On these later visits I saw the Grand Canyon, crossed the Rockies from West to East, drove through Death Valley, and spent a day and a night, with two friends, among the crazy and colourful architectures of Las Vegas. There was the Moab desert, Yellowstone Park, and Monument Valley with its striking contrast between the cathedral-like rocks and the surrounding sands. There was New Mexico and the Kiowa Ranch where D. H. Lawrence had lived for two years and where his ashes are buried in a kind of chapel surmounted by a phoenix, his symbol. In the course of these travels I always spent time at the FWBO centres that had been established by pioneering Order members in New England, San Francisco, Missoula, and Seattle.

Underlying all this were preoccupations that had manifested themselves in the hallucinations I had experienced during the first part of my journey. Of these, some became the subject of conscious reflection. Remembering those cultured Romans, I was reminded of what 'Samurai' William Adams (1564–1620) had said of the no less cultured Japanese. They were very cultured, he had observed, and also very cruel.[644] Cultured or not, the modern Japanese often treated Allied prisoners of war with extreme cruelty, working them to death on the building of the Burma Railway. Earlier, there had been the Nanking Massacre and during the Second World War the Japanese troops had enslaved half a million Korean 'comfort women'. Remembering those cultured Romans, I also remembered how the educated and cultured Germans had, under Nazism, exterminated Jews, homosexuals, and Roma.

In recent years, my main object of reflection has been suffering, especially suffering as inflicted by human beings on one another, as well as on other animals. In particular, I have asked myself why human beings should not only deliberately inflict suffering on other human beings but also delight in so doing. Indeed, there has seemed to me to be something devilish in the enjoyment of another being's suffering, whether or not inflicted by one's own hand. Some have attempted to explain the phenomenon as an inheritance from our animal ancestry, but though animals may kill and eat their prey, they do not, as far as we know, enjoy the infliction of pain as such. Only too often, human beings' enjoyment of the infliction of pain on other human beings is associated with a definite ideology, whether that of Nazism, nationalism, dogmatic religion, Communism, or the Hindu system of hereditary caste.

Suffering can be inflicted not only by bodily action, whether direct or indirect, but also by means of speech or writing, which can be harsh, abusive, or defamatory. It may pour ridicule or find expression in a supposed 'joke'.

To the extent that one deliberately inflicts suffering, and especially when one enjoys inflicting it, one is to that extent morally evil. This is not, of course, the whole story. One is also morally good and can enjoy making other people happy even to the extent of devoting one's whole life to their welfare. Though there is a great deal of suffering in the world, much of it is due not to natural evil but to the morally evil behaviour of other people, especially as supported by this or that ideology. It is not enough, therefore, that we should seek to popularize mindfulness and *mettā*, desirable as this may be. We have also to demolish the wrong views that undergird morally evil behaviour, and I suspect that the work of demolishing them will be one of Triratna's main tasks for a long time to come.

DREAMS OLD AND NEW I

Dreams are part of human experience, and they have certainly been part of mine. I vividly remember a dream I had when I was 8 years old and in hospital with scarlet fever and chickenpox. In my dream I saw a boy of 14 lying full length on a bed. He was brown-skinned, naked, and dead, and I was looking down on him. Reflecting on the dream in my maturer years I have wondered whether the boy was me in a previous life and I was taking my last look at the body I was leaving.

There is only one dream from my years in India that I remember. I had this dream more than once and I used to call it 'the dream of the two ashrams'. The first ashram was situated at the base of a mountain and was open to all. Various religious activities went on there. At the back there was a small door, and this door led to a flight of what seemed to be hundreds of steps. At the top of the steps was the secret ashram, the existence of which was known to a very few. Standing before the ashram there was a stout, middle-aged man, clad in brahminical white, whom I knew to be the rishi Agastya, who had led the Aryans from the Himalayas down into South India.[645] Immediately behind him there was a kind of showcase in which were many golden figures of the Buddha. To the rear there was a courtyard on the right-hand side of which ran a low wall. Looking over this wall I saw in the distance, silhouetted against the sky, a row of factories, some of which had chimneys.

I had the dream about the dead boy only once, but about the two ashrams I dreamed many times, including once or twice when I was back in England. Another dream that came to me more than once I called the dream of the deserted church. Just around the corner from one of our Triratna centres there stood a large church, seemingly built in the Victorian age. No one seemed to go there, and one day, noticing that there was no lock on the back door, I went in. The interior was quite spacious and bare and there were no pews or chairs. Looking round, it occurred to me that it was a good place for a meditation centre and I started holding classes there. People came to the classes and soon I had a little congregation. I also gave lectures from time to time. These lectures attracted a group of young men, and with their help I built a shrine at the far end of the church. On special occasions the young men decorated the shrine, at the apex of which stood a figure of the Buddha. What with all the flowers, lighted candles, and other offerings, it was an inspiring sight. One day, when I had been using the church for several months, I arrived to find a clergyman there. The church was his, he explained. He did not mind my using it, even telling me that it had been deconsecrated, so that it was no longer a church but just a big building. In the course of the next few months we met several times and became good friends, and we kept up our friendship even after he moved to another town. There were also dreams in which I told different people about the deserted church and how I had turned it into a kind of Buddhist centre. I also told them about my friendship with the clergyman. So vivid were all these dreams that the church seemed actually to have an objective existence on another plane.

In yet another of my deserted church dreams I arrived to find a small group of clergymen there. They had been meditating in a tiny room in one corner of the church that I had not noticed and we got into a friendly discussion. One of the clergymen had his wife with him, and she was so medieval in her views that I told her husband that he ought to have a word with her about it. At the time I happened to be listening to John Robinson's *Honest to God* and a recollection of this may have found its way into my dream.[646] There was also a dream in which a neighbour took me to see a church to which there was direct access from the street. Supporting the roof there were two rows of red marble pillars the capitals of which were carved and gilded. It was a magnificent sight but it left me cold.

Around the time of my deserted church dreams I was having many dreams about London, where I was born and grew up. More than once I dreamed that I was standing on the southbound platform of the Tube, waiting for the train that would take me to Tooting Broadway. The train came at last, the name of its destination brightly lit on the front. Once, having arrived at the Broadway, I set out for my old home, perhaps expecting to find my parents there. Instead of my parents I found my grandmother, who in actual life had never lived there, at least not when I did. Indeed, that particular house had never been lived in by me and existed only in that dream. In another dream I was waiting for the Tooting Broadway bus at a bus stop somewhere in North London. It arrived at last and I took a window seat from which I looked out at the shops and other buildings we passed. They were all familiar to me though they did not correspond to anything in my actual life. There were also times when I wandered round central London with a friend. Once we walked right through Westminster Abbey entering through the front door and leaving it by the back door. The vast interior differed in all sorts of ways from the real thing. We also visited the National Gallery, which had a very different layout from the one in Trafalgar Square, and was filled with very different pictures. Once we came upon a tower which was several hundred miles high, and for the cost of a ticket one could go to the top and enjoy the panoramic view. My sister happened to be there and I offered to treat her to a trip. But she declined and I went on my own. In a matter of minutes I had reached the top of the tower which was circular and surrounded by a balustrade. I looked down expecting to see the whole of London spread out far below me, but I saw nothing as we were high above the clouds. On the way down we stopped halfway and I was told that Princess Margaret had recently stopped there and been presented with a bouquet. These dreams were all relatively clear and I did not find it difficult to remember them when I woke up. There were other dreams about London that were confused and unsettling. In them I wandered, sometimes with a friend, among the foundations of the buildings above. Some of these foundations were very complex and for various reasons difficult and unpleasant to negotiate. Once I was being driven through them by a colleague, but eventually the obstacles were such that we had to abandon the car and proceed on foot.

There was a dream in which I saw the tower from somewhere out in space. At that distance it looked no bigger than a needle. At times the needle rose out of London and at times it rose from the summit of a great mountain, such as I often saw in my dreams. The mountain was irregular in shape, with deep valleys and steep pathways. Sometimes I trod those pathways myself, and sometimes, from above, I watched the tiny figures of others negotiating them. One side of the mountain swept down to the sea where there were yellow beaches with which I was familiar. Beyond the beaches there was the dark blue sea, and beyond the sea a vast expanse of brilliant blue sky. This harked back to a much earlier dream in which I was high above the earth. The blue of the sky was not only above me but all around me and beneath me. The sea was far below, and on the sea, its intense whiteness contrasting with the surrounding dark blue, there was a cruise ship, and I was about to allow myself to drop straight down onto its deck.

DREAMS OLD AND NEW II

I've always loved second-hand bookshops, and some of the happiest hours of my life have been spent in them, whether looking for a particular book or simply browsing. It is not surprising, therefore, that there should be bookshops in the world of my dreams or that I should visit them. As in actual life, they were usually situated down obscure side streets and more often than not consisted of no more than a single room crammed with books. There would also be an elderly, overalled proprietor, whom in the course of my visits I would get to know. During the last few years I have dreamed of huge leather-bound volumes as well as of daintily produced volumes of more recent date. On waking up in the morning, I have sometimes even remembered the titles of books bought in my dreams. There was one dream in which I bought so many books that I had to ask friends to help carry them home. Besides bookshops, there were also tea shops in my dreams, where I sometimes had a cup of tea and a piece of cake. These dreams were more frequent during the years I was having acupuncture, first twice a week and eventually once a month. I had dreams of children and small animals, especially white kittens, which my acupuncturist took to mean that I was getting better. There was also a big, angry, black bull and I had to run fast to shut the gate and prevent him from getting out.

The American Indians are said to distinguish between 'big dreams' and 'little dreams', and perhaps my bookshop and tea shop dreams were of the latter kind. There were also dreams, especially after I moved from Madhyamaloka to Adhisthana, which could be considered as being more like 'big dreams'. These began with a series in which I lived in dark, gloomy, caves, sometimes on my own and sometimes with others, the others being either Tibetan monks, or yogis, or even yellow-clad *bhikkhus*. Once or twice I was myself a *bhikkhu*, living with other *bhikkhus* in India or Thailand. In these dreams I had friends among the *bhikkhus*, though they were all dream friends, some of whom I had known for a long time, and not any of the *bhikkhu* friends I had known in actual life. Alternating with these dreams there were dreams of an initiatory nature. What I was being initiated into I do not know but the atmosphere of the place was solemn, mysterious. And in one dream the initiation was also an ordination. I very much wanted this ordination and I received it thanks to the intervention of someone I knew, who approached the giver of the initiation on my behalf. At one point the latter was standing beside me and squeezed my arm as a sign that he would be giving me the initiation, whereupon I burst into tears. In actual life I am unable to shed tears whether of joy or sorrow, as my current medication makes me feel 'detached', as my GP warned me it could do. It was a relief to know that the medication did not operate in the world of my dreams.

Not all my dreams at this period were of a religious or spiritual nature. Some were very mundane, not to say worldly, and in at least two of them I was myself being quite worldly. In such dreams I was in my late teens or early twenties, and in one of them I had come to know an extremely rich man, probably an American. This man, who was about the same age as my father, gave me a million pounds (or was it a million dollars?), at the same time telling me that if within three years I could double the amount by my own efforts he would take me into partnership in his business. I did not succeed in doubling the amount, so was not taken into partnership; but I did not mind this, as I was having other interesting dream experiences. In one dream I was exploring the extent of a vast American university, in another I was buying a new suit, while in another I was travelling about in space on some business of my own. The craft in which I travelled was white, and I was surrounded by the same blue sky as in other dreams. Sometimes I experienced a sense of expansion, of unknown possibilities, and even of freedom from cares.

The London of the seventeenth century was not the London I knew. In several dreams I looked at it from above. It was busy and bustling and more like an anthill than a truly human habitation. At times I looked down, not at the city itself but at a great map in which every single building and every single person was distinctly depicted. In later dreams this London was overwhelmed by tribes coming from the north, and there seemed to be a pattern. People of various kinds moved not only from north to south but also from south to north, the latter being more widespread and more diverse. I saw little bands from Nepal moving up into Tibet as well as individuals making their solitary way from south to north in a variety of geographical contexts. Sometimes there would be fighting between individuals as well as between groups, and this would sometimes take place on the upper slopes of the great mountain that was often the focus of my dreams. In dreams of this kind there was darkness rather than light and the sense of everything human being at an early stage of development.

In some dreams I visited places of which I had dreamed before so that it seemed that the place possessed a kind of existence in the dream world. Such was the hill with which I became very familiar. It was covered with trees and bushes and there was a deserted stone cottage from which I had a view down the hillside, as well as having a glimpse of white houses below. With the stone cottage as my base, I wandered about on my own. The ground was very uneven, and I had to be careful where I trod. Only rarely did I meet anybody. Once it was an old woman gathering sticks, while on another occasion it was a young French couple, tourists, who had lost their way and whom I directed to the nearest road.

Though there were places which I have visited more than once in my dreams there was at least one place which I visited only once and which had, moreover, a unique conclusion. This place was a tract of English woodland far from any habitation. It was not only quiet and peaceful but had an atmosphere that could only be described as spiritual. As I wandered about I became aware that I was not alone for there were *arhants* living in the woodland, and though I could not see them I could feel their presence. I do not know how long I wandered there, whether for hours or days, and whether as reckoned by earth time or dream time, but suddenly there was a great change. The dream woodland vanished and was replaced by a memory that had been submerged for decades.

When I was seven my father took me to see a work friend called Arthur Govey. He lived in Morden at the southernmost end of the Northern Line and on leaving the Tube I noticed that the houses were all newly built. Arthur lived in one of these with his wife Elise and son Roy, a boy of my own age, but all I remember of the visit was that the house had a billiard table and that Arthur and my father spent the evening playing billiards. It was not long before our two families were meeting on Wimbledon Common on Sundays. We had a favourite spot and while our elders talked, Roy and I would wander off into a stretch of woodland, where the trees made a pleasant shade and where the green ferns grew breast high. Roy and I made a clearing in the ferns which we regarded as our headquarters, and we investigated the rotted underside of a great log where there were to be seen tiny snails of various colours. When my dream of a tract of English woodland ended, it was the memory of the time I had spent with Roy that succeeded it. I had not thought of Arthur Govey for years, nor of Roy, nor of the part of Wimbledon Common in which Roy and I wandered more than eighty years ago. Now I remembered them clearly, the memory having been nudged into existence by my dream of that tract of English countryside where *arhants* dwelt.

6
SCIENCE AND POETRY, BUDDHISM AND ISLAM

Science and Poetry: A Note · Buddhism and Islam · Islam and the Buddha · My Muslim Friend

SCIENCE AND POETRY: A NOTE

On 15 March I woke up to the news that Stephen Hawking had died the previous day. In the course of the following days and weeks tributes to him poured in from all over the world. I then knew very little about him. My interests were confined largely to religion and philosophy and the fine arts, whereas Stephen Hawking was a theoretical physicist and cosmologist of whose discoveries in connection with black holes I had heard but vaguely. In my teens, when I had read so much, the only book of popular science with which I was acquainted was Sir James Jeans' *The Mysterious Universe*,[647] which touched my imagination more than my intellect. This did not mean that I was 'against' science, but as I came to know more about Buddhism I became aware that some modern Buddhists, in their eagerness to propagate the Dharma, were taking the name of science in vain. Buddhism was scientific, and the fact that it was scientific proved that it was true. Indeed some went so far as to claim Buddhism had in its own way anticipated important scientific discoveries. My own view was that Buddhism could be described as scientific only in the sense that it was based, like science, on reason and observation, rather than on authority, whether that of the Bible or Vedas.

Besides tributes to his achievements as a theoretical physicist and cosmologist there were also tributes to the courage and determination with which he had overcome extreme physical disabilities. He had even written books. One of these was frequently mentioned in the tributes paid him. This was the best selling *A Brief History of Time*, which had been translated into many languages and of which even I had heard. I therefore decided that I ought to read it and ordered an audiobook version. Having gone through it once, I decided that I ought to go through it a second time, for though the book was clearly – even beautifully – written, the territory it covered was strange to me and called for more reflection. Indeed, I was about to go through it a for a third time, when a friend reminded me that *A Brief History of Time* had been published in 1988, more than thirty years ago, and that it was not the last word on its subject. He therefore recommended that I read Carlo Rovelli's *Reality Is Not What It Seems*, published in 2014.

This was even better written than *A Brief History of Time*. Moreover, in his preface Rovelli more than once speaks of the beauty of the world in a way that suggests he sees it aesthetically as well as scientifically. Later on, in the body of the work, he brings poetry and science closer together doing this by referring to Einstein's idea of the 3-sphere and a passage in Dante's *Paradiso*. 'I believe', Rovelli writes:

> that this example demonstrates how great science and great poetry are both visionary, and may even arrive at the same intuitions. Our culture is foolish to keep science and poetry separated: they are two tools to open our eyes to the complexity and beauty of the world. Dante's 3-sphere is only an intuition within a dream. Einstein's 3-sphere has mathematical form and follows from the theory's equations. The effect of each is different. Dante moves us deeply, touching the sources of our emotions. Einstein opens a road towards the unsolved mysteries of our universe. But both count among the most beautiful and significant flights that the mind can achieve.[648]

This could hardly be better put, especially as he describes 'the flights of the mind' as beautiful. Nor is that all. When he comes to describe Faraday's discovery of the electromagnetic field he does so with the help of such terms as insight, intuition, inspiration, and imagination, all of which are as applicable to a poem, a painting, a musical composition, as they are to a scientific discovery. The Buddhist may well wonder whether the insight or intuition of which Rovelli speaks in connection with Faraday's discovery is the same as the insight developed by the Buddhist in meditation. In other words, is it an insight that liberates from greed, hatred, and delusion? Perhaps time alone will tell, as Buddhists study science and scientists practise meditation.

BUDDHISM AND ISLAM

'As a Buddhist, I am utterly opposed to the encouragement of violence and discrimination against Muslims in Burma and elsewhere in the name of Buddhism.' Such was the opening sentence of a statement which, in my personal capacity, I signed on 19 September 2013. The statement went on to declare that there could be no Buddhist justification for such violence. 'To engage in or incite violence motivated by hatred and prejudice goes against the teachings of the Buddha and is a fundamental breach of Buddhist ethical principles, including Buddhist monastic vows.'[649]

What had particularly shocked me was the fact that Buddhist monks had encouraged the violence and even taken part in it themselves. They had, of course, their apologists, some of whom had created a history according to which Islam, having been responsible for the disappearance of Buddhism from India, was now threatening the Buddhist countries of South-east Asia.

My awareness of the existence of Islam goes back to my early years. Madame Blavatsky's *Isis Unveiled* having opened my eyes to the existence of religions other than Christianity, I set myself to investigate as many of them as I could, and Islam, one of the world's major religions, naturally attracted my attention. As my custom was, I went straight to the source, reading three different translations of the *Koran* (Sale's, Rodwell's and Palmer's).[650] The reading left me with a rather confused impression. Islam was clearly monotheistic but it was also preoccupied with such subjects as divorce, which was of no interest to me. Yet it also contained short, poetic passages of extreme beauty which appealed to me. Later on I came across the works of Hafiz, Attar, and Rumi,[651] much of whose poetry was saturated with Sufism and therefore with Islam. When I was 18 the army took me to India where I saw some of the great monuments of Islamic architecture in Delhi, Agra, and Lucknow. This contact with the cultural side of Islam continued many years later when, with a friend, I visited Córdoba, Granada, and Seville.

It was at about this time that I came across the writings of Henri Corbin, beginning with *Avicenna and the Visionary Recital*, and going on to *Creative Imagination in the Sufism of Ibn 'Arabi*, and *The Man of Light in Iranian Sufism*.[652] These works made a deep impression on me, revealing as they did that there was a philosophical and mystical side to Islam of which the Western world was largely ignorant. In 1982 I therefore led a seminar on Al-Ghazali's *The Duties of Brotherhood in Islam*, a translation of which was readily available.[653] We soon discovered similarities between the Buddhist ideal of spiritual friendship and Islam's ideal of brotherhood. We also learned that according to Al-Ghazali there were three degrees of brotherhood, the first being when you gave your friend whatever you could, the second when you shared with him equally, and the third when you were delighted when he took something of yours without even asking. For Islam, as for Buddhism, friendship was part of the spiritual life.

Twenty years later, however, the Western world was destined to see another side of Islam. The Jihadists were seen beheading their captives on video and on 11 September 2001 there came the unexpected and horrific attack on the Twin Towers in New York. I had seen those towers from Central Park and a day or two after the attack I wrote a short poem.

Proudly they stood, those towers, a monument
To money, and the power that money brings.
But hate was stronger. Now they lie in dust,
And impotent hands a mighty nation wrings.

Like millions of other people I felt deeply for the nearly 3,000 people who had lost their lives in the attack, and images of men and women throwing themselves from upper storey windows have haunted me ever since. I also realized that what came to be called simply '9/11' would affect the attitude of the Western world towards Islam for years to come.

A few days ago a friend drew my attention to a book that presaged a more hopeful relation between Buddhism and Islam than what at present exists in Burma and Thailand. The book was *Common Ground between Islam and Buddhism* by Reza Shah Kazemi, a specialist in comparative mysticism, Islamic Studies, Sufism, and Shi'ism. According to the publishers, 'this groundbreaking book explores the scriptural and spiritual tenets of Islam and Buddhism in relation to one another, creating a basis for comparison and analysis of the two traditions.' It 'discusses metaphysical traditions and philosophical studies born of Islam and Buddhism, places them in context with each other, thus encouraging understanding, and providing a point of reference for continued learning and cooperation.' I have not read the book, but I have ordered a copy, and look forward to getting a friend to read me extracts from it.

In the UK we have 2.7 million Muslims, the vast majority of whom live at peace with their non-Muslim fellow-citizens. There are Muslims in almost every walk of life and it is difficult for us to avoid contact with them, even if we had wanted to do so; and the more that contact is informed by a knowledge of Islam and its culture the better it will be for us all.

ISLAM AND THE BUDDHA

Shah Kazemi's *Common Ground Between Islam and Buddhism* having arrived, I lost no time in dipping into it with the help of friends. In particular I looked into the section on Koranic premises of dialogue between Islam and Buddhism. Before following this up, however, I want to recount two memories that came to me after I had written my article 'Buddhism and Islam'. These related not to Islam but to the Prophet Mohammed. As readers of *The Rainbow Road* will be aware, from the age of 8 I was well acquainted with the pages of the multi-part *Children's Encyclopaedia*.[654] In one issue there were pictures of the founders of the various world religions. One of these showed Mohammed, depicted wearing a turban and with a sword in his hand. The other memory is of a picture postcard that represented Mohammed in a very different way. He wears a green coat and a turban and is sitting astride Buraq, the mule with the head and face of a woman, and I particularly remember her expression of extreme intelligence. She is guided through the air by the archangel Gabriel, and angelic figures holding censers and other objects hover around the Prophet. Years later I learned that this representation of Mohammed depicted his famous 'Night Journey' from Mecca to Jerusalem and back.

With the help of quotations from the Koran, Shah Kazemi establishes that like the Jews and the Christians the Buddhists have a Book (*Kitāb*) in the form of the Buddhist scriptures, as well as a messenger in the form of the Buddha.[655] He therefore believes that it should be possible to say that the Buddha was a Messenger, inspired by God with a message that was destined to become the basis of a global religious community. Though not specifically mentioned by name in the Islamic revelation, like Noah, Abraham, and Ishmael, the Buddha was nonetheless a prophet in the Islamic sense. This argument is strengthened, he believes, in view of the fact that ten percent of the world is Buddhist and that according to the Koran a messenger has been sent to every community. Moreover, the messenger will speak the language of that community.

Sixty or more years ago, I published an article with the title 'Religion as Revelation and as Discovery',[656] in which I described both religion as revelation and religion as discovery in what I called their 'chemically pure' state. Christianity and Islam were examples of religion as revelation whereas Buddhism was an example of religion as discovery. At the conclusion of the article I attempted to mitigate the absoluteness of the difference between the two forms of religion by declaring that in the case of the Buddha, religion as discovery ultimately contained religion as revelation. By this I meant that the Buddha, having discovered the truth, proceeded to reveal it to humanity. Shah Kazemi sees things differently. He believes that the Buddha, like Mohammed, was the recipient of a revelation from on high and he therefore does not see the Buddha as discovering the truth at a deeper level of his own being. Indeed, he sees the fact that the Buddha is called the Tathāgata as supporting his position. According to Bhikkhu Ñāṇamoli and Bhikkhu Bodhi, whom he quotes, Tathāgata means, 'thus come' (*tathā āgata*) and 'thus gone' (*tathā gata*), that is, the one who *comes* into our midst bearing the message of deathlessness to which he has *gone* by his own practice of the path.[657]

Thus Shah Kazemi sees the Buddha as being like Mohammed, a messenger from God, and his message as being a true religion or *dīn*. Besides seeing the Buddha as a prophet like Mohammed, Shah Kazemi also sees him as both messenger (*rasūl*) and saint (*walī*). As he explains,

> the Buddha's enlightenment comprises two aspects, one of which was proper to him alone, the other which is universally accessible. The first aspect can indeed be regarded as the source of his 'prophecy', to use Islamic terms, the 'message' or *sāsana* which formed the basis of the Buddhist tradition; in this respect, no other sage or 'prophet' is conceivable in the Buddhist tradition, and none can attain to his status, as regards what in Islam would be called his *risāla*, his message.[658]

Like other books of an ecumenical nature, *Common Ground Between Islam and Buddhism* contains a foreword by the Dalai Lama. 'This is an important and pioneering book, which seeks to find common ground between the teachings of Islam and of Buddhism', the Tibetan leader writes. 'It is my hope that on the basis of this common ground, followers of each tradition may come to appreciate the spiritual truths their different paths entail and from this develop a basis for respect for each others' practice and beliefs.'

As Shah Kazemi looks for common ground between Islam and Buddhism, the government and army of Buddhist Myanmar continue to persecute the Rohingya Islamic minority. 'Last week I returned from refugee camps in Bangladesh,' writes Hozan Alan Senauke in the May–August *Seeds of Peace*, 'where 700,000 people have fled Myanmar – a country where Buddhism is the state religion – crossing into precarious exile in southern Bangladesh.' He continues:

> The Rohingyas are a Muslim ethnic minority, who have lived in Myanmar's western Rakhine state for many generations. The roots of this conflict are complex and arguable. But the sheer scale of Rohingya suffering goes beyond all argument and justification. What I saw of the camps was a seemingly endless, sprawling, dusty tangle of tents fashioned from bamboo strips and plastic sheets. There are open sewers running in thick streams beside the dirt pathways. The refugees, among them huge numbers of children, are everywhere. I heard stories of their villages burning just miles away in Myanmar. I was told of unimaginable violence, of mass rape and murder, of soldiers throwing babies into the flames. Satellite imagery shows the devastation of villages in Myanmar, but nothing can convey the realities of frightened and broken

> people, bereft of families, land and livelihood. The Rohingya people I met speak of this as the 'Buddhist terror', an unholy alliance of the Myanmar army, monks and Rakhine Buddhists. The terrible irony is that a decade ago, the world's Buddhists witnessed Myanmar's 'Saffron Revolution'. Monks and nuns courageously faced down the military's guns and bayonets, chanting the Metta Sutta, the Buddha's ancient verse of lovingkindness, which includes this verse: '… as a mother at the risk of her life watches over and protects her only child, so with a boundless mind should one cherish all living things, suffusing love over the entire world.…'[659]

MY MUSLIM FRIEND

During my years in India I made many friends. Most of them were Hindu or Buddhist, but I also had Christian and Jewish friends, as well as friends who were Zoroastrians or followers of the Bahá'í faith. It was only in 1964, towards the end of my stay, that I acquired a Muslim friend. I was paying a farewell visit to Bombay and giving lectures in various parts of the city. Bombay was a cosmopolitan place, and as usual people of all faiths and none came to hear me. After one of these lectures I was approached by a tall, handsome young man in western dress. His name was Ramzam Ali, he told me, and in the course of the next few weeks he became my first Muslim friend. Besides coming to other lectures he visited me at the flat in Malabar Hill where I was staying and as he was rather communicative I soon knew quite a lot about him. He lived with his widowed mother who wanted him to take over the running of the family business, marry, and beget children, but he wanted to do none of these things. He was an innocent child of God, he declared, and he wanted to lead a spiritual life. He had no desire for worldly prosperity or for sex, and had his mother not insisted on stuffing him with mutton he would have been a vegetarian long ago.

In the course of our friendship he often spoke of himself as being an innocent child of God, and I came to associate the phrase with him. What he meant by it was not always clear and its connotation seemed more negative than positive. By birth he belonged to the Ismaili branch of Shi'ite Islam and he had a great devotion to its leader, the Aga Khan. The present holder of the office was a young man like himself, he once told me, and a few years earlier he had written to him about some doubts he was experiencing and had received a sympathetic reply signed by the Aga Khan himself. Though devoted to the Aga Khan, Ramzam Ali was hardly an orthodox follower of his branch of the Shi'ite tradition. He believed that the Aga Khan was identical with the Kalki avatar of Hinduism. It would seem that in some quarters there was a partial overlap between popular Hinduism and popular Islam. According to Hindu tradition Kalki was the tenth and last avatar of the god Vishnu and riding a white horse he would purge the earth of unbelievers and establish the reign of righteousness.

One day Ramzam Ali brought his mother to see me. She did not wear a veil and her corpulent person was swathed in layer upon layer of white Koranchikan work. She was not in the least shy and at once came straight to the point. Her husband had died some years ago, she told me, leaving her to run the family business and to bring up their only son. That son was now of age and it was time he took the running of the family business off her hands and married, yet whenever she spoke to him about his responsibilities he would only laugh and say that he wanted to lead a spiritual life. Could he not run a business, and raise a family, and lead a spiritual life, she wanted to know. All this she said at great length and with many repetitions, and since she spoke in Koran Gujarati, Ramzam Ali was obliged to translate. This he did rather ungraciously, laughing whenever his mother spoke of his responsibilities in a way that showed no respect for her feelings. I was left wondering why she had been willing to see me. Perhaps she had hoped that, as an older man, I would agree with her and try to persuade her son to change his mind and accept his responsibilities.

A few days later I paid a farewell visit to Poona where as usual I stayed with friends and gave talks on Buddhism. Ramzam Ali went with me, and in Poona, as in Bombay, he attended my talks. By this time he knew something about Buddhism, due partly to attending my talks and partly to our spending much of our time together discussing the Dharma. He particularly liked hearing about my experiences as a freelance wandering ascetic. One day a local guru of whom I had not heard before invited me to visit his ashram. He was a very modern guru and his ashram was situated in the most fashionable part of Poona. It consisted of a large bungalow furnished and decorated mainly in modern western style. The guru was a youngish man clad in the traditional *gerua* and except for his long black hair he could have passed for a monk of the

Ramakrishna Mission. He was not a follower of Ramakrishna, however, but of Sri Aurobindo and of Anandamayi, whose silver-framed portraits decorated his comfortable sitting room. Ramzam Ali was fascinated by the guru and the fascination must have been mutual, for a few days later the guru invited Ramzam Ali to stay with him and I had to return to Bombay without my young Muslim friend.

7
LAST WORDS

Rebirth Revisited · A Word on the Mantrayāna

REBIRTH REVISITED

Buddhism has assumed a variety of forms over the centuries, but basically there are two forms, the *śrāvakayāna* and the *bodhisattvayāna*, otherwise known as the Hīnayāna and the Mahāyāna. Each has its own ideal, that of the *śrāvakayāna* being the *muni* or *arhant*, while the ideal of the *bodhisattvayāna* is that of Supreme Perfect Buddhahood. Both ideals, together with the spiritual practices associated with them, are undergirded by a basic common principle without which they would be meaningless. This principle is that of karma and rebirth. Christianity and Islam teach that a man or woman has only one life, after which he or she goes to heaven or hell, or spends some time in purgatory prior to admission to heaven. Buddhism, Jainism, Sikhism, and post-Vedic Hinduism teach that a man is born and dies and is reborn again and again, the process having no perceptible beginning, and ending only when, in the case of the *śrāvaka*, Nirvāṇa is attained or when, in the case of the bodhisattva, Supreme Perfect Buddhahood is attained.

In recent times doubts have arisen regarding karma and rebirth. It has even been questioned whether the Buddha himself taught the doctrine to his disciples. In a recent publication, *Rebirth in Early Buddhism and Current Research*, Bhikkhu Anālayo seems to have settled the matter once and for all. 'The doctrine of rebirth is an integral and essential component of early Buddhist thought,' he writes, 'and cannot be reduced to a taking over of popular notions from ancient Indian background. Tradition considers rebirth and its working mechanics to have been verified by the Buddha himself on the night of his awakening. Rebirth is also intrinsically intertwined with the different levels of awakening recognised in early Buddhist thought.'[660] He further writes:

> The early Buddhist doctrine of rebirth does not involve a simple mind-body duality, nor does it posit an unchanging entity to be reborn. Instead, continuity during life and beyond is conceived of as a changing process of a plurality of interrelated mental and physical phenomena that operate under the overarching influence of a complex set of causes and conditions. Centrally important conditions here are one's own intentional actions (karma) at the bodily, verbal and mental level. Operating within a wider network of conditions, karma and its fruit are not deterministic, and the time period for a deed to produce its fruit can vary greatly, such that karmic fruition can take place at a time far removed from the original deed.[661]

By its very definition the *bodhisattvayāna* implies the existence of rebirth. Whatever his level of attainment may be, the bodhisattva sees himself as working towards the attainment of Buddhahood not simply in his present existence, but for aeons upon aeons of lives. One cannot, therefore, claim to follow the bodhisattva path or even to be a follower of the Mahāyāna and at the same time be unwilling to accept the reality of rebirth. Similarly, by its very nature the *śrāvakayāna*, too, implies the existence of rebirth. As Anālayo points out, 'Rebirth is also intrinsically intertwined with the different levels of awakening recognised in early Buddhist thought.' Thus, the Stream Entrant, who destroys the first three fetters, will be reborn no more than seven times; the once-returner, having weakened two more fetters, will be reborn only once more; and the non-returner, having destroyed those two fetters, is reborn in one of the 'pure abodes'. As for the *muni* or *arhant*, having destroyed all ten fetters, he has attained Nirvāṇa and is reborn no more. Thus the path of the *śrāvaka*, like that of the bodhisattva, is unthinkable without the doctrine of rebirth.

It should not be thought, however, that the *śrāvakayāna* and the *bodhisattvayāna* are mutually exclusive in every respect. In the ten *pāramīs* the *śrāvakayāna* has its own version of the bodhisattva path, while many of the Mahāyāna *sūtras* are replete with the doctrinal formulas of the *śrāvakayāna*. Moreover, the *śrāvakayāna*'s path of generosity, ethics, meditation, and wisdom can be seen as corresponding to the six *pāramitās* of the *bodhisattvayāna*, it being necessary only to add energy and patience, both of which are in any case to be found within the *śrāvakayāna* tradition.

The two *yānas* can also be seen as complementary. This became obvious as Buddhism spread and developed, and as the two *yānas* sought to embody their respective spiritual ideals in human form. Thus, there appear statues and paintings of *arhants* and bodhisattvas. The *arhants* are generally depicted as elderly monks. They are shaven-headed and carry a staff, and their bearing is mindful and austere. It is evident that they have spent many years meditating in caves and jungles and that they are true individuals. Indeed, in Chinese and Tibetan art their individuality is often greatly exaggerated, even to the point of caricature. Thus we have the laughing *arhant*, the grimacing *arhant*, and even the 'mad' *arhant*. The bodhisattvas, on the other hand, are generally represented as beautiful young men. They are clad in diaphanous silken garments of various colours, have jewelled diadems on their heads, and are hung about with strings of jewels, as are their no less beautiful female counterparts. A gentle smile hovers about their lips and their expression is one of compassion. It is evident that they feel for the sufferings of sentient beings and are prepared to give whatever help they can. Perhaps the best-known depiction of a bodhisattva is the painting of Padmapāṇi in one of the Ajanta caves. He holds an open blue lotus and his graceful body is bent as though he is listening to the cries that come from the world below. The more we tread this or that spiritual path, the more vivid does its spiritual ideal become, especially if we practise one of the traditional *sādhanas* and repeat the corresponding mantra.

Besides statues of *arhants* and bodhisattvas there are statues of the Buddha, some of them a hundred feet or more in height. Whether followers of the Hīnayāna or the Mahāyāna, Buddhists alike believe that ages ago the ascetic Sumedha, in the world period of the Buddha Dīpaṅkara, vowed to attain Supreme Perfect Enlightenment for the sake of all beings. This vow he eventually fulfilled in the present world period when, as the historical Siddhārtha Gautama, he achieved Supreme Perfect Enlightenment seated under the *bodhi* tree at what became Bodh Gaya. Thereafter he taught the way to Nirvāṇa and hundreds of men and women became *arhants*. He did not teach the bodhisattva path, or at least there is no record of his having done so in the scriptures of early Buddhism, the *pāramīs* being a later accretion.

When talking about the goal of Buddhism, we should be careful to make it clear whether we are talking about Nirvāṇa or Supreme Perfect Enlightenment, the Buddha himself being, of course, both *arhant* and *samyak-sambuddha*, as the traditional salutation to the Three Jewels makes clear. Otherwise, people may be talking at cross-purposes.

A WORD ON THE MANTRAYĀNA

There are two principal forms of Buddhism, the *śrāvakayāna* and the *bodhisattvayāna*, otherwise known as the Hīnayāna and the Mahāyāna. The Mahāyāna has two divisions, the *pāramitāyāna* and the *mantrayāna*. The *pāramitāyāna* consists in the practice of the six *pāramitās* over a huge number of successive lives and for an inconceivable period of time. Its goal is Supreme Perfect Enlightenment. The follower of the *mantrayāna*, also known as the Vajrayāna, may practise the *pāramitās* and even the ethics and meditation of the *śrāvakayāna* but what really propels him or her along his or her chosen path is the fact that he or she practises with the help of mantras. It is the mantras that do the work, so to speak. Not only do they do the work, but mantras have the effect of shortening the time the bodhisattva or *mantrin* takes to achieve his or her goal. Indeed, with the help of mantras one may be able to achieve Supreme Perfect Enlightenment within the compass of a single human lifetime, as Milarepa is believed to have done.

But what is a mantra? In the Vajrayāna or *mantrayāna* it is a group of words or sounds imbued with a certain spiritual power. A mantra may also consist of a single word, or even a single sound, and it may or may not possess a meaning in the ordinary sense of the term. A Western scholar has therefore suggested that the *mantrayāna* should be known in English as the Path of Magic. A mantra 'works' by virtue of the fact that it is the locus of a power or energy which is unknown to science and cannot be measured by ordinary means. To the non-Buddhist observer and even to the follower of the *śrāvakayāna*, the *mantrayāna* may seem to be little more than a web of fantasies and delusions and even a means of exploiting the credulous and gullible. It may also be charged that the Mantrayāna represents, sociologically speaking, a regression to the old pre-Buddhist, Vedic way of thinking. However, there are people who find this 'magical' Buddhism very attractive, especially when the mantra is experienced within a context of light and colour and in association with an archetypal Buddha or bodhisattva.

With the help of a mantra or mantras one passes through the various stages of the Vajrayāna path. These stages correspond to the stages of the bodhisattva path, to which they are in fact equivalent. What would take a bodhisattva thousands of lives to achieve is achieved by the *mantrin* within a comparatively short period, and it is for this reason that the path of the mantra is said to be the short path. Thus, between the path of mantra and the bodhisattva path there is a correlation similar to that between the stages of the *śrāvakayāna* and the number of lives remaining to the practitioner, except that for the *arhant* who attains Nirvāṇa there are no further lives. One therefore sees that, from a certain point of view, the *mantrayāna* path parallels the *śrāvakayāna*. At the same time, there is an important difference, and that difference gives rise to a difficulty. The goal of the *mantrayāna* is Supreme Perfect Enlightenment. This is also the goal of the *bodhisattvayāna*, but the *mantrin* achieves it much more quickly than the bodhisattva, which is probably one of the reasons for the popularity of this path.

But what is a *samyak-sambuddha*? A *samyak-sambuddha* is a bodhisattva who, after traversing the entire bodhisattva path, achieves *samyak-sambuddha*-hood in his last existence and thereafter teaches the Dharma in a world where all trace of it has been lost. Thus, there can be only one Buddha at a time in the world. There can no more be two Buddhas at once than there can be two suns in the sky or two universal rulers on earth. But where does this leave Milarepa? He is believed to have achieved the highest goal of the Vajrayāna, which of course is *samyak-sambuddha*-hood, and this would appear to contradict the general Buddhist teaching about the nature of *samyak-sambuddha*-hood. So far as I am aware, no Vajrayāna teacher has addressed this problem, but there may well be a solution to it hidden away in the esoteric depths of the tradition.

There is also Maitreya Buddha, i.e. Maitreya Samyaksambuddha, who is thus styled proleptically, he not having yet attained to the end of the bodhisattva path. Nonetheless, many Buddhists worship and meditate upon him. Indeed, it has been pointed out that the worship of Maitreya is common to both the Theravāda and the Mahāyāna, so that his worship could be a means of union for all Buddhists.

A mantra does not come to one by accident. It comes to one from a qualified guru who has received it from their own teacher and so on, back along a line that may begin with an archetypal Buddha or bodhisattva. The transmission of the mantra from guru to disciple generally takes place within a ritual context and creates between them a *samaya* or bond which binds the disciple to the guru for life and even beyond. It pledges the disciple to accept whatever treatment they receive at the hands of the guru, however contrary the treatment may be to the usages of society. A breach of *samaya* on the part of the disciple entails serious, even terrible, consequences. According to some authorities it entails rebirth in the Vajra Hell and a stay there for a very long time, but I find it difficult to believe how a teaching of this kind could have arisen within the Vajrayāna, however serious some teachers may have considered any breach of *samaya* by the disciple to be.

There is also the question of whether the occult energy or 'power' generated by the practice of the *mantrayāna* could be used for the furtherance of mundane interests or for the protection of Buddhism. In the early 1950s I was living in Kalimpong, a small town in the foothills of the eastern Himalayas. The Chinese troops had crossed the border with Tibet and were on their way to Lhasa, the capital. Kalimpong was then full of Tibetans, some of whom told me that the Dalai Lama had ordered the lamas of the Tantric College, who were advanced practitioners of the *mantrayāna*, to employ ritual magic to prevent the Chinese troops from reaching the holy city. On 9 September 1951, however, the first contingent of Chinese troops reached Lhasa. For me, this did not mean that the ritual magic of the Tantric College had necessarily failed or was a fantasy. White or black, magic depended upon the power of thought which undoubtedly could be either positive and beneficial or negative and destructive. The practice of the *mettā bhāvanā*, in which *mettā* or loving-kindness is directed first to oneself and finally to all living beings, is a positive example of the power of thought, which can transform for the better relations between individuals and between groups.

SOURCES

REFLECTIONS AND APHORISMS

These were first published in three earlier publications: *Sayings, Poems, Reflections*, Windhorse Press, Purley 1976; *Peace is a Fire*, first published by Windhorse Publications in 1979; *A Stream of Stars*, published by Windhorse Publications in 1998. All three publications originally contained poems and photographs not included here.

The sayings and aphorisms were derived from Sangharakshita's books, talks, seminars, and private correspondence. They sometimes take a slightly different form from the way they appear elsewhere in the *Complete Works* editions. Sources include:

Books, talks, and poems

The Bodhisattva Principle (*Complete Works*, vol. 4); Breaking Through into Buddhahood (*Complete Works*, vol. 11); *The Buddha's Noble Eightfold Path* (*Complete Works*, vol. 1); *Buddhism, World Peace, and Nuclear War* (*Complete Works*, vol. 12); *Buddhism and the West* (*Complete Works*, vol. 11); *Buddhism and William Blake* (*Complete Works*, vol. 26); *Crossing the Stream* (*Complete Works*, vol. 7). 'Fifteen Points for Buddhist Parents' (in *What is the Sangha?*, *Complete Works*, vol. 3); *Fifteen Points for Old – and New – Order Members* (*Complete Works*, vol. 12). *The FWBO and 'Protestant Buddhism'* (*Complete*

Works, vol. 13). 'Meditation: the Expanding Consciousness' (in *What is the Dharma?*, *Complete Works*, vol. 3); 'A Method of Personal Development' (in *Buddhism for Today and Tomorrow*, *Complete Works*, vol. 11); *Mind – Reactive and Creative* (*Complete Works*, vol. 11); *New Currents in Western Buddhism* (*Complete Works*, vol. 11); *The Path of the Inner Life* (*Complete Works*, vol. 7); 'The Path of Regular Steps and the Path of Irregular Steps' (in *The Taste of Freedom*, *Complete Works*, vol. 11); 'The Stages of the Spiritual Path' (in *What is the Dharma?*, *Complete Works*, vol. 3); *The Ten Pillars of Buddhism* (*Complete Works*, vol. 2); *A Survey of Buddhism* (*Complete Works*, vol. 1); 'A System of Meditation' (*Complete Works*, vol. 5); *The Three Jewels* (*Complete Works*, vol. 2); *Wisdom Beyond Words* (*Complete Works*, vol. 14); 'The Veil of Stars' (*Complete Works*, vol. 25).

Seminars

At the time of writing (2022) transcripts of most seminars are available at www.freebuddhistaudio.com, and are to be published in forthcoming new editions. Those quoted in this volume include seminars on the following texts:

Trevor Ling's *The Buddha* (Aryatara, 1976); the *Dhammapada* (n.d.); Zhiyi's *Dhyāna for Beginners* (Sussex, 1975); Geshe Wangyal's *The Door of Liberation* (n.d.); *The Duties of Brotherhood in Islam* (Padmaloka, 1983); *Milarepa's Heartfelt Advice to Rechungpa* (Padmaloka, 1980; an edited version appears in *Complete Works*, vol. 19); the *Itivuttaka* (1975); the *Mahāparinibbāna Sutta* (Padmaloka, 1982); 'The Nature of Existence', chapter 11 of Sangharakshita's *The Three Jewels* (Sukhavati, 1982); D. T. Suzuki's *Outlines of Mahāyāna Buddhism* (Abhirati in Norfolk, 1974); the *Precepts of the Gurus* (four seminars held at Padmaloka from 1978 to 1980); Nāgārjuna's *The Precious Garland* (Padmaloka, 1976); the *Ratnaguṇa-saṃcayagāthā* (Padmaloka, 1976); the *Sāmaññaphala Sutta* (Sukhavati, 1982); the Sevenfold Puja (n.d); the *Stability of Societies* (Wellington, New Zealand, 1979); the *Sutta-Nipāta* (Padmaloka, 1976); the *Sūtra of Golden Light* (n.d); the *Tibetan Book of the Dead* (Padmaloka, 1979); the *Udāna* (Millbrook, Cornwall, 1974). An edited version of the seminar on *The Way to Wisdom* is included in *Complete Works*, vol. 17.

THE ARTS

The Religion of Art is a collection of four essays first published by Windhorse Publications in 1988; a new, slightly revised edition was published in 2010. The publication history of the essays is as follows:

'The Meaning of Buddhism and the Value of Art' was first published in 1956 by the Maha Bodhi Society under the title 'Buddhism and Art'. 'The Religion of Art' was first published in 1973 by the Arya Maitreya Mandala in a book celebrating the 75th birthday of Anagarika Govinda. 'Advice to a Young Poet' was first published in two issues of *The Aryan Path* in 1953. 'Paradox and Poetry in *The Voice of the Silence*' was first published in 1958 by the Indian Institute of World Culture. *In the Realm of the Lotus*, Sangharakshita's conversation about art, beauty, and the spiritual life with the Finnish visual artist, musician, and critic J. O. Mallander, originally the basis of a television documentary, was published by Windhorse Publications in 1995. 'The Journey to Il Convento', 'Saint Jerome Revisited', 'A Note on *The Burial of Count Orgaz*', and 'Criticism East and West' were all published in *The Priceless Jewel* (Windhorse Publications, 1993). 'Buddhism and William Blake' was published in *Alternative Traditions* (Windhorse Publications, 1986).

This part also includes articles from *Urthona*, a 'journal of Buddhism and the arts', which takes its name from William Blake's zoa or archetypal spirit of the creative imagination, was founded in 1992 by Dharmachari Ratnagarbha (then Ambrose Gilson). Over the years Sangharakshita was interviewed for the magazine several times; many thanks to Ratnagarbha for permission to include the interviews in this volume.

LATE WRITINGS

A Moseley Miscellany: Prose and Verse 1997–2012 was published by Ibis Publications in 2015. *Adhisthana Writings* is a collection of short pieces composed during the last years of Sangharakshita's life. They have not appeared in print before, but were posted online as they were written.

NOTES AND REFERENCES

REFLECTIONS AND APHORISMS

1 H. R. Maturana and F. J. Varela, *The Tree of Knowledge*, Shambhala, Berkeley 1987, p. 245.

2 Friedrich Nietzsche, *Thus Spoke Zarathustra*, part 1, 'Of Reading and Writing,' trans. R. J. Hollingdale, Penguin Books, London 1961, p. 67.

3 Sue Prideaux, *I am Dynamite,* Faber and Faber, London 2018, p. 175.

4 Karl Kraus, 'Die Fackel' no. 270/71 (19 January 1909), translated in Thomas Szasz, *Anti-Freud: Karl Kraus's Criticism of Psychoanalysis and Psychiatry,* Louisiana State University Press, Baton Rouge 1976, p. 157.

5 Samuel Johnson, quoted in James Boswell, *The Life of Samuel Johnson*, edited by Birkbeck Hill, vol. 2, Clarendon Press, London 1887, p. 407, entry for 1775.

6 Pablo Picasso, quoted in 'Picasso Speaks', in *The Arts*, vol. 3, ed. Marius de Zayas, New York, May 1923, p. 315.

7 Joseph Joubert, quoted in Auden and Kronenberger, *Faber Book of Aphorisms, Faber and Faber, London* 1962, p. 357.

8 Subhuti, *Women, Men and Angels*: an Inquiry Concerning the Relative Spiritual Aptitudes of Men and Women, Windhorse Publications, Birmingham 1995.

9 The three *lakṣaṇas* are the 'characteristics' or 'marks' of conditioned existence: *anitya* or impermanence, *anātman* or insubstantiality, and *duḥkha* or suffering or unsatisfactoriness.

10 Buddhists traditionally undertake ethical training principles known as precepts (*śikṣāpada*).

11 These are the *brahma vihāras* or positive emotions of friendliness (*maitrī*, Pāli *mettā*), compassion (*karuṇā*), sympathetic joy (*muditā*), and equanimity (*upekṣā*, Pāli *upekkhā*), all of which have to be developed to a limitless extent.

12 The Three Jewels, so called because they represent the highest values in Buddhism, are the Buddha, the personified spiritual ideal, the Dharma, the teaching of the Way to the realization of the spiritual ideal, and the Sangha, the community of the Buddha's Enlightened followers.

13 *Bhikṣu* (Pāli *bhikkhu*), a Buddhist monk.

14 Bodhisattva, literally 'Enlightenment-being'. Someone committed to the attainment of Perfect Enlightenment for the sake of all living beings.

15 *Upāsaka*, a lay devotee. At the time of this talk, members of the Western Buddhist Order were styled *upāsakas* (m.) and *upasikās* (f.), a traditional lay ordination. Because the lay–monastic division was not relevant to ordination within the WBO, this was later changed to *dharmacāri* (m.) and *dharmacāriṇī* (f.) (literally, 'Dharma-farer').

16 Three Refuges: the Three Jewels as objects of personal commitment.

17 Mitra, literally 'friend'. In the Triratna Buddhist Community, one formally engaged in its teachings and activities as their personal spiritual path.

18 Beyond a certain point on the spiritual path, one's practice has sufficient momentum to guarantee that one will continue to progress towards Enlightenment; there is no further danger of falling back. This point was called by the Buddha 'Stream Entry', and someone who has reached it is thus a 'Stream Entrant'. For more on Stream Entry, see, for example, chapter 6, 'The Gravitational Pull and the Point of No Return' in Sangharakshita, *What is the Dharma?*, *Complete Works*, vol. 3, pp. 241–57. Among the many references to Stream Entry in the Pāli canon, the *Saṃyutta Nikāya* has a whole section devoted to the subject. See Bhikkhu Bodhi (trans.), *The Connected Discourses of the Buddha*, Wisdom Publications, Boston 2000, pp. 1788–1837; or F. L. Woodward (trans.), *The Book of the Kindred Sayings*, part 5, Pali Text Society, London 1979, pp. 296–351.

19 The phrase 'dragon's head, snake's body' is found in Japanese Buddhism. For example, Dōgen, the thirteenth-century Zen teacher, uses the expression in his *Eihei Kōroku*. In a note, the translators explain that 'a dragon head with a snake's tail' refers to something that begins

impressively and fades in the end'. See *Dōgen's Extensive Record: a Translation of the Eihei Kōroku*, trans. Taigen Dan Leighton and Shōhaku Okumura, Wisdom Publications, Boston 2010, vol. 1, pp. 77–8.

20 Vajrayāna, the Adamantine Way or Diamond Path, the third phase of the historical development of Indian Buddhism.

21 The Dharma, the Truth, the Buddha's teaching.

22 The *Dhammapada*, an ancient and very popular Buddhist scripture, in its Pāli form consists of 423 verse aphorisms (*pada*) on the Buddha's teaching (*Dhamma*).

23 *Śūnyatā*, literally voidness or emptiness; ultimate Reality.

24 *Śamatha*, literally 'calm'; the progressive unification of (mundane) consciousness. *Vipaśyanā*, literally 'clear seeing'; insight into ultimate Reality.

25 The quotation is from H. P. Blavatsky (trans.), *The Voice of the Silence*, Theosophical Publishing Company Limited, London 1889, p. 27.

26 Suchness, *tathatā* or ultimate Reality.

27 *Saṃsāra*, conditioned (mundane) existence; the process of repeated rebirth.

28 See Gampopa, *The Jewel Ornament of Liberation*, trans. Herbert V. Guenther, Shambhala Publications, London and Boston 1986, pp. 32–3.

29 The quoted expression is from *The Diamond Sūtra*. For Sangharakshita's commentary, see *Complete Works*, vol. 14, p. 477.

THE ARTS

30 Sangharakshita, *The Rainbow Road from Tooting Broadway to Kalimpong*, *Complete Works*, vol. 20, p. 451.

31 Sangharakshita, *Facing Mount Kanchenjunga*, *Complete Works*, vol. 21, p. 434.

32 Ibid. p. 436.

33 Anagarika Govinda, *Art and Meditation*, Book Faith India, Delhi, 1999 (originally published in 1936).

34 The visit is described in Sangharakshita, *Facing Mount Kanchenjunga*, *Complete Works*, vol. 21, pp. 248–56.

35 Ibid. p. 251.

36 Anagarika Govinda, *Art and Meditation*, Book Faith India, Delhi, 1999, pp. 7 & 12.

37 C. L. Stevenson, 'Persuasive Definitions', *Mind*, 47 (1938), p. 331.

38 Evidence of Sangharakshita's immersion in the world of art abounds in his letters and memoirs; some of his essays on art and literature can be found elsewhere in this volume.

39 Sangharakshita's poems have been published in *Complete Works*, vol. 25.

40 Arthur Schopenhauer mentions this idea in his Preface to

The World as Will and Representation (1818):

> I surmise that the influence of Sanskrit literature will penetrate no less deeply than did the revival of Greek literature in the fifteenth century.

Arthur Schopenhauer, *The World as Will and Representation* vol. i, trans. E. F. T. Payne, Dover Publications, New York 1969, p. xv.

41 *The Complete Works of Swami Vivekananda*, seventh edition, Advaita Ashrama, Mayavati, Almora, pp. 2–3. This parable is also contained in the Chinese *Zhuangzi*, probably originating in the fourth century BCE.

42 Plato, *The Republic*, trans. J. L. Davies and D. J. Vaughan, Macmillan, London 1923, pp. 235–7.

43 *Udāna* 6.4 in F. L. Woodward (trans.), *The Minor Anthologies of the Pāli Canon*, part 2, Pali Text Society, Oxford 1994, pp. 82–3.

44 O Bhikṣus, my words should be accepted by the wise, not out of regard for me, but after due investigation – just as gold is accepted as true only after heating, cutting and rubbing. *The Tattvasaṅgraha of Shāntarakṣita*, trans. Ganganatha Jha, Motilal Banarsidass, Delhi 1986, vol. ii, p. 1558, text 3588.

45 The quotation is from the first stanza of John Dryden's poem to music, 'A Song for St Cecilia's Day, 1687'.

46 Herbert Read, *The Meaning of Art*, Penguin Books, Harmondsworth 1951, p. 70.

47 Sri Aurobindo, *Letters on Poetry and Art, The Complete Works of Sri Aurobindo*, Sri Aurobindo Ashram, Pondicherry 2004, vol. 27, p. 6.

48 This was the French nun Thupten Chhokyi (Ani-la) whom Sangharakshita knew in Kalimpong, and of whom he writes extensively in his memoirs. See note 342.

49 Rainer Maria Rilke, *Requiem and Other Poems*, trans. from the German with an Introduction and Notes by J. B. Leishman, Hogarth Press, London 1949, p. 115.

50 Sri Aurobindo, *Letters on Poetry and Art, The Complete Works of Sri Aurobindo*, Sri Aurobindo Ashram, Pondicherry 2004, vol. 27, p. 727.

51 Ibid. p. 715.

52 Ibid. p. 590.

53 Ibid. pp. 714–5.

54 For a discussion of the first three terms, see T. W. Rhys Davids, *Dialogues of the Buddha*, part 1, Pali Text Society, London 1973, p. 7.

55 Sri Aurobindo, *Letters on Poetry and Art, The Complete Works of Sri Aurobindo*, Sri Aurobindo Ashram, Pondicherry 2004, vol. 27, p. 730.

56 *Sakkapañha Sutta*, *Dīgha Nikāya* 21 (ii. 264–7). This translation is by Dhivan Thomas Jones. For other translations, see M. Walshe (trans.), *The Long Discourses of the Buddha*, Wisdom Publications, Boston 1995, pp. 321–34; or T. W. Rhys Davids (trans.), *Dialogues of the Buddha*, part 2, Pali Text Society, London 1971, pp. 310–21.

57 *Vaṅgīsasaṃyutta*, *Saṃyutta Nikāya* (i.195–6). This translation is by Dhivan Thomas Jones. For other translations, see Bhikkhu Bodhi (trans.), *The Connected Discourses of the Buddha*, Wisdom Publications, Boston 2000, p. 292; or C. A. F. Rhys Davids (trans.), *The Book of the Kindred Sayings*, part 1, Pali Text Society, London 1979, p. 247.

58 *Vaṅgīsasaṃyutta*, *Saṃyutta Nikāya* (i.193). This translation is by Dhivan Thomas Jones. For other translations, see Bhikkhu Bodhi (trans.), ibid. pp. 289–90; or C. A. F. Rhys Davids (trans.), ibid. pp. 245–6.

59 *Mahāparinibbāna Sutta*, *Dīgha Nikāya* 16 (ii.96). This translation is by T. W. and C. A. F. Rhys Davids (trans.), *Dialogues of the Buddha*, part 2, Pali Text Society, London 1971, p. 103. See also M. Walshe (trans.), *The Long Discourses of the Buddha*, Wisdom Publications, Boston 1995, p. 243.

60 C. A. F. Rhys Davids, *Psalms of the Brethren*, Pali Text Society, London 1980, p. xxxvi.

61 C. L. A. de Silva, *The Four Essential Doctrines of Buddhism*, Associated Newspapers of Ceylon, Colombo, 1948, p. 155.

62 In 1938, Europe was rearming, but Frank Buchman was convinced that military rearmament alone would not reduce the increasing threat of war with Germany. At a meeting in London on 29 May 1938, he launched a campaign for Moral Re-Armament at which he said:

> The crisis is fundamentally a moral one. The nations must re-arm morally. Moral recovery is essentially the forerunner of economic recovery. Moral recovery creates not crisis but confidence and unity in every phase of life.

Frank N. D. Buchman, *Remaking the World*, London, 1955, p. 46. The movement was renamed Initiatives of Change in 2001.

63 This is the second stanza of Percy Bysshe Shelley's 1820 poem 'To a Skylark'.

64 This much-quoted aphorism is attributed to many sources, but not evidently to the Latin poet Horace.

65 Percy Bysshe Shelley, 'The Poet's Dream'; the lines appear

in Act I of Shelley's four-act drama *Prometheus Unbound*, first published in 1820.

66 In his poem 'The Gardener's Daughter', first published in 1842, Alfred, Lord Tennyson describes a painting in which the subject's hair is 'More black than ash-buds in the front of March'. And in the second stanza of 'Dejection: an Ode', written in 1802, Samuel Taylor Coleridge writes:

> All this long eve, so balmy and serene,
> Have I been gazing on the western sky,
> And its peculiar tint of yellow green.

67 This is presumably a reference to a passage in Plato's *Symposium*. See p. 313 below.

68 This is from Aldous Huxley's introduction to *The Selected Letters of D. H. Lawrence*, William Heineman, London 1932.

69 These are the last two lines of William Wordsworth's 'Ode on Intimations of Immortality from Recollections of Early Childhood', first published in 1807.

70 The description of the ascending scale of beauty in the *Symposium* (sections 210–2) was (according to the *Symposium* itself) a report of the words of a woman called Diotima of Mantinea, who is said by Socrates to have taught him the philosophy of love.

71 P. B. Shelley (1792–1822), from his essay 'A Defence of Poetry' written in 1821 and first published in *Essays, Letters from Abroad, Translations and Fragments* in 1840.

72 From a letter to Benjamin Bailey, 22 November 1817.

73 This is a line from the eighth book of Edwin Arnold's long poem about the Buddha, *The Light of Asia*, first published in 1879; see, for example, Edwin Arnold, *The Light of Asia*, Windhorse Publications, Birmingham 1999, p. 170.

74 Friedrich von Hügel (1852–1925) was an influential Austrian Roman Catholic. This quotation is from *Letters from Baron von Hügel to a Niece*, ed. Gwendolen Greene, J. M. Dent & Sons, London 1927, p. xxi.

75 The poet and critic Matthew Arnold described Percy Bysshe Shelley as 'a beautiful and ineffectual angel, beating in the void his luminous wings in vain' in an essay on Byron in his 1888 collection *Essays in Criticism*.

76 See note 127.

77 Walter Bagehot (1826–77), *Shakespeare the Man: an essay*, The University Society, New York 1901, p. 29.

78 This appears in William Wordsworth's preface to the *Lyrical Ballads*, published in 1802. In the twenty-sixth paragraph of the preface, he says:

I have said that poetry is the spontaneous overflow of powerful feelings: it takes its origin from emotion recollected in tranquillity: the emotion is contemplated till, by a species of reaction, the tranquillity gradually disappears, and an emotion, kindred to that which was before the subject of contemplation, is gradually produced, and does itself actually exist in the mind.

79 This is from the seventh stanza of Robert Browning's poem 'Abt Vogler', which was about the German organist Georg Joseph Vogler, known also as Abbé (or Abt) Vogler; the poem was published in 1864.

80 Aldous Huxley, *Stories, Essays and Poems* (Everyman's Library), Dent, 1960, p. 284.

81 Alfred, Lord Tennyson (1809–1892) first published his poem 'The Palace of Art' in 1832.

82 The Aesthetic Movement of the late nineteenth century championed pure beauty and 'art for art's sake', emphasizing the visual and sensual qualities of art and design over practical, moral, or narrative considerations. Oscar Wilde was a prominent member of the movement. The fashion was for green carnations to be worn in the buttonhole, signifying sexual ambiguity.

83 '*L'amor che move il sole e l'altre stelle*': Dante Alighieri, *La Divina Commedia*, *Paradiso* 33.145.

84 Isn't it time that, loving, we freed ourselves from the beloved, and, trembling, endured as the arrow endures the bow, so as to be, in its flight, something more than itself?

From the First Elegy, Rainer Maria Rilke, *Duino Elegies*, trans. A. S. Kline.

85 In a letter to Ernest Collings written on 24 December 1912, D. H. Lawrence wrote:

I always say, my motto is 'Art for my sake'. If I *want* to write, I write – and if I don't want to, I won't. The difficulty is to find exactly the form one's passion – work is produced by passion with me, like kisses – is it with you? – wants to take.

The Letters of D. H. Lawrence, vol. 1, ed. James T. Boulton, Cambridge University Press, Cambridge 1979, p. 491.

86 Aldous Huxley, *Stories, Essays and Poems* (Everyman's Library), Dent, 1960, p. 260.

87 *Bhayabherava Sutta*, *Majjhima Nikāya* 4 (i.20–1). See Bhikkhu Ñāṇamoli and Bhikkhu Bodhi (trans.), *The Middle Length Discourses of the Buddha*, Wisdom Publications, Boston 1995, p. 104; or I. B. Horner (trans.), *The Collection of the Middle Length Sayings*, vol. i,

Pali Text Society, London 1976, pp. 26–7.

88 The quotation is from John Milton's *Paradise Lost*, book I (lines 553–5); it describes how the fallen angels now in Hell, soothed by the music of flutes and recorders, move forward

> in stead of rage
> Deliberate valour breath'd, firm and unmov'd
> With dread of death to flight or foul retreat,...

89 For example, 'Māra retreated, sad and discomfited' is the last line of all the stories of Māra's encounters with *bhikkhunīs* in the *Bhikkhunīsaṃyutta* of the *Saṃyutta Nikāya*. See Bhikkhu Bodhi (trans.), *The Connected Discourses of the Buddha*, Wisdom Publications, Boston 2000, pp. 221–30; or C. A. F. Rhys Davids (trans.), *The Book of the Kindred Sayings*, part 1, Pali Text Society, London 1979, pp. 160–70.

90 For more on this, see *A Survey of Buddhism*, *Complete Works*, vol. 1, p. 20.

91 For example, section 38 of the *Alagaddūpama Sutta*, *Majjhima Nikāya* 22 (i.140); see Bhikkhu Ñāṇamoli and Bhikkhu Bodhi (trans.), *The Middle Length Discourses of the Buddha*, Wisdom Publications, Boston 1995, p. 234; or I. B. Horner (trans.), *The Collection of the Middle Length Sayings*, vol. i, Pali Text Society, London 1976, p. 180.

92 'There can be no difference that doesn't make a difference.' William James, *Pragmatism* (1907).

93 'The Devil is God turned upside down': an ancient kabbalistic motto. H. P. Blavatsky discusses it in *The Secret Doctrine*, vol. 1, Theosophical Publishing Company, London 1888, p. 411.

94 Vinaya Piṭaka ii.258–9 (*Cullavagga* 10.5); see I. B. Horner (trans.), *The Book of the Discipline*, part 5, Pali Text Society, London 1975, p. 359. Also *Aṅguttara Nikāya* iv.280 (8.53), in E. M. Hare (trans.), *Gradual Sayings*, vol. iv, Pali Text Society, Oxford 1995, pp. 186–7; or Bhikkhu Bodhi (trans.), *The Numerical Discourses of the Buddha*, Wisdom Publications, Boston 2012, p. 1193.

95 *Sutta-Nipāta* 1.3.

96 For the story of Ajātasattu's visit to the Buddha, see *Sāmaññaphala Sutta*, *Dīgha Nikāya* 2 (i.47–86); M. Walshe (trans.), *The Long Discourses of the Buddha*, Wisdom Publications, Boston 1995, pp. 91– 109; or T. W. Rhys Davids (trans.), *Dialogues of the Buddha*, part 1, Pali Text Society, London 1973, pp. 65–94. This translation is from F. L. Woodward, *Some Sayings of the Buddha*, Oxford University Press, Oxford 1973, pp. 61–2.

97 See *Dhammacakkappavattana Sutta*, *Saṃyutta Nikāya* v.421; Bhikkhu Bodhi (trans.), *The Connected Discourses of the Buddha*, Wisdom Publications, Boston 2000, p. 1844; or F. L. Woodward (trans.), *The Book of the Kindred Sayings*, part 5, Pali Text Society, London 1979, p. 357.

98 J. Evola, *The Doctrine of Awakening*, trans. H. E. Musson, Luzac, London 1951, p. 5.

99 *Alagaddūpama Sutta*, *Majjhima Nikāya* 22 (i.134–5). Bhikkhu Ñāṇamoli and Bhikkhu Bodhi (trans.), *The Middle Length Discourses of the Buddha*, Wisdom Publications, Boston 1995, pp. 228–9; or I. B. Horner (trans.), *The Collection of the Middle Length Sayings*, vol. i, Pali Text Society, London 1976, pp. 173–4.

100 *Udāna* 6.4. See also pp. 108–10 above.

101

> That the glory of this world in the end is appearance leaves the world more glorious, if we feel it is a show of some fuller splendour; but the sensuous curtain is a deception and a cheat, if it hides some colourless movement of atoms, some spectral woof of impalpable abstractions, or unearthly ballet of bloodless categories.

F. H. Bradley, *Principles of Logic II*, Oxford University Press, Oxford 1922 (second edition), p. 591.

102

> In self-restrained and unrestrained people we approve their principle, or the rational part of their souls, because it urges them in the right way and exhorts them to the best course; but their nature seems also to contain another element beside that of rational principle, which combats and resists that principle.

Aristotle, *Nicomachean Ethics*, book 1, chapter 13, section 16.

103 Tulsidas was a sixteenth-century Indian poet. His epic poem the *Rāmacaritamānasa* tells the story of the Hindu god Rama. For Sangharakshita's review of a translation of the work, see *In the Sign of the Golden Wheel*, *Complete Works*, vol. 22, p. 71.

104 Rainer Maria Rilke, *Requiem and Other Poems*, translated from the German with an Introduction and Notes by J. B. Leishman, Hogarth Press, London 1949, p. 115.

105 Herbert Read, *The Meaning of Art*, Penguin Books, Harmondsworth 1951, p. 64.

106 Rainer Maria Rilke, *Requiem and Other Poems*, translated from the German with an Introduction and Notes by J. B. Leishman, Hogarth Press, London 1949, p. 149.

107 'Art is an attempt to create pleasing forms.' Herbert Read, *The Meaning of Art*, Faber

and Faber, London 1943. 'Art is significant form.' Clive Bell, 'Art', 1914. 'Art is intuition.' Benedetto Croce, *The Essence of Aesthetic*, Heinemann 1921.

108 For the first statement, see Herbert Read, *The Meaning of Art*, Faber and Faber, London 1943, p. 19. The second seems to come from the beginning of chapter 5, 'Art and Beauty', in Jacques Maritain, *Art and Scholasticism* (trans. J. F. Scanlan, Charles Scribner's and Sons, New York 1954):

> To say with the Schoolmen that beauty is *the splendor of the form on the proportioned parts of matter*, is to say that it is a flashing of intelligence on a matter intelligibly arranged.

109 In the sixth Proposition of part 3 of *Ethics* (published posthumously in 1677), the Dutch philosopher Baruch Spinoza proposes, and goes on to assert proof, that

> Everything, in so far as it is in itself, endeavours to persist in its own being.

110 Percy Bysshe Shelley, *Prometheus Unbound*, Act IV, lines 477–8.

111 This is from William Wordsworth's long autobiographical poem 'The Prelude', book I, line 393:

> For many days, my brain
> Worked with a dim and
> undetermined sense
> Of unknown modes of
> being.

112 The quote is from Aldous Huxley's introduction to *The Selected Letters of D. H. Lawrence*, William Heineman, London 1932.

113 See p. 135 above.

114 See p. 137 above.

115 *The Notebooks of Malte Laurids Brigge* is the only novel of Rainer Maria Rilke. Published in 1910, it is semi-autobiographical, relating to the time the author spent living in Paris. This is the section called 'For the Sake of a Single Poem', translated by J. B. Leishman in his introduction to his translation of Rilke's *Requiem and Other Poems*, Hogarth Press, London 1949, p. 48.

116 Rainer Maria Rilke, *Later Poems*, Hogarth Press, London 1938, p. 243.

117 This is a note to Proposition 13 in part 3 of Spinoza's *Ethics*, published posthumously in 1677.

118
> Par l'opération d'un mystère
> vengeur
> Dans la brute assoupi un
> ange se réveille.

From 'L'aube spirituelle' ('Spiritual Dawn') in *Fleurs du Mal* (*Flowers of Evil*) (1857) by the French poet Charles Baudelaire (1821–1867). We haven't been able to trace this translation.

119 These lines are from Tennyson's dedication to his poem 'The Palace of Art', first published in 1833 and extensively altered for republication in 1842.

120 Bhagavan Das, *Science of the Emotions*, third edition, Theosophical Publishing House, Adyar, Madras 1924, p. 218.

121 B. M. Barua, 'Buddhism as Personal Religion', in *Maha Bodhi*, vol. 52, nos. 3–4, March–April 1944, Calcutta, pp. 63–4. See also B. M. Barua, *Ceylon Lectures*, second edition, Sri Sat Guru Publications, Delhi 1986, pp. 157–62; and also *A Survey of Buddhism*, *Complete Works*, vol. 1, pp. 117–18.

122 For example, in the *Ratnaguṇa-saṃcayagāthā* or 'Verses on the Accumulation of Precious Qualities', it is said of bodhisattvas that 'without a home they wander, dharmas never hold them....' For Sangharakshita's commentary on this text, see *Complete Works*, vol. 14, pp. 548–9. And the *Heart Sūtra* declares that there is no attainment and no non-attainment; for Sangharakshita's commentary see ibid. p. 362.

123 Rainer Maria Rilke, *Briefe aus Muzot*, pp. 83–4. Quoted in *Sonnets to Orpheus: the German text, with an English Translation, Introduction and Notes by J. B. Leishman*, Hogarth Press, London 1949, Introduction, p. 13.

124 Lama Anagarika Govinda, 'The Relativity of Perfection', *Stepping-Stones*, vol. 1, no. 6, Kalimpong, pp. 135–6.

125 The 'philanderings' are famously those of the poet George Gordon, Lord Byron (1788–1824), and Reading Gaol was the prison where the poet and playwright Oscar Wilde was imprisoned in 1895 for most of his two-year sentence 'with hard labour' for the crime (as it then was) of homosexuality.

126 'Heroes and Hero Worship, in Thomas Carlyle, *English Critical Essays*, selected and edited by Edmund D. Jones, Oxford University Press, p. 218.

127 'Art and Morality', in D. H. Lawrence, *Four Essays on Art and Painting*, Bureau of Current Affairs, London, p. 9.

128 See Plato, *The Last Days of Socrates*, Christopher Rowe (trans.), Penguin Books, Harmondsworth 2010, p. 43.

129 For the first of these, see Matthew 12, and for the second, Mark 7.

130 For an example of the Buddha questioning the purifying power of bathing, see the *Saṅgārava Sutta*, *Saṃyutta Nikāya* v.90–3 in F. L. Woodward (trans.), *The Book of the Kindred Sayings*, part 5, Pali Text Society, London 1979, pp. 76–8; or Bhikkhu Bodhi (trans.), *The Connected*

Discourses of the Buddha, Wisdom Publications, Boston 2000, pp. 1611–3.

For an example of the Buddha's denying the value of animal sacrifice, see the *Kūṭadanta Sutta*, in which the Buddha explains to Kūṭadanta, who has planned a great sacrifice of cows, goats, and sheep, that a much more profitable sacrifice is Going for Refuge to the Three Jewels and practising the precepts. Convinced, Kūṭadanta sets free the animals he had intended to slaughter:

> I grant them life, let them be fed with green grass and given cool water to drink, and let cool breezes play upon them.

Kūṭadanta Sutta, *Dīgha Nikāya* 5; M. Walshe (trans.), *The Long Discourses of the Buddha*, Wisdom Publications, Boston 1995, pp. 133–41; or T. W. Rhys Davids (trans.), *Dialogues of the Buddha*, part 1, Pali Text Society, London 1973, pp. 173–85.

131 This is a quotation from the Bible, Acts 3:2 (King James version), although that context is not relevant here.

132 *Saṃyutta Nikāya* iii.66. For this translation, see F. L. Woodward (trans.), *The Book of the Kindred Sayings*, part 3, Pali Text Society, London 1975, p. 58; see also Bhikkhu Bodhi (trans.), *The Connected Discourses of the Buddha*, Wisdom Publications, Boston 2000, p. 901.

133 See Aristotle's *Nichomachean Ethics*, book 10, chapter 9. The theme is developed in his *Politics*.

134 This was the Greek poet Pindar's epithet for Athens.

135 Aldous Huxley, *Music at Night*, Penguin Books, Harmondsworth 1950, p. 87.

136 Immanuel Kant, *Critique of Judgement*, sect. 42, trans. J. C. Meredith, Oxford University Press, Oxford 1911, pp. 297–8.

137 D. H. Lawrence, *Selected Essays*, Penguin Books, Harmondsworth 1950, pp. 118–19.

138 Herbert Read, *The Meaning of Art*, Faber and Faber, London 1943, p. 70.

139 Irwin Edman, *Arts and the Man: A Short Introduction to Aesthetics*, Norton, NewYork 1939, p. 128.

140 P. B. Shelley (1792–1822), from his essay 'A Defence of Poetry' written in 1821 and first published in *Essays, Letters from Abroad, Translations and Fragments* in 1840.

141 Irwin Edman, *Arts and the Man: A Short Introduction to Aesthetics*, Norton, NewYork 1939, p. 49.

142 Thomas Carlyle, 'The Hero as Poet', *English Critical Essays*, p. 220.

143 Herbert Read, *The Meaning of Art*, Faber and Faber, London 1943, p. 39.

144 This is a quotation from the poem 'The Unknown Eros: To the Body' by the nineteenth-century poet Coventry Patmore.

145 Erich Heller, 'Why Modern Poetry is Obscure', second talk, *The Listener*, London, 12 March 1953; also published in Erich Heller, *The Hazard of Modern Poetry*, Bowes and Bowes, Cambridge 1953.

146 William Shakespeare, *Henry V*, Act I, Scene ii, line 221. The whole passage is an extended metaphor suggesting the ordered life of honeybees as a model for the governance of a kingdom.

147 This is to be found in Jonathan Swift's *Thoughts on Various Subjects, Moral and Diverting*, published in 1703.

148 Sangharakshita, *A Survey of Buddhism*, *Complete Works*, vol. 1, pp. 297–9.

149 *The Voice of the Silence* is the title of a book of verses, many of which are of Mahāyāna Buddhist character, composed by H. P. Blavatsky on the basis of an original Tibetan text (by her own account, one she encountered during her studies in the East, called *The Book of the Golden Precepts*) and published in 1889.

150 Thomas De Quincey, 'The Literature of Knowledge and the Literature of Power', first published in *North British Review*, August 1848, as part of a critical essay on Alexander Pope.

151 H. P. Blavatsky, *The Voice of the Silence*, Theosophical Publishing House, Adyar 1959, section 111, p. 147.

152 For more about this, see *A Survey of Buddhism*, *Complete Works*, vol. 1, pp. 209–10 & 312–4.

153 In his essay 'Tradition and the Individual Talent' Eliot doesn't say quite this, but does say:

> Only those who have personality and emotions know what it means to want to escape from these things.

T. S. Eliot, *The Sacred Wood: Essays on Poetry and Criticism*, Alfred A. Knopf, New York 1921.

154 The origin of the traditional laws of thought are obscure, but the first can be traced back to Antonius Andreas, a scholar of Scotus, who flourished at the end of the thirteenth century CE. The others can be traced back to Plato in the fourth and fifth centuries BCE.

155 See *A Survey of Buddhism*, *Complete Works*, vol. 1, p. 206. Also Nāgārjuna, *Mūlamadhyamakakārikā*, xxiv.8–10; see K. Inada (trans.), *A Translation of the Mulamadhyamakakarika*, Hokuseido Press, Tokyo 1970, p. 146.

156 Edward Conze, *Selected Sayings from the Perfection of Wisdom*, Buddhist Society, London 1968, p. 79.

157 Ibid. p. 105.

158 Madame Guyon (1648–1717) was accused by the Catholic church of Quietism, the pejorative name they gave to a set of beliefs they regarded as heretical, and on this account she was imprisoned in the Bastille from 1695 to 1703. But it was the Spanish mystic Miguel de Molinos, another key figure in the Quietist movement, who seems to be the source of this reflection on the kinds of silence, although intriguingly the source material (chapter 8 of de Molinos' work *The Spiritual Guide*, published in 1675) suggests that he referred to three kinds of silence, which did not include the will:

> Silence from words is good, because inordinate speaking tends to evil. Silence, or rest from desires and passions, is still better, because it promotes quietness of spirit. But the best of all is silence from unnecessary and wandering thoughts, because that is essential to internal recollection, and because it lays a foundation for a proper reputation and for silence in other respects.

159 *Saṃyutta Nikāya* ii.273 (21.1). This translation is from F. L. Woodward (trans.), *Some Sayings of the Buddha*, Oxford University Press, Oxford 1973, p. 63. See also Bhikkhu Bodhi (trans.), *Connected Discourses of the Buddha*, Wisdom Publications, Boston 2000, p. 713; or C. A. F. Rhys Davids (trans.), *The Book of the Kindred Sayings*, part 2, Pali Text Society, Oxford 1997, p. 184.

160 Henri de Lubac, *Aspects of Buddhism*, Sheed and Ward, New York 1954, p. 40. The additions in square brackets are by the author. Henri de Lubac does not reveal the source of this classification.

161 H. P. Blavatsky, *The Voice of the Silence*, The Theosophical Publishing House, Adyar 1959, section 300, p. 208.

162 Ibid. section 58, p. 131.

163 Ibid. section 309, p. 210.

164 This is the eleventh definition of 'image' (the one specifically relating to the use of the word in rhetoric) in Webster's *New International Dictionary*, second edition, 1937.

165 Sangharakshita, *A Survey of Buddhism*, *Complete Works*, vol. 1, pp. 373–8.

166 The 'idle singer of an empty day' is from the first verse of the Prologue to William Morris's epic poem *The Earthly Paradise*, produced between 1868 and 1870.

'The hierophants of an unapprehended mystery' is from Percy Bysshe Shelley's essay 'A Defence of Poetry', written in 1821 and first published in *Essays, Letters from Abroad, Translations and Fragments* in 1840.

167 Thomas Carlyle, 'The Hero as Poet: Dante, Shakespeare';

Lecture 3 (12 May 1840) of the series 'On Heroes, Hero Worship, and the Heroic in History', published in a book with the same title.

168 H. P. Blavatsky, *The Voice of the Silence*, The Theosophical Publishing House, Adyar 1959, section 69, p. 135.

169 Ibid. section 36, p. 126.

170 Ibid. section 282, p. 201.

171 E. M. Hare (trans.), *Woven Cadences of Early Buddhists*, Oxford University Press, London 1945, pp. 181–2.

172 H. P. Blavatsky, *The Voice of the Silence*, The Theosophical Publishing House, Adyar 1959, sections 59–61, pp. 131–2.

173 From Shelley's 'Ode to the West Wind'.

174 See above p. 133.

175 J. O. Mallander, born 1944, has spent most of his adult life in the realm of the arts, as an artist, writer, critic, art gallery manager, film maker, and editor of four cultural journals.

176 Lama Govinda and Li Gotami's first meeting with Sangharakshita is described in *Facing Mount Kanchenjunga*, *Complete Works*, vol. 21, ch. 13, pp. 243–62. In Lama Govinda especially Sangharakshita felt he had found a kindred spirit. Their friendship continued even after both men had left India. Lama Govinda's last letter to Sangharakshita, written from California, was dated 10 January 1984. 'What a joy to have your dear long letter…' he wrote. He died just four days later.

177 Lama Anagarika Govinda, *The Way of the White Clouds*, Rider, London 1966, pp. 63–4.

178 A number of colour reproductons can be found in Lama Anagarika Govinda, *Bilder aus Indien und Tibet*, Irisiana Verlag, Haldenwang 1978. Some of his pastels can also be seen, albeit in black and white, among the illustrations in the centre of *The Way of the White Clouds*, Rider, London 1966.

179 Aldous Huxley began his talk 'Visionary Experience' (given in August 1961 at the Fourteenth Annual Congress of Applied Psychology in Copenhagen) by addressing the question 'Why are precious stones precious?' and considering the ideal world of Plato:

> not a mere metaphysical construction, a kind of inference from the facts of our present world and its imperfection. It *is* a visible world, a world which can be seen with the inner eye, and which has certain describable peculiarities – such as the colours being much brighter and it being filled with stones which are very like our precious stones. And I find here probably what is the basic psychological reason for our

immensely high valuation of precious stones, which is this: that these are the objects in the natural world which most nearly resemble things which are seen with the inner eye by people who have the gift of vision – and which even those who do not consciously have the gift of vision – have some kind of unconscious inkling of.

180 Nicholas Roerich mentions Maitreya many times in, for example, *Shambhala*, Frederick A. Stokes Company, New York 1930; see, for instance, pp. 74–7. His 1926 paintings 'Maitreya the Conqueror' and 'Banners of the Coming One' are held by the Museum of Fine Arts in Nizhny Novgorod, Russia, and the collection of the Nicholas Roerich Museum in New York includes a sketch of Maitreya.

181 See *Facing Mount Kanchenjunga*, *Complete Works* vol. 21, pp. 319–20.

182 The rishi Agastya is traditionally said to be the author of many Sanskrit texts and appeared in many Hindu legends. The mythical explanation of his journey south is that according to the *Skanda Purāṇa*, everyone on earth visited the Himalayas at the time of Shiva's marriage to Parvati, putting the earth out of kilter, so Shiva asked Agastya to go south to restore its equilibrium.

183 *The Rainbow Road from Tooting Broadway to Kalimpong*, in *Complete Works*, vol. 20, p. 345.

184 Chattrul Sangye Dorje died in 2015 at the age of 102.

185 Yeshe Tsogyal, *The Life and Liberation of Padmasambhava*, Dharma Publishing, Emeryville 1987.

186 This exhibition, 'Wisdom and Compassion: the Sacred Art of Tibet', was held at the Royal Academy in London in 1992. The catalogue is Marilyn M. Rhie et al., *Wisdom and Compassion: the Sacred Art of Tibet*, Thames and Hudson, London 1991.

187 Henry Miller, *The Colossus of Maroussi*, Penguin Books, London 2016, p. 162. It was first published in San Francisco in 1941.

188 Sangharakshita tells the story of *Ion* as part of his account of this visit to Delphi in *Moving Against the Stream*, *Complete Works*, vol. 23, pp. 278–81.

189 See below pp. 267 and 281.

190 This scene is very often depicted in Tibetan Buddhist art. We see a great ocean and a raft on which Nāgārjuna is sitting, and coming up from the depths is a serpent maiden with the books in her hands. Nāgārjuna (who flourished in India between 150 and 250 CE) is regarded as the founder of the Madhyamaka school.

191 The Yogācāra school was founded by the great teacher

Asaṅga, who, we are told, ascended in meditation to the Tuṣita *devaloka*, the heaven or state of continued happiness, and there encountered the future Buddha, Maitreya, from whom he received five books of teachings, and these form the basis of the Yogācāra school.

192 *The Wounded Angel* was painted in 1903 by the Finnish symbolist painter Hugo Simberg (1873–1917) and is considered one of Finland's most important paintings.

Cecil Collins (1908–1989) was an English artist whose paintings include *The Great Happiness* and many fools and angels; some of his sketches and paintings of angels can be seen in London's Tate Britain.

Rainer Maria Rilke's angel appears at the beginning of the first of the *Duino Elegies*, trans. J. B. Leishman and Stephen Spender, Chatto & Windus, London 1977, p. 25:

> Who, if I cried, would hear me among the angelic orders? And even if one of them suddenly pressed me against his heart, I should fade in the strength of his stronger existence.

193 Section 32 of the *Diamond Sūtra*, from Edward Conze (trans.), *Buddhist Wisdom Books*, HarperCollins, London 1988, p. 68.

194 This is Sappaka or Sabbaka, whose story is told at *Theragāthā* 307–11; see K. R. Norman (trans.), *The Elders' Verses*, Pali Text Society, Oxford 1995, p. 35; or C. A. F. Rhys Davids (trans.), *Psalms of the Brethren*, Pali Text Society, London 1980, pp. 186–7.

195 This is the *Gandhatthena Sutta*, *Saṃyutta Nikāya* i.204; see Bhikkhu Bodhi (trans.), *The Connected Discourses of the Buddha*, Wisdom Publications, Boston 2000, p. 303; or C. A. F. Rhys Davids (trans.), *The Book of the Kindred Sayings*, part 1, Pali Text Society, London 1979, pp. 260–1.

196 This is from William Wordsworth's poem 'The Tables Turned', which is addressed to a friend, urging him to leave his books and go out into the natural world.

197 See p. 185 above.

198 Later published as *The Rainbow Road from Kalimpong to Tooting Broadway*. See *Complete Works*, vol. 20, p. 451.

199 Salman Rushdie's fourth novel, *The Satanic Verses*, led to protests from Muslims in several countries, some of which were violent. Faced with death threats and a fatwa (religious edict) issued by Ayatollah Ruhollah Khomeini, then Supreme Leader of Iran, which called for him to be killed, he spent nearly a decade in hiding, appearing in public only sporadically. The lecture referred to here was

the Herbert Read memorial lecture, 'Is Nothing Sacred?', given on 6 February 1990, when it was read by Rushdie's friend Harold Pinter, as Rushdie himself was in hiding. It was subsequently published by Penguin Books, London 1990.

200 This is one of Sangharakshita's aphorisms, included above; see p. 22.

201 This is the French landscape painter Claude Lorrain (1600–1682).

202 *The Calumny of Apelles* is a panel painting in tempera by the Italian Renaissance painter Sandro Botticelli. Based on the description of an ancient lost painting by Apelles, the work was completed in 1494–5, and is now in the Uffizi, Florence.

The book referred to would have been *The FWBO and 'Protestant Buddhism'*; see *Complete Works*, vol. 13, pp. 365ff.

203 See *Complete Works*, vol. 25, pp. 544–53.

204 This short story, by the Pre-Raphaelite painter and writer Dante Gabriel Rossetti, tells the tale of a fictional Renaissance poet who realizes that the artist's only duty is to express what is in his soul. It was first published in 1850, in a magazine called *The Germ* produced by the Pre-Raphaelite Brotherhood.

205 This engraving, made in 1813 as one of twelve illustrations for *The Grave, a Poem* by Robert Blair, is now held by the Royal Academy in London.

206 This appears in William Blake's introduction to his illustration of Ruth, in the catalogue of his 1809 exhibition:

> The great and golden rule of art, as well as of life, is this: That the more distinct, sharp, and wiry the bounding line, the more perfect the work of art; and the less keen and sharp, the greater is the evidence of weak imitation, plagiarism, and bungling.

See, for example, Alexander Gilchrist, *Life of William Blake*, vol. 2, Macmillan, London 1880, p. 162.

207

> It was during this year [1836] that the then young critic [John Ruskin] emerged as Turner's most eloquent and knowledgeable supporter. Turner had exhibited at this year's Academy exhibition three paintings.... They became the object of a vitriolic attack in which an anonymous reviewer described them variously as 'a strange jumble', 'absurdities', 'a most unpleasant mixture' and altogether 'childish'. Ruskin, then only seventeen but already gifted with a preternatural alertness to art akin to genius, was enraged

> by the criticism. He drafted a reply, and sent a copy of it to Turner himself. Turner thanked him for the 'zeal, kindness and the trouble you have taken in my behalf' but added that 'I never move in these matters'. He pretended never to notice criticism, in other words, and dismissed the article as 'of no import'.

Peter Ackroyd, *J. M. W. Turner*, Random House, London 2006, pp. 132–3.

208 Lama Govinda describes how he came to this realization in *The Way of the White Clouds*, Rider, London 1966, p. 149, though in that context he does not mention Novalis by name.

209
> A novel is, or should be, also a thought adventure, if it is to be anything at all complete.

D. H. Lawrence, *Kangaroo*, Cambridge University Press, Cambridge 1994, p. 279.

210 See *Complete Works*, vol. 14, pp. 285–304.

211 The architect was Christopher Benninger, who in 1971 moved from Harvard to India, and became one of India's leading architects. He moved to Pune in 1976 and designed the Mahavihara there, several hostels, and Nagaloka, the Buddhist training college in Nagpur.

212 See above, p. 164.

213 See Malcolm Woodfield (ed.), *Defending Romanticism: Selected Essays of John Middleton Murry*, Bristol Press, Bristol 1991, p. 145.

214 Il Convento di Santa Croce, in Tuscany, Italy, was established as an Augustinian monastery in 1620. In 1790 it was taken over by Franciscans who remained there until they were turned out by Napoleon's troops in 1805. In the twentieth century it was used as a setting for operatic productions, and on several occasions its owner lent it to the Western Buddhist Order for ordination retreats.

215 This is from Alfred, Lord Tennyson's poem 'Ulysses'.

216 They are evidently more usually known as the Illuminationists. Illuminationist philosophy stems from the Arabic term *ishrāq*, meaning 'rising', in particular the rising of the sun. Also linked to the Arabic for 'east', the term is used, especially in the context of Persian poetic literature, to represent a form of thought which contrasts with cognitive reason; that is, it is taken to be intuitive, immediate, and atemporal knowledge. The source of this form of thought is often identified with the *Eastern Philosophy* (*al-hikma al-mashriqiyya*) of Ibn Sina (known in the West as Avicenna), a text about which there is a great deal of discussion, though it may never have existed.

217 Hermann Hesse (1877–1962) was a German writer whose novels include *Siddhartha*, *The Glass Bead Game*, and *Narziss and Goldmund*, all of which explore philosophical and spiritual themes. His *Journey to the East* was first published in 1932.

218 This is a reference to the Saddhamma Pradeep Retreat Centre, Triratna's first retreat centre in India, which is very near the ancient Buddhist rock-cut caves of Bhaja, in Maharashtra.

219 This is from the Irish poet W. B. Yeats' 1919 poem 'Tom O'Roughley'.

220 This is a reference to the painting 'Philosopher in Meditation', dated 1632, traditionally attributed to the Dutch painter Rembrandt. It is held by the Louvre art gallery in Paris. Recent scholarship suggests that the painting originally had another title: 'Tobit and Anna waiting for their son Tobias'.

221

> Who, if I cried, would hear me among the angelic orders? And even if one of them suddenly pressed me against his heart, I should fade in the strength of his stronger existence.

Rainer Maria Rilke, *Duino Elegies*, trans. J. B. Leishman and Stephen Spender, Chatto & Windus, London 1977, p. 25.

222 The National Gallery attributes this famous painting to the workshop of Andrea del Verrocchio, a fifteenth-century sculptor and painter who lived and worked in Florence, Italy.

223 Peter Lamborn Wilson, *Angels*, Thames & Hudson, London 1980.

224 See *Complete Works*, vol. 25, pp. 521ff.

225 *Tao Te Ching*, chapter 47.

226 W. Holman Hunt (1827–1910), one of the founding artists of the Pre-Raphaelite Brotherhood, spent time in Palestine in the mid-1850s and made a number of paintings. He went out to paint in the desert to create the atmosphere of the Scapegoat. There are two versions of this painting, the smaller version with the rainbow in the Manchester City Art Gallery, the other in the Lady Lever Gallery, Port Sunlight, near Liverpool. The image of the scapegoat had a powerful significance for Sangharakshita, as he describes in *Forty-three Years Ago* (see *Complete Works*, vol. 2, pp. 609–12); see also his poems 'Scapegoat' and 'The Scapegoat' (*Complete Works*, vol. 25, p. 328 and pp. 350–1).

227 In 1486 Pico della Mirandola, an Italian scholar and philosopher, wrote his *Oration on the Dignity of Man*, in which he placed the human quest for knowledge in a Neoplatonic framework:

The idea that men could ascend the chain of being through the exercise of their intellectual capacities was a profound endorsement of the dignity of human existence in this earthly life.

228 The 'Teaching Buddha' is Vairocana, whose name means 'illuminator'. Occupying the centre of the mandala of the five Buddhas, he is represented as brilliant white in colour, and holds his emblem, the eight-spoked golden wheel of the Dharma. His fingers make the 'wheel-turning gesture', which is associated with the Buddha's first teaching at Sarnath and represents the dissemination of truth in all directions, like the sun shining in all directions of space; and he is indeed depicted supported by lions.

229 Mañjuśrī is the protector of the Buddha 'family' of which the 'Teaching Buddha', Vairocana, is the head, and he too is associated with the lion; he is a golden amber colour, said to be the colour of a lion's eye.

230 The Summer Palace in Beijing was sacked by the British in 1900 during what was called the Boxer Rebellion. Sangharakshita briefly describes his grandfather's involvement in *The Rainbow Road from Tooting Broadway to Kalimpong*, *Complete Works*, vol. 20, p. 3.

231 The phrase 'Doing evil that good may come of it' is from St Paul's Letter to the Romans (3:8); Paul says that those who accuse the Christians of taking that attitude are slandering them. St Jerome was born in Stridon (in modern north-east Italy) in 347 CE. He began to collect a library as a student; most of his books then were pagan classics, but he later committed himself to Christianity and joined a community of Christian hermits in the desert outside Antioch in 375 CE. After he was ordained as a priest, he helped to establish a papal library in Rome and then moved to Bethlehem, where he continued to work on his Latin translation of the Bible and to expand his library, considered to be the most important private collection of that period, though it was destroyed in 416, when Bethlehem was sacked by bandits. Jerome died in 420 CE.

232 Andrew Marvell (1621–1678) was a metaphysical poet, a satirist and politician, a supporter of Oliver Cromwell, and a friend and colleague of John Milton. 'To His Coy Mistress' was published posthumously in 1681, but may have been written in the 1650s.

233 William Shakespeare, *Sonnet* 60.

234 Sir Walter Raleigh (1552–1618) was the famous explorer

who sailed to America in the reign of Elizabeth I. In an illustrious but chequered career he fell out of favour with the queen and then was accused of treason by her successor James I and eventually executed.

235 John Milton, *Sonnet* 7.

236 John Blofeld (Chu Ch'an) (trans.), *The Sūtra of Forty-Two Sections*, The Buddhist Society, London 1977, p. 15.

237 Nāgārjuna (flourished in India between 150 and 250 CE) is regarded as the founder of the Madhyamaka school. His *Mūlamadhyamaka-kārikā* (*Fundamental Verses of the Middle Way*) is a Sanskrit text, in part a commentary on discourses of the Buddha, to demonstrate the futility of metaphysical speculation and to affirm the Middle Way the Buddha taught as a direct perception of *śūnyatā* or the 'emptiness' of all things.

238 James A. Michener, *Iberia: Spanish Travels and Reflections*, Random House, New York 2013, p. 156.

239 W. Hamilton (trans.), *The Symposium*, Penguin Books, Harmondsworth 1981, p. 83.

240 Ibid. pp. 90–1. The author has made a few small changes to the translation.

241 The story of Nanda's ordination on what would have been his wedding day is told in the *Dhammapada Commentary*: see Eugene Watson Burlingame (trans.), *Buddhist Legends (Dhammapada Commentary)*, part 1, Pali Text Society, London 1969, pp. 218–9. The better-known sequel, in which Nanda, now ordained, is pining for his wife and wants to leave the order of monks, is told in the same volume, pp. 220–3, also at *Udāna* 3.2.

242 Gerald Brenan, *The Face of Spain*, Penguin Books, Harmondsworth 1987, p. 239.

243 W. Hamilton (trans.), *The Symposium*, Penguin Books, Harmondsworth 1981, pp. 90–1.

244 'Criticism East and West' was written in the spring of 1988. It was to have been read at a weekend school on 'Criticism in Crisis' organized by the Manchester University's Department of Extra-Mural Studies. In the event the school had to be cancelled.

245 Frank Raymond Leavis (1895–1978) was a renowned literary critic, for three decades a lecturer at Downing College, Cambridge. His first book, *New Bearings in English Poetry* (1932) identified the achievements of a number of new poets including T. S. Eliot and W. B. Yeats. This sentence echoes lines from John Keats' poem 'On First Looking Into Chapman's Homer':

> Oft of one wide expanse had
> I been told
> That deep-browed Homer
> ruled as his demesne.

246 Robert Graves, *The Crowning Privilege*, Penguin Books, Harmondsworth 1959, p. 109.

247 *The Times*, 15 February 1988, p. 10.

248 'The thought of thinking Souls' is from Thomas Carlyle's essay, 'Sir Walter Scott', first published in the *London and Westminster Review*, no. 12, in 1838.

The 'grand line of demarcation between the human and the animal kingdoms' is from William Godwin's essay 'Of an early taste for reading', essay V in *The Enquirer: Reflections on Education, Manners and Literature*, G. G. and J. Robinson, London 1797, p. 31.

Robert Louis Stevenson wrote 'Literature in many of its branches is no other than the shadow of good talk.' in *Memories and Portraits*, Chatto & Windus, London 1912, chapter 10, 'Talk and Talkers: First Paper'.

Pound's 'language charged with meaning' is from Ezra Pound, *ABC of Reading*, Faber and Faber, London 1961, p. 28.

249 John William Mackail, *Classical Studies*, John Murray, London 1926, p. 214.

250 Cyril Birch (ed.), *Anthology of Chinese Literature*, Penguin Books, London 1967, pp. 231–2.

251 The quotation is from John Keats' long poem 'The Fall of Hyperion: a Dream'.

252 John Dryden, *An Essay of Dramatic Poesy*. The essay was probably written in 1666, when the London theatres were closed due to plague, and can be read as a defence of drama as a literary form. John Dryden (1631–1700) was an English poet, critic, and dramatist, who was appointed England's first Poet Laureate in 1668.

253 V. Raghavan, *The Number of Rasas*, third revised edition, Adyar Library and Research Centre, Adyar 1975, p. ix.

254 *Words International*, vol. 1, no. 1 (November 1987), p. 19.

255 Dr A. K. Warder, *The Science of Criticism in India*, Adyar Library and Research Centre, Adyar 1978, p. 16.

256 Ibid. pp. 16–17.

257 Ibid. pp. 69–70.

258 Ibid. p. 29.

259 Sushil Kumar De, *History of Sanskrit Poetics*, second revised edition, Calcutta 1960, vol. ii, p. 45.

260 John Middleton Murry, *Countries of the Mind: Second Series*, Collins, London 1931, p. 181.

261 Ernest G. Griffin, *John Middleton Murry*, Twayne, New York 1969, p. 42.

262 Ibid. pp. 42–3.

263 F. A. Lea, *The Life of John Middleton Murry*, Methuen, London 1959, p. 86.

264 John Middleton Murry, *Discoveries*, Collins, London 1924, pp. 13–14.

265 Ibid. p. 14.

266 Richard Rees (ed.), *J. Middleton Murry: Selected Criticism 1916–1957*, Oxford University Press, London 1960, p. 4.

267 *Words International*, vol. 1, no. 3 (January 1988), p. 42.

268 *Words International*, vol. 1, no. 5 (March 1988), p. 34.

269 These lines are from the dedication to 'The Palace of Art', by Alfred, Lord Tennyson (1809–1892), the great Victorian Poet Laureate. The lines are dedicated to Richard Trench who, like Tennyson, belonged to the Cambridge University 'Apostles', a secret society founded in 1820.

270 Richard Rees (ed.), *J. Middleton Murry: Selected Criticism 1916–1957*, Oxford University Press, London 1960, p. 9.

271 This is one of the many notes Blake wrote in the margin of a copy of the *Works of Sir Joshua Reynolds* (now in the possession of the British Library).

272 Blake died in his rooms at Fountain Court, the Strand, London, on 12 August 1827. These words were written by George Richmond, who was a member of The Ancients, a group of Blake's followers, in a letter to the artist Samuel Palmer.

273

> Once I saw a Devil in a flame of fire, who arose before an Angel that sat on a cloud, and the Devil utter'd these words: 'The worship of God is: Honouring his gifts in other men, each according to his genius, and loving the greatest men best: those who envy or calumniate great men hate God; for there is no other God.'

These are the opening words of Blake's 1790 work *The Marriage of Heaven and Hell.*

274 For an explanation of the 'turning about', the *parāvṛtti*, see Sangharakshita, *The Meaning of Conversion in Buddhism*, ch. 4 (*Complete Works*, vol. 2, pp. 275–85).

275 For the yoga of the long *hūṃ*, see W. Y. Evans-Wentz (ed., *Tibetan Yoga and Secret Doctrines*, Oxford University Press, London 1958, book VI, pp. 334–41.

276 These words are from a letter the 20-year-old Blake wrote in response to one from Reverend John Trusler, who had commissioned a work from Blake but had written to him to criticize it.

277 These are lines 146 and 147 of Blake's long poem 'The Everlasting Gospel', found in fragmentary form after his death.

278 These are the first two lines of 'The Everlasting Gospel'.

279 For his comment on Blake's use of 'religion' as a smear word, see Samuel Foster Damon, *A Blake Dictionary: the Ideas and Symbols of William Blake*, Brown

University Press, Providence 1965, p. 345. We haven't been able to trace the reference to 'decayed poetry'.

280 The biography was Hilary Spurling, *Paul Scott: A Life*, Hutchinson, London 1990.

281 Simon Heffer, *Moral Desperado: A Life of Thomas* Carlyle, Weidenfield and Nicholson, London 1995. The writer, philosopher, and historian Thomas Carlyle (1795–1881) was born in Scotland but spent most of his working life in London.

282 The Croydon arts centre, known as Independent Arts, ran as part of the FWBO's Croydon Buddhist Centre during the 1980s. The centre put on a wide range of educational arts events, exploring the spiritual value of many artists and artistic movements.

283 Damien Hirst is an English artist who achieved notoriety by displaying a variety of dead animals preserved in transparent cases; the reference here is to the 1994 work *Away from the Flock*.

American artist Carl Andre's famous pile of bricks, entitled *Equivalent VIII*, was purchased by the Tate Gallery, London, amid much controversy in 1972.

284 Friedrich Schiller's *Letters on the Aesthetic Education of Man* is a seminal treatise on culture and philosophy, written not long after the French Revolution.

285 Francis Beaumont and John Fletcher were English dramatists who collaborated on writing plays in the Jacobean period of the early seventeenth century.

286 Plotinus' *Enneads* are a large collection of pithy philosophical essays, which set forth his ideas on Soul, Intellect, and ascent to the One. Thomas Taylor's translation was first published in 1794.

287 This is quoted in *Readings from the Refuge Tree of the Western Buddhist Order*, compiled and edited by Lokabandhu, 1992, p. 17, but this compilation doesn't give any more details about the source.

288 *Udāna* 8.1. For Sangharakshita's commentary, see *Complete Works*, vol. 10, pp. 632–3.

289 *Ariyapariyesanā Sutta, Majjhima Nikāya* 26 (i.163); see Bhikkhu Ñāṇamoli and Bhikkhu Bodhi (trans.), *The Middle Length Discourses of the Buddha*, Wisdom Publications, Boston 1995, p. 256; or I. B. Horner (trans.), *The Collection of the Middle Length Sayings*, vol. i, Pali Text Society, London 1976, p. 207.

290 From Samuel Johnson's *Lives of the Poets*.

291 See p. 307 above.

292 Richard Holmes' works include biographies of Shelley and Coleridge.

The American biographer Richard Ellmann wrote biographies of W. B. Yeats and James Joyce as well as Oscar Wilde.

293 For an account of Sangharakshita's connection with Allen Ginsberg, see 'With Allen Ginsberg in Kalimpong', *Complete Works*, vol. 22, pp. 563–8.

294 This refers to the Swiss philosopher Jean-Jacques Rousseau (1712–1778). For more on 'Rousseauism' see, for example, *Ritual and Devotion in Buddhism*, Windhorse Publications, Birmingham 1995, pp. 15–16 (*Complete Works*, vol. 11):

> We must beware of a generalized romantic Rousseauism or old-fashioned communism: the notion that people would be really good and happy and healthy and positive and friendly, if you only removed the social restrictions; if you only changed the political system; if you only took them out of the big evil cities and settled them down in some Utopia or some Eden. This view is simply not justified. Although Buddhism suggests that the right conditions will help people develop in a positive way, changes in external conditions are not always enough.

295 This translates the German '*Gesamtkunstwerk*'; Richard Wagner uses the term in his 1849 essays 'Art and Revolution' and 'The Artwork of the Future', in which he speaks of his ideal of unifying all works of art via the theatre.

296 See T. S. Eliot, *The Use of Poetry and the Use of Criticism*, Faber and Faber, London 1980, p. 150.

297 *The Call of the Forest* was published by Windhorse Publications in 2000. The poems can now be found in *Complete Works*, vol. 25, pp. 408–22.

298 Ibid. p. 416.

299 The sculpture is thought not to be by Michelangelo, but to have been made in antiquity and rediscovered in the Renaissance period. It was installed in the Vatican, where it now is again, though it was seized by Napoleon and placed in the Louvre in Paris for a time. William Blake made an engraving of it (he must have worked from someone else's drawing) and surrounded it with writing; this is part of what he wrote.

300 See p.128 above.

301 This is from W. B. Yeats' memoir *Four Years*, first published in 1921, chapter 2.

302 For an account of this visit, see *Moving Against the Stream*,

Complete Works, vol. 23, pp. 260–1.

303 *The Rainbow Road from Tooting Broadway to Kalimpong, Complete Works*, vol. 20, p. 10, p. 36, p. 100.

304 From the long poem 'The Awakening of the Heart'; see *Complete Works*, vol. 25, p. 468.

305 *In the Sign of the Golden Wheel, Complete Works*, vol. 22, p. 186.

306 *The Rainbow Road from Tooting Broadway to Kalimpong, Complete Works*, vol. 20, p. 63.

307 *Facing Mount Kanchenjunga, Complete Works*, vol. 21, pp. 78–9.

308 This is from John Milton's 1644 pamphlet *Of Education*.

309 The Buddha says this in chapter 3 of the *White Lotus Sūtra*, just before he tells the parable of the burning house. See, for example, W. E. Soothill (trans.), *The Lotus of the Wonderful Law*, Curzon Press, London 1987, p. 86.

310 George Herbert (1593–1633) was one of the so-called Metaphysical Poets. This is from the first stanza of his poem 'The Church Porch'.

311 This is the ninth stanza of Thomas Gray's 'Elegy in a Country Churchyard' (1750).

312 *The Rubáiyát of Omar Khayyám*, (1048–1131) translated into English by Edward Fitzgerald, appeared in various editions from 1859. This is verse 38.

313 'The House Beautiful' was a lecture given by Oscar Wilde during his tour of America in 1882; the title was not metaphorical, because the lecture was an actual critique of interior design.

314 Thomas Aquinas (1225–1274) was an Italian theologian, philosopher, and Dominican priest whose writings were hugely influential in the development of Roman Catholic theology. This statement is from his most famous work, the *Summa Theologica*, a compendium for theological students setting forth the reasoning for the main Christian tenets of belief. In the first part of the work, in chapter 5, 'Of Goodness in General', one of the questions he raises about goodness is whether it 'has the aspect of a final cause'. He raises three possible objections to that proposition, and his statement about beauty is in the reply to the first of those objections.

315 This is the main theme of *Either/Or*, Søren Kierkegaard's first published work (1843).

316 In 1945 the American Philip Kapleau (1912–2004) was court reporter for the first of what became known as the Nuremberg trials, which was held in Tokyo. While in Japan he made the acquaintance of the writer on Zen, D. T. Suzuki, and later Kapleau became a teacher of Zen Buddhism in the Sanbō

Kyōdan tradition, a blending of the Japanese Sōtō and Rinzai schools.

317 These are the last four lines of Rupert Brooke's 1913 poem 'Heaven'.

318 This is from the seventh stanza of *Tam O'Shanter*, Robert Burns' narrative poem, written in 1790.

319 In 1895 Oscar Wilde was sentenced to two years' hard labour at Reading Gaol for 'gross indecency'. On release in 1897 he wrote his poem about the experience. One of the incidents it describes is the hanging of a fellow prisoner.

320 'The mass of men lead lives of quiet desperation'; from chapter 1, 'Economy', in American writer Henry David Thoreau's 1854 work *Walden*, which describes his two-year stay in a cabin on the shore of Walden Pond.

321 This is from the beginning of the second 'epistle' of the long poem *An Essay on Man* by the poet and satirist Alexander Pope (1688–1744), in which, as the opening lines say, he seeks to 'vindicate the ways of God to man' (an echo of Milton's *Paradise Lost*, which seeks 'to justify the ways of God to man').

322 In a letter to his brother George written on 21 April 1819, John Keats referred to the world as a 'vale of Soul-making'.

323 The world where the Dharma is taught by perfume and the contrast with our own world are both described in the tenth chapter of the *Vimalakīrti-nirdeśa*, 'The Buddha of the Fragrant Land'; see, for example, Charles Luk (trans.), The *Vimalakīrti Nirdeśa Sūtra*, Shambhala Publications, Boston 1972, pp. 101–8. For Sangharakshita's commentary, see chapter 7, 'The Mystery of Human Communication', in *The Inconceivable Emancipation*, *Complete Works*, vol. 16, pp. 551–66.

LATE WRITINGS

324 Harmsworth's *Children's Encyclopaedia* appeared initially in fortnightly parts, and in 1910 was published as an eight-volume set before being extensively revised and brought out in ten volumes in 1922. It was presumably the earlier version which the Hartnells gave to Dennis Lingwood in sixty-one unbound parts. (*The Rainbow Road from Tooting Broadway to Kalimpong*, *Complete Works*, vol. 20, pp. 22–4.)

325 The Rechabites were a non-conformist Christian sect that emerged in the mid-nineteenth century whose principal tenet was teetotalism. Sangharakshita writes about attending a Rechabite meeting with his mother in *The Rainbow Road from Tooting Broadway to Kalimpong*, *Complete Works*, vol. 20, p. 21.

326 From 'English Lullaby', by Alfred, Lord Tennyson in Archibald Watson Bain, *Poetry for Children*, Cambridge University Press, paperback edition 2011, p. 2 (first published 1927).

327 *The Rainbow Road from Tooting Broadway to Kalimpong*, *Complete Works*, vol. 20, pp. 313–4.

328 *From Genesis to the Diamond Sūtra*, *Complete Works*, vol. 13, p. 609.

329 At the time of composing this piece, the plan to move to a larger, more rural setting was very much in the air although in the event it was only in September 2012, after a three-year search, that a property was finally purchased. Sangharakshita himself moved to Adhisthana in February 2013.

330 From 1976 to 1989 Sangharakshita was based at Padmaloka, a men's community and retreat centre in the village of Surlingham, Norfolk.

331 From 1989 to 1994 Sangharakshita lived in a small flat above the London Buddhist Centre in Bethnal Green, London.

332 See *Complete Works*, vol. 25, pp. 395–7.

333 'The Pilgrim' recounts Tannhäuser's legendary visit to Pope Urban IV. See *Complete Works*, vol. 25, p. 428. 'Love and Duty', composed on 24 May 2001, is one of three Arthurian Poems. Its theme is the illicit love of Queen Guinevere (wife of King Arthur) for 'gallant Lancelot'. Ibid. p. 98.

334 'Old King Cole' is a traditional nursery rhyme.

'Lycidas' is an elegy written in 1637 by John Milton (1608–1674) on the loss of his friend, Edward King. Sangharakshita first came across Milton's poetry at the age of 12 when he received *Paradise Lost* as a Christmas present, the reading of which gave him 'the greatest poetic experience' of his life. (*The Rainbow Road from Tooting Broadway to Kalimpong*, *Complete Works*, vol. 20, p. 36.)

'Onward Christian Soldiers' was a popular Victorian hymn whose music was composed by Arthur Sullivan in 1871. It was sung with gusto at the meetings of the Boys' Brigade that the young Dennis Lingwood attended.

'Sister Helen' is a long poem in the form of a ballad by Dante Gabriel Rossetti (1828–1882), a poet whose 'intensely fused sensuousness and mysticism … went to my head like some subtle and dangerous perfume'. (Ibid. p. 36.)

335 The English poet Philip Larkin (1922–1985) worked as librarian at the University of Hull for more than thirty years. Andrew Motion's

biography, *Philip Larkin: A Writer's Life*, was published by Faber & Faber in 1993.

336 Il Convento di Santa Croce, near the Tuscan village of Batignano, was formerly an Augustinian monastery. (See note 214 above.) From 1981 until 1985 it was the venue for the three-month ordination retreats for men entering the Western Buddhist Order. During these retreats Sangharakshita gave talks, notably including *The Journey to Il Convento* and *St Jerome Revisited* (both given on the 1984 course, and included in this volume), led seminars, answered questions, wrote letters – and some poems – and, of course, performed ordinations.

337 'Bavarian Gentians' was included in Lawrence's *Last Poems* published in 1932. Sangharakshita first came across Lawrence's poetry when he was a teenager. He wrote later (in 1997) that since that time 'rarely have I been without a copy of at least a selection from his poems'. (See 'Travels of a Bibliophile in North America and Australasia' in *Complete Works*, vol. 24, p. 525.)

338 Titian or Tiziano Vecelli (c.1488–1576) was an Italian painter of the Venetian school; Joan Miró (1893–1983) a Spanish painter, sculptor, and ceramicist. The Pre-Raphaelite painters include William Holman Hunt (1827–1910), John Everett Millais (1829–1896), and Dante Gabriel Rossetti (1828–1882).

Sangharakshita's love of art began during his years confined to bed between the ages of 8 and 10 when he took especial pleasure in the art section of the *Children's Encyclopaedia*. He subsequently took up drawing and painting so that for a while 'the feeling became general that I was going to be an artist'. (*The Rainbow Road from Tooting Broadway to Kalimpong*, *Complete Works*, vol. 20, pp. 27–8.)

339 See *Moving Against the Stream*, *Complete Works*, vol. 23, p. 422.

340 The empiricist philosopher David Hume (1711–1776) published *A Treatise of Human Nature* anonymously in 1739–40. Its reception was such that he wrote later that it had 'fallen dead-born from the press'. *An Enquiry Concerning Human Understanding*, was a much shorter revision of the treatise published in 1748 and went on to become a classic of the western philosophical tradition.

341 Rabindra Kumar Banerjee was born in Manipur, India, in 1922. He and the future Sangharakshita met in Singapore in 1946. Banerjee came from a brahmin family but had renounced the caste system in favour of political

activism. Of very different temperament, the two became friends (see Sangharakshita's poem, 'To a Political Friend', *Complete Works*, vol. 25, p. 166) and through their discussions, Banerjee became interested in Buddhism. From 1947, for two years, they were constant companions, walking the roads of India (see *The Rainbow Road from Tooting Broadway to Kalimpong*, *Complete Works*, vol. 20, chapters 16–47). In May 1949 they received *sāmaṇera* ordination at Kusinara where Banerjee (or Satyapriya as by then he was calling himself) became Buddharakshita. Their paths diverged from 1949, Buddharakshita going on to study in Sri Lanka. He later based himself in Bangalore where he developed a branch of the Maha Bodhi Society. Buddharakshita died in 2013.

342 When Sangharakshita first met 'the French nun' she was Dominique Delannoy, an alumna of the Sorbonne, studying in Calcutta. He was introduced to her again when she visited Kalimpong in early 1953 (*Facing Mount Kanchenjunga*, *Complete Works*, vol. 21, pp. 445–6). Later that year, she took from him the Refuges and Precepts and received ordination from a Bengali monk, becoming Anagarika Dharmarakshita (*In the Sign of the Golden Wheel*, *Complete Works*, vol. 22, p. 48). In 1954 she received ordination as a *getsulma* or novice nun from Dhardo Rimpoche, taking the name Thupten Chhokyi (ibid. p. 184). 'Ani-la', as she was now addressed, was a frequent visitor to Sangharakshita's residence, where she would pour out her troubles, involve herself in activities, and was sometimes an embarrassment (ibid. pp. 193–5). Both he and Dhardo Rimpoche sought ways to help her (ibid. pp. 219–24) but in the end her behaviour became so bad that Dhardo Rimpoche was forced to deprive her of her status as nun (*Precious Teachers*, *Complete Works*, vol. 22, pp. 424–7).

> When next heard of she was in Calcutta, where she was seen with bobbed hair, in a short skirt, and puffing a cigarette.

(ibid. p. 428.)

343 Martin Amis, *Experience: A Memoir*, Hyperion, New York 2000, pp. 176–7.

344 Sacheverell Sitwell (1897–1988), brother of writers Edith and Osbert, wrote extensively on art and architecture. The book referred to here was probably either *Southern Baroque Art: a Study of Painting, Architecture and Music in Italy and Spain of the 17th & 18th Centuries* (1924) or *Spanish Baroque Art, with Buildings in Portugal, Mexico, and Other Colonies* (1931).

345 See 'Travels of a Bibliophile in North America and Australasia' in *Through Buddhist Eyes*, *Complete Works*, vol. 24, pp. 523–5, and *My Five Literary Heroes* in this volume (pp. 481 ff. below).

346 Omar Khayyám (1048–1131) was a Persian polymath. Famous as mathematician and astronomer, he wrote on many other subjects from music to mineralogy. He became known in the English-speaking West chiefly as a literary figure when the poet and writer Edward Fitzgerald (1809–1883) published a translation of his poetry: *The Rubáiyát of Omar Khayyám* (first edition 1859), a collection of quatrains (*ruba'i*).

347 Dante Gabriel Rossetti (1828–1882) was both painter and poet. His *The Early Italian Poets*, which included a translation of Dante Alighieri's *La Vita Nuova*, was first published in 1861.

348 *Poèmes* is a bilingual edition of sixty-three of Sangharakshita's poems, translated by Barbara-Laure Desplats, Christian Richard, Varadakini, and Vassika, and published by Amis de l'Ordre Bouddhiste Occidental, Paris, in 2009. The poems were chosen to give as complete a picture of the author as possible: the mystic, the friend, the philosopher, his life in India and in Britain, and his founding of a new Buddhist movement.

349 Attributed to the king and emperor Charlemagne (c.747–814).

350 The introduction and first chapter of the *Survey* was published in German in 1999 by Do Evolution with the title *Buddha-Dharma – Einheit und Vielfalt des Buddhismus, Band I*.

351 A Spanish translation was brought out in 2008 under the title *Una panorámica del budismo* by Ediciones Dharma, Alicante. The Polish version, *Wprowadzenie do buddyzmu*, was published by Wydawnictwo A, Kraków, in 2002.

352 The friend was Paramartha, and their travels are recounted in Sangharakshita's 'Fourth Letter From London' written in November 1990, included in *Through Buddhist Eyes*, *Complete Works*, vol. 24, pp. 404ff.

353 Guhyaloka, or the 'secret realm', is a valley in the Sierra Aitana mountains of southern Spain. Here, since 1987, men's ordination retreats have been held. At the top of the valley is the retreat centre, a house for the resident community is at the bottom, and midway between the two is a bungalow where Sangharakshita stayed whenever he visited the valley.

354 Solidarity or *Solidarnosc*, founded in 1980 at the Gdansk shipyard, became widely known as the first trade union of any Warsaw

pact country not under the control of the communist party and it quickly grew in power. After the fall of the communist regime, its first leader, Lech Walesa, took up office as President of Poland in 1990.

355 From the first stanza of William Wordsworth's 'Ode: Intimations of Immortality from Recollections of Early Childhood', first published in 1807.

356 'In Krakow', three poems written on 20 May 2002, see *Complete Works*, vol. 25, p. 442.

357 Michal Balik (b. 1973), who went on to play a crucial part in Sangharakshita's life, was ordained as Nityabandhu by Sangharakshita in 2004. Nityabandhu means 'eternal friend'.

358 The painter of the murals was Stanislaw Wyspianski (1869–1907) who was also an architect, writer, and musician.

359 John Sobieski (1629–1696) was king of Poland from 1674. He is famous for his military victory over the Turks in 1683.

360 Karol Jozef Wojtyla (1920–2005) became Pope John Paul II in 1978. He was not only the first Polish pope, but the first non-Italian pope since 1523. He was canonized in 2014 and is now known as Saint Pope John Paul II.

Ignacy Jan Paderewski (1860–1941) was an internationally acclaimed pianist and composer, as well as a politician, who was briefly prime minister of independent Poland in 1919.

Henryk Górecki (1933–2010) was first a composer of avant-garde classical music. His third symphony, *Symphony of Sorrowful Songs*, composed in 1976, is in a more tonal vein. Its theme is the separation of mother and child through war. After the fall of communism, the symphony was played widely on the radio in western Europe and the USA.

Nicolaus Copernicus (1473–1543), mathematician and astronomer, was widely read in many other fields. He published his *De revolutionibus orbium coelestium* (*On the Revolutions of the Celestial Spheres*) just before his death, putting into motion a revolution of ideas with his model of the sun, and not the earth, at the centre of the (known) universe.

361 This was the Kalkscheune, a venue for events of all kinds.

362 Friends Organic (originally Friends Foods) was founded by Ratnaguna in c.1976. It continued trading until 2009 when, owing to ongoing financial losses, it had to close.

363 The Katyn Massacre refers to a series of mass executions of Polish nationals, in particular officers of the Polish army, politicians, members of the intelligentsia, and clergy of

the Roman Catholic church, by the Soviet secret police in April and May 1940. The largest number of executions took place in the Katyn Forest in Russia. It is estimated that some 22,000 people were killed. The Auschwitz concentration camp (in fact a series of connected camps), created by the Nazis, took its first prisoners in May 1940. It went on to become one of the main camps for the extermination of Jews and other unwanted peoples. Over a million people were killed, 90% of whom were Jews, mostly Hungarian or Polish. Others who lost their lives were Roma, Sinti, homosexuals, and Russian prisoners of war. There were also many non-Jewish Poles who died in Auschwitz. The camp was liberated on 27 January 1945, now commemorated as Holocaust Remembrance Day.

364 The perception of the loathsomeness of food (*āhāre paṭikkūla-saññā*) is one of the forty *kammaṭṭhānas* cited by the fifth-century Theravādin commentator, Buddhaghosa, as a support for the development of meditative concentration, see Buddhaghosa, *Visuddhimagga* 258–9; Bhikkhu Ñāṇamoli (trans.), *The Path of Purification*, Buddhist Publication Society, Kandy 1991, p. 252; or Pe Maung Tin (trans.), *The Path of Purity*, Pali Text Society, London 1975, pp. 295–7. See also Sangharakshita, *A Survey of Buddhism*, *Complete Works*, vol. 1, p. 160.

365 Sangharakshita was an avid reader of the poetry of Arthur Rimbaud, and the title of this chapter is a reference to his long prose poem *A Season in Hell* (1873), which had a considerable influence on subsequent artists and poets.

366 Sangharakshita had celebrated his 77th birthday on 26 August 2002.

367 Dhardo Rimpoche (1917–1990) was one of Sangharakshita's eight main teachers.

368 Amritakula – which could be rendered 'the brotherhood of the nectar of the deathless' – was a men's community in East London which at this time had some seven or so members, including Order members and men training for ordination.

369 'The Silver Spoon': see *Complete Works*, vol. 25, p. 444.

370 Padmadaka was at this time the chairman of Padmaloka Retreat Centre.

371 I (Vidyadevi) am the editor of this volume and of many of the other volumes of these *Complete Works*. I was ordained into the Triratna Buddhist Order in 1993 and worked closely with Sangharakshita on his writings over many years, producing

books edited from lectures and seminars and compiling *The Essential Sangharakshita* and *The Purpose and Practice of Buddhist Meditation* (volumes 6 and 5 of the *Complete Works*).

372 Paramartha (b. 1960) grew up in the remote town of Invercargill in New Zealand. He first met the FWBO in 1982 and moved to England in 1987 before his ordination retreat at Guhyaloka the following year. From 1989 to 1996 he lived with Sangharakshita in the small flat above the London Buddhist Centre in Bethnal Green during which time he trained as an osteopath. For a brief period in 1997, and then from 2008 onwards, he lived with Sangharakshita in his flat in Moseley, Birmingham, moving with him in February 2013 to Adhisthana in Herefordshire.

373 For an account of these travels see the last three letters in *Through Buddhist Eyes*, *Complete Works*, vol. 24, pp. 493ff.

374 Bishop George Berkeley (1685–1753) was an Anglo-Irish philosopher whose chief work, *A Treatise Concerning Human Knowledge*, was published in 1710. His last major work, *Siris* (1744), begins by advocating the medicinal use of tar-water.

375 Samuel Johnson (1709–1784) – one of Sangharakshita's 'literary heroes' (see 'My Five Literary Heroes', pp. 483–4) – according to his biographer, Boswell, once spoke of a glass of claret thus:

> No, Sir, claret is the liquor for boys; port, for men; but he who aspires to be a hero (smiling), must drink brandy.

James Boswell, *The Life of Samuel Johnson*, Penguin Books, London 1986, p. 264.

376 Subhuti, Sona, and Mahamati were three of the most senior Order members living at Madhyamaloka at this time.

377 Vajragupta writes about this period in *The Triratna Story: Behind the Scenes of a New Buddhist Movement*, Windhorse Publications, Cambridge 2010.

378 *Living with Awareness: A Guide to the Satipaṭṭhāna Sutta* was published by Windhorse Publications in 2003. See *Complete Works*, vol. 15.

379 Thomas Tallis (c.1505–1585), the great organist and composer of choral music who served four English monarchs, composed his *Spem in Alium* around 1570. It is a unique work, being a motet written for five choirs of eight voices, i.e. there are forty parts.

380 *The Tibetan Book of Living and Dying* was published by Harper Collins in 1992. Its author, Sogyal Rimpoche (b. 1947) is a Tibetan lama of the Nyingma school, founder and spiritual director of Rigpa,

a Buddhist organization with centres all over the world. Sangharakshita met Sogyal Rimpoche when the latter was still a small boy (*Precious Teachers*, *Complete Works*, vol. 22, p. 406). As a teenager the Rimpoche came to visit Sangharakshita at his Kalimpong vihara during his farewell tour of India in 1966 (*Complete Works*, vol. 23, p. 384). The two met again many years later in Berlin at the European Buddhist Congress in 1992 when they shared a platform with other leading Buddhist teachers including Thich Nhat Hanh and Ayya Khema (see note 517).

381 Saraha (b. 1968) came across the FWBO during a building project in Manchester in 1995. He was ordained in 2001 and spent some years living at Padmaloka retreat centre before moving to Madhyamaloka in early 2003 in response to a request from Sangharakshita to whom he was able to offer some companionship during this crucial time and afterwards. His love of meditation has taken him on two occasions to spend three months living in a remote cave in the Pyrenees in the tradition of the hermits and *siddhas* of old. (Saraha is the name of one of the early Indian *siddhas* or yogis.) He is now (2022) an International Order Convenor.

382 Mahamati (b. 1955) was ordained in 1977. He was manager of Friends Foods from 1980 to 1982 and director of the Karuna Trust from 1983 to 1992. He went on to become the charity's overseas director, spending seven years living and working in India, during which period he was also involved with TBMSG (the Indian Order and movement). He returned to the UK at the end of 1999 and lived at Madhyamaloka for the remainder of the time Sangharakshita was based there. He became a member of the College of Public Preceptors and from 2006 to 2014 was an International Order Convenor, visiting Triratna centres and bringing together Order members from all over the world. He now lives in Malvern, not far from Adhisthana, and is chair of the Urgyen Sangharakshita Trust.

383 This report was published in the October 2003 issue of *Shabda*, the monthly newsletter distributed to all Order members.

384 Nityabandhu continued living with Sangharakshita until 2008 when he returned to Poland, along with Santaka, another Polish Order member, and Jenny, who was ordained in 2006 and known as Sassirika. Together they inaugurated the Triratna Buddhist Order and Community in a country

where over 94% of the population consider themselves Roman Catholic. That same year Sangharakshita cut the ribbon to mark the opening of Sanghaloka, the new Triratna (then FWBO) centre in Kraków. Since then the sangha has grown with activities in Kraków and in Warsaw, and several men and women are training for ordination.

385 See note 226.

386 The Pre-Raphaelites were a group of young men, primarily painters but including poets and critics, formed in 1848 by William Holman Hunt, John Everett Millais, and Dante Gabriel Rossetti with the intention of transforming British art, reintroducing a spiritual dimension that they felt had been lost since the time of Raphael. They emphasized keen observation of nature, and drew on medieval and, especially in the case of Holman Hunt, biblical themes.

387 'Scapegoat' was written around 1970 (see *Complete Works*, vol. 25, p. 328). 'The Scapegoat' was written around a decade later (ibid. pp. 350–1).

388 J. M. W. Turner (1775–1851) completed *The Bridge of Sighs, Ducal Palace and Custom-House, Venice* in 1833. Today it is on display at the Tate Gallery, London.

389 There is a brief account of this visit in *Moving Against the Stream*, *Complete Works*, vol. 23, pp. 257–8.

390 i.e. to Birmingham and the flat at Madhyamaloka.

391 Joan Grant (1907–1989) went on to write many other books but *Winged Pharaoh* (published 1937) was her most famous.

392 The Ptolemies were a dynastic family of Greek Macedonian extraction who succeeded the pharaohs in ruling over Egypt, establishing an empire that lasted 275 years (305–30 BCE). In 30 BCE the Roman ruler Octavius (later emperor Augustus) defeated his rival, Mark Antony, and deposed Mark Antony's lover, the Ptolemaic queen Cleopatra, annexing the kingdom of Egypt to the Roman empire. Egypt remained under Roman rule, later becoming part of the Byzantine Eastern Roman empire, until the Muslim invasion of 639 CE.

393 Hermopolis, 'city of Hermes', was the name given by the Greeks to the ancient Egyptian city of Khmun. It was a main centre of the cult of Thoth whom the Greeks identified with Hermes. (Today the town is known as El Ashmunein.)

394 Homer, *Odyssey*, Book V.

395 *The Book of the Dead* was the name given to a collection of ancient Egyptian funerary texts meant as a guide to one who has died, and, with its spells, as a protection. An alternative rendering of the title is 'Book of Emerging Forth into Light'.

396 Virgil, *Aeneid*, Book IV, lines 330–6.

397 George Chapman (c.1559–1634) was a dramatist and poet who is most widely famed for his translations of Homer's *Odyssey* and *Iliad*. A copy of Chapman's *Iliad* was one of the first purchases made by the young evacuee, Dennis Lingwood, when he arrived in Barnstaple, Devon in the summer of 1940.

> Though the poem had long been familiar to me in prose translation, and though I knew all the episodes, it was a new poem that burst upon me that afternoon...

The Rainbow Road from Tooting Broadway to Kalimpong, *Complete Works*, vol. 20, p. 49.

398 The Chapman version of the *Iliad* begins:

> Achilles baneful wrath resound, O Goddess, that imposed
> Infinite sorrows on the Greeks, and many brave souls los'd
> From breasts heroic ...

c.f. a modern – prose – translation:

> The Wrath of Achilles is my theme, that fatal wrath which, in fulfilment of the will of Zeus, brought the Achaeans so much suffering and sent the gallant souls of many noblemen to Hades....

E. V. Rieu, first published 1950.

399 From the sonnet by John Keats (1795–1821), 'On First Looking into Chapman's *Homer*' written in 1816.

400 *Paradise Lost*, Book V, lines 285–7.

401 *Mahāgovinda Sutta*, *Dīgha Nikāya* 19 (ii.241); see M. Walshe (trans.), *The Long Discourses of the Buddha*, Wisdom Publications, Boston 1995, p. 308; or T. W. & C. A. F. Rhys Davids (trans.), *Dialogues of the Buddha*, part 2, Pali Text Society, London 1971, pp. 273–4.

402 *Dhammapada* 21.

403 *Ariyapariyesanā Sutta*, *Majjhima Nikāya* 26 (i.163); see Bhikkhu Ñāṇamoli and Bhikkhu Bodhi (trans.), *The Middle Length Discourses of the Buddha*, Wisdom Publications, Boston 1995, p. 256; or I. B. Horner (trans.), *The Collection of the Middle Length Sayings*, vol. i, Pali Text Society, London 1976, p. 207.

404 *Mahāgovinda Sutta*, *Dīgha Nikāya* 19; see M. Walshe (trans.), *The Long Discourses of the Buddha*, Wisdom Publications, Boston 1995, pp. 301–13; or T. W. & C. A. F. Rhys Davids (trans.), *Dialogues of the Buddha*, part 2, Pali Text Society, London 1971, pp. 259–81.

405 An account of this initiation, which took place in October

1957, is given in *Precious Teachers*, *Complete Works*, vol. 22, pp. 401–3. Jamyang Khyentse Rimpoche (1893–1959), also known as Dzongsar Khyentse Chökyi Lodrö, was born in the eastern Tibetan province of Kham. At the age of seven he was officially recognized as the 'action emanation' of Jamyang Khyentse Wangpo, the great founder of the Rimé tradition. His training meant studying the teachings and performing practices from all four Tibetan schools of Buddhism, in line with the Rimé tradition of his predecessor. In due course he became himself highly renowned as a teacher. His last years were spent in the eastern Himalayas, both in India and Sikkim. It was in Kalimpong that Sangharakshita first met him at the home of a mutual friend, Burma Raja (*Precious Teachers*, *Complete Works*, vol. 22, p. 399).

406 Michelangelo (1475–1564) painted the huge fresco of the Last Judgement on the altar wall of the Vatican's Sistine Chapel in the years 1536–1541.

407 Oliver Cromwell (1599–1658), who became a convinced Puritan after a religious conversion in 1630, was one of those who led the Parliamentarian armies to victory in the English Civil War (1642–1651). After the execution of King Charles I in 1649 he became for nearly five years (1653–1658) Lord Protector of England, Scotland, and Ireland.

408 From John Milton's Sonnet 18, 'On the Late Massacre in Piedmont' written after the brutal massacre in northern Italy in April 1655 by troops belonging to the Duke of Savoy of more than 1,500 peaceful Waldensians who refused to convert to Roman Catholicism:

> Avenge, O Lord, thy slaughter'd Saints, whose bones
> Lie scatter'd on the Alpine mountains cold,
> Ev'n them who kept thy truth so pure of old
> When all our Fathers worshipped stocks and stones....

409 Leonardo da Vinci's cartoon, *The Virgin and Child with St Anne and St John the Baptist* is a charcoal and chalk drawing dating to around 1500. It was acquired by the National Gallery in London in 1962. In July 1987 a visitor to the gallery pulled out a gun he had concealed beneath his coat and fired at the drawing, shattering the protective glass and causing significant damage. Richard Cambridge, the perpetrator of this deed, told the police that he wanted to express his disgust with 'political, social, and economic conditions in Britain'. The

restoration took more than a year to complete.

410 The Royal Pavilion in Brighton was built between 1787 and 1823 as a residence for the Prince of Wales, later King George IV. Its architects included John Nash who was responsible for the introduction of its characteristic Indo-Islamic architecture. The arson attack was carried out in 1975 by a 23-year-old art student because it was 'the sort of place people looked up to'. The attack led to the Music Room being closed for eleven years. In fact the arsonist, who suffered serious burns, was later sentenced to six years imprisonment.

411 Tracey Emin (b. 1963). *My Bed* – an installation consisting of her unmade bed with used condoms, blood-stained underwear, and other paraphernalia – was exhibited at the Tate Gallery in London in 1999 and shortlisted for the Turner prize. In October 1999 two half-naked men jumped onto the bed with the intention of adding to the art experience. They called their act *Two Naked Men Jump into Tracey's Bed*. *My Bed* sold at Christie's for over £2.5 million.

412 Graham Sutherland (1903–1980) was an English artist who not only painted but worked with glass and fabric. (He designed the tapestry for the rebuilt Coventry cathedral.) He was commissioned to paint a full-length portrait of Churchill towards the end of the great wartime leader's second period as prime minister. It was presented to him at a public ceremony celebrating his 80th birthday. Churchill hated the portrait.

413 Francis Bacon (1561–1626) was an English philosopher and statesman, scientist, and essayist who has been called the father of the empirical scientific method. His *Novum Organum* or *Novum Organum Scientiarum* ('new instrument of science') was published in 1620. *Organum* is a reference to Aristotle's treatise of that name on logic and syllogism. Bacon's work puts forward a new system of logic. This includes an exploration of the four *idola* or idols that impede the mind's capacity for objective reasoning. Sangharakshita also wrote about the four idols in an article, 'Idols of the Marketplace' for *Golden Drum* (issue 33, May–July 1994); see *Complete Works*, vol. 11.

414 Buddhaghosa's *Visuddhimagga* 102 (iii.76), quoted in *Buddhist Scriptures*, selected and translated Edward Conze, Penguin Books, Harmondsworth 1959, pp. 116–7. See also Bhikkhu Ñāṇamoli (trans.), *The Path of Purification*, Buddhist

Publication Society, Kandy 1991, p. 102; or Pe Maung Tin (trans.), *The Path of Purity*, Pali Text Society, London 1975, p. 119.

415 Friedrich Nietzsche (1844–1900) wrote his *Twilight of the Idols or How to Philosophize with a Hammer (Götzen-Dämmerung, oder, Wie man mit dem Hammer philosophirt)* in 1888. *Götzen-Dämmerung* is a pun on Wagner's *Götterdämmerung*, the Twilight of the Gods. *Götze* means false god or idol and may be a reference to Francis Bacon's *Novum Organum*. It is a devastating critique of those aspects of contemporary culture that Nietzsche saw as nihilistic and life-denying.

416 The attack took place on 11 September 2001.

417 René Magritte (1898–1967) was a Belgian painter whose early impressionist style was succeeded by his sometimes shocking surrealism where unexpected images were juxtaposed to make the observer question the nature of reality. The reference here is to his *Golconda* (1953), which depicts businessmen in suits falling like raindrops from the sky.

418 This friend was Kulananda, author of *Principles of Buddhism* (2003) who, with Dominic Houlder (Mahaprabha, now Adjunct Professor in Strategic and Entrepreneurial Management at the London Business School) co-authored *Mindfulness and Money: the Buddhist Path to Abundance*, published by Broadway Books in 2002.

419 Sangharakshita did refer to this topic a few months later at the launch of *Dear Dinoo: Letters to a Friend*, in a talk given at the Birmingham Buddhist Centre on 10 December 2011. See 'Mingling Souls' in *Complete Works*, vol. 12, pp. 694–5.

420 From the prologue of *The Epic of Gilgamesh*, Penguin Books, Harmondsworth 1973, p. 61.

421 Publius Vergilius Maro (70–19 BCE), the great Roman poet and friend of the emperor Augustus, composed his epic poem, the *Aeneid*, from 29 BCE until his death, when it was left unfinished. Modelled on the earlier Greek epics by Homer, the poem tells the story of the founding of the Roman empire, with its themes of love versus duty, and the role of destiny in human life.

422 Charles Kingsley (1819–1875) was a clergyman (at one time chaplain to Queen Victoria and in later life canon of Westminster Abbey), as well as academic, historian, and novelist. *The Heroes* (1856) was a book for children about Greek mythology. Among his historical novels are the well-known *Westward Ho!* (1855), set in the reign of Queen Elizabeth I, and

Hypatia (1853), a fictionalized account of the Alexandrian Neoplatonic philosopher of that name – a book that gave Sangharakshita, who read it as a boy, his first acquaintance with mystical religion 'never to be forgotten'. (*The Rainbow Road from Tooting Broadway to Kalimpong*, *Complete Works*, vol. 20, p. 20.)

423 This was probably by Alfred Church (1829–1912), a classical scholar who brought out various editions retelling the stories of Homer and Virgil for children. His *The Story of the Iliad* was first published in 1881 with 'illustrations after Flaxman'.

424 Thomas Carlyle (1795–1881), the Scottish philosopher, historian, and satirist whose influence was widely felt in Victorian England through his social commentary. *On Heroes, Hero-Worship and the Heroic in History* was published in 1841, based on six lectures given the previous year. This quotation is from the first page of the first lecture.

425 Jean-Jacques Rousseau (1712–1778), the Genevan political philosopher, writer, educationalist – and composer – whose writings were so influential on thinkers and various movements from the French Revolution onwards.

Robert Burns (1759–1796), the most famous of Scottish poets, and collector of Scottish ballads.

426 Samuel Johnson (1709–1784) is known for his essays, poetry, literary criticism, and his *Dictionary of the English Language* (1755). His *Lives of the Most Eminent English Poets* was published 1779–1781, comprising short biographies and critical appraisals of no fewer than fifty-two English poets of the seventeenth and eighteenth centuries. Birkbeck Hill's edition was published in three volumes in 1905.

427 *The Rambler* was a periodical published on Tuesdays and Saturdays from 1750 to 1752 in the tradition of Richard Steele's *The Tatler* (1709–1711) and Joseph Addison and Richard Steele's *The Spectator* (1711–1712). This regular publication gave Johnson the opportunity to write on a wide variety of themes – morality, literature, society, politics, and religion. The most famous of *The Rambler*'s successors was *The Idler*, published in the London periodical *The Universal Chronicle* from 1758 to 1760.

428 *The Vanity of Human Wishes* (1749), a poem in heroic couplets, is in style an imitation of the Latin poet Juvenal.

429 Dr Johnson's friend and apothecary, Robert Levet, who had a room in the great man's house, died in 1782 (Johnson was 72). They had been friends for some thirty-six years. The

poem has nine stanzas of which the fourth runs:

> When fainting nature call'd
> for aid,
> And hov'ring death prepar'd
> the blow,
> His vig'rous remedy
> display'd,
> The power of art without
> the show.

430 Thomas Wolsey (1473–1530) became a cardinal of the Roman Catholic church in 1515. Favoured by King Henry VIII, he became his chief adviser with huge powers as Lord Chancellor, but fell from favour when he was unable to negotiate an annulment of the king's first marriage. He died while travelling to London to face charges of treason.

431 Charles XII of Sweden (1682–1718) led his armies to military defeat in the Great Northern War. These two quotations are from Johnson's *The Vanity of Human Wishes*, lines 219–22 and 342–5.

432 James Boswell (1740–1795) met Dr Johnson in 1763 and they remained life-long friends. His *Life of Samuel Johnson* was published in 1791 to an acclaim that has accompanied it ever since. The account of Dr Johnson's death is given in Boswell's *Life of Samuel Johnson*, Penguin Books, London 1986, p. 341.

433 In 1983 Sangharakshita led a study seminar at Padmaloka on Johnson's poem 'Ode to Friendship'. This was the first occasion on which he led study for his western disciples not on a Buddhist text but on a text from the Western tradition that expresses Dharmic values.

434 Algernon Charles Swinburne (1837–1909), was a poet, playwright, novelist, and critic, whose critical essay on Blake appeared in 1868.

435 William Blake (1757–1827) composed *The Marriage of Heaven and Hell* between 1790 and 1793 in the aftermath of the French Revolution. The title is a reference – an ironic one – to Swedish theologian Emanuel Swedenborg's *Heaven and Hell* (1758).

436 See *The Rainbow Road from Tooting Broadway to Kalimpong*, *Complete Works*, vol. 20, p. 104.

437 Allen Ginsberg (1926–1997), the American poet and social activist, is best known for his poems 'Howl' (1956) and 'Kaddish' (1961). Along with William S. Burroughs and Jack Kerouac he was a central figure of the 1950s Beat Generation of poets. In later life he was drawn to Eastern religion, both to Buddhism (through meeting Tibetan teacher Chögyam Trungpa) and the Hare Krishna movement. He first met Sangharakshita in Kalimpong in June 1962 when he was eager to discuss Tantric initiation. Sangharakshita took him to meet his teacher,

Yogi Chen (see 'With Allen Ginsberg in Kalimpong (1962)' in *In the Sign of the Golden Wheel*, *Complete Works*, vol. 22, pp. 563–8). Three years later Ginsberg visited Sangharakshita at the Hampstead Buddhist Vihara and recounted some of the Indian adventures that had befallen him since they last met. Shortly afterwards the American poet arranged for Sangharakshita to give a Buddhist poetry reading (*Moving Against the Stream*, *Complete Works*, vol. 23, pp. 123–4). A decade later Ginsberg visited Sangharakshita at his flat above the London Buddhist Centre. On this occasion he sang a version of Blake's 'The Tyger' while accompanying himself on finger cymbals.

438 *Vala, or the Four Zoas* (subtitled 'The Death and Judgement of Albion, the Fallen Man') was written from 1797 to 1807, but left unfinished. Albion was originally fourfold but 'self divided'. The four Zoas are Urthona, Urizen, Luvah, and Tharmas. The nine books that make up the work show the interactions of the Zoas, their fallen forms, and their emanations.

439 William Blake, *Milton*, ed. Kay Parkhurst Easson and Roger R. Easson, Shambhala Publications, Boston 1978, Book the First, p. 81.

440 Samuel Taylor Coleridge (1772–1834), poet, philosopher, and literary critic, wrote *The Rime of the Ancient Mariner* in 1797–8. It was published in *Lyrical Ballads* (1798), a collection of work by Wordsworth and Coleridge. *Christabel*, a poem in two parts, with its haunting atmosphere and theme of innocence and corruption, was composed in 1797 and 1800 but never completed. It was first published in 1816 alongside *Kubla Khan*, to which Coleridge gave the subtitle, 'A Vision in a Dream: A Fragment'. The lines of *Kubla Khan* came to him in an opium-induced sleep after reading a description of the wonders of Xanadu (Shangdu), the summer capital of Mongol emperor Kublai Khan. On awaking, he set to recording the lines that had come to him but was famously interrupted by 'a person from Porlock'. By the time his visitor had left, the lines had faded and only the fragment remained.

441 *Biographia Literaria* (subtitled, 'Biographical Sketches of my Literary Life and Opinions') was first published in two volumes in 1817. The Everyman edition was published in 1956.

442 Friedrich Schelling (1775–1854), the German philosopher, was a student of Fichte and a contemporary of Hegel – from whose

philosophy he diverged. Coleridge travelled to Germany in 1798, staying in university towns, learning German, and studying German philosophy, especially idealist philosophy, and literature.

443 *Biographia Literaria or Biographical Sketches of my Literary Life and Opinions and Two Lay Sermons*, George Bell & Sons, London 1891, p. 145.

444 Oscar Wilde (1854–1900), Irish writer, poet, and playwright.

445 Walter Pater (1839–1894) was an Oxford don. (Among his students was Gerard Manley Hopkins.) In the course of his life he wrote both fiction and non-fiction. Of the latter, his writings on art and artists, literature, and writers influenced literary and artistic life both during his life and after. Most controversial during his life (and of particular interest now to Buddhists) was the conclusion to his *Studies in the History of the Renaissance* (1873). In his unfinished novel, *Gaston*, Pater engaged with some of the figures of the 'Yellow Nineties' including Oscar Wilde whose *Picture of Dorian Gray* he reviewed in 1891 in the *Bookman* magazine.

446 Alfred, Lord Tennyson (1809–1892), the great Victorian Poet Laureate. These lines are from an early work, 'a kind of allegory' entitled 'To— with the following poem' (see *Tennyson's Poetry*, ed. Robert W. Hill Jr., W. W. Norton 1971, p. 26). The lines are dedicated to Richard Trench who, like Tennyson, belonged to the Cambridge University 'Apostles' (a secret society founded in 1820).

447 Wilde's 'Requiescat' (a prayer for the dead) is in five short verses. It was first published in a collection of *Poems* (1881). It begins:

> Tread lightly, she is near
> Under the snow,
> Speak gently, she can hear
> The daisies grow.

The poem of the same name by Matthew Arnold (1822–1888) was first published in 1853. In four verses, it begins:

> Strew on her roses, roses,
> And never a spray of yew!
> In quiet she reposes;
> Ah, would that I did too!

448 'The Harlot's House', composed probably in Paris in 1883, was published only once during Wilde's lifetime in 1885. The last of the twelve verses runs:

> And down the long and
> silent street,
> The dawn with silver-
> sandalled feet,
> Crept like a frightened girl.

449 *An Ideal Husband* was first staged early in 1895 at the Haymarket Theatre, London, when it had 124 continuous

performances. Despite his arrest in April, his conviction for 'gross indecency', and subsequent incarceration, the play continued to be performed, without the author's name being advertised. It continues to be one of Wilde's most popular plays.

450 *The Picture of Dorian Gray* was first published as a serial in *Lippincott's Monthly Magazine* in 1890. It was revised and brought out as a book edition in 1891.

451 *Oscar Wilde: Letters and Essays*, ed. Merlin Holland, Folio Society, London 1993.

452 This lecture was given in 1971, four years after the founding of the FWBO. See Sangharakshita's *What is the Sangha?*, chapter 5, *Complete Works*, vol. 3, pp. 434–44.

453 Written in the first months of 1897 towards the end of his imprisonment in Reading Gaol, the early published editions were expurgated. The full text appeared only in 1962 in *The Letters of Oscar Wilde*, edited by Rupert Hart-Davis.

454 *The White Peacock* was Lawrence's first novel, published in 1911. The story is set in the Eastwood of his own childhood. *Lady Chatterley's Lover*, his last novel, was printed privately in Italy in 1928. The first unexpurgated version to be published in England was only published in 1960.

455 Mabel Evans Dodge Sterne Luhan (1879–1962) – she was married four times – was a patron of the arts. From 1919 she lived in Taos, and with her then husband, started a literary colony. D. H. Lawrence and his wife Frieda were invited to visit in 1922. They returned in 1924 for eighteen months, living on land given to them by Mabel. *Lorenzo in Taos*, published in 1932, is a memoir of Lawrence's visit.

456 In *Through Buddhist Eyes*, Sangharakshita writes, 'It was also as a teenager that I first read *The Rainbow*, which affected me like an emotional depth charge....' (*Complete Works*, vol. 24, p. 525). See also *Facing Mount Kanchenjunga*, *Complete Works*, vol. 21, p. 261. For Sangharakshita's novel see 'A Room with a View' above, p. 444, and *The Rainbow Road from Tooting Broadway to Kalimpong*, *Complete Works*, vol. 20, p. 88.

457 *Kangaroo*, set in Australia, was published in 1923 after Lawrence's visit there with his wife Frieda. The story is of an English writer and his German wife and their visit to New South Wales. *The Plumed Serpent* is set in Mexico. The plumed serpent of the title is Quetzalcoatl, an indigenous deity. Lawrence began writing it during his stay in New Mexico on the ranch at Taos. It was published in 1926. *The*

Woman Who Rode Away was written in Taos in 1924 and published the following year. *The Man Who Died* was first published in 1929 as *The Escaped Cock* (Lawrence's preferred title). Its protagonist is Christ, who survives his crucifixion, returns to the world, and goes in search of the meaning of life, a search which takes him to a temple of Isis. 'The Ship of Death' was written not long before Lawrence's own death and published posthumously in 1933.

458 Dr Johnson's epitaph for Oliver Goldsmith (1728–1774) translates from the Latin:

> Oliver Goldsmith: A Poet, Naturalist, and Historian, who left scarcely any style of writing untouched, and touched nothing that he did not adorn....

459 'Lines Composed on Acquiring "The Works of Samuel Johnson, LL.D.", in Eleven Volumes, MDCCLXXXVII', written in 1983. See *Complete Works*, vol. 25, pp. 370–2.

460 See pp. 341ff. above.

461 'D. H. Lawrence and the Spiritual Community' appears in *Complete Works*, vol. 8.

462 Cecil Blanche Woodham-Smith (1896–1977) whose first historical work, *Florence Nightingale*, was published in 1950. She went on to write on other historical themes including the Irish famine of the 1840s and the life of Queen Victoria.

463 Marcel Proust (1871–1922), the great French novelist, composed *Remembrance of Things Past* (*À la recherche du temps perdu*, more recently translated as *In Search of Lost Time*) – a novel in seven parts – from 1909 until his death. A theme of the novel is an exploration of what Proust called voluntary and involuntary memory, the first being partial, the second bringing one much closer to the 'essence' of the past. An example of the latter occurs in a scene in which the narrator tastes a madeleine (a kind of small cake) and immediately a complete experience from childhood fills his mind – a memory of eating a piece of madeleine given to him by an aunt. In fact in the novel it is the taste rather than the smell of the delicious cake that evokes the memory; but the meaning of Sangharakshita's train of thought is clear.

464 See *The Rainbow Road from Tooting Broadway to Kalimpong*, *Complete Works*, vol. 20, pp. 316–17 and 377–9.

465 Sangharakshita and Buddharakshita (see note 341 above) received their *sāmaṇera* or 'lower' ordination together at Kusinara on 12 May 1949 (*Complete Works*, vol. 2, pp. 417–19). Soon afterwards their paths

diverged: Sangharakshita went to Benares to stay with Bhikkhu Jagdish Kashyap while Buddharakshita left for Ceylon (*The Rainbow Road from Tooting Broadway to Kalimpong*, *Complete Works*, vol. 20, p. 443). From March 1950 Sangharakshita was based in Kalimpong and that autumn he travelled to Sarnath where on 24 November 1950 he received the *bhikṣu* or 'higher' ordination (*A History of My Going for Refuge*, *Complete Works*, vol. 2, pp. 420–2).

466 As told in *In the Sign of the Golden Wheel*, *Complete Works*, vol. 22, chapter 1, pp. 5–17, 'The Scent of Gardenias'.

467 Plutarch (46–120 CE) was born near Delphi and educated in Greece, then under Roman rule. In the later part of his life he was a priest at the temple of Apollo at Delphi. He visited Egypt, and this information about the Egyptian temples is to be found in section 52 of 'Isis and Osiris', included among the seventy-eight essays and speeches of his *Moralia*.

468 Samuel Taylor Coleridge (1772–1834), the great English poet, literary critic, and philosopher, lived from 1816 with the physician James Gillman and his wife in Highgate where, despite the struggle with opium addiction, he managed to complete his *Biographia Literaria* and produce some other work. Sangharakshita has regarded Coleridge as second only to Shakespeare among the greats of English literary history. See also 'My Five Literary Heroes' in this volume (pp. 481ff. and also note 440 above).

469 The art students called themselves the English Mystical School, or New English Mystical School. It was with them (and others) that Sangharakshita visited Glastonbury Tor in 1969. The experiences they had are recounted in his poem, 'On Glastonbury Tor' (*Complete Works*, vol. 25, pp. 499–504).

470 See *1970: A Retrospect* in *Complete Works*, vol. 23, pp. 465–9.

471 See 'Living with Carter', pp. 607–16 below.

472 Parliament Hill Fields (from which one could at one time see the Houses of Parliament) are at the south-east corner of Hampstead Heath, that great green and open space that runs from Hampstead to Highgate in North London. Kenwood House, a former stately home, now restored and open to the public, is at the northern edge of the Heath.

473 Burton Watson (trans.), *The Vimalakīrti Sūtra*, Columbia University Press, 1997, chapter 10: 'Fragrance Accumulated', p. 117. See also note 323 above.

474 Aśvaghoṣa (attrib.), *The Awakening of Faith*, trans.

Yoshiko S. Hakeda, Columbia University Press, New York 1967, p. 56.

475 Sangharakshita writes of Auntie Kate and other aunts to whom 'only the creator of the Aunts in *Mill on the Floss*' could do justice in *The Rainbow Road from Tooting Broadway to Kalimpong*, *Complete Works*, vol. 20, p. 10.

476 From the second canto of Tennyson's poem 'The Princess', published in 1847.

477 Sung widely since Victorian times as a Christmas carol and still popular today.

478 By hymn writer Isaac Watts (1674–1748) based on Psalm 90. It is often sung to the tune 'St Anne' by William Croft (1678–1727) who composed it whilst organist at St Anne's Church, Soho.

479 *The Pirates of Penzance; or, the Slave of Duty* is a comic opera by librettist W. S. Gilbert (1836–1911) and composer Arthur Sullivan (1842–1900). It was first performed in 1879.

480 Felix Mendelssohn Bartholdy (1809–1847) composed the overture (also known as *Fingal's Cave*) in 1830 after visiting the cave on the Hebridean island of Staffa. Sangharakshita writes about the concert in *The Rainbow Road from Tooting Broadway to Kalimpong*, *Complete Works*, vol. 20, pp. 31–2.

481 George Gershwin (1898–1937), the American composer and pianist, wrote *Rhapsody in Blue* for solo piano and jazz band in 1924.

482 See *The Rainbow Road from Tooting Broadway to Kalimpong*, *Complete Works*, vol. 20, chapter 4, pp. 34–44, 'Here Comes the Boys' Brigade'.

483 This hymn by Sabine Baring-Gould (1834–1924), an Anglican priest and scholar, was written in 1865 originally as a processional hymn for children. The tune, 'St Gertrude', through which it became famous, was composed by Arthur Sullivan in 1871.

484 Perhaps only the last of these well-known composers and their works requires a note. Christian Sinding (1856–1941) was a Norwegian composer who wrote for the piano, both solo and in combination with other instruments. His 'Rustle of Spring' for solo piano was written in 1896 and became a huge success beyond his own country.

485 Sangharakshita's poem was based on a story told by Goethe's friend, Bettina von Arnim (its veracity has been questioned) about the meeting of the two German geniuses in Teplitz (then part of the Austro-Hungarian empire) in 1812. As the two men strolled along together they were met by the empress Maria Ludovica of Austria

and her entourage. Whilst Goethe politely bowed and stepped aside, Beethoven strode straight through their midst, afterwards berating his companion for his servile behaviour. 'There are countless nobles,' he remonstrated, 'but only two of us!'

486 Charles Baudelaire (1821–1867), the French poet, essayist, and art critic. *Les Phares* or 'The Beacons' is a poem of eleven verses, the first eight of which celebrate one of the great European artists. It was included in his collection *Les Fleurs du Mal* (*The Flowers of Evil* or *The Flowers of Suffering*) first published in 1857.

487 Johann Sebastian Bach (1685–1750) composed the *Toccata and Fugue in D Minor* (BMV 565) for organ. No autograph manuscript survives to give the date of composition. (It was published only in 1833, owing to the efforts of Felix Mendelssohn.) Sangharakshita recalled first hearing the piece when he was 15 or 16.

> Stunned, overwhelmed, annihilated by those majestic chords, I went about for several days in a kind of waking trance.

(*The Rainbow Road from Tooting Broadway to Kalimpong*, *Complete Works*, vol. 20, p. 72.)

488 It seems it was, in fact, George Bernard Shaw (1856–1950), the Irish playwright, essayist, and writer, in his play *Man and Superman*, 1903, act 3.

489 Victory over Japan Day. This was 15 August 1945 when the Allies announced that Japan had surrendered, signalling the end of the Second World War. On 2 September a treaty was signed. Conscript Dennis Lingwood (later Sangharakshita), who was at that time stationed in Calcutta for a few weeks, was sent to Singapore to await demobilization (*The Rainbow Road from Tooting Broadway to Kalimpong*, *Complete Works*, vol. 20, pp. 153–7).

490 *Fantasia* is an animated film released by Walt Disney in 1940. Its eight sections feature the music of classical composers from Bach to Stravinsky played by the Philadelphia Orchestra. Leopold Stokowski (1882–1977) was the orchestra's musical director from 1912 to 1940.

491 During a trip to visit the Essen Buddhist Centre and Order members and Mitras in the area in autumn 1989 (*Through Buddhist Eyes*, *Complete Works*, p. 370). The performance was given by the Deutsche Oper am Rhein with a female singer taking the lead role.

492 Richard Strauss (1864–1949), the German Romantic composer especially of operas

and Lieder. His *Four Last Songs* (*Vier Letzte Lieder*) for soprano and orchestra were written in 1948, the year before he died. The fourth is 'Im Abendrot' or 'Sunset'.

Jeremiah Clarke (c.1674–1707) was organist at the Chapel Royal. He composed *The Prince of Denmark's March* around 1700. The piece came to be associated with Henry Purcell and known as the *Trumpet Voluntary* (so called because, though played on the organ, it makes use of the organ's trumpet stop). More recently an orchestral arrangement including trumpet, organ, and kettledrums was devised by conductor Sir Henry Wood (1869–1944). Both these works were indeed played in the course of Sangharakshita's funeral at Adhisthana on 10 November 2018.

493 FWBO activities in Ipswich began in 1986 with meditation classes run by Rex Smart (Saddharaja). From these small beginnings a thriving FWBO (Triratna from 2010) community has grown that over the years has seen the establishment of chapters of Order members, residential communities, a right livelihood business, and, in January 2009, the purchase of premises at 4 Friars Bridge Road to permanently house the Buddhist centre. Sangharakshita officially opened the new centre in July that year.

494 Swadipa (b. 1947) was working as Consultant Obstetrician and Gynaecologist at Ipswich Hospital when he attended a talk at Ipswich Public Library. The talk was on Dr Ambedkar; the speaker was Order member Sumana. In 2008 he himself was ordained. He and Carol were delighted to offer accommodation to Sangharakshita both on the visit referred to here and the previous year when Sangharakshita opened the Ipswich Buddhist Centre.

Carol (b.1947 in Ipswich) was ordained as Charumani in 2014. She was a reception class teacher in an independent girls school in Ipswich when, in 1999, she went along to the Ipswich Buddhist Centre to learn to meditate. She retired in 2007 and asked for ordination the same year.

495 Harshaprabha (b. 1953) went along to an FWBO class in London in 1974, and the following year attended a lecture given by Sangharakshita, 'Enlightenment as Experience and Non-Experience'. They met not long afterwards when Sangharakshita visited the men's community where Harshaprabha was living. With mutual visits, letters, and cards, a friendship sprang up between them. In 1981

Harshaprabha, a trained architect, founded Octagon Architects and Designers, a Buddhist right livelihood business that continued until 2002. In 1991 he started FWBO (Triratna) activities in Colchester. In 2004 he spent a year in Guelph, Ontario, sowing the first Triratna seeds in eastern Canada. That it was Guelph and no other Canadian town is rather striking for Guelph is the place to which some of Sangharakshita's forebears had emigrated (see p. 526 and note 507 below). Furthermore, when the great Buddhist missionary Anagarika Dharmapala visited North America for the second time in 1896, he made a visit to just one Canadian town. That town was – Guelph! (*Anagarika Dharmapala: A Biographical Sketch*, Sangharakshita, Ibis Publications 2013, p. 51, and *Complete Works*, vol. 8.)

496 Norman Foster (b.1935), the English architect, designed the Willis Building soon after founding the now famous Foster Associates in 1967. The Willis Building was constructed between 1970 and 1975, one of Britain's first hi-tech developments. Notable for its lack of right angles, it is coated in smoky glass and topped by a roof garden.

497 See note 430.

498 Heinrich Heine (1797–1856), the German poet and writer, made several visits to the East Frisian island of Nordeney where he wrote many of the verses included in his cycle, *The North Sea* (*Die Nordsee)* written 1825–6. Kate Freiligrath Kroeker's *Poems Selected from Heinrich Heine* was first published in London in 1887.

499 The Knights of St John, also known as the Hospitallers, originated in the eleventh century in a Jerusalem hospital dedicated to St John the Baptist for the tending of sick and weary pilgrims. At the time of the First Crusade (1096–1099) they ceased humanitarian work to become a military order with a papal charter for the defence of the Holy Land. When the Holy Land came under Islamic rule, the Knights' headquarters were removed first to Cyprus, then Rhodes, and then to Malta – their emblem is the Maltese Cross. The first record of the Order's activities in Battisford is under Henry II (1133–1189) and refers to a preceptory or hospital of the Knights. Under Henry VIII the property was confiscated and given in 1544 to one Sir Richard Gresham.

500 The phrase is from John Keats' 1816 sonnet 'On First Looking into Chapman's *Homer*'.

501 This material is summarized in the following chapter.

502 The name of the room was intended to echo the chapter rooms in cathedrals and

was to be used for study and discussion, especially by members of the Order.

503 In January 2010 the Western Buddhist Order and its Indian counterpart, Trailokya Bauddha Mahasangha, were renamed the Triratna Buddhist Order and Triratna Bauddha Mahasangha respectively.

504 From John Keats' *The Eve of St Agnes* (1819), second stanza.

505 Proverbs 10:9.

506 The Fenian Brotherhood (named after a legendary band of Irish warriors) were Irish Republicans based in the United States who carried out raids on British army forts and customs posts in Canada in a bid to bring pressure on Britain to withdraw from Ireland.

507 A town on Lake Huron in south-western Ontario.

508 General John O'Neill (1834–1878), a member of the Fenian Brotherhood, led a number of the Fenian raids.

509 During his year living in Guelph, Harshaprabha (see note 495 above) visited nearby Fergus and looking round the graveyard there discovered the gravestone of Robert Lingwood. Next to Robert Lingwood's grave was the grave of his daughter Jessie (1865–1866) and son Henry (1867–1880). Nearby was the grave of Florence Evelyn Lingwood, fourth daughter of John Campbell Ross (died 21 November 1924).

510 Anna Butters of Besthorpe is the 'Nana' of whom Sangharakshita writes in *A Mosaic of Memories* (see p. 429 above).

511 The Voluntary Aid Detachment was founded in 1909. During the First World War tens of thousands of volunteers – two-thirds women and girls – provided field nursing services at home in Britain and abroad. Vera Brittain's *Testament of Youth* (1933) recounts her experiences as a VAD nurse in the First World War.

512 Named after Field Marshal Earl Roberts (1832–1914) these workshops were for the retraining of wounded ex-servicemen.

513 This stone cottage was the Triyana Vardhana Vihara in Kalimpong (the name was given by Sangharakshita's teacher, Chattrul Sangye Dorje). It came with four acres of terraced hillside which Sangharakshita cultivated as described here (see *Precious Teachers*, *Complete Works*, vol. 22 pp. 429–33). The Vihara was his base from 1957 until he left India for England in 1964.

514 Uncle Tom also appears in *My First Eight Years*, see Neighbours and Early Friends, p. 416–17.

515 Dennis Lingwood left the army demobilization camp where he had been stationed

in Singapore early in 1947 and, in search of a context to lead a spiritual life, returned to India, where he had first landed in 1944. From the spring of 1947 he adopted the name 'Dharmapriya' (he who loves the Dharma – see *The Rainbow Road from Tooting Broadway to Kalimpong*, *Complete Works*, vol. 20, p. 207). It is with this name that he 'went forth' and spent his two-year wandering period. On 12 May 1949 at Kusinara he received the *śrāmaṇera* monastic ordination from U Chandramani, who gave him the name 'Dharmarakshita' ('he who is protected by the Dharma'). However, another disciple of U Chandramani who had been given the same name protested until the elderly preceptor decided the newly ordained *śrāmaṇera* should be Sangharakshita (Ibid. pp. 410–1). 'Urgyen' is a variant of 'Uḍḍiyāna' the place where Padmasambhava was born. (He is sometimes known as Urgyen Padmasambhava.) This name was given to Sangharakshita by his Tibetan teacher Kachu Rimpoche on 21 October 1962 in the context of a Padmasambhava *abhiṣeka* or initiation held at the Triyana Vardhana Vihara (*Precious Teachers*, *Complete Works*, vol. 22 pp. 472–4).

516 Ibid. p. 33.

517 The European Buddhist Union, founded in 1975, is an umbrella association for Buddhist groups and organizations from all Buddhist schools. In 1992 it organized a congress on the theme of 'Unity in Diversity' which was attended by leading Buddhist teachers in Europe including Ayya Khema, Sogyal Rimpoche, Thich Nhat Hanh, and Sangharakshita and which drew some 2,000 visitors. The congress was held in former East Berlin in the Werner-Seelenbinder-Halle shortly before it was demolished. During the event with its talks and discussions and its many stalls representing the different Buddhist groups and schools, Sangharakshita gave a talk on 'Buddhism and the West: the Integration of Buddhism into Western Society'; see *Complete Works*, vol. 11.

518 A Berlin vegetarian restaurant founded in 1982, run by Rinzai Zen practitioners and specializing in Japanese food.

519 The panel discussion on Emptiness and Compassion took place on 27 September 1992. In responding to a question from the floor, Thich Nhat Hanh emphasized the importance of being happy. Sangharakshita pointed out that one cannot always be happy – not even Dharma teachers – but one can always be friendly.

520 Venerable Myokyo-ni (Dr Irmgard Schlögl) (1921–2007) was an Austrian-born

Rinzai Zen nun. She was a member of the Zen group associated with Christmas Humphreys at whose London house she lived after undergoing Zen training in Japan. She went on to become head of the London Zen Centre and author of a number of books on Zen.

521 Dennis Lingwood's first job when he left school in late 1940 was with Parkes' Coal Company in Torquay. One of their customers was Agatha Christie (*The Rainbow Road from Tooting Broadway to Kalimpong*, *Complete Works*, vol. 20, p. 64).

522

> If a man does not make new acquaintance as he advances through life, he will soon find himself left alone. A man, Sir, should keep his friendship in constant repair.

According to his biographer, James Boswell, the remark was made by Dr Johnson in 1755 to the painter, Sir Joshua Reynolds. See 1755: *aetat.* 46 in James Boswell, *The Life of Samuel Johnson*, first published in 1791.

523 See p. 61 above.

524 8 May 1945: the Nazi forces surrendered to the forces of the Allied armies bringing the war in Europe to an end.

525 See note 475 above.

526 Mallika was ordained in 1974. She spent most of her Dharma life in the sangha of the London Buddhist Centre, and in old age (as mentioned here) returned to her native Scotland, where she died in 2018.

527 Since 2013 Adhisthana, in rural Herefordshire, has been at the heart of the Triratna Buddhist Community. It includes the Sangharakshita Library, a retreat and study centre, and a large residential community and was Sangharakshita's home for the last six years of his life.

528 Vidyaruchi, from Norfolk, England, was ordained in 2009. He was Sangharakshita's personal secretary for several years.

529 Buddhadasa (Australian), Suvajra (Scottish), and Ashvajit (English) were all ordained in the 1970s. They all did much to support Triratna activities in many parts of the world – Buddhadasa in England, Finland, and Australia; Suvajra in England and India; and Ashvajit in New Zealand, England, India, and Sri Lanka. They were all members of Sangharakshita's support team in the final years of his life.

530 These are both Mahāyana *sūtras*. The *Saṃdhinirmocana Sūtra* is the key text of the Yogācāra school, available in English translation as John Keenan (trans.), *The Scripture on the Explication of Underlying Meaning*, Numata Center for Buddhist

Translation and Research, Berkeley 2000.

Sangharakshita describes the *Śūraṅgamasamādhi Sūtra* in *The Eternal Legacy*; see *Complete Works*, vol. 14, pp. 195–8. For an English translation, see, for example, Sara Boin-Webb, *Śūraṃgamasamādhisūtra: The Concentration of Heroic Progress*, Curzon Press, Richmond, Surrey, 1998.

531 Sthanashraddha was ordained in 2013 and was Sangharakshita's secretary for the last few years of his life.

532 Kalyanaprabha had edited *A Moseley Miscellany* and several other books published in Sangharakshita's later years, and she also worked closely with him on preparing his library for its move to Adhisthana. She has edited several volumes of the *Complete Works*.

Subhuti, to whom Sangharakshita had handed on the responsibility of being the Order's first chair after himself, was in the UK, but at this time he was spending a lot of his time with the Triratna community in India.

At the time of this event Parami and Lokeshvara were living at Adhisthana as the International Order Convenors, after many years supporting projects elsewhere: Parami (from Scotland) had lived in Spain for many years and Lokeshvara (from Norfolk, England) had been chair at Padmaloka Buddhist Retreat Centre.

Yashodeva, having spent much of his Triratna career supporting the movement's growth in the Hispanic world, was also a key member of the Adhisthana community.

533 More money came in after the ninetieth birthday celebrations so that the final count was around £135,000, some of which was dedicated to the translation of Sangharakshita's works.

534 Saddhanandi, who was Adhisthana's chair at the time of this exhibition (after many years as chair of Tārāloka Retreat Centre), had interviewed Sangharakshita about the objects in this collection, and in the course of doing so formed a close friendship with him.

Danasamudra, who also lived in the women's community at Adhisthana at this time, was the first librarian of the Sangharakshita Library there.

535 See *The Rainbow Road from Tooting Broadway to Kalimpong*, *Complete Works*, vol. 20, pp. 1–2.

536 Sir Harry Lauder lived at 46 Longley Road, Tooting, from 1903 to 1911.

537 For more about this, and reflections on the role of the Manu, see the talk 'The Manu, the Buddha, the Guru, and the

Terton', in *Complete Works*, vol. 12, pp. 319–21.

538 Alaya, ordained in 1975, was a carpenter, and worked on many projects in the Triratna Buddhist Community, including the Glasgow Buddhist Centre, the shrine at the London Buddhist Centre, and the shrine at Vajraloka. In 1988 he moved with his family from London to Norwich where he was involved with the Norwich Buddhist Centre until his death in 2015.

539 The centre in Bethnal Green opened in 1978, and became known as the London Buddhist Centre. Sukhavati was adopted as the name for the men's community above the Centre.

540 The 'gee-gees' is slang for racehorses.

541 See *What is the Sangha?*, *Complete Works*, vol. 3, chapter 5, pp. 434–44.

542 *The Rainbow Road from Tooting Broadway to Kalimpong*, *Complete Works*, vol. 20, p. 52.

543 Ibid. pp. 328–34.

544 Ibid. p. 345.

545 William Lygon, Seventh Earl of Beauchamp, of Walmer Castle, Kent, was embroiled in scandal in connection with his homosexuality and in 1931 King George v was told of this and reportedly responded, 'Why, I thought people like that always shot themselves.'

546 The six emphases are the centrality of Going for Refuge to the Three Jewels, a unified Order, a non-sectarian approach, the importance of spiritual friendship, right livelihood, and the spiritual value of the arts. The talks are amalgamated in 'Forty Years On: The Six Distinctive Emphases of the FWBO' in *Complete Works*, vol. 12, pp. 663–73.

547 Anthony Trollope (1815–1882) juggled his career as a novelist with long service working for the General Post Office. His novel *The Prime Minister*, the fifth of the Pallisers series, was first published in 1876. *Doctor Thorne*, first published in 1868, is the third in the series *The Chronicles of Barsetshire*.

548 For something of Sangharakshita's friendship with Claire Cameron, see *The Rainbow Road*, *Complete Works*, vol. 20, pp. 100 and 103. See also in *Dear Dinoo: Letters to A Friend*, *Complete Works*, vol. 21, pp. 479–82.

549 PEN is an international association of writers. The PEN Club was founded in London in 1921, the initials standing for 'Poets, Essayists, Novelists'; this was later expanded to include playwrights and editors. It is now known as PEN International and has branches in many countries; among its aims is 'to create a

world community of writers that would emphasize the central role of literature in the development of world culture'.

550 Sangharakshita gave this article the title 'A Bird's Eye View of Indian Buddhism'. Not having heard anything about it from Oxford University Press and assuming (wrongly, as it turned out) that they no longer wanted it, in 1980 he included it as the introduction to the fifth edition of *A Survey of Buddhism*. It now appears in *Complete Works*, vol. 7, pp. 485–513.

551 The article 'Rights and Duties' appeared in *Crossing the Stream*; see *Complete Works*, vol. 7, pp. 276–80.

552 The Buddha speaks of the mutual duties of parents and children, employees and employers, and so on in the *Sigālaka Sutta*, *Dīgha Nikāya* 31; see M. Walshe (trans.), *The Long Discourses of the Buddha*, Wisdom Publications, Boston 1995, pp. 461–9; or T. W. & C. A. F. Rhys Davids (trans.), *Dialogues of the Buddha*, part 3, Pali Text Society, London 1971, pp. 173–84.

553 The shipping forecast is broadcast by BBC radio several times a day. Its list of thirty-one placenames (all of them coastal or offshore sites around the British Isles) with associated weather conditions make a kind of soothing litany ('Shannon, Rockall, Mallin, Hebrides') which many British people are fond of, and it has been the subject of poems and artworks.

554 *Moving Against the Stream*, *Complete Works*, vol. 23, p. 264.

555 Neoplatonism is a term used to describe a succession of philosophers in the Platonic tradition from the third to sixth centuries CE, beginning with the Egyptian Plotinus. According to Plotinus, God is the highest reality and consists of three parts or hypostases: the One, the Divine Intelligence, and the Universal Soul.

The three *svabhāvas* of the Yogacārā are *pariniṣpanna*, absolute nature, *paratantra* or dependent nature, and *parikalpita*, imputed nature or mere illusion. For an introduction to these, see *A Survey of Buddhism*, *Complete Works*, vol. 1, pp. 370–1.

556 This is very much the figure seen in Sangharakshita's piece 'Four Visitors'; see below p. 619.

557 This refers to the tradition of the British tabloid press of publishing a full-page image of a topless model on page 3 of their daily newspapers.

558 This phrase translates the Latin *mens sana in corpore sano*, first used in the *Satires* of the Roman poet Juvenal and adopted as a motto in some English schools as expressive of the ideal education.

559 *The Rainbow Road from Tooting Broadway to Kalimpong*, *Complete Works*, vol. 20, p. 344.

560 For the whole poem, see *Complete Works*, vol. 25, pp. 198–9.

561 In chapter 6 of Anthony Trollope's 1855 novel *The Warden*, a young man playing the flute is three times referred to as 'Apollo'.

562 Plotinus, *Enneads* 1.6, trans. A. H. Armstrong, Loeb Classical Library, Harvard University Press, Cambridge MA 1969, p. 233.

563 Thomas Aquinas (1225–1274) was an Italian theologian, philosopher, and Dominican priest whose writings were hugely influential in the development of Roman Catholic theology. This statement is from his most famous work, the *Summa Theologica*, a compendium for theological students setting forth the reasoning for the main Christian tenets of belief. In the first part of the work, in chapter 5, 'Of Goodness in General', one of the questions he raises about goodness is whether it 'has the aspect of a final cause'. He raises three possible objections to that proposition, and his statement about beauty is in the reply to the first of those objections.

564 See Eugene Watson Burlingame (trans.), *Buddhist Legends (Dhammapada Commentary)*, part 1, Pali Text Society, London 1969, pp. 218–23; and *Udāna* 3.2. For Sangharakshita's commentary on the latter, see *Complete Works*, vol. 10, pp. 504–7.

565 *Pāṭika Sutta*, *Dīgha Nikāya* 24 (iii.34). See M. Walshe (trans.), *The Long Discourses of the Buddha*, Wisdom Publications, Boston 1995, pp. 382–3; or T. W. & C. A. F. Rhys Davids (trans.), *Dialogues of the Buddha*, part 3, Pali Text Society, London 1971, pp. 31–2.

566 This poem is one of those in the section dated 1793 which William Blake jotted down in a notebook called the Rossetti manuscript because it was once owned by the poet Dante Gabriel Rossetti. The book is now held by the British Library.

567 This unpublished article has not been found.

568 For Sangharakshita's encounters with Jinaratana in India see *Facing Mount Kanchenjunga*, *Complete Works*, vol. 21, pp. 266, 568 *et passim*.

569 *The Theology of the Pain of God*, first published in Japan in 1946 and in America in 1965, is the work of the Japanese theologian Kazoh Kitamori (1916–1998).

570 Peggy Kennett (Jiyu Roshi) (1924–1996) was an English student of Zen. She spent a number of years in Japan training in the Sōtō Zen school before moving to

the USA, where she founded the Zen Mission Society (later the Order of Buddhist Contemplatives) and Shasta Abbey in California, where she lived and was the abbess until her death. She was one of the first women to hold the title of roshi or authorized teacher.

571 See also pp. 496–7 above. Sangharakshita describes a second trip in *1970: A Retropect*; see *Complete Works*, vol. 23, pp. 466–9.

572 Both Ananda and Abhaya were involved in the Triratna Buddhist Community (then the FWBO) from its earliest days, and Ananda was one of the first twelve people to be ordained. A dedicated poet, one of Ananda's later projects was the founding of the Wolf at the Door writing workshops, and Abhaya, after a period working and studying in Japan, returned to the UK and was involved in teaching the Dharma at several Buddhist centres, including Cambridge, Vajrakuta, and Brighton.

573 See, for example, 'In the New Forest', *Complete Works*, vol. 25, p. 329.

574 See 'On Glastonbury Tor', *Complete Works*, vol. 25, pp. 499–504.

575 The poet is John Dryden (1631–1700) and this line is from the fifth stanza of his poem 'Alexander's Feast, or, the Power of Music'.

576 The Welsh poet Dylan Thomas (1914–1953) lived with his family in the Boathouse at Laugharne (which is in south-west Wales, on the estuary of the river Tâf) from 1938 until his death in 1953. The shed in which he did a lot of his writing is now a museum, preserved just as it was when the poet used it.

577 These were the Pendine Sands, on which Malcolm Campbell broke the land speed record in 1924 in his Sunbeam car Blue Bird.

578 The six-winged Raphael is described in John Milton, *Paradise Lost*, book 5, lines 275–87.

579 Ibid. book 4, lines 109–111:

> So farewell hope, and, with hope, farewell fear,
> Farewell remorse! All good to me is lost;
> Evil, be thou my Good …

580 See p. 593 above.

581 For a description of Dr Dinshaw Mehta, and his life and friendship with Sangharakshita, especially during the 1950s, see 'The Monk and the Prophet' in *Dear Dinoo: Letters to a Friend*, *Complete Works*, vol. 21, pp. 599–619.

582 *Gārava Sutta, Saṃyutta Nikaya* i.138–40 (6.2); see Bhikkhu Bodhi (trans.), *The Connected Discourses of the Buddha*, Wisdom Publications, Boston 2000, pp. 233–5; or C. A. F. Rhys Davids (trans.), *The Book of the Kindred Sayings*, part 1, Pali

Text Society, London 1979, pp. 174–6.

583 This work, first published in 1841, was based on a series of lectures given by Thomas Carlyle (1795–1881), a Scottish philosopher and historian who moved to London in 1831 and became known as 'the Sage of Chelsea'.

584 Sangharakshita describes his initiation into these three practices in *Precious Teachers*; see *Complete Works*, vol. 22, pp. 554–6.

585 The Latin saying *Corruptio optimi pessima* is found in English writings from the seventeenth century onwards.

'Lilies that fester smell far worse than weeds' is the last line of Shakespeare's *Sonnet* 94.

586 These are the last two lines of Stephen Spender's poem, 'The Truly Great', which begins 'I think continually of those who were truly great'.

587 *Maggasaṃyutta*, *Saṃyutta Nikāya* v.2; see Bhikkhu Bodhi (trans.), *The Connected Discourses of the Buddha*, Wisdom Publications, Boston 2000, pp. 1524–5; also F. L. Woodward (trans.), *The Book of the Kindred Sayings*, part 5, Pali Text Society, London 1979, p. 2.

588 This is the first line of a prose work (originally a sermon) published in *Devotions upon Emergent Occasions* in 1624. The famous passage begins, 'No man is an island, entire of itself' and ends,

> Any man's death diminishes me, because I am involved in mankind. And therefore never send to know for whom the bells tolls; it tolls for thee.

589 See the *Sigālaka Sutta*, *Dīgha Nikāya* 31 (iii.190); M. Walshe (trans.), *The Long Discourses of the Buddha*, Wisdom Publications, Boston 1995, pp. 467–8; or T. W. & C. A. F. Rhys Davids (trans.), *Dialogues of the Buddha*, part 3, Pali Text Society, London 1971, p. 182.

590 The story is told at Vinaya Piṭaka i.301–3 (*Mahāvagga* 8.26); see I. B. Horner (trans.), *The Book of the Discipline*, part 4, Pali Text Society, Oxford 1996, pp. 431–4. See also Sangharakshita, *The Buddha's Victory*, chapter 4, 'A Case of Dysentery' (*Complete Works*, vol. 11).

591 The story of Soṇa Koḷivisa, who walked up and down so vigorously that his feet bled, is to be found at Vinaya Piṭaka i.181–2 (*Mahāvagga* 5.11–13); see I. B. Horner (trans.), *The Book of the Discipline*, part 4, Pali Text Society, Oxford 1996, pp. 239–41. The story is also told in the *Soṇa Sutta*, *Aṅguttara Nikāya* iii.374 (6.55), though this does not include the detail of Soṇa's bleeding feet. See Bhikkhu Bodhi (trans.), *The Numerical*

Discourses of the Buddha, Wisdom Publications, Boston 2012, pp. 932–4; or F. L. Woodward (trans.), *The Book of the Gradual Sayings*, vol. v, Pali Text Society, Oxford 1996, pp. 266–8.

592 Abanindranath Tagore (1871–1951) and his pupil Nandalal Bose (1882–1966) were pioneers of modern Indian painting. Nephew of the poet Rabindranath Tagore, Abanindranath Tagore was influential in promoting contemporary interpretations of traditional Moghul and Rajput styles as a counterbalance to the spread of Western art. Bose also contributed to the cause of Indian nationalism through art, focusing mainly on traditional subjects but with the innovative use of non-traditional techniques such as linocut.

593 Sir Edwin Arnold (1832–1904) was an English poet and journalist. His epic poem recounting the life of the Buddha, *The Light of Asia: the Great Renunciation*, is based on the *Lalitavistara Sūtra*. He was principal of the British government college in Poona, India, from 1856 to 1861, before returning to England to join the staff of the *Daily Telegraph*.

594 Published in English translation as Gwendolyn Bays (trans.), *The Voice of the Buddha: The Beauty of Compassion*, Dharma Publishing, Berkeley 1983.

595 The text, known as the Tiratana Vandanā, is found in several places in the Pāli canon, notably in the *Mahāparinibbāna Sutta*, *Dīgha Nikāya* 16 (ii.93), in the section called the Mirror of the Dharma. See M. Walshe (trans.), *The Long Discourses of the Buddha*, Wisdom Publications, Boston 1995, p. 241; or T. W. & C. A. F. Rhys Davids (trans.), *Dialogues of the Buddha*, part 2, Pali Text Society, London 1971, pp. 99–100. Buddhaghosa discusses the elements of the text in great detail at *Visuddhimagga* 198–221: see *The Path of Purification*, trans. Bhikkhu Ñāṇamoli, Buddhist Publication Society, Kandy 1991, pp. 192–218; or Pe Maung Tin (trans.), *The Path of Purity*, Pali Text Society, London 1975, pp. 227–56.

596 Vera Brittain (1893–1970) was a nurse during the First World War and later became a noted socialist and pacifist. It was her memoir of the First World War, *Testament of Youth*, that made her famous. It was followed by *Testament of Friendship: The Story of Winifred Holtby* (published in 1940), and a third work, *Testament of Experience*.

597 For a little about Sangharakshita's connection with Ginsberg, see 'With

Allen Ginsberg in Kalimpong', in *Complete Works*, vol. 22, pp. 563–8); and Sangharakshita's poem, 'In Memory of Allen Ginsberg', *Complete Works* vol. 25, p. 413. See also note 437 above.

598 See *Complete Works*, vol. 12, pp. 338–62.

599 See *Complete Works*, vol. 11.

600 In 2002 the FWBO made a submission to the United Kingdom Parliament in support of the proposal to abolish the offence of blasphemy made that year by Lord Avebury (1928–2016), a humanist and 'secular Buddhist'; perhaps it was he who quoted *Buddhism and Blasphemy* in Parliament.

601 *Vatthūpama Sutta*, *Majjhima Nikāya* 7 (i.37). See Bhikkhu Ñāṇamoli and Bhikkhu Bodhi (trans.), *The Middle Length Discourses of the Buddha*, Wisdom Publications, Boston 1995, p. 119; or I. B. Horner (trans.), *The Collection of the Middle Length Sayings*, vol. i, Pali Text Society, London 1976, p. 47.

602 See *Facing Mount Kanchenjunga*, *Complete Works*, vol. 21, p. 300; see also *Transforming Self and World*, *Complete Works*, vol. 16, pp. 273–4.

603 This is from the Sevenfold Puja, which is recited throughout the Triratna Buddhist Community. Its verses are adapted from Śāntideva's *Bodhicaryāvatāra*, and it was first published in *FWBO Newsletter* no. 4 (March 1969) with the explanation that the verses had been 'translated by Mrs A. A. G. Bennett. Selected and arranged by Ven. Sthavira Sangharakshita'. For a little about Mrs Adrienne Bennett, see *Moving Against the Stream*, *Complete Works*, vol. 23, pp. 54–5.

604 For more about the traditional teaching, see 'The Buddha's Victory', in the collection of that name in *Complete Works*, vol. 11.

605 These are the sixth and second (respectively) of 'The Proverbs of Hell'. William Blake's *Marriage of Heaven and Hell* was published in the author's own illustrated edition in 1793.

606 These are the first two lines of the Prologue to William Blake's 'For the Sexes: The Gates of Paradise,' in *Complete Writings*, Oxford University Press, Oxford 1966, p. 761.

607 *Sutta-Nipāta* 1.4. Andrew Olendzki's translation.

608 *Vision and Transformation* was later republished as *The Buddha's Noble Eightfold Path*. For its chapter 'Perfect Livelihood: the Ideal Society', see *Complete Works*, vol. 1, pp. 538–51.

609 The Arts and Crafts movement emerged from the attempt to reform design and decoration in mid-nineteenth-century Britain. It was a reaction

against a perceived decline in standards that the reformers associated with machinery and factory production. It drew on the ideas of the architect A. W. N. Pugin and the critic John Ruskin, but it was mainly influenced by William Morris.

610 This is a reference to the work of the Indian statesman Dr B. R. Ambedkar. See *Complete Works*, vols. 9 and 10.

611 This is the twenty-seventh 'Proverb of Hell'; see plate 8 of William Blake's *Marriage of Heaven and Hell*, which was published in the author's own illustrated edition in 1793.

612 Friedrich Nietzsche, *Thus Spoke Zarathustra*, chapter 73 ('The Convalescent'). This translation has not been identified.

613 See p. 565 above.

614 The talk, based on the occasion described in the Pāli canon when the Buddha helped a sick monk, was originally published in *The Buddha's Victory*; see *Complete Works*, vol. 11. For the Pāli canon incident, see Vinaya Piṭaka i.301–2 (*Mahāvagga* 8.26); I. B. Horner (trans.), *The Book of the Discipline*, part 4, Pali Text Society, Oxford 1996, pp. 431–4.

615 This seminar, or retreat, was held at Adhisthana on 21–28 July 2017, and co-created by Ananda, Atula, Dhivan, Ratnaprabha, Saccanama and Satyalila.

616 Satyalila was one of the main inspirations behind the series of retreats on the work of William Blake that took place at Adhisthana in these years. The curation of '50 years, 50 voices', a collection of interviews with Order members, is another of her many creative projects, and yet another is the indexing most of the volumes of the *Complete Works*, including this one.

617 Sanghadeva, after involvement in many Triratna projects, became gardener and cook at Madhyamaloka in Birmingham when Sangharakshita lived there, and later moved to Adhisthana, where he took charge of creating the gardens that surround the retreat centre.

618 This was indeed the spot where Sangharakshita was buried, his funeral taking place on 10 November 2018. His burial mound is covered in green turf and surrounded by a garden of white flowers.

619 Dante Gabriel Rossetti (1828–1882) was an English poet and painter and a co-founder of the Pre-Raphaelite Brotherhood. Rossetti is not among the 'five literary heroes' mentioned in Sangharakshita's piece about the writers he most admired ('My Five Literary Heroes', pp. 481–90 above), but Rossetti was one of his favourites from the early days, the 'intensely fused sensuousness and mysticism' of Rossetti's

poetry 'went to my head like some subtle and dangerous perfume' (*The Rainbow Road from Tooting Broadway to Kalimpong*, *Complete Works*, vol. 20, p. 36).

620 The quotation is from canto 17 of the *Paradiso* of Dante's *Divine Comedy*.

621 Shelley's 'Julian and Maddalo' was written in 1818–19, and published in 1824, after the poet's death.

622 The 'Rossetti Manuscript', which Rossetti bought from Samuel Palmer's brother William (to whom Blake's widow had given it), is now held by the British Library in London, and can be seen there.

623 'Napoleon on Board the Bellerophon' can be seen at Tate Britain in London; the painting was given to the gallery in 1880. It is the work of Sir William Quiller Orchardson, who specialized in painting historical scenes.

624 'The Golden Stairs', by Sir Edward Coley Burne-Jones, can be seen at the Tate Britain gallery in London.

625 This print, 'William Caxton showing specimens of his printing to King Edward IV and his Queen', was first published in a magazine called *The Graphic* in 1877, to celebrate the four hundredth anniversary of the first printed book in England, Chaucer's *Canterbury Tales*, which was printed by William Caxton, who lived in Belgium for a while and observed the progress of printing in mainland Europe, and in 1476 is said to have imported the first printing press ever seen in Britain.

626 See p. 616 above.

627 In this *sūtra* Māra pretends to arouse the *bodhicitta* in order to be released from his bonds; then he thinks,

> Now that I am delivered from the bonds, I shall go to the Buddha and disturb the instruction of the Dharma.

Sara Boin-Webb, *Śūraṃgamasamādhisūtra: The Concentration of Heroic Progress*, Curzon Press, Richmond, Surrey, 1998, p. 178.

628 See *Precious Teachers*, *Complete Works*, vol. 22, p. 402.

629 This verse is at the top of plate 77 ('To the Christians') of William Blake's 1815 illustrated work *Jerusalem*.

630 The stages are described in the *Satipaṭṭhāna Sutta*, *Majjhima Nikāya* 10 (i.58). See I. B. Horner (trans.), *The Collection of the Middle Length Sayings*, vol. i, Pali Text Society, London 1976, p. 74; or Bhikkhu Ñāṇamoli and Bhikkhu Bodhi (trans.), *The Middle Length Discourses of the Buddha*, Wisdom Publications, Boston 1995, p. 148.

631 The story of Nanda is told in Eugene Watson Burlingame (trans.), *Buddhist Legends*

(*Dhammapada Commentary*), part 1, Pali Text Society, London 1969, pp. 218–9; also at *Udāna* 3.2. For Sangharakshita's commentary on the *Udāna* text, see *Complete Works*, vol. 10, pp. 504–7.

632 *Symposium*, sections 210–2.

633 See note 562.

634 *Complete Works*, vol. 25, p. 223.

635 From chapter 16, 'The Glorious Company of Bodhisattvas', in *The Three Jewels*; see *Complete Works*, vol. 2, pp. 154–5.

636 This article was originally published in *The Path of the Inner Life*, and later in *Crossing the Stream*; see *Complete Works*, vol. 7, pp. 405–10.

637 For more about Dinshaw Mehta and the 'guidance', see *In the Sign of the Golden Wheel*, *Complete Works*, vol. 22, pp. 284ff.

638 *The Rainbow Road from Tooting Broadway to Kalimpong*, *Complete Works*, vol. 20 p. 226.

639 See *Precious Teachers*, in *Complete Works*, vol. 22, pp. 472–4.

640 In May 2009, Dhammarati, then the chair of Triratna's Preceptors' College, reported on Sangharakshita's meeting with the public preceptors in March of that year:

> It felt like Bhante was saying something of real significance about the Order and how we understand it: at one point he talked about it as almost as a 'refounding' of the order.

This is probably the remark referred to here.

641 See p. 623 above.

642 *The Agony in the Garden of Gethsemane* on display at the National Gallery in London is given the attribution 'The Studio of El Greco', and the gallery states that it is based on an original El Greco now held by the Toledo Museum of Art, Ohio.

643 The Isenheim Altarpiece was painted and sculpted in the early sixteenth century. It is on display at the Unterlinden Museum, at Colmar, Alsace, in France.

644 For the story of William Adams, see, for example, Giles Milton, *Samurai William: the adventurer who unlocked Japan*, Sceptre, London 2002; for examples of cruelty see, for example, pp. 118, 229, 354.

645 See note 182.

646 Sangharakshita was revisiting *Honest to God* having considered the text in great detail many years before in his talk 'Buddhism and the Bishop of Woolwich' (John Robinson was then the bishop); see *Complete Works*, vol. 12, pp. [illegible]–11.

647 Sir James Jeans was an English scientist. *The Mysterious Universe*, which was first

published in 1930, starts with an account of Plato's allegory of the cave.

648 Carlo Rovelli, *Reality Is Not What It Seems: The Journey to Quantum Gravity*, trans. Simon Carnell and Erica Segre, Penguin Books, London 2017, p. 88.

649 This was a statement on 'Buddhist-led violence against Muslims in Burma', and was signed by Sangharakshita and six other members of the Triratna Buddhist Order, and posted on thebuddhistcentre.com in October 2013.

650 George Sale published the first English translation of the *Koran* in 1734, and in 1861 Rev. J. M. Rodwell produced a version in which he rearranged the chapters into what he considered to be chronological order and interpreted the work through Mohammed as its author. In 1880, as part of the 'Sacred Books of the East' series pioneered by Max Müller, Edward Henry Palmer produced an 'erudite, relatively un-polemical' *Qur'an* in two volumes – a first attempt to bring the Arabic scripture into a more colloquial English.

651 Hafiz, Attar, and Rumi, together with Saadi, are known as the quartet of great Sufi master poets. All of them were Persian. Attar (c.1145–c.1221), one of the most ancient and highly revered poets of Persia, inspired later Sufi poets such as Rumi and Hafiz. Rumi (1207–1273) was born in Balkh (now in Afghanistan) and died in Konya (now in Turkey), where his tomb is visited by many pilgrims. He wrote in Farsi (Persian), Arabic, Turkish, and some Greek, and is loved throughout the East and increasingly in the West as well. And Hafiz or Hafez (1315–1390) was a Persian poet whose works are regarded by many Iranians as the pinnacle of Persian poetry. He was born in Shiraz, and some years after his death a mausoleum to him was placed in the Musalla Gardens in the city; to this day, Iranians gather there to recite and sing his words.

652 Henri Corbin (1903–1978) was a philosopher, theologian, Iranologist, and professor of Islamic studies in Paris.

653 The text is Al-Ghazali, *The Duties of Brotherhood in Islam*, trans. Muhtar Holland, Islamic Foundation, Leicester 1975. A transcript of Sangharakshita's seminar on it is available at freebuddhistaudio.com.

654 *The Rainbow Road from Tooting Broadway to Kalimpong, Complete Works*, vol. 20, pp. 15–25.

655 Reza Shah Kazemi, *Common Ground Between Islam and Buddhism*, Fons Vitae, Louisville 2010, pp. 8–9.

656 This was published in *Crossing the Stream*; see *Complete Works*, vol. 7, pp. 364–71.

657 Reza Shah Kazemi, *Common Ground Between Islam and Buddhism*, Fons Vitae, Louisville 2010, p. 14.

658 Ibid. pp. 20–1.

659 *Seeds of Peace* is published by the INEB (International Network of Engaged Buddhists). This article is from *Seeds of Peace*, vol. 34, no. 2, May–August 2561 (2018), p. 4. Hozan Alan Senauke is a Sōtō Zen priest and poet, currently (2021) Abbot at the Berkeley Zen Center.

660 Anālayo, *Rebirth in Early Buddhism and Current Research*, Wisdom Publications, Boston 2018, p. 35.

661 Ibid. p. 163.

INDEX

A GUIDE TO THE COMPLETE WORKS OF SANGHARAKSHITA

Gathered together in these twenty-seven volumes are talks and stories, commentaries on the Buddhist scriptures, poems, memoirs, reviews, and other writings. The genres are many, and the subject matter covered is wide, but it all has – its whole purpose is to convey – that taste of freedom which the Buddha declared to be the hallmark of his Dharma. Another traditional description of the Buddha's Dharma is that it is *ehipassiko*, 'come and see'. Sangharakshita calls to us, his readers, to come and see how the Dharma can fundamentally change the way we see things, change the way we live for the better, and change the society we belong to, wherever in the world we live.

Sangharakshita's very first published piece, *The Unity of Buddhism* (found in volume 7 of this collection), appeared in 1944 when he was eighteen years old, and it introduced themes that continued to resound throughout his work: the basis of Buddhist ethics, the compassion of the bodhisattva, and the transcendental unity of Buddhism. Over the course of the following seven decades not only did numerous other works flow from his pen; he gave hundreds of talks (some now lost). In gathering all we could find of this vast output, we have sought to arrange it in a way that brings a sense of coherence, communicating something essential about Sangharakshita, his life and teaching. Recalling the three 'baskets' among which an early tradition divided the Buddha's teachings, we have divided Sangharakshita's creative output into six 'baskets' or groups: foundation texts; works originating in India; teachings originally given in the West; commentaries on the Buddhist scriptures; personal writings; and poetry, aphorisms, and works on the arts. The 27th volume, a concordance, brings together all the terms and themes of the whole collection. If you want to find a particular story or teaching, look at a traditional term from different points of view or in different contexts, or track down one of the thousands of canonical references to be found in these volumes, the concordance will be your guide.

1. FOUNDATION

What is the foundation of a Buddhist life? How do we understand and then follow the Buddha's path of Ethics, Meditation, and Wisdom? What is really meant by 'Going for Refuge to the Three Jewels', described by Sangharakshita as the essential act of a Buddhist life? And what is the Bodhisattva ideal, which he has called 'one of the sublimest ideals mankind has ever seen'? In the 'Foundation' group you will find teachings on all these themes. It includes the author's *magnum opus, A Survey of Buddhism*, a collection of teachings on *The Purpose and Practice of Buddhist Meditation*, and the anthology, *The Essential Sangharakshita*, an eminently helpful distillation of the entire corpus.

2. INDIA

From 1950 to 1964 Sangharakshita, based in Kalimpong in the eastern Himalayas, poured his energy into trying to revive Buddhism in the land of its birth and to revitalize and bring reform to the existing Asian Buddhist world. The articles and book reviews from this period are gathered in volumes 7 and 8, as well as his biographical sketch of the great Sinhalese Dharmaduta, Anagārika Dharmapala. In 1954 Sangharakshita took on the editing of the *Maha Bodhi*, a journal for which he wrote a monthly editorial, and which, under his editorship, published the work of many of the leading Buddhist writers of the time. It was also during these years in India that a vital connection was forged with Dr B. R. Ambedkar, renowned Indian statesman and leader of the Buddhist mass conversion of 1956. Sangharakshita became closely involved with the new Buddhists and, after Dr Ambedkar's untimely death, visited them regularly on extensive teaching tours.

From 1979, when an Indian wing of the Triratna Buddhist Community was founded (then known as TBMSG), Sangharakshita returned several times to undertake further teaching tours. The talks from these tours are collected in volumes 9 and 10 along with a unique work on Ambedkar and his life which draws out the significance of his conversion to Buddhism.

3. THE WEST

Sangharakshita founded the Triratna Buddhist Community (then called the Friends of the Western Buddhist Order) on 6 April 1967. On 7 April the following year he performed the first ordinations of men and women within the Triratna Buddhist Order (then the Western Buddhist Order). At that time Buddhism was not widely known in the West and for the following two decades or so he taught intensively, finding new ways to communicate the ancient truths of Buddhism, drawing on the whole Buddhist tradition to do so, as well as making connections with what was best in existing Western culture. Sometimes his sword flashed as he critiqued ideas and views inimical to the Dharma. It is these teachings and writings that are gathered together in this third group.

4. COMMENTARY

Throughout Sangharakshita's works are threaded references to the Buddhist canon of literature – Pāli, Mahāyāna, and Vajrayāna – from which he drew his inspiration. In the early days of the new movement he often taught by means of seminars in which, prompted by the questions of his students, he sought to pass on the inspiration and wisdom of the Buddhist tradition. Each seminar was based around a different text, the seminars were recorded and transcribed, and in due course many of the transcriptions were edited and turned into books, all carefully checked by Sangharakshita. The commentaries compiled in this way constitute the fourth group. In some ways this is the heart of the collection. Sangharakshita often told the story of how it was that, reading two *sūtras* at the age of sixteen or seventeen, he realized that he was a Buddhist, and he has never tired of showing others how they too could see and realize the value of the '*sūtra*-treasure'.

5. MEMOIRS

Who is Sangharakshita? What sort of life did he live? Whom did he meet? What did he feel? Why did he found a new Buddhist movement? In these volumes of memoirs and letters Sangharakshita shares with his readers much about himself and his life as he himself has experienced it, giving us a sense of its breadth and depth, humour and pathos.

6. POETRY, APHORISMS, AND THE ARTS

Sangharakshita describes reading *Paradise Lost* at the age of twelve as one of the greatest poetic experiences of his life. His realization of the value of the higher arts to spiritual development is one of his distinctive contributions to our understanding of what Buddhist life is, and he has expressed it in a number of essays and articles. Throughout his life he has written poetry which he says can be regarded as a kind of spiritual autobiography. It is here, perhaps, that we come closest to the heart of Sangharakshita. He has also written a few short stories and composed some startling aphorisms. Through book reviews he has engaged with the experiences, ideas, and opinions of modern writers. All these are collected in this sixth group.

In the preface to *A Survey of Buddhism* (volume 1 in this collection), Sangharakshita wrote of his approach to the Buddha's teachings:

> Why did the Buddha (or Nāgārjuna, or Buddhaghosa) teach this particular doctrine? What bearing does it have on the spiritual life? How does it help the individual Buddhist actually to follow the spiritual path?... I found myself asking such questions again and again, for only in this way, I found, could I make sense – spiritual sense – of Buddhism.

Although this collection contains so many words, they are all intent, directly or indirectly, on these same questions. And all these words are not in the end about their writer, but about his great subject, the Buddha and his teaching, and about you, the reader, for whose benefit they are solely intended. These pages are full of the reverence that Sangharakshita has always felt, which is expressed in an early poem, 'Taking Refuge in the Buddha', whose refrain is 'My place is at thy feet'. He has devoted his life to communicating the Buddha's Dharma in its depth and in its breadth, to men and women from all backgrounds and walks of life, from all countries, of all races, of all ages. These collected works are the fruit of that devotion.

We are very pleased to be able to include some previously unpublished work in this collection, but most of what appears in these volumes has been published before. We have made very few changes, though we have added extra notes where we thought they would be useful. We have had the pleasure of researching the notes in the Sangharakshita Library at 'Adhisthana', Triratna's centre in Herefordshire, UK, which houses his own collection of books. It has been of great value to be able to search among the very copies of the *suttas*, *sūtras* and commentaries that have provided the basis of his teachings over the last seventy years.

The publication of these volumes owes much to the work of transcribers, editors, indexers, designers, and publishers over many years – those who brought out the original editions of many of the works included here, and those who have contributed in all sorts of ways to this *Complete Works* project, including all those who contributed to funds given in celebration of Sangharakshita's ninetieth birthday in August 2015, and to a further outpouring of generosity after Sangharakshita's death in October 2018. All these donors have made the publication of this series possible, and we are very grateful. Many thanks to everyone who has helped; may the merit gained in our acting thus go to the alleviation of the suffering of all beings.

Vidyadevi and Kalyanaprabha
Editors

THE COMPLETE WORKS OF SANGHARAKSHITA

I FOUNDATION

VOLUME 1 A SURVEY OF BUDDHISM / THE BUDDHA'S NOBLE EIGHTFOLD PATH
A Survey of Buddhism
The Buddha's Noble Eightfold Path

2 THE THREE JEWELS I
The Three Jewels
The Meaning of Conversion in Buddhism
Going for Refuge
The Ten Pillars of Buddhism
The History of My Going for Refuge
My Relation to the Order
Extending the Hand of Fellowship
Forty-Three Years Ago
Was the Buddha a Bhikkhu?

3 THE THREE JEWELS II
Who is the Buddha?
What is the Dharma?
What is the Sangha?

4 THE BODHISATTVA IDEAL
The Bodhisattva Ideal
The Endlessly Fascinating Cry (seminar)
The Bodhisattva Principle

5 THE PURPOSE AND PRACTICE OF BUDDHIST MEDITATION
The Purpose and Practice of Buddhist Meditation

6 THE ESSENTIAL SANGHARAKSHITA
The Essential Sangharakshita

II INDIA

7 CROSSING THE STREAM: INDIA WRITINGS I
Early Writings 1944–1954
Crossing the Stream
Buddhism in the Modern World: Cultural and Political Implications
The Meaning of Orthodoxy in Buddhism
Buddhism in India Today
Ordination and Initiation in the Three Yānas
A Bird's Eye View of Indian Buddhism

VOLUME 8 BEATING THE DHARMA DRUM: INDIA WRITINGS II
Anagarika Dharmapala and Other 'Maha Bodhi' Writings
Dharmapala: The Spiritual Dimension
Beating the Drum: 'Maha Bodhi' Editorials
Alternative Traditions

9 DR AMBEDKAR AND THE REVIVAL OF BUDDHISM I
Ambedkar and Buddhism
Lecture Tour in India, December 1981–March 1982

10 DR AMBEDKAR AND THE REVIVAL OF BUDDHISM II
Remembering Ambedkar
Buddha and the Future of His Religion
The Mass Conversion and the Years After, 1956–61
Lectures in India and England 1979, 1982–92
Wisdom before Words: The Udāna

III THE WEST

11 A NEW BUDDHIST MOVEMENT I
Ritual and Devotion in Buddhism
The Buddha's Victory
The Taste of Freedom
Buddha Mind
Human Enlightenment
New Currents in Western Buddhism
Buddhism for Today – and Tomorrow
Buddhism and the West
Aspects of Buddhist Morality
Dialogue between Buddhism and Christianity
Buddhism and Blasphemy
Articles and Interviews

12 A NEW BUDDHIST MOVEMENT II
Previously unpublished talks

13 EASTERN AND WESTERN TRADITIONS
Tibetan Buddhism
Creative Symbols of Tantric Buddhism
The Essence of Zen
The FWBO *and 'Protestant Buddhism'*
From Genesis to the Diamond Sūtra

IV COMMENTARY

V MEMOIRS

WINDHORSE PUBLICATIONS

Windhorse Publications is a Buddhist charitable company based in the UK. We produce books of high quality that are accessible and relevant to all those interested in Buddhism, at whatever level of interest and commitment. We are the main publisher of Sangharakshita, the founder of the Triratna Buddhist Order and Community. Our books draw on the whole range of the Buddhist tradition, including translations of traditional texts, commentaries, books that make links with contemporary culture and ways of life, biographies of Buddhists, and works on meditation.

To subscribe to the *Complete Works of Sangharakshita,* please go to: windhorsepublications.com/sangharakshita-complete-works/

THE TRIRATNA BUDDHIST COMMUNITY

Windhorse Publications is a part of the Triratna Buddhist Community, an international movement with centres in Europe, India, North and South America and Australasia. At these centres, members of the Triratna Buddhist Order offer classes in meditation and Buddhism. Activities of the Triratna Community also include retreat centres, residential spiritual communities, ethical Right Livelihood businesses, and the Karuna Trust, a UK fundraising charity that supports social welfare projects in the slums and villages of India.

Through these and other activities, Triratna is developing a unique approach to Buddhism, not simply as a philosophy and a set of techniques, but as a creatively directed way of life for all people living in the conditions of the modern world.

For more information please visit thebuddhistcentre.com